Fundamentals of Substance Abuse Practice

JERRY L. JOHNSON
Grand Valley State University

BROOKS/COLE
CENGAGE Learning™

Australia • Brazil • Japan • Korea • Mexico • Singapore • Spain • United Kingdom • United States

BROOKS/COLE
CENGAGE Learning™

Fundamentals of Substance Abuse Practice
Jerry L. Johnson

Executive Editor: Lisa Gebo

Assistant Editor: Alma Dea Michelena

Editorial Assistant: Sheila Walsh

Marketing Manager: Caroline Concilla

Marketing Assistant: Mary Ho

Advertising Project Manager: Tami Strang

Project Manager, Editorial Production:
Cathy Linberg

Print/Media Buyer: Rebecca Cross

Permissions Editor: Sarah Harkrader

Production Service: Hal Lockwood,
Penmarin Books

Copyeditor: Janet Tilden

Cover Designer: Andy Norris

Compositor: UG/GGS Information
Services, Inc.

For product information and technology assistance, contact us at
Cengage Learning Customer & Sales Support, 1-800-354-9706
For permission to use material from this text or product,
submit all requests online at **cengage.com/permissions**
Further permissions questions can be emailed to
permissionrequest@cengage.com

Library of Congress Control Number: 2003100451

ISBN-13: 978-0-534-62667-9

ISBN-10: 0-534-62667-X

Brooks/Cole
10 Davis Drive
Belmont, CA 94002-3098
USA

Cengage Learning is a leading provider of customized learning solutions with office locations around the globe, including Singapore, the United Kingdom, Australia, Mexico, Brazil, and Japan. Locate your local office at:
international.cengage.com/region

Cengage Learning products are represented in Canada by Nelson Education, Ltd.

For your course and learning solutions, visit **academic.cengage.com**

Purchase any of our products at your local college store or at our preferred online store **www.ichapters.com**

Printed in United States
7 8 9 10 11 10

In Memory of Charlie Lundy,
Counselor to the Angels

Brief Contents

I THEORETICAL FOUNDATION

1 Social Work and Substance Abuse Practice   1

2 Pharmacology   28

3 Models of Chemical Dependency   56

II CLIENT ENGAGEMENT

4 The Art of Client Engagement   92

5 Understanding the Family   128

6 Macro Context for Substance Abuse Assessment   153

III SCREENING AND ASSESSMENT

7 Introduction to Screening and Assessment   181

8 Substance Abuse Assessment   200

IV TREATMENT

9 The Substance Abuse Treatment System   245

10 Substance Abuse Treatment Methods   284

11 Populations at Risk   310

Appendixes   331

References   357

Index   389

Contents

To the Instructor   xv

To the Student   xviii

About the Author and Contributors   xx

I   THEORETICAL FOUNDATION

1   SOCIAL WORK AND SUBSTANCE ABUSE PRACTICE   1

Challenges of Working with Substance Abusers   1
Professional Challenges   2
Personal Challenges   3
    Reasons for Keeping a Substance Abuse Journal   4

An Attempt to Clarify Key Terms   4
Working Definitions: Use, Abuse, and Dependency   6
Traditional Concept of Addiction   10
The Difference Between Dependency and Abuse   11

Drug Use Trends   13

Substance-Related Accidents and Death   15

Prevalence of Substance-Related Problems in Practice   16
Substance Abuse and Psychiatric Disorders   17
Gender Considerations   18
Substance Use During Pregnancy   20
Age and Risk of Substance Abuse   20
Human Diversity   21
Social Class (Education, Employment, Income)   22

Fields of Practice   23

Do You Know What Chemical Dependency Feels Like?   26

Summary   27

2   PHARMACOLOGY   28

Pharmacology (Drug Effects)   28

Drug Variability   29
   Individual Factors   30
   Environmental/Situational Factors   31
   Dose   32
   Drug Mixing   32

Methods of Administering Drugs   33
   Oral   33
   Inhalation or Smoking   34
   Injection (IV)   34
   Mucous Membranes   35

Drug Tolerance   35
   Physical Tolerance   35
   Psychological Tolerance   36
   Behavioral Tolerance   36
   Cross-Tolerance   36

Drug Categories   36
   Central Nervous System (CNS) Depressants   37
      Drugs in This Category   37
      Routes of Administration   38
      Major Effects   38
      Overdose   39
      Tolerance   39
      Withdrawal   39
   CNS Stimulants   40
      Drugs in This Category   40
      Routes of Administration   42
      Major Effects   42
      Overdose   43
      Tolerance   44
      Withdrawal   44
   Cannabis   44
      Drugs in This Category   45
      Routes of Administration   45
      Major Effects   45
      Overdose   46
      Tolerance   47
      Withdrawal   47
   Opiates   47
      Drugs in This Category   48
      Routes of Administration   48

        Major Effects   48

        Overdose   49

        Tolerance   49

        Withdrawal   50

    Hallucinogens   50

        Drugs in This Category   51

        Routes of Administration   51

        Major Effects   51

        Overdose   52

        Tolerance   53

        Withdrawal   53

    Inhalants   53

        Drugs in This Category   54

        Routes of Administration   54

        Major Effects   54

        Overdose   54

        Tolerance   54

        Withdrawal   54

Summary   55

3   MODELS OF CHEMICAL DEPENDENCY   56

What Approach Will You Choose?   57

    Problems with Clinical Specialization   58

The Models   61

    Moral Model   62

        Discussion   63

    Community Model   65

        Discussion   67

    Biological Model   68

        Are Chemically Dependent People Different from Everyone Else?   69

        Is There an Addictive Personality?   70

        Discussion   70

    Social Learning Theory Model   71

        Discussion   73

    Cognitive-Behavioral Model   74

        Discussion   75

    Disease Model   76

        Origins of the Disease Model   77

        Basic Tenets of the Disease Model   78

        Discussion   79

        Evaluation of Jellinek's Research   80

        Media and Public Opinion   80

The Power of the Drug   80

Inevitable Progression?   81

Gateway Drugs   82

Loss of Control   82

The Disease Model as Gospel   83

Summary of Models   84

Substance Abuse from a Multi-Systemic, Ecological Perspective   84

Systems and Ecological Systems Theory   84

A Multi-Systemic Framework for Substance Abuse Practice   86

Biological Dimension   86

Psychological Dimension   87

Family Dimension   88

Religious/Spiritual/Existential Dimension   88

Social/Environmental Dimension   89

Macro Dimension   90

Summary   90

II   CLIENT ENGAGEMENT

4   THE ART OF CLIENT ENGAGEMENT   92

Definition of Engagement in Substance Abuse Practice   93

Client Engagement as an Art   93

How Well Do You Communicate?   94

Paulo Freire and Dialogue   95

Semiotic of Communication   97

Sign   98

Marker   98

Sight Involvement   99

Tourism as Metaphor for Self-Exploration   102

How Should We Treat Our Clients?   105

Five Characteristics of Effective Helping Professionals   106

1. Worldview Respect   107

2. Hope   108

3. Humility   109

4. Trust   112

5. Empathy   114

Special Issues Involved in Engaging Substance Abuse Clients   115

Denial   115

Defining Denial   116

Minimization   116

Rationalization   117

Projection   117

Assessing Client Motivation   118
    1. Precontemplation   118
    2. Contemplation   119
    3. Determination   120
    4. Action   120
    5. Maintenance   121
    6. Relapse   121
The Use of Confrontation to Deal with Denial   122
An Alternative Way to Approach Denial   124
    Dilemma of Change   124
    Compliance or Engagement?   125

Summary   126

5   UNDERSTANDING THE FAMILY   128

Why Do We Need to Understand Families?   128

What Is a Family?   130

The Changing Role of Families in Substance Abuse
  Treatment   131

Working with Family Systems   132
  Definitions of Terms   133
  Family System   133
  Subsystem   133
  Boundaries   134
  Family Structure   135

What Is a Functional Family?   135

The Competing Demands of Stability and Change   136

How Families Adapt to Chemical Dependency   137

Family Resilience   138

Chemically Dependent Families   139
  Family Survival Roles   141
    Chemically Dependent Person   141
    Chief Enabler   142
    Hero   142
    Family Scapegoat   143
    Lost Child   144
    Family Mascot   144

The Family Life Cycle   145

Other Issues to Consider in a Family Assessment   147
  Codependency   148
  Shame   149

Effects of Parental Substance Abuse on Older Children   150
Emotional Abuse   150
Sexual Abuse   150
Domestic Violence   151
Substance Abuse in Family History   151

Summary   151

**6   MACRO CONTEXT FOR SUBSTANCE
ABUSE ASSESSMENT   153**

The Power of Community   153

What Is "Community"?   155

Symbolic Interactionism and Community Influence   155
The Social Self   156
Self and Others   157
*Is the Right to Self-Determination Equally
Available to Everyone?*   158
Self and Community   160

Local Community   161

Assessing Multiple Communities   162
Geographic Community   163
Communities of Identification   163
Community Resources   164
Professional Treatment and Support   164
Institutions and Associations   164
Social Relationships   165

Macro Influences on Substance Abuse Treatment   165
*Structural and Historical Systems of Oppression:
Who Holds the Power?*   165
Drug Laws and Public Opinion   167

Drug Control Policy—A Primer   168
Comprehensive Drug Abuse Prevention and Control Act   169
Federal Sentencing Reform Act of 1984   171
The Anti-Drug Abuse Act of 1986   171
The Anti-Drug Abuse Act of 1988   173
Impact of Anti-Drug Legislation on Substance Abuse Practice   174

Macro Influences on Social Work Practice   175
Reimbursement Policies in Substance Abuse Practice   175
The Role of Social Workers in the Substance Abuse Field   177
Is It Necessary for Helpers to Be in Recovery?   178

Summary   180

III SCREENING AND ASSESSMENT

7 INTRODUCTION TO SCREENING AND ASSESSMENT 181

Definition of Assessment 182

How Screening Differs from Assessment 183

Substance Abuse Screening Instruments 184
    The Michigan Alcoholism Screening Test (MAST) 184
    CAGE 186
    Addiction Severity Index (ASI) 187
    Substance Abuse Subtle Screening Inventory-3 (SASSI-3) 188
    Other Substance Abuse Screening Instruments 188

Screening for Problems Related to Substance Abuse 189
    Physical Problems 190
    Depression 191
    Suicidal Ideation 193

How Assessment Differs from Diagnosis 196

Operating Principles of Substance Abuse Assessment 198

Summary 199

8 SUBSTANCE ABUSE ASSESSMENT 200

Dimensions of Assessment 200

Step-by-Step Assessment Process 201
    Dimension 1: Client Description, Presenting Problem, and Context of Referral 201
        What to Look for 202
        Key Questions 202
    Dimension 2: Treatment History 204
        Key Questions 205
    Dimension 3: Substance Use History 205
        Screening Instruments 209
        Family History of Substance Use 209
        What to Look for 209
        Key Questions 210
    Dimension 4: Medical History 210
        What to Look for 211
        Key Questions 211
    Dimension 5: Basic Needs 211
        What to Look for 212
        Key Questions 212

Dimension 6: Psychological and Emotional Functioning   212
    Mental Status Screening   213
    What to Look for   217
    Key Questions   218
Dimension 7: Family History and Structure   218
    What to Look for   220
    Key Questions   222
Dimension 8: Community/Macro Context   222
    Local Community   223
    Key Questions   224
    Sub-Dimension 1: Cultural Context   224
    Sub-Dimension 2: Social Class   226
    Sub-Dimension 3: Social-Relational   229
    Sub-Dimension 4: Legal History and Involvement   230
    What to Look for   232
Dimension 9: Motivation   232
    Key Questions   232
Dimension 10: Diagnosis   233
    The Diagnostic Process   234
    Multiaxial Assessment Using DSM   236
    Key Questions   240

The Case History Report   240

Summary   243

IV   TREATMENT

9   THE SUBSTANCE ABUSE TREATMENT SYSTEM   245

Levels of Substance Abuse Treatment   246
Education/Prevention Services (Early Intervention)   246
    Youths and Adolescents   247
    DWI Schools   248
    Education as an Alternative for the "Resistant" Client   249
    Education as a Component of Other Treatment Services   250
    Effectiveness of Educational Programs   251
Intervention   252
    The Johnson Model of Intervention   252
    The Intervention Process   253
    Effectiveness of Intervention   255
Twelve-Step Support Groups   256
    Core Elements of the AA Model   258
    The Twelve Steps   258
    Spirituality   260

Sponsorship 261
Effectiveness of Twelve-Step Groups 262
Outpatient Treatment 263
Effectiveness of Outpatient Treatment 264
Intensive Outpatient/Day Treatment 265
Effectiveness of Intensive Outpatient Programs 267
Inpatient Treatment 267
Types of Inpatient/Residential Services 269

Making a Referral for Substance Abuse Treatment 275
Least Restrictive Environment 275
Matching Treatment to Client Needs 276
Confidentiality 278
Assessing Substance Abuse Treatment Providers 279
Provider Location 280
Funding Sources 281
Transportation 281
Goodness-of-Fit 281
Follow-Up to Referral 282

Summary 283

10 SUBSTANCE ABUSE TREATMENT METHODS 284

Recovery: The Holy Grail of Substance Abuse Treatment 284
Stage One: Abstinence 286
Stage Two: Confrontation 287
Stage Three: Growth 288
Stage Four: Transformation 289
Recovery for the Substance Abuser 290

General Principles of Substance Abuse Treatment 290
Chemical Dependency Is an Illness 290
Engagement Is Necessary for Successful Treatment 291
A Multi-Systemic Approach Works Best 291
Aftercare Is Essential 292
Clients Need Help in Developing a Social Support Network 292

Treatment Planning 292
Treatment Plan Format 293
Issues in Treatment Planning 296
Treatment Goals: The Abstinence–Controlled Use Continuum 296
Principles of Harm Reduction 297

Specific Treatment Methods 299
Individual Therapy/Counseling 299
Group Therapy/Counseling 300

Family Therapy/Counseling   302
   Disease Model   303
    Family Systems Theory   303
Community Practice   304

Relapse Prevention   306
  Treatment Issues   308

Summary   309

11   POPULATIONS AT RISK   310

African Americans   310
  Treatment Issues   312

Latino Americans   313
  Treatment Issues   314

Native Americans   315
  Treatment Issues   317

Gay, Lesbian, Bisexual, and Transgendered (GLBT) Persons   317
  Treatment Issues   318

Adolescents   320
  Treatment Issues   322

Older Persons   324
  Treatment Issues   325

Persons with Co-occurring Disorders   325
  Treatment Issues   327
   Integrated Treatment   328

Summary   329

Appendixes   331

Appendix A: Substance Abuse Assessment/Case History Format   331

Appendix B: Sample Substance Abuse Assessment/Case History Report   336

Appendix C: African American Women: Oppression, Depression, Rage, and Self-Medication, by Lois Smith Owens   349

References   357

Index   389

To the Instructor

Based on more than 20 years of practice in the substance abuse field, I believe that information from micro, mezzo, and macro system levels should be taken into account in assessment, planning, and treatment decisions. Accordingly, this book is designed to teach students how to gather and use multi-systemic and multi-level client data when assessing and treating individuals and families. Readers will learn how to collect and apply information from individual clients, family members, the local community, and macro levels in substance abuse practice.

This book provides resource material for graduate-level social work students as well as upper-level undergraduate students who are about to enter (or have already entered) a field practicum setting.

You will notice that this book includes topics that most of your students will have explored in social work practice classes. This is especially true in Chapters 4 and 5 (see descriptions below). I have found that a certain amount of repetition is required to master social work knowledge, values, and skills. Moreover, information learned in general practice classes assumes new meaning and relevance when considered in the context of substance abuse practice. Whenever possible, I relate knowledge that may have been covered in general practice classes specifically to substance abuse practice, primarily through case examples.

OVERVIEW OF THE BOOK

This text is organized into four parts that parallel practice processes. Part I (Chapters 1, 2, and 3) provides the theoretical foundation for the rest of the book. Chapter 1 offers a general overview of the substance abuse field, including information about the prevalence of substance abuse problems in practice and important definitions of use, abuse, and addiction that are critical to the remainder of the text.

Chapter 2 gives an overview of the various pharmacological, psychological, emotional, and social effects of specific drugs within major drug categories. The focus is on the reciprocal effects of substances on individuals, including behavioral and emotional symptomatology, potential withdrawal risks, drug interaction risks, and other indicators to use in developing an accurate substance abuse assessment.

In Chapter 3, we explore six prominent theories and models used in substance abuse practice. Existing literature and research are combined with specific practice examples to demonstrate the impact of these models on substance abuse assessment and treatment. The models are then placed into a multi-systemic framework to be used in assessment and treatment.

Part II (Chapters 4, 5, and 6) focuses on client engagement across different systemic levels. Chapter 4, on client engagement, describes the processes of communication and itemizes several helper characteristics that contribute to building successful helping relationships. Drawn from information across several disciplines, Chapter 4 provides a comprehensive look at client engagement.

Substance abuse has a dramatic impact on the families and extended kin of the affected individual. In Chapter 5, contributor Rodney Mulder and I focus on family dynamics, processes, and practices important to engagement, assessment, and treatment of substance abuse clients.

To remain consistent with the multi-systemic approach advocated in this text, Chapter 6 explores the influence of the community on individuals and families seeking substance abuse services. Factors such as diversity (race, gender, class, age, and so on), rural versus urban setting, living conditions, crime and drug prevalence, law enforcement, availability of transportation, community support, and treatment resources play significant roles in substance abuse work at the individual and family levels.

Part III (Chapters 7 and 8) covers screening and assessment in substance abuse practice. This part of the text offers practical and usable information for substance abuse screening or comprehensive, multi-systemic substance abuse assessment. Chapter 7 provides a general overview of the screening and assessment processes. A clear distinction is made between assessment and both screening and diagnosis, while demonstrating the crucial role of assessment as an ongoing aspect of the treatment process. Chapter 8 serves as a comprehensive and practical resource for performing a multi-systemic substance abuse assessment. In this chapter, we cover 10 specific assessment dimensions, providing readers with specific questions and examples that clearly demonstrate how to carry out a substance abuse assessment.

Part IV (Chapters 9, 10, and 11) focuses on substance abuse treatment. Chapter 9 provides an overview of the substance abuse treatment system, organized by level of care. Chapter 10 offers specific information about substance abuse treatment, encompassing multiple theories, models, and methods into a multi-systemic treatment framework. Additionally, in this chapter readers learn about multi-systemic treatment planning, as well as relapse prevention as part of aftercare services. Chapter 11 supplies invaluable treatment information for working with several unique populations. Included are issues to consider when treating African Americans; Latino Americans; Native Americans; gay, lesbian, bisexual, and transgendered (GLBT) persons; adolescents; persons with co-occurring disorders; and older persons.

The book concludes with three appendices that are designed to augment the material presented earlier. Appendix A offers readers a sample case history/assessment format, while Appendix B provides a sample case history report of a client assessment. In Appendix C, Lois Smith Owens gives the reader a compelling glimpse into the lives of African American women, providing a better understanding of the contributing factors to substance abuse in this population.

ACKNOWLEDGMENTS

This book reflects the help and support of many people. I want to thank Rod Mulder and Lois Smith Owens for their invaluable contributions. I also want to thank Patty Stowe-Bolea, Ph.D., for her time, energy, and valuable feedback on Chapter 4.

Of course, without the support and patience of my wife Cheryl, this book could not have been written. Additionally, I would like to thank Dick Welna and Ted Peacock for having faith in me to write this text and for their patience with this deadline-impaired author. The book benefited greatly from the comments and suggestions of reviewers Allan Barsky of Florida Atlantic University and Sanford Schwartz of Virginia Commonwealth University. I also want to thank Janet Tilden for her tireless work in helping shape the final product, and Lisa Gebo at Wadsworth for having faith in this text.

Finally, I must thank Richard Smith, who gave me the chance of a lifetime more than 20 years ago. Dick, you gave me the opportunity to become a professional. I will never forget your patience, trust, and energy. Without your confidence in me, this book would never have been written.

Wadsworth is pleased to welcome Jerry Johnson to our publishing family through the recent acquisition of the former F. E. Peacock Publishers, Inc. We also thank Ted Peacock, Richard Welna, and their entire staff for their contribution to this work and to the field.

To the Student

This book is the culmination of more than 20 years of personal experience in the substance abuse field, along with the accumulated learning gained from being surrounded by interesting and knowledgeable staff, colleagues, and, of course, thousands of clients. My goal was to write a textbook that would be readable, approachable, and broad in its scope and background, while simultaneously providing specific information for use in daily practice. Regardless of whether or not you intend to specialize in substance abuse practice, I believe you will find that this text covers the field of substance abuse practice in sufficient depth and detail to be helpful.

THE MINIMUM REQUIREMENT

Before we begin, I want you to know what my graduate students learn at the beginning of every semester. It will be essential for you to develop two practice principles, each requiring specific knowledge, values, and skills. You will soon discover that refining these principles is easier said than done. Minimally, what I ask and hope for does not take hundreds of words to state, but it will take hundreds of hours of training, supervision, and additional training to accomplish. It is much easier to describe these practice principles in a book than it is to master them in practice.

My hope is that you will apply the following principles *with every client on your current caseload and all new clients you meet in the coming months and years:*

1. *Ask:* At the appropriate moment, *ask* your clients about substance use and abuse—their own use as well as that of family members and peers.
2. *Act:* If you discover a substance use or abuse history (defined here as past and/or present abuse), depending upon the nature and scope of that history, know how to *act* in a competent, well informed, and helpful manner. Somebody's life may be depending on you at that moment. This book is designed to teach you how to help your clients as effectively as possible.

If everyone in the human service professions who has contact with clients were to utilize these two principles, we would create a professional environment that supports social workers reaching beyond clinical specialty or agency mandate. It would be an environment where social workers relish the chance to develop new skills for the holistic betterment of the clients they serve and the highest application of this noble profession. My goal is to ensure that no agency or social worker, regardless of personal beliefs or funding strategy, will allow even one client (even the most resistant) to go underserved—or worse yet, unserved—because the extent of their substance use and abuse issues is unknown. If you join me in this endeavor, never again will "individualized" treatment plans be based on incomplete assessment data.

Learning and applying these two new practice principles will lead to a plethora of new skills. It is my job in the remainder of this text to provide you with the knowledge, values, and skills necessary to carry out these principles in your daily practice.

ABOUT THIS BOOK

This textbook is intended to be a resource that will outlive your time in the classroom—a reference guide for practice. If I have been successful, you should be able to refer to this book at any time, in any practice setting, regardless of your level of knowledge or experience, and find it useful. Some elements of the book are grounded in practical realms, while others are theoretical. At certain points, you will learn specific questions to ask your clients, while other sections will force you to think and reflect on your own ideas, attitudes, beliefs, and practices. Yet even the most theoretical aspects of this text ultimately end in discussions about their practical application with clients in the field. This book provides a comprehensive and multi-systemic look at how to perform substance abuse assessment and treatment.

Wherever it fits, I wrote this book in the first person. Since the material flows directly from material I have used to teach substance abuse practice courses, it seemed natural to write as if I were speaking to you in class. Hence, this text is designed to be interactive. That is, I want to interact with you, while you interact with the material and your peers in a way that fosters critical thought and reflection. Therefore, this book should not be viewed as a "lecture" but as a foundation for dialogue.

Many textbooks simply offer a compendium of existing information, packaged to provide an overview of what others have already said about a particular subject. While the theory and methods presented here are firmly grounded in the literature, my goal is to do more than summarize what everyone else has already said. I have tried to combine previously written information with personal experience to demonstrate how theory, method, and critical thinking can combine to produce unique approaches and methods for working with clients in daily practice. After reading and reflecting on this book, you are encouraged to develop and refine an approach that best suits your clients, practice settings, and personal style. Far from the final word on the subject, this book should serve as a foundation upon which you can begin to build and refine your work with clients in whatever practice setting you choose.

About the Author
and Contributors

Jerry L. Johnson, Ph.D., is an Assistant Professor of Social Work at Grand Valley State University in Grand Rapids, Michigan. He received his Ph.D. in sociology from Western Michigan University and his master's degree in social work from Grand Valley State University. Johnson has been in social work practice for more than 20 years, primarily in the substance abuse field, as a family therapist, consultant, program administrator, and teacher. He has developed substance abuse prevention and treatment programs in Michigan, the Republic of Armenia, and the Republic of Belarus. In 2000, he taught substance abuse practice to professors at the first national meeting of social work professors in Shanghai, China.

Rodney Mulder, Ph.D., is Professor of Sociology and Social Work at Grand Valley State University. He has taught at GVSU for 35 years, and since 1995 he has been the Dean of the School of Social Work. Mulder has taught courses in substance abuse since 1975, has been involved in substance abuse research since 1974, and has done clinical work with alcoholics and drug addicts for the last 20 years.

Lois Smith Owens, MSW, is Director of Admissions for the School of Social Work at Grand Valley State University. For more than 40 years, Smith Owens has been involved in the substance abuse field as a police officer, university administrator, and professor. Smith Owens is a well-regarded diversity consultant and professional storyteller, as well as a published author.

1

Social Work
and Substance
Abuse Practice

Few areas of practice encompass as wide a range of situations and people as substance abuse practice. Nearly everyone in the United States has at one time or another experienced substance use, abuse, or chemical dependency among friends, family members, or acquaintances. Many of us (including those of us who are social workers) have personally used or abused substances at some time in our lives (Johnston, O'Malley, & Bachman, 1998; SAMHSA, 1998; Community Epidemiology Work Group, 1998).

This book is dedicated to teaching the science and art of substance abuse practice, including client engagement, assessment, treatment planning, referral, and intervention. Unlike other books about substance abuse practice, this one focuses on engagement, assessment, and treatment planning, while still offering three chapters on treatment. Why the focus on pre-treatment stages? Primarily because comprehensive (holistic and multi-systemic) assessment is becoming a fading art in the wake of managed care limitations on practice. The prospect of reduced time in treatment leads many to cut back on the time spent assessing client problems and strengths, often basing treatment decisions, legal recommendations, and even child custody issues on the results of simple screening instruments (see Chapter 7) rather than a comprehensive assessment. Managed care limitations are no excuse for a lack of thoroughness in client engagement, assessment, and treatment planning. Among other topics, the first nine chapters of this book argue this important point.

CHALLENGES OF WORKING
WITH SUBSTANCE ABUSERS

Clients with substance abuse problems challenge social workers in a variety of ways. Inevitably, each of us will bring our personal perspectives, biases, beliefs, and attitudes to bear on the subject. Therefore, unlike other client-based problems, working with substance-abusing or chemically dependent clients presents challenges on both professional and personal levels.

Professional Challenges

Individuals and families with substance-abusing members are among the most difficult clients to identify, assess, and engage because of their ability to hide the existence or extent of their problem(s) from others (Johnson, 1973, 1986). The personal defense system of a chemically dependent person or family can be formidable and frustrating to even the most experienced social worker (van Wormer, 1995).

For social workers new to dealing with chemically dependent persons or families, their seemingly intractable and obsessive relationship with their drugs-of-choice and lifestyle appears to defy all common sense and logic. They continue to abuse substances or protect and defend their substance-abusing member despite obvious and substantial risks to health, career, personal safety, relationships, freedom from incarceration, and even parental rights. Even more insidious are clients whose substance abuse problems go unnoticed by unsuspecting or untrained social workers in an unrelated field of practice, such as mental health or gerontology.

In graduate social work courses, I routinely state that many clients' treatment needs go unmet because of a failure to identify and assess substance abuse. Often, students will disagree with this statement, claiming instead that substance abuse is so easy to identify that only the most uninformed and/or uncaring social worker could overlook it. By the end of the semester, many of the same students who scorned the incompetence of "other" social workers discover that they and/or their agency routinely forget to consider substance use and abuse.

CASE EXAMPLE   "My Clients Aren't Substance Abusers"

During the late 1980s, I started a new substance abuse treatment program for adolescents in my home city. At first, the program was a "hard-sell" to other service providers because it broke the traditional 28- to 45-day inpatient treatment paradigm that was prevalent at the time. As the director, I spent a lot of time visiting agencies, trying to convince workers to refer adolescents needing substance abuse services. The referrals did not come, despite my program being the only substance abuse treatment option for adolescents in the region.

Once I learned how the local juvenile court and community mental health centers operated, the reason became clear. In these large systems, social workers and other professional staff did not ask about substance use behavior by the client, family members, or immediate peer groups. These organizations—with a combined total of more than 1000 adolescent clients annually—neither required professional staff to inquire about substance use and abuse, nor

provided training on how to use substance abuse information in an assessment.

Community mental health workers believed that it would be inappropriate for them to assess clients for substance abuse, because they were operating a mental health center and not a substance abuse clinic. Besides, as more than one worker told me, substance abuse was a behavioral symptom indicating a deeper mental health issue. Therefore, according to their logic, why should they worry about it? Once the client's mental health was "restored," his or her substance abuse symptoms would quickly subside.

The story was similar at the juvenile court. Neither probation officers nor court intake workers routinely inquired about substance use and abuse. It may seem difficult to believe, but workers did not obtain even the most simple substance abuse history, even with adolescents adjudicated for drug-related offenses! And, while it may seem like a difficult issue to broach with clients in a court setting, it is a critically important issue if

---

CASE EXAMPLE   *continued*

rehabilitation or prevention of future problems is a goal. In time, I was hired to present a series of training sessions with juvenile court staff. Within two years, probation officers and intake workers were doing a basic substance abuse screening on all clients of the court and referring for a comprehensive assessment when problems were indicated by the screening process.

Another professional challenge arises from two related sources. First is the fact—mentioned earlier—that nearly everyone in the United States has, at one time or another, been in close contact with a substance abuser. Moreover, most Americans over 18 years old have used an illegal drug, consumed alcohol, or failed to follow doctor's orders when using a prescribed medication. In other words, nearly everyone has either done it or been close to someone who has (Walker, 1998). Second, alcohol consumption in particular and drug use in general is a longstanding part of American culture and folklore (Musto, 1999; Peele, 1998). Attitudes and behaviors range from teenagers drinking with parental consent as a "rite of passage," to the many popular myths about how much to drink, how to avoid hangovers, and what constitutes problem drinking. The use of mind-altering substances, especially alcohol, is viewed as a personal and sacred "right" that has been part of American culture since the country's inception. In the context of an anti-drug media blitz occurring since the early 1980s ("Just Say No!"), one can safely say that every American—unless they live in a cave—has some knowledge, experience, or at least a strong opinion about substance use, abuse, and chemical dependency.

What is our challenge, you ask? Because of its pervasiveness in American society, nearly everyone believes they are an "expert" about substance use and abuse. Their perceived expertise derives from exposure to substance use or abuse through personal experience or relationships, the socialization processes, television and radio talk shows, popular myth, or religious and spiritual beliefs and practices. Therefore, substance abuse practice holds a unique position in social work. As a social worker, you will often deal with people confident that they know the "Truth" even if it is based on myth, folklore, and anecdotal personal experience. Nevertheless, clients' knowledge should not be ignored, because many clients do know more about substance use and abuse than the general public. This knowledge—what Freire (1994) calls *class knowledge*—must be understood and respected. Rarely will you face the same kinds of challenges from clients with other problems that you will face when working with many substance abuse clients.

Personal Challenges

Working with substance abusing clients is also personally challenging—whether you specialize in substance abuse or not—because they often blur the line between professional knowledge, values, and skills and personal values, beliefs, experiences, and myths. When these lines blur, you cease being a social worker in a professional sense, becoming just another person lost in the confusing maze of myth and contradiction. When and if you cross this line, clients are better off talking to a friend or their hair stylist than a boundary-impaired social worker.

Reasons for Keeping a Substance Abuse Journal Many students and practicing social workers do not like to admit that their personal beliefs and experiences shape their professional attitudes and practices. These people strongly believe that they can be value-neutral with clients. Maintaining boundaries between the professional and personal *is* critical, but it is not as easy as it sounds. Therefore, during the first class session, I ask my students to begin writing a *substance abuse journal*, initially focusing on their personal relationship with substance use, abuse, and chemical dependency. Students document their personal experience, but also the experience of friends, family, and partners. The substance abuse journal is more than a written account of events. Students interact with themselves about their personal feelings, attitudes, and beliefs about substance use and abuse. They also comment on the potential impact of these issues on their current worldview.

The substance abuse journal is a personal account, covering a broad range of questions, issues, attitudes, and beliefs that are raised in each class session. Certainly, some students do not take their journal seriously, and some do not write in it at all. This is similar to the casual approach many take toward training, supervision, and continuing education. The decision to keep a substance abuse journal is yours. However, in class—and here—I appeal to the most important quality you have: professional integrity. Do you want to be truly helpful to your clients, or just earn a paycheck? Competent education, training, and supervision are the only way to overcome the boundary issues discussed here (Kirst-Ashman & Hull, 1999). Social workers equipped with suitable training can overcome the power of popular culture, myth, and folklore to remain in a professional helping role with substance abusing clients, regardless of personal background and experience.

Topic for Your Journal: Your Relationship with Substance Use

Why not begin your substance abuse journal right now? In the first entry, focus on your personal relationship with substance use, abuse, and chemical dependency. Throughout the remainder of the text, periodically I will ask you to write about other subjects. I hope you take the opportunity to participate.

Please ... take 15 minutes right now.

AN ATTEMPT TO CLARIFY KEY TERMS

There is confusion in the substance abuse field about the differences between substance use, abuse, and dependence. Knowing the difference between these terms is more than an academic exercise; it is central to substance abuse practice. Recommendations for treatment and/or level of intervention are based largely on how well you can distinguish between clients who are using or abusing substances, and those who are chemically dependent.

To begin, let's look at where the confusion originates—in the media, with politicians, and among high-profile substance abuse professionals. Confusion begins with the reporting of drug use statistics. As we discuss later in this chapter, media reports usually cover only the total number of users in each drug category, meaning that drug use statistics treat first- or one-time users the same as those who are chronically chemically dependent. For example, if 80 percent of teens say they use alcohol, how do we know what part of that 80 percent only used once? Speculation about the extent of abuse and addiction from these results is inappropriate to the intention of the research.

Why are the statistics reported in this way? One reason is that drug use survey results make exciting and enticing media stories that elicit public pressure for stricter drug laws. Another is that they relegate drug users to a lower social level in society. This allows the federal government to pursue the "War on Drugs" as a criminal justice war, and creates the impression that there are millions of Americans mindlessly running through life ruled by the demon drug, each ready to steal from law-abiding citizens to satisfy their cravings.

Others who take a more conservative position believe the statistics foretell a difficult future. Simply put, they believe that drug addiction will ruin the leadership potential of future generations of Americans. Accordingly, any use of drugs inevitably leads to chemical dependency. This position is remarkable, given that most of these same people regularly drink alcohol, smoke, or take prescription medication.

A close look at statistical trends over the past 25 years does not support the former position, while the latter is based on the notion that drugs—and not the people who use—cause chemical dependency. That is, once people ingest a drug, a biological and chemical force outside of human control overtakes them, leading to loss of control. The public opinion that shapes these perspectives is based on partial and vague information, leaving people—including opportunistic political leaders—free to act as if substance *use* is synonymous with substance *abuse* or chemical *dependency*.

The definitions of use, abuse, and dependency (or addiction) are indeed a difficult problem to settle, because each concept is bound up in culture, history, personal experience and subjectivity, folklore, and myth. Everybody has their own definition of use, abuse, and dependence/addiction, including social workers. To confound the discussion, if one truly adopts a perspective based on individuality and human diversity, it is possible that everybody's definition is more or less correct.

The most common theory used to explain chemical dependency is the disease model (Jung, 1994; Doweiko, 1993; Peele, Brodsky, & Arnold, 1992; Peele, 1998; Vaillant, 1983; Jellinek, 1960). According to this model, drug addiction is a disease similar to diabetes, with a distinct biological and medical origin. Accordingly, anyone who drinks or uses drugs is at risk of contracting the disease, because nobody knows for sure what genes or biological or social phenomena are involved in its origins. The disease of addiction, characterized by specific behavioral symptomatology (see Chapter 3), is believed to act the same in everyone, no matter who they are; where they come from; their age, race, gender, and so on (Peele, 1998). That is, since the disease of addiction is the same for everyone, it follows that the definitions of use and abuse are identical for everyone, as are treatment considerations.

Yet writers like Peele (1998) and others (Denning, 2000; Fingarette, 1988) vigorously dispute the universalist claims of the disease model. Basing their critique on a wealth of secondary research, these authors suggest that addiction is not a disease, but originates in people's subjective experience of life, expectations about drug effects, the setting or environment where the drugs are taken, and their actual experience with the drugs they use. According to this argument, there are as many different definitions of use, abuse, and addiction as there are people using drugs of all kinds.

Have I cleared up the confusion yet? The answer, obviously, is "no." Although this is a brief presentation of the factors involved, it should be easy to see why this topic is so confusing. When you get to Chapter 3, remember these terms and, in your substance abuse journal, discuss how each of the different theories define use, abuse, and dependency.

Working Definitions: Use, Abuse, and Dependency

Use: *The ingestion of substances (alcohol or drug, legal or illegal) with any regularity (once or repeatedly over a lifetime) that results in little or no significant negative life consequences.*

The important concepts in this simple definition of substance use are "any regularity" and "no significant negative life consequences." The degree to which someone does or does not have a substance abuse problem has nothing to do with the amount or regularity of use. There are many people who drink alcohol, take prescription pain medication, or even smoke marijuana daily or weekly while experiencing no problems because of their use. Likewise, it is impossible for people to use a drug once and immediately become dependent. This fact is important enough to repeat: the amount or frequency of use alone—no matter what the drug—does not constitute the existence of a substance abuse problem. The reality is more complicated than that.

Another important element in this definition is the phrase "negative life consequences." If someone uses drugs with any frequency without demonstrable negative life consequences, then, according to this definition, they do not have a problem. What are "negative life consequences"? They are problems that occur in a person's life and/or environment because of substance use. Negative life consequences can involve personal, social, vocational, health, daily practices, sexual, affective, or cognitive considerations. These consequences can directly affect the substance user or people close to the user. While there are few limits to the potential areas in which negative life consequences can emerge, there is no objective definition that applies to all people using drugs. What constitutes a negative life consequence is unique to every person. Clients determine what their negative life consequences are based on their unique life circumstances. That is, the definition and meaning attached to the concept emerge through a collaborative, working partnership between client and worker. A negative life consequence for one person may make no difference to another. It is futile to impose an objective definition of negative life consequences on every client you see.

If your goal is to help change people's perspectives and life circumstances, a unique definition of negative life consequences must emerge through dialogue in order for the definitions to have personal and cultural meaning in your client's daily life (Giroux, 1997; McLaren, 1995; Freire, 1994). As we discuss later, it is not your role to gather information and then impose problem definitions "from on high," but to move toward an individual definition of negative life consequences in collaboration with clients, whether you are working with an individual, couple, family, or community. For example, to some clients the potential for physical withdrawal from a particular drug may constitute a negative life consequence. However, physical withdrawal potential is not negative for everyone. Consider people living with chronic pain. Without daily doses of morphine (a highly addictive opiate derivative) and thus the potential for severe withdrawal, these people may be unable to function from day to day. These people make a trade-off based on life circumstances; physical addiction is better than chronic and debilitating pain. In other cases, some people will react negatively to the physical sickness of withdrawal, while some will not appear to experience it at all. This does not suggest that the latter persons do not suffer some form of physical withdrawal. It simply means that the fact of physical withdrawal is not serious to them personally (because of high pain tolerance, *machismo*, or something else). To assume physical withdrawal as a negative life consequence for everybody, simply because the professional literature says it is or because it would be negative if it happened to you, is inappropriate. From a social work perspective, people in their environment subjectively define what constitutes negative life consequences. These personal definitions may or may not match what you believe is true in their lives.

Of course, the idea of negative life consequences is not immune to extreme interpretations by people interested in being extreme. It is possible to believe that everyone who uses any drug experiences negative life consequences, even if they do not know it yet. For example, drug use damages the body, alcohol affects the liver, and tobacco causes cancer. In the strictest sense, all of these statements are true. However, strictly speaking, anyone who eats fast food, red meat, and vegetables treated with insecticides, or inhales air pollution in big cities will experience negative life consequences, too. Use and apply common sense when working with clients regarding *their* lives. Although you may believe people are damaged by use, it is important to leave your beliefs where they belong—in your personal life and not superimposed onto the lives of your clients.

The definition of "use" offered here is simple to understand. However, the word "use" becomes complicated when mixed with ideology and politics. For example, one common definition claims that "use" means ingestion of any drug only in the amounts appropriate for its intended use (Hanson & Venturelli, 1998; Ray & Ksir, 1993). Therefore, "use" of a prescription medication, for example, means using it only in strict accordance with a doctor's written instructions. Any use that does not fit this strict definition is abuse. This stipulation sounds simple and sensible.

Nonetheless, this definition has problems. What is the "intended" use of marijuana? Heroin? Alcohol? If there is an intended use for alcohol (i.e., for thirst quenching), does this mean that everyone who has ever drunk enough alcohol to feel minimally intoxicated is a substance abuser? Even the most conservative people, perhaps with the exception of the Woman's Christian Temperance Union (WCTU) or certain religions, would disagree with this strict definition of alcohol use. Why? Primarily because alcohol is a legal drug for people over 21 years old, and surveys suggest that more than 90 percent of all adults drink alcohol at some point in their lives and more than 50 percent drink weekly (SAMHSA, 1998).

Now apply the "intended use" criterion to illegal drugs. By definition, there is no "intended use" for illegal drugs such as marijuana or heroin. Therefore, according to this definition, anyone who ingests these drugs for any reason and in any amount, even if they use the drug only once, is abusing that drug. If every one of the more than 13 million Americans who used an illicit drug in 1998 actually abused those drugs, then, by definition, every one of these drug "abusers" probably requires some form of social work intervention. This applies to us as well. If you or I ever smoked marijuana or, for that matter, ever took one more pill than our doctor prescribed to kill pain, then we would be classified as a drug abuser.

Topic for Your Journal: Misuse Versus Abuse

Hanson and Venturelli (1998, p. 7) try to explain the difference between misuse and abuse by claiming that misuse is drug use for anything but medicinal purposes, or using drugs in ways other than how they were intended. However, using the word "misuse" avoids the issue of abuse entirely. Consider, for a moment, the difference between misuse and abuse. Beyond semantics, is there a difference? Perhaps you can consider this issue in your substance abuse journal by looking up definitions from various other text. Using this information, along with your own reasoning, decide for yourself whether a difference exists. If there is little or no difference between definitions, could the differences in connotation be political or social in nature? What did you conclude? Here's another question for your substance abuse journal: **What is your definition of use?**

One problem with the intended use definition is that without repeated use and some demonstrable level of negative personal or social consequences, it does not meet the minimum criteria for *Diagnostic and Statistical Manual (DSM)* diagnosis of substance abuse (American Psychiatric Association, 2000). Even the *DSM* recognizes, without saying it explicitly, that people can use legal and illegal drugs without problems. According to Peele (1998), most people who use drugs experience no negative consequences at all. Their use meets the criteria, under the definition offered in this book, of "normal use."

Why should you care about this topic? The concept of use is more than semantics. When it comes to drugs, use is the positive side of the mythical yet profoundly important social distinction between "normal" and "abnormal." People who use drugs are normal, while people who abuse or become dependent are abnormal. This dichotomy goes directly to the heart of the issue. By what criteria do we assess people's substance use behavior as problematic?

Abuse: *The use of drugs—legal or illegal—with some regularity or pattern, that results in persons experiencing a pattern of negative life consequences resulting from their substance use.*

Again, this definition is simple and straightforward. People who fit the criteria for substance abuse must use drugs with regularity. Indeed, it is possible to use a substance one time and experience negative life consequences, even death. However, if individuals survive their one-time use, only by applying the strictest definition of substance abuse could they be determined to have a substance abuse problem. It is highly unlikely that you would ever see these people, unless you are a medical social worker and saw them at a hospital after an accident.

Please note that there is no inevitability about an individual moving from substance use to substance abuse (Akers, 1992), just as not all substance abusers move to chemical dependency. In fact, most people use drugs or drink alcohol without moving beyond the use stage (see Chapter 3). The same is true for people fitting the definition of substance abuse. Far more people move in and out of use and abuse patterns over the course of their lives without moving to chemical dependency than those who progress to the more serious stage (Peele, 1998).

According to the *DSM-IV-TR* (American Psychiatric Association, 2000), not only must people use drugs with some regularity, but they must meet one (or more) of four distinct criteria in order to be classified as substance abusers, each of which describes an element of negative life consequence. Included is "failure to fulfill major role obligations" (p. 182); use in situations where it is "physically hazardous" (p. 183); "recurrent substance-use-related legal problems" (p. 183); and continued use despite "persistent or recurrent social or interpersonal problems caused or exacerbated by the effects of the substance" (p. 183). Additionally, the diagnostic label of substance abuse is not historical. The client must exhibit one or more of the criteria during a continuous 12-month period. (See Chapter 8, where we discuss using the *DSM* for diagnosis in some detail.)

In other words, people who are considered substance abusers, unlike those who simply use, must demonstrate a *pattern* of negative life consequences. The key word here is "pattern." One or two incidents are not a pattern. A pattern is repeated or recurrent; it happens regularly. People who are arrested for first-offense driving while intoxicated (DWI) or who have an argument with their spouse once after using drugs may not fit the definition of substance abuse. They simply may have terrible luck or have made a dreadful mistake. Over the years, I have seen many instances where clients were over-diagnosed, leading to treatment that was too intensive for their needs. These people clearly did not demonstrate a pattern of substance abuse or negative life consequences.

What I call substance abuse, Akers calls "habitual use" (1992, p. 16). While his definition is similar to the one presented here, he warns that abuse, like use and dependence, falls along a continuum from light to heavy abuse:

> Habitual use is the regular use of a drug continued over time. A sustained or increasing substantial dosage of a drug taken every day is the clearest indication of a habit. However, there may be great variability in the size and frequency of a habit. Habituation may be to small dosages and the time between doses could be long. Therefore, light or moderate nonhabitual use of some substance often shades into or overlaps habitual use (Akers, 1992, p. 16).

The major problem with Akers's definition is that he omits any reference to negative life consequences. It is easy to believe that negative life consequences are implied, given the improbability that someone could use an "increasing substantial dosage of a drug" (sic) every day and not experience negative life consequences. However, it is inconsistent with social work values and ethics to base assessment and treatment on unstated and unproven assumptions or implied states. Therefore, it is important to develop advanced engagement skills to create a trusting and mutually respectful environment where your client can talk openly about his or her life circumstances, saving you from the temptation to rely on hunches, stereotypes, or illusory correlations (Gambrill, 1997).

Chemical Dependency or Addiction: *Recurrent or chronic use (often daily), that results in a physiological and/or psychological "need" (real or felt) for the drug as a matter of survival, causing severe and/or chronic negative life consequences. The chemically dependent person's life is fully encompassed by the obsession to use drugs and live the accompanying lifestyle.*

Before exploring this definition, it will be helpful to read the following brief discussion regarding the concept of addiction. The professional definition of addiction has changed over the last century, and these changes directly influence the working definition of dependency/addiction provided above.

Traditional Concept of Addiction

Historically, the term *addiction* referred to the physiological effects of certain drugs. If the repeated use of drugs led users to experience physical withdrawal symptoms, then the drug was addicting, and users were addicted to the drug. In Chapter 2, you will learn that withdrawal symptoms occur after people develop a tolerance for the drug. Tolerance, in this sense, means that the body becomes progressively "immune" to the toxic effects of the drug; hence, users must increase dosages to achieve the same level of feeling or intoxication (Akers, 1992; Goode, 1989). Withdrawal symptoms from physical dependence occur after the body builds up a tolerance to a drug to the point that it needs periodic doses of the drug to function "normally." When people do not take the needed dosage within a particular time period, their bodies begin readjusting to life without the drug. That is, users become physically sick. Thus, addiction in the traditional sense could occur only if people experienced physiological changes caused by a drug. If not, then people were not addicted, nor was the drug addicting. The traditional concept of addiction pertained primarily to opiate use (heroin, morphine, etc.), which was a major social issue in the United States from the end of the Civil War (1865) to the early 1900s, as well as to alcohol use.

The problem with this definition should be obvious. Certain drugs do not cause physiological tolerance, but they still can be abused to the point that persons become addicted. It does not take physical tolerance and withdrawal symptoms before people experience a powerful "need" for the drug on a regular basis. For example, while there is considerable debate about this subject (Leshner, 1997; Lukas et al., 1996), cocaine, marijuana, and LSD are not believed to cause physiological tolerance and therefore do not lead to physical withdrawal symptoms. Yet few can deny that users of marijuana, LSD, and especially cocaine experience significant negative life consequences. (See Chapter 2 for specific information about the effects of drugs on the human body.)

To incorporate the psychological with the physiological, scholars developed the term *chemical dependency*. It is widely accepted that people can develop, through repeated use in their social environment, a psychological dependence on (or a created sense of need for) certain drugs (Levinthal, 1999, Hanson & Venturelli, 1995; Ray & Ksir, 1993; Akers, 1992). People can meet the criteria for dependence through psychological means, physiological means, or both. Persons need not experience physical withdrawals to be considered dependent. Do not discount the seriousness of psychological withdrawal; it can be, and often is, as "real" as physical withdrawal. Perhaps the only significant difference between physical and psychological withdrawal is that people experiencing physical withdrawal will need medical supervision during their withdrawal period (i.e., detoxification services).

CASE EXAMPLE Cocaine Dependency

I once had a client who, after two years of significant powder cocaine abuse, heard voices, saw fictitious people in his hospital room, awoke feeling as if bugs were crawling on him, beneath his skin, and suffered from severe and debilitating headaches during the three days following cessation of use. Fortunately, he was in a setting where his symptoms could be managed and where he did not have access to drugs for self-medication.

The Difference Between Dependency and Abuse

The key to an accurate assessment often hinges on your ability to recognize and distinguish between dependency and abuse. On paper, there is a fine line between the two states. In practice, however, the differences are vast, both quantitatively and qualitatively. When you interview someone who fits the description of a substance abuser versus someone who is chemically dependent, you will know the difference, although at first glance the distinction may not be apparent.

What is the difference? Chemically dependent persons will show significant psychological, behavioral, and/or physiological impairment. People classified as substance abusers rarely experience physiological impairment and usually have low to nonexistent levels of psychological impairment. Much of the problem for substance abusers is found in social relationships (love, work, and play). Usually, substance abusers have not reached the stage where psychological and physiological changes and problems are a significant issue.

The difference between abuse and dependency is often qualitative, measured in intensity, patterns of negative life consequences, and the pervasiveness of drugs and drug use in people's lives. Often, the only clue that people have progressed from abuse to dependency is a sense or feeling you have while listening to their story. People will not walk into your office and simply spout the details of a destroyed life in order to convince you of their addiction. The story will be revealed gradually through connecting themes from information gathered across the life history of the persons being interviewed.

Despite the existence of negative life consequences, the relationship between substance abusers and their drugs is only one part of a full life. During an interview, you do not get the sense that drug use is more important to them than other aspects of life. People classified as substance abusers may indeed have weekends or days when the abuse and its effects become their sole focus (e.g., someone gets drunk and loud at a wedding, or they miss work because of a bad hangover, etc.). Outside of these intermittent periods, however, substance abusers usually are able to maintain their life roles (job, relationships, friendships, etc.) with some degree of competence.

The life of a chemically dependent person is a different story. Once you circumvent clients' denial systems and engage them in trusting relationships, you will hear the differences. Chemically dependent people's attention, emotions, thoughts, and actions—their entire existence—is involved with the many aspects of addicted life. Drugs, drug use, and the people and activities involved with recurrent or chronic drug use become a chemically dependent person's main—if not *only*—true interest. These individuals believe that using drugs is as important as breathing or eating—it's a matter of daily survival. Their personal relationships with friends and loved ones come second to drug use, unless the relationships are with people who use drugs with them or sell drugs to them (bartender, server, or illegal drug dealer).

Chemical dependency is a lifestyle. It defines relationships with the people, organizations, and institutions in people's lives. Chemically dependent people's primary relationship has shifted from people to drugs. Fisher and Harrison (2000) claim that chemically dependent people form an "intimate and monogamous relationship" with their drugs of choice (p. 8). This is an apt characterization. Often, their list of drugs used, length of time used, and the frequency of use will not appear much more significant than similar information for someone who is not chemically dependent. The difference, again, is in the lifestyle of chemically dependent persons: how they approach daily life and drugs, the role drugs and drug use plays in their lives, and their relationship to drugs versus their relationship with the rest of the world. When you talk to a chemically dependent person, it becomes clear that his or her problems are more pervasive than a simple drug history can tell.

You will find the difference between chemical dependency and substance abuse in the entirety of people's lives, including those parts of the assessment that are beyond and behind a substance use history. The true tale is told in relationships and the priorities clients place on different life spheres. The keen social worker learns how to make connections between seemingly distinct events and understands that literally no aspect of a chemically dependent person's life is untouched by drugs and the drug culture.

DRUG USE TRENDS

Substance use, abuse, and dependency have received so much public attention since the 1980s that it seems all too obvious to restate that the abuse of legal and illegal substances poses a threat to personal and public health in the United States and abroad (Johnson, 2000; Denning, 2000; McNeese & DiNitto, 2000). While substance abuse causes significant problems for many people, perhaps the most prominent public issue is the so-called War on Drugs (Musto, 1999; Walker, 1998; Levinthal, 1999; Akers, 1992). From a public policy perspective—especially related to the public funding of military-style interdiction and the booming prison industry—the War on Drugs continues to have more impact on American life than individual substance use and abuse. Certainly, these laws, policies, and funding priorities shape the role and function of social workers in the substance abuse field and determine how users and drug offenders are treated by the public, criminal justice system, health care industry, and the treatment profession.

Shedding new light on the scope of substance use in the general population is not the goal of this discussion. Other authors cover the subject in significant detail (Levinthal, 1999; Fisher & Harrison, 2000; SAMHSA, 1998; Inciardi & McElrath, 1995; Johnston, O'Malley, & Bachman, 1998). There appears to be little disagreement about the number of people who have used drugs at some point or are using drugs now. Below is a brief presentation and analysis of the data to serve as a backdrop for the remainder of the book.

As we begin, recognize the limitations inherent in any drug use survey. For example, in the Monitoring the Future study, only youths currently enrolled and attending school were surveyed, thereby excluding all youths who were not enrolled in school or were absent on measurement day. While this is not an indictment of the study, it does limit its utility. One could easily speculate that youth drug use reports would rise if the excluded youth were somehow located and surveyed, given that educational level significantly affects drug use (SAMHSA, 1998). Unfortunately, the "missing" respondents are often the same people who comprise our caseloads. Nevertheless, since this group is not measured, this is pure speculation.

Millions of Americans—adolescents and adults—use and abuse legal and illegal drugs. The Substance Abuse and Mental Health Services Administration (1998) in its annual survey of legal and illegal drug use found that more than one-half (50 percent) of all adult Americans drink, with approximately 5 percent reporting "heavy" use and 16 percent reporting binge-drinking tendencies. The same study reported more than 11 million underage alcohol users (12 to 20 years old), the age group where binge drinking is most common (SAMHSA, 1998). People who are considered to be heavy and/or binge drinkers are more likely to use illegal drugs than other drinkers are, with up to 25 percent of these drinkers using illegal drugs in addition to drinking. This tendency, combined with binge drinking statistics, suggests that adolescents and young adults (aged 12 to 20 in the studies) are more likely to use illegal drugs then older drinkers (SAMHSA, 1998).

Other studies show that drug use decreases with age, suggesting that many people "mature out" of substance use and abuse by 29 years of age (Peele, 1998). While this does not mean Americans should stop worrying about adolescent drug use, it does suggest that the next generation's drug use—as adults—will probably be similar to that of previous generations.

Moreover, 6.4 percent (more than 13 million) of all Americans over the age of 12 reported illegal drug use in the month before completing the survey. Among 12- to 20-year-olds, 30-day use climbed to 11.4 percent. The vast majority (77 percent) of this group used marijuana, and, while some reported using other drugs as well, more than half used only marijuana. Comparing these statistics with a high-water mark of 25 million drug users in 1979 clearly demonstrates that overall drug use has been on the decline for more than 20 years. In fact, surveys show a steady decline in drug use until 1992, when it rose again before stabilizing in 1995. However, the trend among youth is quite different. Drug use in this age group has nearly doubled since 1992 (Community Epidemiology Work Group, 1998).

While the rising rate of youth drug use is noteworthy, do not hit the "panic button" just yet. The oft-cited report about youth drug use doubling since 1992 is a prime example of how statistics can present a less than holistic picture of current trends. For example, according to the Monitoring the Future study (Johnston, O'Malley, & Bachman, 1998), youth drug use reached its lowest level since the study began in 1992, leveling off at a rate of approximately 50 percent of its 1979 high. Therefore, the "doubling" of use since 1992 means that youth drug use is still approximately 66 percent of what it was in 1979. *This means that illegal drug use by youths has dropped 33 percent in less than 20 years!* This does not signal a victory in the War on Drugs, but it is a clear sign of improvement. I am sure that anti-tobacco groups would have been thrilled with figures like these in the first 20 years following the Surgeon General's 1964 report connecting tobacco use to cancer.

Equally important, but not nearly as often cited, is the fact that alcohol use by young people remained nearly the same (approximately 88 percent having consumed alcoholic beverages at some point in the previous 30 days over the same 20-year period). An interesting question to ask yourself is why we hear so much about illegal drug use among young people despite a nearly 20-year downward trend, but we rarely hear about alcohol use (unless a teenager is killed while driving under the influence of alcohol or dies from an alcohol overdose at a party). What do you think about this? This is an interesting topic to write about in your substance abuse journal.

Similar trends are reported among college students. Drug use peaked in 1980 (first year of the study), with 38.4 percent reported having used in the previous 30 days. By 1993, these rates had fallen to 15.1 percent, or 39 percent of the 1980 high-water mark. Meanwhile, alcohol use inched down to a level of 88 percent of previous highs (from 82.8 percent in 1982 to 71.4 percent in 1992). Drug use rates have gradually increased since 1992 but remain well below reported highs for all drugs except alcohol (Johnston, O'Malley, & Bachman, 1998).

SUBSTANCE-RELATED ACCIDENTS AND DEATH

To make the data about substance-related accidents and death meaningful, we must look at the variables in the survey and its political and social context. It is clear that substance-related accident and death statistics alarm the public, inflame politicians, and force insurance executives to lose sleep. These incidents helped begin social movements like Mothers Against Drunk Driving (MADD) and Students Against Drunk Driving (SADD) that spearheaded a nationwide movement to toughen drunken driving laws (Jung, 1994).

Accident and death statistics involving substance use do not, however, indicate whether the accidents or deaths involved persons with substance abuse problems. These surveys only report about victims or perpetrators who were under the influence of a drug at the time of the accident or death. It is possible (and quite probable) that some people represented in these surveys were "normal" or first-time users, while others were substance abusers or chemically dependent. Therefore, although accident and death statistics speak to the tragic social and human cost of substance use in general, they do not speak to the prevalence of substance abuse problems. Not every victim or perpetrator of a substance-related accident or death is chemically dependent, although this is often the conclusion of lay readers.

With this warning in mind, substance use is involved in about 40 percent of all hospital admissions and up to 25 percent of all deaths. Estimates place drug-related deaths (other than nicotine) at about 100,000 annually (American Psychiatric Association, 1995). Twenty-four percent of these deaths happen in drunken driving accidents, 11 percent from homicide, and 8 percent from suicide. The Centers for Disease Control and Prevention (1998) reported 430,000 annual deaths resulting from legal tobacco use, with a yearly medical cost amounting to more than $50 billion.

Indeed, one could fill volumes with a breakdown of drug use statistics, but these numbers are not always relevant to social workers in the field. Perhaps it is enough to say that substance use and abuse are widespread. It is, however, pertinent to determine the extent to which substance abuse and chemical dependency affect the lives of real people and how often social workers find these issues in practice.

PREVALENCE OF SUBSTANCE-RELATED
PROBLEMS IN PRACTICE

While current use patterns provide a glimpse of the American culture, these data do not address the problems associated with substance abuse or dependence. According to the definitions of use, abuse, and dependency discussed earlier, we can say that substance-related problems for individuals, families, and communities occur when people abuse or become dependent on substances. These problems do not stem (with the exception of an accident after first use) from substance use. Below, we explore the relevant trends that demand the attention of social workers in the field: statistical indicators of the extent to which you may find substance abuse problems in your daily practice. Used correctly, these trends can help you know what to look for in certain situations. Keep in mind, however, that these trends cannot predict what you will find with any particular client.

One such study is the National Comorbidity Study (Anthony, Warner, & Kessler, 1997). This extensive study attempted to determine the lifetime prevalence of *DSM* (American Psychiatric Association, 2000) diagnosed substance abuse problems based on clinical data collected from more than 8000 participants. Among the findings, this study definitively showed that most people who use drugs do *not* go on to develop problems because of their use (Anthony, Warner, & Kessler, 1997). In fact, the drug most people are likely to become dependent on is tobacco (24 percent, or one in four users). One in seven alcohol users (14 percent) reported becoming alcohol dependent, while one in 13 (7.5 percent) moved from drug use to drug abuse or dependency. One figure that may astound you involves cocaine use. According to this study, only 2.7 percent of people who use cocaine develop a problem (abuse or dependence) at some point during their lifetime (Denning, 2000, p. 20), calling into question the public perception that cocaine (and its derivative, crack) is a "one-hit" addictive drug.

"Scary Drug of the Year": Cocaine

Cocaine's potential for a "one-hit" addiction is a myth dating back to the era when it was, as Akers (1992) calls it, the "Scary Drug of the Year" (pp. 35–36). This simply means that certain drugs, even if the drugs have been around for a long time, suddenly take on new and different use patterns (real or contrived) and acquire an almost faddish status in society (Akers, 1992) through intense focus by the media and, often, legislative bodies.

During the late 1980s (and still today in some circles), people believed that cocaine was the "most addicting substance known to man" (*Reader's Digest*, 1987, p. 32). Horror stories circulated claiming, among other things, that people became addicted when they used it the first time. Earlier, we demonstrated just how untrue that is. At different times, heroin, marijuana, LSD, crack cocaine, and, more recently, "ice" (smokeable form of methamphetamine) and ecstasy (designer drug) have reached this status in American society.

From my discussion here, do not conclude that I believe substance use to be safe, for that is not the case. Without question, substance use can be harmful to individuals, families, and communities. We must bring perspective to the subject, however, and understand the scope of the problem in real terms to avoid becoming part of the system that promulgates false and misleading information to clients or the public. Remember, too, that the small percentages of people who become dependent on various drugs (2.7 percent of cocaine users become abusers, for example) represent literally millions of individuals, each with families and peer groups who are undoubtedly affected by their substance abuse. In the forthcoming discussion, it will become clear just how prevalent substance abuse problems and chemical dependency are among those who comprise our caseloads, regardless of field of practice.

Substance Abuse and Psychiatric Disorders

Psychiatric disorders and substance abuse problems often occur simultaneously, although one or the other is often overlooked depending on the agency or specialty of the practitioner (Evans & Sullivan, 2001). Recent research suggests there are large numbers of individuals with a dual diagnosis in the general population and on professional caseloads. According to the Epidemiologic Catchment Area Study (Regier et al., 1990), of those people in the general population with a mental disorder, 29 percent also have substance abuse problems at some time in their lives. When researchers screened for people with alcohol problems, 37 percent also had a mental disorder. People who abuse or are dependent on drugs other than alcohol or tobacco are seven times more likely to have an alcohol disorder, and 53 percent had a co-occurring mental disorder (Brady & Lydiard, 1992).

When looking exclusively at client populations, the number of co-occurring disorders increases dramatically. Data suggest that a staggering 78 percent of all people in treatment for a substance abuse problem also have a co-occurring mental disorder, the most prevalent of which is depression (Denning, 2000). These figures should not be surprising. Often, the very effects of drugs mimic or reverse the effects of mental disorders. For example, people suffering from untreated major depression are more likely to use stimulant drugs (such as cocaine) to overcome their illness, while people with anxiety disorders may use depressant drugs (such as alcohol) for the same reason (Grinspoon, 1993).

Women who drink excessively are more likely than men to suffer from increased levels of shame and guilt, interpersonal problems, and financial difficulty (Hughes, 1990; Leibenluft, 1994). Moreover, women who are substance abusers tend to have low self-esteem, feelings of stigmatization, sexual abuse victimization, lack of social support (Morris & Bihan, 1991), relationship issues, inadequate coping skills, and vocational and legal needs (Reed, 1987). Additionally, substance abuse among women often coincides with eating disorders (van Wormer, 1995). Studies of women hospitalized for substance abuse disorders demonstrate a significant relationship between substance abuse and long-term diagnoses of bulimia and/or anorexia (Hughes, 1990).

It is clear from the research in this area that psychiatric disorders are prevalent in the substance abusing population (Ries & Consensus Panel Chair, 1994). However, one cannot tell from this research whether the psychiatric disorders are substance-induced or exist independently of the substance abuse. Therefore, social workers in a variety of systems such as psychiatric hospitals, case management services, adult foster care, private practice, parole, probation, or jail/prison settings, or youth mental health treatment must understand the high rate of co-occurring disorders. In fact, social workers in any field of practice where clients may be experiencing some form of mental health disruption must be ready, willing, and able to "ask" about substance abuse and then—if necessary—know how to "act" on this information in a professional manner.

Gender Considerations

Generally, men are more likely than women to be diagnosed with a substance abuse problem (Peele, Brodsky, & Arnold, 1992; SAMHSA, 1998; Community Epidemiology Work Group, 1998). Despite the widespread agreement of every survey of drug use on this point, however, some believe the gender gap is closing rapidly (*American Journal of Public Health*, 1998), while others believe that lower diagnosis rates for women result from systemic biases leading to misdiagnosis (i.e., with depression).

Women with substance abuse problems differ from male substance abusers in many ways. For example, women experience a more virulent physiological and psychological dependence (Blume, 1986; Evans & Sullivan, 2001). According to the National Institute on Alcohol Abuse and Alcoholism [NIAAA] (1990), women tend to have a shorter onset of drinking-related problems, to be older at the point of assessment, to experience a higher rate of physiological impairment at an earlier point in their drinking careers, to experience more significant negative consequences in a shorter time period, and to become intoxicated more quickly on less alcohol because of lower body water content, hormone fluctuations, and reduced enzymes used to metabolize alcohol. Moreover, women have a 50 to 100 times higher mortality rate from alcohol and drug abuse. The decrease in life expectancy for the average alcohol-dependent woman is 15 years (Blume, 1986).

Interestingly, until the 1970s, women were not included in research samples on substance abuse and addiction (Blume, 1992; Brown & Alterman, 1992; Westermeyer, 1992). Furthermore, society's sex-role stereotyping and gender socialization of women contribute to denial and ignorance surrounding women's problems with substance abuse disorders (Abbott, 1994; Blume, 1992). Even today, much of American society frowns on substance abuse in women more than in men. For example, the widespread media coverage given to fetal alcohol syndrome (FAS) has created an increased level of stigmatization for mothers with alcohol problems (van Wormer, 1995), although little attention is given to the potential role alcoholic fathers play in FAS development because of damaged sperm or testicular atrophy (Ettore, 1992).

Many people blame the helping professions (particularly psychiatry) for marginalizing women in substance abuse because the professions tend to be male-dominated and patriarchal in the use of *DSM*. That is, some scholars believe women and men receive different diagnoses for similar behavior based on sexist criteria and assumptions by those empowered to make life-changing decisions. According to Smith (1990),

> There are…"female and male disorders." This means simply that women predominate markedly over men in some types of psychiatric diagnosis (notably in affective psychoses and to a lesser extent in paranoid states) whereas men predominate (very markedly) in the diagnostic categories of alcoholism (and) drug dependence (p. 115).

According to Smith, this bias oppresses women, keeping them subservient to men in the social world. Following this line of thinking, psychiatrists and social workers diagnose men with the more socially acceptable (masculine) condition of substance abuse, whereas mostly male doctors subjugate women to lifelong dependence on the mental health system by attributing their condition to mental illness. A substance abuse diagnosis is acceptable and temporary, while mental illness is perceived as a more negative and lifelong problem.

CASE EXAMPLE   Fewer Girls Referred for Treatment

When I was a program director, my staff noticed that we received few referrals of adolescent girls for treatment from local sources. Through an informal investigation, we demonstrated that more than 80 percent of females admitted to a local juvenile court received treatment through community mental health programs, while we (in substance abuse) treated the males. Interviews with probation officers confirmed that the females used drugs, but the probation officers believed that they needed help with depression and childhood abuse more than substance abuse. In fact, this perception may have been based on gender bias rather than true need.

Gender-biased treatment, according to van Wormer (1995), can be traced to public myths about women and substance abuse, including many that are conflicting. For example,

> We hear both that alcoholism is not hereditary for the female *and* that it is inherited mother to daughter; that the female alcoholic works outside the home *and* tends to be hidden in the closet; that there are as many female alcoholics as there are male *and* that there are fewer female than male alcoholics. Responsibility for fetal alcohol syndrome is placed solely with the mother (van Wormer, 1995, p. 165).

It is important to remember that simply because men appear more likely to have substance abuse problems than women, this should not preclude you from looking closely for substance abuse problems among women. To ensure that you do not impose a patriarchal perspective onto your clients, get into the habit of self-critical reflection about the extent to which gender bias and stereotypical gender-based expectations affect your life. This is another excellent topic for your evolving substance abuse journal. How would your parents view a daughter with a substance abuse problem? How would they regard a son in the same situation?

Substance Use During Pregnancy

You must be especially vigilant to inquire about substance use among women who are pregnant or could become pregnant, especially if you are working in a child welfare setting. Of the more than four million women who give birth each year in the United States, some 760,000 (19 percent) drank alcohol, 500,000 (12.5 percent) used illicit drugs, and nearly 21 percent smoked cigarettes during pregnancy (National Center on Addiction and Substance Abuse, 1996).

When a mother smokes, drinks, or uses drugs during pregnancy, medical costs skyrocket. According to the U.S. General Accounting Office (1990), hospital charges for drug-exposed infants are up to four times greater than charges for drug-free infants. According to veteran child welfare workers, maternal substance abuse and dependency play significant roles in child abuse, neglect, and out-of-home placements (Teichart, 1996).

This issue becomes even more serious and difficult when we realize that by the time a woman knows she is pregnant, the damage caused by substance use may already have taken place. In the period of time between conception and confirmation of pregnancy, a woman who uses substances—including nicotine and caffeine—may have already caused significant harm to her developing fetus. Therefore, it is essential to focus on prevention and education in an effort to help women of childbearing age avoid drugs in case they become pregnant.

Age and Risk of Substance Abuse

Age is a determining factor in the incidence of substance abuse problems. People between 25 and 44 years old comprise the largest group with alcohol and other drug problems (Denning, 2000). However, it is important to note a couple of interesting points. First, early onset of drug use is a good statistical predictor of later substance abuse potential. For example, according to Anthony, Warner, and Kessler (1997), youths who use cocaine between the ages of 15 and 24 are nearly twice as likely to become chemically dependent as people who use cocaine for the first time between 25 and 44. Second, despite the common belief that there are millions of untreated chemically dependent adolescents, experience does not bear this out. While early onset of drug use (among a host of other variables) is a predictor of later chemical dependency, most adolescents—even those in substance abuse treatment—do not meet the diagnostic guidelines for chemical dependency (Peele, Brodsky, & Arnold, 1992). Over the course of 20 years of working in adolescent substance abuse, I rarely met a client (in either outpatient or residential treatment) who met the criteria for chemical dependency. This was true despite the fact that adolescents are the "largest single age group of people undergoing hospital treatment today for chemical dependency" (Peele, Brodsky, & Arnold, 1992, p. 34).

Keep in mind that even though most adolescents do not meet *DSM* criteria for chemical dependency, they may still require social work services for problems involving substance abuse. Persons abusing or dependent on drugs of any kind find themselves involved in a multi-faceted problem that affects and is caused by multiple issues in individual and family life (Denning, 2000; Anthony, Warner, & Kessler, 1997). As such, individuals or families—even if they do not meet the *DSM* criteria for chemical dependency—can benefit from well-planned and competently implemented social work services that meet the client's level of need with the appropriate intensity. We discuss the treatment needs of adolescent clients in Chapter 11.

Human Diversity

The category of human diversity may encompass factors such as race, ethnicity, culture, sexual orientation, gender, physical and mental ability, to name a few. In this section, our focus is primarily on race, ethnicity, and culture. Pertaining to this and other discussions in this text, race and ethnicity do not mean the same thing, despite their interchangeable usage in everyday language. Ethnicity refers to a group descending from a particular region or country in the world, regardless of race, while race refers to groups whose affiliation is determined by skin color and other physical features. Culture is partly determined by a combination of both aspects. See Chapter 8 for a working definition of culture in substance abuse assessment and treatment.

Contrary to popular myth, African Americans are less likely to use drugs than European Americans (SAMHSA, 1998). However, the research does not agree on the level of abuse and dependency found among African Americans. Some researchers report less abuse and dependency among this group (Anthony, Warner, & Kessler, 1997) while others report more (Peele, 1998; Brunswick, Messeri, & Titus, 1992). We discuss some of the reasons for the difference in the section on social class.

People of Latino descent report levels of use and dependency similar to those among European Americans for all drugs except tobacco. As a group, Latinos appear to become dependent on tobacco at lower levels. Native American people report more alcohol dependence than any other group, with a lifetime prevalence of anywhere from 25 to 60 percent (Westermeyer, 1996). Again, the discussion about social class later in this chapter may shed light on this interesting finding.

People in different ethnic groups vary tremendously in their likelihood of developing a substance abuse problem. Most research finds that Irish and Native Americans have very high alcohol abuse rates, and that Slavs, the English, and other American Protestants are at high risk for developing alcohol problems (Vaillant, 1983). Italians, Jews, and Greeks (and those from other Mediterranean cultures), along with the Chinese, have "exceedingly low rates of alcoholism" (Peele, Brodsky, & Arnold, 1992, p. 51). In my work in Eastern and Central Europe and China, I found evidence to support Peele's findings. In countries such as Armenia, Albania, and China, the rates of substance abuse (alcohol and other drugs) appear to be quite low, while in Russia and Belarus, the opposite appears true (Johnson, 2000).

Social Class (Education, Employment, Income)

Education, employment, and annual income play important roles in determining the likelihood of substance abuse and chemical dependency. People who are unemployed, who have lower educational levels, and who earn less than $20,000 per year are significantly more likely to become chemically dependent (Anthony, Warner, & Kessler, 1997). Peele (1998) states that chemical dependency strikes the poor more than the rich, with especially high levels of dependency in urban centers populated by people of color. Moreover, despite statistics showing that fewer African Americans use drugs in the general population, as a group they have higher incidences of chemical dependency, primarily related to social class and life opportunities limited by a discriminatory and racist social system (West, 1999). According to Peele, Brodsky, and Arnold (1992),

> Addiction thrives most in barren, frightening environments, some of which seem uncontrollable (like war zones) and even permanent (like urban ghettos)... all individuals are most susceptible to addiction when their lives place them in such valleys (p. 192).

This observation brings up an interesting issue. If the results just reported are true, then the notion that chemical dependency is an "equal opportunity affliction" (Hanson & Venturelli, 1998, p. 10) is questionable at best. There is a widespread notion that nobody is immune from chemical dependency, and this is mostly true. Chemical dependency does affect people in all segments of society. However, the level of risk is different for people who live in different circumstances and/or belong to different demographic groups. Moreover, not only is the level of risk higher for some, but the opportunities to receive competent, quality substance abuse services are more limited for people who live in lower socio-economic situations. While some of the differences may relate to race and ethnicity, class considerations play a significant role in increasing the risk for chemical dependency and the opportunity to receive competent, professional treatment services (Sklar, 1995; Peele, 1998).

It is true that general use statistics report that people of all races, classes, and locales use drugs, but this has little to do with which groups are most at risk for substance-related problems. While drugs may be "... as seductive to the poor as they are the wealthy, to the highly educated and the school dropout, and to the young and the old" (Hanson & Venturelli, 1998, pp. 10–11), it appears that people with the greatest class struggles develop substance-related problems most often.

Critical Thinking Exercise

Related to the discussion about the effects of social class on chemical dependency, let's take a moment to engage in a critical thinking exercise.

Many people believe that substance abuse problems strike everyone equally, regardless of personal background or circumstances. Moreover,

---

Critical Thinking Exercise *continued*

there are just enough high-profile rich people on the "recovery" circuit to make this statement believable. Nevertheless, we have statistics that say otherwise. So, before we change our minds about this issue, what are the possibilities?

1. *The statistics reported above are true*. The poor, undereducated, and urban dwellers are more susceptible to chemical dependency.

2. *The statistics are misleading*. Perhaps we know about these groups only because they are the ones most highly represented on treatment caseloads. According to this line of thinking, people who have adequate incomes and educational attainment do not end up in publicly funded treatment programs and are thus left out of the studies.

3. *The belief that everyone is a potential addict is ideological propaganda put forth by government and anti-drug forces as a scare-tactic prevention method*. If everyone believes they are at risk of dependency, then fewer will use drugs (according to this line of thinking). Indeed, the United States has a long history of attempting to scare people away

from behavior that is considered harmful (Musto, 1999).

4. *There is a political and social reason for wanting us to believe that only the poor, undereducated, and urban dwellers are susceptible to chemical dependency*. In much of the public's mind, these three characteristics apply to people of color. As such, "proving" that these groups are the most chemically dependent serves to further separate "us" from "them." The process of "Othering" shows up throughout this country's history as a primary prevention method (Musto, 1999).

These are only four possibilities. Now, some of my readers may think that I have been watching too much television, because the examples (primarily numbers 3 and 4) may seem outlandish. However, exploring a range of possibilities is part of the process of critically thinking and analyzing any particular subject. Take some time now and discuss these issues fully, listening to the diverse viewpoints in your class or workplace. Read literature that agrees and disagrees with each perspective. Can you think of additional possibilities? What are your conclusions?

This is certainly not our last word on human diversity and populations-at-risk in relation to substance abuse practice. Throughout this book, we discuss the impact of issues such as race, culture, gender, age, class, and sexual orientation on substance abuse assessment and treatment. One operating premise of this book, consistent with professional social work values and ethics, is the concept that assessment and treatment are greatly affected by an individual's background and worldview (Kirst-Ashman & Hull, 1999; Davis & Proctor, 1989). As such, this brief statistical overview is only an introduction to an important, understudied, and under-appreciated aspect of the substance abuse field.

FIELDS OF PRACTICE

As I said earlier, this book is intended for social workers, some of whom have no intention of specializing in substance abuse practice. Regardless of whether or not you choose to specialize in substance abuse practice, you will be seeing clients with substance abuse issues nearly every day of your professional career (Gray, 1995; Raskin & Daley, 1991).

The following discussion looks briefly at different fields of practice and offers case examples in which substance abuse coexisted with other issues. For review, Kamerman (1998) states that a field of practice consists of

> the context for practice that is shaped and developed in response to the settings in which social workers practice, the social problems in which social workers intervene, and the client populations whom social workers help (p. 297).

Looking at this definition, fields of practice can involve the setting in which you work (such as government and nongovernmental agencies, private or public social service agencies, hospitals, or industrial sites), what issues you routinely see as a specialty (domestic violence, mental health, medical social work, homelessness, poverty, child abuse, and so on), or the people you normally serve in the agency (children, adolescents, adults, women, refugees, or members of some other group). According to Raskin and Daley (1991):

> The addicted person may seek help in a medical setting, a crisis clinic, a mental health agency, a family service agency, or from a private practitioner. In the medical setting, the presenting problem may be pancreatitis, liver disease, traumatic injury, or broken bones. In the mental health setting, the person may present depression, suicidal feelings, self-destructive behavior, anxiety, or psychotic symptoms. Each of these problems may be the result of alcoholism or drug addiction (p. 25).

It should be clear that wherever you practice, whether it be at a particular setting, with a particular problem, a particular population, or a combination of all three (most common), you will have a significant number of clients who may need a planned and organized course of substance abuse treatment. Here are a few case examples to demonstrate the point.

Gerontology

I was seeing a family of four adult sisters. Their presenting problem was to decide what to do with their 72-year-old mother. The mother had gradually become unable to care for herself. She was showing symptoms of Alzheimer's Disease. Two sisters wanted to put her in a nursing home, while the other two wanted her to continue living at home with family support.

One day during a particularly intense session in which the sisters were discussing mother's deteriorating condition, I overheard one sister casually mention to another that she should not forget to take mom her gallon of wine later that day. Upon further questioning, the sisters revealed (without any resistance, I might add) that every two days Mom needed her gallon of wine or she would wander off by herself toward the store trying to buy her own. This triggered their taking Mom to a doctor to look for Alzheimer's Disease. Later, the sisters stated that mom had "always liked her wine" and they had been providing it for her for "many years." I asked if their mother's doctors knew about her wine consumption. The sisters asked why that would be of concern to the doctor, because Mom had Alzheimer's Disease, after all. As such, I received permission to call the mother's doctor to suggest they do a substance abuse assessment, which they did. Chronic alcohol dependence often mimics the signs and symptoms of Alzheimer's Disease.

Medical Social Work

In a local emergency room, a man in his 40s arrived seeking treatment for a head injury after falling from a ladder at his home. During his medical treatment, one of our social work graduate students decided to look closely at his medical history. She discovered that this was the man's fifth accident requiring emergency room treatment in 18 months.

As the man waited for his X-rays, the student decided to collect a biopsychosocial history, including a substance use history. As part of the interview, she discovered that the man had a long history of heavy drinking and marijuana use. She consulted with her supervisor, who referred the man and his family to a local substance abuse facility for a substance abuse assessment. As it turned out, the man was not "accident-prone" but chemically dependent.

Mental Health

A local social worker called about a particularly difficult case at a local outpatient mental health facility. The client, a woman in her late 20s, exhibited signs of schizophrenia, complete with hallucinations, delusions, paranoid thoughts, and bizarre behaviors in public. The psychiatrist in charge of the case had diagnosed her one year earlier as suffering from schizophrenia and placed her on a series of medications to relieve her symptoms. Unfortunately, the medication did not work.

I asked the social worker about weight loss and if there was any pattern to her bizarre behavior. Indeed, the woman had lost significant weight and her symptoms appeared to "come and go." I recommended that she be assessed for stimulant abuse, especially cocaine, since the chronic effects of cocaine mimic schizophrenia. The social worker convinced the psychiatrist (and it took some convincing, I was told) to refer her for a substance abuse assessment. It turned out that the woman was periodically using powder cocaine and smoking crack cocaine on a daily basis. What appeared to be signs of schizophrenia were indeed cocaine-induced. The mental health agency referred the woman to a long-term residential substance abuse treatment program for appropriate help.

Family Practice

A single father requested family treatment because his daughter and son, both adolescents, were causing significant problems. The daughter, at 15 years old, was "dating" a 20-year-old man, while the son was experiencing significant health problems. While interviewing the family, we learned that the family had considerable issues pertaining specifically to substance abuse. The adolescent son's health problems were directly related to his drug use, and the father had "overcome" alcoholism 14 years earlier. After using circular questioning (see Chapter 8) in a family interview, we learned that the daughter's problems corresponded almost exactly with the date when her father had begun drinking again. The family was both baffled and resistant to the notion that substance use and abuse were an integral part of their current difficulties.

Community Practice

I was invited by a local neighborhood association to do a community assessment of a particular neighborhood in the central city. After interviewing community leaders, local residents, the police, and representatives from local associations and institutions, conducting a door-to-door survey of neighborhood strengths and issues, and surveying public records, we learned that this particular neighborhood had significant problems related to substance use and abuse. Not only were neighbors concerned about the inordinate number of drug houses in the area, but they also noted that there were a significant number of households in the area with substance abusing or chemically dependent members.

DO YOU KNOW WHAT
CHEMICAL DEPENDENCY FEELS LIKE?

At some point, most of you have fallen in love or become infatuated with another person. Remember what that was (or is) like? Waiting for telephone calls that never come, picking up the phone to see if the dial tone is working, or ruminating for hours over whether the person actually loves you back. Remember, if you will, staring at his or her picture for hours, trying to capture a slight whiff of cologne or perfume on your clothes, scribbling her or his name on your notebooks, telephone bills, or your latest term paper. Remember driving by his or her house hoping to see her or him, but trying not to be seen in the process? Remember sitting in class in a daze, daydreaming about your new love? You ignored your grades, friends, family, and restricted your schedule in order to free up every moment so you could be with, or be available on a minute's notice to, the "love of your life."

Also, remember your reaction when someone, such as a friend or parent, tried to suggest that you were obsessed with this new person and perhaps you should see him or her less often? I am sure your reaction to these suggestions was not one of the proudest, most in-control emotional moments in your lifetime. It never is, when someone—who you are convinced does not understand you—accuses you of being obsessed with another. What was your reaction when this happened? Did you become angry, even to the point of denying that you were obsessed with the person? At some point, deep in your mind, you probably knew that the relationship—or at least your obsession with it—was bad for you. However, you could not act. The thought of breaking up with the object of your love seemed impossible. How could you live without her or him? You felt compelled to stay with it, rationalizing all the reasons (whether they made sense or not) why you were doing the right thing.

If any of this sounds familiar, then you have a clue about what chemical dependency feels like. You have experienced, first-hand, something akin to chemical dependency. Fortunately, for most of you, the obsession waned and the relationship became part of a healthy, balanced life. However, some people remain obsessed or move from obsessive relationship to obsessive relationship until the pattern becomes personally destructive. Remember how you felt, how crazy and out-of-control the sensation and your life was? Now, imagine this condition lasting for years! This is similar to the chemical dependency experience. If you have experienced the thoughts and feelings of an obsessive relationship—even for one day in your life—then you have an experiential "window" into the life of a chemically dependent person, something to draw upon during your next interview with a chemically dependent client.

SUMMARY

Substance use, abuse, and chemical dependency are pervasive in the United States and across the globe. Many people have either used or abused substances or been in close relationship with someone who has done so. Social workers need to examine their personal beliefs, values, attitudes, and stereotypes about substance use, abuse, and chemical dependency. This is especially true when considering the fate of clients or potential clients in social work practice.

In this chapter, we began exploring the subject from several viewpoints. You should review the various definitions related to the substance abuse field and the various models and theories used to explain addiction. This is important because personal values, beliefs, and attitudes often lead to practice models that, in turn, guide the assessment and treatment process. While there is little agreement on models, theories, definitions, and methods, there is agreement that much of the substance abuse field is controversial and generates much discussion and consternation among the various schools of thought.

What is easy to agree upon is the need for social workers—especially those not specializing in substance abuse treatment—to become competent at recognizing the potential for substance abuse problems and at engaging clients around the issues in order to complete a thorough and professional substance abuse assessment. Putting forth the effort to acquire these skills will help ensure that your clients receive the type, intensity, and form of social work services they need.

2

Pharmacology

This chapter provides an overview of the drugs (including alcohol) you will most often encounter in substance abuse practice. Before we begin, please understand that reading one chapter about drug effects will not provide you with a thorough understanding of this topic. Acquiring in-depth knowledge of this complicated, complex, and rapidly changing subject requires considerable time and effort. Other texts provide a more detailed look at pharmacology and brain function (Ray & Ksir, 1993; Fishbein & Pease, 1996; Grilly, 1994; Inciardi & McElrath, 1995; Hanson & Venturelli, 1998; Levinthal, 1999; Maisto, Galizio, & Connors, 1995). My purpose here is to offer practical information that you can apply in your everyday substance abuse practice, helping you to properly assess a client's substance abuse problem, to understand the degree of health and safety risks involved, and to know what your clients are likely to experience when (and if) they abstain.

A secondary goal is to dispel commonly held myths about drugs, drug effects, and drug use. For example, taking aspirin before going to bed after a night of heavy drinking will not prevent a hangover. Nor, for that matter, will ingesting bread or any other starchy food. In fact, it is unwise to eat before sleeping after a night of heavy drinking, because of the threat of asphyxiation. After a drinking binge, it is safer to sleep on an otherwise empty stomach. After reading this chapter, not only will you be prepared to assess and treat clients with substance abuse problems, you will also be more informed about drugs in general.

We begin by exploring *pharmacology*, or the effects of various drugs on the human body. You will be introduced to several key concepts to help you understand drugs and perhaps gain a better idea of why drugs are so attractive. Later, we will look at specific drugs, focusing on their effects (normal and acute), potential withdrawal symptoms, and the dangers posed by each.

PHARMACOLOGY (DRUG EFFECTS)

Since 95 percent of social workers will not specialize in substance abuse practice (van Wormer, 1995), most of the readers of this book will not need to be experts in pharmacology. Therefore, the primary reason for the following discussion is fundamental: to help you understand *how to save someone's life!* In any field of social work practice, it is essential to possess a working knowledge about the

effects of specific drugs on the human body, what overdose and physical withdrawal look like, when drug mixing can be fatal, and when it is mandatory to get
your client emergency medical services. To begin, here are six truths to counter
some of the prevailing misinformation about drugs.

1. *Drugs are harmless.* Contrary to what many people believe, neither alcohol
   nor illicit drugs are the enemy. Alone, a drug has no inherent value (Szasz,
   1996, 1997). Drugs (including alcohol) are not predatory substances that
   magically or aggressively attack the human body from without. People must
   ingest drugs for the action to begin. Until people actually put drugs into
   their bodies, drugs hurt nobody.

2. *Drugs have a physiological and neurological effect on human beings.* This is the reason people use drugs for recreation, abuse, or medical treatment. The physiological and neurological changes that drugs produce—getting high, killing
   pain, easing anxiety, and so on—are the reason these chemicals exist. If drugs
   did not have these effects, people would find another way to satisfy their desire to change how they think, feel, and act, either for fun or for survival.

3. *Before a person will experience a drug's effect, the drug must get to the brain.* People
   feel the effects of a drug—any drug—only when it reaches the brain. The
   faster a drug gets to the brain, the more intense is its effect. To accomplish
   this, users (and doctors) manipulate the way they take (or administer) drugs.

4. *Generally, drugs in the same category act in similar ways.* That is, depressant drugs
   depress and stimulants stimulate, and so on. How a person reacts to a drug—
   or combination of drugs—is unique, within the bounds of the drug's primary action. In addition to the drug's pharmacological properties, people
   experience a drug based on genetic and biological factors, psychological
   characteristics, and social influences (Peele, 1998).

5. *It is difficult to predict exactly how a particular drug—or combination of drugs—will
   react in the same person from one episode of use to another.* Drug effects are unpredictable. This phenomenon is especially problematic when experienced users
   introduce someone to a drug for the first time. The "normal" dose for an
   experienced user can kill a first-time user.

6. *Mixing drugs can be deadly.* You will rarely meet a client with a substance
   abuse problem who uses only one drug at a time. Minimally, most people
   mix alcohol with other drugs. The practice of mixing alcohol with other
   drugs, especially legally prescribed medications, can cause overdose and
   death. Predicting the effects of a combination of drugs is even more difficult
   than predicting the effects of a single drug.

DRUG VARIABILITY

In relation to drug use, *variability* means that all drugs affect all people differently
(Levinthal, 1999). How people react to drugs is unpredictable, even in controlled
conditions. In the "uncontrolled" environment of parties or the streets, variability increases dramatically. Inability to determine the exact dose, level of purity, or

the strength of the drug—often combined with poor health and nutrition—puts the drug user at risk for accidental overdose. All things being equal (which they never are), a person will experience the same drug differently each time he or she uses it.

Perhaps you have experienced this phenomenon. On a Friday night, you drink three cans of beer and feel excited, confident, and happy. The next Friday, you drink five cans of beer in a shorter time and do not experience the same pleasurable effects that three cans caused only a week earlier. This is what is meant by drug variability. Now, the difference did not occur because on the second night the alcohol somehow became dormant in your system. In fact, you were actually more intoxicated the second night than the first, simply because you ingested one additional ounce of alcohol (there is half of one fluid ounce of alcohol in a single 12-ounce can of non-light beer). The fact that your mood did not improve does not mean that your motor skills and impulse control were unaffected. You simply did not *feel* the alcohol the same way. As we explain later, there is always a difference between what the user perceives (effect) and his or her actual level of intoxication. Users' perceptions are irrelevant to their actual level of intoxication.

What causes drug variability? There are many factors involved in how drugs (including alcohol) affect users, only one of which is the drug itself. These factors are discussed below.

Individual Factors

Several individual factors determine how drugs affect users. Physiologically, the amount of sleep people get, what they eat, and how healthy they are on a particular day influence how they experience a drug *on that particular day*. The more a person eats before using, the slower the effect of that drug, especially if it is taken orally (swallowed). How rested a person is also determines drug effects. Generally, the more tired people are, the more a drug will affect them. If users do not feel well, drugs will have stronger effects that day. Physical size also determines variability. Generally, heavier people need larger doses of a particular drug to reach a desired effect.

Issues such as age, gender, culture, and the user's expectations about the drug play a role in its effect. People's expectations and beliefs about drugs—their mental set (Peele, 1998)—strongly influence drug reactions. Research demonstrates that psychological factors (along with environmental/situational factors discussed later) can actually reverse specific pharmacological properties of a drug (Peele, 1998; Zinberg, 1972, 1974, 1984; Lennard et al., 1971; Lasagna, von Felsinger, & Beecher, 1954). For example, in one experiment, male subjects became aggressive and sexually aroused when they believed they were drinking liquor (placebo effect), but not when they actually drank liquor in a disguised form (Marlatt & Rohsenow, 1980; Wilson, 1981). Similarly, alcohol-dependent individuals lost control of their drinking when they believed they were drinking alcohol, but not when they actually ingested alcohol in a disguised form (Engle & Williams, 1972; Marlatt, Demming, & Reid, 1973). Marlatt (1982) identified several cognitive and emotional factors (expectations, beliefs, and feelings) as the major determinants of relapse during chemical dependency treatment.

Gender also plays a significant role in pharmacology. Even if a male and female are the same weight, drugs are metabolized differently. Females have, on average, a higher proportion of fat-to-muscle and a lower proportion of water in their bodies than males. Primarily because of lower water content, a woman drinking the same amount of alcohol as a man will become more intoxicated. Because women tend to have lower levels of the particular enzymes needed to metabolize alcohol in the liver, they will often have higher blood alcohol levels (BAL), indicating a higher level of intoxication (Frezza et al., 1990).

Environmental/Situational Factors

Drug use is often related to social group influences (Peele, 1998). Jessor and Jessor (1977) and Kandel (1978) identified the instrumental role of peer pressure on the initiation and continuation of drug use among adolescents. Moreover, the immediate social group strongly influences the style of drinking (light, moderate, or excessive). According to Falk (1981, 1983; Falk, Dews, & Schuster, 1983) a person's environment influences drug-taking behavior more than the reinforcing properties of the drug itself. The social environment also influences the way people react to drugs (Johanson & Uhlenhuth, 1981). Much of the research in this area involved returning Vietnam veterans who had become addicted to heroin during the war. The results were astounding. Researchers found that the majority of servicemen and women addicted to heroin in Vietnam did not become re-addicted to heroin after returning home (Robins, Davis, & Goodwin, 1974; Robins, Helzer, Hesselbrock, & Wish, 1975, 1980). According to the researchers, these results proved the influence of the social environment on drug use and drug effects. It should be noted that the researchers did not explore the extent to which the study subjects became addicted to drugs other than heroin. Yet nearly everyone who has drunk alcohol or experimented with a drug can probably testify as to the power of the social environment on their experience (i.e., going to a dance club versus sitting alone on the couch watching television).

Topic for Your Journal: Impact of Your Social Environment

In your substance abuse journal, reflect on a time (or times) when your use of alcohol or other drugs (legal or not) was affected by your social environment or personal expectations about the drug's effects. For example, did it feel different to drink alcohol when you were with friends at a dance club, as compared to drinking while you were sitting in your living room watching television? Can you remember a time when you drank more than normal but still did not feel intoxicated? In the context of the preceding discussion, speculate about the reasons for differing experiences with substance use.

Dose

The size of the dose (how much a person ingests) is a major determinant of how a drug affects the user. Higher doses generally produce more intense effects (Jung, 2001). The effects are small at low doses, gradually increase as the dose increases, and level off at even higher doses. This "leveling off" of a drug's effect is its maximum effect. Most drugs have a maximum effect; at some point, an increase in dose will not increase the effect of the drug (Ray & Ksir, 1993). For example, many people believe that taking three or more aspirin will relieve headaches faster than taking two aspirin tablets. This is untrue. After two aspirin, the individual's expectation about the power of the aspirin produces any extra effect he or she may feel. The same holds true for drugs that are abused, such as alcohol and cocaine. At some point as the dose increases, the user does not become more intoxicated but only closer to overdose.

Another important term in pharmacology that is often misunderstood is *potency* (Ray & Ksir, 1993). Potency simply refers to the size of the dose required to reach the "normal" effect of the drug. For example, LSD is the most potent drug because it takes only .004 milligrams (on average) for a person to reach "normal" effect. Alcohol, on the other hand, takes one or more ounces for the user to reach the normal level of effect. Therefore, while LSD is the most potent drug, other less potent drugs are more dangerous because of the properties and amounts that people consume. Therefore, potency has nothing to do with strength of effect, how fast it occurs, or how intoxicated the user becomes.

Drug Mixing

Drug mixing occurs when people use two or more drug(s) at the same time. Always look for evidence of drug mixing because the results are unpredictable and can be deadly. Many people mix drugs under the mistaken impression that it is safe to do so, since most of the time nothing bad happens. They overlook the fact that it takes only one bad experience to end a life.

When people mix drugs from the same or similar categories, the drugs can interact to produce stronger effects (for example, alcohol and muscle relaxants are both depressants). In these cases, the effect of the mix is synergistic rather than additive. That is, mixing two or more drugs from the same or similar classifications can multiply the effect of each to an unpredictable and serious level. In some synergistic combinations, the effects of one drug may double or triple the effects of another.

For example, under doctor's orders people sometimes use a central nervous system depressant drug to ease anxiety (i.e., Valium or Xanax). Alone, this is fine. However, trouble can begin when people mix alcohol with the prescription medication. Perhaps it is a glass or two of wine with dinner or a few drinks with friends after work. It all seems harmless enough, but combining prescription medication with even a small amount of alcohol can lead to serious intoxication. What makes the situation even more serious is that it is impossible to predict when, and if, drugs will interact synergistically. On some days, everything is fine; on other days, the person becomes highly intoxicated, passes out, or even lapses into a coma. The cumulative effects of the individual and social factors discussed earlier interact differently each day to determine how combinations of drugs will affect the user. During an assessment, become aware of possible drug mixing and the potential for problems as a result. Because of variability, even if an individual has mixed drugs for years with few side effects, the danger remains.

METHODS OF ADMINISTERING DRUGS

Also called routes of administration, there are several different ways to deliver drugs to the brain. In fact, nearly every drug, with the possible exception of alcohol, can be administered in more than one way. Remember, the goal of a substance user—whether recreational or under medical supervision—is to deliver drugs from outside the body into the bloodstream and to the brain in the most efficient way possible. Only when drugs reach the brain do they affect the user. Often, people's desire to experience intense and sudden drug effects influences the route of administration they choose.

The method of use (mainly for recreational users) can also be an important indicator about the depth and/or seriousness of a substance abuse problem. For example, few people inject drugs into their veins unless under doctor's orders. Hence, if your client uses needles to inject cocaine, this can be a reliable indicator that he or she has, or is about to develop, serious problems. During an interview, always ask how clients administer each drug they use. Injecting drugs does not necessarily mean that people have problems, but it should trigger the need to inquire more seriously into their drug history and the reasons for their chosen route of administration. In twenty years of practice experience, I have rarely met a "recreational" IV drug user, despite many client claims to the contrary.

There are four main methods for administering drugs. Not all methods are appropriate for all drugs. Below, we discuss the different methods of administration. The most commonly used routes of administration for each specific drug are discussed later under each drug classification.

Oral

Oral administration, or drinking/swallowing a drug, is the most common route of administration. It is also the slowest route to the brain. Before becoming active, drugs taken orally must be metabolized by several organs, including the stomach and intestines, and moved into the bloodstream before reaching the brain. As a result, several characteristics of the user have a greater influence on drug effects with this method than with other methods of administration. For example, drugs taken orally work more rapidly when the stomach is empty. If users want drugs to act rapidly, they take drugs before or instead of eating, to reduce dilution.

For example, if people drink alcoholic beverages on an empty stomach, they will begin feeling intoxicated rather quickly. Drinking water before or during drinking episodes also slows the effects. However, drinking carbonated beverages such as club soda before or during alcohol consumption speeds up the process. The air bubbles in carbonated beverages move the alcohol through the bloodstream and into the brain more quickly because the body handles it as if it is oxygen instead of food. This explains, at least in part, why champagne seems to "hit" people quicker than other alcoholic beverages.

Inhalation or Smoking

Next to drinking and swallowing, inhaling and/or smoking drugs is the most common route of administration. One reason it is so common is that inhalation is the fastest way to deliver drugs to the brain, even faster than injection (Ray & Ksir, 1993; Levinthal, 1999). When a drug is smoked or inhaled, it is processed immediately in the lungs, which contain surface blood vessels that are designed to quickly deliver oxygen throughout the body. Smoking and inhaling use the same delivery system as oxygen, making it an extremely efficient delivery system. Most drugs of abuse can be smoked (cocaine, heroin, or marijuana) or inhaled (common household chemicals, gasoline, or model glue). The drug that is most commonly used in this manner is nicotine.

Injection (IV)

By injecting drugs directly into the bloodstream through a vein (mainlining), users (and doctors) bypass the digestive system, speeding the drug's journey to the brain. Intravenous (IV) administration delivers the drug directly to the bloodstream. When drugs are injected, the effects are rapid and intense. Other methods of injection include intramuscular injections (into a large muscle) and subcutaneous (injected into the tissue just under the skin). However, by far the most common method of injection among substance abusers is directly into a vein.

IV drug use can lead to serious problems for users. Outside a doctor's office, needle hygiene and sterilization is lax. Therefore, people are exposed to infectious diseases such as HIV/AIDS and hepatitis because of reused dirty needles. The most common problems occur when veins become damaged or blocked from overuse or bacterial infection. Overused veins collapse and bacteria causes serious infection and abscesses. When this happens, people move to other veins. It is common to observe needle "tracks" on veins in the hands, legs, neck, feet, and groin areas. I have seen clients who were injecting drugs under their fingernails and toenails and into veins in the genitals. When they reach this stage of dependency, users are so desperate that any vein in any location is acceptable.

Learn to recognize the signs of IV use and do not be judgmental when you see them. One indicator is people's clothing. Clients who always wear long-sleeved shirts or turtlenecks, especially in warm weather, may be trying to hide needle tracks. When you notice this, inquire about it in a direct, open, and accepting manner.

Mucous Membranes

Another route of administration is saturation of mucous membranes, allowing a drug to dissolve into the bloodstream. Like inhalation and injection, the use of mucous membranes bypasses the digestive system. Most commonly known as "snorting," this route of administration is quicker than drinking/swallowing, but slower than either inhalation or injection. Users chop a drug into fine powder and quickly inhale it into the nose. Powder cocaine is commonly used this way; however, most drugs can be snorted. Any drug that can be crushed into powder can be snorted. Many people choose to snort heroin instead of injecting it. People also use the mucous membranes in the eye (LSD), genital areas, and the rectum via suppositories.

A client's chosen route of administration is important assessment information. Not only does it provide clues about the potential seriousness of the drug use, but also about medical issues that may require attention. For example, people who drink heavily often irritate the inside of the mouth, esophagus, and stomach lining. People who smoke or inhale drugs often develop lung infections, oral infections, or impaired breathing. IV drug users can develop a number of dangerous health problems, and those who regularly snort drugs can severely damage their nasal passages and sinuses.

DRUG TOLERANCE

People have developed drug *tolerance* when they need larger doses to produce an effect that was originally achieved with smaller doses (Fishbein & Pease, 1996). With regular use, people can gradually grow less responsive to a drug. Tolerance levels may vary greatly, depending on a drug's unique effects, dose, route of administration, and frequency of use (Ray & Ksir, 1993), along with the user's genetic makeup, gender, culture, and other physiological characteristics.

Physical Tolerance

Physical tolerance occurs when brain cells begin functioning "normally" in the presence of certain drugs (Royce, 1989). Under conditions of repeated or chronic use, the brain can become insensitive to a drug, even when high dose levels are present in the bloodstream and brain. That is, the brain begins functioning as if the presence of the drug is normal, thereby reducing the drug's effect on the user. In many instances, physical tolerance develops slowly. However, certain drugs can produce relatively quick and high tolerance levels (opiates), while other drugs produce only mild tolerance (marijuana) over a longer period. How rapidly tolerance develops is a function of a drug's half-life, or the time it takes the body to metabolize half of the active portion of a drug.

Psychological Tolerance

Drugs may also lead to psychological tolerance, although this issue is hotly debated in medical research circles (Levinthal, 1999). In terms of effect, psychological tolerance is similar to physical tolerance. That is, users require higher doses over time to achieve the same effects. The difference between the two types of tolerance is that psychological tolerance is not physical. Although users may feel as if they are experiencing physical withdrawal symptoms, these effects are psychological in nature. In many ways, psychological tolerance is more difficult to overcome. Depending on the drug, people often develop both physical and psychological tolerance, making it difficult to distinguish between the two.

Behavioral Tolerance

Behavioral tolerance occurs when people learn to act normally while under the influence of drugs (Ray & Ksir, 1993), learning to "walk with a limp," as it were. Nearly everybody knows people who drink heavily and do not appear drunk. These highly tolerant people look, talk, and act as if they are perfectly sober, despite having consumed large quantities of alcohol. While physical and psychological tolerance play a role in this process, the ability to act sober often indicates behavioral tolerance.

Even though these people appear sober, the opposite is true. They are often highly intoxicated people who have learned to act normally in controlled social environments. Behaviorally tolerant individuals learn which behaviors they can perform and where they can perform them. These people arrange their life so that their social movement is limited to routine, well-rehearsed actions and environments. Have you noticed that many alcohol and/or drug dependent people stay at home most of the time? If these people were suddenly placed in an environment where non-routine behaviors were necessary (such as a driving emergency), they would demonstrate their true level of impairment.

Cross-Tolerance

Cross-tolerance occurs when tolerance to one drug transfers to other drugs, diminishing the effect of the other drugs as well. This usually occurs between drugs in the same category (Levin, 1990). Growing insensitivity to one drug (i.e., alcohol) generalizes to other drugs in its classification (i.e., benzodiazepines such as Valium) reducing the effect of both drugs (Sexias, 1975). Tolerance developed to one drug in the CNS depressant classification (see below) means that users build up tolerance to other drugs in that classification. The same holds true for the opiates such as heroin or morphine.

DRUG CATEGORIES

There are several different methods for classifying drugs (Hanson & Venturelli, 1998; Jacobs & Fehr, 1987). In this discussion, similar pharmacological properties (drug effects) are used to classify the various drugs. For each category, I give several examples of the most common drugs in that category, street names, routes of administration, major and acute effects, signs of overdose, potential for tolerance, and withdrawal symptoms.

Central Nervous System (CNS) Depressants

CNS depressants are the most commonly used drugs. People have always used substances to induce sleep, relieve stress, and reduce anxiety. Alcohol is the most popular CNS depressant. Other drugs in this category are labeled "downers," sedatives, hypnotics, minor tranquilizers, and anti-anxiety medications. Unlike other drugs, CNS depressants that reach street level are rarely produced in illegal laboratories. Instead, legally prescribed medications are diverted to the "streets" for recreational use, or individuals abuse (or sell) prescription medications.

CNS depressants slow the central nervous system to induce relaxation, drowsiness, or sleep. Drugs in this category include alcohol; drugs prescribed for anxiety, sleep disturbance, and seizure control; and over-the-counter medications for sleep disturbance, colds, allergies, and coughs. When they are abused, depressants can be extremely dangerous. In 1990, more than 100,000 deaths were alcohol-related, making this the third leading cause of death in the United States (McGinnis & Foege, 1993). Alcohol, in combination with other depressants, accounted for nearly one-third of drug-abuse-related emergency room episodes in 1992 and 39 percent of deaths from drug overdose (SAMHSA, 1998).

Drugs in This Category Alcohol is the best-known CNS depressant because of its widespread use, legal status, public availability, and social acceptance in most cultures of the world. Many myths are circulated about what type of alcohol is safest (beer, wine, or liquor). Assuming there is a difference is the main myth. Alcohol is alcohol; the only difference between types is the amount of water and other non-alcoholic ingredients such as hops and grains added to make the beverage contain more liquid. Adding these extra ingredients does not reduce the amount of alcohol in a beverage; it simply dilutes the alcohol that is there. The amount of pure alcohol in one 12-ounce can of beer equals the amount of pure alcohol in a 4-ounce glass of wine. Both equal the amount of pure alcohol in one standard "shot" (1.5 ounces) of liquor.

What about the old adage that says "wine is fine, but liquor is quicker"? This is true, but only in relation to alcohol's effect. As stated above, water dilutes alcohol and slows its effects. The more water and other non-alcoholic ingredients are present in a beverage, the longer it takes alcohol to reach the brain. However, just because it takes longer to feel the effects does not mean there is less alcohol in the bloodstream. Whether people drink six shots of whiskey, six cans of beer, or six glasses of wine, their blood alcohol level will ultimately be the same, and the level of intoxication will be similar.

Barbiturates were often used in the early twentieth century to aid with sleep, seizures, and pain. In moderate amounts, these drugs produce intoxication similar to alcohol. Depending on the dose, frequency, and duration of use, these drugs cause a rapid development of physical tolerance. Additionally, the margin of safety between the normal and lethal dose is quite narrow. That is, it is easy for users with high tolerance to overdose on barbiturates. Although many people have taken barbiturates therapeutically without harm, the increasing number of fatalities associated with these drugs led pharmaceutical companies to develop alternative medications (benzodiazepines). Today, barbiturates account for only 20 percent of all prescriptions for depressant drugs in the United States (Drug Enforcement Administration, 1997).

The barbiturate category includes seconal (reds, red devils), nembutal (yellows, yellow jackets), tuinal (rainbows), amytal (blues, blue heaven), and phenobarbital. Specific drugs in this category end with "al," making barbiturates easy to identify. There are also nonbarbiturate drugs with similar effects, including Doriben (goofballs), Quaalude (ludes), Miltown, and Equinil.

As a so-called "safe" version of barbiturates, the **benzodiazepines** greatly reduced the number of prescriptions for barbiturates. Benzodiazepines now account for more than 30 percent of all prescriptions for controlled substances in the U.S. (Drug Enforcement Administration, 1997). When these drugs first appeared in the 1960s, experts considered them to have little abuse potential. However, use of benzodiazepines produces many of the same side effects as barbiturates. Although it is not as easy to commit suicide with these drugs, the potential for abuse is significant, and the actual abuse of these drugs is well documented (Drug Enforcement Administration, 1997). Popular drugs in the benzodiazepine family are Valium, Librium, Dalmane, Halcion, Xanax, Tranxene, Resitoril, and Ativan.

Recently, one drug in the benzodiazepine family has become infamous. Rohypnol (roofies) is also known as the "date rape" drug. Rohypnol is illegal in the United States but is widely prescribed in Europe as a sleep aid. When combined with alcohol, Rohypnol produces disinhibition and amnesia, making it easy for perpetrators to sexually assault their victims. Perpetrators slip Rohypnol into the drink of an unsuspecting victim and attack as soon as the drug takes effect.

Over-the-counter medications also may contain depressant drugs. For example, sleep aids such as Nytol and Sominex, many cold and allergy products, and cough medicines may contain scopolamine, antihistamines, or alcohol. Substance abuse clients put themselves in danger of relapse after drinking an over-the-counter cold medication that can contain as much as 20 percent alcohol. Several over-the-counter cold and flu medications do not contain alcohol. Take care to recommend these alternatives to clients instead of those containing alcohol.

Routes of Administration Obviously, people drink alcohol. Some over-the-counter medications are sold in the form of liquids. Barbiturates and benzodiazepines are pills, although some users convert pills into liquid for injection or powder for snorting.

Major Effects The effects of CNS depressants (and all drugs, for that matter) are related to the dose, method of administration, an individual's tolerance level, and several social factors including the setting, expectations of the user, and mindset of the user (Peele, 1998). At low doses, depressants produce relaxation and calmness, inducing muscle relaxation, disinhibition, and reduced anxiety. Judgment, motor coordination, and impulse control are impaired, and the reflexes are slowed, along with the pulse rate and blood pressure. At high doses, users demonstrate slurred speech and staggering, and eventually they fall asleep. Chronic effects of alcohol abuse include permanent loss of memory, gastritis, esophagitis, ulcers, pancreatitis, cirrhosis of the liver, high blood pressure, and weakened heart muscles. Damage is especially acute to a developing fetus, often resulting in fetal alcohol effect (FAE) or fetal alcohol syndrome (FAS).

Overdose Being drunk is considered a form of alcohol overdose. Other symptoms include staggering, slurred speech, extreme disinhibition, and in some people, blackouts (an inability to recall events that occurred while they were intoxicated). Generally, the human body naturally helps people avoid alcohol overdose by inducing vomiting or sleep. However, rapid ingestion of alcohol, particularly in people with low tolerance or little experience, can result in coma or death. When this outcome occurs, it usually happens when young people participate in drinking contests or binge drinking, defined as five or more drinks in a row in one drinking occasion (Levinthal, 1999). Rarely will you find experienced drinkers (or alcoholics) suffering from extreme alcohol overdose.

As these drugs depress the central nervous system, overdose is extremely likely and can be fatal. Typical symptoms include shallow respiration, clammy skin, dilated (wide) pupils, weak and rapid pulse rate, coma, or death. Since a fatal dose is only 10 to 15 times the effective dose, barbiturates are popular "suicide" drugs. This is why barbiturates are no longer widely prescribed. It is far more difficult to overdose on benzodiazepines, although it is possible. The probability of overdose increases if drugs from this category are mixed. As stated earlier, people often mix alcohol with a depressant drug prescribed by their doctor. It is common to have clients with more than one doctor prescribing the same or different depressant drugs for real or mythical illnesses or pains. Because alcohol use is so common, mixing it with other prescribed medication often goes unnoticed.

Tolerance Physical, psychological, behavioral, and cross-tolerance develop rapidly with all CNS depressants, explaining why the potential for overdose is so high. For example, Suzy, a heavy drinker, is anxious. To calm her nerves, her doctor prescribes Valium. However, because Suzy has developed a tolerance for alcohol, she also has a tolerance for Valium. Therefore, in the amounts prescribed, Valium has no effect on her anxiety. Not feeling the effects of Valium, Suzy takes three or four pills (instead of the prescribed one or two) and has a glass of wine. The synergistic effects of the two depressant drugs put Suzy in a coma in less than one hour.

Withdrawal Physical withdrawal from CNS depressants can be dangerous. Symptoms may range from anxiety, irritability, loss of appetite, tremors, insomnia, delirium, and seizures, to coma or death. Symptoms of the most severe form of alcohol withdrawal—called delirium tremens (DT's)—include fever, rapid heartbeat, and hallucinations. Because of the potential for serious medical consequences, the detoxification process must include medical supervision. Anyone under your care who is a chronic or high-dose user of CNS depressants must be discouraged from detoxifying without medical supervision.

Relapse is another issue to consider. Whether or not you are responsible for your client's treatment, clients often need support to avoid relapse because withdrawal symptoms are unpleasant. Because depressant drugs alleviate the unpleasant symptoms of withdrawal, relapse (often with very high doses) is highly likely during this period. We discuss strategies for relapse prevention in Chapter 10.

CNS Stimulants

Often referred to as "speed" or "uppers," stimulant drugs increase people's energy level and alertness. As the name implies, these drugs stimulate the central nervous system to produce increased levels of mental and physical energy, and they affect all systems and functions of the body. The most prominent stimulant drugs of abuse are cocaine and amphetamines, while the two most commonly used stimulants are nicotine and caffeine. While many stimulant drugs are available by prescription (to treat obesity, narcolepsy, and attention deficit hyperactivity disorder), most stimulants are drugs of abuse.

CNS stimulants cause increased respiration, heart rate, motor activity, and alertness. They provide users with a sense of exhilaration, enhanced self-esteem, improved mental and physical performance, increased activity, and reduced appetite. Researchers believe that stimulants offer the most significant psychological and physical reward and reinforcement, which is the mechanism believed to be at the heart of the chemical dependency process (Drug Enforcement Administration, 1997, p. 29).

Drugs in This Category Cocaine and its derivative, crack cocaine, have received widespread attention over the past 20 years, yet the substance was first scrutinized many years ago. Sigmund Freud wrote "Uber Coca" in the early twentieth century to describe the benefits of using cocaine to treat a number of medical illnesses, including opiate (morphine) withdrawal. Cocaine was first available in the 1880s as a legal drug. As the public slowly became aware of its dangers, public opinion quickly changed, making it unpopular by the early 1900s. Soon its use dissipated considerably.

While cocaine remained available and was popular in arts communities, it reemerged in the 1980s as a popular drug of choice among young urban professionals. Again, cocaine was considered relatively harmless and its use became associated with wealth and success. Public attitudes changed in the mid-1980s with the advent of crack cocaine and the associated media attention. Again, cocaine quickly became "public enemy number one," primarily because of crack cocaine and, according to some, the people who were purported to be its main users (Musto, 1999). Cocaine and its derivatives (crack, rock, freebase) are derived from coca, a chemical substance found in the leaves of the coca shrub, grown in Central and South America. Coca leaves are processed (squashed and mashed with water and other solvents and allowed to dry) to produce coca paste. The paste is then processed into the white powder that most recognize as cocaine.

Cocaine powder has the texture of baking soda. Before it is sold on the streets, cocaine is "cut" with substances such as powdered sugar, talc, arsenic, lidocaine, or baking soda to increase its weight and profit margins.

When cocaine powder, baking soda, and water are heated, the result is crack cocaine paste. After the paste hardens, it is cut into pieces, or "rocks," for smoking. The name "crack" comes from the crackling sound the drug makes when it is smoked. Because the heating process removes most of the impurities, crack cocaine is a more pure form of the drug. Additionally, because it is smoked, the speed and power of its effects increase dramatically.

Amphetamines were first used during World War II to alleviate combat fatigue. Following the war, they became available to the public as the primary ingredient in asthma inhalers. Historically, long-haul truck drivers, students cramming for exams, athletes striving to improve performance, and individuals trying to lose weight have used amphetamines. These drugs were prescribed in the 1950s and 1960s for weight control and energy enhancement. In the late 1960s, amphetamines emerged as a popular drug of abuse before the return of cocaine. Interestingly, cocaine and amphetamine abuse are negatively correlated. That is, during periods of high amphetamine abuse, cocaine abuse drops, and vice versa (Ray & Ksir, 1993). Today, amphetamines are prescribed mostly for life-threatening obesity and narcolepsy.

Included in the amphetamine family of drugs are Benzedrine (crosstops, black beauties), Methedrine or methamphetamine (crank, meth, crystal meth), Dexedrine (dexies), and Desoxyn. In recent years, methamphetamine has emerged as a popular drug of abuse. It comes in either powder form that is snorted like cocaine, or in a smokeable form known as "ice." Its effects are similar to cocaine but last longer. Moreover, it is easier and cheaper to obtain methamphetamine because it is produced in clandestine laboratories from a mixture of easy-to-obtain chemicals. In many communities, methamphetamine has surpassed both alcohol and cocaine as the primary drug of abuse (Center for Substance Abuse Research, 1997; Center for Substance Abuse Treatment, 1997). Barry (1998) stated that methamphetamine use and abuse are a significant problem among women, gay men, and Asians and Pacific Islanders in the United States. On a national level, approximately 80 percent of people treated for methamphetamine abuse are European Americans, although there has been a recent increase in the number of Latino and Native Americans treated for methamphetamine abuse, particularly in the western United States (Shoptaw et al., 1997).

Other stimulant drugs have properties that mimic those of amphetamines. For example, methylphenidate (Ritalin) is widely used to treat attention deficit hyperactivity disorder (ADHD). This drug has recently become a popular drug of abuse as young people sell their prescription medications on the streets for profit. Other stimulants include Preludin (used in the treatment of obesity), Tepanil, and Didrex.

Several stimulant drugs are available without prescription. For example, caffeine is an active ingredient in coffee, teas, colas, and chocolate as well as in some over-the-counter products designed to keep people awake (i.e., No Doz, Alert, and Vivarin). Phenylpropanolamine is a stimulant found in weight control products sold over the counter (i.e., Dexatrim).

A new drug that has emerged recently among the stimulant family is Methcathinone. Known on the street as "cat," the drug was placed under federal control by the DEA in 1993 (Levinthal, 1999). Methcathinone acts similarly to methamphetamine and is usually sold as a powder. It has a high abuse potential and produces amphetamine-like effects. Although it is not yet widely used, cat is popular in many rural areas, especially where illegal laboratories are easy to conceal.

Although it has only mild euphoric properties, nicotine is the most highly addictive drug available. According to the American Heart Association (1999), more than 430,000 Americans die each year from smoking-related illnesses, four times as many deaths as those caused by alcohol. By a wide margin, nicotine is the most deadly drug of abuse worldwide (Fishbein & Pease, 1996).

Routes of Administration   Stimulant users take advantage of every route of administration. Cocaine is snorted, smoked, and injected. Amphetamines are most commonly swallowed as pills, injected, or snorted. Methamphetamine is usually snorted or "cooked" into rocks and smoked, similar to crack cocaine. Methcathinone is usually snorted but is also injected or dissolved into beverages. Obviously, nicotine is usually smoked, although smokeless tobacco products are quite popular.

Major Effects   At low doses, stimulants produce a sense of euphoria, exhilaration, extended wakefulness, and loss of appetite. Users report an increased sense of self-confidence, self-assurance, and self-esteem. Some users claim that being high makes them feel "bulletproof." Stimulants increase psychomotor stimulation, alertness, and sexual stimulation (physical and mental), while they reduce inhibitions, weaken impulse control, and elevate the user's mood. There is an increase in heart rate and blood pressure. Many users believe that amphetamines enhance physical performance, which is one reason why athletes often use stimulants.

Stimulant users feel a sudden sensation known as a "rush" or "flash." However, the intensity of the rush is determined by the route of administration. Smoking or injecting stimulants produces the most intense rush. The quicker a drug "hits" the user's brain, the more likely it is to have positive psychological effects (rewards). For this reason, cocaine is a highly attractive drug. An amphetamine high is usually less intense (unless it is injected) but longer lasting.

The acute effects of stimulant abuse can be dramatic and fatal. These include heart attacks, strokes, and seizures. The dependency-causing properties of these drugs are quite high (mostly psychological), primarily because of the euphoric reward. Chronic users encounter an increased risk of stroke, cardiovascular problems, and depression. Symptoms resembling psychosis, including paranoia and hallucinations (visual and auditory), can occur during an overdose, also known as an amphetamine or cocaine psychosis. This type of psychosis is easily reached and quite common among stimulant abusers.

Why Is Cocaine So Attractive?

Perhaps we should talk more about cocaine. Students often ask why cocaine is so attractive to people. Although a cocaine high is relatively intense, it is short-lived. Withdrawal (the "crash") is very unpleasant, having been described by my clients as intense feelings of panic and anxiety, as if the user suddenly crested the peak of a roller coaster. Despite this, people seem so attracted to cocaine that a myth has developed claiming that cocaine is a "one-hit" addiction. According to this myth, people who try cocaine or crack cocaine become immediately addicted. As we discussed in Chapter 1, however, most people who try cocaine do not become addicted (Denning, 2000).

The following analogy seems to best explain some people's overwhelming attraction to cocaine. To experience the full effect of this analogy, please close your eyes for a moment. I know this makes reading more difficult, but let's see how talented you really are. Remember, if you will, how you felt during your most exciting and powerful sexual experience. Remember how you felt, the sensations you experienced, and how you probably wished it would never end. Also, remember how much you wanted to reach that peak again, and soon! Do you have the mental picture yet?

Now, imagine being able to intensify that peak sensation ten-fold, perhaps even twenty-fold. Can you sense how *that* would feel? If it could happen, wouldn't you want to experience it again, perhaps even crave the feelings? The flash or rush from cocaine feels like the sexual experience we just described, especially when it is smoked or injected. Can you begin to understand why this drug is so attractive? You will often hear users speak of cocaine in sexualized terms, describing it as their "lover." This is because the cocaine "flash" mimics the peak sensation of a sexual experience. Moreover, just as in sex, the peak is gone as quickly as it arrived.

To reach that peak we just described, however, cocaine users must make two deals with the "devil," so to speak. First, they must "agree" (although they will not know it at the time) that they will never again reach that euphoric peak, although they will try. Second, the intense sensations are followed almost immediately (inside of 10 minutes) by the "crash." As stated above, the crash is what causes intense cravings to occur. Think about it—in a span of approximately 10 minutes, individuals feel better and worse than they have ever felt before. Moreover, they believe it will happen again, the next time they use.

If you have ever enjoyed a sexual experience to the point that you wanted to try it again, were willing to act out of character, or worse, become assaultive or forceful in your pursuit of that feeling, then you know what it feels like to experience the attraction to cocaine. This, my friends, is why people are willing to subject themselves to the dangers of cocaine.

Overdose CNS stimulants ignite the pleasure center of the brain, tricking users into believing that they are not hungry, thirsty, tired, or in pain. There is no built-in saturation point, so people can continue using until they run out of drugs or die. Therefore, the compulsion to use, the desire to maintain the high, and the unpleasantness of withdrawal make overdose common and relatively easy to reach. Symptoms of overdose include tremors, sweating, flushing, rapid heartbeat, anxiety, insomnia, delusions, hallucinations, paranoia, convulsions, heart attack, or stroke. Clients often report feeling their heart beat so fast and hard that their chest moved; being so hot that they went without a coat in the middle of winter; seeing people coming after them; hiding from police sirens heard miles away; and so on. One client reported that he was so numb from extended cocaine use that his partner kicked him in the groin and he did not feel it (until the next day). Deaths caused by stimulant overdose (especially cocaine) have been widely reported (Drug Enforcement Administration, 1997).

Tolerance Stimulant users rapidly develop a psychological tolerance to the pleasurable effects of cocaine and amphetamines, as well as a physical tolerance for tobacco and caffeine. This tolerance can lead to major problems. These drugs feel so rewarding, particularly when smoked or injected, that users are prone to compulsively use in an effort to recapture the euphoric effects and in response to altered brain chemistry (Nestler & Aghajanian, 1997; Leshner, 1997). People often use to prevent the feelings of "coming down." Users, having developed a high tolerance for stimulants, no longer feel the pleasurable effects. They use stimulants simply to alleviate the negative feelings of "coming down" and to feel "normal."

There is debate about whether tolerance to stimulants is psychological or physical (Levinthal, 1999). Some believe that most stimulants cause only psychological tolerance, some believe it is physical, and some believe it is both. For us, this argument is irrelevant, since all clients are referred to a medical doctor as a first priority in treatment. What matters more are people's reasons for chronic use and understanding their mindset, lifestyle, culture, and environment in order to make an accurate assessment and proper referral, or to provide the appropriate level of treatment. It is important to know that tolerance develops and that people begin taking stimulants in larger doses in an attempt to recapture the first exhilarating flash and resulting enhanced sense of self. If they continue taking larger doses, eventually they will overdose and possibly die.

Withdrawal Withdrawal from CNS stimulants is usually not medically dangerous. Nevertheless, it is extremely unpleasant, creating a significant potential for relapse to alleviate the discomfort. Common withdrawal symptoms include chronic headache, irritability, restlessness, and anxiety, along with sleep disturbance and difficulty concentrating. With cocaine, the intensity of its peak effect makes withdrawal miserable and produces overwhelming cravings for more of the drug. With chronic or heavy use, symptoms usually last two to three days and include (in addition to those mentioned above) irritability, depression, anxiety, possible short-term memory loss, lethargy, psychomotor discomfort (aches, pains, itching, etc.), and a reduced ability to experience pleasure. The latter often leads to sexual dysfunction (especially in males), flat affect, and lingering depression (Castro et al., 1992). During withdrawal, suicidal thoughts and fantasies often pose a significant threat.

While the most intense withdrawal symptoms subside in a few days, please note that depression, drug craving, and an inability to experience pleasure may last several months or years (Center for Substance Abuse Treatment, 1999a). Stimulant abusers are at high risk for relapse, even after many weeks, months, or years of abstinence. Specific sounds, smells, seasons of the year—almost anything can lead people to seek the pleasurable effects of the drug. (See Chapter 10 for a discussion of relapse prevention.)

Cannabis

Marijuana, a member of the cannabis family, is the most widely used illegal drug. More than 22 percent of adults between 18 and 25 years old use marijuana at least annually (Jung, 2001), and 12.8 percent report using at least monthly (Johnston, O'Malley, & Bachman, 1998). In addition to being popular, marijuana is one of the oldest known psychoactive drugs. Despite (or because of) its popularity and widespread use, marijuana is also the most controversial drug in the United States.

The earliest reference to cannabis dates to 2700 BC (National Institute on Drug Abuse, 1998). During the 1700s, the hemp plant (cannabis sativa) was the largest cash crop in the American colonies. Before the cotton gin, hemp was used to make clothing and rope. In the 1800s, people began experimenting with marijuana as a psychoactive drug. In 1926, states began outlawing it, believing that marijuana use caused criminal behavior, violence, and sexual perversion. For the next several years, marijuana was the subject of an intensive prevention campaign, based mostly on misleading information about its effects. Marijuana use moved underground until the 1960s, when it reemerged as a drug of choice for mainstream young people. Since that time, it has remained the most available and popular illegal drug, especially among young people.

Drugs in This Category The drugs in the cannabis family include marijuana, hashish, charas, bhang, ganja, and sinsemilla. The active ingredient is delta-9-tetrahydrocannabinol (THC), found in the resin that develops on the leaves of the cannabis plant. Hashish and charas have a THC content of 7 to 14 percent; ganja and sinsemilla, 4 to 7 percent; and bhang and marijuana, 2 to 5 percent.

Routes of Administration All of the drugs in this category are usually smoked in a "joint" or a pipe ("bong"). These drugs are either smoked alone or combined with other drugs. For example, some people mix cocaine or hallucinogens with marijuana for an enhanced effect. Cannabis is also eaten as part of various foods (such as hash brownies or cookies).

Major Effects Within 10 to 30 minutes, users feel euphoric, with an enhanced sense of taste, touch, and smell. They also become relaxed and experience an increased appetite (the "munchies"). Other effects include an altered sense of time and the loss of some short-term memory skills. Marijuana creates a sense of heightened awareness, along with a mildly euphoric state that makes users feel dreamlike. The physiological effects of marijuana include increased pulse rate and blood pressure, dilated blood vessels in the cornea (bloodshot eyes), and dry mouth. Motor skills and reaction time slow, with impairment lasting after the effects wear off, especially imperiling the user's ability to operate a vehicle. Marijuana use is linked to a significant number of vehicular and non-vehicular accidents (Soderstrom, Trifillis, Shankar, & Clark, 1988).

The experience of using marijuana depends on user expectations, personal experience, and input from the social environment. Low doses induce a sense of well-being and relaxation, accompanied by a vivid sense of sight, smell, taste, and hearing. Contrary to popular belief, marijuana does not cause paranoia. Because users become more keenly aware of the environment, they often quickly and suddenly to noises, sounds, and other social stimuli. Users believe that they can hear, smell, and feel everything going on around them. The enhanced senses put users "on edge." This is not paranoia, but hypervigilance. As with other drugs, higher doses intensify its effects. Individuals may experience shifting sensory images, rapidly fluctuating emotions, fragmentary thoughts with disturbed associations, an altered sense of self-identity, impaired memory, and a dulling of attention despite the illusion of heightened insight. At high doses, marijuana users often experience image distortion, fantasies, and hallucinations.

The long-term effects of marijuana use are still largely unknown (Ray & Ksir, 1993). For example, chronic marijuana use has an adverse effect on lung function, although there is no direct evidence that it causes lung cancer or other lung diseases (NIMH, 1997). Although users experience an increased heart rate, there is no evidence that marijuana adversely affects the heart (Schwartz, 1987). Similar to CNS depressants, marijuana suppresses the immune system, exposing users to infectious diseases and viruses. Chronic marijuana use decreases the male hormone testosterone and damages sperm formation, although there is no direct evidence that it affects male fertility or sexual potency. In females, extensive marijuana use reduces estrogen levels, impairs ovulation, and has been linked to increased incidence of miscarriage (Levinthal, 1999). The National Institute on Drug Abuse (1998) found evidence that marijuana produces adverse effects on the brain, lungs, reproductive system, attention, memory, and learning. However, other investigators reviewing the same research have arrived at different, often contradictory conclusions (Zimmer & Morgan, 1997).

Over the years, marijuana use has been linked to "amotivational syndrome" (Jung, 2001; Levinthal, 1999; Fishbein & Pease, 1996). Many have claimed that marijuana use "causes" people to become apathetic, lose goal directiveness, and have dulled emotions—all characteristics of amotivational syndrome. In reality, however, no causal relationship between marijuana use and amotivational syndrome has been established (Ray & Ksir, 1993; Schwartz, 1987). Marijuana use is one of many factors correlated to amotivational syndrome, along with family divorce, parental substance abuse, and others. While there is anecdotal evidence that chronic users of marijuana become apathetic, there is no direct empirical link between marijuana use and amotivational syndrome.

On a more positive note, the National Institutes of Health (1997) reports that marijuana is medically useful in reducing nausea and vomiting from chemotherapy, stimulating appetite in AIDS patients, treating spasticity and nocturnal spasms that complicate multiple sclerosis and spinal cord injuries, controlling seizures, and managing neuropathic pain. Further clinical studies are necessary to reach conclusions on the ultimate value of marijuana in medical treatment, but these findings only add to the controversy over marijuana. Several states have approved the medical use of marijuana. Currently, these policies are being challenged in court by the federal government.

Finally, unlike drugs that are water soluble, THC is fat soluble. Therefore, THC lingers in the body's fat cells and organs anywhere from several days to several months, depending upon the user's habits. Indeed, marijuana can be detected in urine or blood tests for approximately seven days for infrequent users and as long as 60 days for frequent or heavy users (Levinthal, 1999). There is no credible way to predict how long THC will remain detectable to drug tests.

Overdose   Overdose is unusual, if not impossible, because of the raw amount one would have to consume. As stated earlier, intensified emotional responses and mild hallucinations can occur, and the user may feel out of control. Many reports of overdose are simply panic reactions to the normal effects of the drug. In individuals with preexisting mental disorders, high doses of marijuana may exacerbate symptoms such as delusions, hallucinations, disorientation, and depersonalization (Julien, 1998). However, anyone reporting a marijuana overdose probably had an intense emotional reaction to the drug or mixed it with other drugs that were actually responsible for the overdose. There are no reported or known deaths from marijuana overdose (Ray & Ksir, 1993).

Tolerance Tolerance is a controversial issue with respect to marijuana. According to Palfai and Jankiewicz (1997), mild tolerance may develop. However, Inaba, Cohen, and Holstein (1997) stated, "Tolerance to marijuana occurs in a rapid and dramatic fashion" (p. 245). Despite these differences of opinion, it has been established that chronic users become accustomed to the effects of the drug and develop a capacity to administer the proper dosage to produce the desired effects. Cross-tolerance to CNS depressants, including alcohol, has been demonstrated (Palfai & Jankiewicz, 1997).

Withdrawal A withdrawal syndrome does occur in chronic high-dose cannabis users who abruptly discontinue use. The symptoms include irritability, restlessness, decreased appetite, insomnia, tremor, chills, and increased body temperature. The symptoms usually last three to five days but pose no serious medical threat unless the user has preexisting medical conditions that are exacerbated by the withdrawal syndrome.

Marijuana use and abuse will consistently be detected among clients during substance abuse assessments. Despite the controversy surrounding its use, people do become dependent on marijuana, although the social consequences are usually more significant than the medical or physiological effects. Do not overestimate or underestimate the problems that frequent or chronic marijuana use causes among users. While it may not be as deadly as alcohol, nicotine, or other drugs, marijuana causes a plethora of negative life consequences. Therefore, regardless of what you believe about marijuana or have experienced personally with marijuana, you must take it seriously in a substance abuse practice context.

Topic for Your Journal: Legalization of Marijuana

Here is an interesting and timely subject for your substance abuse journal. Many people believe that marijuana should be legalized, for a variety of reasons. What is your opinion on this subject? As you discuss your beliefs, be sure to critically evaluate the reasons for your opinion.

Opiates

Drugs classified as opiates are naturally occurring substances harvested from the opium poppy plant and/or synthetic drugs prepared in private laboratories. Originally, drugs extracted from opium were used for pain relief. Egyptian, Greek, and Arabic cultures used opium to treat diarrhea, as a sleep aid, and for recreational purposes (Julien, 1998). The plant is grown in many countries around the world, and the milky fluid that seeps from incisions in an unripe seedpod of the poppy plant is scraped off and dried to produce opium. Opium is sold in liquid, solid, or powder form, although most commercially available opium is a fine brownish powder (Drug Enforcement Administration, 1997).

Morphine was isolated from opium in the early 1860s during the American Civil War. Heroin was developed in 1874. Both drugs were widely available without prescription until the early 1900s, when the United States banned non-medical use because of the number of people addicted to morphine and heroin. During that period, morphine addiction was called the "soldier's disease" (Musto, 1999). Since that time, opiate abuse has ebbed and flowed, with heroin use peaking in the 1960s and 1970s. Heroin reappeared in the late 1990s, verifying Julien's (1998) statement that

> The use of opiates is deeply entrenched in society; it is widespread and impossible to stop. Opiates exert pleasurable effects, produce tolerance and physiological dependence, and have a potential for compulsive misuse, all liabilities that are likely to resist any efforts at legal control. Also, the opiates will continue to be used in medicine because they are irreplaceable as pain-relieving agents (p. 286).

Drugs in This Category The "natural" opiates include opium, morphine, codeine, and heroin. The synthetic opiates include Meperidine, Fentanyl (the most potent opiate), Vicodin, Dilaudid, Percodan, Methadone, Darvon, Demerol, and Dalwin. All of these drugs, whether natural or synthetic, have similar tolerance and abuse potential. That is, the synthetic drugs are not safe, despite the pharmaceutical industry's continuing efforts to find an opiate-like drug that is non-addicting.

Routes of Administration Drugs in the opiate classification are swallowed as pills, smoked, snorted, and/or injected. Heroin, the most abused "street" drug in this category, is injected, smoked, and snorted. More heroin users than ever before are now smoking and snorting the drug because of the danger of HIV/AIDS. Millions of people around the world have smoked opium for centuries in low dosages. Many of the synthetic drugs come in pill form. For example, the use of Vicodin (a pain reliever) has grown in popularity in recent years.

Major Effects The effects of opiate drugs depend heavily on the dose, route of administration, tolerance, and the expectations of the user. Aside from clinical uses for pain relief, cough suppression, and treatment of acute diarrhea, opiates produce a general sense of well-being—an almost dreamlike state that reduces tension, anxiety, and aggression. These effects, while helpful in a medical sense, account for the attraction of opiates as recreational drugs. Opiates create a number of other effects, including nausea, vomiting, itching, drowsiness, inability to concentrate, apathy, lessened physical activity, constriction of the pupils, dilation of blood vessels causing "flushing" of the face and neck, and respiratory depression. As doses increase, the user's feelings, level of sedation, and the pain-relieving effects of the drugs become more pronounced. Except in cases of acute intoxication, there is no loss of motor coordination or slurred speech.

Among the many hazards of opiate use are the risk of infection and disease from unsanitary administration (dirty needles), a rapid tolerance build-up leading to a difficult withdrawal syndrome, and a significant risk for overdose. Medical complications often arise from the chemicals used to "cut" the drug for resale and the unpredictable potency of drugs purchased on the street and prepared in illegal laboratories. Opiate abusers commonly report skin, lung, and brain abscesses, endocarditis, hepatitis, HIV/AIDS, and tuberculosis.

Methadone is a synthetic opiate used to treat opiate dependence. Methadone does not have the dramatic euphoric effects of heroin, has a longer duration of action (12 to 24 hours compared to 3 to 6 hours for heroin), and blocks the symptoms of withdrawal from heroin. Under medical supervision, heroin addicts are given daily, decreasing doses of methadone over a long period to wean them from heroin without causing a withdrawal syndrome. Theoretically, methadone maintenance is time-limited, meaning that eventually people using methadone as part of treatment should become drug-free. However, because of lax program management, this outcome is often not achieved (Musto, 1999). The popularity of methadone maintenance programs has waxed and waned over the last 30 years in the United States. Currently, methadone maintenance programs are in vogue as a way to treat opiate addiction.

Overdose Death from overdose (especially injected heroin) occurs when a user's respiratory system shuts down. It is relatively simple to overdose on opiates, given the wide variation in purity and the inexact ways that doses are determined on the streets. Symptoms of overdose include slowed breathing, decreased blood pressure, decreased pulse rate, lower body temperature, dulled reflexes, and clammy skin. Depending on the dose, individuals become extremely drowsy, lose consciousness, and/or lapse into a coma. Many opiate overdoses are fatal.

Tolerance Tolerance to opiates develops rapidly and results in the addict using amounts that would kill a non-addict. Regular users grow accustomed to using high doses, accounting for a relatively high death rate in longtime opiate users who relapse after periods of abstinence. These individuals often begin using doses equal to what they were accustomed to using before detoxifying. Cross-tolerance among the opiates occurs, but there is no cross-tolerance with CNS depressants. The combination of moderate to high doses of opiates and alcohol or other CNS depressants can (and often does) result in respiratory depression, coma, or death. While cross-tolerance does not occur, because of the similarity of effects, mixing opiates and depressants can be deadly.

There are two primary categories of opiate abusers. One group comprises people who become dependent through legally prescribed medications, primarily for pain management (Vicodin, Demerol, morphine). For example, physical tolerance often develops even when morphine is used according to medical prescription (Jung, 2001). As the user's tolerance builds, he or she often begins recruiting several doctors to prescribe opiates at the same time, ensuring an unlimited supply.

The second group of people begins using for experimentation or recreation, often building into a full-blown dependence in a relatively short period. It is possible to develop tolerance to opiates in a two-week period of daily use (Jung, 2001; Ray & Ksir, 1993). People who use opiates daily or more than once within a 48-hour period (the time it takes to fully metabolize the drug) can develop physical tolerance quickly. However, not all people who use opiates develop tolerance. Many people (perhaps more than those who become addicted) use opiates for many months and years without developing a physical tolerance. These people are called "chippers." As long as more than 48 hours elapses between doses, allowing the drug to be metabolized, tolerance does not develop (Levinthal, 1999). It is possible to chip and never experience the physical problems associated with opiate addiction. While some periodic users do ultimately become dependent, many do not. According to the DEA (1997), dependence on opiates usually occurs within one to two years of first use.

Withdrawal When opiates are used on a continuous basis, there is rapid development of physical dependence, leading to inevitable withdrawal symptoms. Withdrawal symptoms are unpleasant and uncomfortable but rarely life threatening, yet addicts often fear withdrawal to the point that they will risk their lives through continued use, rather than undergo the flu-like symptoms of withdrawal. The fear of withdrawal sickness is far more significant than the actual experience of the withdrawal syndrome.

Opiate withdrawal feels like a bad case of influenza, with running eyes and nose, restlessness, goose bumps, sweating, muscle cramps or aching, nausea, vomiting, and diarrhea, along with intense cravings for the drug to relieve the symptoms. Withdrawal symptoms peak after 48 hours and dissipate thereafter. Despite the relatively harmless nature of withdrawal, opiate-dependent individuals must always be referred for medical assistance because of the potential for other medical conditions that can—when combined with withdrawal syndrome—lead to serious medical complications.

Opiate addiction is serious. Addicts go to great lengths to hide their habit and fear that they will be unable to survive the withdrawal syndrome. Do not lose sight of the fact that opiates are dangerous. Overdose can happen even to the most experienced user, and often occurs with first- or second-time users. Moreover, the lifestyles of many opiate addicts place these individuals at severe risk of illness or death through exposure and vulnerability to tuberculosis, HIV/AIDS, and other infectious diseases, as well as medical complications from poor nutrition, blocked or damaged blood vessels, and extremely potent versions of the drugs that can instantly kill even the most hardened opiate addict. Be sure to consult medical personnel in all cases of opiate dependency.

Hallucinogens

The category of drugs known as hallucinogens is among the oldest known groups of drugs. Historically, people from cultures around the world have used various hallucinogenic substances—most of which occur naturally—for a variety of reasons. Today, most hallucinogens are synthetic drugs produced in laboratories.

While the biochemical, pharmacological, and physiological basis for hallucino-genic activity is not well understood, the potent and powerful effects of these drugs are well known.

Many hallucinogenic drugs (especially lysergic acid diethylamide, better known as LSD or "acid") became popular in the 1960s and 1970s. Usage of hal-lucinogens declined in the 1980s but has recently resurfaced among adolescents and young adults. As an illustration, the number of twelfth-graders reporting hal-lucinogen use in the previous 12 months was 11.2 percent in 1975. There was a gradual decrease to 5 percent in 1992, but in 1997, 9.8 percent reported use (Johnston, O'Malley, & Bachman, 1998).

There is a considerable body of literature linking the use of some hallucino-genic substances to brain damage in animals; however, there is no conclusive evi-dence linking brain or chromosomal damage to hallucinogen use in humans. The most common danger of hallucinogen use is impaired judgment that often leads to rash decision-making and accidents (Drug Enforcement Administration, 1997, p. 34). This evidence contradicts many of the myths and legends claiming that LSD causes "brain fry." In the late 1960s and 1970s, at the height of its popular-ity, people believed that hallucinogenic drugs caused significant brain damage. Obviously, the research cited above suggests otherwise. While these drugs do not cause permanent brain damage, they are not safe to use. On the contrary, hallu-cinogenic drugs produce many harmful and troubling side effects.

Drugs in This Category As Julien (1998) points out, hallucinogens comprise a heterogeneous mixture of drugs, including LSD (acid), psilocybin (magic mush-rooms, shrooms), peyote, morning glory seeds, mescaline, STP, MDMA (ec-stasy), ketamine, and PCP (angel dust). LSD is the most potent drug available, requiring only .004 milligrams (a small drop from an eyedropper) to achieve its full effects. Ecstasy has recently become the most commonly used hallucinogen, especially at "Rave" parties for young adults.

Routes of Administration Most of the time, users take hallucinogens orally. LSD is a liquid. Over the years, users have found ingenious ways of disguising its use. For example, LSD can be put on stamps, stickers, and paper—nearly any-thing that allows people to put the drug into their mouths. In our adolescent res-idential treatment center, we began removing stamps from client mail because kids were getting LSD sent from the outside. The recipient would tear the stamp and place it in his or her mouth for a quick dose of LSD. Hallucinogens can also be snorted, smoked, or injected. PCP is often sprinkled on a marijuana joint and smoked. Ecstasy usually comes in pill form.

Major Effects Hallucinogens, taken in non-toxic doses, produce dramatic changes in mood, thought, and perception. These drugs—depending on the dose and the expectations of the user—produce an altered state of consciousness, in-cluding distortion of the visual, auditory, olfactory, and/or tactile senses and an increased awareness of thoughts and impulses. Sensory experiences may cross into one another (i.e., seeing odor or hearing color), and inanimate objects may seem to move, talk, or change shape. Other psychic effects include distortions of time and space. Time may appear to stand still, while forms and colors seem to change and take on new significance. Common sights and sounds may be perceived as exceptionally intricate and astounding, one reason why strobe lights, glow-sticks, and black lights are often found where people use hallucinogens. These light sources enhance the user's experience of the drugs. In the case of PCP and ketamine, there may be increased suggestibility, delusions, depersonalization, and dissociation.

Physiologically, hallucinogens produce increased pulse rate, blood pressure, and dilated pupils. Other side effects include high body temperature and dizziness. Hallucinogenic "trips" are long lasting, taking approximately 20 minutes to one hour to begin and lasting eight hours or longer. Because of the powerful physical, emotional, and mental effects of hallucinogenic trips, users are exhausted after the experience. This is why parties where ecstasy is used provide "cool down" rooms. As a result, it is difficult for people to use hallucinogens daily, perhaps preventing people from becoming dependent (Ray & Ksir, 1993).

Hallucinogenic experiences can be pleasurable or frightening. Which way a "trip" goes—good or bad—has to do with the user, his or her attitude, mood, expectations, and the surrounding environment. "Bad trips" involve acute anxiety, paranoia, fear of loss of control, heightened and intense emotional responses (i.e., unexplained, uncontrollable crying), and delusions. Individuals with preexisting mental disorders may experience more severe symptoms. Bad trips can be terrifying. Many people quit using LSD after experiencing a bad trip.

A well-publicized adverse effect of LSD is flashbacks. Flashbacks are fragmentary recurrences of the effects of the drug (mostly LSD) experienced in the absence of actually taking the drug (DEA, 1997). Flashbacks are unpredictable, but more likely to occur during times of heightened stress. Young people seem to experience flashbacks more frequently than adults do. Over time, these episodes diminish and become less intense. Some people have reported flashbacks occurring more than five years after last taking LSD, although this is uncommon. Flashbacks usually cease after several months of abstinence (Fishbein & Pease, 1996).

Overdose With the exception of PCP, ketamine, and ecstasy, the concept of overdose does not apply to hallucinogens. For example, Julien (1998) reports that the lethal dose of LSD is 280 times the normal dose. Bad trips or panic reactions do occur and may include paranoid ideation, depression, undesirable hallucination, and/or confusion. These are usually managed by providing a calm and supportive environment.

An overdose of ecstasy can result in acute intoxication, psychosis, coma, or death (Drug Enforcement Administration, 1997). Acute intoxication or psychosis causes people to become agitated, confused, and excited, while exhibiting a blank stare and/or violent behavior. Analgesia (insensitivity to pain) occurs and may result in self-inflicted injuries and injuries to others when attempts are made to restrain the individual. Since the intended effect of hallucinogenic drugs is to cause users to "lose touch" with their reality, users may become involved in serious or even fatal accidents. For example, a user may step off a balcony under the mistaken, drug-induced belief that he can fly like a bird.

Tolerance   Tolerance to the hallucinogenic properties of these drugs does occur, as well as cross-tolerance between LSD and other hallucinogens. No cross-tolerance effects have been discovered between hallucinogens and other drug classifications.

Withdrawal   Withdrawal symptoms include extreme exhaustion and continued mental, emotional, and cognitive distortions. As stated earlier, the hallucinogenic trip is tiring; it is not an easy drug to use. While the effects are often quite powerful and challenging, it takes most of a full 24-hour day to use, experience the drug, and recover from the trip. If a user experiences a bad trip, it can take longer. People withdrawing from a hallucinogenic trip need rest and people in supportive roles to assist with their return to "reality." When bad trips occur, users should be taken immediately for medical services, as bad trips can result in accidents that harm self and others.

Hallucinogens are powerful drugs that challenge the user's connection with reality. They are unpredictable, causing users to experience either intensely pleasurable or wickedly unpleasant effects, depending on the mood and attitude of the user. While most people do not become dependent on hallucinogens in the same way as other drugs (Ray & Ksir, 1993), they do go through periods of intensive use followed by longer periods of non-use. My clinical experience suggests that most people grow out of hallucinogen use in early adulthood. Most of the clients you will see in practice who are abusing hallucinogens will be adolescents and/or college-age young adults.

Inhalants

Drugs classified as inhalants consist mainly of legally purchased household and industrial chemicals. Typical users of inhalants are young adolescents or children, and/or the desperately poor of all ages. Because of their availability, inhalants are easy for youngsters to use in early experimentation and for people to obtain if they are too poor to purchase other mind-altering substances. While the sudden national concern about inhalants appears new, the use of inhalants is not a recent phenomenon. For years, people (often the very poor) have inhaled toluene, gasoline, airplane glue, and other chemicals. What is new is the prevalence of use by young children in the middle and upper classes of the United States. Over the last decade, treatment centers and hospital emergency rooms have seen a dramatic rise in inhalant overdose and/or resulting medical complications from inhalant use by children (Levinthal, 1999). In our treatment center, we treated a number of serious cases of childhood inhalant abuse.

One of the biggest issues of inhalant use for parents, significant others, and social work professionals is detection. There is no urine test to detect these chemicals, and parents often overlook inhalants while looking for traditional drugs of abuse. Many parents are not aware that their son or daughter inhales gasoline, cleaning chemicals, or butane from cigarette lighters. What parents do know is that their child acts intoxicated and smells of chemicals. These are the telltale signs of inhalant abuse: behavior that resembles alcohol intoxication, coupled with the smell of chemicals.

Drugs in This Category The industrial solvents and aerosol sprays that are used as drugs include gasoline, kerosene, chloroform, airplane glue, lacquer thinner, acetone, nail polish remover, lighter fluid, fluoride-based sprays, metallic paints, butane, correction fluids, and almost anything else that comes from an aerosol spray container. Perhaps the most common of the solvents used as a drug is toluene. This is a common industrial degreaser kept in and around machine shops and factories. Users saturate a rag and seal it in a plastic bag, keeping it fresh and ready to use for many days. Other chemicals of abuse include amyl nitrite (poppers, rush), butyl nitrite and isobutyl nitrite (quicksilver). Additionally, nitrous oxide (laughing gas), a substance used by dentists, is also widely used as a recreational drug.

Routes of Administration As the name implies, inhalants are inhaled. This practice is referred to as "huffing." Industrial solvents and aerosol sprays are poured or sprayed on a rag or into a bag and inhaled deeply through the mouth and nose.

Major Effects Chemicals used as inhalants reduce inhibition and produce euphoria. People under the influence of inhalants will appear to be drunk but smell of chemicals or gasoline, rather than alcohol. Other symptoms include slurred speech and unsteady gait (impaired motor skills) and drowsiness. The nitrites (rush, etc.) alter consciousness and enhance sexual pleasure. The user may experience giddiness, headaches, and dizziness.

The most critical acute effect of inhalants is death. Users can experience loss of consciousness, coma, or death from a lack of oxygen, respiratory arrest, or asphyxiation. Many of these substances are highly toxic (poisons), and chronic use may damage the vital organs, especially the liver, brain, kidneys, and lungs. In our treatment centers, we have seen 11- and 12-year-old kids who have inhaled so much gasoline that they developed severe upper respiratory conditions. Many older, chronic users have severely damaged the lining of the nose, throat, and lungs from heavy use of inhalants. Emergency room doctors report seeing cases where people inhaled so much spray paint that they literally painted the inside of their lungs, leading to death (Drug Enforcement Administration, 1997).

Overdose Overdose on these substances may produce hallucinations, muscle spasms, headaches, dizziness, loss of balance, irregular heartbeat, and coma or death. Overdose is relatively easy to accomplish, given the toxicity of the chemicals being used and the inability of users to judge dosage. Unfortunately, it is a relatively common occurrence in communities across the United States to hear reports of teenagers or children dying from an overdose of inhalants.

Tolerance Research into the use of household and industrial chemicals as drugs of abuse is relatively new. Therefore, there is no credible evidence that tolerance develops for any of the substances in this category used as drugs of abuse, although this may change. Stay informed of new research findings in this area.

Withdrawal Researchers and/or practitioners have yet to report withdrawal symptoms caused by inhalants.

Inhalant abuse (or huffing) is not new. What is new is how prevalent it has become among young children and adolescents. These chemicals are dangerous and can do significant physical damage to users. They are toxic poisons that are inhaled into the developing body and brain of a child. Because of the nature of the products used as drugs of abuse, detection is difficult. It is your job to ask about inhalant abuse, especially with clients who are children, adolescents, or profoundly poor. These are the primary populations in which inhalant abuse is prevalent.

SUMMARY

In this chapter, we looked at how drugs, including alcohol, interact with the human body and mind (pharmacology) to create the potential for abuse. The intent was to provide enough relevant information about drugs and their effects to let you perform a competent substance abuse assessment, prepare an appropriate treatment plan, and make an appropriate referral for services or provide services yourself. At this point, you should be familiar with the various drug categories and the general pharmacological effects of drugs within these categories.

Discovering a client's individual response to drugs should be part of a clinical interview in which you remain mindful of the concept of variability and all of the non-pharmacological forces that influence the way drugs affect people. Factors such as gender, tolerance level, body type and weight, food intake, rest, and overall physical condition affect a person's response to drugs, along with other issues such as the person's mood, expectations about the drugs, social setting, dose used, and route of administration. As a result, it is impossible to predict with any certainty how a drug—or combination of drugs—will affect clients from day to day.

Clients will often know more than you know about drugs and drug effects; do not feel threatened by this fact. Their lives often depend on advanced knowledge of chemicals and doses. Clients know the latest street names, effects, and combinations of drugs being used on the streets. When taking a substance use history, do not be afraid to ask for clarification, definitions, or explanations about drugs. Believe me, if you pretend to know more than you do, your client will realize it and use that information to his or her benefit in the session. Even if you are a recovering addict, the drug culture changes rapidly. If you have been in recovery for any significant period, your client's drug culture will not be the same as your drug culture was. If you are not a recovering person or are without significant experience in the drug culture, use your client's expertise to help with the engagement process.

3

Models of Chemical Dependency

here are several theories and models that purport to explain the causes and treatments for chemical dependency. As you will see, the various models described in this chapter are quite different, yet each one addresses the same problem—chemical dependency. Our task is to understand each model, determine its efficacy with different clients, and make informed choices about which model or combination of models to apply in social work practice. We also look at how these different models can come together to form a professional approach based on systems theory that is consistent with the foundations of social work practice.

Do not be surprised by the wide variety of explanations for the same phenomenon. This type of variance is common when it comes to theories that apply to human behavior. Different approaches can be traced to research findings, practice experience, hunches, and personal beliefs. For example, professionals use many different models to explain mental illness, family problems, and child abuse. Theoretical and/or methodological differences are common, and the often-heated debate and dialogue created by these differences lead to advances. This is the way a "profession" develops a body of knowledge over time.

In relation to substance abuse, however, proponents of certain models insist on the "rightness" of their ideas with a fervor and inflexibility that is uncommon in other fields of practice (Peele, 1998), causing significant controversy among scholars, researchers, and practitioners. In some professional circles, for example, publicly questioning the notion of chemical dependency as a disease is tantamount to questioning the basic teachings of the Bible or other sacred texts. On one occasion, I was literally "shouted down" by seminar participants after suggesting that the disease model, applied through a twelve-step approach (see below), may not work for adolescents.

Moreover, the topics of substance use, abuse, and chemical dependency generate interest and involvement from government, the criminal justice system, medical community, mental health professionals, child welfare agencies, religious communities, businesses, and the media, not to mention a chorus of strong and passionate beliefs based on personal self-interest and experience (by those in recovery). As we discussed in Chapter 1, no other field of social work practice involves as many different systems operating with the same levels of passion and intensity as does substance abuse. The differing goals and interests of the various groups, as well as the professional and personal perspectives of these systems, create sharp differences of opinion about the origins, prevention, and treatment of substance abuse. Consequently, there is little agreement about the best way to approach people with substance abuse problems.

If you are like many other helping professionals, your choice of the model you will use in practice is likely to be based more on personal values and beliefs than professional training and experience, although this should not be the case. As you read this chapter, stop periodically to critically evaluate each model. Write your thoughts and reflections in the substance abuse journal you began in Chapter 1. It is important to know and understand the origins of your ideas, beliefs, and attitudes in order to maintain appropriate professional boundaries and improve practice outcomes.

WHAT APPROACH WILL YOU CHOOSE?

There are as many theoretical approaches in the social work profession as there are individual social workers. Which approach or approaches you abide by depends on many factors, including which graduate school you are attending (or attended), the agency where you work, your practice specialty, or your unique personal preferences. Perhaps your favorite professor swore by a certain approach, or, as is often the case in substance abuse practice, a loved one was a client of a certain professional or program that used a particular approach. For example, many social workers, regardless of the perspective of their graduate or undergraduate program, believe that the disease model (described later in this chapter) most effectively describes chemical dependency because a certain program uses it, most people seem to believe in it, or a family member found "recovery" through this approach. These workers' beliefs are based more on personal experience than on professional study, experience, research, and critical thinking (Gambrill, 1997).

Because of the central role of personal perspectives in social work practice, it is crucial for you to critically analyze and discuss (with people you trust) what you believe and why you believe it. This analysis will help you understand why you chose—consciously or unconsciously—one perspective, model, approach, or method over others, and it will uncover potential reasons for your experiences with clients, either successful or unsuccessful.

Discovering the "roots" of your perspective is consistent with Phillips' (1987) "theory ladenness of perception," whereby "the observer's background knowledge (including theories, factual information, hypotheses, and so forth) serves as a 'lens' helping to 'shape' the nature of what is observed" (p. 206). In addition to your professional perspective, your personal life experiences, shaped by your life-learning (Johnson, 2000), also influence the professional lens through which you perceive clients. It is important to understand your perspective about how people "should" manage their lives and solve their problems. Additionally, what you believe about the people you work with, especially people whose race, gender, ethnicity, class, or sexual orientation differ from your own, informs which approaches you will choose in practice.

Topic for Your Journal: Are Drug Abusers Different from Alcoholics?

As a young person, what were you told about people who abuse drugs? What about people who drank too much? Do you believe they are different? Is alcohol abuse more acceptable than heroin or crack cocaine abuse? Do substance abusers lack will power or firm moral footings, *or do they suffer from a disease over which they have no control? Take a few minutes to answer these questions in your substance abuse journal, remembering to reflect on the potential sources of your beliefs and how your beliefs compare to the literature in the substance abuse field.*

The perspective you believe in, combined with your own life-learning, helps to determine how you view clients and their problems. It influences your beliefs about the causes of substance abuse problems or issues, how the problems are demonstrated in a client's life, and what treatment methods will best address the issue. In short, your worldview affects everything in practice, and, by association, each client's prospects for receiving help under your care. This is such an important issue that we will begin discussing it here and continue the discussion in Chapter 4.

Problems with Clinical Specialization

Because of a trend in social work education toward specialization (or concentration) by model (disease, cognitive, psychoanalysis, etc.) and/or modality (individual, family, group, etc.), clients with multiple problems often do not receive the help they need because the social worker's specialty does not match a particular client's situation. That is, social workers or programs often try to jam the proverbial square peg into a round hole, and if clients are not helped by that approach, they blame the client rather than the method (Miley, O'Melia, & DuBois, 1995). This is especially true in the substance abuse field with respect to the disease model of addiction (Peele, 1998; Miller & Rollnick, 1991; van Wormer, 1995). If clients do not find recovery by abstaining from all substances, they are said to be in denial or "not ready for treatment" and are denied further service in many programs across the country (Peele, 1998). Little thought is given to the approach taken by the helper and its impact on client "readiness" for treatment or level of denial (Brehm & Brehm, 1981).

Rarely are the personal style, beliefs, and attitudes of a social worker examined when clients do not succeed in treatment. This lack of scrutiny raises an interesting question. What if we are responsible for client denial or a lack of readiness for treatment? Do we have a responsibility to see that our clients receive every possible opportunity to engage in a trusting and open professional relationship, where they can freely discuss and reflect on their lives, problems, and possible remedies? Think about this topic and write about it in your substance abuse journal.

Often, problems with specialization occur when we invest, for a variety of reasons, in a single approach or theory as if we have discovered an absolute "Truth." Truth, in this sense, is defined as the one approach that works best for all people, all of the time, but only if they accept the "Truth." Therefore, when clients do not respond, instead of looking to other approaches, some specialists prescribe more of the method that has already been unsuccessful. If a more intensive application of the method does not work, it is time to blame clients.

To further understand the scope of the problem, we need to discuss theory in general. Far from being a concrete representation of the truth, a theory is a set of myths, expectations, guesses, and conjectures about what might be true (Best & Kellner, 1991). A theory is hypothetical—a set of ideas and explanations that needs proving. No single theory can explain everything. According to Popper (1994), a theory ". . . always remains guesswork, and there is no theory that is not beset with problems" (p. 157). As such, specialization can encourage people to believe they have found the truth in a theory that, if you believe Popper, is only hypothetically true.

"Wait a minute," you may exclaim, "I'm not a specialist, I'm an eclectic." According to Gambrill (1997), eclecticism is "the view that we should adopt whatever theories or methodologies are useful in inquiry, no matter what their source and without worry about their consistency" (p. 93). While some have managed to develop consistency in their eclecticism, in my experience, most do not. Too often, an eclectic social worker specializes by modality and uses a variety of modality-specific methods, randomly putting ideas together when a particular approach does not "work." This often leaves him or her searching (mostly in vain) for a "magic bullet" intervention that will work as it did for the treatment "guru" at last week's workshop. Moreover, while using interventions from various "schools," practitioners are still wedded to one general method while experimenting with techniques borrowed from other approaches. The problem with this approach is its inconsistency. Many "eclectic" social workers end up confusing themselves and their clients as they search for the "right" approach. They rarely look beyond a chosen modality to see what might lie outside their self-imposed, theoretical cage.

A specialist in individual therapy may try Reality Therapy (Glasser, 1965), a Rogerian approach (Rogers, 1957), or a Freudian approach, for example. A family therapy specialist may use a structural (Minuchin, 1974), strategic (Haley, 1976), or solution-focused approach (de Shazer, 1988). However, in the end, little has changed. These "eclectic" social workers still believe their clients need individual or family treatment, never considering potentially useful ideas from different modalities that might be used instead of, or in combination with, an individual or family approach. For example, sometimes simultaneously addressing issues in local communities is needed if clients are to live successfully sober after treatment.

While eclecticism is a noble goal, it can be difficult to find a common thread of consistency. The most successful eclectic practitioners, through experience, find a unifying theory or approach that serves as the basis for using different models or methods. What is important, according to clinical outcome research, is the consistency of approach in helping facilitate successful client outcomes (Gaston, 1990; Miller & Rollnick, 1991; Harper & Lantz, 1996). Trying to be eclectic makes consistency difficult.

What we need is a perspective that offers consistency while simultaneously exposing the practitioner to a variety of methods, models, theories, modalities, and levels of assessment. This unifying approach requires advanced practice knowledge and skill across theories, modalities, and systemic levels. It should provide practitioners with a unifying perspective that is consistent throughout the treatment process, from assessment to follow-up and evaluation. Later in this chapter, we discuss an approach that is multi-systemic and holistic, based on the ecological systems theory so prevalent in the social work profession. This type of advanced systems perspective allows you to utilize information from the totality of your client's life and circumstances, applying it in a way that can generate treatment methods that best suit your client's assessment and treatment needs.

CASE EXAMPLE   "They Just Don't Understand My Situation"

As this example illustrates, a multi-level perspective can help explain individual behavior that appears "resistant" and/or "pathological." At the time of her assessment, Sandra was a 25-year-old single, Caucasian mother of two, pregnant with her third child. She reportedly had a long history of substance abuse, including periodic heavy drinking as well as marijuana and crack cocaine use. She had been admitted for substance abuse treatment twice following arrests for prostitution. Her former counselors characterized both courses of treatment as "failures." Sandra reportedly began using alcohol and drugs immediately after discharge. Thus, the counselors labeled Sandra a resistant client, not ready for "serious" treatment.

The reports also stated that she was chemically dependent and exhibited a strong sense of denial about the depth of her problem. In fact, she had never been willing to admit to a counselor, aloud, that she was chemically dependent. The substance abuse programs she attended worked strictly from a disease model approach, believing that she had a primary disease of addiction. According to this model, Sandra could be helped only if she would admit her addiction and seek daily, lifetime support in Alcoholics Anonymous (AA) or Narcotics Anonymous (NA) to achieve and maintain abstinence. Neither program reported any professional contact with family, friends, or other social service providers as part of the personal history taking or treatment process. Recovery was viewed as her responsibility.

In our initial interview, Sandra again presented as a resistant, involuntary client unwilling to consider, even for a moment, that she had substance abuse problems. She complained bitterly about her previous social workers, claiming, "They just don't understand my situation." Upon further inquiry, I learned that she was correct.

Two years earlier—unbeknownst to previous social workers—Sandra had been reported to Child Protective Services (CPS) when doctors

---

CASE EXAMPLE   *continued*

discovered that her second child was born with cocaine in her blood. At the time, CPS referred Sandra to substance abuse treatment, placing her children with Sandra's mother. Upon further questioning, Sandra admitted that her mother had always believed that Sandra was a "bad parent," and was—according to Sandra—seeking ways to "steal" legal custody of her grandchildren.

At this point, I began to consider issues in the political system to see if there was anything to explain Sandra's apparent unwillingness to seek help. In Sandra's home state, a new set of child welfare laws had given CPS the ability to terminate parental rights for any child (existing and subsequent) if the mother was discovered to have used drugs during pregnancy. In other words, Sandra believed (correctly) that if she admitted to a substance abuse problem, she would give the state and her mother the ammunition they needed to terminate her parental rights and take her children.

There were additional pertinent factors in this case. For example, Sandra was on welfare, which meant that she had to attend public treatment facilities. A third treatment "failure" would make her ineligible to receive state support benefits. She lacked formal education or job skills, and she was unable to locate or afford adequate and safe child care. Additionally, as is often the case, the substance abuse treatment programs provided no special services for women with children (Hughes, 1990).

Thus, because of factors at the macro level (child welfare laws and mandatory reporting) and the mezzo level (local CPS workers and substance abuse "specialists"), and the micro level (her mother), Sandra refused to admit she had problems, would not seek treatment, and was

labeled a resistant client. In fact, she was not in denial of anything. She was acutely aware of her problems with substance abuse, the legal system, her mother, and the state. She was pursuing the only strategy she knew at the time (refusal), hoping that somehow, everything would magically work out in the end.

The problems in this case are self-evident. Sandra had the misfortune to be referred to professionals who found Truth in only one perspective. These professionals overlooked the "keys" to the case, choosing instead to label her resistant and "in denial." By using a multi-systemic approach, I was able to see how the various systems mutually elicited Sandra's seemingly intractable behavior. Sandra was caught in a paradox: to get better and keep her children she had to admit using drugs. However, admitting that she had a substance abuse problem would place her at risk of permanently losing her children to the State. This paradox was created by her counselors' insistence on applying one model that demanded she admit her addiction. They did not recognize that Sandra might have good reasons for being "resistant."

The professionals were correct in one instance—Sandra had a serious substance abuse problem. However, she was never going to admit it. In her mind, she could not admit it, although continuing in the same way (not admitting her addiction and prostitution) would put her at even greater risk of losing her children.

After reflecting on the above case, please answer the following question in your substance abuse journal: *What is the value of a correct diagnosis if a social worker does not understand clients and engage them in a successful assessment and/or treatment process?*

THE MODELS

In this section, we discuss several of the most commonly used models in substance abuse practice, beginning with the least used and ending with the most popular. Please understand that there are nearly as many theories and models as there are individual professionals in the substance abuse field. Therefore, a comprehensive look at the models and theories would require a separate volume. The models discussed here are the moral model, community model, biological model, social learning theory model, cognitive-behavioral model, and the disease model.

Moral Model

Elements of what is commonly known as the moral model (Fisher & Harrison, 2000; Doweiko, 1999; van Wormer, 1995; Akers, 1992) are pervasive in the United States, primarily in the form of substance abuse policy, laws and punishment, religious teachings, and public opinion (Miller & Hester, 1995). Rooted in eighteenth-century England (Doweiko, 1999), the moral model greatly affects the way Americans view substance use and abuse. The moral model was the foundation for the temperance movement that led to national prohibition of alcohol consumption in 1919. Strong elements of this perspective remain in place today. Proponents of the moral model believe that substance use, abuse, and chemical dependency are caused by poor (or immoral) personal decision-making. Hence, individuals choose to abuse substances, and their behavior leads to chemical dependency. Substance abusers are viewed as weak-willed and immoral people, unable to make "proper" choices in life. As a result, these people cannot contribute to a healthy and prosperous family and/or community. The moral model has contributed many of the derogatory and stereotypical social labels used to characterize substance abusers (i.e., drunks, boozers, dope fiends, losers, criminals, the unwashed, etc.). These labels give voice to the moral indignation many Americans direct toward this population. The moral model is characterized by polarized thinking: normal versus abnormal, right versus wrong, and moral versus immoral.

According to the moral model, if people become substance abusers by making poor decisions or improper choices, then solving their problems is also a matter of choice. Accordingly, people can reform themselves by choosing to change, either alone or with religious and/or spiritual guidance. Sometimes "immoral" abusers need help making the decision to change. This type of help usually takes the form of criminal punishment for drug selling, possession, or other illegal acts, because punishment motivates the immoral person to seek redemption. To proponents of the moral model, personal will power and decision-making are the keys to ensure that one does not become—or remain—a substance abuser.

The idea that substance abuse is a function of inappropriate moral decision-making is associated with beliefs about race, class, ethnicity, sexual orientation, and gender as a central part of the moral equation. According to the moral model, there are different levels of immorality in substance abuse and addiction, depending upon who is abusing substances. For example, middle- or upper-class European American substance abusers (even drug sellers) are treated differently from poor people, people of color, or immigrants who abuse or sell drugs (Sklar, 1995; Walker, 2001). One must only look at the prevalence of people of color incarcerated for drug offenses and the different laws pertaining to powder versus crack cocaine possession (Sklar, 1995) to realize that less-privileged people are viewed with more disdain for their behavior than are affluent European American males.

The difference between moral and immoral behavior is defined by the most pow-erful members of society, who tend to look favorably on members of their own group and exclude those who are different.

Many religious groups take the moral model further, believing that substance use and abuse is sinful. Certain religions ban substance use (for example, Islam and the Mormon Church), believing that chemical dependency and the associ-ated behavior occurs because of a disruption in one's relationship with God. As such, spiritual and/or religious intervention is seen as a necessary prelude to ref-ormation. These organizations also believe that acceptance of a particular reli-gious persuasion is the necessary first step in changing a substance-abusing lifestyle (Miller & Hester, 1995). In this way, substance abuse and the pathway to redemption are an inexorable part of the human politics of religion. The fact that the moral model has strong religious ties is a main reason that this set of beliefs still thrives today (Miller & Hester, 1995).

The moral model also provides the foundation for policies of the criminal justice system. Jail and prison populations have increased dramatically over the last 20 years (Sklar, 1995), spurred by a 1988 U.S. Supreme Court decision ruling that crimes committed by an alcoholic were willful misconduct and not the re-sult of a disease (Miller & Hester, 1995). Arrests and incarceration for drug- and alcohol-related crimes have skyrocketed since the mid-1980s, filling the jails and prisons with mostly nonviolent offenders (Akers, 1992). While I am not suggest-ing that substance-related offenses are "victimless" crimes, the desire to severely punish drug and alcohol offenders reflects the depth of the moral indignation American society holds for people who abuse or become dependent on alcohol and other drugs.

Discussion   As you will see later, the disease model is the most common treat-ment model in the United States. However, the most pervasive set of beliefs can be traced to the moral model. This model underlies public sentiment, social pol-icy, and drug laws. It is the basis for how much of the public view people who abuse drugs. It is based on the belief that people who live outside the boundaries of what the majority constitutes as moral cannot be good, productive, moral people. It also includes issues related to what constitutes moral behavior, and who—or which group—has the power to define what is "moral." It is incumbent upon society, through formal systems of social policy and laws—and the informal sys-tem of public opinion—to deal with these individuals in a way that is consistent with the moral beliefs of the majority. In the case of the chemically dependent, this often means punishment, pity, paternalism, and exclusion.

Even Alcoholics Anonymous, the most prominent organization in the world dedicated to helping people with alcohol problems, and Narcotics Anonymous for drug-dependent people base their beliefs and practices on elements of the moral model. For example, members are considered to have "defects of charac-ter" (Narcotics Anonymous, 1986, p. 15). Furthermore, these organizations ac-tively encourage members to see themselves as different from the remainder of society, believing that only those who have "been there" can understand and as-sist people with substance abuse problems. While these methods may be helpful, they serve to perpetuate the belief that substance abusers are different—in a negative way—from the majority of American citizens.

While many social workers disparage the moral model, there are elements that can be helpful when it is consistent with the client's worldview. Do not dismiss a model that suits a client's overall perspective, unless it constitutes a breach of the NASW Code of Professional Ethics (National Association of Social Workers, 2000). Many people have found freedom from a substance-abusing or chemically dependent lifestyle through attendance at churches, mosques, synagogues, and other forms of religious participation, without ever setting foot in a therapist's office, treatment center, or AA meeting. To dismiss the possibility that religious conversion—or a return to one's religious roots—might be an effective strategy for a particular client would be a narrow approach to social work at best. In fact, many religious organizations such as the Nation of Islam are effective at helping their members change their lives. I know many people whose personal recovery through religious involvement is testimony to this fact. Therefore, do not overlook the potential positive outcome from religious involvement, especially if the client's religion is different from your own.

Having affirmed the potential benefits of religious involvement, I must add that it is not our place to insist on any one particular religious affiliation or to insist on any religious affiliation at all unless it stems from information obtained from the client during an interview. The moral model becomes dangerous—and unethical—when we insist that clients follow *our* personal religious teachings. For example, even if you consider yourself a "Christian" social worker, it is ethical to recognize that not all clients will benefit from exposure to your Christian beliefs and practices. You must be willing to allow a client to disavow religion or to attend services at the local Buddhist temple, Jewish synagogue, or Islamic mosque if it will be helpful.

Social work practice is not the place to spread one's personal beliefs and attitudes. This includes beliefs about religion, AA doctrine, or opinions on abortion, homosexuality, or any other controversial public issue. Problems with the moral model often stem from this practice. Like everyone else, social workers are individuals, socialized within families and environments that promote certain beliefs. Therefore, before we learned the models, theories, and practices of the social work profession, we learned lessons from family, friends, media, and culture. These are deep-seated beliefs that are difficult to discern until they reveal themselves during client interaction. As you will read in Chapter 4, a person's "life-learning" (Johnson, 2000, p. 3) is difficult to overcome, but this task is essential to ethical social work practice.

Topic for Your Journal: How Does the Moral Model Influence You?

What are your deep, hidden, and often-unconscious beliefs about people who are chemically dependent? Participating in negative *stereotyping, name-calling, and the disparagement of people who have substance abuse problems, or who participate in the activities that*

Topic for Your Journal *continued*

many chemically dependent people engage in during their addiction (crime, prostitution, violence, and so on), is harmful and unethical behavior. We will discuss this topic in depth in Chapter 4, but at this point you should begin thinking about a question that goes beyond "politically correct" *classroom or agency speech. It is a deeply personal question requiring serious personal reflection. In your substance abuse journal, respond to the following question: In your most private moments outside the classroom or agency, what part(s) of the moral model do you believe and practice?*

Community Model

Advocates of a community theory of substance use and abuse fall into several different, yet related camps. While the various theories suggest different specifics, they share a common understanding that substance abuse and chemical dependency are best explained in terms of macro (global, national, state, and local levels in terms of policy, laws, and public opinion) and mezzo (local community, institutions, and neighborhood environment) influences on individuals and families.

Some community models—including radical and/or progressive models (De Maria, 1992; Galper, 1980; Mullally, 1993)—consider issues such as racism, sexism, homophobia, classism, and ableism to explain the influence of oppressive systems on people in their community. That is, communities can be nurturing environments or hostile places where inequity and hatred contribute to individual and family problems, especially substance abuse (Brueggemann, 2001; Anderson & Carter, 1984).

For example, as stated in Chapter 1, Native Americans report significantly higher rates of alcoholism than the general population. Many have theorized that there might be a genetic predisposition to alcoholism among Native Americans, but few have considered the possibility that stripping tribes of their land, culture, and religion might have created an emotional and cultural wasteland in which alcohol abuse is a realistic outcome. Since no researcher has proven an undeniable genetic link, perhaps the high rates of addiction in Native American communities are community-based in their origin and maintenance, or both. What do you think? See Chapter 11 for a more detailed discussion of these issues.

The field of social work has adopted most of its community theories from sociology and anthropology. Over the years, a wide range of theories have emerged, including anomie/strain theory (Akers, 1992; Merton, 1938, 1957; Cloward & Ohlin, 1961), social control/bonding theory (Hirschi, 1969; Gottfredson & Hirschi, 1990), labeling theory (Braithwaite, 1989; Becker, 1963), selective interaction/socialization theory (Goode, 1989), and many variations of Marxist theory, including work by Paulo Freire (1994).

Given the number of theories and models of community analysis, it is important to define "community," although this can be an arduous task. Cohen (1985) catalogued more than 90 different definitions used in the social science literature. One prominent definition suggests that a community exists when people form a social group based on common location, interest, identification, culture, and/or activities (Fellin, 1995; Garvin & Tropman, 1992). Therefore, people belong to more than one community. While *community* means different things to different people, it can signify a geographic space, geopolitical or civic entity, or a place of emotional identity (Hardcastle, Wenocur, & Powers, 1997).

Fellin (1995) defines three different types of communities: those based on geographical or physical location, non-place communities of identification (race, gender, sexual orientation, and so on), and personal communities that are an integration of the multiple communities in an individual's life. Of the three (geographical, identification, and personal), an individual's emotional identification with a community usually gives it significant meaning (Hardcastle, Wenocur, & Powers, 1997; Lasch, 1994; Cohen, 1985; Fellin, 1995).

According to Cohen (1985), a community is "the arena in which people acquire their most fundamental and most substantial experience of social life outside the confines of the home" (p. 15). Pardeck, Murphy, and Choi (1994) suggest that the ". . . community is the domain where certain assumptions about reality are acknowledged to have validity" (p. 345). When considering community theories of substance use and abuse, the interplay of all three categories mentioned earlier is important to note in any comprehensive analysis (see Chapter 6).

A community approach to substance abuse suggests that substance abuse and/or chemical dependency flourishes where there is disintegration, disorder, and inequities at the local (micro and mezzo), state, or national/global (macro) level. Additionally, in many disrupted and oppressed urban communities (although not only urban communities), drug selling on the streets or in drug houses contributes to and is a direct result of multiple community problems (Anderson, 1990), including higher rates of chemical dependency (Peele, Brodsky, & Arnold, 1992). According to Akers (1992), under these conditions, high rates of substance abuse and other forms of "deviant behavior" are expected (p. 7). Substance abuse and chemical dependency flourish in communities that lack cohesion, social controls, and close-knit family structures, and in which physical decay, poor housing, unstable populations, and individual and/or group oppression prevail (Peele, Brodsky, & Arnold, 1992; Peele, 1998). That is, areas and groups that suffer from the violence of oppression, discrimination, poverty, and a lack of opportunity have the highest risk for substance abuse.

People working from a Marxist tradition attribute inequity, oppression, and alienation to the prevailing capitalist economic system in the West and the drive for profit by multinational corporations around the world (Longres, 2000). According to this view, society's elite groups own most of the wealth (means of production), and, in order to maintain their elite position, exploit the populace (masses) through low wages and other means, causing widespread disruption and feelings of worthlessness. This sense of alienation and hopelessness ultimately leads to severe social dysfunction, including substance abuse and chemical dependency as a means of coping with an unfair and oppressive environment.

If substance abuse results from community disruption, then individual change requires intervention at the community level (Rothman, 1995a; Hardcastle, Wenocur, & Powers, 1997; Homan, 1999; Netting, Kettner, & McMurtry, 1993) in addition to intervention with individuals and/or families. The context for people's beliefs and actions must change if individuals living in these communities are to change. Rothman (1995b) suggests that the change process occurs in the "pattern of macro relationships to micro practice" (p. 4). Going further, he states (1995b),

> This final contextual factor relates macro-oriented community intervention, with its emphasis on structural change, prevention, and social reform, to micro-oriented intervention (casework, counseling, clinical treatment), with its emphasis on personal renewal and psychological repair. We know that problems and systems are interconnected: society and community can cause or exacerbate the troubles of individuals, and distorted values and detrimental behaviors of individuals can undermine the common good. (There are) various generic practice approaches, wherein the skills of individual and community intervention are combined (p. 4).

There are many approaches to promoting community change based on the problem-solving method (Rothman, 1995a; Pincus & Minahan, 1973; Glaser, Abelson, & Garrison, 1983; McMahon, 1994). Community assessment and intervention can also be practiced from a strengths perspective (Saleebey, 1997), focusing on community assets rather than problems (Kretzmann & McKnight, 1993). The latter approach, which is quite popular in many urban districts, is called asset mapping. Kretzmann and McKnight (1993) suggest surveying a community to locate preexisting assets among its people, organizations, and institutions, building upon these strengths to develop a local strategy for change.

Discussion Community theories provide a framework that is critical to understanding a client's life from a multi-systemic perspective. These models point out the ways in which individual and family problems are influenced by aspects of the broader community, including the local neighborhood. C. Wright Mills (1959) promoted this perspective when he stated that a true understanding of social circumstances must base itself on an understanding of an individual's "personal troubles" in the context of the "public issues of social structure" (p. 8). The community models, when applied to substance abuse practice, allow you to understand client behavior in a more holistic manner. According to Mills (1959),

> We have come to know that every individual lives, from one generation to the next, in some society; that he (or she) lives out a biography, and that he (or she) lives it out within some historical sequence. By the fact of his (or her) living, he (or she) contributes, however minutely, to the shaping of this society and to the course of its history, even as he (or she) is made by society and by its historical push and shove (p. 6; words in parentheses have been added).

Without an understanding of community models, particularly related to mechanisms of oppression and discrimination, it would be impossible to develop a multi-systemic view of clients with substance abuse problems. Community models emphasize the challenges faced and the strengths possessed by each individual in terms of race, gender, class, and sexual orientation. They help us to understand why some people seem to give up hope, while others never had hope in the first place.

At a personal level, community models provide insight into the causes of behaviors that might otherwise be labeled as resistant, and they help to explain why some people act out criminally while others do not. Understanding the influence of community opens a window into the ways in which a client's life may differ from that of the social worker. These issues can be understood only if we realize that "attention must be directed everywhere at once. The skilled social worker, like the anthropologist, seeks pattern in the chaos, the method in the madness" (van Wormer, 1995, p. 11).

Yet, as informative as these models are, they do not account for individual substance abusing behavior, or an individual's unique, individual interpretation of culture and environment and how these beliefs and attitudes translate into personal behavior. While community models are an integral part of acquiring a multi-systemic understanding, they are but one part of the overall process.

Biological Model

For several decades, researchers have searched for a genetic link to addictive behavior. While there is consensus about a genetic loading for addiction, the exact nature of predisposition and whether one even exists is debatable (Leshner, 1997; Goodwin & Warnock, 1991). Thus far, the propensity of research into addictive behavior has focused on alcoholism (Doweiko, 1999). However, it is widely believed that if such a genetic link exists for alcoholism, then one must also exist for other forms of chemical dependency. If a genetic link is discovered, chemical dependency, like other genetically inherited disorders, could be considered a disease. The extent to which a genetic predisposition to addictive behavior can be proven will affect the degree to which a disease model will be as widely accepted by scientists as it is by substance abuse treatment providers and the public.

According to biological theories (including genetic hypotheses), chemical dependency has a physical beginning, stemming largely from the physiological or genetic characteristics of an individual. Certain people have a genetic and/or biophysiological predisposition that causes them to become chemically dependent (Hanson & Venturelli, 1998; Doweiko, 1999). Over the last 20 to 30 years, an impressive body of research suggests that this theory may be true. Many scientists now believe that the addictive use of drugs is mediated by the individual's genetic heritage (Hill, 1995). What scientists cannot determine is the extent to which familial addiction, environmental influences, and other characteristics such as gender, race, and ethnicity influence the development of addiction.

Much of the research conducted up to this point has focused on studies involving twins and adopted children. In perhaps the most well-known group of studies, Cloninger, Gohman, and Sigvardsson (1981) claimed that children born to alcoholic parents were likely to become adult alcoholics, even if non–alcoholic parents adopted them at birth. In this study, the authors classified alcoholics into two groups—Type I and Type II—with Type I, mostly nonviolent alcoholics, being the most common (Cloninger et al., 1981). Cloninger et al. (1981) also found a strong environmental impact on the development of adult alcoholism, suggesting that children of Type I alcoholics who were adopted by a middle-class family in infancy had a 38 percent chance of becoming alcoholic in adulthood. Children adopted by lower-class families had a significantly higher possibility of becoming alcoholic (Goodwin & Warnock, 1991).

For children of Type II alcoholics (violent alcoholics who were most often male), there was a 50 percent chance of becoming alcoholic, no matter what the economic status of the adopting family. In 1996, the same authors found that Type I and Type II patterns of alcoholism were independent subtypes (Sigvardsson, Gohman, & Cloninger, 1996; Cloninger, Sigvardsson, & Gohman, 1996). Additionally, they found evidence that women could also become Type II alcoholics (Del Boca & Hesselbrock, 1996).

While proponents of genetic inheritance theories use Cloninger's work to support their belief in predisposition, others question the study (Hall & Sannibale, 1996), claiming that it was seriously flawed. Cloninger et al. (1981) based their classification of parents on records collected by local social workers and not on interviews, leading to questions about the extent to which alcoholic parents were, in fact, alcoholic. Moreover, the same researchers (Hall & Sannibale, 1996) found that the distinction between Type I and Type II alcoholics was flawed. More than 90 percent of the alcohol-dependent people in Hall and Sannibale's study had characteristics of both Type I and Type II alcoholism.

Researchers continue to search for clues about the extent to which genetic predisposition and environmental factors influence the onset of addictive substance use. It seems that as one study arises to prove genetic prevalence, another follows that proves the opposite. For example, one research team sought to isolate the impact of genetic inheritance on the development of addictive drinking in pairs of male and female twins (Pickens et al., 1991). The authors concluded that the influence of genetic factors was weaker than the influence of shared environmental factors, especially for females.

These results contradicted a study conducted by Kender et al. (1992). These researchers studied 1000 pairs of female twins and determined that genetic inheritance accounted for 50 to 60 percent of the potential for alcoholism among women. The authors concluded that genetic inheritance was a major factor in women developing alcoholism. Of course, if 50 to 60 percent of the variance was genetic inheritance, then 40 to 50 percent must be environmental. These findings still suggest that whether a female becomes alcoholic or not is a matter of chance.

Are Chemically Dependent People Different from Everyone Else? For many years, researchers have believed that alcohol or drug dependent people must be different somehow from those who are not. While the range of research is too great to fully discuss here, there are noteworthy themes that require attention. One area of investigation has been brain chemistry, based on a theory that the reward sensors in the central nervous system (CNS) are more sensitive to drugs in some people, making the experience more pleasurable and alluring to these individuals (Mathias, 1995; Jarvik, 1990).

Recently, researchers have confirmed that the pleasure center of the brain involves the limbic system and that recreational drugs of abuse seem to cause pleasurable effects by altering normal brain activity within this system (Hystad, 1989). While many researchers suggest that different regions of the brain are involved in the addictive process (Fischbach, 1992; Restak, 1994; Nestler, Fitzgerald, & Self, 1995; Anthony, Arria, & Johnson, 1995), all agree that the limbic system is involved in the pleasurable response induced by drugs of abuse.

As stated above, there appears to be solid evidence suggesting that a genetic predisposition exists for addictive substance use, making some people biologically different from others. However, clinical research has uncovered no biochemical or genetic difference that inevitably produces addiction. Many researchers now believe that genetic predisposition interacts with environmental factors to make an individual vulnerable to chemical dependency. Some have suggested that addiction rests on a foundation of 30 percent genetic predisposition and 70 percent environmental factors (Uhl, Persico, & Smith, 1992).

All observers seem to agree, however, that even if a genetic predisposition does exist, without environmental factors influencing the individual toward addiction, "they won't become addicted" (Uhl, Persico, & Smith, 1992, p. 4). Genetic predisposition alone does not lead to chemical dependency without other conspiring factors, even if the individual drinks or experiments with drugs (Kahn, 1996; Restak, 1995). An individual's genetic code is but one of many factors that determine his or her behavior (Cattarello, Clayton, & Leukefeld, 1995). While there may be a biological basis for addictive behavior (Leshner, 1997; Nash, 1997; Cowley & Underwood, 1997; Halloway, 1991), it is important to remember that whether an individual becomes chemically dependent still depends mostly on factors beyond genetic makeup.

Is There an Addictive Personality? Without question, the most frequently asked question during classes, workshops, and seminars on substance abuse has to do with the existence of a so-called "addictive personality." In fact, many people do not ask about it but simply assume that it exists. Belief in an addictive personality has kept researchers busy for more than 50 years looking for proof that exposure to dysfunction in early childhood or some combination of inherited traits shape an individual's personality such that he or she is more likely to become addicted in adulthood. Despite the search, such a personality pattern has never been proven (Miller & Kurtz, 1994; Schuckit, Klein, Twitchell, & Smith, 1994; Metzger, 1988). It seems that whenever one research study identifies a set of personality characteristics that compose the addictive personality, another comes along to refute it, often posing a different set of characteristics.

Discussion Social workers seeking a multi-systemic perspective must understand the emerging evidence that there is a genetic loading or a biological predisposition for addictive behavior. This knowledge should lead to an exploration of the family dynamics, looking for information about whether a particular client may have a significant substance abuse problem now or is at risk for developing such problems in the future. However, there is no scientific agreement about the specifics of genetic predisposition or the extent to which these biological factors contribute to an individual's chemical dependency. Therefore, genetic information may be helpful when trying to prevent the onset of addiction. Beyond these two functions, whether a person is genetically loaded for addiction is insignificant outside the assessment process. It is more important to develop a working knowledge of the physiological and biological effects of drugs—to understand what drugs do to the brain, central nervous system, and other critical systems of the body. We need to be aware of withdrawal effects and the risks inherent in drug mixing. Because of the potential for serious illness or even death, it is essential to become knowledgeable about the ways in which drugs affect the human body and to utilize this knowledge in forming questions during the assessment process and in referring clients to physicians for medical examinations early in the substance abuse assessment process.

Social Learning Theory Model

Social learning theory (SLT) is derived from the more famous general approach to social learning pioneered by Albert Bandura (1969, 1977, 1986) and is compatible with a wide range of social learning and control theories (Jessor & Jessor, 1977; Kandel & Adler, 1982; White, Bates, & Johnson, 1990). While several different social learning theories have been published over the years, all of them emphasize individual learning that occurs in the social environment both directly (by personal experience) and indirectly (by modeling of others). SLT also focuses on cognition as a major factor in determining individual behavior (Petraitis, Flay, & Miller, 1995; Akers, 1977) and integrating principles of learning with cognitive and social psychology. This model explains how social and personal "competencies" (Hilgard & Bower, 1975, p. 599) develop from the social context in which learning occurs (Maisto, Carey, & Bradizza, 1999). According to Bandura (1969),

> Human functioning . . . involves interrelated control systems in which
> behavior is determined by external stimulus events (social environment),
> by internal processing systems and regulatory codes, and by reinforcing
> response-feedback systems (p. 19; parenthetical remark added).

There are four general principles essential to understanding social learning theory: differential reinforcement, vicarious learning, cognitive processes, and reciprocal determinism (Maisto, Carey, & Bradizza, 1999). Differential reinforcement refers to the "application of consequences for a behavior dependent on stimulus conditions" (p. 108). In other words, people respond differently to occurrences in their social environment based on individual differences and on what they learn from observing others. Therefore, depending upon the environment and the person, people respond according to the type of reinforcement they receive (or vicariously invoke) from the environment. For example, it is socially acceptable to drink to intoxication at some holiday parties because it is positively reinforced by the environment (others do it and have fun), while it is unacceptable to do the same at Sunday church services because the environment does not tolerate and/or support this type of behavior.

Also called modeling (Maisto, Carey, & Bradizza, 1999), vicarious learning means that people learn new behaviors by observing and communicating with others. In other words, observation of a model being reinforced for a particular behavior increases the likelihood that the observer will utilize that behavior in similar circumstances. Likewise, observing others being punished for a particular behavior can decrease the likelihood that the observer will adopt that behavior (Bandura, 1986). For example, if a child sees Dad drinking to relax, and it seems to consistently work for Dad, it is more likely that the child will grow up believing that drinking is the best way to relieve the stress of a given day.

Cognitive processes (thought and thinking) mediate events that occur in the environment. According to Bandura (1986), cognitive processing allows us to use our environment to identify probable consequences of a particular behavior. Thus, our expectations help to guide later behavior. Individuals regulate their behavior through various cognitive processes—they are not mindless dupes, controlled by external environmental conditions. According to Bandura (1986), people have forethought capability and self-reflective capability, in that they can plan and evaluate their behavior. Another important concept from SLT is the notion of self-efficacy, which refers to an individual's beliefs about the likelihood that he or she can enact a behavior competently (Maisto, Carey, & Bradizza, 1999). In substance abuse treatment, a sense of self-efficacy increases the client's chances of success.

Reciprocal determinism is similar to the person-in-environment construct in social work theory. According to Bandura (1977), the person, environment, and behavior are "interlocking" (pp. 9–10). The environment affects people's behavior, but people also affect their environment. A person's thoughts and the resulting behavior are influenced by the environment, and his or her behavior affects the environment. Specifically related to substance abuse and/or chemical dependency, SLT suggests that addictive behavior is a socially influenced, learned behavior acquired and sustained through a social learning process. Learning occurs through imitation, trial and error, and other cognitive mental processes in social relationship with an individual's primary (highly intimate) and secondary (less intimate) groups.

According to Maisto, Carey, and Bradizza (1999),

> Cultural and subcultural norms define whether alcohol use will be encouraged at all and, if so, in what quantities and under what social conditions. These group norms are learned by observation of socializing agents, such as the drinking behavior of adults and the presentation of alcohol use in the media (p. 112).

People learn attitudes and beliefs about drugs through the influence of their social groups and larger social systems, including the media. If a person's primary group(s) define the use of a particular drug as good, that person will be likely to use that drug repeatedly (Bandura, 1969; Akers, 1992).

Maisto, Carey, and Bradizza (1999) also discuss how individuals begin to use substances and, according to SLT, how substance use disorders develop.

> Drinking behavior typically is begun by youth under nonstressful conditions as part of a more general socialization process, but in the course of experimenting with alcohol, the individual will experience the negative reinforcement of stress reduction through drinking alcohol on a number of occasions. If alcohol use is intermittently reinforced by stress reduction, it will tend to be used on future occasions when the individual experiences stress. If these stressful occasions of use become frequent enough and begin to interfere with the individual's life, then it becomes likely that an alcohol use disorder will develop (pp. 112–113).

Drawing on tenets of operant conditioning, Bandura (1969) believed that the probability of an individual experimenting with or continuing to use drugs is increased by actual or anticipated reward or positive consequences and avoidance of punishment or negative consequences. Whether individuals abstain or use drugs depends on the past, present, and anticipated future rewards and punishments attached to abstinence or use (Akers, 1992; Becker, 1963, 1967). As such, modeling plays a major role in the development of substance abuse and chemically dependent behaviors.

Proponents of SLT view addictive behaviors as a category of bad habits or learned maladaptive behaviors. While SLT recognizes that biological factors may contribute to individual substance abuse, the specific patterns of use are learned. SLT proponents believe that the same principles of learning apply at all points on the continuum between substance use and chemical dependency (Marlatt & Gordon, 1995).

Accordingly, SLT is a "coping deficits model" (Maisto, Carey, & Bradizza, 1999, p. 113). That is, substance use in stressful conditions occurs when alternative coping behaviors are not available to the individual. If an individual has not learned how to behave in healthier ways, substance abuse becomes their only option in stressful situations. In this way, social learning theory shares many of its tenets with the cognitive-behavioral approach (Marlatt & Gordon, 1995; Cooper, Russell, & George, 1988; Dimeff & Marlatt, 1995), which is discussed next.

Discussion Social learning theories focus primarily on the individual and how he or she learns to cope in everyday life. SLT utilizes mezzo and macro level analysis to explain individual behavior at the micro level. Because social learning theories influence much of the substance abuse field in treatment and prevention, these ideas (along with the cognitive-behavioral models discussed below) must be taken seriously.

In substance abuse treatment, the focus on stress, learned behavior, modeling, cognitive processes, and coping mechanisms originated with the social learning theories. SLT has contributed many treatment strategies commonly used in substance abuse treatment programs across the country. For example, stress management programs, life skills training, parent training, and coping skills training programs are used in all fields of social work practice, especially in substance abuse treatment. Additionally, the idea of providing positive mentors for troubled youths is a direct result of social learning theory. When theorists discuss the impact of the family and social environment on the behavior of an individual, they are utilizing elements of the social learning theory because it speaks directly to the socialization process.

The field of substance abuse prevention owes its beginning and theoretical foundation to SLT. For example, the combination of SLT and the moral model (see above) has led to the practice of using public figures in "just say no" advertising and anti-drug speeches across the United States, along with attempts to use "scare tactics" as a method of preventing drug use and criminal behavior among young people. The use of positive role models, substance abuse prevention strategies, and peer support programs testifies to SLT's preeminence in the substance abuse field.

Cognitive-Behavioral Model

Cognitive-behavioral theories maintain that people respond to life events through a combination of cognitive, affective, motivational, and behavioral responses. These theories are based on analysis of the ways in which individuals perceive, interpret, and assign meaning to events (Beck & Weishaar, 2000, p. 241). Traditionally, cognitive and behavioral theories were separate schools. Within the substance abuse field (as well as other fields of practice), however, the two have melded into one approach (Payne, 1997). Here, we treat the two as one model for assessment and treatment of substance abuse and chemical dependency.

Cognitive-behavioral approaches deal with the way people think and act. They are based on the assumption that people's thoughts, beliefs, attitudes, and perceptual biases are learned behavior that influences which emotions will be experienced and the intensity of these emotions. All of these cognitive processes together determine what behavior an individual will exhibit in his or her social world (Beck, Wright, Newman, & Liese, 1993). The focus of substance abuse assessment and treatment with these approaches is on how people think and act, the interaction between the two, and how this interaction has led them into a substance-abusing lifestyle. Treatment, therefore, focuses on changing people's thought processes and behavior to exclude substance abuse from their personal repertoire (Akers, 1992). This model is the most grounded in research of all the models discussed in this text (van Wormer, 1995), and the United States government recommends using cognitive-behavioral approaches with most people suffering from what it calls a "treatable brain disease" (National Institute on Drug Abuse, 1999, p. viii).

Proponents of cognitive-behavioral theory believe that substance abuse and chemical dependency represent a category of "bad habits" (Marlatt & Gordon, 1995, p. 9) driven by destructive and abusive patterns of thinking and perception. Since addictive behavior is learned, it can be analyzed in the same way as any other learned habit. That is, addictive substance use is not different from other issues. This approach represents a stark contradiction to the common understanding of addiction as a disease. Additionally, addictive behavior is not seen categorically, but rather on a continuum of quantity and frequency of occurrence (Marlatt & Gordon, 1995). Addictive behaviors are strongly affected by the individual's expectations of achieving desired effects when using substances. Furthermore, perceived self-efficacy levels (especially low for abusers and high for treatment successes) increase or decrease the likelihood that an individual will engage in addictive substance use. Cognitive-behavioral theory proponents believe that addictive behavior represents a pattern of maladaptive coping behaviors (Marlatt & Gordon, 1995, p. 10).

People who abuse substances develop a set of addictive core beliefs such as "I am helpless" or "I need drugs to feel better" (Beck et al., 1993, p. 52). These core beliefs interact with life stressors to produce excessive anxiety, depression, or anger that activates their drug-related beliefs, leading first to a craving (perceived "need" for the drug) and then to use. It is important to note that cognitive-behavioral proponents do not suggest that an individual who has a craving for drugs must be experiencing physical withdrawal. In fact, there is considerable evidence that the experience of craving does not require physical withdrawal in order to exist (Kassel & Shiffman, 1992).

People who adopt drug-related addictive beliefs come to define certain life stressors as being so severe or troublesome that the only way to gain relief is to abuse alcohol and other drugs. As such, individuals learn to expect that emotional and cognitive relief can occur only when they are under the influence (Goldman, Del Boca, & Darkes, 1999; Sayette, 1999), which can lead the individual to experience psychologically based cravings when drugs are unavailable.

While many in the substance abuse field are critical of this approach because it does not focus on labels such as "addict" or "alcoholic," or on the "disease" process, most mainstream substance abuse treatment programs incorporate many of the ideas, techniques, and practices of the cognitive-behavioral approaches. For example, various techniques for cognitive restructuring, used to teach clients to replace unhealthy thoughts with healthier ones, are part of most relapse prevention programs. Additionally, coping and stress management techniques are widely used, including elements of Ellis's Rational Emotive Therapy (RET) (Ellis, 2000; Ellis, McInerney, DiGiuseppe, & Yeager, 1988) and Reality Therapy (Glasser, 1965; Payne, 1997).

Discussion The substance abuse field owes a great deal of its present beliefs and techniques to cognitive-behavioral theories. In fact, methods adopted from cognitive-behavioral approaches are widely used in the substance abuse field, even if the underlying belief system of chemical dependency as learned behavior is not. These models are mostly concerned with the individual (micro level), but do explain in a comprehensive way how individuals come to use and abuse substances. Because of the individual focus of cognitive-behavioral theories, social workers must learn to use this model in the context of a more broad-based systemic understanding of individual clients. We discuss this model as it pertains to substance abuse treatment and relapse prevention in Chapter 10.

Disease Model

In the United States, the disease model is, unquestionably, the most prominent and widely applied theory within the professional substance abuse treatment field; it has become "virtually the gospel in the field of alcohol (and other drug) studies" (Lender, 1981, p. 25). The disease model is a theory and not a model per se. It is widely applied to define chemical dependency, while methods of treatment are normally taken from other theories and models, such as the cognitive-behavioral and social learning theories. The disease model is also the primary paradigm for treating other forms of addictive behaviors (such as gambling, sex, and overeating). Because of the prevalence of this approach, a lengthier discussion will be provided for it than for other theories introduced in this chapter.

Over the last 20 years, many people (especially popular psychology leaders) have come to believe that virtually everything people do with regularity, dedication, single-mindedness, or compulsion is a disease. People are said to be addicted to chocolate, coffee, exercise, sex, shopping, people, the Internet, and food. Recently, a popular psychology guru on a highly rated television talk show claimed that it is possible to become addicted to suicidal thoughts! The twelve-step model pioneered by AA is now applied to more than 100 conditions other than alcohol and drug abuse (*Harvard Mental Health Letter*, 1992). The proliferation of new addictions—or "pseudo ailments" (Leo, 1990, p. 16)—stems from the fact that in contemporary America, the term "addiction" has become synonymous with "disease."

Perhaps the most prominent new form of addictive disease occurs when people become addicted to other people and/or relationships. In this addiction, children who grow up with alcoholic parents—because of the trauma of that type of upbringing—become "addicted" to choosing alcoholic and abusive partners in adulthood. These people (mostly women) act out their disease by consistently developing intimate relationships with chemically dependent partners. They maintain these relationships through "enabling" behavior that allow adult children of alcoholics (ACOA) to satisfy their needs by attempting to control their alcoholic partner's substance abuse (Hobe, 1990; Cruse, 1989; Ackerman, 1989; Gravitz & Bowden, 1987; Woititz, 1983; Black, 1981). Recently, a more general codependency movement emerged, based on the tenets of the ACOA movement. This perspective views codependency similarly to the ACOA perspective, but its cause is related to trauma experienced during childhood that results from bad parenting or destructive adult relationships (Beattie, 1987). Depending on one's personal definition of "bad parenting," it is feasible that nearly everyone could be classified as codependent and therefore likely to engage in unhealthy and destructive relationships that will ultimately become an addictive disease.

The common denominator between all the various diseases is the disease model of addiction (Doweiko, 1993; Vaillant, 1983; Johnson, 1973; Jellinek, 1960). Since the days of E. M. Jellinek's original research in 1952—and bolstered by the American Medical Association's classification of alcoholism as a formal disease in 1956 (Musto, 1999)—the belief in the notion of addiction as a disease has become commonplace, mainly in the United States.

Origins of the Disease Model Abusive alcohol and opiate use was called a disease beginning in the early nineteenth century (Musto, 1999). This viewpoint came into prominence in the 1950s and was expanded to include compulsive and destructive use of all drugs. In 1952, Jellinek described the disease model in terms that remain relatively unchanged today. He suggested in his landmark research that alcohol addiction progressed in four stages (prealcoholic, prodromal, crucial, and chronic). In the *prealcoholic* phase, individuals use alcohol primarily for relief from social tensions. In this phase are the roots of the person's eventual loss of control. That is, people no longer drink socially, but to relieve tension and anxiety. If individuals continue to drink, they progress to the *prodromal* phase. During this phase, people develop blackouts, begin drinking secretly, become preoccupied with alcohol use, and feel guilty about their behavior while intoxicated (Jellinek, 1952). With continued use, they advance to the *crucial* phase. In this phase, individuals begin developing a physical dependence on alcohol. Additional symptoms of the crucial phase include loss of self-esteem, loss of control over drinking, social withdrawal, self-pity, and nutritional neglect. During this phase, people attempt to reassert control over drinking by entering into periods of abstinence, only to relapse later (Jellinek, 1952).

According to Jellinek (1952), the final and most serious stage occurs if people continue to drink. During the *chronic* phase, individuals are lost in the alcoholic lifestyle. They experience symptoms such as physical and emotional deterioration, drinking with social inferiors, motor tremors (shakes), obsession with drinking, loss of control, and the need to use other drugs when alcohol is unavailable. At this point, if their drinking goes untreated, these people will ultimately die of disorders related to addiction, such as liver failure.

In 1960, Jellinek extended the disease concept by classifying various patterns of addictive drinking. These included five subtypes of additive drinking: Alpha, Gamma, Beta, Delta, and Epsilon. The most severe subtype is the Gamma-type alcoholic. People who fall into this category, after progressing through Alpha, Beta, or Delta categories, exhibit symptoms such as physical withdrawal, craving, medical complications, decreased tolerance to alcohol, blackouts, and loss of morals (Jellinek, 1960). One of the major changes in Jellinek's later work was a description of Alpha pattern drinking. Jellinek identified Alpha drinking patterns as relatively stable, often lasting for many years. However, consistent with earlier beliefs about inevitable progression, if Alpha drinkers continued to drink, they would become Gamma alcoholics.

There is some research to support Jellinek's claims. Schuckit et al. (1993) examined the drinking patterns of 636 male alcoholic clients admitted to inpatient programs. In this study, there was significant variation in specific problems related to alcohol use, and a consistent progression in the severity of problems caused by addictive drinking. While these findings offer some support for inevitable progression, there is far more research suggesting otherwise (discussed below). In light of the paucity of supporting evidence, it is remarkable that the disease model has survived without major modification for more than 50 years. Moreover, proponents have generalized the disease model to include drugs other than alcohol and non-substance-related destructive behaviors (process addictions).

Basic Tenets of the Disease Model Proponents of the disease model claim that addiction is a biological, psychological, and spiritual disease that is incurable and progressive. Often comparing addiction to diabetes and more recently, heart disease, proponents believe that once a person develops the disease, it inevitably progresses through a series of stages until the person dies. The only way to arrest the disease is by abstaining from all substance use. Therefore, the goal of treatment is remission, not cure. The only way to achieve remission (or recovery) is via lifelong support—primarily through twelve-step groups such as Alcoholics Anonymous (AA)—to help monitor the personal and social "triggers" that could cause a return to drug use (relapse).

Since the disease is incurable, the goal is recovery (or *control* of the disease through abstinence). Recovery (versus cure) is an important concept, because disease model proponents believe that the recovering addict is merely one drink or drug use episode away from triggering the disease anew, dragging the person back onto the inevitable course of addiction. In fact, a common understanding in the professional and recovering community suggests that if a person relapses after an extended period of abstinence—because of inevitable progression—he or she will be more severely dependent than before.

Several other factors characterize the disease of addiction, including inevitable loss of control (people cannot control their use once they begin), moral and spiritual bankruptcy, and denial of the existence of a problem (Denning, 2000; van Wormer, 1995; Johnson, 1973). While nobody knows for sure where the disease originates or how to tell if it actually exists, it is an all-or-nothing endeavor. Either people have the disease and all its attendant behaviors, or they do not (Peele, 1998).

In fact, people who are thought to have the disease and later find that they can stop abusing drugs without twelve-step support or who successfully return to "normal" social drinking or drug use are not viewed as exceptions to the disease model, but are considered to have been initially misdiagnosed. Therefore, diagnosis is based on circular thinking. Individuals who have the disease are expected to show certain behaviors, and if individuals demonstrate these behaviors, they have the disease. There is no other way to appropriately test for or diagnose the disease of addiction.

One of the most interesting tenets of the disease model—especially as it is practiced in AA—pertains to the role of professional helpers. According to this model, recovering people are the best source of help for "practicing addicts," because people who have experienced addiction and recovery are better suited to help than professionals who lack the necessary "life experience." This issue is discussed again in Chapter 6.

Why You Should Visit a Twelve-Step Group

Perhaps the best way to understand the disease model is to familiarize yourself with the twelve-step process of Alcoholics Anonymous (AA), Narcotics Anonymous (NA), and other community support programs based on the twelve-step model. In fact, you should visit an AA or NA meeting in your local community. The programs offer three different types of meetings, two

Why You Should Visit a Twelve-Step Group *continued*

of which you, as a nonmember, will be permitted to attend. These two are called "open" or "speaker" meetings. The third type—a closed meeting—is not open to outside attendance. Closed meetings are the main working meetings of the organization, reserved for individuals seeking help for personal substance abuse issues. As a matter of professional ethics, you should not attempt to participate in a closed meeting unless you are seeking personal help.

Local AA and NA organizations all over the world host open or speaker meetings that are specifically designed to make it possible for interested people from the community to learn about the workings of the organization. Locally, meeting times and dates are available through the AA or NA telephone number found in every telephone directory in the United States. Many regions, especially those located in and around larger metropolitan areas, post meeting information on the Internet.

I urge you to attend at least one AA or NA meeting (preferably two), for a couple of reasons. First, attendance is the best way to understand the disease model and its application. What you hear and observe in these meetings is consistent with what occurs in disease-model-based substance abuse treatment programs across the country. Second, because you refer clients to community resources, it is important to have a working knowledge and understanding of any program to which you send vulnerable clients. All graduate students in my substance abuse practice courses are required to attend and report on at least one AA or NA open/speaker meeting during the semester. It is, by far, the most powerful and enlightening assignment in that particular class. For a more in-depth look at the workings of AA and other twelve-step groups, see Chapter 9.

Discussion The disease model is the most widely accepted explanation for chemical dependency in the United States, but it remains controversial outside the circle of people who fervently believe in it. While many substance abuse professionals believe in absolute fidelity to the disease model, many experts in the substance abuse treatment field question the notion of chemical dependency as a disease. Even among those who question the validity of the disease model, the range of opinion is remarkable. At one extreme are authors like Szasz (1972, 1991), Peele (1998), and Fingarette (1988) who believe the disease does not exist. Each suggests that it is inappropriate to classify what amounts to personal "bad habits" as diseases, lest everyone in the world be classified as having one disease or another (Szasz, 1972, p. 84). Kaiser (1996) and Szasz (1988) call the disease of addiction a "mythical disease" (p. 319). Prominent family therapist David Treadway (1990) suggests that the disease model may be useful as a "metaphor or reframe for many clients," but warns that mental health professionals become uncomfortable "when it is presented as scientific fact" (p. 42). Even Vaillant (1983), a longtime supporter of the disease model, claims that one needs to use a "shoehorn" to make addiction fit into the disease model concept (p. 4). The disease model can be characterized as a community response to the moral model, in that it offers some improvement in the way people with alcohol and other drug problems are socially defined. However, the disease model continues to promote stigmatizing effects (i.e., addicts are viewed as "sick" and "different" people with "moral defects") that are contrary to social work values of respect and understanding the person and environment. Regardless, most programs across the United States are adamant about the need for client and professional fidelity to this particular theory of addiction.

Evaluation of Jellinek's Research   Many authors have uncovered a number of flaws in Jellinek's original research. For example, Jellinek gathered his original data from questionnaires distributed to AA members through the organization's international newsletter. Of the 158 questionnaires returned, 60 were discarded because members had pooled and averaged their responses. To draw his conclusions, Jellinek took the 98 remaining survey responses and generalized the results to describe the behavior of both AA members and nonmembers. Given the extremely low number of responses and the gross violations of accepted research protocol (sampling procedures, for one), it is surprising that Jellinek's concept of addiction as a disease received such widespread acceptance. I doubt that his research could even be published in a professional journal today.

Media and Public Opinion   Just how did Jellinek's research become so popular, despite the flaws in the research? One reason may be the way mainstream advertisers, even the alcohol producers themselves, have propagated the disease model. For example, "because the majority of treatment programs are based on the disease concept, their lobbying, public relations, and advertising efforts inevitably propagate the disease theme" (Fingarette, 1988, p. 23). Dreger (1986) stated that one of the reasons that this disease is unique and questionable is the fact that alcohol (the agent of the disease) is "promoted by every Madison Avenue technique and by every type of peer pressure one can imagine. No other disease is thus promoted" (p. 322). Taking a different approach, Fingarette (1988) accuses the alcohol industry of contributing to the public perception of alcoholism as a disease:

> By acknowledging that a small minority of the drinking population is susceptible to the disease of alcoholism, the industry can implicitly assure consumers that the vast majority of people who drink are not at risk (p. 27).

Another possible reason for the proliferation of the disease model is its consistency with the philosophy of AA. This has helped the disease model become accepted by the political and medical establishments, as well as the public. Anytime addiction is featured in the mainstream media, television talk shows, even local and national news broadcasts, it is ultimately referred to as a disease. Returning to an earlier theme, Peele (1998) noted:

> The disease model has been so profitable and politically successful that it has spread to include problems of eating, child abuse, gambling, shopping, premenstrual tension, compulsive love affairs, and almost every other form of self-destructive behavior. . . . From this perspective, nearly every American can be said to have a disease of addiction (p. 67).

The Power of the Drug   Another problem with the disease concept involves how the disease is characterized. The whole notion of addiction as a disease hinges on the idea that people who are addicted are "powerless" to control their use of drugs. Drug use completely takes over their daily life until the moment they quit using, end up in jail or a mental hospital, or die. Hence, drugs are seen as the cause of addiction, not people who use drugs compulsively. The demon drug renders the user powerless to stop voluntarily or as an act of personal will. Some drugs, such as crack cocaine, are believed to be so powerful that anyone who tries them even once will immediately become addicted and willing to give up everything to get more of the drug.

What is often overlooked is that neither alcohol nor drugs are the enemy; by itself, a drug has no inherent power (Szasz, 1996, 1997). Moreover, nearly every drug that is now widely abused was once legal, appropriate, and considered safe by the medical profession and mainstream society (Musto, 1999). In actuality, drugs are harmful only when people use them in abusive and harmful ways. In this way, the disease model attributes too much power to the drug, removing elements of personal responsibility for the effects of drug dependency on people, families, or communities. As Siegel (1989) states, the disease model gives "credit to the disease rather than the person" (p. 12). Chemical dependency requires the active participation of the "victim" to exist. That is, it occurs only when individuals put drugs into their bodies (Savage, 1993). Drugs (including alcohol) are not predatory substances that aggressively attack the human body at will. People must administer them first.

Inevitable Progression? An area of contention between proponents and critics of the disease model involves the question of whether people who use drugs inevitably progress from one stage to another (i.e., from use to abuse to dependency). Many authors do not believe in inevitable progression (Skog & Duckert, 1993). George Vaillant (1983), a supporter of the disease model, has stated that progression from one stage to the next is not inevitable:

> The first stage is heavy social drinking. . . . This stage can continue asymptomatically for a lifetime; or because of a change of circumstances or peer group it can reverse to a more moderate pattern of drinking; or it can progress into a pattern of alcohol abuse. . . . At some point in their lives, perhaps 10–15 percent of American men reach this second stage. Perhaps half of such alcohol abusers either return to asymptomatic (controlled) drinking or achieve stable abstinence. In a small number of such cases . . . such alcohol abuse can persist intermittently for decades with minor morbidity and even become milder with time (p. 309).

Similarly, Royce (1989), another supporter of the disease concept, stated,

> Even when progression occurs, it does not follow a uniform pattern. The steps may be reversed in order, or some steps may be omitted. Symptoms progress, too; something that was minor in an early stage may appear later in a different form or to a greater degree. . . . Rate of progression varies also (p. 89).

Toneatto et al. (1991) found that a *minority* of drinkers, approximately 25 to 30 percent, progress through all the stages of alcoholism. Schuckit et al. (1993) also found that alcoholics tend to alternate between periods of abusive and nonabusive drinking, and another group found that addiction is "often, but not automatically progressive" (Morse & Flavin, 1992, p. 1013).

It is apparent that progression from substance use to abuse to chemical dependency is not inevitable. While nobody knows for sure why some people remain in the abuse stage while others progress to dependency, it is clear that there is no inevitability to the progression through the stages. Nevertheless, it is also true that all chemically dependent people had to begin somewhere, so those who ultimately become chemically dependent do progress through stages. The fact that chemically dependent people progress through the stages, however, does not mean that every user does (Peele, Brodsky, & Arnold, 1992; Peele, 1998; Akers, 1992; Jung, 1994). The fact that people believe in inevitable progression becomes even more mystifying when one considers that most adults drink alcohol but do not find themselves pulled down the inevitable path toward addiction.

Gateway Drugs　The misguided belief in the inevitability of chemical dependency contributes to the widely held notion of the importance of "gateway drugs" (Hanson & Venturelli, 1995, p. 8). "Gateway drugs" refer to the drug(s) people normally use first, often as young people—alcohol, tobacco, and marijuana. It is obvious why these drugs are normally the first to be used. Alcohol and tobacco are readily available, while marijuana is probably the most available illegal drug in the United States. Simply stated, nearly everyone who becomes chemically dependent, no matter what drug(s) they ultimately prefer, probably began by using alcohol, tobacco, and/or marijuana.

Over the years, this phrase, as simple and straightforward as it seems, has become loaded with misperception and political ideology. For example, Hanson and Venturelli (1995) state that, "the word gateway suggests a path leading to something else" (p. 8). While this is true, over the years it has come to mean that the use of so-called gateway drugs inevitably leads people to move along the continuum from simple use to chemical dependency, and from the gateway drugs to "harder" drugs. What is the political usefulness of this misperception? It provides the "grounds" for drug prevention strategies based on scare tactics: "Don't drink alcohol or smoke pot, because you'll end up shooting heroin later in life." In reality, all available evidence says otherwise. Even the kids these messages are targeted toward rarely believe this myth.

Loss of Control　The concept of loss of control is, perhaps, the most contentious issue between proponents and critics of the disease model. The notion that addicts lose control of their use, thus making use involuntary, is a fundamental tenet of the disease model. In fact, it is the first of the twelve steps of AA: "We admitted that we were powerless over alcohol and that our lives had become unmanageable" (Alcoholics Anonymous, 1981, p. 5).

The idea of inevitable loss of control (powerlessness) has been disputed by many (Skog & Duckert, 1993), including researchers who, under experimental conditions, were unable to prove that it occurs (Marlatt, Demming, & Reid, 1973). Defenders of the disease model point out that researchers "took too literally the idea that one drink always means getting drunk," and "many research projects set out to disprove the 'one drink' hypothesis in laboratory or hospital settings so artificial and with criteria so wooden that nobody with real experience in alcoholism could take the results seriously" (Royce, 1989, p. 135). Vaillant (1983) found that drinking patterns often change over time, suggesting that alcohol-dependent people do experience a measure of control over their drinking. Moreover, Peele (1998) states that many scientists now believe that alcohol-dependent people regulate their drinking to achieve a desired emotional state.

It is possible that alcoholics may have inconsistent control over their drinking or drug use, consuming different amounts of alcohol and other drugs at different points in their lives (Toneatto et al., 1991; Vaillant, 1990). Still, there is no direct evidence to suggest that addicts experience consistent loss of control, as suggested by Jellinek (1952, 1960). As a result, some proponents of the disease model modified the definition of loss of control to mean the alcoholic or addict cannot predict the situations in which he or she will lose control. The loss of predictability is now thought to define the alcoholic or addict (Keller, 1972). In light of the fact that this modification was made in reaction to criticism and not as a result of research, many remain skeptical.

The Disease Model as Gospel One of the most interesting and sometimes troubling aspects of the disease model is the expectation that addicts and professionals will adopt the beliefs, philosophies, and methods of the disease model without question, giving the impression that the disease model is like a religious cult (Kaiser, 1996). In some circles, the disease model is dogma, with proponents determined to avoid all forms of criticism, often resorting to name-calling and personal attacks, as if anyone who dares to disagree must be an uneducated cave dweller.

In the professional substance abuse community, the demand for unquestioned loyalty to any model or perspective is dangerous. This extreme level of narrow-mindedness often leads professionals to be uninterested in and/or unaware of new research, unable to benefit from frank and critical professional debate, and closed to treatment possibilities that do not fit the model. In addition, clients are often required to assume the values and beliefs of the program or professional helper, even if these values and beliefs are inconsistent with the client's personal values and beliefs. Proponents often tell clients that there is only one way to recover, excluding all other possibilities for treatment. The "childlike faith" requirement in many substance abuse programs alienates many potential clients who want help with their substance abuse problems, leading to exceedingly high dropout rates from substance abuse treatment (DeLeon, 1994). While disease model proponents proclaim that millions of people have found successful recovery with this model (Alcoholics Anonymous, 1981), it is impossible to determine the number of people who have been driven away from potential treatment by a single-minded, dogmatic approach that fervently resists any attempt to modify the model to fit a particular client's circumstances.

While there are many problems with the disease model, it is widely used as a basis for treatment. In Chapter 10, we discuss several ways that the disease model is useful in substance abuse treatment. As with the moral model, multi-systemic social workers do not discard a model or theory that may be helpful to some clients.

Summary of Models

Obviously, there is no agreement about what causes some people to use substances, some to abuse substances, and some to become dependent on substances. Any model—or combination of models—can accurately describe chemical dependency if a person believes in it. There is no single Truth to behold in substance abuse assessment and treatment. Nevertheless, the disease model is the most commonly held theory in professional substance abuse practice. Therefore, it is incumbent upon you to study the issue to determine the best way to approach clients with substance abuse problems.

For those working from a multi-systemic perspective, each model, or combination of models, is but one part of the comprehensive, systemic, and holistic equation to be used when trying to sort through a substance-abusing client's life, history, beliefs, attitudes, and actions. Multi-systemic practitioners view substance abuse in the context of a broader ecological systems model, whereas the models presented in this chapter explain substance abuse and treatment from primarily one point of view. In the following discussion, substance abuse and chemical dependency are placed into a multi-systemic framework that considers client problems in the context of micro, mezzo, and macro influences. This approach considers issues of human diversity and cultural competence, social work values and ethics, and the need to promote social and economic justice for all clients in our care and all groups that experience oppression and discrimination.

SUBSTANCE ABUSE
FROM A MULTI-SYSTEMIC,
ECOLOGICAL PERSPECTIVE

Throughout the first three chapters of this text, you have been introduced to small tidbits of what I call a multi-systemic approach to substance abuse assessment and treatment. Here, we look at this approach in relation to substance abuse, the models discussed earlier, and substance abuse engagement, screening and assessment, treatment planning, and treatment. First, I offer a primer on ecological systems theory in social work. While this may be a repeat of information gained in earlier social work practice courses, some level of repetition is useful in reinforcing key points.

Systems and Ecological Systems Theory

The foundation of a multi-systemic approach to substance abuse is the ecological systems perspective. Ecological systems theory (Germain & Gitterman, 1996; Germain, 1981) originated from the general systems theory offered first by von Bertalanffy (1971). Systems theory is a biological theory that proposes that all organisms are systems, composed of subsystems, and in turn belong to larger systems. This theory applies to social systems (groups, families, communities) and, according to Hanson (1995), has value in social work because it deals with the holistic instead of parts of human social behavior.

Systems theory began having an impact on social work in the 1970s, primarily through the work of Pincus and Minahan (1973). Later developments by Siporin (1975) and Germain and Gitterman (1996) increased the popularity of systems theory, making it one of the hallmarks of social work practice. Perhaps the biggest boost to the application of systems theory to social work practice came from the family therapy movement. In family therapy, systems theory is the basis for most contemporary models of assessment and treatment. The first practitioners to apply systems theory to substance abuse practice were, in fact, family therapists (Satir, 1964; Haley, 1976; Stanton et al., 1982).

The ecological systems approach evolved from an integration of a biopsychosocial model with systems theory (Gambrill, 1997; Kirst-Ashman & Hull, 1999; Sheafor, Horejsi, & Horejsi, 2000). The ecological systems approach is interactionist; it looks at the person and environment as constantly interacting in daily life (Howe, 1981). According to van Wormer (1995),

> The ecological approach is holistic, biopsychosocial in its understanding of the person-in-the-environment and the environment-in-the-person. In ecology, emphasis is on adaptation of the individual organism and of the system (such as the family system) to internal and external stress. Alcoholism in the family can be understood in terms of internal (illness within the individual) stress with a strong external environmental component. The focal point of study would be the interaction among various parts of the alcoholic system (p. 7).

The ecological systems approach to substance abuse proposes that individual addictive behavior is shaped by the biological, psychological, social, and cultural realms, along with the larger systems of laws, policies, and oppressive mechanisms in society. It stresses adaptation of the person to the environment. In this way, ecological systems theory can be interpreted as a passive model, whereby humans adapt to the given environment, regardless of its inequities and oppression. Issues related to culture, race, gender, class, and sexual orientation make substance abuse mean different things for each particular individual within her or his biopsychosocial environment. It is your responsibility, as a multi-systemic practitioner, to understand each person's "multi-dimensional experience" (van Wormer, 1995, p. 9).

Those who employ an ecological systems approach work in the here-and-now toward improving coping skills, enhancing functioning, and evoking radical systems change to promote social and economic justice. The multi-systemic approach adds to ecological systems theory by expecting that encouraging change will involve more than helping people adapt to their environment. It also proposes radical system change (Rojek, 1986). This counteracts one of the most significant criticisms of the ecological systems approach, mentioned earlier—that it implies slow and manageable change toward integration and adaptation, with little provision for radical change (Payne, 1997).

In the language of systems theory, the difference between ecological and multi-systemic approaches represents the difference between first- and second-order change (O'Hanlon & Wilk, 1987). First-order change occurs when individuals or families adapt to an existing social situation without necessarily changing the overall system, while second-order change occurs when radical change in the system requires people to interact with each other and outside systems in an entirely new and often unpredictable manner.

For example, in substance abuse treatment, a first-order change may result in a person becoming sober and clinging to recovery in the face of lingering poverty caused by a lack of job skills. In this example, the treatment focus would be entirely on sobriety, instead of sobriety and the development of job skills to provide the individual with the tools to lift himself or herself out of poverty. Second-order change would entail training and/or education that would empower the newly sober client to fundamentally change the way he or she lives, relates to the social environment, and responds to new challenges. In this example, the social worker may advocate for admission into a school or training program and provide assistance in finding a suitable position worthy of the person's skills and abilities.

A multi-systemic approach alleviates the tendency to attribute an individual's behavior solely to internal personality traits. It looks at problems and behaviors in the context of multi-dimensional influences in the social environment (van Wormer, 1995), including deficits and strengths. This approach also suggests that changing one aspect of an individual's functioning will have reverberating influences on other segments of the system. While Siporin (1980) claims that this does not seem to happen in practice, my clinical experience has been filled with examples of clients who, having gained confidence and/or experienced success in one area of life, have gone on to apply these changes to other social interactions, forcing others to relate differently to the newly confident client.

A Multi-Systemic Framework
for Substance Abuse Practice

Each of the models discussed in this chapter can be adapted into a multi-systemic practice framework. As a multi-systemic practitioner, I neither accept any one model fully, nor disregard a model entirely if there is potential for helping a client succeed in a way that is compatible with professional social work values and ethics. The following discussion looks at substance abuse and chemical dependency at multiple levels to demonstrate how each of the models can be applied to better understand and assess client substance abuse problems. Generally, the following six dimensions (biological, psychological, family, religious/spiritual/existential, social/environmental, and macro) encompass the information needed to complete a comprehensive, multi-systemic substance abuse assessment.

Biological Dimension   As we discussed earlier, chemical dependency has biological components, including the significant involvement of the brain (Center for Substance Abuse Treatment, 1999a; Leshner, 1997). Research into genetics demonstrates a genetic loading for addictive behavior, although its exact nature and the extent to which it is a determining factor are unknown. Moreover, because of lifestyle factors and the effects of drugs on the human body, knowledge about how drugs affect the body and the many potential health considerations is essential for anyone who carries out substance abuse assessment and treatment.

You must understand the potential impact of drug mixing and exposure to other types of disease (i.e., TB, hepatitis, HIV, etc.) that may occur as a result of a substance abusing or chemically dependent lifestyle. Additionally, you should understand the impact of potential co-occurring mental disorders and consider how these illnesses—and the medication used to treat mental illnesses—may interact to influence the client's behavior.

Individuals who reach the stage of chronic chemical dependency have a chronic illness (not disease) that is primary, progressive, and potentially fatal, although this end is not inevitable. At this advanced stage, you must know how to apply elements of the disease model as it relates to chronic addiction. For example, all substance-abusing clients, whether or not they are chemically dependent, require a thorough physical examination by a physician to assess the effects of drug use, as well as neglect of nutrition and preventive health care. However, clients who have not reached late-stage addiction may not have an illness but may instead be involved in adaptive, coping behavior that was learned and has become a routine part of their approach to daily life (see below).

Psychological Dimension If you opt for a multi-systemic perspective, you will need a working knowledge about how elements of the psychological dimension are involved in addictive behavior and how addictive behavior affects the psychology of the client (and that of significant others). Hence, you must understand various theories and models, not one prevailing model, because a model that works for one client will not necessarily be effective for another (McMahon, 1994; van Wormer, 1987).

Therefore, you must know the disease model in order to understand the formidable psychological defense mechanisms (such as denial) that chemically dependent people and their families present. You must also understand how drugs are used to alleviate physical and psychological pain and how self-medication can lead to serious and significant psychological consequences. Additionally, an advantage of the disease model is that it tends to alleviate guilt feelings and provides a reason for an individual's behavior. Yet, the same mechanism that offers relief for the addict can cause guilt among family members. Keep this in mind when working with chemically dependent clients and their families, especially when discussing codependent or so-called enabling behavior (Wegscheider, 1981). It is easy, when trying to introduce these concepts, to create or enhance family members' feelings of responsibility for the addict's behavior.

Understanding the social learning and cognitive-behavioral models focuses on issues such as self-esteem, coping mechanisms, life stressors, and the role they play in addictive behavior. Both of these prominent models explain substance abuse as a coping mechanism for dealing with life's stressors. Proponents of each model believe that the substance abuser approaches substance use as a primary way of dealing with psychological pain and stress. A comprehensive assessment and treatment plan would be lacking in depth and efficacy if these models were excluded.

Another area where social learning and cognitive-behavioral theories may prove helpful, along with the genetic predisposition models, is with clients who have a real or potential co-occurring mental disorder. Keep in mind that addictive behavior and mental illness often run in families. Therefore, a glimpse into family history for evidence of these issues is critical in any assessment process. Moreover, you must also know that people use alcohol and other drugs to treat serious mental illness. Become adept at understanding the relationship between mental illness and substance abuse; learn how to determine whether mental illness predated addictive behavior or occurred as a result of addictive behavior; and be able to anticipate when clients may need a second-level mental health assessment performed by a licensed psychiatrist with knowledge about substance abuse and chemical dependency. See Chapter 8 for information on co-occurring disorders pertaining to assessment and Chapter 11 for information pertaining to treating clients with co-occurring disorders.

Family Dimension Familiarity with the disease model, genetic model, social learning, and cognitive-behavioral models, along with an understanding of systems theory, is necessary in assessing the family in substance abuse practice. The disease model and systems theory are both helpful in understanding the reciprocal impact an individual's personal addictive behavior has on the family and individuals within that family. Genetic models, as mentioned earlier, suggest that preparing an extensive family history and looking for patterns of addictive behavior and/or mental illness may be helpful. Social learning and cognitive-behavioral models focus on the learned aspects of addictive substance use and therefore must be considered when assessing the client's family as part of a comprehensive assessment. As van Wormer (1995) states so eloquently,

> The family has a pattern, a rhythm that is more than the sum of its parts. From generation to generation, the rhythm persists. So, the culture of addiction— the urges, the emotions, and the escape—is echoed down the line (p. 197).

Each of the models presented, in the context of systems theory, allows you access to this rhythm and the generational transmission processes of addictive behavior. Knowledge about how to engage and assess family systems is essential. See Chapter 5 on the family system and Chapter 8 on assessment details for more in this area.

Religious/Spiritual/Existential Dimension Proponents of the disease model believe that chemical dependency is a disease that is caused by, and is the cause of, spiritual and moral bankruptcy among the people it affects (Alcoholics Anonymous, 1981). Discovering and accepting spiritual beliefs has been shown to be central to recovery from chemical dependency (Peck, 1993). Therefore, understanding how AA and the other twelve-step support groups operate pertaining to religion and spirituality is important for several reasons. First, many people find comfort in the idea of relying on a higher power to help in the recovery process. Second, others will be resistant to any mention of spirituality, God, or a higher power, thus making engagement in twelve-step groups difficult.

With the latter group of clients, you must be prepared to openly discuss these issues as a way of easing their entry into an appropriate twelve-step group. Third,
many clients blame religion for their current condition. This, too, represents an
area of significant concern that you must be prepared to process in an open and
accepting manner. Fourth, many clients may find benefit from re-engaging in a
religious or spiritual tradition from their past. Your job, in this instance, is to encourage clients to approach whatever religious or spiritual tradition they believe
will help.

Because of the prevalence of the moral model in American society, exploring
people's religious beliefs as they pertain to their definition of self in relation to
the world is often a critical part of the substance abuse assessment and treatment
process. As we discuss in Chapter 8, how clients view themselves in relation to
others provides a window into understanding the inner-workings of their individual interpretation of culture. That is, you will need to find out to what extent
your clients have internalized negative messages about their behavior from the
environment. Based on these beliefs, what are their beliefs about the potential for
change, especially as it relates to the many moral and religious messages conveyed
about people with substance abuse problems? Please see Chapter 4 and Chapter 8
for more about the importance of this issue in substance abuse assessment. In
Chapter 9, we discuss the centrality of spirituality in twelve-step recovery in
more detail.

Social/Environmental Dimension Community models, along with social
learning theory and cognitive-behavioral theories, provide keys to understanding
the role of the social, political, and economic environment in an individual's
addictive behavior. Issues here revolve around peer influences (social learning
theory), the neighborhood, various organizations and associations within the
community, and the environment of the community in general. Social learning
theory emphasizes the impact of peer influences on substance abuse behavior, in
that people learn to use substances by watching and learning from others in their
environment—family, friends, and other models in the community. An assessment from this perspective can be quite instructive indeed.

Community models look at the broader environment and its impact on people. At issue is the general atmosphere of the neighborhood and the client's living
environment. Are there drug houses on every corner? Do the police and other
social service agencies recognize the needs of this community? Also at issue are
the nature and availability of organizational support, including the role of social
service organizations, and your presence as a social worker in a client's life. For example, can clients find a program to serve their needs, or what does seeing a social
worker mean within their community or culture? What are the conditions of the
schools and the influence of churches, neighborhood associations, and block clubs?
More importantly, what is the prevailing culture of the local environment? Are
neighbors supportive or afraid of each other, and can a client expect to reside in
the present situation and receive the support needed to change?

An assessment of social class, personal safety, and security of a local environment is critical to a comprehensive substance abuse assessment. See Chapter 6 for

a more thorough discussion of this dimension in relation to the community's influence on individual clients and their families. Readers are encouraged to read the plethora of materials available about community assessment strategies, as the details of community assessment outside the context of individual and/or family practice are outside the scope of this text.

Macro Dimension Community models provide access into the realm of macro influences on a client and his or her problems and potential for change. Knowledge of various drug laws (local, state, and national) is critical, as well as an understanding of how various relevant social policies are interpreted and enforced in a particular client's life. For example, a multi-systemic approach demands an understanding of how child welfare policies affect the life of a chemically dependent mother and whether local police target African American males for drug offenses more than members of other races.

Moreover, issues at this level include public sentiment, stereotypes, and mechanisms of oppression that play a significant role in the lives of people who are not European American, male, middle-class (or more affluent) citizens. Racism, classism, homophobia, and sexism, to name a few, are real threats to people who are attempting to live a "normal" life. As a multi-systemic practitioner, you must understand this reality and learn from clients what their individual perceptions are of these mechanisms and how they affect clients' problems and potential for change. The macro dimension also involves issues such as housing, employment, and public support, along with the dynamics of the criminal justice system. For example, if your client has been arrested for drug crimes, what is the chance that he or she will get fair and just legal representation in the court system?

SUMMARY

While there are many different models to explain substance abuse at all levels, a multi-systemic approach to substance abuse practice does not allow you to subscribe to any one model to the exclusion of others. There is something in every model that may help you understand clients, assess their needs, and prepare a treatment plan that is culturally and personally consistent with their problems, culture, individual characteristics, beliefs, and strengths.

Many students new to a multi-systemic approach become confused because the requirements seem so diverse and complicated. However, as you will see in Chapter 8, an organized and efficient social worker who has learned to think multi-systemically can gather large amounts of critically important information about a client in a relatively short period. For this to happen, you must have a deep understanding of the various models and be willing to accept the fact that no single model is completely right or wrong. It is easier to latch on to one model and "go with it." Indeed, any of the aforementioned models claim to explain all aspects of addictive behavior. However, the goal of substance abuse practice is not to be correct or to promote our own ease and comfort, but to develop an assessment and treatment plan that is right for each client, whether or not we would ever use it in our own lives. Social work practice is not about the social worker, but the client. It is important never to lose sight of this fact.

To close this discussion, I return to the writings of sociologist C. Wright Mills, who inadvertently created an apt description of a multi-systemic approach for social work when he stated in 1959,

> Whether the point of interest is a great power state or a minor literary mood, a family, a prison, and a creed—these are the kinds of questions the best social analysts have asked. They are the intellectual pivots of classic studies of (person) in society—and they are the questions inevitably raised by any mind possessing the sociological imagination. For that imagination is the capacity to shift from one perspective to another—from the political to the psychological; from examination of a single family to comparative assessment of the national budgets of the world; from the theological school to the military establishment; from considerations of an oil industry to studies of contemporary poetry. It is the capacity to range from the most impersonal and remote transformations to the most intimate features of the human self—and see the relations between the two. Back of its use is always the urge to know the social and historical meaning of the individual in the society and in the period in which he (or she) has his quality and his (or her) being (p. 7; parentheses added).

A multi-systemic approach to substance abuse practice provides a unifying framework for social work practice with individuals and families experiencing substance abuse problems. It is not a model per se, but an organizing framework for understanding. It provides the context for a wide-ranging and comprehensive inquiry into a client's life circumstances. It provides understanding and direction, not method. It leads you onto the path toward a comprehensive and holistic approach. However, it does not come without a price. You must train yourself to appreciate the complex and to embrace the comprehensive. Are you up to the challenge?

In this chapter, we looked at six models that attempt to explain the whole of substance abuse and addictive behavior. While there are many models and theories that claim to own the truth, each can contribute in one way or another to a comprehensive understanding of every client. When placed in a multi-systemic framework, elements of each model can be used to help assess a client's substance abuse issues and formulate a plan for successful treatment.

4

The Art of Client Engagement

The first three chapters established a theoretical foundation for work with substance-abusing and chemically dependent clients. Starting with this chapter, we move beyond theory and into the skills and techniques required for substance abuse practice.

This chapter lays the practice foundation for everything that will follow. Our focus is on client engagement: how to develop a productive, professional relationship with substance-abusing clients, their families, and communities. All aspects of substance abuse practice are important, but client engagement is fundamental—without it, no progress is possible. Engagement is important with other client populations, but it is even more foundational to successful treatment of substance abuse clients because of the way they arrive for services (usually under pressure) and the strength of their personal defense systems.

The ways in which you will engage clients with substance abuse problems are largely determined by the qualities and characteristics you bring to the professional relationship, as well as your personal beliefs and attitudes about substance use, abuse, chemical dependency, and people involved with these issues. That is, engagement involves your professional use of self.

Developing superior client engagement skills requires more than classroom participation. You can learn these skills through reading, dialogue, personal reflection, and action (practice), followed by further reflection and supervision. Action and reflection on action—or "praxis" (Freire, 1994, p. 48)—leads to a deeper understanding of what it takes to successfully engage clients in a relevant and meaningful assessment and treatment process. If you are serious about developing a multi-systemic approach with substance-abusing and chemically dependent clients, you will need to work hard to develop and refine your engagement skills. While certain skills and techniques are helpful, relying too heavily on technique presents problems of authenticity. Taking an approach that involves appropriate use of self liberates you from over-reliance on techniques and instead allows you to become a genuine helper, able to engage clients in life-changing, meaningful dialogue.

Throughout this chapter, we will discuss various personal and professional characteristics that skilled social workers bring to substance abuse practice. These qualities determine your overall approach and perspective toward people with substance abuse problems. They comprise much of what it means to be an effective "social" worker, in the sense that competent practitioners possess well-developed engagement or social skills, as well as advanced skills in other elements of the sequential helping process (Miley, O'Melia, & DuBois, 1995; Sheafor, Horejsi, & Horejsi, 2000).

DEFINITION OF ENGAGEMENT
IN SUBSTANCE ABUSE PRACTICE

Client engagement occurs when you develop, in collaboration with clients, a trusting and open professional relationship (Gelso & Hayes, 1988; Ridgeway & Sharpley, 1991; Walborn, 1996) that promotes hope and presents viable prospects for change. Successful engagement occurs when you create a social context in which vulnerable people (who often hold jaded attitudes toward helping professionals) can share their innermost feelings, as well as their most embarrassing and shameful behavior with you, *a total stranger.*

For example, chemically dependent clients of all ages, races, and classes bring tales of embarrassing, dangerous, and even personally repulsive behavior. Men and women who are dependent on cocaine or crack cocaine may have acted out sexually in ways that they would not have considered if they had not been under the influence of this powerful stimulant. Whether they have traded sexual favors for drugs or money, engaged in unprotected sexual activities with multiple partners, or (if they are heterosexual) engaged in homosexual activities as a way of fulfilling cocaine-related fantasies, clients have often lived a lifestyle that most have only read about. Clients may need to reveal past sexual abuse, criminal behavior, or other incidents they would prefer to forget.

These experiences are not shared easily. Information such as this is disclosed only in the context of a relationship that involves trust. It takes more than the promise of confidentiality or pressure from a spouse, partner, or probation officer for this type of personal information to be shared. Intensely personal information is usually revealed in layers, as a relationship of trust and openness develops, or it is not revealed at all. When seemingly insurmountable barriers are overcome and clients are successfully engaged in a helping process, they become open to the possibility of change as a function of the relationship (Mallinckrodt, 1993; Reandeau & Wampold, 1991). Clients not only trust that they can reveal themselves, but that they might find a path toward a different life.

CLIENT ENGAGEMENT AS AN ART

Fundamental to the substance abuse assessment and treatment process is your ability to engage clients in an open process of sharing and dialogue (Miley, O'Melia, & DuBois, 1995). Like a talented qualitative researcher, you must learn to hear and understand a client's life story. Similar to the "invention stage" of naturalistic research, you must learn the art of "getting into" the client's world and "getting along" with the individual or family (Kirk & Miller, 1986, p. 22). In fact, qualitative research skills—especially the skills of new ethnography (Goodall, 2000; Ellis & Bochner, 1996)—apply directly to client engagement because of the need to "tune-in" to the client's life experiences and needs (Ragg, 2001, p. 102). Here, the term *engagement*, or tuning-in, is similar to what narrative therapists refer to as making a connection between social worker and client (Monk, 1997; Winslade, Crocket, & Monk, 1997).

Because engagement skills are related to personal qualities, it is easy to believe that these skills are innate—either you have them or you don't. In reality, engagement skills can be learned by anyone who chooses to work on them. To have advanced engagement skills does not mean that you must be gregarious, funny, talkative, or the life of the party. You do not have to be witty, clever, or a great conversationalist outside the professional social work context. It is not important how you behave in your private life. What matters are the qualities, attributes, characteristics, and style you exhibit the moment your office door closes, you enter a client's living room, or, in the case of community practice, you participate in a formal or informal meeting of community members.

There is more to successfully engaging clients than knowing which questions to ask, in what order, and how to analyze the answers given to each question. Displaying proof of numerous degrees, certifications, and awards in plain view can provide positive symbols of your competence and engender hope in your clients (Harper & Lantz, 1996; Torrey, 1986), yet these symbols can only provide a platform from which competent practice originates. Let's face it—almost anyone can learn to ask questions. The integration of skill and art in substance abuse practice comes from understanding how to engage people who are seemingly "programmed" not to trust, and knowing what to do with their life stories during and after each interview. Hence, the goal of client engagement in substance abuse practice is to create a situation in which clients feel free to respond, discuss, question, and reflect in a dialogue about their lives and personal history.

HOW WELL DO YOU COMMUNICATE?

Successful engagement depends on your ability to communicate with clients. In this context, "communication skills" are narrowly defined. Often, communication skills are judged by a person's writing or speaking ability. In substance abuse practice, however, communication demands more: you must be able to communicate in a way that allows clients to understand what is being asked and said, while providing a context where clients and social workers can exchange information honestly and freely, despite the barriers that are naturally in place during an interview (i.e., power differential, culture, class, gender, denial mechanisms, and so on). Communication is the proverbial two-way street. In addition to being a good speaker and writer, you will need to be a good listener with the ability to listen to and respect the people with whom you are communicating.

To illustrate this point about effective communication, think about presentations you have attended. Have you ever attended a workshop or lecture in which the presenter knew the subject matter thoroughly and was able to speak easily and well, yet you lost interest, grew bored, or fought the urge to leave? At the end of the day, after reflecting upon the presentation, you found it difficult to remember anything you could translate into tangible social work practice skills. Was the presenter actually a good communicator, or were they simply a good presenter? There is a big difference between the two.

The same distinction applies to social work practice. It does not matter how verbal you are, or what kind of witty conversationalist you may be in a social environment. It does not matter if you can get your client laughing or crying. What matters is the extent to which your client feels *heard, respected,* and *understood.* In substance abuse practice, good communicators create this context with clients, despite the psychological defense mechanisms clients employ during a session. Good communicators speak in relevant and meaningful ways that "fit" within the context of clients' lives, education levels, and overall levels of experience and sophistication. Clients walk away feeling important and believing that they participated in a useful and relevant experience. They may even want to return, or follow through on a referral for treatment.

Paulo Freire and Dialogue

Paulo Freire's (1973/1998, 1994, 1996; McLaren & Leonard, 1996) philosophy and methods for teaching literacy offer invaluable insight for communicating effectively with substance-abusing clients. Freire developed a program for teaching literacy to oppressed peoples in Latin America that engaged students by discovering ways—through communication—to make learning relevant to the students' life and culture.

Who Are the Oppressed?

A short primer on Freire's basic assumptions will provide a context for the remainder of this chapter. According to Freire, any act or action by one group against another is considered oppressive "when it prevents people from being more fully human" (Freire, 1994, p. 39). Based on this definition, Freire describes how certain groups in society (mostly the poor, people of color, and people living lifestyles outside the social "norm," i.e., gays and lesbians, etc.) are trapped by personal troubles (e.g., illiteracy, poverty, crime, substance abuse, etc.) and imprisoned within a "culture of silence" (1994, p. 12). The oppression of these individuals and groups is a direct product of economic, social, and political domination by the majority culture.

Who Are the Oppressed? *continued*

Rather than being encouraged and equipped to know and respond to the concrete realities of their world, oppressed people are kept submerged in a situation where critical awareness, empowerment, and the ability to be active agents in their lives are practically impossible. As a result, they become "domesticated" (Freire, 1994, p. 20) by their oppression. They learn to define themselves, their world, and their personal potential in terms set forth by an oppressive, demoralizing system; they become victims of a "circle of certainty from which they cannot escape" (Freire, 1994, p. 20). Members of these groups learn to internalize the socially defined messages about themselves, thus becoming objects or instruments of an oppressive social system that degrades, prescribes behavior, and limits their ability to change. In their present state, these victims cannot stand up for themselves or foster change to increase their well-being. They learn to comply with their oppressors—to "go along to get along." This compliance is part of the culture of silence.

How does the oppression take place? The prevailing system uses several instruments in its quest to domesticate people, including the media, the educational system, academic and scholarly accounts of history, political science, as well as racist, sexist, and classist social policy (Wilson, 1987) and unjust use of the criminal justice system. Any vehicle (including, in some instances, social workers) that galvanizes public opinion about certain people and groups is used to the advantage of the system to ensure that there is stratification between the sexes, races, and classes, creating an "us" versus "them" mentality.

The oppressed are forced into the role of the "Other" (Johnson, 2000, p. 36), in that they become the scapegoat for social and economic problems, turmoil, or disruption in American life. Moreover, the oppressed are considered personally responsible for their own pain (i.e., people are homeless because they choose to be homeless). Michelle Fine refers to this process as the "colonizing discourse of the Other" (Fine, 1994, p. 70). Through the process of circumscribing the Other, elite levels of society separate and merge personal identities, using the Other as part of a larger goal of social domination (Johnson, 2000).

Living a domesticated life runs contrary to what Freire calls the "ontological vocation" of people (Freire, 1994, p. 14). People who become demonized are not, in fact, the way they are portrayed. We come to believe certain negative stereotypes about them (i.e., mothers who receive public assistance are "welfare queens," all African American men sell crack cocaine, etc.). More insidiously, the people targeted by this systematic oppression and demonization come to believe these falsehoods about themselves; in other words, they live in the "House of the Oppressor" (Freire, 1994, p. 27).

Contrary to the belief system imposed on them, people can improve their lives and become a factor in determining their own future. People can understand their oppression through dialogue that encourages them to question, analyze, and reflect upon their lives. During this process, the oppressed become a force in their own lives, and their inherent strengths, gained through personal experience and "class knowledge," become the primary motivating force in their liberation from past domination (Freire, 1994, p. 26).

In his book, *Education for Critical Consciousness* (1973/1998), Freire explains,

For the act of communication to be successful, there must be accord between the reciprocally communicating Subjects. That is, the verbal expression of one of the Subjects must be perceptible within a frame of reference that is meaningful to the other Subject (p. 138).

In order to create a context of understanding, we need to employ a "problem-posing" approach (Freire, 1994, p. 47) to client work. To do this, we adopt a nonexpert position while reflecting people's lives back to them by asking probing questions in a way that forces critical thinking. The good communicator learns about people's lives, upbringings, and environments and re-presents the information back to them as a problem to be analyzed and solved, rather than a permanent by-product of domestication. Problem-posing dialogue occurs when you challenge clients to reconsider beliefs, discover the origins of beliefs, reconsider how they act, and begin to realistically see the possibility of change.

If done properly, this approach leads to a dialogue between you and your clients that allows you to inquire, explore, and learn about each other. Dialogue begins the process of moving clients from domesticated "peasants" to active agents of change in their own lives: "Dialogue is the encounter between men and women, mediated by the world, in order to name the world" (Freire, 1994, p. 69).

Throughout the remainder of this book, "dialogue," as defined above, is the goal for client engagement. Dialogue is a joint endeavor, developed between people (in this case, you and your client) that moves clients from their current state of hopelessness ("I cannot stop using drugs") to a more hopeful, motivated position in their world ("Perhaps I can, indeed, achieve sobriety"). When this movement occurs, you have engaged your client.

For example, if your client states during an interview, "My grandfather was alcoholic, my father was alcoholic, and all of my older brothers are alcoholic," problem-posing responses might include, "So your situation is hopeless—is that what you are saying?" or "Do you believe that your future is already decided because of your family history?" or "Does that mean you are destined to do the same?"

In these examples, the client's statement about the history of alcoholism in his family is re-presented in the form of a question that simultaneously supports his statement, exposes a belief system of hopelessness, and challenges him to re-think his underlying belief systems in the context of his substance-abusing family system. Problem-posing questions force clients to examine themselves and their operating premises in a way that can lead them to rethink beliefs and practices.

Semiotic of Communication

Let us take a slightly different, yet related look at communication. Elsewhere, I described a communication model based on my experience working in foreign countries where language differences often seemed insurmountable (Johnson, 2000). Many of you will face this same problem in social work practice with substance-abusing clients. Their language and lifestyle will seem foreign, as if you suddenly found yourself in a different country and/or culture, with people speaking a different language. Yet, your task is to understand their language, culture, and lifestyle.

I surmised that it was possible to communicate (albeit, not completely or fluently) across different languages if certain conditions were met. These conditions pertained mostly to the level of personal adjustment to (or, comfort with) the "host culture" by the visitor. This communication model (Johnson, 2000, p. 113) can be depicted as follows:

Sign [understanding] = Marker [social context recognition]
+ Sight Involvement [ability to attend]

Communication is defined as a cultural experience—an active production of people that is influenced by the culture in which it occurs (MacCannell, 1976) and the people participating in the conversation. Each client interview is a unique cultural production, similar to what we encounter when traveling to a foreign culture with different values, beliefs, and socially constructed meanings for events in daily life. Below is an explanation, with examples, of the diagram above.

Sign A sign represents a jointly constructed meaning—an understanding—between people speaking different languages. When we are attempting to communicate with people who speak a different language, the goal is to jointly agree upon a common meaning (sign) that is understandable to both. Understanding means more than just knowing the words; it also involves grasping the culturally intended meanings of the words in a particular context.

For example, what does it mean when clients claim that they are "fine" or "good"? Does it mean that they abstained from using drugs, or that they managed to use and not overdose? Either definition of "fine" or "good" could represent an honest response to the question, "How was your week?" The intended meaning depends on the unique cultural intention of the person describing her or his week, and what a "good" or "fine" week means to him or her.

Marker A marker represents the immediate social context in which communication occurs. It refers to information about the purpose of the conversation as defined by the setting, agenda, and topic, and the social positioning of the people involved in the conversation.

For example, when you meet with a client for a substance abuse assessment, you should understand all the features of the marker—purpose (substance abuse assessment), setting (your office or client's home), agenda (we ask personal questions, and they answer honestly), and social positioning (we have power over them). You also need to ensure that your clients understand and accept these elements of the marker. What is their understanding of why they are there (to get a judge off their back)? What do they see as the agenda (to tell you what you want to hear)? What influence does the setting have on your client's ability to understand (sterile office in a government building, or in a hospital)? What are their reactions to the imbalance of power that is present in all social work interviews (So, what's new? I need to protect myself or they will take my children.)?

As you can see, failure to consider these fundamental factors as part of any client interview is a prescription for communication breakdown. Without a shared understanding of the marker, the necessary trust will never develop, dooming your work from the start. Your job is to explore these factors with clients to ensure that you are both on the same page, as it were. Here is an example of a misunderstood marker:

When I was working with adolescent substance abusers, parents often would bring their daughter or son for a substance abuse assessment without telling the child where they were going, or why. The parents' reasoning was that their son or daughter would refuse to come if he or she knew the agenda.

I remember parents telling their children that they were going to a movie, or explaining the suitcase of clothing by saying they were headed on a short vacation. Instead, they drove to our clinic for an "ambush assessment." You can imagine the youth's reaction upon discovering that he or she was going for substance abuse treatment instead of a movie! In these examples, the parents and worker understood the marker, but the adolescent did not. Hence, communication was usually ineffective because the marker was not jointly defined, accepted, and understood.

Sight Involvement Sight involvement refers to the degree that participants are interested in the communication. I define "interested" in a broader sense than is commonly understood. Here, interest means attraction, especially to the social worker. That is, you will need to present yourself in a way that is interesting (attractive) to clients. Do you inspire hope, confidence, and trust? These factors lead to joint sight involvement.

More importantly, interest refers to clients' ability to understand a marker, yet without interest the marker will never be understood. Several issues related to being with unfamiliar people influence this capacity to understand, including differences in language, culture, daily norms, and beliefs about the meaning of drug use. Therefore, the degree of sight involvement is determined by clients' cognitive, emotional, and physical ability to focus on the marker. It is directly related to their comfort and familiarity with their surroundings, determining the extent to which they can concentrate on the conversation at hand.

If clients are intoxicated, suffering the aftereffects of chronic chemical dependency, or forced to talk in professional substance-abuse-speak instead of common language, they probably will not understand the marker, leading to low sight involvement. The example above of teenagers who were "ambushed" into substance abuse treatment demonstrates some of the difficulties associated with little or no sight involvement. Because of their anger, humiliation, or personal denial, these teens lacked interest and attraction, meaning they had little or no sight involvement. Therefore, sight involvement is related to ability and motivation, and without it, there will be no understanding of a marker and, therefore, no sign agreement. This is a prescription for treatment failure.

Your ability to communicate—and understand—within the foreign culture of substance-abusing clients is a function of your social and cultural adjustment to them and all parties' understanding, interest, and involvement in the social work interview. Unless you have a history with substance abuse and/or have experience involving people from this world, these clients are likely to represent a "foreign culture" to you. The dynamics of cultural adjustment are the same for you in a practice setting as they would be if you were visiting a foreign country. Hence,

A person cannot learn to communicate in a foreign culture (mutually construct the meaning of signs) until she or he recognizes the social context of the conversation (marker), which is determined by their ability to attend to the conversation, gained through familiarity with the social-cultural setting (sight involvement) (Johnson, 2000, p. 113).

In substance abuse practice, the elements of successful communication described in this model pose significant barriers unless these issues are attended to in a professionally competent manner. The elements of communication apply to you and your client. As the social worker, you are responsible for facilitating the communication process. When communication occurs, client engagement occurs. If only one participant (usually you) is clear about the marker, sight involvement, and sign, then clients will drop out.

Here is an example to illustrate what must be managed in order to achieve communication based on a joint understanding of the sign.

A new client walks into your office for an assessment for potential substance abuse problems. You have not had much experience with substance-abusing clients (that you know of, anyhow), so as you wait, you begin to wonder. If you do not use drugs or drink, do you think people who do this are morally wrong? Perhaps you have drunk alcohol, smoked pot, or experimented with several other drugs in the past (and may continue today), and you did not become addicted. Do you think people who do become addicted are weak, ignorant, or lacking in personal control?

You have worked your whole career with the mentally ill. Do you think substance abuse problems mask mental illness? You inevitably paint a picture of the person that will appear. What does the person look like? Is your client male or female, Caucasian or African American, rich or poor, clean or dirty?

The individual who appears for the meeting is a male in his mid-20s. He has long, matted hair, smells bad, and is disheveled in appearance and generally dirty. Do you immediately assume, at some level, that a substance abuse problem exists? This person reminds you of an old friend, your brother, the street person on the corner, or someone you saw featured on a television show last week, all of whom had serious drug problems. Would you hesitate to ask this person about any part of his life, such as his sex life? In other words, because of this person's appearance, would you feel free to ask him about anything you want?

On the other hand, your client is in his mid-50s, dressed in a dapper business suit with perfect grooming and an imposing, CEO-like demeanor. Does he remind you of your boss, father, or rich uncle? What does this do to the directions you take during the interview, questions you ask, and assumptions you make before the interview begins? Would you feel that questions about sex and HIV risks are inappropriate, or do you assume that he is safe either because he is not promiscuous or has sex with a safer crowd?

Would you make different assumptions if the client looked like a stereotypical prostitute, your mother, or your first-grade teacher? What if you heard that the client had a criminal record (as many substance-abusing clients do) or was on welfare, gay or lesbian, or the owner of a business in your town?

These thoughts are difficult to manage, and we have not even discussed the psychic emergency (Johnson, 2000) clients are going through at the same time. In order for you to engage your client, you must wade through all of these thoughts before you can conduct a meeting in which reciprocal communication can occur. You must grow comfortable with the person that you are interviewing, adjusting yourself to the individual, family, or group from a "foreign culture" that walks through your office door, waits for you at a local restaurant, or invites you into their living room. This is your adjustment task.

At this point, you may be saying, "Wait a minute there! I don't make assumptions about my clients. I am a social worker who has learned not to prejudge any of my clients. I have taken a cultural diversity class as part of my curriculum, so I am able to work with people who are different from me. I approach every client with a clean slate, always starting where the client is. I do not have these kinds of thoughts. What do you have to say about that?"

Well, unless you are a cyborg, you *do* have thoughts like these (and so do I). Perhaps not these specific thoughts, but judgments, biases, prejudices, beliefs, and attitudes, nonetheless. It is part of the human condition, and being a social worker does not exempt us from being human. While our profession promotes a unifying set of values, beliefs, and ethics that seek to counter these issues (Fong, 2001; Kirst-Ashman & Hull, 1999; Johnson & Yanca, 2001; Hepworth, Rooney, & Larsen, 1997; Appleby, Colon, & Hamilton, 2001), social workers are just as "human" as the rest of society.

Before becoming social workers, we are socialized according to our environment—one that has opinions about race, class, gender, culture, sexual orientation, and chemically dependent people, to name a few. Stumbling over our own "baggage," as it were, is inevitable and inescapable in social work practice. The aspect that should separate us from the rest of society is our willingness to work at understanding ourselves in order to limit the potentially damaging effects that our personal prejudices, biases, and attitudes have on clients. Because we have chosen this profession and its associated role in society, it is our personal and professional obligation to examine our biases and minimize the damage they cause.

We can summarize the elements of communication in this way: if sign agreement is the ultimate goal of communication, then marker and sight involvement are the ingredients that make this happen. The presence or absence of a marker and sight involvement is the responsibility of the person who is in unfamiliar territory. In a foreign land, that means it's the foreigner's responsibility, not the host's. In substance abuse practice, you are the foreigner. Although your clients may come to your office (culture), it is your responsibility to adjust to them, not they to you. Why? Because mastery of these ingredients is directly related to the ability to gain a sense of comfort or adjustment in the host culture, or, in our case, to the culture of clients who need help.

To most readers, this explanation probably sounds reasonable. It does not always happen that way in practice. The communication process is affected by social stratification and a sense of importance or power in relationships. The following example illustrates this point about power imbalances.

Recently I traveled with a colleague to China to train Chinese social work professors about teaching substance abuse practice in their respective schools. While we were there, the Chinese students and professors wanted to use

"American" names to make it easier to know them. Therefore, my good friend Su Bin (his full Chinese name) wanted to be called "Robert." While this was a nice gesture and consistent with their culture, I insisted they use their given names and hold me accountable for learning to pronounce them correctly. My colleague from the U.S. insisted they use American names.

A couple of months later, two Chinese faculty members came to our university as students. During a faculty meeting, several social work faculty members (led by the colleague who went to China earlier in the year) decided that we should ask them to use "American" names to make it easier on us. After a lengthy discussion (no social work faculty meeting ever has short discussions), the faculty began moving toward this consensus.

Now, you may be wondering why I had a problem with this. Did I not just state that they (the Chinese students) should adjust to us? Well, yes, I did. However, when we were in China, never once had it crossed my mind to use a Chinese name to make it easier on them! We used our American names, although the Chinese had difficulty pronouncing them. As Americans, we are rarely expected to adapt to others because of our perceived status in the world. Our culture, unlike that of the Chinese and other groups, does not place importance on showing humility and respect for others. The Chinese visitors used their Chinese names and everybody seemed fine with it.

Unfortunately, we often demand that substance abuse clients use the drug names and other terms that we understand. I once overheard a social worker insist that her client use the word "hallucinogen" instead of "acid," a common street name for the same drug. It does not stop there. Sometimes there is little effort to learn and use a client's language; instead, the worker demands that the client learn and use social workers' language, especially acronyms (AOD, ADHD, OCD, etc.). Again, because of perceived status imbalances (and real differences in power) in the relationship, along with deep-seated beliefs that "street language" is inappropriate, we as professionals sometimes demand adjustment, instead of adjusting ourselves.

Tourism as Metaphor for Self-Exploration

The communication model described above can be used to determine the amount of self-work you will need to do in adjusting to the culture of substance-abusing and/or chemically dependent clients. Fundamental to that work—and what gives it relevance—is the fact that client cultures (i.e., youth gangs, culture of substance abuse, and so on) require the same level of adjustment and understanding as traveling abroad to a different culture. This adjustment must take place before treatment can proceed. I prefer to use tourism as a metaphor in explaining successful client engagement as an intercultural project between individuals, or between an individual social worker and a family, group, or community with potential or real substance abuse issues. Briefly defined, tourists are

(often) middle-class sightseers traveling the world in search of lived experience and authenticity. They embark on a personal journey to locate themselves and their history, by participating in non-modern worlds and cultures with people who inhabit these strange places (Johnson, 2000, p. 14).

Yet there is a catch. The desire to experience "reality" has limits. Tourists want a real experience, but not one that compromises their idea of what is normal. They maintain a sense of personal security by knowing they can return "home" when the experience gets too real. As such, tourists are not required to adjust to new cultural environments; they observe it as if they were enjoying a day at the zoo. Zygmunt Bauman (1995) calls this being "in" instead of being "of" the host culture (p. 95). Being in a culture—or a client's world—is superficial, limiting one's ability to understand and respect that culture. This often leaves tourists upon returning home, or social workers after a session with a client, exclaiming, "I'm so grateful for what I have." This is a patronizing response stemming from a lack of understanding, serving only to further the separation between "us" and "them."

Becoming "of" a culture, or part of a client's world, does not mean that you must become a drug user to understand your client. In reality, you will never be able to completely understand—you can only do the best you can, given the limitations of time, setting, roles, and personal differences. However, you must make the effort. Begin by critically examining yourself in relation to your clients and exploring internalized myths, stereotypes, and beliefs about your clients in an effort to open yourself to new realities, experiences, understanding, and respect for differences. Become keenly aware of the possibility that we, as social workers, can unwittingly perpetuate a culture of silence through our attitudes and/or actions toward clients, acting as "agents of the state," as it were, and disempowering clients instead of empowering them to take constructive action on their own behalf.

When social workers become "of" another culture or world to the best of our ability, we cease believing in "normal" versus "abnormal," deeply understand the negative and limiting effects of Othering in people's lives, and appreciate the fact that our good fortune is based more on an accident of birth, and sometimes luck, than anything else. We learn that our lives are not "better" than our clients' lives, but different. Hard work, desire, drive, or intelligence alone did not make our lives different from theirs, but more opportunity leading to more choices, in the context of different social expectations based on race, class, gender, family, community, and/or country of origin. Hence, in this context, being "of" represents intercultural adjustment. Anything less is tourism (Johnson, 2000, pp. 14–15).

To avoid the trappings of "tourism" in substance abuse practice, engage yourself—as you want to engage clients—in a dialogue about your own beliefs, attitudes, prejudices, and biases about your clients and their world. Use your substance abuse journal to engage in this dialogue. After every session or class period, dialogue with yourself in writing about any issues, comments, feelings, or beliefs that surfaced during that particular session or class. Describe the client you met with, avoiding clinical generalizations. What were your personal, emotional, and physical reactions to him or her, and what were the reasons for your reactions? For maximum effect, let someone you trust read and comment—either in writing or in person—about what you wrote. Then, reflect upon his or her comments and respond in your next journal entry.

It is also good practice to find a group of trusted colleagues to meet with periodically to discuss cases and/or practice issues. These meetings don't have to be formal. You can meet over dinner, coffee, or at an overnight retreat. The setting is not as important as the people involved. They must be people you trust and respect—people who are willing to tell you the truth and risk angering you. Along the same lines, either engage in this type of dialogue with your supervisor, or arrange for professional supervision and consultation with a respected and experienced member of the practice community.

Family gatherings can be a fruitful setting for discovering what may be hidden in the deepest regions of your psyche. Learn to listen differently to conversations among family members. What do your mom, dad, brother, uncle, sister, or partner say—or hint—about minorities, substance abusers, welfare recipients, social policy, and politics? Listen for clues, and examine privately what you discover. Do family gatherings contain racial jokes or disparage people with substance abuse problems as being immoral or weak? What is your response? Even if you do not participate or your outlook on the world differs from your family's, often those thoughts, beliefs, prejudices, and attitudes are still rumbling around inside, waiting—like pent-up steam—to escape under pressure. I know this might take some of the fun out of family gatherings, but it will—I promise—prove helpful in your quest to understand yourself in relation to your clients.

It is not important (for the most part) for you to be issue-free or without biases and prejudices. Complete neutrality would be impossible. Instead, you need to be consciously aware of your issues, biases, and prejudices, knowing what they are about and how they could become a barrier if left unattended. For example, it is possible to perform competent substance abuse treatment after growing up in a chemically dependent household, to perform couple's therapy while going through a divorce, to work with people of color despite having been raised by racist parents, or to work with gay and lesbian clients even if you are not gay or lesbian yourself (van Wormer, Wells, & Boes, 2000). However, success is only possible if you are willing to put considerable time and energy into critical self-reflection by participating in dialogue with yourself and others. To assume you are unbiased or objective simply because you are a social worker, or to realize you have these feelings and beliefs but to be afraid to discuss them with anyone, would be a recipe for disaster.

If you think you are "supposed" to believe certain things about people because a textbook says so, because other students in your class or cohort seem to, or because your professor demands that you hold certain beliefs—but you still believe differently—take comfort in knowing that you are not alone. Social workers who are willing to risk being politically incorrect in order to sort through potentially damaging beliefs, prejudices, and biases will, in the end, be more effective with clients from all walks of life.

So take the risk. Do not give in to the natural tendency toward "group-think" (Janis, 1971, 1982; Meyers, 1996) that occurs in this or any other profession. You are a human being, with human flaws and human emotions. No one in the profession—including your professor, supervisor, or the author of this book—can claim differently, despite what we might say in public.

HOW SHOULD WE TREAT OUR CLIENTS?

There is really no secret to becoming an effective social worker with substance-abusing or chemically dependent clients and families. Effectiveness lies in the personal qualities that you genuinely exhibit in the human relationships that are at the foundation of professional social work practice. How you treat clients on a daily basis is the key to being an effective substance abuse practitioner. There are certain personal qualities that enhance client engagement, thereby reducing dropouts and/or unsuccessful outcomes. On the other hand, there are also certain characteristics (or the lack of certain characteristics) that lead to ineffective client engagement.

The characteristics discussed below must be understood in the context of culturally competent practice principles. Cultural competence is a perspective that focuses on the strengths and abilities of all people to contribute to society (Parham, 1993; Pinderhughes, 1989) and is designed to facilitate the breakdown of cultural barriers, to address the issues of difference, and to increase access to resources (Cross, Bazron, Dennis, & Isaacs, 1989). Models of culturally competent practice are designed to address the fact that some members of the dominant culture are insensitive to the culture and history of people in non-majority groups (Boyd-Franklin, 1989; Lee, 1994; Wilson, 1992). Cultural competence is central to any cross-cultural experience that involves power differences (Manning, 2001)—a category that, as we stated earlier, includes every social work interview.

Cultural competence *begins* with learning about different cultures, races, personal circumstances, and structural mechanisms of oppression (Browne & Mills, 2001). It *occurs* when you master the interpersonal skills needed to move beyond general descriptions of a specific culture or race to learn specific individual, family, group, or community interpretations of culture, ethnicity, and race. The culturally competent social worker knows that within each culture are individually interpreted and practiced thoughts, beliefs, and behaviors that may or may not be consistent with group-level information. That is, there is tremendous diversity *within* groups, as well as *between* them. Individuals are unique unto themselves, not simply interchangeable members of a specific culture, ethnicity, or race who naturally abide by the group-level norms often taught in graduate and undergraduate courses on human diversity.

Particular facets or representations of oppression within oppressed groups are unique to families and to individuals within specific families. You cannot know, with any degree of certainty, an individual's chemical dependency experience until you know the individual and/or family, at a minimum. Before clients will reveal their stories, which include highly personal and often painful information, they must trust and respect you. You cannot acquire this information simply by asking, although asking is a good place to begin. True cultural competence stems from your ability to engage clients in dialogue that allows for a free discussion of their unique experiences with chemical dependency. How does the client sitting before you uniquely experience chemical dependency in his or her life? How do social, economic, and/or political systems limit or drive your client's beliefs, attitudes, and behaviors?

Everyone interprets culture differently. Their personal interpretations of the larger culture ultimately become the specific culture of an individual and/or family. For example, a culturally competent social worker not only knows about how "the Mexican family" views a woman's use of alcohol and other drugs, but also is able to discover how a specific Mexican family treats a female member who is abusing drugs and, within that frame, how an individual woman in a particular Mexican family is treated, and internalizes that treatment, as a result of her substance abuse. To avoid stereotyping, a culturally competent social worker uses group-level knowledge as a guide for information gathering, approaching this information with a skepticism that allows him or her to understand that group-level knowledge may, in fact, be inaccurate when applied to a particular client, family, group, or community.

This discussion brings us back to the original point about culturally competent social work practice. Although it is beneficial to know the latest drug use data by social group, and it is certainly important to know particular cultural norms, styles, and practices (Acevedo & Morales, 2001), this knowledge does little good unless you have mastered the skills discussed in this chapter. The ability to acquire meaningful information from clients is the best demonstration of culturally competent practice (Lum, 1999).

Before moving on to the next topic, I want to acknowledge that some of the information below will be familiar to you. Much of it has been covered in other social work practice courses. However, I firmly believe that learning and integration come from a certain level of repetition and by placing learned knowledge into a new practice context. My challenge to you is to place this information into the context of substance abuse practice, providing something new to add to your practice repertoire.

Five Characteristics of Effective Helping Professionals

Research demonstrates that across a broad range of practice methods, certain characteristics are associated with successful substance abuse treatment (Miller & Rollnick, 1991; Harper & Lantz, 1996). Social workers and other helping professionals working in the same settings and offering the same treatment approaches show dramatic differences in rates of client dropout and successful outcome, exceeding differences caused by practice methods (Lantz, 1993; Lantz & Pegram, 1989; Luborsky et al., 1985). Specifically, the ability to successfully engage clients in a helping relationship distinguishes effective from less effective social workers (Gaston, 1990; Jennings & Skovhodt, 1999; Najavits & Strupp, 1994; Pritchard, Cotton, Bowen, & Williams, 1998).

Below we look at five characteristics associated with competent and successful helping in substance abuse practice. These qualities—worldview respect, hope, humility, trust, and empathy—should be the foundation for your work with substance abusing clients. While there are other characteristics of effective helpers, these five provide the foundation for successfully engaging, assessing, and treating people with substance abuse problems.

1. Worldview Respect Perhaps the most important quality we can bring to the helping relationship with substance-abusing clients is worldview respect (Winslade, Crocket, & Monk, 1997; Harper & Lantz, 1996; Torrey, 1986). Worldview respect is defined as the ability to understand and accept the overall approach, perspectives, background, actions, and beliefs of your client, and to ensure that any activities in the social work context are compatible with that worldview (Lum, 1999). Whatever you do in your work with a client must make sense within the framework of the client's worldview, which is shaped by all aspects of his or her person, including race, ethnicity, sexual orientation, class, etc., and the accompanying perceptions, beliefs, and lifestyle choices.

For example, first-generation German or Russian Americans may not view drinking six cans of beer or a bottle of vodka every night as abusive, based on cultural practices in their home countries, families, or local communities. Moreover, many clients coming from the substance abuse culture do not understand that using vulgar language to describe their activities is considered inappropriate and/or impolite in conversation.

Worldview respect occurs when you accept people's lives, behaviors, and beliefs without personal or moral indictment or negative reactions. Those who demonstrate acceptance (and, by definition, respect) affirm the worth of others as human beings "without necessarily condoning (their) actions" (Barker, 1999, p. 2). Social workers with this characteristic treat their clients as partners or co-authors (Winslade & Smith, 1997) in the practice process, listen to their opinions and beliefs, communicate cordially and freely, and give credit to clients for their accomplishments, strengths, and potential (Miley, O'Melia, & DuBois, 1995), even in the face of client hostility and denial.

Respect is important when it comes to people's individual problems or behaviors, but it also applies to the broader category of human diversity. This means that you must respect the culture, race, gender, class, ethnicity, sexual orientation, religious background, and the unique and individual belief systems, attitudes, and practices of each client (Miley, O'Melia, & DuBois, 1995; Appleby, Colon, & Hamilton, 2001). Understanding and respecting diversity ultimately occur at the individual level. Without fundamental respect grounded in an ecological model that recognizes the importance of person-in-environment, diversity, and strengths perspectives in social work practice (Meyer, 1993; Hepworth, Rooney, & Larsen, 1997; Germain, 1991; Compton & Galway, 1994), client engagement does not happen, and professional relationships cannot flourish.

For example, you must understand and accept the fact that some substance abuse clients will believe that "sex work" (prostitution) is an acceptable way to support their existence, or that it is acceptable to steal from family members or the public. Some clients will insist that using needles to inject drugs is reasonable, despite the obvious health risks associated with this behavior. You can demonstrate respect by not outwardly marginalizing people's perspectives, but by actively trying to understand more about how and why they believe and act as they do, despite your personal repulsion or disgust with what you hear and see in sessions with clients.

Substance abuse clients are particularly sensitive to negative value judgments (Shorkey & Rosen, 1993), as are the family members of chemically dependent clients (Cermak, 1986). It is critically important to avoid any action or response that feeds into this sensitivity. Sometimes, clients will use language and describe behaviors that seem intended to elicit these judgments (i.e., graphically describing IV use, sickness, or sexual behavior). Others will exhibit a rigid and seemingly impenetrable wall of personal denial (Denzin, 1987; Johnson, 1973). These behaviors are used for protection from harsh or moralistic judgments. Hence, striving to avoid any behavior that can be interpreted or misinterpreted as judgmental is critical in early engagement efforts with substance-abusing clients and their families.

2. Hope For clients with substance abuse problems, a sense of hope is fundamental to the pursuit of change and betterment (van Wormer, 1995; Harper & Lantz, 1996). According to Freire (1994), "Hope is rooted in people's incompletion [sic], from which they move out in constant search—a search which can be carried out only in communion with others" (p. 72). The capacity to feel hope is based on the belief that people are essentially "unfinished" (Freire, 1998, p. 51) and that today's problems are temporary as long as there is more life to live and, thus, time to change. Hope is contingent on clients' awareness that they are unfinished people, with possibilities for change (Torrey, 1986; Frankl, 1973; Dixon & Sands, 1983). A sense of hopefulness greatly supports people's motivation to engage in a helping process.

On the other hand, hopelessness is a form of silence. It denies the possibility of growth, and it allows people to flee from themselves and avoid seeing future possibilities in life. It is based on the notion that people are, in fact, finished in life. They have nothing to look forward to, and no chance to achieve a different life. Hope stems from relationships with other people and with the world; hopelessness surges when people are alone, really and/or figuratively, which is often the case with clients who are involved in substance abuse or chemical dependency.

Hope generates the desire and ability to discover, create, and experience meaning in life (Harper & Lantz, 1996), and these drives are also missing from the lives of clients with substance-related problems. Because of the extent of their domestication, clients do not—or cannot—realize that their lives have meaning and that their present state is not unchangeable. They experience what Frankl (1973) called an existential vacuum. According to Peele, Brodsky, and Arnold (1992),

> A person is vulnerable to addiction when that person feels a lack of satisfaction in life, an absence of intimacy or strong connections to other people, a lack of self-confidence or compelling interests, or a loss of hope. . . . Situations in which people are deprived of family and the usual community

supports; where they are denied rewarding or constructive activities; where they are afraid, uncomfortable, and under stress; and where they are out of control of their lives—these are situations especially likely to create addiction. The relationship between hopelessness, lack of opportunity, and persistent addiction is, of course, a template for lives in America's ghettos (pp. 42–43).

Substance-abusing clients often present with a profound sense of hopelessness, as well as other symptoms of depression. These depressive tendencies are particularly prevalent among people with alcohol problems (van Wormer, 1995). In Chapter 1, we mentioned that depression often accompanies substance abuse and chemical dependency. (This topic will be covered in more detail in Chapter 8.) Elements in a chemically dependent client's personal approach to the world often foster a sense of hopelessness that must be addressed during the practice process. Three elements seem to contribute to feelings of hopelessness: a general sense of negativity, distorted thinking, and self-defeating self-talk (Murphy, 1992), such as "I am a born loser," or "I'm destined to die young." You will often encounter a deep and sometimes overwhelming sense of hopelessness in clients. If left unattended, prospects for change evaporate. Creating a sense of hopefulness in clients where little or none exists is our primary job in substance abuse practice.

Developing a relationship with substance-abusing clients and their families that promotes hopefulness begins in the initial stages of engagement (Ragg, 2001; Curtis, 1999). The important concept here is "begins," since client engagement is a dynamic, continuous process that continues throughout the assessment and/or treatment stages (Gaston, 1990; Gelso & Hayes, 1988). Hopefulness grows out of how you present yourself in initial client interviews. While this quality is often described as self-confidence without arrogance, promoting a sense of hopefulness is also related to your level of humility, ability to engender trust, and what Carl Rogers called "helper attractiveness" (1957). According to Rogers, helper attractiveness is determined by the client's perception of your ability to help. This attractiveness is bolstered by qualities such as warmth, the appearance of competence, concern, integrity, and empathy. Hope stems from your ability to engage clients in an open and trusting discussion of their lives, including both problems and strengths (Saleebey, 1997; van Wormer, 1995).

3. Humility A few years ago, a mother and father called me seeking help for their 12-year-old daughter. She had a long history of being unruly in school and inattentive to nearly everyone around her, especially her parents and numerous previous therapists. Her parents and school officials suspected drug use, but nobody could prove it and the daughter vehemently denied it. What occurred in the opening minutes of the first session with this family demonstrates one aspect of humility.

As they entered my office, both parents were dressed formally, the father in a business suit and the mother in an expensive dress. The daughter was also dressed formally. The family looked more like they were headed to church than a therapist's office. After brief introductions and social pleasantries, the father looked at me solemnly and said, "Dr. Johnson, we have taken our daughter to [he proceeded to name five prominent psychiatrists and psychologists in the area] and they haven't been able to help her. If they couldn't help, what makes *you* think that you can help?"

How you conduct yourself in moments like this one will determine whether you will get the chance to help. That is, in the face of a challenge early in a session, whatever you say first may be the most important words you will speak to a particular client. I could have rattled off a list of my "greatest hits," as it were: years of experience, degrees held, clients seen, success statistics, etc. However, this family had already been to five distinguished colleagues, including one psychologist who went on to host a nationally syndicated television talk show for many years. I had a nice resume, but not *that* nice! The truth is that I did not know if I could help. In fact, I never know if I can help any client who walks through my door.

After a long pause, I sat back in my creaking old rocking chair, looked down as I crossed my legs, took a deep breath, and replied rather quietly, "You know, I was just sitting here wondering the same thing myself. But since you're here, we might as well give it a shot." The parents sat down, and we proceeded with the session. The family continued to be my clients until they attained a successful resolution to their problems.

My initial response to the father's question was genuinely humble—it was not a calculated technique, such as a "one-down" maneuver (Haley, 1976), but an honest expression of my thoughts and feelings at the time. My humility was probably the only reason the family decided to work with me. I often wonder whether I can help clients, and never act as if I am sure of any outcome. The only thing we can guarantee any client is that we will try to help.

One way to express humility is to communicate the belief that you are not superior to your client—both of you are human beings with strengths and weaknesses. Your professional training and knowledge provide expertise, but they do not confer elite status. Social workers hold unique skills, but not a special place in the universe that makes us better than those who seek our help. While the social worker and client are not equal in terms of power in the relationship, they are equal as human beings; both are unfinished people, with room to learn and grow. Clients learn from social workers, and social workers learn from clients. Or, as Freire (1994) so aptly states, "at the point of encounter there are neither utter ignoramuses nor perfect sages; there are only people who are attempting, together, to learn more than they now know" (p. 71).

You can exhibit humility by showing an intense curiosity about people's lives, despite years of experience and training. Statements such as, "I know a lot about addiction, but I know very little about *your* addiction" demonstrate a willingness to work together toward mutual understanding and respect. Seeking understanding by asking questions, even if you think you know the answer or their story seems outrageous, demonstrates humility. Humility demands that every client's story be respected and gross generalizations avoided. For example, each client's "journey" from substance use or experimentation to chemical dependency is different (Peele, 1985/1998). Your job is to discover these differences.

Topic for Your Journal: How Humble Are You?

Humility is rooted in your fundamental beliefs about yourself and your clients. To explore your level of humility, respond to the following questions in your substance abuse journal:

- Why do some people become chemically dependent (or imprisoned, poor, unemployed, uneducated, etc.), while others (including you) do not?

- Do you feel that you (or people without problems) are personally "one-up" on your clients, in a sense that goes beyond the professional power imbalance?

- Do you believe that clients have the right to challenge and/or question your tactics, knowledge, training, and experience, even if they are mandated by the criminal justice system to come to you for treatment?

Humility is also demonstrated by the words you and others in the profession use to describe clients. Do you treat "dope fiends"? Is your next client a drunk, a junkie, or a "perp"? Or are your clients people who have been diagnosed with a substance abuse problem? There is a subtle yet powerful difference between believing your client is a person who happens to have substance abuse problems and believing that your client *is* the problem—that his or her identity is encompassed by a diagnostic label (O'Hanlon & Wilk, 1987). What if the diagnostic label is wrong?

> I once had a client who had been diagnosed as schizophrenic 17 years earlier. After having been forced into multiple psychiatric hospitalizations over the years, it turns out that he had been diagnosed incorrectly, based on a personal reference to Jesus Christ he had made years earlier. This man had lived in a world that treated him as a "psychotic" for 17 years of his life.

Language is a powerful force in social stratification, creating differences between people and groups in society (Gil, 1998; Meyers, 1996; Kirk & Kutchins, 1992; Szasz, 1974). The language used to describe self and others helps determine place in society, not unlike labeling people by race and gender (i.e., famous black author, female editor, etc.). People use labels to put a distance between themselves and the Other: healthy and sick, sane and insane, moral and immoral (O'Hanlon & Wilk, 1987). The language you use to describe clients and the words that clients use to describe themselves are critically important. According to Postman (1976),

> This is why in discussing what words we shall use in describing an event, we are not engaging in "mere semantics." We are engaged in trying to control the perceptions and responses of others (as well as ourselves) to the character of the event . . . the way in which "it" is named reveals not the way it is but how the namer wishes to see it or how he is capable of seeing it. In addition, how it has been named becomes the reality for the namer and all who accept the name. But it need not be our reality (p. 57).

The language you use to describe or label your clients becomes reality—the basis for your beliefs, assessment results, and action. If a client agrees or is convinced to agree with a label, it becomes the client's reality. This can be positive (in the case of reframing) or negative. More importantly, the language you use to describe or label clients, even under peer pressure from colleagues, provides a glimpse into your level of humility. If you disparage clients when you are with colleagues, it will be difficult to prevent those attitudes from creeping into your sessions with clients.

True humility leads to a belief that it is an honor to be allowed into your client's life in an intimate and trusting capacity. It is an honor to have the privilege to be "with" someone during difficult times, and it is an honor to receive the trust and respect of that person during these times. Clients who trust you enough to engage in a dialogue about their lives under the influence of chemicals are according you the highest form of honor and respect. Freire (1994) puts it best:

> Dialogue, as the encounter of those addressed to the common task of learning and acting, is broken if the parties (or one of them) lack humility. How can I dialogue if I always project ignorance onto others and never perceive my own? How can I dialogue if I regard myself as a case apart from others— mere "its" in whom I cannot recognize other "I's"? How can I dialogue if I consider myself a member of the in-group of the "pure," the owners of truth and knowledge, for whom all non-members are "those people" or "the great unwashed"? How can I dialogue if I start from the premise that naming the world is the task of an elite? How can I dialogue if I am closed to—and even offended by—the contribution of others? How can I dialogue if I am afraid of being displaced, the mere possibility causing me torment and weakness? People who lack humility (or have lost it) cannot come to the people, cannot be their partners in naming the world (p. 71).

4. Trust Trust is an important and multifaceted concept (Miley, O'Melia, & DuBois, 1995) that moves along a continuum from "no trust" to "complete trust." You must actively participate in the process of establishing trust. It will not happen if you passively observe and judge whether your client trusts you. Your job is to facilitate trust in the relationship, beginning with the first contact (usually by telephone) and continuing throughout the relationship. While some elements of a client's ability to trust are personal (e.g., the client may have had multiple treatment failures or been mandated for treatment by the criminal justice system), the strongest influence is the unique social worker-client relationship.

Much has been written about the need for trust in a social work relationship (Johnson, 1997; Hepworth, Rooney, & Larsen, 1997; Denning, 2000; Moore-Kirkland, 1981; Appleby, Colon, & Hamilton, 2001; Longres, 2000; Fossum & Mason, 1986). For the most part, these writers focus only on the client's trust in the social worker, or one-way trust. The client's ability to trust is often characterized (rightly so in some cases) as a function of self-esteem or the transference of distrustful qualities onto the social worker because of past relationships with people who remind the client of the social worker (Hepworth, Rooney, & Larsen, 1997; Mark & Faude, 1997; Moore-Kirkland, 1981). While it is often true that clients have negative life experiences with previous helpers, trust in the social worker–client relationship must be reciprocal. That is, "to get it you must give it" (Miley, O'Melia, & DuBois, 1995, p. 131).

Trust reflects the quality of your relationship with your client. It is based on your client's perception of your trustworthiness (Miley, O'Melia, & DuBois, 1995) and is earned through ongoing interaction with your clients. More importantly, your clients will not develop trust in you unless you exhibit trust in them, regardless of how they act or what their background might be. It is important that you learn to trust your clients. This means that you are willing to trust clients to do what is best for them: to know themselves and what they need to do. You must also communicate the belief that your clients have the capacity to change. Freire (1994) calls this "an intense faith in humankind, faith in their power to make and remake, to create and recreate. Faith in people is an *a priori* requirement for dialogue" (p. 71). Each person knows his or her own experience best (Miley, O'Melia, & DuBois, 1995). When this experience is understood and validated by others, trust emerges.

Similarly, you can demonstrate trust in your clients by recognizing that they have the right to decide *not* to change. Clients can decline services or refuse to change, if that is their choice. In the end, it is the client's life, not yours. Clients can *always* do better than we think they can. Members of the social work profession can, unless we are careful, unduly confine a client's potential improvement within artificially imposed limits defined by our professional knowledge, beliefs, and experience. I cannot begin to count the number of adolescent substance abuse clients I have encountered over the years who were told, both subtly and directly, that they had little chance of success, only to go on to become productive citizens (often earning more money in their chosen professions than their pessimistic social workers).

Your job, then, is to facilitate a relationship that puts clients—even court-mandated clients—in charge of their lives. Voluntary clients have the right to stop using drugs, abusing family members, and/or committing crimes. More difficult for some to understand is the idea that court-mandated clients also have the same rights. They also have the right to refuse services, lose their parental rights, or remain in jail if that is their choice. You demonstrate trust in clients when you communicate that you have no personal stake in their decisions beyond an obligation to engage in a dialogue that allows them to make informed choices, whether or not it is the choice you would want them to make.

Here is an example of clients' freedom of choice that you are likely to face at some point, if you haven't already. It is common for clients to choose jail or prison over treatment. This choice is unthinkable for many social workers, because the possibility of preferring jail or prison to treatment is outside their life experience. Therefore, many try to talk clients out of this choice (which is acceptable) and may even express anger at them (which is inappropriate), as if the client's choice affects the social worker. Often, these helpers try to make it seem as if substance abuse treatment is easier than jail or prison, in an attempt to get clients to comply. However, for many clients, the prospect of exploring the deepest parts of life, facing confrontation, and being held accountable for difficult and often painful changes appears far less attractive than the prospect of three square meals a day, weightlifting, and television that 90 or 180 days in jail entail. For many clients, jail seems to be the easier alternative. They have "done" jail or prison before, but not treatment.

The truth is that substance abuse treatment can be a difficult, painful, and sometimes lengthy ordeal. If clients participate seriously in treatment, it could (and probably will) seem that their lives have become worse than before treatment, at least in the short term. In addition, there are no guarantees that life will be different after treatment, no matter how hard they work. It is also true that jail, for people who have been there before, is relatively easy to survive. There are no expectations, few alternatives, and even fewer demands, beyond compliance with a few rules and a time schedule. Yet, one thing is certain. If clients remain in treatment, there is a chance—however small and remote—that their lives will change. Unless they are fortunate enough to land in a jail or prison that offers substance abuse treatment, there is little chance for similar changes to occur while they are incarcerated. Regardless of this reality, it is ultimately the client's decision.

5. Empathy Earlier, we established that the social worker's style is a major factor in determining practice success (Cartwright, 1981). Of the qualities and characteristics that promote client engagement, the social worker's ability to show empathy accounts for the largest part of the difference between successful and unsuccessful outcomes, as indicated by several clinical studies (Lafferty, Beutler, & Crago, 1989; Ridgeway & Sharpley, 1991; Miller, Taylor, & West, 1980; Miller and Baca, 1983; Miller & Sovereign, 1989; Valle, 1981).

Empathy is "the helper's ability to perceive and communicate, accurately and with sensitivity, the feelings of the client and the meaning of those feelings" (Fischer, 1973, p. 329). Similarly, Ragg (2001) states that empathy is the "ability to accurately understand the client's experience within each of the response systems (affect, thinking, action, and interaction)" (p. 87). Shulman (1999) describes the mental process needed to respond with empathy to client disclosures as "tuning in" to the underlying messages and emotions, instead of the words. For example, a substance abuse client might say during a first interview, "Stop telling me that I have a problem." Your tuned-in response to this might be, "It can be frightening to consider that possibility," or "It sounds like you are tired of people telling you how you act." Tuning in is contingent on your ability to arrive at a mental and emotional space where you can listen to, reflect, and respond to client concerns in an open and accepting manner (Keith-Lucas, 1972). According to McCrady (2001),

> Developing genuine empathy for a client requires that the clinician be able to look beyond the client's behavior when using alcohol or drugs to understand the nature of substance use disorders and the difficulties inherent in changing what are often long-standing and pervasive patterns of thought and behavior (p. viii).

The crucial aspect of an empathetic response is "skillful, reflective listening" (Miller & Rollnick, 1991, p. 55). In other words, communicate to your clients that you understand their feelings, perspectives, and opinions without taking a position that could be perceived as judgmental, critical, or blaming. An empathetic social worker seeks to let clients know that their concerns are understandable and valid. Returning to earlier discussions about communication and trust, you should respond in a manner that is consistent with a client's frame of reference and compatible with the client's communication style and social context.

SPECIAL ISSUES INVOLVED
IN ENGAGING SUBSTANCE ABUSE CLIENTS

All of the topics we have discussed up to this point occur in all helping relationships, but they take on special relevance in substance abuse practice. In addition, there are certain issues that arise in substance abuse practice that have not been previously covered. Below, we look at several of these issues, including denial, motivation, treatment compliance versus engagement, as well as the role of confrontation in substance abuse assessment and treatment. The skills that were discussed earlier, when applied consistently in the early stages of your relationship with substance-abusing clients, will help overcome many of the issues discussed below.

Denial

If you have ever discussed substance abuse or chemical dependency with anyone in the professional or recovering community, undoubtedly you have heard about the persistent and pervasive personal defense system known as denial. In some circles, denial takes on mythical proportions, as if it were a separate pathology reserved exclusively for people who abuse chemicals. Many observers believe, like Yablonsky (1989), that "almost all substance abusers in the early phase of the addiction process, when confronted about their addiction, deny they are addicted" (p. 4). It is true that substance-abusing clients—and their family members—often present a formidable denial system (Doweiko, 1999; Jung, 2001). However, denial is neither pathological in a clinical sense, nor reserved exclusively for those who are chemically dependent (Miller & Rollnick, 1991). Remember that denial is the first of Kubler-Ross's stages of grief. Actually, the tendency to deny the existence or severity of a personal problem is a normal personal defense mechanism employed by many people when they are confronted with something they find embarrassing or painful. It is also a common response if people become used to being confronted and, in their mind, accused of having a problem by others (spouse, friends, parents, and/or other helping professionals). When people are accused of possessing an undesirable personal characteristic or identity ("You are an addict" or "You are a liar") and are told that they must or should change, they are likely to argue about—or, deny—whatever they are accused of (Miller & Rollnick, 1991; Miller, 1983). Perhaps this is a way for clients to assert their personal freedom—in other words, denial is a normal response based on normal psychological principles. Orford (1985) suggests that normal psychological phenomena such as denial are often labeled as pathological when they are associated with addictive behaviors.

Defining Denial The traditional view of substance abuse and chemical dependency suggests that the behavior is supported by a series of psychological defenses that have all been subsumed under the general category of denial. As we have stated before, there is no single pattern of development for the transition from use, to abuse, and to dependence. However, because of the existence of denial, users and their family members are often—apparently—the last to know about the existence or severity of the problem.

According to Denzin (1987), alcohol-dependent people develop a lay theory of drinking that is based on denial. They believe that alcohol conveys power and control in and over their lives. Any challenges to their use evoke rationalizations and a stiff defense of their drinking. They try to shift the blame away from their behavior, blaming others who "made" them drink. Instead of seeing alcohol as the problem, they often see it as the solution ("It's the only way I can cope"). Periodically, you will hear chemically dependent clients telling "war stories" in which they routinely associate drinking with positive experiences. Moreover, many chemically dependent clients insist that they could return to use, if only people would leave them alone. They seem to long to return to a time when they had power over their use, despite a history of personal setbacks related to substance use (Denzin, 1987).

Denial is a psychological defense mechanism comprising at least three characteristics: minimization, rationalization, and projection. These defense mechanisms, like all psychological defenses, are considered healthy when used temporarily (van Wormer, 1995). Denial protects individuals and/or family members from a conscious awareness of a difficult problem and the stress, anxiety, and potential harm that may result from this awareness. For example, a chemically dependent person and his or her family will use denial to avoid recognizing an addiction, primarily because as soon as the reality is recognized, there becomes an obligation to do something about it (Doweiko, 1999). Denial protects the individual and/or family from having to deal directly with the problem.

Denial in chemical dependency may differ from denial in other areas (for example, grief) in that it often continues indefinitely (van Wormer, 1995). In fact, denial of a growing problem with alcohol is considered the most common reason why the individual does not seek professional help (Wing, 1995). By definition, denial is "a disregard for a disturbing reality" (Kaplan & Sadock, 1990, p. 20). It prevents the chemically dependent person from being aware of his or her problems, while simultaneously allowing these problems to grow and become more dangerous and/or life threatening. Accordingly, denial is a form of self-deception (Shader, 1994). It allows chemically dependent persons to continue using by shielding them from the guilt and shame associated with continued use.

Minimization Substance-abusing and chemically dependent clients often minimize the extent of their use in an attempt to convince themselves and others that they can continue to use. For example, statements such as "I only drink beer" or

"If I ever use as much cocaine as Henry, then I'll have a problem" are common examples of minimization. Minimization is so prevalent that many substance abuse professionals routinely multiply the amount of alcohol and other drugs the client admits to using by three or four (van Wormer, 1995). I agree that minimization is typical of adult clients, but my clinical experience suggests that sometimes the opposite is true with adolescents, especially males. Sometimes I have divided the reported amount in half to compensate for the males' need to present themselves as big, strong, macho users.

Family members and close friends also tend to minimize the client's use, even after the chemically dependent family member has admitted the extent of his or her use. I have had spouses of chemically dependent clients insist that their spouse was lying about his or her use: "No way, I would have known about it." You will also find parents of adolescent substance abusers minimizing their son's or daughter's use (e.g., "My son would not do that"). This minimization is indicative of what Wegscheider (1981; Wegscheider-Cruse, 1985) calls the family disease: when chemical dependency exists in families, all or most members of the family assume protective roles that help them deny the existence of a threatening problem.

Rationalization   The ability to *rationalize* use is an important component of denial and can be a barrier to the assessment and treatment process. Rationalizing often begins with statements such as "I use drugs to ease the pain of a troubled childhood," or "I have to stay drunk to live with my husband." With adolescents, "Everybody does it," or "It's only pot, and you probably did it when you were young, too" are commonly heard. Rationalizing presents an interesting dilemma for family members and professionals alike. There may be elements of truth in the "reasons" for using, thereby eliciting sympathy or pity. For example, some people who abuse substances did have a troubled childhood, or do live with difficult partners. However, the goal of rationalizing is to convince others that the user is fine, and that he or she should be pitied, not confronted.

Projection   A client is *projecting* when he or she places blame for substance abuse anywhere other than on self. For example, a client may explain, "My wife is such a complainer, she makes me drink," or "It's my job . . . I have to party with my boss to keep her happy." According to van Wormer (1995), projection is "widely used among aggressive and antisocial" (p. 123) addicts, and less so among those with strong feelings of guilt and remorse. I have observed that projection is common among adolescent clients.

My clinical experience suggests that the significance of any client's level of personal denial is directly related to his or her level of motivation to change. I also agree with van Wormer's (1995) observation that the level of denial may also be related to the level of desire to continue using the drug and the extent of guilt and shame associated with its use. These issues are intertwined to the extent that an individual's perceived need to use a drug and the extent to which he or she feels guilty or ashamed about its use play significant roles in helping or hindering a client's motivation to change.

Assessing Client Motivation

Determining your client's motivation for change during a substance abuse assessment and throughout the treatment process will help you to make decisions about how to approach him or her in practice. Miller and Rollnick (1991) and others (Davidson, Rollnick, & MacEwan, 1991) suggest that clients with different levels of motivation require helpers to approach them differently. The authors further believe that "problems of clients being unmotivated or resistant occur when a counselor is using strategies inappropriate for a client's current stage of change" (Miller & Rollnick, 1991, p. 16).

During the 1980s, Prochaska and DiClemente (1982, 1984, 1986; DiClemente & Prochaska, 1985) developed the *transtheoretical* model based on their work with people who were trying to quit smoking. This model helps us understand how and why clients—either alone or with the help of a counselor—change their addictive behavior. Subsequently, the transtheoretical model was applied to other addictive behaviors such as overeating and abuse of alcohol and other drugs (Connors, Donovan, & DiClemente, 2001; DiClemente & Hughes, 1990; DiClemente, 1991).

According to the transtheoretical model, there are six levels of motivation or stages of change that can be identified during substance abuse practice. It is important to note, however, that these stages are fluid, meaning that clients move from one to another, often needing between four and six "trips" through the stages before achieving long-term abstinence from alcohol and other drugs (Miller & Rollnick, 1991). The stages of change are precontemplation, contemplation, determination, action, maintenance, and relapse. These stages are described below, together with assessment indicators.

1. Precontemplation When people are in the precontemplation stage, they have not yet considered—or refuse to consider—the possibility that they have a problem. Most often, these clients present with classic denial, and are labeled as resistant, recalcitrant, or unmotivated. Moreover, they usually refuse to participate in an assessment or make it difficult for the social worker to perform the assessment. Hence, rarely will people in the precontemplation stage present themselves for substance abuse treatment. Most often, clients in this stage are coerced into the process by outside systems or significant others, or they are identified through medical examinations or other screening instruments (discussed in Chapter 7). As you read the following discussion, see if you can locate each of the elements of denial discussed in the previous section.

DiClemente (1991, p. 192) suggests that there are four primary types of people in the precontemplation stage: reluctant, rebellious, resigned, and rationalizing. People who fit into the category of *reluctant precontemplators* genuinely do not understand that they have a problem or even need to consider changing. According to DiClemente (1991), these individuals are not resistant so much as they are reluctant. If clients appear genuinely surprised, baffled, or taken aback by the suggestion that they may have a substance abuse problem, or seem to have never considered the issue despite addictive behavior and significant negative life consequences, they may be in the reluctant precontemplation stage.

People in the *rebellious precontemplation* stage are invested in their problem, their lifestyle, and in making their own decisions. Rebellious precontemplators are resistant—resistant to being told what to do, to having their problems pointed out to them, and to most anything you do in relation to them. If clients argue with nearly every question, refuse to respond or respond only in a hostile manner, and/or exhibit other oppositional behavior, it is quite possible that you are dealing with a rebellious precontemplator. DiClemente (1991) and others (Prochaska and DiClemente, 1982, 1984, 1986) believe that the best approaches are to present them with choices or give the appearance that you are not really trying to change them.

Resigned precontemplators usually have given up on their prospects for change and appear overwhelmed by their problems. Often these individuals will want to tell you how many times they have tried and failed to quit, how nothing seems to work, and/or how they may be "destined" to be a drug addict. These clients lack hope. Throughout your conversation with them, they make it known that it is too late for them to change. Previously, we discussed the importance of instilling hope in our clients. This is especially true when working with people who seem resigned to a lifetime of chemical dependency.

Finally, *rationalizing precontemplators*, according to DiClemente (1991), "(have) all the answers" (p. 193). These individuals do not consider the possibility of change because they "have it all figured out." They know someone who has bigger problems, they have plenty of reasons why their problem is not a problem, or they believe that they would be fine if people would simply leave them alone. Rationalizing precontemplators can sound a lot like rebellious precontemplators, with one exception: rationalizing precontemplators will be intellectual, while rebellious precontemplators will be quite emotional in their presentation. If you begin to feel as though you're in an intellectual debate with your client about the extent of her or his problems, you are probably dealing with a rationalizing precontemplator.

2. Contemplation While most clients will probably present in one of the precontemplation stages, you will also find some who are in the contemplation stage. The contemplation stage is characterized by ambivalence (Miller & Rollnick, 2002). Clients in this stage are open to the possibility that they have a problem and are willing to consider the idea that change may be needed. However, they have not yet made a decision to change and appear hesitant to make a commitment. This is a critical stage to recognize and one that can be quite frustrating, especially when you misread your client and act as if she or he is ready to change immediately. Miscalculations of this type often drive clients away or push them back into the precontemplation stage.

Clients in this stage will often state that they know they should change and that they understand they have a problem. They will give several reasons why they should change, but do not. These individuals will often have been through unsuccessful treatment several times in the past and can easily sound like resigned precontemplators. The major difference is that people in the contemplation stage acknowledge that a problem exists and that something should be done about it. To use this ambivalence as a catalyst for a productive relationship, you will need to help clients explore past treatment failures and examine their fears about changing or staying the same, while offering hope that they can succeed in treatment. Clients in this stage, according to DiClemente (1991), lack a sense of self-efficacy needed to commit to a life-changing process. In this case, not only is it our job to assess this stage, but to enhance it by employing approaches that help clients believe they have the capacity to succeed.

3. Determination Rarely during an assessment will you meet clients who are in the determination stage. Exceptions to this general statement can occur if you are doing assessments for admission into inpatient or residential treatment centers. Sometimes clients entering inpatient or residential treatment have moved into the initial phases of the determination stage, but it is a tenuous move at best. Clients in the determination stage are already in the process of deciding "to stop a problem behavior or to initiate a positive behavior" (DiClemente, 1991, p. 197). These individuals have made a concrete decision to change. These people are highly motivated and ready to put forth a serious effort to overcome their problems. Clients in the determination stage normally have already begun making changes or recently tried to change. They bring a serious commitment to their situation that is unseen in earlier stages. Your challenge is to enhance their motivation, to offer support and linkages to resources needed to further their chances of success, and to discuss with them the potential barriers to change that may have to be confronted along the way. Helping clients through their anxiety and normal hesitation is critically important during this stage.

As stated above, outside an inpatient or residential treatment context, rarely will you do an initial assessment for a client who is in the determination stage (or the action stage below, for that matter). Clients normally progress to the determination stage as a function of the substance abuse assessment and early treatment processes. Occasionally clients present with what appears to be high motivation to change, leading you to misread their level of motivation. These clients say the correct things, use recognized slogans and familiar jargon, talk about all that they are willing to do to change, and, most importantly, discuss their need to change. Yet they never seem to follow through. Thus, they belong in the contemplation or precontemplation stage, but have learned to disarm us by saying what we want to hear.

People in the determination stage worry less about jargon and more about what to do. How can you tell the difference between clients who are in the determination stage and those who are not? Listen for reports about previous actions taken, concrete plan development, and whether or not the client has reasons for not beginning the process immediately. People in the determination stage will have misgivings, hesitancies, and fears about what they are trying to accomplish. They will not usually be adamant about the need to change, nor will they dismiss the notion that change is difficult and frightening. Therefore, if clients are adamant about the need to change and unwilling to address the challenges involved in change, it is likely that they have not reached this stage.

4. Action People in the action stage do not present for a substance abuse assessment. By definition, these people are committed to their present course of action toward change. They have passed the point of decision-making and are actually taking steps to change their lives, perhaps by attending AA or NA meetings. If clients in the determination stage commit to a plan of action (DiClemente, 1991; Prochaska and DiClemente, 1982, 1984, 1986), they move from that stage to the action stage. Hence, the action stage is characterized by clients actually implementing their plans. Until or unless the client's plan of action does not succeed (see below), you will not see the client in a substance abuse assessment context.

5. Maintenance Occasionally clients will present in the maintenance stage, primarily for reinforcement of their sobriety. However, many of these clients find the support they need in groups such as AA or NA, in their churches, synagogues, or mosques, or among family and friends. The maintenance phase is the last stage of successful change. Over time, clients slowly replace old ineffective behaviors with new patterns. As the new behavior patterns, attitudes, and beliefs become firmly entrenched, old patterns dissipate. It is important to note that this process takes time, perhaps years to accomplish. Clients who submit themselves for assessment at this point are usually trying to avoid and prevent a relapse, a stage that is discussed next.

6. Relapse This is another stage in which you will often find clients coming for assistance. They have cycled through the other stages, often more than once, and achieved a period of maintenance through action. However, in substance abuse treatment, relapse is a common and normal occurrence (Denning, 2000). People, for one reason or another, often "slip" back into substance abuse behaviors as they try to solidify their hold on their new lifestyle. These clients often come for assistance just after relapsing, with a weakened sense of self-efficacy, guilt feelings, and an attitude of resignation. The indicators of someone in the relapse stage are obvious. These are people who have been abstinent for any period and who want to prevent a full-fledged relapse, while continuing to make progress. We will discuss relapse and its prevention in Chapter 10.

It is important to identify your client's level of motivation during a substance abuse assessment. However, identifying his or her level of motivation does not stop with the assessment. It is an ongoing part of the substance abuse treatment process. Clients do not cycle smoothly through the stages, and relapse is a regular and expected occurrence in substance abuse treatment. Also, remember that clients should be approached differently based on their motivation stage. For example, a client in the rebellious precontemplation stage should not be approached harshly and directly. It is more effective to use an indirect approach that relies on slowly and gently pointing out discrepancies in the client's story.

Typically, professionals in the substance abuse field have relied on direct and even harsh confrontation methods in the early stages of treatment—and even during an assessment—as the primary method of overcoming denial and enhancing motivation. In fact, confrontation and substance abuse treatment often seem to go hand-in-hand. Below we look at this issue, with an eye toward finding more creative and respectful ways to confront denial while still enhancing the clinical relationship. There are better ways to overcome denial or a lack of motivation than to figuratively hit clients between the eyes with a stick.

The Use of Confrontation to Deal with Denial

Now that we have looked at the interface between denial and your client's level of motivation, it is time to discuss the specifics of how to engage clients in the precontemplation and early contemplation stages. That is, how do you engage clients who exhibit seemingly impenetrable walls of personal denial? Typically, substance abuse professionals believe that direct confrontation is the way to proceed.

In the United States, it is common practice to use direct and harsh confrontation to overcome denial. This practice is a holdover from the Synanon therapeutic community model of the 1960s and 1970s (Denning, 2000). It advocates what some have called "attack therapy" or the "hot seat," and it is frequently used with "involuntary" clients (Miller & Rollnick, 1991, p. 6). The goal is to break through people's denial with direct, stern, and harsh confrontation. Often, these sessions involve yelling and personal accusations reminiscent of a street fight. One adult residential program I know of periodically covers the windows and forces its clients into "marathon" group sessions, where it is common for counselors to literally and figuratively "get in the face" of their clients.

Here is an example. I heard the following story from a 16-year-old male client who had recently left a residential treatment program for substance abusers. His parents admitted him for treatment at my clinic after pulling their son from the residential program. Instead of helping him become drug free, the program had produced a bigger problem: for two months, their once lively and talkative adolescent refused to speak with anyone.

Josh, a healthy-looking young man, sat in my office and stared silently out the window or looked at the floor. For three weekly sessions, we sat in silence. However, based on his demeanor and physical actions (i.e., eye contact, etc.), I did not believe that Josh was suffering from early-onset mental illness. Finally, during our fourth session he began to speak, ever so slowly:

> Everyone at the program was assigned a mentor, someone who had been in the program a while. For the first 30 days in the program (it lasted upwards of one year, at about $5000 per month—cash only), I was tied to this guy with a rope. They literally tied a piece of rope from his belt loop to mine and I couldn't go anywhere without him. They even made us be tied together when we slept.
>
> During community meetings (these happened at least twice per day), all of the senior clients would be in a room with the counselors and my mentor dragged me in. I had to stand alone in the middle of the room while counselors and my mentor asked me questions in front of everybody, sometimes even parents. When I began to answer, the whole room—clients and staff—would scream "Liar, liar, liar—you're a liar!" This would go on so long and loud that I couldn't even finish my answer. People would get up in my face yelling "Liar!" so loud that I could not say anything. Wherever I went

some days, I couldn't talk or someone would tell me to shut up because I was a liar.

This went on for weeks. They thought that I lied about everything because I abused drugs. I was so scared and embarrassed. I lied sometimes but not always. They didn't even care. Therefore, after a while I just quit talking.

The negative result of intense group confrontation on this young man's life is consistent with clinical research demonstrating that confrontational group therapy may cause more harm than good (Lieberman, Yalom, & Miles, 1973). These methods are particularly detrimental to people with low self-esteem (Annis & Chan, 1983). Josh certainly fit into this category. What adolescent does *not* have low self-esteem?

While this level of hostility in group sessions may sound extreme, Miller and Rollnick (1991) and Yablonsky (1989) report that is actually quite common. Why? Many substance abuse professionals (and the lay public) mistake denial for lying, and they believe that substance-abusing individuals need such treatment because of their tendency to be pathological liars. Many professionals believe that substance abuse clients are unaffected by ordinary treatment methods and that confrontation is the only effective treatment strategy (Jung, 2001). According to Miller and Rollnick (1991),

Approaches such as these would be regarded as ludicrous and unprofessional treatment for the vast majority of psychological or medical problems from which people suffer. Imagine . . . this approach being used as therapy for someone suffering from depression, anxiety, marital problems, sexual dysfunction, schizophrenia, cancer, hypertension, heart disease, or diabetes. Aggressive confrontational tactics have been largely reserved for those suffering from alcohol and other drug problems, and other groups like criminal offenders (p. 6).

Despite the beliefs and practices of mainstream substance abuse professionals, the use of confrontational strategies has not been supported by research. In fact, these strategies often lead to treatment failure (Denning, 2000; Peele, 1985/1998). There is no credible evidence, beyond a set of common beliefs within the field of practice, to indicate that harsh confrontation is helpful when treating people with substance abuse problems.

Certainly there is a time and place for confrontation in substance abuse practice. That is not the issue. Instead, I (and others) take issue with the harsh style of confrontation that is often used and the belief that all clients "need" it. There are times when a client's behavior or attitude can benefit from well-timed and appropriate confrontation (Sheafor, Horejsi, & Horejsi, 2000; Doweiko, 1999), but it need not be harsh or "personal." For example, there are many direct ("Last week you said 'X,' and now you say 'Y.' Which is correct?") and indirect ("Wow! A .45 blood alcohol level would kill most people; how did you survive?") methods of confrontation that fit within the worldview and presentation of individual clients.

What If Your Client Seems Evasive?

I do not recommend directly confronting what you believe to be evasive client behavior in the first session. Nor should you worry if you suspect that your client is lying. We are not human lie detectors, and not all substance-abusing clients lie, contrary to popular belief (Mark & Faude, 1997). Our job is not to hunt down, search out, and confront lies and partial truths. If you do your job well and engage your client based on the principles described in this book, whether your client lies or omits information is irrelevant because the truth will "come out" eventually. In other words, we must learn to trust the process. (Don't we give our clients the same advice?)

If you suspect that your client is denying or minimizing, note it, ask for clarification, and move on. Later, when the time is right based on your assessment of the relationship, you can return to the issues and point out discrepancies or what appear to be partial truths. Eventually, most clients will cease believing they must—or can—lie to you. I am not suggesting that you should believe everything your client says. I am simply saying that the beginning of a professional relationship is usually not the time for direct confrontation. At this stage, you have no way to tell if your client is lying anyway, because you do not yet know them. Therefore, any direct confrontation at this stage would be based on your assumptions about the client, rather than valid information. Be patient! Early confrontation usually results in client dropout (Miller & Rollnick, 1991). As someone once said to me many years ago, sometimes the only achievable goal in a first interview is to have a second. There is wisdom in this statement.

An Alternative Way to Approach Denial

It is helpful to remember that clients in the precontemplation and contemplation stages are grappling with an important decision. They are not only focused on their immediate problems, but also on the potential problems that abstinence might produce. The anxiety caused by the prospect of giving up the life they may have known for many years can discourage participation or cause a total refusal to accept help. Therefore, beyond focusing on the presenting problems and the benefits of change, do not overlook what might be the most significant issue: the dilemma clients face when contemplating change.

Dilemma of Change Consider, if you will, the following definition: a dilemma occurs when a person is presented with two or more options, neither of which appears good. In this light, your client's hesitancy to change is understandable. Clients often say, "My life may be difficult now, but what if I go through all that work to change and my life is still miserable? At least now I'm high and don't worry about life as much." This remark is not a function of resistance or denial, but an accurate appraisal of a real possibility. Ambivalence (Miller & Rollnick, 2002; Connors, Donovan, & DiClemente, 2001) in the face of change is an expected part of the assessment and treatment process.

Clients are not the only people who are ambivalent about change. Most of us experience a similar dilemma whenever we contemplate changing something significant in our lives. Perhaps you have remained in at least one dead-end relationship long after knowing it was doomed. Why? For the same reason that clients hesitate about giving up drugs. "This relationship is not what I want, but maybe it is better than nothing" or "Maybe if I just try harder, the relationship will improve." Does this rationalization sound familiar?

Do not overlook the anxiety and fear associated with change. Instead, learn to embrace it and use it. Clients are not eager to change, nor is it certain that they will reap benefits from achieving sobriety. In fact, many recovering substance abusers have said that it took a significant period of abstinence, sometimes years, before their lives became better. For some, this improvement never happens. People do not change without pain (guilt, shame, embarrassment), struggle (multiple relapses), and/or without considering a permanent return to their previous life ("It wasn't *that* bad . . . I had some great times on cocaine").

Compliance or Engagement? Earlier, I stated that you should learn to embrace and use the ambivalence that comes from the dilemma of change to benefit your clients. Traditionally, counselors have tried to "blast" through it with confrontation. Sometimes, when clients are confronted harshly and directly in the early stages of a professional relationship, they learn to "put up" with this behavior, especially if they were mandated to attend treatment. They develop an attitude of compliance, or they learn how to act in order to get what they want. Typically, what clients want is to be left alone. While compliance is a necessary first step in a process that can result in engagement in treatment, it is not an end-state. Whenever a social worker or counselor demands compliance (i.e., "go along to get along") beyond a first step, it is no longer a first step but a static state of being. My experience suggests that when consistent compliance is demanded, it is usually for the comfort of the worker rather than a client's well-being. Compliance leads clients to talk and act as they believe we want them to do, instead of how they need to act in order to change.

Clients who quietly and meekly comply with your demands without putting up a fight have either decided to agree with you in order to "get by" or tuned you out completely. Demands for compliance deepen their level of domestication to include conformance with what *we* want them to feel, believe, and say, leaving the client—when social work contact ceases—no better off than before. The only difference is that they now have another "failure" to live with. Meanwhile, we move on to the next client with the same unsuccessful approach as before.

When clients are struggling to change, they rarely comply smoothly with an assessment or treatment process. Engaged clients will argue, complain, and challenge. Many are discovering themselves—their feelings, beliefs, and attitudes—for the first time without drugs to mediate their experience. This struggle is often indicative of people finding their voice and learning to live in the world without chemical assistance. Forgoing a lifestyle of chemical dependence is neither easy nor smooth. In fact, it can be downright difficult and frightening. Do not expect clients to act as if the process is easy, because it is not. Clients who are invested in a recovery process must fight against the urge to maintain the status quo nearly every step of the way. Sometimes they will blame you or the program for their struggle. This is part of the process, and it is something you should look for as the professional relationship grows and the level of client engagement deepens.

I encourage you to look upon combative and challenging behavior as a gauge for how your work is progressing, especially if your client is in the determination stage of change. Clients who consistently "go along" with everything you say are probably not making progress. They are not challenging themselves, stretching their perspectives, or truly trying to make life-changing decisions. Have you ever made a major life-altering decision against your will without putting up a good fight? If not, why expect clients to be any different?

On the other hand, clients who challenge, show discomfort (even extreme discomfort), and are willing to argue are often grappling with themselves, their worldviews, and the earth-shattering possibility of long-term sobriety. Coming to grips with a lifetime of domestication, a lack of hope, and the daily problems caused by living under a cloud of chemicals is "messy." Giving up longstanding beliefs, attitudes, and behaviors is a struggle, and it is the kind of "serious business" people should be expected to resist at first. Hence, indications of a deep and serious struggle can reflect progress. In most cases, this behavior does not indicate that your clients are resistant to treatment, but that they at least have a passing investment in the substance abuse assessment and treatment process.

Topic for Your Journal: Alternative Explanations for Client Behaviors

In your substance abuse journal, make a list of so-called "normal" but stereotypical client behaviors that could be labeled as resistance or denial (e.g., refusing to admit they have a drug problem or being argumentative). Next, generate several alternative explanations for each behavior in your list. You will have to use your imagination *on this one. The only rule for this exercise is that no alternative explanation is ruled out because it sounds too far-fetched—at least not yet. Then, when the listing is complete, discuss with your colleagues and classmates the issues and alternatives you discovered and what they could mean in substance abuse practice.*

SUMMARY

In this chapter, we looked at how to engage clients in a substance abuse assessment and treatment process. When clients are engaged, they meaningfully participate in their own assessment, treatment planning, and treatment. Engagement fosters empowerment, honesty, and truth in the social work relationship. The methods of engagement described here were primarily drawn from the work of Paulo Freire about the state of oppressed people and the way to enlist their participation in a life-changing, liberating dialogue with helpers. Based on Freire's work, our job is to create a relationship with clients that allows them to trust us enough to reveal their attitudes, beliefs, and behaviors related to substance abuse.

We also looked at the qualities of successful helpers in substance abuse practice. These qualities—worldview respect, hope, humility, trust, and empathy— are the foundations on which clients are successfully engaged as active participants in assessment and treatment. To embody these qualities, explore the depths of your own person to discover your biases, perspectives, attitudes, and beliefs about your clients and their place in the social world. Only through the parallel processes of personal reflection and action—praxis—can you ever hope to become the kind of social worker who can work successfully with substance abusing and/or chemically dependent clients.

As you have discovered in this chapter, there are also several issues that are related specifically and sometimes uniquely to substance abuse practice. Learning to handle a client's level of denial, to enhance his or her motivation as part of the professional interview, and to approach the client's story in an appropriate way that promotes engagement are critically important skills to develop in substance abuse practice. When applied together, the issues and ideas discussed in this chapter will help you to work more effectively with substance-abusing or chemically dependent clients and their families. To repeat what was said in the beginning of this chapter, without successful client engagement, assessment and treatment cannot occur.

5

Understanding
the Family*

Because the family is the primary source of socialization, modeling, and nurturing of children, the family system has a significant impact on the current
behavior of your client. When you integrate a family systems perspective
into your overall practice approach, you will often be able to make sense of behavior that would otherwise be difficult to explain. In this chapter, we will look
at the general characteristics of families and the impact of family relationships,
rules, roles, and structure on a client's daily life. We also look at ways to engage a
family system, whether your client is an individual or the family as a whole. In
Chapter 8, we will place this information into a specific assessment context, and
in Chapter 10, we will look at the role and function of family therapy in substance abuse treatment.

WHY DO WE NEED
TO UNDERSTAND FAMILIES?

There can be little doubt that substance abuse and chemical dependency affect
both individuals and families. You may believe a particular family is a victim of
the substance use of one or more members or that the substance abuser is a victim of a troubled family. In either case, you will need to understand family structure, relationships, and dynamics and know how to engage the entire family as
your client instead of focusing solely on the individual. These skills are central to
the substance abuse assessment process. As Steinglass et al. (1987) stated, "It is
possible for an entire family to have alcoholism" (p. 46). Others have described
chemical dependency as a family disease (e.g., Goodwin & Warnock, 1991). The
phrase "family disease" has at least two main meanings in the substance abuse
field. First, there seems to be a genetic predisposition toward chemical dependency in some families. It is estimated that first-generation children of alcoholics

---

*I am indebted to Rodney Mulder for his collaboration in preparing this chapter.

are seven times more likely to develop alcoholism, with the risk being particularly high for the sons of alcoholics (Pollock, Schneider, Gabrielli, & Goodwin, 1987; Merikangas, 1990). These genetic connections are found more often with alcohol problems than with other drugs of abuse (Bierut et al., 1998) and more often for sons of alcoholics than for daughters (McGue, 1997).

A second meaning of "family disease" pertains to the environmental context in which individuals are raised and socialized. As stated in Chapter 3, while ge... ...ogy of chemical dependency... ...ed risk of chemical depende... ...lly develops within a family... ...ther drug use and abuse by... Hence, any assessment of... ...the context of the family, a... ...g the family system (Curtis, ...

Uno... ...in the United States are affect... ...ven adult Americans has at le... ...). Clearly substance use, abus... ...hile some observers believe t... ...behavior (Steinglass et al., 1... ...tionships in chemically dep... ...family systems become c... ...tionship patterns do not, rem...

Because of the... ...standing of how substance abuse affects a family cannot be reduced to a single cause and effect. Assessing a family requires in-depth understanding of how a family manages its developmental tasks in the context of the interpersonal relationships that occur during various stages of the family life cycle (Carter & McGoldrick, 1988; Nichols & Schwartz, 1991; Arnstein, 1984; Eshleman, 1994). These stages include the period when families launch children to create "new" families, or when previously divorced families remarry, creating a new family system. Family therapist Carl Whitaker (1989) once mused that parents procreate so that their children can grow up and recreate their family of origin in their own families. Family relationship traditions, rules, and interaction patterns are transmitted from one generation to the next (Bowen, 1985). When families intersect through marriage, the conflict between competing dynamics brought from the partners' families of origin can lead to disagreements in the new family. Often these disagreements involve methods of child rearing.

Our clinical experience suggests that most clients come individually for an assessment, often referred by family members. Given that most substance abuse clients do not choose to seek treatment on their own, the family plays an important role in the referral process. Despite the problems that substance-abusing or chemically dependent family members generate, they usually maintain frequent and ongoing contact with parents, siblings, and significant others, regardless of their age or marital status (Stanton, 1997). Hence, it is important to understand the individual's place in the family system and discover how to work through the individual to enlist the family in the assessment and treatment process. Because of the ongoing contact between clients and their families of origin, family members can assist the treatment process by increasing an individual's awareness of the problem, facilitating treatment entry, and helping to encourage and support behavioral change.

WHAT IS A FAMILY?

As if family dynamics were not complex enough, the definition of *family* constantly changes, challenging the most skilled social workers to understand what people mean when referring to their families. Here, we define *family* to include any combination of nuclear, extended, single-parent, reconstituted, gay and lesbian couples, and/or any other form of family life (Holsems, 1998). A family is composed of the people—regardless of their actual blood or legal relationship to the client—whom clients consider to be members of their family. If a client refers to a neighbor as "Uncle Joe," then that perception represents your client's reality. What good would it do to argue otherwise? You should seek to understand your client's unique definition of his or her family, rather than imposing a rigid theoretical standard that may not fit your client's life (Karpel & Strauss, 1983).

With that caveat in mind, there is academic value in trying to define a family. We can assume that families are composed of individuals in close relationship to each other (Karpel & Strauss, 1983), regardless of whether or not the members appear close. Moreover, family interactions are patterned, predictable, and stable. Thus, you must attend to several factors when trying to understand the role a family plays in a client's substance use and abuse.

The most important factors to consider are the type and quality of relationships between family members and how these relationships work together systemically to maintain the integrity and coherence of the family system (Nichols & Schwartz, 1991). The dynamics of family relationships can be dizzyingly complex. As a result, it is impossible to characterize the substance-abusing or chemically dependent family according to any simple formula or template. There is considerable variation in how families organize around chemical dependency and the member(s) who are either substance abusing and/or chemically dependent (Steinglass et al., 1987). Family assessment becomes even more complex when you realize that even though you are looking into relationships and patterns of relationships and behaviors, you cannot forget that families are composed of individuals. Moreover, from a multi-systemic perspective, family systems are embedded in a community that introduces and supports relational complexity between family members and between the family and people in the local environment, including other professionals and social service organizations.

Since the mid-1950s, when the family therapy field began applying general systems theory (von Bertalanffy, 1971) to families, the family therapy literature has downplayed the role of individuals within the family, while emphasizing the importance of the systemic dimensions (Karpel & Strauss, 1983). Since families consist of individuals in close relationship with others, any effort to understand family in the context of substance abuse practice must accommodate both individual and systemic dynamics. That is, assessing the role of the family in substance abuse involves looking at what occurs *within* and *between* people in a family context. This approach is consistent with the multi-systemic perspective advanced in this text. Individuals operate within the context of families, which operate within the context of communities, which operate within the context of larger social, political, cultural, ideological, and economic systems (Lowery, 1998). Moreover, people are neither fully defined by their families, nor totally free to self-define and self-determine (Johnson, 2000). There are critical interfaces between individuals and families, and between families and the larger communities, that influence the way individuals think, feel, and act. To accurately assess and treat families, you must learn to determine how families manage the critical interfaces between these various systems.

THE CHANGING ROLE OF FAMILIES
IN SUBSTANCE ABUSE TREATMENT

A brief history of substance abuse treatment may help to place current practices in perspective. Throughout most of human history, individuals with a substance abuse problem were viewed from the moral model perspective (see Chapter 3). Substance-abusing individuals were considered weak-willed, prone to poor decision-making, and/or a product of "bad seed." Most believed that substance abuse problems were the fault of the afflicted individual. "Treatment," when it existed, usually took the form of extended confinement to mental hospitals, church involvement, or when all else failed, social sanctions (Musto, 1999; Peele, 1998).

After the Prohibition era ended in 1933, the disease concept (Chapter 3) began making headway in the United States, gaining some acceptance. In 1935, Alcoholics Anonymous (AA) began using the disease concept as the foundation of its twelve-step program. When spouses of alcoholics began forming Al-Anon groups during the 1940s to provide support for spouses of substance-abusing (mostly alcoholic) persons, the focus remained on the "sick" individual rather than his or her spouse.

At about the same time, the use of psychoanalysis was growing in popularity. It, too, explained addiction as an individual malady. It posited that addiction was a symptom of a deeper, underlying pathology that could change only through long-term psychoanalysis. The research on addiction grew in the 1940s and 1950s but continued to emphasize the emotional and physiological problems of the individual addict. If marital or family problems were identified, these issues were used to determine how the spouse's behavior contributed to the disease. That is, chemically dependent persons and their spouses or partners were blamed for the problem.

During the systems therapy movement of the 1960s and 1970s, adherents of this new approach began to take a more comprehensive look at families, focusing more clearly on the interactions between family members. However, family therapy was slow to enter mainstream substance abuse treatment, primarily because most family therapists viewed substance abuse as a nuisance (Curtis, 1999) and most substance abuse counselors were recovering addicts with no formal training outside of Alcoholics Anonymous. Recovering lay counselors were not trained in family systems issues, family dynamics, or family treatment theories and methods. Recovering counselors mostly subscribed to the disease model of addiction. Accordingly, any focus other than individual recovery through AA took attention away from where these well-meaning counselors thought it should be.

From the 1970s to the 1990s, most substance abuse treatment programs developed some form of family "treatment" by including spouses and children in the treatment process. However, this involvement often took the form of films, classes, or encounter groups where family members could vent their negative feelings toward the addicted family member. Little was done to promote family stability or unity after the chemically dependent person had achieved sobriety. This period also ushered in an era of self-help. Specifically, self-help groups such as Adult Children of Alcoholics (ACOA) encouraged members to examine how family dynamics are affected by addiction. Today, there is a plethora of support groups, each claiming to help members of chemically dependent families "recover" from their disease.

With the onset of managed care, substance abuse treatment programs slowly began employing professionals who held advanced clinical degrees and had been trained as family therapists. While many substance abuse treatment programs across the United States now include professional family therapy services, the field as a whole has been slow to incorporate family systems principles into its regular treatment regimens. Any family treatment that is offered most likely reflects the increasing interdisciplinary nature of the substance abuse field. Many professionals who are now working in the field have been trained in family therapy, producing what has been described as a gradual shift in thought from seeing the family as enemy to the family as potential treatment ally (van Wormer, 1995). Yet many substance abuse treatment programs still relegate family work to aftercare, once clients are relatively grounded in personal sobriety. This attitude is unfortunate, given the importance of family relationships and support in establishing sobriety after a period of substance use, abuse, and addiction (Curtis, 1999; Freeman, 1993).

WORKING WITH FAMILY SYSTEMS

Before describing specific aspects of chemically dependent family systems, we should define several important terms. A complete study of the various systems-based family treatment models would exceed the scope of this book. The following discussion (along with the specifics in Chapter 8) should, however, give you enough information to include family issues as part of substance abuse assessment with individual clients, or to work with entire families to address concerns about the afflicted individuals and themselves. We also revisit this subject in Chapter 10 when discussing the role and function of family therapy in substance abuse treatment.

Definitions of Terms

Family System   A family is made up of individuals in simultaneous and mutual interaction to create a dynamic and evolving system. Critical to understanding family systems theory is an awareness of the importance of organization within the family. A family system can be described as being

> greater than the additive sums of the separate parts. That is, the fit between the elements of the system, the pattern with which the parts come together, produces something that cannot be predicted from a knowledge of the separate characteristics of each of the component parts. Just as we cannot predict the characteristics of a chemical compound from the properties of the separate elements that combine to form it, we cannot predict the behavioral properties of a family simply through knowledge of the separate personalities of the husband, wife, and children. Conversely, we say that no system can be adequately understood or totally explained once it has been broken down into its component parts (Steinglass et al., 1987, pp. 44–45).

Family members perform many reciprocal roles as part of their contribution to overall system behavior. The roles played by family members depend on others playing certain roles simultaneously. Members use feedback from other members' roles to give their individual roles form and purpose. People performing various roles work together to keep the family stable, unified, and functioning. In this way, family roles—including the role played by the substance-abusing or chemically dependent member—are vital to the ongoing existence of a particular family.

Furthermore, no single member or subsystem of members in a family can be said to act independently. Instead, in a family system, "the state of each unit is constrained by, conditioned by, or dependent on the state of other units" (Miller, 1965, p. 68). In the context of their family system, the behavior of family members, including the various roles they play in relation to each other, is shaped and constrained by the simultaneous behaviors of all other members of the family, singly and in combination. When chemical dependency becomes part of daily functioning in families, it can have a dramatic effect on how the system organizes in an effort to cope with the problems caused by chemically dependent members. As stated above, the ways in which chemically dependent families organize around afflicted members vary considerably.

Subsystem   Families separate into subsystems to perform various family functions (Goldenberg & Goldenberg, 2000). Each individual is a subsystem, as are dyads (couples) and larger groupings. The most obvious subsystems are parents, adolescents, children, and grandparents. Age, gender, generation, and family responsibilities, to name a few, define subsystems. In all families, individuals belong to several subsystems, each requiring different roles and behavior. For example, John may be a father, husband, son, brother, and nephew. Administering discipline may be appropriate in John's role as father, but not as husband or son. Subsystems are important in determining family structure and, together with the concept of boundaries, are one major area of family problems (Minuchin, 1974).

Boundaries Individuals, subsystems, and family systems are separated by interpersonal boundaries (Minuchin, 1974; Haley, 1976). Boundaries are invisible barriers that surround subsystems, regulating the amount of contact with others (Minuchin, 1974). Boundaries also serve to protect the separateness and autonomy of the family and its subsystems from its environment. To emphasize the boundary between the parental and child subsystems, for example, a mother might tell her eldest son, "You aren't your brother's parent. If he is drinking, tell me so I can deal with him."

Each subsystem has specific functions that make demands on its members. The development of the interpersonal skills necessary to function competently within these subsystems relies on freedom from interference by other subsystems. Boundaries provide the "room" for this to occur. For example, parents cannot function competently in their parental role if they are constantly receiving "advice" from in-laws, grandparents, or social workers. Proper subsystem functioning relies on the existence of clear boundaries that delineate subsystems and permit contact between them. According to Minuchin (1974), the composition of the subsystems is not as important as the clarity of the boundaries separating them.

Boundaries vary along a continuum between disengaged and enmeshed (Minuchin, 1974). Disengaged boundaries permit little or no contact with other subsystems in the family. Although families with disengaged boundaries permit growth and autonomy, members do not feel loved and supported.

Enmeshed boundaries represent overly close families. Within an enmeshed family, the lines between subsystems are blurred or do not exist, allowing free interaction between members of different subsystems. When this unrestricted interaction occurs, families engage in cross-generational coalitions (Minuchin, 1974; Goldenberg & Goldenberg, 2000; Nichols & Schwartz, 1991). To establish such a coalition, an individual from one subsystem (say, a parent) forms a close alliance with an individual from another subsystem (say, a child) against an individual from one of their subsystems (such as the other parent). Cross-generational coalitions are also called triangulated relationships (Bowen, 1985). Enmeshed families are emotionally close, but family members are not allowed freedom, independence, or room for growth.

Ironically, family systems with enmeshed internal boundaries tend to maintain rigid external boundaries with their environment, while the opposite is true for families with internally disengaged boundaries. Few families are at either extreme on the disengaged–enmeshed continuum. However, according to Minuchin (1974), most families that seek help are more enmeshed than disengaged.

In chemically dependent families, boundaries quickly shift, become blurred, or disappear as a function of substance use (Elkin, 1984). For example, children often become primary parents for each other, or serve as intimate counsel for the non-addicted parent. More insidiously, the blurring or removal of boundaries in chemically dependent families can lead to the reported high rates of domestic violence and sexual abuse (Sheafor, Horejsi, & Horejsi, 2000). Boundaries— physical and moral—disappear, making these types of abuse more likely in chemically dependent families (Boyd-Franklin, 1993; Lowery, 1998).

Family Structure A family's structure is the organized pattern of interaction between its members. It is composed of the daily, often predictable behavior of family members in relation to each other. Structure, therefore, is an invisible set of demands that organizes how family members interact (Goldenberg & Goldenberg, 2000). Families perform repeated interactional patterns that delineate family structure. For example, when a parent tells her child not to drink and he obeys, the interaction defines who she is in relation to him, and who he is in relation to her, in that context at that time.

Family structure develops within two systems of constraint. The first is generic, based on accepted community and cultural standards pertaining to family organization. For example, in most cultures and communities, parents and children have different levels of authority in the family. The second system is idiosyncratic, involving the mutual expectations of family members. These rules pass through generations of explicit and implicit role negotiations between family members, and between family members and the larger communities. For example, gender roles in terms of who works and who cares for children, the kinds of toys male and female children are allowed to play with, and attitudes toward male and female children with regard to substance use are all examples of idiosyncratic family rules that exist, often outside of conscious awareness. Over time, these patterns become self-perpetuating. In some cases, especially in families with chemically dependent members, these self-perpetuating behavior patterns close off the family from change, leading to a rigid and restrictive family structure. We discuss this topic at greater length below.

WHAT IS A FUNCTIONAL FAMILY?

Family therapists have identified a variety of factors that social workers can use to define a functional family. However, before we can define what is functional, we must recognize the problems inherent in this task, especially in a country as culturally, racially, and ethnically diverse as the United States. Additionally, any mention of family roles and functionality must acknowledge the impact of gender roles and sexism (Avis, 1996), as well as social class (Jones, 1991; Boyd-Franklin, 1993).

Over the last 20 years, many have challenged the underlying assumptions about gender that are part of many family therapy models. For example, a number of female authors (Hare-Mustin, 1978, 1987; Gilligan, 1982; Goldner, 1985; Avis, 1985), to name a few, have criticized existing family therapy models for failing to attend to gender and power differences in male-female relationships, in effect ignoring how these differences influence normal family functioning. The main point of this argument was that social workers, being part of the larger society, tended to reinforce traditional gender roles as part of daily practice (Avis, 1996). A feminist approach to family therapy has been developed to address these issues (Goldenberg & Goldenberg, 2000).

In addition to gender, any definition of a functional family must be considered in the context of culture, ethnicity, and class politics. What is considered "normal" for families in the literature must be interpreted warily when dealing with individual families. As we discussed in Chapter 4, how you engage clients and/or families is filtered not only through your professional knowledge, beliefs, and values, but also through your personal "cultural filters"—attitudes, assumptions, customs, religious beliefs and practices that stem from your particular cultural, ethnic, and family background (Giordano & Carini-Giordano, 1995). For example, what may seem dysfunctional to a European American social worker from a middle-class, two-parent family may not be dysfunctional at all in a poor, African American, single-parent family. Whether related to gender, race, ethnicity, or class, use the following descriptions of a functional family only as a guide, not as a final definition during an assessment.

As stated above, there are many different definitions of what constitutes a functional family. For example, van Wormer (1995) describes functional families as those in which there is respect for individual differences; open communication among members; love for who people are, rather than what they do; stable routines and rituals; a process for resolving guilt and shame; and free expression of feelings. Jay Haley (1976) and Cloe Madanes (1981) believe that functional families have a defined hierarchy (division of power within the family), clear boundaries between subsystems (i.e., parents and children, etc.), and clear lines of communication.

Minuchin (1974) also focuses on subsystems, boundaries, and family closeness (i.e., level of enmeshment), while Bowen (1985) suggests that functional families avoid triangulated communication patterns, allowing family members to mature into interdependent adults. Steinglass et al. (1987) believe that a healthy family is one that has developed an "appropriate balance between morphogenesis (controlled growth) and morphostasis (internal regulation), the key being a coherent fit of regulatory mechanisms and developmental themes" (p. 45), meaning that there is always interplay—a push and pull—between the family's desire to maintain stability and its desire to change and grow (Speer, 1979).

THE COMPETING DEMANDS
OF STABILITY AND CHANGE

In some families, the need for stability is so great that change seems to occur only in response to tremendous pressures. These families rigorously cling to the status quo, stifling developmental changes and growth until they explode, often in the form of a family crisis. For example, in some families, parents and children seem to unconsciously agree that they will continue to relate on all levels (rules, roles, and so on) as if the kids are still young, despite the fact that the kids are in late adolescence. When an adolescent decides to change the rules by staying out late, finding a love interest, or drinking and using drugs, the family erupts into a major crisis. This type of interactional structure is closely related to an enmeshed family system, typical in chemically dependent families.

In other families, change seems to come so rapidly and frequently that family life appears chaotic and disorganized. Members of these families appear almost unaffected by other members, allowing for fluctuating rules, roles, and behaviors with no apparent set of family standards or practices. Members often come and go, including some persons who appear to have little or no connection to the family unit. This description corresponds to Minuchin's (1974) definition of a disengaged family, discussed earlier.

As stated earlier, from a family systems perspective, healthy families maintain a balance between stability and change. Stability comes over the long term, while changes occur as developmentally necessary to allow everyone in the family to reach individual and collective developmental milestones at the appropriate time (Steinglass et al., 1987). Often, chemically dependent families react to problems by striving to maintain short-term stability. When one member of a family is chemically dependent, in many ways, all members are chemically dependent. This is not to say that all family members are substance abusers. Rather, it means that even if only one family member is identified as chemically dependent (either by someone within or outside the family), the lives of all members are constrained by the roles and rules developed out of the inevitable tug-of-war between the need for stability and change.

HOW FAMILIES ADAPT
TO CHEMICAL DEPENDENCY

When working with a substance-abusing family, you will need to discover the extent to which the family has changed to accommodate the substance-abusing or chemically dependent member. In the early stages of addiction, families tend to accommodate very little to the abusing member. However, the family often has expended considerable energy in trying to help or change the substance-abusing member, usually to no avail. Families in this stage often feel considerable anger and resentment, and they cope by means of denial and minimization.

In the middle stages of dependency, family members begin making unconscious and conscious adaptations to life with a chemically dependent member. Family members' roles change. This is usually the stage, before roles and relationships solidify around the chemically dependent member, where families seem the most chaotic and troubled, primarily because members often react to the chemically dependent person in different ways. During this stage, the survival roles discussed below are clearly beginning to take shape in families.

By the late stage of chemical dependency, adaptive roles have become rigid. The family begins actively hiding and/or isolating the chemically dependent member, trying to exclude him or her from routine family functions. Families in this stage begin exhibiting shame and guilt, yet appear to have resigned themselves to the family's seemingly hopeless condition (Curtis, 1999). By this time, the family has become a chemically dependent family system, in which all members of the family are integrally affected by the chemically dependent member and his or her needs.

FAMILY RESILIENCE

Before becoming too enthralled by the terms *functional* and *dysfunctional*, remember that being defined as dysfunctional does not necessarily mean that a family is dysfunctional in everyday life. (After all, it is popular in many social work circles to believe that *every* family is dysfunctional.) Be sure to focus on how individual families manage, cope, or thrive during periods of dysfunction. Instead of believing that every family is dysfunctional, it is more appropriate to claim that every family experiences *periods of dysfunction*, followed by *periods of functionality* after an adjustment period. This cycle includes even the most troubled families on your caseload. So, when evaluating a family's functionality, try to look upon dysfunction as a difficult period rather than a constant state.

Many who have been in the social work field for any length of time recognize that there are some individuals and families who are happier and more stable than others. These families, regardless of structure, number of problems, definition of who is a "family member," boundary characteristics, racial make-up, social class, education, or training, seem more competent, show greater recuperative abilities and flexibility, and are better able to adapt to changing conditions.

To bear out this observation, there is an emerging body of literature about family resilience. According to this perspective, families as a whole—or one or more individual members—may experience dysfunctional behavior during periods of crisis or personal stress. Since this is when individuals or families may come to you for an assessment, it is easy to believe that they are dysfunctional, when they may simply be experiencing a period of dysfunction. While some families may be shattered by this crisis, others emerge after a period of readjustment stronger and closer than before the crisis. Yet, at the time of the crisis a family may appear dysfunctional. Through the professional labeling process, these families become labeled as dysfunctional when in fact they are in the process of transformation.

Resilience can be described as the ability of families (or individuals) to draw upon strengths, resources, relationships, and support when necessary in order to overcome or adjust to threats to their integrity (Hawley & deHaan, 1996). Resilience is not a set of static skills, but a developmental process that enables people to create adaptive responses to stress, and in some cases, thrive and grow in response to stressors (Walsh, 1996). According to Walsh (1996), a family's relational resilience is forged through adversity, not despite it:

> How a family confronts and manages a disruptive experience, buffers stress, effectively reorganizes, and moves forward with life will influence immediate

and long-term adaptation for all family members and for the family unit (p. 267).

Even chaotic, disorganized, abusive, and multi-problem families have resources such as intimacy, support, and personal and/or collective family meaning (Minuchin, 1974). Aponte (1994) stated that poor families exhibit resilience characteristics, even if these characteristics go unrecognized by outsiders. A resilience-focused approach to individuals and families helps identify resources (social networks, etc.) and strengths that could be tapped to help the family adapt and change of its own accord. This approach is embedded within the context of a strengths perspective (Saleebey, 1997), an integral part of social work theory and practice.

As we proceed through this discussion, keep in mind that the labels "functional" and "dysfunctional" have little value in and of themselves. What is important is knowing how a particular family handles daily challenges, stressors, and crises without a social worker's intervention. Even if a family seems to fit the quintessential definition of *dysfunctional*, ask yourself, "How did this family survive long enough to get to my office?"

CHEMICALLY DEPENDENT FAMILIES

We began this chapter by claiming that chemical dependency has a profound influence on families. Now we will explore the general characteristics of chemically dependent families so that you will know what to look for during a comprehensive substance abuse assessment.

In many families, chemically dependent behavior distorts the family's "developmental and regulatory" (Steinglass et al., 1987, p. 46) capacities, meaning that chemically dependent families tend to distort the importance given to substance-related tasks over non-substance-related tasks. For example, some families adhere to highly developed rules about how each member is to act when the father drinks, while paying scant attention to the children's health care or school performance. These families also have trouble balancing stability and change. Often, the process of change and growth is thwarted, resulting in what Steinglass et al. (1987) call inappropriately long periods of phase-related behavior (dominated by the need for stability) and a corresponding tendency to ward off developmentally appropriate transitional behavior. Chemically dependent families tend to favor short-term stability over all other issues. The goal becomes simply to stay together, no matter what the cost to individual members. Any changes or intrusions from outside the family are viewed as threats to the status quo. Therefore, chemically dependent families often present as highly guarded and protective, while being "frozen in time" (Steinglass et al., 1987, p. 56).

In addition to the overwhelming systemic drive for stability, chemically dependent families are often characterized by other problems, including a high degree of conflict, chaos, unpredictability, and inconsistent messages to children about their worth. There is typically a breakdown of traditional rituals and rules

(Hawkins, 1997). Such environments are often associated with poor communication among family members (Murphy & O'Farrell, 1996), high levels of stress (Kurtz, Gaudin, Howing, & Wodarski, 1993), child abuse and neglect (Olsen, 1995), domestic violence (Bennett, 1995), emotional and physical abuse (Famularo, Kinscherff, & Fenton, 1992), and sexual abuse (Gil-Rivas, Fiorentine, Anglin, & Taylor, 1997).

Children from chemically dependent families are at increased risk for adjustment problems, including poor school performance, criminal involvement, depression, suicidality, and substance abuse (Chassin, Curran, Hussong, & Colder, 1996; Ireland & Widom, 1994). Many individuals raised in such homes continue to experience emotional problems into adulthood (Sher, 1997), including depression, anxiety, and post-traumatic stress disorder, as well as substance abuse or chemical dependency.

We propose five basic themes found in many chemically dependent families. By no means do these themes apply to every chemically dependent family. We offer them simply as a guide for interviewing and assessment. When assessing individual substance abuse in a family context, it is important to get a sense of the whole, how the family is organized to interact internally between members and externally with its environment (Lowery, 1998). These basic themes of chemically dependent families are listed below.

1. Chemically dependent families are systems in which substance abuse is the central organizing principle around which the behavior of family members is structured (Elkin, 1984).

2. Chemically dependent behavior in family life can profoundly distort the balance between growth and development (change) and stability within the family. Typically, although not always, this balance is skewed toward an emphasis on preserving short-term stability at the expense of long-term growth (Steinglass et al., 1987).

3. Chemically dependent families tend to have significant boundary and hierarchy problems (Haley, 1976; Price, 1996; Elkin, 1984). These families tend to ignore boundaries between subsystems, creating cross-generational coalitions between parent and child, and the parental function (when the chemically dependent person is an adult) is usually ineffective. These issues are normally expressed through various roles that become fixed and rigid in their presentation (Satir, 1964, 1972; Treadway, 1989; Freeman, 1993; Wegscheider, 1981). This presentation, and its significance in the assessment process, will differ based on race, culture, and ethnicity (Boyd-Franklin, 1989; McRoy, Aguilar, & Shorkey, 1993).

4. Changes that occur in chemically dependent families can profoundly influence the family's individual members and the system as a whole in terms of stunted or frozen growth and development. Families often become stuck in developmental stages of the family life cycle (McGoldrick, 1989).

5. Families with chemically dependent members tend to experience high levels of shame, grief, stress, and guilt (Fossum & Mason, 1986). These emotions

and the behaviors that result often override all other emotions, leading to behavioral problems in the non–chemically–dependent family members, especially children. These issues can last a lifetime, leading to relationship and family problems for children later in life (Bepko & Krestan, 1985; Sher, 1991; Wegscheider-Cruse, 1985).

As mentioned earlier, use these themes with caution. They are generalizations that can provide a guide for assessment, not a roadmap to a certain location.

Family Survival Roles

Since we have referred several times to interpersonal roles in chemically dependent families, it will be helpful to discuss these issues more thoroughly. The application of role theory (Davis, 1996) to the family was pioneered by Virginia
Satir (1964, 1972) and her trainees (Wegscheider, 1981), pertaining specifically to
family therapy with chemically dependent families. Interpersonal roles are part of
all family systems. Because of the stress in chemically dependent families, however, members (and others outside the family) learn to adapt by rigidly adhering
to protective roles that preserve short-term stability.

Family survival roles become encompassing and rigid because adherence to
the negative roles is perceived by family members as the way to remain in the
family and protect the integrity of the system. It is important to remember that
in a system, roles interact with each other; in effect, they "need" each other to
exist. In healthy families, members move in and out of a variety of roles, but in
chemically dependent families, role assignments tend to remain fixed.

Sharon Wegscheider (1981), borrowing from the writings of Virginia Satir
(1964, 1972), depicted six family roles in chemically dependent families: the
chemically dependent person, chief enabler, hero, family scapegoat, lost child,
and family mascot. We have chosen to focus on this configuration of roles, primarily because it is the most recognizable. Larsen (1985) also proposed a constellation of roles for members in chemically dependent families. His roles (also six)
include the caretaker, people-pleaser, workaholic, martyr, perfectionist, and tap-
dancer. While the names are different, Larsen and Wegscheider are describing essentially the same issues. In chemically dependent families, members assume roles
that are "self-defeating, greatly exaggerated and complicated by a pathological
relationship to a chemically dependent person . . . that diminish our capacity to
initiate or participate in loving relationships" (Larsen, 1985, p. 6).

Regardless of what name is given to the roles, as part of a substance abuse
assessment it can be helpful to identify which role or roles clients play in their
family of origin. This exercise is valuable for a family assessment, but it can also
provide insights into other areas of the client's life, because family members tend
to apply the same role behavior at work, school, other organizations, and more
importantly, in their personal relationships. The six roles (Wegscheider, 1981) are
described below.

Chemically Dependent Person   Chemically dependent members exhibit
self-protective and insulating behavior, remaining preoccupied with their own

concerns and, most importantly, with sustaining their behavior. Their life revolves around using substances at sufficient levels to maintain their dependency. To do this, chemically dependent members involve most of their time, money, and friends in the lifestyle. They organize their lives so as to always be able to find and use alcohol or other drugs. That is, any social outlet must allow drinking or drug use, or it ceases to be an option.

Chemically dependent members are often charming and grandiose to outsiders and strangers, while being angry, rigid, and violent toward close friends and family members. Family members living with chemically dependent persons ultimately focus on the addict, whether or not the person is physically present. Loved ones subordinate their personal needs to the needs of the addicted person, whose behavior, attitudes, and moods often dominate family agendas. The addict's behavior, or anticipated behavior, dictates how family members act or react to events, resulting in the formation of complementary family roles to help members cope from day to day.

Chief Enabler   This term has gotten Wegscheider (1981) into trouble with feminist scholars over the years because of the implication that "enabling" means being responsible for the behavior of others, and because this role is often associated with the wife or female partner of a chemically dependent person. However, the role and behavior attached to the label of chief enabler can be applied to males as well as females. Chief enablers are the people whose responsibility it is to manage the family, including paying the bills, attending to children's needs, and, by being over-responsible, seeing to it that the family system remains intact from day to day. Whatever duties chemically dependent persons do not perform, chief enablers assume as their responsibility.

Chief enablers are frequently overwhelmed with stress, guilt, and shame. Their behavior tends to exhibit powerlessness, fragility, self-blaming, and self-pity. They often present with various stress-related physical conditions such as anxiety, stomach and intestine problems, headaches, and fatigue. Their feelings, hidden underneath these behaviors, include hurt, anger, fear, guilt, and pain. Nevertheless, chief enablers cannot access these feelings either because their family demands they be ignored, or because their personal behavior precludes the expression of feelings. Black (1981) says that the chief enabler (often called a codependent person) lives in a world where the system imposes three rules: do not talk, trust, or feel.

Chief enablers are responsible for family stability. Their task is to ensure that families remain stable, together, and functioning. To allow any confrontation of chemical dependency or seek personal help is tantamount to treason. Therefore, living under the unspoken threat of family disintegration, chief enablers continue managing the family, while ignoring or denying the troubles caused by chemical dependency. In helping people self-identify with this role, it is important not to allow them to assume that being an enabler suggests that they are responsible for a chemically dependent family member's behavior.

Hero   Usually a first child, the hero is the child who—by being born—transformed a couple into a family. Often these children carry a family's hopes and aspirations.

They are frequently high-achieving and industrious children who constantly seek approval. Everyone, including the school, church, and extended family, sees this child as the "star," the one who can save the reputation and dignity of the family.

Therein lies the problem: these children are usually praised for *what they do* and not for *who they are* as people. Hero children usually try to be perfect in order to make everyone else feel good. The behaviors that these children show are success, super responsibility, and appearing to have their lives together. By achieving success in school and sports, they are able to give their families someone to look to as evidence of good parenting, even while their families are wracked by internal troubles. Hero children work hard for approval, often developing independent lives outside their families where they may receive more reward and praise.

Hero children learn that it is their job to take care of other people. As adults, these children often become social workers or other helping professionals. They are plagued by chronic low self-esteem. Their feelings, covered up by their behavior, include loneliness, hurt, inadequacy, confusion, and anger. These feelings reflect the fact that the job of hero children cannot be accomplished. No matter how hard they work, their families remain troubled and continue to disintegrate.

Family heroes may have the most difficult task of all in overcoming their role behavior. It can be extremely painful to acknowledge that despite doing everything "right," they still feel bad and have troubles. These children often fall into substance abuse or other destructive behaviors because of the frustration associated with being perfect, yet ineffective. Hero children may also become workaholics, have trouble admitting that they are wrong, and act as caretakers for others. Often, a hero child will marry a chemically dependent person. While this is true for both male and female hero children, according to Black (1981), if a hero child is female, there is a strong likelihood she will marry an alcoholic.

Family Scapegoat These children look at hero children and believe that they cannot do as well in life. Therefore, family scapegoats rebel. Additionally, because they assume a rebel role, everyone else tends to blame these children for family troubles. Hence, scapegoats effectively—at least with outsiders—distract attention from the real troubles in the family.

Family scapegoats are likely to have trouble with their parents and/or extended family members, their teachers, and later with police. These children perform poorly in school, often leading to school refusal. While all children in chemically dependent families are at high risk for substance use, family scapegoats are the most likely to become the next substance abuser in these families, usually beginning at a relatively early age (Wegscheider, 1981). Family scapegoats are the children who are most likely to join gangs and act out sexually at earlier ages. Among girls, there is a strong likelihood of an unplanned pregnancy.

The behaviors shown by family scapegoats include defiance, sullenness, isolation and withdrawal, substance use and abuse, and heavy reliance on peer groups. To outsiders, family scapegoats exhibit hostility, defiance, and anger. Underneath these behaviors are feelings of hurt, guilt, anger, rejection, and loneliness. These children take the focus off chemically dependent members and do not compete with family heroes. Without help, these children will develop little zest for life, be troublemakers (or, dropouts) in school and later at work, and are the children most likely to go to jail.

Lost Child Lost children live mostly in fantasy worlds and almost never cause trouble. They are often unseen and unheard, choosing to remain alone, isolated, and quiet. When there is a fight or struggle in the family, lost children flee to the safety of their bedroom or friends. These are the children who may "get lost" in computer games and/or spend literally hours alone in their rooms. Their behaviors are defensive in nature, including withdrawal, aloofness, quietness, independence, and disaffection. Often, lost children are overweight (Wegscheider, 1981).

To the family, lost children are a relief, since parents do not have to worry about them, especially compared to scapegoats. They have few friends, try to conform and follow the crowd, and have trouble making decisions. The feelings covered up by these behaviors include loneliness, hurt, inadequacy, and anger. The lost child, however, rarely shows anger because to do so would be "out of character." In therapy, a major task is to learn to show anger in a productive way. Most lost children equate anger with rage. Without help, these children show little zest for life, may have sexual identity problems, be promiscuous or never date at all, and have difficulties with adult relationships.

Family Mascot These people are always clowning, making jokes, and pulling pranks. The function of family mascots is to provide relief and distraction. By being funny, they allow families to ignore their troubles, even if only for a few moments. Family mascots often appear hyperactive and have short attention spans. They carry this role, like the others, from home to school, work, and social relationships. Whenever they find themselves in a tense or stressful situation, they use humor as a pressure release. They are expert at making a joke whenever anyone in the family attempts to express feelings or confront behavior. In fact, the role of the family mascot is to stop family members from expressing feelings, including the addict's anger and rage (van Wormer, 1995).

The behaviors shown by these children include hyperactivity, clowning, and trying to attract attention. These children are emotionally fragile, and if they cannot be clowns, they are lost. Clowning around allows family mascots to cover up feelings of fear, insecurity, confusion, and loneliness. These children present as being immature and in need of protection. Without help or therapy they may develop ulcers or other stress-related diseases, remain immature, and be compulsive clowns. With help, these children can learn to take care of themselves without obvious clowning, and to have a good sense of humor.

You may be wondering what happens in families where there are more labeled roles than members. Individuals in families of all sizes adopt more than one role, or aspects of more than one role, in their daily behavior. Rarely are roles adhered to exactly as stated. People tend to fit primarily into one of the six role categories; however, they will include aspects of others in their presentation. For example, it is common for family scapegoats to also be family mascots at times. In the context of a substance abuse assessment, it is important to keep in mind that there is a great divide between the behaviors exhibited and the feelings held inside. You may have noticed that the constellation of feelings associated with each role was essentially the same. With essentially the same feelings bottled up inside, it is not surprising that people would exhibit aspects of more than one role.

While the scientific validity of survival roles is still being researched, our experience convinces us that people who grow up in chemically dependent families immediately recognize these roles and negative effects that the roles have had in their lives. Of course, these roles can develop in families where there is no chemically dependent member. However, when working with chemically dependent families you can help your clients to identify their own roles and those of other family members. Using these role descriptions can be an important part of both the assessment and the treatment process.

THE FAMILY LIFE CYCLE

The earliest mention of the developmental concepts that later became known as the family life cycle took place in the 1950s (Singer & Wynne, 1965; Duvall, 1957). Since that time, use of the family life cycle as a paradigm for conceptualizing troubled families has grown (Liddle, 1991), beginning with the work of Jay Haley (1973). Haley introduced what we now know as the family life cycle as part of the theoretical foundation for strategic and structural family therapy. Since then, others have incorporated it into their work with families. Haley believed that families experienced troubles primarily because they became stuck between stages of the life cycle, especially at the point when adolescents leave home as young adults (Haley, 1980).

The family life cycle can be applied in many contexts. Some helping professionals (Carter & McGoldrick, 1988; Combrinck-Graham, 1983, 1985, 1988; Minuchin & Fishman, 1981; Bowen, 1985; Pittman, 1987) base their family work on different aspects of a family's struggle to develop and grow over the course of the family life cycle. Others apply the concept of life cycle stages to therapy with individuals (Wachtel & Wachtel, 1986).

According to Haley (1973), the family life cycle consists of eight distinct developmental stages. In each stage, families attempt to master several developmental tasks appropriate to that stage. As these tasks are mastered, families are able to move normally from one developmental stage to the next, in concert with the demands and needs of family members. According to Haley (1973, 1980), families unable to master the required tasks in any stage often find themselves stuck between stages. This inability to move forward often causes one or more family members to develop clinical symptoms that can burgeon if not assessed and treated in this context (Carter & McGoldrick, 1988). The stages of the family life cycle and their associated tasks are listed in Figure 5.1 (Haley, 1973).

Some of these stages do not apply to certain families (such as single-parent households, or couples without children), and other writers (Carter & McGoldrick, 1988) have added stages to account for divorce and remarriage, yet the basic stages listed in Figure 5.1 provide a useful framework for social workers considering whether

STAGE	DEVELOPMENTAL TASKS
1. Married couples without children.	Establishing a mutually satisfying marriage. Adjusting to pregnancy and the promise of parenthood.
2. Childbearing families (oldest child up to 30 months of age).	Having, adjusting to, and encouraging the development of infants. Establishing a satisfying home for both parents and infants.
3. Families with preschool children (oldest child $2\frac{1}{2}$ to 6 years old).	Adapting to the critical needs and interests of preschool children in stimulating, growth-promoting ways. Coping with energy depletion and lack of privacy.
4. Families with school-age children (oldest child 6 to 13 years old).	Fitting into the community of school-age families. Encouraging children's educational achievement.
5. Families with teenagers (oldest child 13 to 20 years).	Balancing freedom with responsibility. Establishing post-parental interests and careers.
6. Families launching young adults (first child gone to last child's leaving).	Releasing young adults with appropriate rituals and assistance. Maintaining a supportive home base.
7. Middle-aged parents (empty nest to retirement).	Rebuilding the marriage. Maintaining kin ties between generations.
8. Aging family members (retirement to death of spouse and beyond).	Coping with bereavement and living alone. Closing the family home or adapting it to aging. Adjusting to retirement.

FIGURE 5.1 The Family Life Cycle

or not to apply a life cycle approach to substance abuse assessment. It is easy to see that addictive behavior by one or more members can impede or stop a family's progress through the life cycle. By using the family life cycle as a guidepost, you can compare the current family life cycle stage to the stage the family "should" be at based on age, family structure, and ethnic and cultural background. For example, trouble (such as a family member beginning to use drugs) often erupts when a family becomes "stuck" in a particular life cycle stage (for example, a teenager begins using drugs just before his senior year of high school). It is common to find parents with substance-abusing adult children of any age who, because of the offspring's substance abuse and associated childlike behavior, still treat him or her the same as a teenager living at home, or worse yet, as a child of five or six years old. Here is a clear example of a family that is stuck in an inappropriate stage of the life cycle:

> I once treated a 47-year-old male for alcohol abuse. He was single and living at home with his elderly mother. His mother still packed his lunch each day, sending his food in glass baby-food jars. On a day when she sent him a bacon sandwich, she placing a note in his lunch bag that said "Honey, be careful and do not choke on the bacon rinds." Essentially, this family was stuck in a life cycle stage, with all the relationship qualities and family rules of a family with a young child. As my client began establishing his individuality, his mother threatened suicide.

Jerome Price (1996) details a strategy for assessing individual and family life cycle issues. It was originally developed as an assessment process to work with parents of teenagers who were aggressive and/or had psychiatric symptoms; its purpose was to help parents regain control of their lives. However, given the childlike behavior of many persons with substance abuse problems in relation to their families of origin, this developmental approach can be an invaluable assessment tool.

According to Price, as part of an assessment, it is instructive to gather the following information:

1. What stage of the family's life cycle or the child's development do family members believe they are in? (This is the apparent age in relationship.)

2. Now, attach an age to each level: (a) what age are the parents acting as if the child is? and (b) what age does the child behave as if he or she is?

3. If the (young) adult were actually the age his or her behavior suggests, how would the parents be advised to act in relationship to their child?

4. How could the situation be altered so that it reflects the actual age in relationship?

Here is an example to illustrate these ideas:

1. In a substance-abusing family, family members may believe that they are operating in the stage where the substance-abusing daughter is an independent adult, living on her own.

2. The parents treat the daughter as if she was 15 (giving her an allowance, dropping by her home unannounced, calling her employer to see if she is at work), while the daughter, who is 32 years old, behaves as if she is 17 years old (i.e., always asking for money, arguing with parents about her behaviors, and so on).

3. If their daughter were actually 15 years old, the parents could ground her, discipline her, and feel responsible for her conduct, yet she is 32 years old and living on her own.

4. The parents can be helped to establish age-appropriate and developmentally appropriate boundaries, while the daughter can learn to establish herself as an independent adult, seek help for her substance abuse, and so on.

As part of an overall approach to family assessment, placing the family's current relationships, structure, rules, and roles in the context of the family life cycle can provide invaluable information for assessment and treatment planning.

OTHER ISSUES TO CONSIDER
IN A FAMILY ASSESSMENT

There are several additional issues that can be an important part of your overall substance abuse assessment related to the family system. These issues tend to affect adult clients long after they have ceased living in a chemically dependent family of origin.

Codependency

Since it became part of the American lexicon in the early 1980s, codependency as a constellation of treatable issues has remained controversial. This movement spawned a plethora of community support groups, popular psychology books, tapes, and seminars all over the United States. It has been the target of jokes, ridicule, and disdain by many, including some helping professionals (Cermak, 1986). However, to people experiencing the damaging effects of codependency and to those who are responsible for treating these individuals, codependency is a real, serious, and life-changing set of problems. To them, it is no joke.

When the term *codependency* first appeared, it included every person in a family who had regular contact with a chemically dependent member. Although the term could apply to both men and women, it usually applied just to women (van Wormer, 1995). For many people, the term *codependent* was code for women who remained in long-term relationships with chemically dependent men and, somehow, were responsible for their partner's chemical dependency. When used in this way, it was roundly (and rightly) criticized as sexist. It implied that women had a "disease" of their own, shared responsibility for the dysfunction in the relationship and family, and, most importantly, were partly responsible for their partner's chemically dependent behavior. Once considered positive, the term *codependent* (or *enabler*) became negative in connotation and effect. Many believed that this notion reinforced a past history of oppression of women and an overall pattern of gender socialization that treated woman as passive, self-sacrificing, nurturing caretakers whose worth was determined by their relationships with men (Frank & Golden, 1992).

In systems theory, however, the term *codependency* connotes an interaction of roles and does not comment at all on gender, or assign blame or responsibility. Codependency is used as a way of classifying behaviors to shed light on how problems flow from one role to another as the family system tries to cope with a person who is becoming increasingly problematic. In this text, codependency does not refer to the origins or perpetuation of the problem. It is simply a descriptive term that includes a constellation of behaviors, feelings, and effects that occur regardless of gender, age, or role, in the context of the family. Used this way, codependency changes from a commentary on women versus men, to a concept that is helpful in the assessment of chemical dependency in families.

From a multi-systemic perspective, codependency is not an individual pathology but an adaptive function of a troubled family system. It demonstrates how a person (male or female) can become stuck in a particular role within a family system. In the context of the family, codependency can describe the interplay of interactions for each role, showing how an individual's behavior seems to become increasingly more unproductive—in effect, helping to perpetuate the rules and roles of a system that he or she wishes to change. In this context, it does not assign blame or attach responsibility for others, but provides a means of highlighting behavior patterns within a person's life that may or may not be productive.

Most people in alcoholic families feel stuck and cannot see a way out for themselves and others. By looking at their life through the systemic perspective of codependency presented here, clients can begin to realize that if (consistent with systems theory) one part of a system changes, the whole system must inevitably adjust to it. In this way, your client may begin to understand how powerful the family system is and how difficult it is to change. In the process, your clients can reasonably come to understand that they are not bad, sick, or destined to failure and misery. They can learn, by understanding their role in the family, that they may not be responsible for the origins of their problems, but they can take action to change their own behavior (not the chemically dependent person's behavior) in the future.

Shame

Many social workers do not link codependency and shame. However, the two are closely tied together. In order to complete a comprehensive substance abuse assessment, you will need to understand the connection. There are different types of shame. First, there is normative shame that informs people about how to behave in a healthy and positive way. For example, most people avoid breaking the law for fear of experiencing this type of shame. Normative shame also teaches people how to function in society and tells them if it would be appropriate to act in a way they are contemplating. In the past, experiencing shame was seen as positive. To feel shame was to be honorable, discreet, and modest. A person with a sense of shame was respectful of society's norms, of others' boundaries, and of people's privacy.

Shame in chemically dependent families is not the same as normative shame. Current theories identify shame as a key element in aggression, addictions, narcissism, some depressions, and in some obsessions (van Wormer, 1995). Within families, the presence of parental love defends against shame, while its absence seems to promote shame in children. If parents appreciate each child for who he or she is, and show respect for feelings, differences, and individual peculiarities, then their children will be less likely to develop feelings of shame.

It seems that many people confuse guilt and shame. For example, in normative shame, guilt arises when people do something wrong and feel bad about it. In other types of shame, the individual believes that he or she is defective. That is, shame is associated with developmental defects or failures and is connected to a defective self. It is not connected with doing anything wrong, but is a general state of being. Shame is a more primitive emotion than guilt.

Kaufman (1992) argues that treating addictions, eating disorders, sexual abuse, and dysfunctional family systems involves treating shame. Any time there is physical, emotional, or sexual abuse, there normally is a deep sense of shame. Kaufman (1992) further argues that as a traditional, hierarchical, and religious society has given way to a world shaped by freedom, insecurity, and loneliness, an important psychological change has taken place. That is, guilt, class shame (shame associated with one's socio-economic condition), situational shame (shame associated with specific behavior towards others), and the fear of authority have become less prominent. These issues are no longer the chief forces around which internal personal controls are organized.

In the place of the traditional categories of shame discussed above is narcissistic shame: the kind of shame that says one is "no good," defective in some way. This type of internal, fundamental shame is common within families marred by chemical dependency. During an assessment, your client may not be able to identify the feelings that overpower him or her. Moreover, he or she may be sensitive about being accepted and fear abandonment. Abandonment is feared by many people who live with a deep sense of shame. Adults who are exploited are forced into feelings of shame. If people are constantly humiliated, they may be living out a life script that began with feelings of shame in childhood. These people are often humbled and made to feel inferior. Frequently in adulthood they will continue to react to events as if they were still children.

To overcome narcissistic shame, people must describe their feelings to others and "go through it." People cannot nibble at their shame or refer to it in a peripheral way; instead, they must go through it in a deliberate way. Only then can an individual understand the effects of the family system on self. In a family, if a child's basic needs are understood and met on a regular basis, a sense of trust builds between the child and adults. This is the basis for healthy self-esteem. If parents do not meet their child's needs, the child begins feeling deficient. If this happens on a regular basis, then the resultant shame becomes part of the child's identity.

Effects of Parental Substance Abuse on Older Children

Abusive or addictive substance use by parents often diminishes their ability to nurture and provide guidance for children. Additionally, chemically dependent behavior models inconsistency and/or unpredictability in parenting. Parental inconsistency may negatively influence a child's sense of order, reducing self-esteem and self-efficacy. For young people, especially adolescents, there may be few rules regarding appropriate and inappropriate behavior, inconsistent or nonexistent enforcement of penalties for violating rules, and little monitoring of friendship and peer-group choices. The research literature consistently indicates that higher levels of parental oversight are associated with lower levels of adolescent alcohol and other drug use as well as other forms of delinquent behavior. The point here is that when parents become chemically dependent, their behavior directly undermines healthy adolescent adjustment.

Emotional Abuse

Emotional abuse in chemically dependent families may consist of name-calling, derogatory remarks, criticism, put-downs, ridicule, or emotional withdrawal. Any type of verbal or nonverbal behavior intended to demean or belittle a person is emotional abuse. This type of abuse can cause serious and long-lasting psychological damage, particularly if it is applied to young children. Consistent patterns of emotional abuse can cause the victim to believe that the negative remarks must be true, leading to a poor self-concept and feelings of unworthiness and/or being unloved.

Sexual Abuse

Sexual abuse of minor children and/or partners or spouses is common in chemically dependent families. Between adult partners it can consist of rape and/or withholding sex as a means of attaining something. Children who have been sexually abused experience trauma and considerable psychological and relational difficulties as they emerge into adulthood, if the abuse continues unchecked.

Domestic Violence

Domestic violence is often found in chemically dependent families. It can take the form of any aggressive behavior ranging from a slap or shove to serious injury. It not only has the potential to cause serious psychological damage, but can also lead to significant physical injury and even death. Many victims do not even consider much of what they endure as domestic violence, having been convinced by their abuser that they somehow deserved the assault because of their behavior.

Substance Abuse in Family History

A family history of chemically dependent behavior is a major risk factor for the development of chemical dependency in subsequent generations (Peele, 1998; Fisher & Harrison, 2000). Although the majority of children who have chemically dependent parents do not become chemically dependent, these children are four times more likely to become alcoholics than are children whose parents are not addicted (Cermak, 1986). Moreover, children (or adults) who grow up in a chemically dependent family also report a higher prevalence of mental and behavioral disorders, more family problems, and more severe physiological responses to substances (withdrawal symptoms, etc.), particularly alcohol.

During an assessment, it is important to gather in-depth information about your client's family history of substance use, especially about those family members who were chemically dependent. Yet determining the effects of family history on your client is not as easy as it sounds. For example, familial chemical dependency occurs in different forms. Curtis (1999) identified three subtypes of familial chemical dependency risk: familial chemical dependency combined with low levels of other psychopathology; families with high levels of chemical dependency, antisocial behavior, and violence; and families with high levels of chemical dependency combined with a history of mental health problems such as depression, mania, and anxiety disorders.

It is important to remember that these subtypes are based on family history, which by definition applies to more than one person. While there is no scientific evidence (either socially or genetically) to prove that chemical dependency is transmitted directly through families, evidence over the years suggests that those with a family history of addictive behavior are more likely to spawn addictive behavior in subsequent generations.

SUMMARY

The role a client's family system plays in the development and maintenance of chemical dependency, as well as the potential for change, must be included in a comprehensive substance abuse assessment. Families provide the primary source of care, nurturing, socialization, and modeling for children, and family members affect each other in profound ways. During a comprehensive substance abuse assessment, we must strive to learn as much as possible about each client's family system, including structure, subsystems, boundaries, and interpersonal role development. Additionally, any assessment of a family also includes information about the way the family members react to stressors, changes, and problems, and how each are handled within the family system. In other words, how does the family respond to the inevitable push/pull between short-term stability and long-term growth and development?

In this chapter, we looked at various systemic aspects of so-called functional and chemically dependent families. We explored the central role substance abuse plays in organizing family systems, and how family members, working together to form a holistic entity, organize their feelings, thoughts, beliefs, and actions around a member's chemically dependent behavior. Moreover, we employed a systemic definition of codependency that removes gender bias and social stigma from the label while offering a valuable way of understanding relationship and role patterns in chemically dependent families, illustrating how behavior is mutually shaped and maintained in these families, without assigning responsibility or blame.

We urge you to remember that the description of functional and dysfunctional families offered here is intended as a guide for investigation and not a universal definition of what chemically dependent families look like. A client's culture, ethnicity, gender, race, and class positions, along with other unique personal or lifestyle characteristics, will render these descriptions helpful or irrelevant, depending on the unique situation of your client. Instead of seeking out a universal definition of families, engage each client in a dialogue about his or her unique situation. No two clients are alike, just as no two family systems are alike. Your task is to recognize and understand differences, and to incorporate these unique features into your client's substance abuse assessment and treatment plan.

6

Macro Context for Substance Abuse Assessment

I n previous chapters, we began introducing a systemic approach to assessing clients for substance abuse problems. In this chapter, we examine the impact of communities—local, state, and national—on clients. Unfortunately, helping professionals and textbook authors frequently overlook the influence of community, perhaps because it is more abstract and difficult to identify than other aspects, such as psychological factors. This chapter should help to demystify community issues and clarify their importance within the assessment process.

THE POWER OF COMMUNITY

Each person inhabits multiple communities defined by family ties, location, ethnicity, and other attributes. Our perceptions of the world and our place in it, our view of others in relation to ourselves, and the ways in which we behave reflect the attitudes, beliefs, and social practices of our communities. Each community plays a significant role in determining our self-image and our behavior.

Communities entail more than local norms, attitudes, beliefs, and behaviors. Local communities are subsystems of larger systems that develop and enact laws and policies. Local enforcement of laws and policies that were developed at the state and federal levels influences an individual's substance use and abuse, along with his or her ability to seek and receive professional help. Government policy, culture, and the media influence public opinion, which is reflected in the laws and policies adopted by democratically elected politicians.

From a systemic, person-in-environment perspective (Germain & Gitterman, 1996; Germain, 1991), there are reciprocal influences between the individual, his or her family, and the larger social, political, and economic systems that compose the individual's social environment. As a multi-systemic social worker, you will need to familiarize yourself with these systemic issues to determine how they affect individuals seeking substance abuse services.

The interacting social systems described above also affect the way we carry out our professional duties. Many of the same community factors that affect how clients think, feel, and act also affect how we think, feel, and act in professional practice. We are not immune to the powerful forces of individual socialization, local community standards and beliefs, public sentiment, drug laws and policies, professional socialization, reimbursement regulations, and professional training. For example, third-party reimbursement policies, enforced through the managed care system, often determine the extent to which you can refer clients for treatment, regardless of what your assessment reveals about a client's needs. Policies developed at the national level by legislators and insurance providers inevitably shape assessment, diagnostic, referral, and treatment practices.

Topic for Your Journal: What Would *You* Do?

A 17-year-old girl was referred to our treatment center for an assessment because of her substance abuse problems. We discovered that this girl had been living on the streets as a prostitute for two years. She was using heroin, crack cocaine, alcohol, and marijuana daily. In fact, she reported having been drug-free only two days during the two years prior to the assessment. She presented as a motivated young person, ready for a voluntary admission to residential substance abuse treatment. Clearly, she required immediate, long-term care. Because of her status, her treatment needs were covered by the federal Medicaid program. No problem, right?

Earlier that year, the state had mandated that all Medicaid substance abuse treatment funds would be managed by a privately owned managed care company. After submitting our assessment to the fund manager, the girl's treatment was restricted to three days in residential care and 10 outpatient visits! We decided to admit the girl for treatment and appeal the company's ruling. After losing all appeals, we decided to keep her on as a free client instead of having her turn up dead.

As this case reveals, even if your practice does not deal with private, third-party funders, you need to understand current managed care practices and be able to gauge their impact on client care. This girl was lucky. As the agency director, I had the power to admit her at no charge. How would you have handled this case as a staff member at a public substance abuse agency? What if your director denied your request to admit this client? Take a few minutes to write about this situation in your substance abuse journal.

Reimbursement practices are just one of the many ways in which community factors influence our work with substance abuse clients. Social work training, beliefs, and practices, in conjunction with the mission and practices of your agency—inevitably determined by the requirements of its funding sources—also play integral roles in service provision. Moreover, federal and state drug laws and policies affect how people are received in local treatment centers and practitioners' offices. Obviously, there is much more involved in providing substance abuse services than what you write in a case history report. We discuss each of these issues in more depth later in this chapter.

WHAT IS "COMMUNITY"?

A community exists when people form a social group based on common location, interest, identification, culture, and/or activities (Fellin, 1995; Garvin & Tropman, 1992; Hardcastle, Wenocur, & Powers, 1997). People belong to and simultaneously participate in more than one community. Fellin (1995) defines three types of communities: those based on geographical location, non-place communities of identification (race, gender, sexual orientation, etc.), and personal communities comprising the multiple communities of each individual.

The extent to which an individual is emotionally tied to or identified with a particular community determines the strength of its influence (Hardcastle, Wenocur, & Powers, 1997; Lasch, 1994; Cohen, 1985; Fellin, 1995). When doing a substance abuse assessment, try to discover which communities an individual identifies with most strongly (or is identified with by others).

Poulin (2000) describes three areas that form "a comprehensive picture of how community factors affect the individual" (p. 95), including ethnicity and culture, community conditions, and community resources. A comprehensive substance abuse assessment looks at each area as part of the total assessment picture.

SYMBOLIC INTERACTIONISM AND COMMUNITY INFLUENCE

Symbolic interactionism (SI) is a school of thought that originated at the University of Chicago in the early part of the twentieth century (Mead, 1962; Blumer, 1969; Charon, 1998; Denzin, 1992; Becker & McCall, 1990). SI offers an instructive framework to understand the relationship between the community and individual. Briefly, symbolic interactionism explores how people develop a sense of self through interaction with their social environment (Mead, 1962). While SI was originally developed as a theory to explain individual behavior in the context of family and community, it provides a sound theoretical framework for understanding and assessing families and communities. While our primary focus in this chapter is on the individual in the context of larger systems of influence, the same ideas can be applied to other systemic levels of practice (i.e., community practice).

The individual develops his or her primary sense of self through internal social processes (in the mind, or "minded behavior") that mimic the social processes occurring in the community. According to SI, a sense of self develops through an internal conversation between a person's desire to act (known as the "I") and his or her internalized understanding of the values, beliefs, norms, and expectations of the immediate social environment (known as the "Me"). That is, the "Me," based on expectations from the environment, modifies and moderates the often irrational and inventive tendencies of the "I," thus bringing the individual's attitudes, thoughts, feelings, and behaviors in line with the demands of the social environment.

The struggle between the "I" and "Me" occurs within a person's mind, but it is determined by what the individual believes are the expectations of his or her local community. People learn these expectations through socialization by their families, schools, local communities, and the media. Individuals engage in a constant struggle to reconcile what they *want* to do, think, and feel with what they believe they *should* do, think, and feel, based on feedback from their local community.

To interact successfully, individuals "take the role of others" by acting as they believe others expect them to act in social situations (Mead, 1962, p. 57). Accordingly, individuals incorporate the attitudes, beliefs, and practices of the environment into their daily behavior. Over time, people act more in concert with the context of the environment that molds and shapes their behavior, attitudes, and beliefs. While individuals can influence their own behavior and thus their local environment, over time they gradually assume behaviors, attitudes, and beliefs that mirror their social environment. This is especially true with substance-abusing clients, who are influenced by the drug subculture as well as their family and significant others. The influence of social expectations is eloquently conveyed by Knipe (1995):

> The behavioral outcomes of consuming alcohol depend upon culture. It is true that we as biological beings have a metabolic system that processes alcohol in the same way, no matter where we live or what our culture is. This metabolic process is not learned; it is biologically determined and is constant to us as biological species. The behavioral consequences of drinking alcohol are learned. *We need go no further than any five-year-old child in any culture to learn what that behavior is.* Without the benefit of consuming alcohol, that child will accurately act out appropriate drinking comportment (p. 68; emphasis added).

Alcoholics Anonymous and other twelve-step groups rely on social conditioning to promote the success of their programs. Over time, participants in twelve-step groups gradually relinquish past beliefs, attitudes, and behaviors and begin to fall in line with the norms and behaviors of the group. Those who refuse to change do not remain long in the organization.

Each of us knows someone whose beliefs, attitudes, and behaviors changed to reflect new friends, schools, or other influences. Socialization within families occurs in the same way. As children, we look to our families to teach us about everything from what is considered "breakfast food" to the use of alcohol in daily life. Similarly, substance-abusing clients have often learned their cues and actions from the drug subculture.

The Social Self

Community is the means by which individuals become persons (Mead, 1962). The self is a social self, the result of complex processes of social interaction, participation in groups, and membership in the community as a whole. Contrary to the popular American ideal of rugged individualism and the public worship of self-made individuals, people consist of more than inner thoughts, urges, perceptions, and behaviors; we do not "chart our own course" to the extent many believe. In other words, people are never truly "self-made." This is true of successful business people, parents, athletes, students, or substance abusers. Even the most heralded "self-made" business tycoons did not do it alone. Henry Ford may have invented the automobile and had the internal drive to start a business, but how rich and successful would his company have become if nobody had worked in his factories or purchased his cars? Similarly, people do not become chemically dependent by themselves. Your client did not wake up one day declaring, "I think I'll become a heroin addict." He or she had "help" from friends, drug dealers, and other influences in the beginning to use and, after a time, becoming defined socially as an addict.

People are not slaves of an all-powerful social system, nor are they rugged individualists forging their own paths. As a social self, the individual is shaped through constant interaction between internal impulses and the moderating forces of immediate environment, including the power of culture (Knipe, 1995). Individuals—through their thoughts, beliefs, and actions—influence the social environment while simultaneously being influenced by it. Yet, the fact that it is possible for people to influence their environment does not mean that many—or even most—people actually succeed in doing so. The ability to carve out an existence contrary to powerful (often unspoken) community forces is unequal, determined by an individual's place in the social hierarchy. People who are, for one reason or another, outside the majority culture must overcome more barriers to self-determination than those within the majority culture. It is within this realm of social existence and barriers to self-determination that substance use, abuse, and chemical dependency thrive (Peele, 1998).

Self and Others

Ramsey (1965) believes that the "self arises . . . in relation with others" (p. 141). People live interdependently with others who help construct their beliefs and feelings about their place in the world. According to symbolic interactionism, people see themselves reflected back through the gestures, responses, and actions of others in relation to themselves (Miller, 1967). As people observe others' responses to them, they shape their response and behavior in terms of this feedback. For people to interact successfully, they must incorporate the perspectives and beliefs of others in the community into their personal construction of self. Those who cannot or do not accomplish this task often become labeled as misfits in some way, even to the point of being diagnosed as mentally ill (Szasz, 1974, 1994).

Human beings are social creatures, and the self is a social creation. Many people, institutions, and macro-level systems play an instrumental role in developing one's self-identity. Significant others, including family, close friends, and other role models, along with many less significant people such as employers, social workers, police, the media, and other members of the community, repeatedly confirm or deny an individual's self-identity. Responses from others help individuals define their place in the social hierarchy. For example, after constantly being treated with suspicion by European American merchants, African American children learn that they are not considered to be as trustworthy as European American people, demonstrating their lower rank in the social hierarchy.

As part of their development, people choose peer groups and significant others who confirm their emerging definitions of self (Lauer & Handel, 1983). For example, people with substance abuse problems normally "find themselves" in social circles that both support and oppose their substance-abusing behavior. Those who support the behavior normalize it by providing "standards" that clients can use to gauge the extent and severity of their own use ("I'm not an addict— but my friend George, now *he's* an addict"). At the same time, people also tend to marginally participate in social groups who oppose their substance abuse, perhaps treating them as a perpetual "client" or helpless figure who needs "saving." This bifurcated social existence feeds substance abusers' belief that they are "unfit," "bad," or "troubled," leading them to find solace in the social group that approves and supports their behavior. You will often hear this process described by young people who participate in gangs. Among the members of their gang, these youths report feeling strong, powerful, and respected in ways that are not available to them outside the context of their gang "family." During an assessment, strive to discover how clients choose the people and groups in their immediate social circle. Consider what these choices say about the kind of people they are or those they wish to become (Hewitt, 1997), and think about how substance use helps them to accomplish this goal.

Is the Right to Self-Determination
Equally Available to Everyone?

The right to self-determination is part of American folklore and myth. According to this ideology, every American citizen "can grow up to be President" by working hard and following the rules of society. Is this true? Social workers must grapple with this question on a daily basis. The right to self-determination is central to the social work field (NASW, 2000). Yet, the issue is not whether everyone has the right to self-determine, but the extent to which people have the freedom to accomplish this task. According to George Herbert Mead (1962),

> What a human being *is* depends upon interaction with others. And what a human being *does* depends not simply upon what kind of person he or she is (personality), but upon the person's interaction with others. At the same time, the individual is part of the interaction, acting and not merely reacting, creating and not merely being formed or controlled (p. 6n).

Mead did not account for the power of structural oppression and its limiting effects on an individual's ability to act and create without "being formed or controlled." The freedom to act—to make choices about which part(s) of community culture one will accept or reject—is unequally distributed. Because of race, gender, social class (income, education, professional standing), sexual preference, perceived mental illness or substance abuse problems, and other life situations, many people do not have the same freedom to make choices about their lives as those in the mainstream (i.e., European American, middle-class and above males; or globally, most citizens of industrialized nations).

 People in these non-majority groups are often restricted by the majority culture in the extent to which they can exercise their right to self-determination. This is not to say that people in non-majority groups cannot exercise self-determination. They can indeed, but with great struggle in the face of structural limitations and barriers that majority group members do not confront, and often do not realize exist (Sernau, 2001; Davis & Proctor, 1989). For example, members of the majority culture do not face harsh treatment or suspicion resulting from racism, employment limitations due to sexism, or the inability to live in a safe neighborhood because of poverty.

Many members of the majority culture refuse to acknowledge that people still face discrimination and oppression on a daily basis; instead, they believe that discrimination is a thing of the past. While some aspects of civil and human rights and social and economic justice have improved (at least outwardly), much remains the same. For some groups, conditions have become more difficult. For example, gay men and lesbian women are often treated harshly in the United States (van Wormer, Wells, & Boes, 2000). While conditions have improved in recent years, it remains apparent that some people in mainstream society find it acceptable to subject gays and lesbians to ridicule, beatings, or even murder because of deeply engrained intolerance of personal or group differences. Despite these attitudes being contrary to our profession's values and ethics, unfortunately, some social workers hold similar oppressive attitudes toward gay men and lesbian women.

Outright acts of discrimination, racism, sexism, and homophobia occur daily; they have not disappeared. European American social workers must guard against a tendency to ignore or trivialize reported acts of discrimination and oppression. This attitude dismisses clients and perpetuates their problems through cultural and social blindness. Similarly, social workers of color should try to avoid holding all of their European American clients accountable or responsible for the plight of minorities in the United States.

Other barriers are rooted in oppressive practices that no longer exist. These barriers continue to be treated as if they are real in the present, lingering in a person's life as part of historical memory (Johnson, 2000). They are based on historical acts of oppression, passed down the generations through oral history in families and communities. However, they may not be as pervasive or limiting in the present as they were in the past. Perceived social barriers drive people's feelings, beliefs, and actions just as powerfully as contemporary acts of oppression. Issues from the past, whether real or imagined, should never be ignored, passed off as fantasy, or used by social workers as indications of a lingering mental illness.

It is imperative to give due weight to people's internalized beliefs about the world. These perceptions drive their attitudes and beliefs about themselves and their relative position in the social hierarchy. Regardless of the origins of these beliefs, they play a significant role in how people interact in the world. However, our job is not limited to understanding our clients' internalized oppression.

Understanding does little good without subsequent action on people's behalf. Simple understanding too easily leads to pity and to acts that disempower and infantilize clients. For example, when a person's publicly funded rent check is given directly to the property owner instead of to the recipient, this policy suggests that welfare recipients are too irresponsible to pay their own rent.

Using a multi-systemic approach to social work practice depends on achieving cultural competence and engaging clients in a dialogue about their internalized worldviews, social and personal barriers to self-development, and limits maintained by community expectations. Furthermore, we must be able to create an empowering context in which clients can confront these issues. In other words, we need to help create a context in which clients can advocate for the right to make their own rent payments, rather than being infantilized by the welfare system.

To give another example, if a social worker and Native American client determine that the client would benefit by beginning to practice traditional cultural values, efforts to connect the Native American client to traditional rituals such as a sweat lodge must be considered within the context of the majority culture in order to be successful. In Native American families with a long history of assimilation into European American, Christian culture, there may be little support, even within the family, for efforts to practice traditional Native American values (Weaver, 2001). The fact that adopting traditional values may be generally positive does not mean that you can simply include it in a treatment plan and expect it to happen. You must assess this plan with the client based on his or her location in the social hierarchy, and support your client's efforts to confront and surmount whatever barriers the majority culture may place in the way.

Self and Community

Each individual "is rooted in a biological organism that acquires a self only through its interaction with a community of other selves" (Mead, 1962, pp. 16–17). The community is the shaping force in people's development of their social selves; it is the means by which "the 'me'—my self as social or seen from the perspective of significant others and the community in general—comes to be" (Winter, 1966, p. 21). Creating and maintaining self-identity is a function of community. According to Pantoja and Perry (1998), no individual exists without receiving messages about self-identity from contact with others.

Communities help people to understand themselves, but they do not necessarily determine people's characters or behaviors. Communities offer individuals a variety of meanings, values, and behaviors from which to choose. People are under no obligation to blindly accept what each community has to offer, although—as we discussed above—some people have more freedom to deviate from community standards than others do. Individuals decide, consciously or not, which aspects of the community norms they want to adopt. They accept or reject community standards in a variety of ways, sometimes consciously and directly, other times unconsciously and indirectly through behavior that defies, angers, or frightens others in the community. In this way, individuals reflect communities, but are not fully determined or controlled by them (Brueggemann, 2001).

Communities also play a major role in shaping and maintaining people's substance use and abuse. Specifically, communities help define which drugs are acceptable for use (i.e., alcohol and nicotine); what frequency or amount of use is considered "normal"; when substance use becomes problematic; what action people with substance abuse problems should take, if any; and substance abusers' chances for future recovery and acceptance within the community. Community influences can make people more or less likely to use alcohol and other drugs (Moos, Finney, & Gamble, 1985).

To fully comprehend people's lives, you must understand their relationship to various communities, including the aspects of community that involve "production, distribution, and consumption" (Pantoja & Perry, 1998, p. 226). Central to this category are conditions for employment (Warren, 1972; Engels, 1972), along with a community's ability to satisfy other needs and "support the economic function" (Pantoja & Perry, 1998, p. 226) of the community and its individual members. The community provides socialization, social control, social placement, mutual support, personal defense, and communication. Pertaining to support of the economic function, examples include access to employment, credit, and the capital needed to improve one's personal environment or community conditions. How these functions occur and who (individuals or institutions) will carry them out are based on the geographical, historical, cultural, economic, and other circumstances in a particular community. For example, "poor" communities often have a long history of poverty, crime, and inadequate educational opportunities. That is, over time, these communities develop a culture that makes it difficult, if not impossible, for people to change without considerable outside intervention. Without an understanding of the implications of this dimension of communities for individual clients and their families, any assessment and treatment plan will be lacking, and the chances for successful substance abuse treatment will drop substantially.

LOCAL COMMUNITY

As part of the assessment process, it is essential to consider the impact of people's immediate social environment on their daily life and worldview. This information allows you to understand the limits and barriers your clients face and their strengths to overcome them during treatment and afterward. In the end, after any course of treatment is completed, most clients return to the local environment where they experienced substance abuse problems. Many people cannot and/or will not relocate, even if doing so would be in their best interest. Researchers have found that most substance abuse treatment fails because of the pressures placed on an individual to return to "normal" as defined by the local community (Freeman, 1993; Sernau, 2001). Therefore, planning for the client's reintegration into the home environment as a recovering substance abuser deserves careful attention. This planning must begin during the initial assessment, not in the days (or hours) immediately preceding the client's discharge from primary treatment.

As part of the planning process, we need to help clients to identify various communities, determine which one(s) they have the most significant relationship(s) with, discover the reciprocal influences between clients and their communities, and understand how various community influences are integrated into their own worldviews. As part of a substance abuse assessment, a typical community assessment elicits "information about physical status, economic resources, ethnicity, social class, education, past help-seeking behavior, and available social supports" (Saari, 1991, p. 89). In other words, community assessment is a necessary part of the overall substance abuse assessment process (Kemp, Whittaker, & Tracey, 2002).

It is not enough to know that people live in a rural or urban area, that the homes are mostly rented or owned, or that the community is considered lower, middle, or upper class. This information is only a start. We must also learn about clients' involvement in non-place communities such as race, gender, and sexual orientation; how they "fit" into the geographic community (from clients' perspectives); the level of potential support to change—or to continue abusing drugs—provided by a particular community of location or non-location; and the general physical environment of the residential community. This includes information about friends, social activities, leisure activities, and other aspects of social involvement.

For example, what good is an assessment and treatment plan if you do not know that local drug dealers have "taken over" your client's front yard as their main business location? What are the chances that this client can avoid a relapse with drug dealers standing 10 feet from his front door? To encompass this information in a substance abuse assessment, strive to define people's "personal geographies"—what is meaningful to them in an everyday community context (Fong & Furuto, 2001).

Too often, social workers make plans for treatment based on partial and incomplete client information. Including community aspects as part of a substance abuse assessment may take more time, but the benefits to clients and your practice will be immense. (Incidentally, time limits imposed by managed care providers are no excuse for half-completed substance abuse assessments. Competent social workers learn to gather this information rapidly. Developing this skill requires guidance, feedback from supervisors, and experience.)

This text explores ways of integrating community and environmental information into the context of an individual assessment. For those readers who are interested in additional information about community assessment and intervention, I recommend the works of authors who write exclusively about work at the community level (c.f., Kahn, 1991a, 1991b; Fisher & Karger, 1997; Rivera & Erlich, 1998b; Brueggemann, 2001; Netting, Kettner, & McMurtry, 1998; Rothman, 1995a; Hardcastle, Wenocur, & Powers, 1997).

ASSESSING MULTIPLE COMMUNITIES

Earlier we discussed several forms of community that people participate in daily. In the following discussion, we look at specific community issues that you should inquire about during a substance abuse assessment. To make collecting this information more organized and understandable, consider developing an ecomap (Hartman, 1978) or a social network map (Tracey & Whittaker, 1990). These tools, either together or separately, help the interviewer to understand resources in the client's community and social networks. I recommend that these tools be used together. The ecomap focuses on resources and restraints in the environment from a systems perspective, and the social network map focuses on personal relationships. These two areas are inextricably linked in a client's life. For example, if people's personal networks are depleted by their chemical dependency in the context of a community suffering from chronic poverty and a lack of professional resources, looking exclusively for resources within their communities would be unrealistic. In this instance, you would be forced to look outside the community for resources.

Geographic Community

According to Erlich and Rivera (1998), people's relationships with their geographic communities often provide the most intimate and personal involvement they will experience, with the exception (for some) of familial relationships. Develop a "picture" of people's environments, including employment opportunities, housing quality, transportation, education, leisure activities, crime and safety, levels of personal support and involvement (Young, 1994), and the extent to which they identify with their present communities, or geographic communities of the past. Seek to understand the "fit" between clients and their environment (Germain & Gitterman, 1996), the level and depth of personal involvement with others, and how your client perceives his or her place in relation to others in the local community. Delve into aspects of identity that are related to race, class, culture, language, sexual orientation, religious affiliation, and other subgroups. Going further, learn how these personal and community variables interact with people's kinship patterns, religion, power relationships, gender roles and expectations, and friendships to form their social environment.

The ultimate goal is to understand clients' perceived and/or real place in their communities. Central to this understanding is an awareness of the economic and political configuration of the community and, according to Rivera and Erlich (1998a), "the process of empowerment and the development of critical consciousness" (p. 10) within the client's locality. In other words, are there sufficient resources, support, and opportunities for the client to fundamentally change his or her place in the local community?

Communities of Identification

To assess the impact of communities of identification, inquire into a community's prevailing values, beliefs, and the level to which clients are connected to these values and beliefs, if at all. Cultural beliefs shape a community's value system in the same way that they shape an individual's value system (Poulin, 2000). As we discussed earlier, communities play a significant role in shaping an individual's beliefs, values, and behaviors. To gain an understanding of people's perceptions, and to place their thoughts, feelings, and behaviors in context, you must understand the values and beliefs that prevail within their local communities.

Clients should be assisted to identify and articulate their belief systems, and to discover how their perceptions and beliefs fit into or clash with the belief systems of their community. Areas to discuss include the values and ethics of the local community, as well as your client's local ethnic, racial, religious, or other groups. Moreover, clients can be prompted to articulate the ways in which these communities support or oppose their current lifestyle, belief system, and future attempts to change. Along these lines, it is essential to discuss values, ethics, and beliefs of the drug subculture. Drug subcultures have their own distinct sets of rules, beliefs, and practices, as well as language and value systems that are central to the way an individual and/or local community views the world and the individual's place within it.

Also, keep in mind the impact that community values have on the helping process. These values influence belief systems of the client and helper, treatment approaches, and attitudes toward the helping process. Community values about help-seeking behavior must be understood because some communities of identification marginalize or degrade the professional helping process, while supporting help-seeking within the context of the community itself. For example, Native American, African American, and some rural communities do not believe in seeking help from strangers in a professional setting (Weaver, 1999, 2001; Greene, Jensen, & Jones, 1999; Poole, 1999). This topic will be discussed at greater length in Chapter 11.

Community Resources

Discover what resources exist within a client's community that may be helpful during the client's treatment for substance abuse problems. Community resources generally fall into three categories: professional treatment and support, institutions and associations, and social relationships. These resources are discussed below.

Professional Treatment and Support   Do your clients live in areas with a wide range of treatment and support options? If they require substance abuse treatment, are services available nearby or is travel required? Most urban areas offer a full range of treatment options (inpatient, intensive outpatient, outpatient, and twelve-step support groups). However, accessibility is often limited because of inadequate funding and long waiting lists. Nonetheless, urban areas usually have twelve-step groups such as AA, NA, and Al-Anon that meet every hour of the day, every day of the year, including major holidays. Sometimes twelve-step groups are the only option available to a client needing help.

Clients living in rural areas often have difficulty obtaining treatment because the necessary options are not available in their locale and there are fewer twelve-step meetings offered. These limitations may require you to make significant trade-offs. One option is to try to locate a treatment facility and have people travel to receive treatment. If this is not feasible, clients are often forced to utilize the resources available, whether they meet their needs or not. Another issue in rural areas is the availability of aftercare resources. Even if clients have the means and ability to travel to a nearby urban area to receive primary inpatient treatment, there are few, if any, local treatment options available after primary treatment ends.

Institutions and Associations   What organized resources exist in people's locales to help with recovery? These resources may include community institutions and associations where positive social relationships and activities occur. It is important to locate schools, job training sites, welfare offices, churches, social clubs, bowling leagues, etc., during the assessment process. If clients live in rural areas or in poorer sections of large cities, you must assess their proximity to such institutions and their ability to access the resources. For example, a client may want to enroll in GED classes at a community college, but she may not have a car and public transportation may be unavailable during the times when classes are offered. People who live in some rural areas may have to travel great distances to access such resources.

Social Relationships   Assessing the quality and type of social relationships in people's communities is critical to assessment, planning, treatment, and ultimately (and most importantly), follow-up and reintegration into the community after treatment. Strive to discover individuals and groups with whom clients socialize now or may begin socializing after treatment. As we stated earlier, individuals tend to surround themselves with people who verify and support the image and behaviors consistent with the client's self-identity. Hence, learning about their most intimate social groups is vital to understanding their worldview and seeing how it translates into everyday thoughts, beliefs, attitudes, and behaviors.

You should also simultaneously assess the availability of positive social supports in people's communities. These resources may include non-drug-using friends, neighbors, community or church elders, and so on. Of special importance is discovering whether there are other people in the client's locale who are successfully battling their own chemical dependency. A community of local recovering people, within or outside organized groups, is a critically important resource for people who are going through treatment. If clients begin attending a twelve-step support group, encourage them to locate sponsors. Sponsorship is critical to their chances for success in recovery through these organizations.

MACRO INFLUENCES
ON SUBSTANCE ABUSE TREATMENT

In addition to local communities, issues at the macro level influence whether clients seek and/or accept help. Macro-level issues, such as drug policy and laws, structural inequalities, and public opinion, should be included in a multi-systemic substance abuse assessment.

Structural and Historical Systems of Oppression:
Who Holds the Power?

Often embedded in laws, policies, and social institutions are oppressive influences such as racism, sexism, homophobia, and classism, to name a few. These structural issues play a significant role in the lives of our clients (through maltreatment and discrimination) and in social work practice. How people are treated (or how they internalize historical treatment of self, family, friends, and/or ancestors) shapes how they believe, think, and act in the present. Oppression affects how they perceive that others feel about them, how they view the world and their place in it, and how receptive they are to professional service providers. Therefore, a substance abuse assessment is not complete unless we consider the impact of structural systems of oppression and injustice on the client's problem, and potential for change.

Oppression is a by-product of socially constructed notions of power, privilege, control, and hierarchies of difference. Oppression is created and maintained by differences in power (Pellegrini, 1992). By definition, those who are in power can force people to abide by the rules, standards, and actions the powerful persons deem worthwhile, mandatory, or acceptable. Those who hold power can enforce particular worldviews; deny equal access and opportunity to housing, employment, or health care; define right and wrong, normal and abnormal; and imprison, confine, and/or commit physical, emotional, or mental violence against the powerless (McLaren, 1995; Freire, 1994). Most importantly, power permits the holder to "set the very terms of power" (Appleby, 2001, p. 37). It defines the interaction between the oppressed and the oppressor, and between the social worker and client.

Social institutions and practices are developed and maintained by the dominant culture to meet *its* needs and maintain *its* power. Everything and everybody is judged and classified accordingly. Even when the majority culture develops programs or engages in helping activities, these efforts will not include measures that threaten the dominant group's position at the top of the social hierarchy (Freire, 1994). For example, Kozol (1991) wrote eloquently about how public schools fail by design, while Freire (1994) wrote about how state welfare and private charity provide short-term assistance while ensuring that there are not enough resources to lift people permanently out of poverty.

Oppression is neither an academic nor a theoretical consideration; it is not a faded relic of a bygone era. Racism did not end with the civil rights movement, and sexism was not eradicated by the feminist movement. Understanding how systems of oppression work in people's lives is of paramount importance for every individual and family seeking substance abuse services, including those who belong to the *same* race, gender, and class that you belong to. No two individuals, regardless of their personal demographics, experience the world in the same way. Often, clients are treated ineffectively by professional social workers who mistakenly believe that people who look or act the same will experience the world in similar ways. These workers base their assumptions about clients on stereotypic descriptions of culture, lifestyle, and substance use and abuse patterns. These people take group-level data (e.g., many African American adolescents join gangs because of broken families and poverty) and assume that *all* African American teenagers are gang members from single-parent families. Social work values and ethics demand a higher standard, one that compels us to go beyond stereotypes. Our job is to discover, understand, and utilize personal differences in the assessment and treatment process to benefit clients, not use differences as a way of limiting clients' potential for health and well-being.

We cannot accurately assess people's substance abuse problems without considering the effects of oppression related to race, ethnicity, culture, sexual preference, gender, or physical/emotional status. We need to understand how oppression influences our clients' beliefs about problems and potential approaches to problem-solving, and how it determines what kind of support they can expect to receive if they decide to seek help. Despite the widely held belief that chemical dependency is an equal opportunity disease (Gordon, 1993), it is clear that some people are more vulnerable than others. While some of the general themes of chemical dependency may appear universal, each client is unique. That is, an individual's dependency results from personal behavior, culture (including the history of one's culture), past experiences, and family interacting with larger social systems that provide opportunities or impose limits on the individual (Johnson, 2000; Giddens, 1991, 1993).

To assist in evaluating community influences, Hagan and Smail (1997) described a process called power-mapping, which involves three key steps. The first step is to map the distribution of power and resources in a particular community context. Second, we analyze how conditions of power or powerlessness affect those within this setting. Third, we identify sources of actual or potential power. This type of analysis has several benefits: it enhances critical consciousness (Freire, 1994) of the social and environmental distribution of power and its consequences in the lives of your clients; it provides information about resources to support interventions; and it shapes your perspective on what needs to be done to empower clients in key life dimensions.

Systems of oppression ensure unequal access to resources for certain individuals, families, and communities. However, while all oppressed people are similar in that they lack the power to define their place in the social hierarchy, oppression based on race, gender, sexual orientation, class, and other social factors is expressed in a variety of ways.

Drug Laws and Public Opinion

For nearly 150 years, the United States government has attempted to control drug use through legislation enacted at local, state, and national levels, while attempting to influence passage and enforcement of international drug laws. For example, the U.S. government's support of military-style interdiction in several Latin American countries is an effort to shape international drug policy. Ever since the first drug laws were passed in the early part of the twentieth century, American citizens—and especially, U.S. politicians—have mistakenly believed that stiff legal sanctions alone would solve drug problems in the United States. The history of drug control legislation in the United States—including the Prohibition period—has been cyclical in nature, reflecting phases of public opinion rather than actual outcomes. Musto (1999) encapsulates this dilemma:

> As we look back over the waxing and waning popularity of mood-altering substances, it is difficult to escape the suspicion that, although drug abuse is a real and deeply imbedded social problem, attempts to solve it are sometimes nearly overwhelmed by wars of words. The contest is waged by opposing camps of fiercely committed partisans. As times change, and as drug fads decline and are replaced by health or moral crusades, one camp gains

adherents, new laws are demanded and passed, old ones are abolished, and sometimes still older ones are retrieved, brushed off, and re-implemented as innovations. Meanwhile, the opposition has not entirely disappeared, but continues to fight rearguard actions and wait for the next opportunity to prevail (Musto, 1999, p. 273).

It is clear that drug control efforts in the United States are—first and foremost—a political issue, leading to laws and policies that are dusted off and recycled repeatedly in the vain hope that what did not work before will somehow work now.

For example, the foundational beliefs of contemporary drug policy are a repeat of earlier legislation: recycled (albeit, expanded) legislation from drug policy failures of the 1950s. Inspired by McCarthyism and Cold-War paranoia, many Americans during the 1950s believed that drug selling and abuse were part of a communist conspiracy (Fried, 1997; Whitfield, 1991). During that era, the federal government regarded almost anything outside the "mainstream" as the product of communist influence (Oakes, 1994; Whitfield, 1991). U.S. drug laws and policies are closely linked to prevailing public opinion, regardless of whether or not that opinion and resulting legislative actions are consistent with the medical, social, and behavioral facts about substance use and abuse.

For example, the Drug Enforcement Administration (DEA) lists marijuana as a Schedule I drug (the most restrictive classification) despite a lack of scientific and social evidence to support this designation. Political rhetoric, and eventually laws and policies, match the prevailing mood of the country at the time. Since the early 1980s, this rhetoric has largely been intolerant of drugs, drug sellers, and drug users. If you are interested in an extended analysis of U.S. drug control policy, I recommend Musto's (1999) well-respected historical overview of drug laws and policy in the United States.

DRUG CONTROL POLICY—A PRIMER

Public opinion about alcohol, other drugs, and drug abusers has varied throughout American history. Until the early 1900s, the use of alcohol and other drugs was tolerated. Drugs such as cocaine, heroin, and morphine were legally available on the open market. In fact, the stereotypical heroin user during this period was a middle- or upper-class housewife, since it was not socially acceptable for women to drink alcohol (Ray & Ksir, 1993; Levinthal, 1999). Looking through a contemporary "lens," it is difficult to envision a time when heroin use was as acceptable as alcohol use. Clearly the social context plays a prominent role in defining the appropriate and inappropriate use of drugs in any historical era. What do you suppose social work students in the year 2101 will think about our habits?

Beginning in the early twentieth century, public opinion gradually changed to usher in a period of intolerance, culminating in the passage of a constitutional amendment prohibiting the production and sale of alcoholic beverages in 1919 (the beginning of the Prohibition era). During this era, the federal government invoked strict penalties for drug sales and social sanctions for drug users, marking the first time the federal government enacted drug laws that superseded state and local authority (Musto, 1999). Interestingly, drug use (mostly opiates and cocaine) declined nationwide during this period, causing politicians to believe that severe anti-drug laws caused the reduction. They were wrong. Other factors, such as World War I, had more to do with reduced use than threats of harsh punishment. Nevertheless, politicians of that era wrongly believed that laws drove public opinion, when it was actually the other way around.

Let's look at another historical example. Use of heroin skyrocketed during the 1940s. In response, the federal government enacted legislation that imposed the first round of mandatory minimum prison sentences for drug sellers and users in 1951. In 1956, the government approved the death penalty for some drug offenses. During the 1960s, there was an unprecedented rise in drug use and public tolerance despite the harsh laws. The Nixon Administration abolished these harsh laws in 1970 because it had become clear that the laws were ineffective in reducing drug use (Musto, 1999).

The 1960s and 1970s marked a renewed period of public tolerance for drug use. Beginning with the inauguration of Ronald Reagan in 1980, public opinion changed quickly and dramatically, reawakening the oft-repeated desire for harsh anti-drug legislation. We are still embedded in this historical era today. Stimulated by a growing movement of parents against drugs in the early 1980s, strict drug laws were enacted in 1984, 1986, and 1988. These laws and the resulting policies remain the cornerstone of contemporary anti-drug policy and the "War on Drugs." Among other things, during the 1980s American lawmakers resurrected and expanded many of the failed efforts from the 1950s, including the death penalty for some drug-related offenses. Below is a brief discussion of four major anti-drug legislation packages, three of which were passed during the 1980s.

Comprehensive Drug Abuse Prevention and Control Act

In 1970, the U.S. Congress passed the Comprehensive Drug Abuse Prevention and Control Act (also known as the Controlled Substances Act). In addition to several other important outcomes, the Act officially classified each drug into one of five "schedules," with regulatory requirements associated with each schedule. According to the provisions of the Act, the criterion used to determine whether a particular drug is scheduled (controlled by the Drug Enforcement Administration) is its "potential for abuse" (DEA, 1997, p. 1). If a particular drug has no potential for abuse, this statute does not account for it. Accordingly, the Act established a definition of "potential for abuse," although this critically important concept is not legally defined in the Act (DEA, 1997, p. 2).

A drug has the potential for abuse if:

1. There is evidence that individuals use the drug—or other substance— in amounts sufficient to create a hazard to the health and/or safety of other individuals or the community; or

2. There is significant diversion of the drug or other substance from legitimate drug channels (medical doctors writing prescriptions); or

3. Individuals are taking the drug or other substance on their own initiative rather than on the basis of medical advice; or

4. The drug is a new drug, related in its action to another drug already determined to have a potential for abuse, so as to make it likely that the drug will have the same potential for abuse as the similar drug.

5. Of course, evidence of actual abuse of a substance is indicative that a drug has a potential for abuse.

For example, Schedule I drugs (the most restricted class of drugs):

Have a high potential for abuse; have no currently acceptable medical use in treatment in the United States; and lack accepted safety standards for use of the drug.

Drugs listed on Schedule I include heroin, methaqualone (Quaaludes), hallucinogens (LSD), and marijuana.

Schedule II drugs also have a high potential for abuse and/or dependency. However, Schedule II drugs have an accepted medical use. Schedule II drugs include cocaine, PCP, methamphetamine, and opiates other than heroin (i.e., methadone, morphine).

Schedule III drugs have a lower potential for abuse than drugs listed on Schedules I and II; have currently accepted medical uses; and abuse of these drugs may lead to "moderate or low physical dependence or high psychological dependence" (DEA, 1997, p. 3). Drugs listed as Schedule III drugs include anabolic steroids, codeine, and some barbiturates.

Schedule IV drugs have a low potential for abuse relative to drugs in Schedules I to III; accepted medical use(s); and abuse of the drugs may lead to "limited" physical or psychological dependence (DEA, 1997, p. 3). Drugs on Schedule IV include Valium, Xanax, Darvon, and other benzodiazepines.

Schedule V drugs have the lowest abuse potential of all drugs classified under the Controlled Substances Act. In addition, they, too, have readily accepted medical uses, and abuse of these drugs can lead to limited physical and psychological dependence. Drugs on Schedule V include over-the-counter cough medicines with codeine.

As you review the different Schedules and, more specifically, which drugs fall under each, it should be apparent that politics and ideology play a significant role in the scheduling process. For example, drugs such as marijuana and LSD, while not safe to use, have less potential for dependency (physical and psychological) and medical problems than drugs listed on subsequent Schedules, especially Schedule II (cocaine, PCP, morphine, methamphetamine).

Moreover, the two most dangerous drugs in terms of health consequences and potential for physical and/or psychological dependency—alcohol and nicotine—are *not* "Scheduled." Also not controlled are substances classified as "inhalants."

Inhalants (see Chapter 2) are common household and industrial chemicals (gasoline, spray paint, cleaning agents, etc.) that have become the drugs of choice among children and the desperately poor because of widespread availability and low cost.

Topic for Your Journal: What Makes a Drug Dangerous?

It appears that a problem with scheduling drugs lies in deciding which drugs are "dangerous." Just what is a dangerous drug? More importantly, is the drug itself dangerous, or does it become dangerous only when in the hands of human beings? Take a few moments to reflect on these questions. In your substance abuse journal, respond to the following question at some length: What constitutes a dangerous drug?

Federal Sentencing Reform Act of 1984

The 1984 Federal Sentencing Reform Act established the United States Sentencing Commission to create sentencing guidelines for federal drug offenses. The Act also established mandatory minimum sentences for drug offenses committed near schools, mandatory prison terms for all serious felonies, and "sentencing enhancements" for all drug offenses that involved a firearm (U.S. Sentencing Commission, 1991, p. 8). This legislation marked the return of mandatory minimum sentences as a central feature in anti-drug efforts.

The Anti-Drug Abuse Act of 1986

This legislation expanded mandatory minimum sentences specifically for cocaine offenses. Passage of this Act signaled that the American public had decided that cocaine—especially crack cocaine—was "public enemy number 1." This legislation was a by-product of public fear during the mid-1980s about crack cocaine abuse, violence, and AIDS.

One part of this legislation package contained a controversial provision regarding minimum mandatory prison sentences for certain cocaine-related offenses. The Anti-Drug Abuse Act of 1986 legally mandated a minimum prison sentence of 5 to 40 years for possessing 5 or more grams of crack cocaine, about the average amount carried by youthful street sellers. Why was this controversial? Taken alone, this sentence may sound prudent given the destructive power of crack cocaine and the media frenzy about it over the last 15 years. However, it must be understood in its appropriate context. The mandatory minimum sentence for crack cocaine possession matches (remember, this is based on possession of 5 grams of crack or more) the mandatory minimum sentence for possessing 500 grams of powder cocaine. That is, one must possess 100 times more powder cocaine to get the same mandatory prison sentence as five small "rocks" of crack cocaine, despite the two drugs being essentially the same substance.

To justify this decision, Congress must have decided that crack cocaine and powder cocaine were different drugs, allowing offenders to be treated differently under the law. This conclusion is similar to deciding that injected heroin should be treated differently from heroin that is smoked or snorted, or invoking different prison sentences for possessing different types of marijuana. Sounds silly, right? This silliness is reality in the politics of crack cocaine. While it is true that crack cocaine provides a more intense high and is cheaper to obtain than powder cocaine (Doweiko, 1999), it is still cocaine. Cocaine laws are a prime example of what happens to truth and sanity when anti-drug legislation is driven by media frenzy and the politics of race and class.

The philosophy behind this law is based on two assumptions, both of which are untrue: powder cocaine is less harmful to users, and powder cocaine is always inhaled (snorted) and never smoked or injected. In case you did not know, the original idea for crack cocaine came from what is called "freebase" cocaine. For years, users "cooked" powder cocaine into small "rocks" for smoking, freeing the base (cocaine) from its impurities to create a more powerful effect. Crack cocaine, after all, is made from powder cocaine. Moreover, the fact that crack cocaine is more intense does not mean that the effects of snorted, smoked, or injected powder cocaine are weak. On the contrary, the effects of both powder and crack cocaine are strong and appealing, causing the same damaging effects to users, including the associated violence and risk for HIV/AIDS contraction.

Since there is no evidence that crack cocaine makes users any more violent or dependent than powder cocaine (Jung, 2001), the differential treatment of these two versions of the same drug in the law must have political and social roots. That is, if the difference cannot be found in physiological or psychological effects, then perhaps the difference is related to the persons who typically possess and use the various forms of the drug. Driven mainly by graphic media reports of gang violence and documentary evidence of the powerful effects of crack cocaine, this legislation essentially targets street-level, mainly African American, crack sellers over large-scale, usually European American, drug traffickers. These disparate mandatory minimum sentencing guidelines for crack and powder cocaine have led to justifiable accusations of racism and classism. African American and poor defendants are much more likely to incur harsh mandatory minimum sentences than European American offenders (Musto, 1999).

In recent years, some members of Congress have raised questions about cocaine laws. For example, according to the U.S. Sentencing Commission's special report to Congress (1997),

> While there is no evidence of racial bias behind the promulgation of this federal sentencing law, nearly 90 percent of the offenders convicted in federal court for crack cocaine distribution are African-American while the majority of crack cocaine users is white. Thus, sentencing appears to be harsher and more severe for racial minorities than others because of this law. The current penalty structure results in a perception of unfairness and inconsistency (p. 8).

There were two significant congressional efforts to overturn or modify these sentencing guidelines during the 1990s. On both occasions, the Clinton Administration refused to approve the changes. The gross differences in mandatory minimum sentencing, despite the controversy, remain in place today. In January 2002, a bill was introduced to address this discrepancy. However, even if it is passed, mandatory minimum sentences for powder and crack cocaine will remain vastly different.

The Anti-Drug Abuse Act of 1988

Anti-drug legislation passed after the 1988 presidential election outlines some of the most wide-ranging and harsh penalties in American history. This Act flowed out of strong anti-drug public opinion that would reach its peak in 1989 (Musto, 1999). Among its many provisions, the Anti-Drug Abuse Act of 1988 changed the terminology of drug abuse by including alcohol in its scope. The phrase "alcohol and other drugs" and mandatory government health warnings on all containers of alcoholic beverages reflect the passage of this Act. Additionally, in an effort to reduce drunken driving (driven mainly by the newfound lobbying power of Mothers Against Drunk Driving), the law provided grants to states willing to institute stricter drunken driving laws, including lowering the legal blood alcohol limit from .10 to .08. This Act also reinstated the death penalty for some drug offenses, emphasized the importance of drug-free workplaces, and established a commission to develop the Drug-Free Schools and Communities Act of 1989. This Act also included provisions that addressed money laundering, provided for asset forfeiture, established penalties for selling anabolic steroids, and increased efforts designed to produce international interdiction (Levinthal, 1999; Musto, 1999).

Perhaps the most significant changes this Act instituted were, according to Musto (1999), largely "symbolic" in nature (p. 278). Included was a congressional declaration to reject all proposals to legalize drugs, and a statement that the United States would be drug-free by 1995. (Apparently it takes more than a congressional declaration and anti-drug laws to eliminate America's drug use and abuse problems.)

This Act also created a new vocabulary for alcohol and other drug discussions within government-funded substance abuse prevention programs. For example, automobile accidents were called "crashes," since the word "accident" implies that the event was not the fault of the intoxicated driver; the phrase "responsible use" was replaced with "use" in reference to alcohol; the practice of choosing designated drivers was discouraged because it allowed others to drink uncontrollably; and the phrase "recreational use" was dropped from references to illicit drugs because all use is harmful and, by definition, harmful substances cannot be used recreationally (Office of Substance Abuse Prevention, 1989).

For social workers, the most important element of the 1988 law established new federal funding entities for treatment, prevention, and research: the Center for Substance Abuse Prevention (CSAP) and the Center for Substance Abuse Treatment (CSAT), included in the Substance Abuse and Mental Health Services Administration (SAMHSA). Moreover, this Act also established the Office of National Drug Control Policy, under the control of the so-called "Drug Czar."

CSAP and CSAT provide funding for treatment and prevention initiatives across the country and have led to new research initiatives on treatment outcome and "best practices" in the substance abuse field (National Institute on Drug Abuse, 1999). You should become familiar with the mechanisms of this federal bureaucracy and its funding initiatives. These centers provide most of the funding for treatment and prevention at the local level. Federal funds are granted to states, which are expected to pass it along to treatment and prevention agencies at the local level.

Impact of Anti-Drug Legislation
on Substance Abuse Practice

Social workers performing substance abuse assessments must understand federal, state, and local interpretations of the various anti-drug laws passed in the last 20 years. Since social work practice is a political endeavor (Gil, 1998; Fisher & Karger, 1997; Haynes & Mickelson, 1997), a multi-systemic practitioner must know how the various laws and policies affect a client's daily life.

For example, when working with people abusing crack cocaine, it is helpful to understand the heightened legal risks and the more serious social sanctions placed on these individuals compared to people who use other drugs. Because of the barrage of media attention, much of American society views people using crack cocaine more negatively than it does people using other drugs. This is especially true for African Americans living in urban environments. You must fight the urge to assume that all young people of color standing on any street corner are gun-toting gang members trying to sell crack cocaine to an unsuspecting public, or that any woman who abuses crack cocaine is either a prostitute or willing to sell her children for drugs.

If these comments sound extreme, think about the images engrained in the public consciousness by televised news programs about abuse of crack cocaine. When you think about news accounts and documentaries over the years, what picture comes to mind? Is it a different picture from the one you see when thinking about someone snorting powder cocaine, or abusing alcohol or marijuana? These images affect the way social workers approach their clients, increasing the obstacles individuals confront during treatment.

It is essential to understand how policies at the state and local levels affect your clients, especially clients who rely on the welfare system. Restrictions placed on welfare recipients often represent hidden substance abuse laws and policies. For example, in many states, welfare recipients are required to pass random urine screenings for drugs in order to maintain their benefits (Musto, 1999). In other states, Child Protective Services must immediately intervene when infants are born with drugs in their systems. This same policy allows the state to investigate any subsequent children born to the same mother, for the rest of the mother's life.

Clearly, laws and policies developed in Washington, DC, or in your state capital have a direct bearing on individual clients seeking substance abuse services. These laws and policies infiltrate many aspects of the social welfare system. Social workers who are hoping to assist clients in overcoming drug problems must become familiar with the various laws and policies, striving to understand how these policies affect clients' day-to-day lives as well as their behavior throughout the substance abuse treatment process.

MACRO INFLUENCES ON
SOCIAL WORK PRACTICE

As stated earlier, social workers are not immune to macro-level influences. In the same way that individuals are influenced by their social environment, so too are social workers. Whether these influences come from professors, supervisors, journal articles, or discussions with colleagues at conferences, social workers—individually and collectively—are shaped by their professional environment. The following discussion considers two significant influences on social work practice with substance abusers: reimbursement policies and qualifications for employment in this field.

Reimbursement Policies in Substance Abuse Practice

Many of us hate dealing with the financial aspects of the social work profession. Until managed care revolutionized reimbursement practices beginning in the mid-1980s, social workers and other mental health professionals were, by and large, able to leave fees, reimbursement, and funding to the financial professionals within their organizations. Issues related to service reimbursement have always been an important consideration in practice, but not an issue most practitioners have wanted to consider. Circumstances have definitely changed. No longer can we ignore the details of reimbursement policies and their impact on all aspects of service provision, especially in substance abuse practice.

For years, there have been two distinct classes of clients: those who are fortunate enough to have private health insurance coverage with provisions for substance abuse services and/or the personal wealth to pay privately for services, and those who lack these resources. The latter group includes people on public funding (i.e., Medicare and Medicaid), the working poor, and people whose employers provide inadequate coverage for substance abuse services. Clients in the former group have nearly unlimited treatment options, while the prospects for the latter group are not so bright.

When the latter group needs help with substance abuse problems, they have limited choices. Often, these persons languish on long waiting lists at publicly funded treatment facilities or receive no treatment at all. While there are many well-run publicly funded treatment facilities in the United States, budget shortfalls and low pay cause these facilities to fall short of privately funded facilities in terms of quality of care, physical surroundings, and staff experience and training. Of course, many people—including policy makers, lawmakers, and the public—believe that any treatment, even if it is underfunded and lacks adequately trained staff or decent facilities, is better than no treatment at all.

The disparity in funding and treatment options has led to a debate about equity in health care funding for clients with substance abuse problems. The argument against providing substance abuse and mental health coverage—often called behavioral health care (Buck & Umland, 1997)—for all people is similar to the argument against providing health care for all Americans: How can we afford to cover everyone?

For many years, health insurers and other public and private third-party payers have offered different benefits for substance abuse and mental health services as opposed to physical illness and treatments. Some payers offered equal benefits, some offered reduced substance abuse benefits, and others provided no coverage for substance abuse or mental health services. In 1996, the United States Congress passed and the President signed the Mental Health Parity Act (MHPA, P.L. 104–204). Effective January 1, 1998, this law required that health plans provide the same annual and lifetime benefits for mental health services that they offer for other health care issues.

The purpose of the MHPA sounds good, but it includes loopholes and limitations, especially pertaining to substance abuse services. First, the law does not apply to substance abuse benefits. Therefore, health plans are not required to provide any coverage for substance abuse treatment unless it is mandated by state law. Moreover, the law does not affect service limits. That is, third-party payers may still place strict limits on the number of outpatient mental health visits allowed or the availability of inpatient care (Sherer, 1998).

Even though lifetime or annual spending limits for mental health care may be equal to those for other services, health insurance plans can make it impossible to come anywhere near the limits. The plans often restrict the number of annual or lifetime visits per policyholder, rather than limiting the total expenditure (Sherer, 1998). For example, a private insurer may allow a typical annual limit of $25,000 in substance abuse or mental health care spending (Rand Corporation, 1997), but the client cannot reach this funding limit because a provider can simultaneously restrict the total number of inpatient or outpatient visits to ensure that the annual dollar amount will never be reached. In this context, it does not matter how high the annual or lifetime spending limit may be if insurers will not allow clients to access the funding.

Moreover, the law does not affect "cost sharing" issues, including client deductibles. This loophole is important to understand. The MHPA does not state that providers must provide equal limits for out-of-pocket expenses charged to the client for mental health and physical health care services. For example, an insurance plan may offer a 10-percent deductible for physical health care services while requiring a 50-percent deductible for behavioral health care services. This loophole can make services for substance abuse or mental illness unaffordable for most people.

Recall our discussion about the moral model in Chapter 3. Substance abuse is largely seen by the public (and our elected officials) as the result of poor choices and bad morals. Perhaps this attitude continues to inhibit efforts to achieve parity in health care benefits between substance abuse/mental health problems and coverage for physical illness/disease, leading many to claim that the differences in coverage amount to discrimination against people with substance abuse and/or mental health problems (Hughes, 1996; Melek & Pyenson, 1996; Jensen, Rost, Burton, & Bulycheva, 1998). Yet, while discriminatory practices have reportedly decreased since the MHPA was enacted in 1998 (Buck, Teich, Umland, & Stein, 1999), the depth of coverage has been shrinking (Jensen, Rost, Burton, &

Bulycheva, 1998). An estimated 75 percent of all employer-sponsored health plans in the United States continue to place greater restrictions on behavioral health coverage than on general medical coverage (Buck, Teich, Umland, & Stein, 1999).

Looking at the argument that achieving parity in behavioral health and general health coverage is cost-prohibitive, several researchers have demonstrated that this assertion is unfounded. In fact, most research suggests that full coverage for substance abuse and mental health services would increase premiums less than 1 percent per month (Buck, 1999; Sing, Hill, Smolkin, & Heiser, 1998; Sturm, 1997; Sturm, Zhang, & Schoenbaum, 1999). Some research has even suggested that parity would result in lower total costs (NIMH, 1997).

If these projections are correct, then perhaps cost is not the underlying issue. Perhaps the disparity in coverage reflects the public's attitudes toward people with substance abuse and mental health problems. Despite government agencies' protestations to the contrary, it seems that providing treatment for people with these problems is not a public priority. If, in fact, most Americans believe in the moral model, then there is little motivation to provide benefits for treatment of a problem that is "self-imposed."

The complex and interwoven effects of public sentiment, political will, lobbying efforts, and personal suffering cannot be fully analyzed in this text. However, anyone who provides assessment, treatment, or other services to people with substance abuse problems must understand the socially stigmatizing effect that simply having these problems causes in most of American society, affecting clients and their family members more broadly than insurance coverage. The apparent disdain for substance abusers, exemplified by what appears to be discriminatory insurance practices, permeates families, local communities, and the broader American society.

Simply put, despite public rhetoric about the need to care for people with substance abuse problems and mental illness, recent presidential administrations have been reluctant to legislate against the insurance companies. It appears that ultimately, people with substance abuse problems and/or mental illness are viewed as expendable.

The Role of Social Workers in the Substance Abuse Field

Over the years, professional social workers left the substance abuse treatment field to others. A survey of NASW members during the early 1990s found that only 5.4 percent of social workers identified substance abuse treatment as their specialty (Gibelman & Schervish, 1993). In my graduate social work classes, only 5 to 10 percent of students are interested in the substance abuse field, and most of these students are either recovering from their own past chemical dependency or have lived with chemically dependent significant others.

The primary role of social workers in the substance abuse field has been limited to referring clients with substance abuse problems to specialists from other professions and/or specialized treatment agencies that are staffed mostly by recovering paraprofessionals (Googins, 1984). Few social workers, without the personal connection mentioned above, become involved with substance abuse clients as a primary career choice.

There are signs, however, that this situation may be changing. Health insurance and other third-party funding sources, influenced by managed care, are now demanding that substance abuse specialists have advanced degrees (van Wormer, 1995). Moreover, with the field now open to treating clients simultaneously for co-occurring disorders (substance abuse and mental illness), agencies must employ professionally trained social workers because of their advanced training and experience with mental health issues. As a result, more social workers are entering the substance abuse field. Still, even with these changes in the field, most people who provide primary substance abuse treatment are those who have personal life experience.

Is It Necessary for Helpers to Be in Recovery?

Sooner or later, nearly every social worker in the substance abuse field is asked, "Are you recovering?" For years, a dispute has raged about whether effective substance abuse assessment and treatment can be performed by a professionally trained but non-recovering helper. This debate dates to the earliest days of substance abuse treatment. According to Royce (1989),

> Since the first Yale Plan Clinic in 1944, recovered alcoholics have been part of most treatment teams, whether or not they belonged to a profession or had a college degree. . . . The understanding and empathy those workers gained from their own experience as alcoholics has long been recognized as a valuable contribution to the recovery process (p. 94).

Much of the daily business of chemical dependency treatment is performed by non-degreed, so-called "life-experienced" counselors. In the United States, every state except one requires only a high school diploma or GED as the qualifying academic credential to work as a substance abuse counselor (Fisher & Harrison, 2000). While there are additional requirements beyond academic preparation (certification, minimum number of years clean and sober), the field of substance abuse counseling is dominated by people who are in recovery. The assumption in the field (and, by the way, also in the wider community) is that personal recovery from chemical dependency is, in and of itself, a sufficient "credential" to work as a treatment professional.

Have you ever wondered why life experience is so important in substance abuse, but not in any other field of practice? For example, is it more helpful to have counselors who have been diagnosed with schizophrenia treat clients with the same problem because they have "been there"? How about clients with depression, suicidal ideation, or those near death in hospice? Can only social workers who have "been there" themselves be helpful with any particular problem? For example, must a social worker have attempted suicide to successfully work with a suicidal client? In substance abuse assessment and treatment, many people believe personal experience is a necessary attribute for helping professionals. Do you agree or disagree with this concept?

Topic for Your Journal: Must Helpers Be in Recovery?

In your journal, write about your position on this debate. Look at the literature and discuss it with your peers and professors. Consider the following question: Is personal *recovery necessary to be effective in substance abuse practice? Explain your answer using documented and published positions from the literature.*

All things being equal, helpers who are in recovery can bring a level of insight, understanding, and acceptance to their relationships with substance-abusing clients that cannot be taught in schools of social work. Their depth of understanding, knowledge of the subculture and lifestyle, and personal experience with the hardships of committing to personal change are irreplaceable. Of course, all things are rarely equal in life, meaning that the positive qualities recovering helpers can bring to a therapeutic relationship may also be problematic.

Personal recovery alone, without professional training and education, is not an appropriate qualifying credential for a career as a helping professional. The role of professional helper is not the same as that of a "sponsor" in Alcoholics Anonymous or Narcotics Anonymous. Personal recovery does not train one to assess and treat co-occurring disorders, handle client crises unrelated to alcohol and other drugs, provide relationship or family therapy, or effectively run group treatment sessions. It does not provide knowledge of assessment skills, codes of ethical professional conduct, and professional relationship boundaries. All it gives a person is knowledge of how *he or she* managed to achieve recovery.

Herein lies the catch. Many recovering counselors insist that clients follow the same course of treatment that they did to achieve sobriety. With rare exception, these well-meaning counselors tend to believe in a single path to recovery. Without advanced training in multiple theories and models, a systems perspective, and a variety of treatment skills, recovering counselors often subscribe to a "one-size-fits-all" approach—the disease model. As a result, assessment and treatment usually end up looking and sounding a lot like an Alcoholics Anonymous meeting, with counselor and client sharing the details of their lives with each other. Unfortunately, if clients do not respond to this approach, the recovering counselor usually has no other options, and clients end up being labeled "not ready for sobriety" and dismissed from the program entirely.

Let me be clear on this point. My purpose here is not to suggest that recovering counselors have no place in the substance abuse field. I know many highly skilled recovering counselors without advanced professional training. My issue is with those who believe that personal recovery from chemical dependency is more important than professional education and training. Personal recovery is part of the life experience of the social worker, but not the primary part. It helps (sometimes) to engage some clients in a professional relationship, but it does not help others. In fact, I believe that professional helpers should not even mention their personal recovery to clients unless directly asked or challenged by clients. Counselors who begin a helping relationship with their own recovery story either expect that fact to have a dramatic impact on clients (which it does not), or they do not have much else to offer in the helping relationship. Helpers should no more tell their own recovery story than any other personal story to clients during an assessment or treatment session. Those stories are best left for AA meetings.

The best option is for people in personal recovery to attain professional credentials by attending school, like everyone else in the helping professions. They should not only receive advanced training and education, but also experience other fields of practice besides substance abuse during their field practicum and/or internship experiences. For example, a recovering student who gains experience in a general mental health setting while in school will bring a broad base of experience to her or his work in substance abuse that a paraprofessional cannot possibly have.

Professional training and personal recovery are a dynamic combination that gives clients the opportunity to receive high-quality professional treatment within a context of personal understanding and acceptance. Unfortunately, this combination remains rare. The substance abuse field has developed pseudo-credentials in place of undergraduate and/or graduate degrees, and agencies continue to employ recovering counselors (often at very low wages). As a result, there is little motivation for counselors to return to school.

SUMMARY

In this chapter we explored the impact of community and macro factors in the lives of people with substance abuse problems, discussing why this information is an important part of a comprehensive substance abuse assessment. Individuals are shaped by interactions with their local environment. In turn, local environments are shaped by the macro environment of laws, policies, culture, and public opinion in the context of a historical period.

To prepare you to perform a community assessment as part of an overall substance abuse assessment, we discussed how individuals and communities interact from a symbolic interactionist perspective. We outlined the various types of communities in which individuals participate on a daily basis. One cannot understand these communities and their influence on clients without well-developed skills in culturally competent practice (see Chapter 4).

We looked closely at drug laws and policies in the United States. Depending upon your client's unique circumstances, national and international drug laws and the resulting policies can dramatically affect how he or she presents for an assessment in your office or agency.

Lastly, we discussed how macro systems affect social workers in practice. Topics included managed care, parity in health care funding, and the role of training, education, and personal recovery in the substance abuse field.

7

Introduction
to Screening
and Assessment

In this chapter, we describe the elements of a comprehensive, multi-systemic substance abuse assessment. Additionally, we distinguish the multi-systemic assessment process from screening and diagnosis, while acknowledging that clinical diagnosis is required in most clinical settings (Strom, 1992). Screening and clinical diagnosis are important, but they represent only two parts of the overall assessment process.

Assessment is the foundation of social work services (Gambrill, 1997; Kirst-Ashman & Hull, 1999; Sheafor, Horejsi, & Horejsi, 2000). It provides crucial information about clients, their problems, life histories, and strengths. An accurate and holistic assessment determines whether clients actually have substance abuse problems, and if so, the severity of these problems, the client's need and readiness for treatment, and the level of service required to meet the client's individual needs (van Wormer, 1995; Levinthal, 1999; Jung, 2001; Steinglass et al., 1987; Elkin, 1984; Kaufman, 1984).

A *timely, thorough, and continuous* assessment process lays the groundwork for competent substance abuse practice. If assessment is done well, it will have a positive effect on treatment by providing for successful client engagement (see Chapter 4), identification of problems and strengths (Saleebey, 1997; Cowger, 1992, 1994), and appropriate treatment matching (Denning, 2000; Bower, 1997; McLellan et al., 1997; Project MATCH, 1997). If assessment is done poorly, overlooked, or rushed, the lack of accurate assessment information can negate the potential for effective substance abuse treatment.

When carrying out an assessment, it is important to avoid the "rush to treatment syndrome," in which the assessment process is short-circuited and professionals move too quickly into diagnosis, treatment planning, and intervention. All too often, overzealous social workers base treatment decisions on sparse client data. It is tempting to blame the rush to treatment syndrome on the time parameters imposed by the managed care system. Although it is true that managed care limits the amount of time spent with clients, this has become a contemporary excuse for a longstanding problem. Having been around since before managed care, I am aware that the rush to treatment syndrome has a long history. Managed care—a system with many grave problems indeed—in this case provides a convenient and popular scapegoat for social workers who are willing to bypass or shortcut assessment, thus short-changing their clients. To use a well-worn cliché, you cannot construct a building without a solid foundation. Comprehensive, multi-systemic, and ongoing assessment is a critical element of providing appropriate treatment for clients with substance abuse problems.

DEFINITION OF ASSESSMENT

Assessment is "a process occurring between social worker and client in which information is gathered, analyzed, and synthesized into a multidimensional formulation" (Hepworth, Rooney, & Larsen, 1997, p. 194). During the assessment process, you and your client make important decisions about issues that need attention. Together, you discuss the client's immediate risk of danger (i.e., health risks posed by withdrawal) and identify client characteristics and resources that can be mobilized in a productive manner (Smith, Wesson, & Tusel, 1989). Finally, you determine who is best qualified to provide the treatment indicated by the assessment. If you can provide the appropriate treatment, during the initial assessment you will begin developing a working relationship and treatment plan with your client. If not, you must decide who can provide the necessary services and then facilitate a referral.

Assessment is an evolving process, changing with each client contact. As time passes, the assessment should change to reflect the client's life experiences between contacts, the deepening trust that is developing within the social worker-client relationship, and progress or lack of progress toward client goals. Assessment is not static; it is not a set of forms to be completed, filed away, and never read again. It grows and changes as people change.

One of the major outcomes of assessment is an agreed-upon treatment plan (Smith, Wesson, & Tusel, 1989). Any action on behalf of clients should be based on an updated and revised assessment. If the information recorded in assessment documents does not change over time, it is evidence that you are not paying attention or that you have reached conclusions—either consciously or unconsciously—about the client and his or her capacity for change. An assessment should be thought of "as a complex, working hypothesis based on the most current data" (Hepworth, Rooney, and Larsen, 1997, p. 197).

If you are providing a substance abuse assessment and referral, the assessment you complete follows the client to the treatment agency and its staff. Your assessment will directly influence how other professionals define, approach, and treat the client over the short and long term. Assessment and referral is not a short-term responsibility to be taken lightly. It is a way for you to have a positive impact on people's lives long after they leave your care. If you are responsible for overseeing treatment (for example, as a case manager) your role becomes even more important. You will have to coordinate services with treating agencies or individuals and deal with the success or failure of the substance abuse treatment process that you helped initiate.

Any successful assessment must have value to clients, in that clients must understand the process and what is contained in the assessment report (see Chapter 8). The assessment must include a clear and accurate description of the client's life, problems, and strengths, as well as guidelines (or suggestions) for changing if the client chooses to follow through with the plan (Gambrill, 1997). An assessment should provide clients with helpful views of their problems and allow them to take a different perspective toward their life, problems, strengths, and opportunities for change. It should be presented in a vocabulary that is understandable to clients, and in a way that allows clients to break problems into manageable parts (Stuart, 1980). It should also be framed in terms of clients' strengths (Saleebey, 1997) and assets so they can come to believe that they can contribute to their own treatment. An assessment should build a sense of hope that things can change and that clients can and must play an instrumental role in the change process (see Chapter 8 and Appendix B).

HOW SCREENING DIFFERS FROM ASSESSMENT

A substance abuse assessment is a multi-dimensional process, drawing information about the client's situation from a number of sources and system levels (Sheafor, Horejsi, & Horejsi, 2000). Ideally, it is conducted from a multi-systemic perspective that views client problems in terms of ecological systems. It is holistic—comprehensive in its scope and content. Think of an assessment as the process of learning and bringing new perspective to people's life stories.

Screening, on the other hand, is simply one part of the overall assessment process. It is usually a brief procedure to identify individuals with possible substance abuse problems or people at risk of developing substance abuse problems (Jung, 2001; Fisher & Harrison, 2000; Gambrill, 1997; Hepworth, Rooney, & Larsen, 1997; van Wormer, 1995). Screening tools, which often take the form of standardized tests, are useful in practice settings such as court services, health care, mental health clinics, and the like. It is important to remember that screening instruments simply provide a starting point in the assessment process. They indicate *potential* substance abuse problems and are only one small element of the larger assessment process.

In some practice situations, unfortunately, the only option for assessment is to rely on substance abuse screening instruments. Workers do not have sufficient time to complete a comprehensive substance abuse assessment. While the use of a screening instrument can never be as comprehensive as a multi-systemic assessment, by augmenting the items contained on the instrument with questions about substance abuse history, family, peer groups, and the local community, you can develop a more comprehensive picture of your client's life and problems. However, if the results from a screening instrument suggest that people may have substance abuse problems, it is best to refer them for comprehensive assessment. Do not take the results of a screening instrument to mean that people have definite substance abuse problems. To do so would be to misuse the technology and to do a disservice to your clients.

SUBSTANCE ABUSE
SCREENING INSTRUMENTS

Various screening instruments are available to substance abuse professionals, each with advantages and drawbacks. We will explore the most widely used screening instruments below.

The Michigan Alcoholism Screening Test (MAST)

The MAST (Seltzer, 1971) is one of the oldest screening instruments in the field. Despite having been around for more than three decades, the MAST is still one of the most widely used screening tools by professionals in a variety of settings (Jung, 2001). The MAST (see Figure 7.1) is a 24-item, self-report inventory of common signs and symptoms related to a host of problems stemming from alcohol use. It is quite simple to administer and score, taking no more than 10 to 15 minutes depending on the client's reading level. A shorter ten-item form, the Brief MAST, is also available for use (Allen & Columbus, 1995).

Look closely at the MAST in Figure 7.1. The questions appear straightforward and simple to understand. However, there are problems with the MAST, as there are with any standardized instrument. As you read the questions, it should be obvious that people could easily fake responses, rendering the score invalid and unreliable (Denning, 2000; Storgaard, Nielsen, & Gluud, 1994). Moreover, even truthful responses could lead to false conclusions.

For example, question 8, "Have you ever attended a meeting of Alcoholics Anonymous (AA)?" could produce misleading responses. Clients may answer "yes" to this question if they have attended an AA meeting with a friend or family member, or as part of a class assignment. I have had potential clients honestly answer "yes" to this question, and it later became apparent that their response was meaningless with respect to their personal drinking behavior.

It is important to become familiar with the specific populations for which various screening tools were designed. For example, the MAST is intended for adults and is highly unreliable and invalid when used with adolescents. To understand why this is so, take a moment to re-read questions 3, 6, 9, and 12 and answer them as if you were an adolescent.

Question 3 asks whether family members have ever been concerned about the client's drinking. While this sounds like a reasonable question, an affirmative

POINTS		QUESTION	Yes	No
	0.	Do you enjoy a drink now and then?	_____	_____
(2)	*1.	Do you feel you are a normal drinker? (By *normal*, we mean you drink less than or as much as most other people.)	_____	_____
(2)	2.	Have you ever awakened the morning after some drinking the night before and found that you could not remember a part of the evening?	_____	_____
(1)	3.	Does your wife, husband, a parent, or other near relative ever worry or complain about your drinking?	_____	_____
(2)	*4.	Can you stop drinking without a struggle after one or two drinks?	_____	_____
(1)	5.	Do you ever feel guilty about your drinking?	_____	_____
(2)	*6.	Do friends or relatives think you are a normal drinker?	_____	_____
(2)	*7.	Are you able to stop drinking when you want to?	_____	_____
(5)	8.	Have you ever attended a meeting of Alcoholics Anonymous (AA)?	_____	_____
(1)	9.	Have you ever gotten into physical fights when drinking?	_____	_____
(2)	10.	Has your drinking ever created problems between you and your wife, husband, a parent, or other relatives?	_____	_____
(2)	11.	Has your wife, husband (or other family members) ever gone to anyone for help about your drinking?	_____	_____
(2)	12.	Have you ever lost friends because of your drinking?	_____	_____
(2)	13.	Have you ever gotten into trouble at work or school because of drinking?	_____	_____
(2)	14.	Have you ever lost a job because of drinking?	_____	_____
(2)	15.	Have you ever neglected your obligations, your family, or your work for two or more days in a row because you were drinking?	_____	_____
(1)	16.	Do you drink before noon fairly often?	_____	_____
(2)	17.	Have you ever been told you have liver trouble? Cirrhosis?	_____	_____
(2)	**18.	After heavy drinking have you ever had Delirium Tremens (DT's) or severe shaking, or heard voices or seen things that really weren't there?	_____	_____
(5)	19.	Have you ever gone to anyone for help about your drinking?	_____	_____
(2)	20.	Have you ever been in a hospital because of drinking?	_____	_____
(2)	21.	Have you ever been arrested for drunk driving or driving after drinking?	_____	_____
(2)	22.	Have you ever been seen at a psychiatric or mental health clinic or gone to any doctor, social worker, or clergyman for help with any emotional problem, where drinking was part of the problem?	_____	_____
(2)	#23.	Have you ever been arrested for drunk driving, driving while intoxicated, or driving under the influence of alcoholic beverages? (IF YES, how many times?_____)	_____	_____
(2)	#24.	Have you ever been arrested, or taken into custody, even for a few hours, because of other drunk behavior? (IF YES, how many times?_____)		

* Alcoholic response is negative.
** 5 points for Delirium Tremens.
# 2 points for *each* arrest.

Scoring System: In general, five points or more would place the subject in an "alcoholic" category; four points would be suggestive of alcoholism; and three points or less would indicate the subject was not alcoholic.

SOURCE: D. J. Lettieri, J. E. Nelson, & M. A. Sayers (eds.), Alcoholism Treatment Assessment Research Instruments, *NIAAA Treatment Handbook*, Series 2 (Washington, DC: U.S. Government Printing Office, 1985).

FIGURE 7.1 Michigan Alcoholism Screening Test (MAST)

answer might be meaningless in the context of adolescent assessment. Many parents become concerned if they learn that their adolescent has been drinking, even if their child only drank once. Sometimes parents will bring in their adolescent for an assessment after discovering that he or she drank for the first time. This is responsible parenting, but it is not an indication of a drinking problem.

Question 6 concerns people's perceptions about the normalcy of the client's drinking. What is a "normal" adolescent drinker? Technically, because it is illegal for people under 21 years old to drink, can adolescents ever be considered "normal" drinkers, or are all adolescents abnormal drinkers because of their legal status? As a professional social worker, how does one go about determining the answer to this question? Do you compare the drinking patterns of adolescents to those of adults? To your own drinking behavior when you were an adolescent? Is there a correct answer to this question?

Question 9 implies that if a client ever had a physical fight while under the influence of alcohol, he or she might have a drinking problem. This may be true for adults, because people over 18 are supposed to know better than to get involved in physical fights. However, what about adolescents? Similarly, question 12 asks whether the client has lost friends because of drinking. During adulthood, the loss of a friend over drinking is likely to be a serious matter, but friendships among adolescents are often more easily made and broken.

Thus, it is important to know your audience in order to determine whether certain well-established screening instruments, like the MAST, will be helpful in the assessment process. My experience suggests that adolescents, on average, score much higher on the MAST than do most adults. Does this mean that adolescents have more severe alcohol problems, or is the test providing a high number of false positives? If you rely solely on the MAST for assessment, as I have seen many professionals do, this question is unanswerable.

There are additional problems with the MAST. First, it is a "general screen" (Miller, Westerberg, & Waldron, 1995, p. 62) for alcohol problems. In fact, the MAST is most useful as a screen for severe alcohol problems (Doweiko, 1999; Saunders et al., 1993). Second, it does not detect binge drinking or provide information about an individual's drinking pattern (Smith, Touquet, Wright, & Das Gupta, 1996), which is important to know when working with adolescents. Moreover, the MAST is designed to screen for alcohol problems and cannot be used to screen for drug problems (Lewis, Dana, & Blevins, 1988). There is an instrument patterned after the MAST, called the DAST, that is designed to identify potential drug problems (Skinner, 1982). The same concerns about validity and reliability apply to the DAST as to the MAST.

CAGE

The CAGE was developed by Ewing and Rouse (1974; Ewing, 1984) and is still widely used because of its brevity and simplicity. The CAGE consists of only four questions, which are easily remembered by the acronym:

C   Have you ever tried to **cut** down on your drinking?

A   Have people **annoyed** you by criticizing your drinking?

G   Have you ever felt **guilty** about your drinking?

E   Have you ever used alcohol in the morning as an **eye–opener**?

According to Ewing and Rouse (1974), the client who answers "yes" to two or more of these questions is likely to be alcohol dependent, according to the *DSM-IV*. An affirmative response to one question suggests the need for a more detailed inquiry (Doweiko, 1999). As might be expected from a test this brief containing such obvious content, studies evaluating the effectiveness of CAGE have had mixed results (Cooney, Zweben, & Fleming, 1995). As with other screening instruments, be skeptical about accepting CAGE results outside the context of an assessment interview.

Addiction Severity Index (ASI)

The ASI was originally designed as a research instrument (pre- and post-test) to evaluate substance abuse treatment outcomes (McLellan, Luborsky, O'Brien, & Woody, 1980; McLellan, Luborsky, Cacciola, & Griffith, 1985). Over the years, however, it has become increasingly accepted as a reliable and valid screening tool for substance abusers applying for treatment (Treatment Research Institute, 1990). Because it is used with people already identified as potential substance abusers, the ASI is helpful as a guide for initial treatment planning. The ASI is designed to determine people's need for treatment, based on subjective, interviewer-determined use severity ratings. According to the training manual, the severity ratings are based on people's activities in the 30 days before the interview (Treatment Research Institute, 1990).

The ASI has been used with a variety of adult populations, including the mentally ill (Corse, Zanis, & Hirschinger, 1995), homeless (Drake, McHugo, & Biesanz, 1995), pregnant, gamblers (Lesieur & Blum, 1992), and prisoners (Amoureus, van den Hurd, Schippers, & Breteler, 1994), as well as a variety of racial and ethnic groups (Brown, Alterman, Rutherford, & Cacciola, 1993). Yet no reliability or validity testing has been done to determine its accuracy and effectiveness with these populations (Treatment Research Institute, 1990). Its major use has been with adults seeking treatment for substance abuse problems, including drugs other than alcohol (McLellan, Randall, Joseph, & Alterman, 1991). There is also a modified version of the ASI applicable to adolescents called the Teen Addiction Severity Index (T-ASI) (Kaminer, Bukstein, & Tarter, 1991).

The ASI is administered through a semi-structured interview. It addresses eight potential problem areas including medical status, employment, social support (such as the quality of personal relationships), drug use, alcohol use, legal status, family/social status, and psychiatric status (McLellan et al., 1980). The most current edition (fifth) contains 200 items and requires approximately one hour to complete (McLellan, Kushner, Metzger, & Peters, 1992). The interviewer asks questions and records the answers on the answer form (for a copy of the ASI, look online at http://tresearch.com). It is a self-scoring test, taking a trained interviewer approximately five minutes to complete.

While the ASI is a popular tool in the substance abuse field, like the other instruments discussed here, it should be considered as only one part of the overall assessment process. It is predominately a research instrument and thus is well suited to measure differences in behavior over time. Moreover, because the severity index for each of the eight major areas is based on behavior during a 30-day period, the ASI will not aid in determining substance use history, or severity based on longer-term use. If this instrument is used according to the instructions, clients who have not used substances for 30 days, even if they are chemically dependent (having spent the last 30 days in jail, for example), will not appear to need services.

Substance Abuse Subtle Screening Inventory-3 (SASSI-3)

The SASSI was developed by Miller (1983) and is now in its third version (Miller, 1997). It is a short, inexpensive screening tool based on client self-report of life-time substance abuse activity. Clients complete the instrument alone or through an interview. It combines scales that measure obvious signs and symptoms of substance abuse with questions consisting of subtle attributes and items seemingly unrelated to substance abuse. A series of decision rules are used to categorize the adult client as having a high or low probability for a substance abuse problem, and the adolescent client as chemically dependent or not chemically dependent.

The SASSI-3 comprises two sections. The first section includes a 12-item Alcohol scale and 14-item Other Drugs scale. The remainder of the SASSI-3 consists of 67 true-false items (55 for adolescents) regarding belief, value, and attitude statements, many of which are seemingly unrelated to substance use. These statements were selected to differentiate people with a high probability of having substance abuse problems from those with low probability. Through the scoring system, all SASSI-3 items are categorized into eight subscales including symptoms, obvious attributes, subtle attributes, defensiveness, supplemental addiction measures, family dynamics, involvement with the criminal justice system, and random answering pattern (used to test for randomness, faking, or comprehension problems during test-taking) (Miller, 1997; Kerr, 1994).

There are different versions for adults (18 and above) and adolescents, with separate scoring norms by gender for each version. The SASSI is written for a fifth-grade reading level (Treatment Research Institute, 1990). However, Kerr (1994) believes the actual reading level is much higher. It is used in general mental health centers, university student centers, employee assistance programs, substance abuse treatment centers, and health care settings (Creager, 1989). Where I live, it is used by the local Community Health Department as the primary assessment instrument for individuals referred for publicly funded substance abuse treatment. The SASSI-3 takes 10 to 15 minutes to administer and only a few minutes to score. A review of the SASSI-3 by Kerr (1994) indicates that the test does a good job identifying chemical dependency, but is not adequate to be used alone or as a basis for diagnosis.

Other Substance Abuse Screening Instruments

There are many other screening tools available for use with clients who may have substance abuse problems. One valuable screening tool used by hospitals, health centers, and many substance abuse treatment centers is urine toxicology testing, or urinalysis. This process detects current or recent substance use. However, the results of urinalysis are relatively useless in terms of clinical decision-making. Urinalysis only detects the presence of substances. It provides no information about the existence of a potential problem, use patterns, history, and so on. If urine testing is used where you work, do not read too much into the results.

The Alcohol Use Disorders Identification test (AUDIT) was developed by Saunders et al. (1993) to detect alcohol use problems that have not progressed to the point of addiction or dependency. It was developed by the World Health Organization (WHO) for use by primary health care providers (Babor, de la Fuente, Saunders, & Grant, 1992). The instrument consists of 10 items: three on quantity and frequency of drinking, three on alcohol dependence, and four on alcohol-caused problems. The AUDIT was found to be approximately 90 percent effective in detecting alcohol use disorders (Brown, Leonard, Saunders, & Papasoulioutis, 1997). It has been used in a variety of countries and is available in English, Spanish, Slavic, Norwegian, Swahili, and Romanian (McNeese & DiNitto, 2000), although an assessor must be keenly aware of cultural differences when using this instrument with clients of non-European-American descent.

One of the most important evaluations you must make when working with substance-abusing clients is the extent to which clients might be in physical danger. Most often, immediate health issues revolve around the potential for withdrawal syndrome. As such, the Clinical Institute Withdrawal Assessment for Alcohol Scale-Revised (CIWA-AR) is designed for that purpose. This noncopyrighted scale measures 15 symptoms of alcohol withdrawal such as anxiety, nausea, and visual hallucinations. It takes approximately five minutes to administer and score. It determines the extent to which clients may be in immediate danger of withdrawal symptoms, from low to severe (Doweiko, 1999).

Additionally, the Walmyr Scales (Hudson, 1992) have short self-administered tools for both alcohol and drug use. The Alcohol Use Profile (Hystad, 1989) and the Comprehensive Drinking Profile (Marlatt & Miller, 1984) can be used to screen for potential alcohol and/or drug problems in clients. Additionally, Corcoran and Fischer (1987) and Hersen and Bellack (1976) offer sourcebooks with a variety of screening instruments readily accessible for use.

With any of these standardized instruments, it is tempting for the overburdened social worker or agency to give too much credence to the results of a single screening instrument. This is a mistake. No matter how effective they might be as part of the overall assessment process, these screening instruments should never be used as the sole basis for treatment decisions.

SCREENING FOR PROBLEMS
RELATED TO SUBSTANCE ABUSE

Your first decision during a substance abuse assessment is likely to be determined by an immediate medical need or, in some cases, a client crisis. You must hone your skills to spot indicators of a potential crisis that may pose an immediate health risk or even a life-threatening situation. Substance abuse is associated with serious accidents, short- and long-term health problems, sexually transmitted diseases, communicable diseases such as tuberculosis (Smith, Wesson, & Tusel, 1989), co-occurring mental illness and/or substance-induced mental health problems, child abuse, domestic violence, and suicidal ideation or action (Denning, 2000; Doweiko, 1999; van Wormer, 1995). In fact, the lifetime risk for suicide among people with alcohol problems is almost 15 percent (Hirschfield & Davidson, 1988; Schuckit, 1986), and the risk among adolescents is even higher (Fowler, Rich, & Young, 1986).

Because of the relationship between substance abuse and serious, even life-threatening behaviors, as well as physical, emotional, and mental conditions, it is essential to put "First Things First" (Denning, 2000, p. 94). Begin by screening for the most dangerous issues, making sure that these conditions receive attention before proceeding with the assessment process. Consistent with Maslow's hierarchy of needs (Maslow, 1970), a client's immediate needs must be attended to before it is possible to deal with needs that are more abstract. This is no time to fall victim to the "rush to treatment" syndrome.

Below, we consider several health issues (physical and mental) resulting from a substance-abusing lifestyle. You should screen for these problems with every substance-abusing client. *Never overlook these potentially life-threatening issues*, even with people who do not appear to have problems. To do so would be to place your clients, yourself, and your agency at risk for tragedy.

Physical Problems

Every client you see who is suspected of having a substance abuse problem must immediately be referred to a medical doctor for a complete physical examination. My position is more rigid than most in the field, for good reason. Anything less than a referral to a medical doctor places you in the unethical position of making potentially life-threatening health care decisions that you are not trained to make. Research has made it clear that substance abuse is related to a plethora of medical conditions, injuries, and diseases (CDC, 1998; Anthony, Warner, & Kessler, 1997; Sheafor, Horejsi, & Horejsi, 2000). Chronic substance abusers tend to neglect their overall health and are less likely to be attentive to their nutrition and other preventative health care measures (Smith, Wesson, & Tusel, 1989). Thus, substance abuse clients need expert medical attention, even if they do not have life-threatening conditions.

How many courses on medical diagnostics have you taken as part of your graduate social work education? None, I suspect. Social workers are not medical doctors and do not have the training—no matter how many years of experience we might have in the field—to make an accurate medical assessment. This is why we should live by the creed, "Let doctors be doctors, and social workers be social workers." A substance abuse professional's "best friend" is a physician who is willing to give complete physical examinations to substance-abusing clients. Your agency should make contractual arrangements with a physician, or you should find local physicians who are willing to see your clients, many of whom may be covered by Medicaid or have no private health insurance coverage or funds available to pay for health care.

Making a referral for a physical examination means more than telling a client, "Now, it is important that you contact your doctor immediately for a physical examination." This instruction will often be ignored. You must be assertive. How, you ask? First, make the call to the doctor with the client present, and schedule the appointment. Second, make sure the client has transportation and, whenever possible, ensure that the physician's office is located near her or his home. Asking a client to travel 20 or 30 miles to a doctor's office almost guarantees that the appointment will be missed. Better yet, arrange for the physician to perform physical examinations on the premises of the agency where you work. Third, obtain a signed release of information form that allows you to communicate with the physician. This release form will let you make sure the doctor knows why clients are being referred for a physical. The information that you provide should cue the doctor to connect seemingly unrelated medical conditions. Also, make sure the doctor takes a complete medical history; runs laboratory tests, bloodwork, and/or urinalyses to check for the presence of drugs; checks liver and kidney function; and looks for infectious diseases such as hepatitis and HIV/AIDS. A skin test or chest X-ray is desirable to check for communicable diseases such as tuberculosis (Smith, Wesson, & Tusel, 1989). It is also appropriate to have people's prescription medications reviewed, since drug mixing can have serious or even life-threatening ramifications for substance-abusing clients (see Chapter 2). Moreover, the signed release form allows you to obtain a copy of the physical examination and all test results to place in the client's file for future reference.

Depression

As we discussed in Chapter 1, a significant number of people on social work caseloads have co-occurring mental health and substance abuse disorders (Regier et al., 1990), although one or the other is often overlooked or marginalized in professional practice. This bias occurs because most counselors in substance abuse agencies are "recovering" paraprofessionals without mental health training, and most social workers with mental health training are not trained in substance abuse assessment (see Chapter 6).

Of all the mental health problems that could be present, perhaps the most immediate and pervasive issue is depression. Frequently associated with substance abuse, depression may be both a cause and effect of substance abuse (van Wormer, 1995). Stimulants such as cocaine and depressants such as alcohol deplete the body of natural chemicals and exacerbate the depression people often tried to alleviate by using these drugs in the first place. It is estimated that 10 to 15 percent of individuals who are depressed use substances to self-medicate (Campbell, 1992). Evans and Sullivan (2001) found that depression was one of the major antecedents to problem drinking. Depression not only increases the risk of substance abuse disorders, but it negatively affects recovery (Sisney, 1991). In women, it contributes to higher rates of chemical dependency, more trips to the physician for psychosomatic complaints, and a higher rate of psychiatric admissions (Sandmaier, 1992; Blume, 1986; Gordon & Ledray, 1986; Abbott, 1994; Davidson, 1993).

Whether depression is the cause of substance abuse or substance abuse is the cause of depression is a debate that has raged for decades. In any event, it is not important to know the answer to this dilemma early in the assessment process. What is important is that you understand how serious depression can be for people in the throes of substance abuse, and the mechanisms available to perform a simple screening to test for depression.

The *DSM* (APA, 2000) associates chronic depression with poor appetite or overeating, insomnia, low energy or fatigue, low self-esteem, poor concentration or difficulty making decisions, and feelings of hopelessness. Whereas depression in adults usually results in a slowing of activity, depression in children and adolescents is often expressed by agitated behavior (Sheafor, Horejsi, & Horejsi, 2000). Surprisingly, research suggests that primary depression in substance abusers is actually quite rare. Between 2 percent (Powell et al., 1987) and 5 percent (Schuckit, 1995) of the cases of depression in substance abusers involve primary depression. However, Blume (1994) says that women experience substance abuse and depression differently from men. She noted that because most research into substance abuse has been conducted using male subjects, little is understood about the effects of substance abuse on women. She suggests that 60 to 65 percent of chemically dependent women experience primary depression.

Several scales are available to screen for evidence of depression. They include the Depression Scale in the Walmyr Scales (Hudson, 1992), the Zung Self-Rating Depression Scale (Zung, 1965), and perhaps the best known scale, the Beck Depression Inventory (BDI) (Beck et al., 1961). Each is easy to complete, score, and interpret. The results of these instruments are highly correlated with each other (Hepworth, Rooney, & Larsen, 1997). Rauch, Sarno, and Simpson (1991) also provide specific questions to screen for depression (see Chapter 8).

After screening, what should you do with the information? This is a complicated issue, because depression can be both a cause and effect of substance abuse. The symptoms of withdrawal from many drugs match the symptoms of depression (Jung, 2001). This overlap is not only confusing, but could also lead to inappropriate diagnosis of major depression and perhaps to the inappropriate use of antidepressant medication for clients whose symptoms of depression may subside with time and abstinence from drugs.

Describing the effects of withdrawal, Willoughby (1984) noted that the depressant effects from one drink of alcohol might last as long as 96 hours, while the depressant effects of a two-day alcohol binge may linger for several weeks (Segal & Sisson, 1985). It has been suggested that during the first two weeks of abstinence, most chronic substance abusers meet the diagnostic criteria for major depression (Wolf-Reeve, 1990, p. 72). That is, most depression seen during early substance abuse treatment is substance-induced depression and will likely pass (Miller, 1994). There is no clear rule about how long is "long enough" to wait before making a depression diagnosis. Some claim two to five weeks after abstinence (Evans & Sullivan, 2001; Decker & Ries, 1993; Satel, Kosten, Schuckit, & Fischman, 1993), while others believe social workers should wait "several months" (Decker & Ries, 1993, p. 704). I subscribe to the latter policy (90 days) unless the depression is so severe as to produce a suicide threat (see next page).

The key ingredients in the waiting process are patience and information. You must exercise patience when substance-abusing clients exhibit depressive symptoms, especially if these symptoms are mild to moderate. Wait before recommending psychiatric care and medication, especially if the client is still abusing substances. Moreover, you need to understand that the strong link between depression and substance abuse does not work only in one direction. Not only should you screen for depression when suspecting substance abuse, but also screen for substance abuse when suspecting depression. If clients with depression are secretly abusing substances, there are no medications available to alleviate the disorder; the depression will continue, if not deepen. This is where information is important. Gather as much information about clients as possible, looking for patterns and themes. Look for multi-systemic connections between issues, such as depression and substance abuse. Thoroughness during the assessment process will pay off later.

Suicidal Ideation

Despite my preaching that patience is key when dealing with substance-abusing clients' depressive symptoms, there are cases that require immediate and decisive interventions by the social worker. Substance abuse and chemical dependency with co-occurring depression is cited as a causal factor for attempted suicide (Pages et al., 1997; Malone, Hass, Sweeney, & Mann, 1995). Higher levels of suicidal ideation were found in a hospitalized sample of women with major depressive disorders, and according to NIAAA (1990), suicide rates are higher for female than for male substance abuse clients.

When you discover severe depressive symptoms in clients who are either currently abusing drugs or have only recently become abstinent, you should immediately evaluate for suicide risk so that protective and precautionary measures can be taken if necessary (Gambrill, 1997; Miley, O'Melia, & DuBois, 1995; Hepworth, Rooney, & Larsen, 1997). At the precise moment of assessment, you may have the best opportunity to save people from their own worst impulses.

There is a strong correlation between depression and suicide (Hirschfield & Davidson, 1988; Proctor & Groze, 1994; van Wormer, Wells, & Boes, 2000). Since substance abusers tend to exhibit symptoms of depression either because of their abuse or because of coexisting major depression, this is a high-risk group for suicide (Roy, 1993; Murphy, Wetzel, Robins, & McEvoy, 1992). Suicide is not confined to one particular group in society, although suicide rates tend to be higher among European Americans than people of color (Frankel, 1992).

Further, a review of data collected by the U.S. Bureau of the Census (1995) suggests that suicide rates are higher among European American men than European American women. The highest rate of suicide is among people 65 years of age and older, although it is the leading cause of death in the 15- to 24-year-old age group (Ivanoff & Reidel, 1995). Moreover, lesbian and gay adults and adolescents are "two to three times more likely to attempt suicide than others" (Proctor & Groze, 1994, p. 504). All of these trends are heightened when the individual in question is abusing substances. See Chapter 11 for further discussion in the context of treatment.

Legally and ethically, you must make *every reasonable effort* to prevent your clients from committing suicide, despite the fact that it is difficult to prevent suicides from occurring when the client is intent on following through (Hillard, 1995). Reasonable efforts include, but are not limited to, performing an appropriate screening for warning signs, properly assessing the severity of immediate risk, staying with clients during times of high risk, arranging for family and friends to provide 24-hour supervision, and if necessary, calling the police and committing the client to involuntary hospitalization.

There is some debate about the value of involuntary hospitalization. Some research suggests that hospitalizing suicidal adolescents, for example, to prevent suicide actually increases the risk (Dawes, 1994). Others argue that involuntary hospitalization is both unethical and ineffective (Gomory, 1997; Szasz, 1994). My position is that you must do everything possible to give people opportunities to change their minds—to prevent them for destroying themselves during what might be a moment of intense hopelessness—even if that means making a call to the police for a trip to the emergency room. If people are seriously intent on committing suicide, you cannot stop it, but this cannot be used as an excuse for doing nothing.

CASE EXAMPLE The Family That Dropped the Ball

When John became my client for a significant substance abuse problem, he brought with him an extensive history of unsuccessful suicide attempts. On nine occasions during a two-year period, John had tried to kill himself using a variety of methods, including cutting his wrists lengthwise, using pills, intentionally ramming his car into a bridge, etc. For six months, he seemed to be making progress with his substance abuse issues and gaining a will to live.

Then he called me at home on a Friday night, through the answering service, to tell me that he was killing himself. In fact, he had the razor blade in his wrist while making the call. While I kept him talking, a colleague who happened to be at my home went to another telephone and called the police. I listened as the police arrived and took him to the local emergency room for an assessment.

The next morning, John called again. He told me that the emergency room doctors had treated his cut wrist and sent him home. They did not perform a suicide assessment. He refused hospitalization, and his family was unwilling to support any effort to begin involuntary commitment. Later that day I held a family session. During the session, John agreed that he was "over it" and that he would not be killing himself that day. To be sure, I arranged for his family (parents and older brother) to watch him until his crisis passed. The agreement was that the family would call me before ending the 24-hour guard. Everyone agreed to this arrangement.

Two days later, I received a telephone call from John's father. John had killed himself within hours of the family session. One hour after agreeing to watch him, the parents had left for Florida on vacation and his brother had left town to watch a baseball game, leaving John alone in his brother's house. John asphyxiated himself in his brother's garage, using his brother's car.

Roy (1993) offers the following factors as potential indicators of suicide risk.

1. *Gender.* Men tend to commit suicide more often than women.

2. *Marital status.* Single/divorced/widowed adults are significantly more likely to attempt suicide than married adults.

3. *Coexisting depressive disorder.* See above discussion of depression.

4. *Adverse life events.* An individual who has suffered an adverse life event such as the loss of a loved one or major illness is at increased risk.

5. *Recent discharge from treatment for alcoholism.* The first four years following treatment have been associated with a significantly higher risk for suicide.

6. *A history of suicide attempts.*

Other scholars agree with this list (Murphy et al., 1992; Sheafor, Horejsi, & Horejsi, 2000; Gambrill, 1997; Hepworth, Rooney, & Larsen, 1997). Evans and Farberow (1988) suggest that a clustering of these factors signals an increased risk. Additionally, sudden changes in functioning such as inattention to personal hygiene, changes in appetite, increased use of drugs and alcohol, risk-taking behavior, or school or work failure also may indicate that clients are contemplating suicide (Lamb, 1990; Bloch, 1999). Finally, Lamb (1990) and Ryan et al. (1987) caution that a sudden elevation in mood of a previously depressed person may reflect a feeling of relief at having made the decision to commit suicide.

It is essential to take every suicide gesture or threat seriously. Do not fall into the trap of believing that talking about suicide is simply a way of getting attention. Suicidal clients may be searching for attention, but at that moment they need it badly. So, by all means, *give it to them immediately.* There is nothing more attention-grabbing than having a client commit suicide and realizing that you failed to inquire about it in time, or receiving a summons from civil court and/or a notice of ethics violation from your state licensing board.

When you sense that clients are contemplating suicide, discuss your concerns directly with them. Many social workers hesitate to confront the issue directly, fearing that doing so will foster suicidal behavior. This is not the case. By talking directly to people about your concerns, you give them permission to discuss their thoughts and/or urges. If you hesitate or hint around at the subject, this behavior could leave clients believing that you either did not hear them or that you do not take them seriously. Avoiding the issue may foster suicidal urges by the very act of your omission. As I advise throughout this book, Ask! Do not hesitate; your client's life may be in danger.

When screening efforts uncover suicidal thoughts or urges, it is your job to assess the severity of the risk. Although assessing severity is an inexact science, you can base your risk assessment on the following four elements:

1. Does your client plan to use a relatively lethal method?

2. Does he or she have the means available?

3. Does this person have a plan in mind?

4. How specific is the client's plan?

The most important factor for determining the seriousness of a suicide threat is the individual's plan (Aguilera & Messick, 1982). Risk increases when the plans are detailed and specific, and when the chosen methods are lethal and readily available (Hack, 1995). If you determine that suicide is imminent or the risk is relatively high, it is time to take action. First, do not take full responsibility for people's well-being by acting as though you are the only one in the world who can help. Locate social support among family, friends, and other professionals. Social support is the most effective way to prevent suicide. Putting family and friends on a suicide watch, as described in the case study above, can be an effective intervention if there is sufficient follow-through. Since being alone is one of the primary risk factors for suicide, it is important that suicidal people not be left alone during their crisis. If friends and family are not able or willing to help, you can turn to involuntary hospitalization.

Following John's suicide (see case example above), my agency instituted a new policy. If we determined that a client might become suicidal, the client was required to sign releases of information allowing us to contact friends, family members, and neighbors if he or she needed support during a suicidal crisis. Clients were told that if they became suicidal, we would immediately (after calling the police) call their friends and relatives asking them to support the client through the crisis. Over the years, this policy was quite effective. It resulted in a "win-win" situation for clients and staff. If clients were lonely and wanted attention, they got it. If people were seriously in crisis, we saved their lives. Some have suggested that our policy might inhibit clients from calling during a crisis, thus defeating the policy's purpose. My response is twofold. It did inhibit non-serious calls, but it did not stop people who were seriously in crisis from seeking support. In fact, after a while, many clients stopped calling me, and simply called their support people. So not only did clients not kill themselves, but they became empowered to help themselves instead of relying on professional help—a significant step in the recovery process.

As stated earlier, it is impossible to prevent a suicide if the individual is seriously intent on the act. Our responsibility is to act—directly, quickly, and decisively—doing everything we can to try to save our client's life. It is our responsibility ethically, legally, and as members of the human race. I hope you will not have to experience the dreadful aftermath of a client suicide to learn how serious the issue is, particularly with substance-abusing clients.

HOW ASSESSMENT
DIFFERS FROM DIAGNOSIS

As we have already mentioned, an assessment describes the evolving lives of clients, and it is written in narrative form. It summarizes our understanding of the role of substance use and abuse in clients' lives. Therefore, assessment describes the *process* of a client's life. It requires us to describe the context in which people's troubles occur, searching out patterns of related behaviors that occur over time and, when taken together, are used to understand what and how certain problems exist. It is based on their problems and strengths in the context of (or the fit between) the person-in-environment.

Diagnosis, a term borrowed from medicine, takes observed behavior and assigns a label or set of labels that represent that behavior. Diagnosis intends to communicate a frame, or snapshot, of the client's presenting problem (Appleby, Colon, & Hamilton, 2001), by providing a generally agreed-upon meaning to the client's behaviors and experiences, usually in pathological terms (Gambrill, 1997). In social work practice, all diagnoses and the criteria for making a diagnosis are contained in the *DSM* (APA, 2000). Diagnosis, in this context, describes a person's *state of being*.

Diagnosis, unlike assessment, gives a snapshot of what people "have" (chemical dependency), with no concern for the context, history, or multi-systemic involvement of various factors in the problem's development. Moreover, diagnosis does not provide clues about client strengths or suggest how to change their diagnosed state of being. It is based on a "psychobiological" (Denning, 2000, p. 71) perspective that does not consider systemic influences beyond the micro level. Since the *DSM* process is based on the disease model, it places little or no emphasis on broader systems, strengths, or empowerment, all of which are hallmarks of social work assessment (Kutchins & Kirk, 1995). Petersen (1987) likens the difference between assessment and diagnosis to the difference between a motion picture and still photograph, while Gambrill (1997) explains it as follows:

> Trait labels (e.g., aggressive personality) are not used (in an assessment), since they do not offer information about what people do in specific situations and what specific factors affect their behavior. Attributing the cause of problems to character traits ("She is lazy") or to thoughts or feelings increases the likelihood of "pseudoexplanations" (circular explanations that are not helpful). You may say, "She is lazy," referring to the fact that she does not complete her homework. When asked, "Why doesn't she complete her homework?" you may say, "She is lazy." (p. 211)

In the approach to substance abuse assessment that is advocated here, diagnosis is only one part of the assessment process and is given no more weight than any other part. In fact, Kanter (1985) observes that the "traditional psychiatric diagnosis has little bearing on rehabilitative potential" (p. 66), recommending instead a focus on skill capacities for functioning in important situations. Moreover, labeling substance-abusing clients by diagnosis has little positive impact on the assessment or treatment process (Amodeo et al., 1997; Peele, 1998; Brown, 1985).

Perhaps the only reason to learn the *DSM* system and to include a diagnosis in a client assessment is for third-party reimbursement. Kirk and Kutchins (1988; Kutchins & Kirk, 1988) conducted a study of clinical social workers that indicated that their use of the *DSM* was primarily for reimbursement purposes rather than a guide to treatment. As a funding tool, *DSM* skills are required by many government programs and insurance companies (Schamess, 1996). Given the pressure to use the *DSM* for diagnosis (Kirk & Kutchins, 1988, 1992), it is important to keep its limitations in mind. I advise students to think of the *DSM* as a "payment voucher" that is necessary to make money, but not helpful—at least by itself—for client assessment and treatment planning.

OPERATING PRINCIPLES
OF SUBSTANCE ABUSE ASSESSMENT

Before diving into the specifics of assessment in the next chapter, here are a few general guidelines to follow during an assessment. These guidelines are applicable regardless of your client, agency, or practice setting.

1. *Every client is unique, and so is his or her story*. Never believe that all clients are the same, or even similar. Regardless of which model (see Chapter 3) or models you believe in, not all substance-abusing or chemically dependent clients experience the same or similar processes, experiences, or stages. Do not base your approach on the general characteristics described in social surveys about a culture, race, ethnicity, sexual orientation, gender, or other classification. Try to understand each client's personal interpretation and practice of culture, race, and so on, rather than relying on stereotypic assumptions about individuals or families.

2. *Successful client engagement is fundamental.* Client engagement is the key to successful social work practice, regardless of field, setting, or population (Chapter 4). There are no shortcuts or creative ways to circumvent the need for sound client engagement in the assessment process. Do not fall into the trap of believing that work on engagement skills is "too basic" or simple for your energies. These skills are never completely mastered, regardless of one's experience. Everyone's relationship skills need work—yours, mine, and those of every other social worker who is currently practicing in the field.

3. *Ask (always) and act (if needed)*. Since substance abuse and chemical dependency are so prevalent and studies show that a high percentage of social work clients have substance abuse issues, I implore you to always—with every client on your caseload—ask about substance use and abuse by clients and/or their significant others. Then, if abuse is present, know how to act on the information. Chapters 8 through 11 should make this possible.

4. *There are significant differences between use, abuse, and chemical dependency.* Please review Chapter 1 for definitions of these confusing terms. There are major differences—quantitatively and qualitatively—between using substances, abusing substances, and being chemically dependent. You must know these differences, in theory and practice, so that clients are not under/over diagnosed or under/over treated.

5. *Chemical dependency (or addiction) is not inevitable.* If there is one myth that I hope is "exploded" in this text, it is the wrongheaded assumption that people who use drugs inevitably progress through distinct and similar stages from use, to abuse, and ultimately to chemical dependency. As we discussed in Chapter 3, there is no credible research to support what was supposedly proven by Jellinek's research (1946, 1952, 1960). Contrary to this popular view, most people who use or abuse substances do not become chemically dependent.

6. *No single model or theory explains chemical dependency*. Many theories claim to define substance abuse and chemical dependency. While some theories share ideas, most are distinctly different. You should be conversant with all of the various practice methods and prepared to utilize different models as needed. You will need to apply the model that best fits the client and his or her needs, perspectives, and presentation, depending upon the seriousness of the problem and what the client will tolerate.

7. *Work toward developing a multi-systemic approach*. A multi-systemic approach to substance abuse practice, in the context of successful client engagement, offers the best opportunity to perform an assessment and provide treatment that meets each client's unique needs.

8. *Be aware of your own prejudices, biases, beliefs, or need for power.* Throughout this text, you have been encouraged to keep a personal substance abuse journal to head off problems caused by unchecked and free-floating personal beliefs about people who abuse substances, or your conscious or unconscious need to exercise the power inherent in the therapeutic relationship (Carpenter, 1994). Because attitudes toward substance abuse are such a pervasive part of people's life-learning, along with the myths and untruths that constitute so-called common knowledge, you must sort through your feelings to be effective with substance abuse clients. If you have resisted keeping a substance abuse journal, I encourage you to rethink your resistance and begin now. It will make your work with substance abuse clients more effective. If you need a good topic to begin your journal—here's one to consider: Why were you so resistant to begin keeping a journal when everyone else did back in Chapter 1?

SUMMARY

In this chapter, we described substance abuse screening and assessment as an effort to develop a fluid, yet comprehensive look at a client's problems and strengths. We contrasted assessment with screening and diagnosis, showing how the latter two functions are but two parts of the larger assessment process. As we progress through the remaining chapters, think of assessment as the most important process in a client's treatment, in that any treatment recommendations and plans that may be needed flow from a comprehensive assessment. Despite the time limits imposed by managed care in private and public funding arenas, those who are skilled in the assessment process—rooted in a multi-systemic approach—understand that no treatment model (even those purported to be very brief) can be successful without a comprehensive assessment of the client's situation.

8

Substance Abuse
Assessment

In the first seven chapters we explored various elements of a substance abuse assessment. Chapters 1 through 3 provided a theoretical and knowledge base, while Chapters 4 through 6 focused on skills involved in multi-systemic client engagement. Chapter 7 introduced screening and assessment in substance abuse practice. In this chapter, we bring together all of this information to demonstrate how to perform a comprehensive, multi-systemic substance abuse assessment and how to write a case history report.

DIMENSIONS OF ASSESSMENT

In a substance abuse assessment, you will need to collect several dimensions of information (Hepworth, Rooney, & Larsen, 1997; Miller & Rollnick, 1991; Fisher & Harrison, 2000; McNeese & DiNitto, 2000; Rothman & Sager, 1998; Smith, Wesson, & Tusel, 1989). Each dimension requires different information, but it will appear that some of the information overlaps. On the surface this may be true, yet certain dimensions demand that the same information be considered in a different context, making it different information. For example, when discussing a client's interpretation of his or her culture, you must consider information about the client's family, peer group, and social activities.

In addition to the typical client data collected in any assessment, your goal is to uncover deeper and richer elements of clients' feelings, beliefs, and attitudes in an effort to understand how they relate to others. A comprehensive assessment considers more than behavior—it means getting to know clients better than anybody has ever known them before, in a way that allows them to participate as active partners in the process. This approach goes beyond traditional social work rhetoric about empowerment and "starting where the client is"; instead of giving lip service to these goals, you will be expected to accomplish them.

As stated above, information from the previous chapters is woven together in this chapter to give you a sense of the whole. We will look at what information is needed in each assessment dimension. Comprehensive assessment is a multi-systemic process that is easy to learn but difficult to master. To learn this method takes knowledge, experience, supervision, and consultation—followed by more experience and critical self-reflection to master the nuances of performing a comprehensive, multi-systemic substance abuse assessment. This skill cannot be mastered quickly.

STEP-BY-STEP ASSESSMENT PROCESS

The time has come to begin putting the assessment together in a way that makes sense. This discussion contains three parts: (1) a general description of each dimension and the type of information needed for assessment purposes; (2) specific questions and/or lines of inquiry to help clarify indicators of potential problems in each dimension; and (3) a review of the more important aspects of each dimension that must be considered in the final case history report.

Dimension 1: Client Description, Presenting Problem, and Context of Referral

The first step in the substance abuse assessment process is to discover the nature of the presenting problem. The presenting problem is the issue that clients identify as the most pressing at the time of the interview. This issue usually prompted the clinical contact. If you do not work in a substance abuse agency, many people will not mention substance abuse. If you work in a substance abuse agency, some clients may not mention it even if they have been referred for a substance-related crime. They may do this to distract your attention from their substance-abusing behavior or because they honestly believe that substance abuse is not a major problem. Whatever issue your client presents, you must discuss it at length. It does not matter whether you believe what they are saying is true. If you begin by ignoring clients in the first moments of the first session, your chances for successful engagement are slim.

At this early stage in an assessment, strive to understand people's presenting problem(s) from *their* perspective. At this time, your beliefs about the presentation are irrelevant, and expressing them will only slow the process of engagement. Moreover, do not assume clients believe that their presenting complaint is problematic. Even if clients present what sounds like problems, they may not believe these issues are problematic. Perhaps these people learned to act as if they have problems so that you will "bend over backwards" to help, forgetting to discover whether they are serious or not. Once you both agree there are issues to discuss, follow up with a series of questions that allow you to understand their opinion about their presenting problems, how they began, how long they have been occurring, and how clients came to believe that they had problems in the first place.

Additionally, ask about the referring agency's perspective about the presenting problem. This question leads to an important discussion about the context of the referral. Is it a voluntary referral or did the court system, other official agency, employer, or spouse/partner/parent mandate the assessment? Why did clients decide to seek help now instead of three months earlier, one year earlier, or next week, for that matter? Did someone threaten to leave, throw them out on the street, or fire them from their job? Let's face it: rarely do people wake up in the morning and suddenly—over coffee—decide to get a substance abuse assessment. There is usually an important or painful factor motivating them to do so. You will need to know (and understand) this factor if you are to place people's presenting problems in their proper context and assess people's motivation (see Dimension 9 below).

What to Look for After completing this dimension, you should have a clear understanding of what clients believe are their problems at this time, how they came to see the issues as problems, and their opinion about the seriousness of the problems. It should also be clear what factor or factors prompted them to seek an assessment at this moment, instead of some other time in the past or future. Information from this dimension illuminates people's perspectives about their lives, problems, and the conditions under which they chose to seek help. More importantly, what you should look for at this stage is an early glimpse into people's motivation for seeking help.

Key Questions When you have completed this dimension, you should be able to answer the following questions:

- Who is your client? (Describe age, race, physical stature, appearance, clothing, hygiene, and any other physical, psychological, or relational issues related to how your client presented for the interview.)

- What problem or problems does your client believe are the most troublesome right now?

- What motivated your client to schedule an assessment at this time?

- What strengths and resources does your client exhibit with regard to this dimension?

What If My Client Seems Intoxicated?

Students often ask two important questions: how can I tell if clients are under the influence, and what should I do if they are intoxicated? The answer to the first question is not as obvious as it may seem, while the answer to the second is controversial. Let's take them one at a time.

Is My Client Intoxicated?
Clients rarely show for a professional appointment grossly intoxicated, to the point where they are stumbling, slurring their words, or throwing up all over everything. In more than 20 years of practice encompassing thousands of clients,

What If My Client Seems Intoxicated? *continued*

I have experienced this perhaps five or six times. Moreover, while I cannot prove it scientifically, the people who did appear sloppily intoxicated usually did not have serious substance abuse problems.

People with serious or chronic substance abuse problems rely on being able to "pass" without detection. As we discussed in Chapter 2, chemically dependent persons often develop a behavioral tolerance that allows them to be intoxicated while acting relatively normal, especially around people they do not know well. On the other hand, contrary to popular belief, most chemically dependent people can stop using drugs for an appointment (Peele, 1998). Many will even stop for a certain number of days prior to the assessment in case they are required to take a urine test to detect drug use. They know exactly how many days it takes to metabolize particular drug(s) from their system. Hence, determining whether your client is under the influence during a session is not as easy as it may seem.

First, you need to become familiar with what intoxication looks and smells like, for a wide variety of substances. If you smell the odor of alcohol or marijuana, or a strong aroma of mints or mouthwash, this should be a cue that your client may be intoxicated. If your client is acting manic, or if about 10 to 15 minutes into a session his or her mood switches from agitation and energy to sadness and lethargy, it is possible that your client used cocaine in the parking lot before the session. (Review Chapter 2 on drug effects for information about behavioral and physiological effects of certain drugs.)

If you suspect that your client is intoxicated, it is best to ask if he or she is under the influence. Make sure, however, that you do this in a nonjudgmental and professional manner. This is no time to be angry, offended, or outraged. In fact, you have no right to react this way. These reactions, if you have them, suggest that you may have issues to work out, not your client! Explore why a stranger's drug use makes you angry, offended, or sad before imposing your feelings onto your client.

If My Client Is Intoxicated, What Should I Do?

This is the controversial part of the equation. Many substance abuse professionals believe that the client should not be seen by a social worker if she or he is intoxicated. I believe the decision to cancel or continue the session depends on several factors. I do not believe the appointment should automatically be canceled. I know social workers who will terminate a session with a substance abuse client if the client admits having had a drink that day, but will meet with a client with other problems, even if the client admits having just left a "three martini" business lunch. Intoxication is intoxication, regardless of whether a person admits to having a substance abuse problem.

Before deciding whether to meet with an intoxicated client, you should assess three issues: (1) Can the client participate, or is he or she too intoxicated to understand the session? (2) Is the client's behavior or attitude so erratic that you may be at risk for attack or abuse of some kind during the session? (3) Does your client need immediate medical attention because of the potential for withdrawal symptoms? If the answers to these questions indicate that the client can understand, is not erratic, and is not sick, then it is perfectly acceptable and helpful to interview the client, even for a few minutes. It can be an enlightening experience to interview a client who is intoxicated because you can compare it with your experience of him or her sober. This is especially true if your interview includes significant others and/or family members (Steinglass, 1980). Therefore, I suggest that you go ahead and meet with the intoxicated client, but make sure to ask him or her about it directly. Do not pretend that you do not know what is going on, because this will make you appear untrustworthy in your client's eyes.

If you choose to cancel the appointment or send your client home early, do not just pack the person off, especially is he or she drove to your agency. If you believe your client is intoxicated and he or she gets into an accident after leaving your office, you could be liable. Instead, offer to call a taxi (even if your agency must pay for it), offer bus fare, or call someone to pick your client up.

Moreover, if your client is intoxicated and you choose to send him or her home, do not scold the client as if you were dealing with an acting-out child! This is *not* the time to tell your client that he or she should learn to act more appropriately and is probably not suited for treatment, or that you

Continued

What If My Client Seems Intoxicated? *continued*

will report the offense to his or her probation or parole officer. If you feel compelled to lecture or scold your client (although this should never be the case), wait until the next session. Simply cancel the appointment, make sure to write down the next appointment time in case your client's memory fails, and move on to your next session. If the client pushes you for an explanation, simply say that you can discuss it at the next session.

As stated earlier, this is a controversial topic, and one that elicits strong opinions. Social workers and other professionals get angry at the thought that someone who might have an un-controllable disease would have the audacity not to control it for the professional's benefit! More practically, it is not punishment to send the client home without a session—it is a reward. What is the motivation for the client to come sober the next time? Before making universal statements about what you will do in this situation, think it through and clearly decide what your motivation is for sending the client home without help.

Dimension 2: Treatment History

The information gained from investigating people's treatment history and, more importantly, their experience with other professional helpers is an important part of assessing motivation. How people experienced previous treatment providers sheds light on the approach you should take to engage them in the assessment and/or treatment process.

What is their history and experience with treatment and treatment professionals? Have they ever been in treatment—voluntarily or involuntarily—and, if so, with whom, for how long, and what was their perception of the outcome? Ask the same about family members. Was the treatment inpatient or outpatient; individual, family, group, or support group centered? After collecting this information, ask which treatments people preferred, and why. Explore their ideas about the value of treatment, what was gained from the experience(s), and what they could have gained, but did not, and why.

Going further, what do your clients perceive as their previous helpers' "theories" about their problems? What explanations were offered (if any), and what did your clients think about these theories? Did clients agree, disagree, or ignore these theories? Regardless of how people respond, ask for an explanation. Listen for clues about which issues clients might be willing to address and which they would rather avoid. Clients often leave treatment because a helper avoided or ignored their stated problems, not because they did not want to cooperate. In Chapter 4, we discussed the need to trust clients to do what is in their best interest. Here, trust translates into a belief that clients know their problems and what works best for them. For example,

> I once knew someone who attended outpatient therapy for substance abuse. She mentioned in the first session that she had been molested as a child. Instead of investigating this issue further, the therapist ignored it, focusing instead on abstinence from drugs. Over the next five sessions, the therapist never brought up the issue of childhood sexual abuse, even in passing. The client dropped out of therapy.

It is also helpful to ask clients about their previous helper's style and approach. The answers to this inquiry provide valuable information about the engagement process. Even if the previous helper's theory and approach sound reasonable, do not forget that it was unsuccessful. Most likely, something in the client-helper relationship did not work. Perhaps the client was not ready to engage or the previous helper made mistakes, or both. It is too easy (and common) to assume that clients cause treatment failure. Sometimes—in fact, many times—it is the helper's fault. Since the majority of people seeking help have a history of unsuccessful treatment attempts, your ability to act differently from others is often the crucial difference between successful engagement and client dropout.

The client-helper relationship is built through process more than content. For example, if their previous social workers believed they were chemically dependent—and you agree with that assessment—the secret to engaging them around the issue is to find a more effective way to approach them about the issue. Clients do not engage with techniques or methods, they engage with human beings who happen to be social workers. In this instance, the content (client is chemically dependent) is less important than the process (your approach) in your effort to engage clients in a productive professional relationship.

Key Questions When you have completed this dimension, you should be able to answer the following questions:

- What are the client's (or family members') histories in professional treatment for any problem, and how does the client view the outcome of that treatment?

- What is your client's opinion of the previous helper's theory?

- How does your client define the approach of previous helpers, and what is the client's opinion about the previous helpers' approaches, styles, and personas?

- From this discussion, what did you learn about how you should approach your client in your professional relationship?

- What strengths and resources does your client exhibit with regard to this dimension?

Dimension 3: Substance Use History

The most obvious dimension of a substance abuse assessment is the substance use history, although rarely is it completed in a comprehensive manner. Too often, I have reviewed what were purported to be complete substance use histories, only to discover that people's use history was omitted. While it is true that people's current use is probably the most important factor, omitting information about historical use restricts your ability to see patterns across a lifetime. This omission often leads to under- or over-diagnosis of the extent of their problem(s). Collecting a comprehensive substance use history means discovering which drugs clients use, or have *ever* used at any time (including legal drugs such as nicotine and prescription medications).

Style Tips

If you are not careful, this is one area where your interview can "bog down" into boring minutia or begin sounding like an interrogation. Most pre-designed assessment formats include a form for recording a person's substance use history. If you must use the form or take a use history all at once, my suggestion is to apologize in advance for having to do this, and move forward. Most clients do not mind this type of questioning, as long as it is not your overall style and you explain it as a necessary and brief experience.

In addition to a list of substances used in a person's lifetime, you should also collect the following information *for each substance reported.*

1. *Frequency of use.* When people used a particular drug (or are currently using it), how often, and on average, did/do they use it? Asking for an average may seem like an imprecise way of obtaining information about frequency. However, you will be surprised by how precise substance abusers or addicts can be about each substance they have ever used.

2. *Dosage used.* How much of the drug, on average, did/does the person use? Were there times the person can remember using more or less of the drug than average, and what was the result? Why did the client increase or decrease the dose? The answer to this question sheds light on issues such as tolerance, motivation for using, and whether or not the individual has or had control over use.

3. *Age at first use.* This is important information, because of the direct relationship between age at first use and the development of later substance abuse patterns (van Wormer, 1995; Denning, 2000; Jung, 2001). Here, you will get a picture of the extent and depth of people's substance use history and whether their use has escalated as they aged. For example, have your clients "graduated" from cigarettes, alcohol, and marijuana as teens, to cocaine, heroin, methamphetamine, or other so-called "harder" drugs as young adults? This pattern suggests a deepening reliance on substances and an increased desire to find a more powerful and fulfilling effect.

   Not all adults began using alcohol and other drugs as teenagers. It is common to find many adults with substance abuse problems who did not begin using until adulthood. Many people do not begin using drugs until the late 20s, 30s, or even later. Many older people do not begin drinking until they reach retirement age (Moody, 2000). When you discover that a client began using a substance during adulthood, you should wonder about what happened in the client's life to motivate them to begin using it.

4. *When was the drug last used?* When did clients stop using particular drugs and move on to others? More importantly, why did they stop using particular drugs at that time? If people have continued to use the drug, why have they continued? What do your clients "get" from use of these substances?

5. *Routes of administration*. From our discussion in Chapter 2, how a person administers a drug is an important assessment indicator. People with more serious problems usually move from the simplest, most common route of administration to ones that are specifically designed to speed up onset of the drug's effects and increase the power or intensity of the effects. Which routes of administration people choose may indicate serious problems related to specific drugs. For example, smoking cocaine (as crack cocaine or freebase) indicates more serious use for this drug, while smoking marijuana is the most common route of administration for that drug.

Because of these nuances, become familiar with each drug, its typical and potential routes of administration, and what each means in terms of potential seriousness. Many prescription medications are commonly swallowed as pills, yet you should not assume that this is how clients administer the drugs. Some clients chop pills into powder and snort them, "cook" them in water and inject them directly into their veins, or smoke them in pipes. Ritalin, commonly used to treat ADHD, is one example of a drug modified from its original form to increase the speed and power of its effects to the user.

6. *History of overdose or bad reactions.* For each drug, it is important to know if your clients have overdosed or had a bad reaction. If so, when did the reaction take place, what happened, and how did the experience affect their future use of that or other drugs? Did your clients require medical attention, and, if so, what happened? I categorize legal entanglements while under the influence of a particular drug as a "bad reaction."

The following information should be obtained about people's substance use in general.

1. *Drugs used in the previous 30 days*. Inquire about what drugs, in what combinations, how often, and in what dosage clients have taken in the 30 days prior to the assessment. The goal here is to build a timeline from 30 days ago to the day of the assessment, ending with information about the client's most recent use of drugs, including moments before the assessment interview. When compared to lifetime use patterns, the timeline allows you to discover any recent patterns that suggest increased, decreased, or "normal" use.

Be thorough, especially about the combinations and categories of drugs most recently used. What you are looking for, aside from changes in use intensity, is the possibility for withdrawal syndrome and the need for medical attention. You can also use this information to help explain erratic behavior during the session, up to and including evidence of hallucinations, delusions, and/or manic or depressed mood. If your clients used a hallucinogen or stimulant drug in the previous 24 hours, these behaviors are probably related to their use, rather than an Axis II diagnosis.

2. *Favorite substances (usually the top three)*. Here, you want to ascertain people's three "drugs of choice"—that is, the drugs clients use the most, would use the most if they had access to them, or like the best, but for some reason do not use as frequently as others. The reason for asking about preferences is

obviously to determine which drugs clients are most likely to use, but more importantly, to better understand their behavior and the potential dangers of drug mixing (see Chapter 2).

You should also discover if their list of favorite drugs has changed recently, and if so, what (or who) influenced the change. Additionally, for each drug of choice, ask people what route of administration they like best for that particular drug. Here, as in other sections, look for patterns of behavior and attitude changes to suggest an intensifying problem, strong influences from particular people or peer groups, and a desire to find a more intoxicating drug or more efficient ways of administering drugs to enhance their effects.

3. *Patterns of substance/drug mixing.* It is important to understand what combinations of drugs people use simultaneously, and in what dosages, to assess the potential for overdose. Additionally, if clients are considering abstinence, knowing which drugs they take, in what combinations, can lead you to make an appropriate medical referral for withdrawal symptoms.

4. *Longest period without using substances.* This information is important for several reasons. First, periods of abstinence, depending on the reasons, help determine the extent to which people have control over their use, a key indicator about the severity of a client's problem. If your clients have weekly or monthly periods of abstinence, the chances are great that they are not chemically dependent. People's reasons for abstinence are important. If they were abstinent for one year while in jail or for the month they spent as an inpatient in a substance abuse program, then the nature of these periods of abstinence may indicate that your clients have little or no control over their use.

As in other dimensions, you will need to collect information that goes beyond dates and times. Explore the reasons for people's abstinence, how it felt (or, what they thought about that period), how their lives changed during these periods, and why they began using substances again. You also want to explore their attitude about abstinence: whether it is desirable, undesirable, or of no consequence. If you can get people to discuss their attitudes about abstinence, then you should be able to discuss their beliefs and attitudes about substance use and abuse. If handled correctly, this discussion can be the most important part of your work in this dimension. Listen for clues about the relative importance people place on substance abuse, but more importantly, on being intoxicated. What does being intoxicated provide or offer some people that they find difficult to obtain otherwise? Do they feel better, think more clearly, relax more easily, or feel more competent, attractive, and potent, for example?

During this conversation, you are asking people to reveal important aspects of their worldview, in an effort to determine if substance use and intoxication are a central part of their perspective and the extent to which being under the influence defines "normal life." Back in Chapter 1, we discussed the qualitative differences between people classified as substance abusers and chemically dependent. The greater the importance of using substances to people's daily existence, the more likely it is that they are approaching (or have already arrived at) chemical dependency. Do your clients talk about use as a hobby, or does it sound like a full-time job? Is it a casual pastime, even if it brings some negative life consequences, or is it their life's passion? Chemical dependency is a lifestyle that is as all-encompassing as any other lifestyle.

Information about people's worldview is not usually stated directly; you cannot elicit it through direct questions about the role substance use plays in their life, although this is a good question to ask. Worldview information is gleaned from an individual's responses, facial expressions, affect changes, body language, and other subtle cues that occur during an interview. In Chapter 1, we equated addiction to "crazy-in-love" relationships, suggesting that chemically dependent persons believe they need to use drugs in order to live, just as non-addicted persons believe they must breathe to live.

Most clients cannot grasp this fact about themselves to the extent that they can verbalize it. Look and listen for words, actions, and expressions that indicate these feelings. For example, sometimes sullen and reserved clients will suddenly energize and animate when asked about their favorite drugs. Some clients will refer to their drugs as living beings, while some simply tell you that they only feel alive when they are high. Listen closely for these clues. They will be useful later in the assessment process.

Screening Instruments It is sometimes appropriate to employ one of the screening instruments discussed in Chapter 7, or other instruments available in the professional literature (Miller & Marlatt, 1984; Sobell, Sobell, & Ward, 1980). I often ask clients to keep a record of their substance use during the assessment period (Miller & Munoz, 1982; Wilkinson & LeBreton, 1986) as a way of highlighting the extent of their use. A written record is useful as part of the assessment, and it can also help clients to recognize their own use patterns.

If you choose to use a screening instrument, remember to consider the results in the context of the entire assessment. Because these instruments are quick, easy, and appear definitive, too many social workers and other service providers consider the results final. Re-read the discussion on screening instruments in Chapter 7 to revisit how unreliable many of these instruments are, especially for people outside the European American male majority culture.

Family History of Substance Use In addition to a personal use history, also collect substance use information about family members, friends, co-workers, etc., because of the social influence of people's immediate environment on their behavior. Moreover—in the case of family members—a substance use history is important because of the potential for genetic influences on substance abuse behavior (Jung, 2001; Swan, Carmelli, & Cardon, 1997; Wallace, 1989). Understanding people's cultural and ethnic background can also put their substance use, and attitudes and beliefs about various substances, in its proper context (Appleby, Colon, & Hamilton, 2001).

What to Look for As in all aspects of an assessment, no single piece of information is important unto itself. Each bit of information must be considered in the context of the whole. The substance use history is a prime example. No single occurrence or drug used is important outside the context of people's lives. When making sense of information in this dimension, search for patterns and trends occurring over time.

As we discussed earlier, the younger the age at which people begin using drugs, the more likely it is that they will develop substance abuse problems as adults (Jung, 2001). However, you should not take age of first use as an absolute predictor of the seriousness of the problem. Trends and patterns tell the story in an assessment. Look for a trend towards increased doses, increased drug mixing, more frequent use, and changes in routes of administration. Do people appear to be progressing from use to abuse to addiction? Do they rely on being intoxicated to function in daily life more now than in the past?

Key Questions When you have completed this dimension, you should be able to answer the following questions:

- What is the complete history of the client's lifetime use of legal and illegal drugs, including all of the information described above for each drug used?

- What are the client's beliefs, attitudes, and feelings about substance use, abuse, and addiction? What are his or her beliefs, attitudes, and feelings about intoxication, abstinence, treatments, and professional help? Does your client believe her or his use is below normal, normal, or above normal compared to others?

- Is there a family history of substance abuse, and what do family members and close friends think about the person's use?

- Has the client's substance use moved from social to a lifestyle in its presentation?

- Does your client fit the criteria for a substance abuse or substance dependence diagnosis? Which criteria are applicable, and which ones are not?

- What strengths and resources does your client exhibit with regard to this dimension?

Dimension 4: Medical History

We have already discussed how important it is for every substance abuse client to complete a medical history and physical examination as part of a substance abuse assessment. In addition to identifying emergency needs, a physical examination identifies short- and long-term health care needs. For example, poor nutrition, liver disease (Lieber, 1994; Maher, 1997), stomach ulcers (Cook, 1981), high blood pressure and congestive heart failure (Regan, 1990), seizures (Patterson et al., 1987), and kidney failure (Maher, 1997) are a few potential short- and long-term medical effects of substance abuse.

Substance abuse adversely affects the immune system (Cook, 1998), heightening the client's susceptibility to communicable diseases such as tuberculosis, viral infections, and sexually transmitted diseases such as HIV/AIDS (Jung, 2001). It also affects reproductive systems in males and females (Mello, 1988), and can harm a developing fetus (Mattson & Riley, 1998). As part of the medical history, also explore people's sexual history for indicators of potential health concerns. Substance abuse—especially chronic dependence—has wide-ranging effects on people's health. Because of the potential for serious illness, chronic disease, and death, one of your first actions with your substance-abusing clients should be to ensure that they receive a complete physical examination.

What to Look for   In this dimension, look for evidence of unmet medical needs, including withdrawal symptoms. Over the longer term, referring all of your clients for a medical examination will ensure that they receive the type of medical care they need. Since substance abuse is correlated with many chronic medical conditions, helping people find a way to get their medical needs met will, in the end, improve your relationship with them and help make treatment success more attainable. Remember—everyone gets a medical examination.

Key Questions   When you have completed this dimension, you should be able to answer the following questions.

- Based on the substance used, is your client at risk for withdrawal symptoms or other immediate medical complications?
- What is the client's history of medical attention and examinations?
- What other health problems is your client at risk for, including HIV/AIDS, tuberculosis, or other diseases that may be associated with a substance-abusing or chemically dependent lifestyle?
- What strengths and resources does your client exhibit with regard to this dimension?
- Did you remember to refer your client for a complete medical examination?

Dimension 5: Basic Needs

Basic needs are defined as safe housing, adequate food, appropriate clothing for the season, and reliable transportation (Rothman & Sager, 1998). Be sure to assess the extent to which your clients can meet their basic needs, along with the basic needs of their dependent children, even if clients do not "appear" to be lacking in this area.

A look at people's ability to provide for basic needs is fundamental to the overall assessment process. After all, it is difficult, no matter how serious a substance abuse problem may be, to focus on substance abuse or mental health issues—or even physical health problems—if people cannot meet their basic needs on a daily basis. This is especially true when dependent children are involved (Mather & Lager, 2000). Many practitioners overlook these issues in their eagerness to move forward with substance abuse treatment. It is fruitless to expect people to enter substance abuse treatment, no matter how needed it may be, if they are worried about feeding, housing, and clothing their children. While you may see substance abuse problems as a threat to basic needs, if people cannot eat, feed their children, or sleep in a warm bed, chemical dependency, prostitution, or drug selling will undoubtedly be the least of their worries.

Do not assume that clients are getting their basic needs met by other professional services. Find out for sure whether their needs are being met somewhere, somehow. You may need to act immediately on these issues, offering a connection to resources for housing assistance, food, clothing, emergency services for victims of domestic violence, and so on. When clients are in your office, it is your ethical responsibility to see that these issues are addressed in a timely and respectful manner.

What to Look for   Do your clients have places to live? Are they and their children getting adequate food? Do they have appropriate clothing for the local climate? Are they able to utilize community resources in order to meet these needs independently? If basic needs are not met, what immediate course of action is necessary to assist them to get their needs met?

Key Questions   When you have completed this dimension, you should be able to answer the following questions:

- Are your client's (and family members', if applicable) basic needs being met?
- If so, how? If not, which needs are not being met and why?
- What strengths and resources does your client exhibit with regard to this dimension?
- Is a referral necessary to ensure that the client's basic needs are met tonight?

Dimension 6: Psychological and Emotional Functioning

Assessing people's psychological and emotional functioning is essential (Hepworth, Rooney, & Larsen, 1997) because of the number of people you will see with co-occurring substance abuse and mental health problems (Anthony, Warner, & Kessler, 1997; Brady & Lydiard, 1992). The reverse is also true; many people with mental health disorders also have co-occurring substance abuse problems (Community Epidemiology Work Group, 1998). Therefore, substance abuse practitioners must know how to assess both substance abuse and mental health problems. To assess one area without accounting for the other almost guarantees that clients will not receive the type and intensity of services they require.

Our coverage of this area will not train you to make psychiatric diagnoses or sophisticated clinical judgments. In many states, MSW-level practitioners are only allowed to make diagnostic impressions, leaving final diagnostic certification to psychiatrists. After reading this discussion, you will know when it is appropriate to refer people to a psychiatrist or psychologist for a second-level assessment and possible diagnosis of a co-occurring disorder. Since it is common for some level of psychological and/or developmental disorders to go undetected in substance abuse assessments (Evans & Sullivan, 2001), many clients are set up to fail. This discussion will help you detect potential psychological and/or developmental problems so that appropriate measures are taken to ensure that people have the extent and depth of their problems accurately assessed and treated.

Earlier, we discussed how substance use, abuse, and/or chemical dependency make it difficult to diagnose co-occurring mental health problems. Below, we discuss the different relationships that can occur between substance use and mental health symptoms or disorders (Landry, Smith, & Steinberg, 1991; Lehman, Myers, & Corty, 1989; Meyer, 1986). All of these possibilities must be considered during the assessment and screening process:

1. Substance use can cause psychiatric symptoms to occur and/or mimic psychiatric disorders. Acute and chronic substance use can cause symptoms associated with many psychiatric disorders. The type, duration, and severity of these symptoms are usually related to the type, dosage, and chronicity of the substance use.

2. Acute and chronic substance use can lead to the development of mental disorders, provoke their reemergence, or worsen the severity of preexisting psychiatric disorders.

3. Substance use can mask psychiatric symptoms and disorders. Moreover, individuals often use substances to reduce psychiatric symptoms (self-medication) and to rid themselves of the unwanted side effects of psychotropic medications. That is, substance use may hide or change the character and nature of psychiatric symptoms and disorders.

4. Withdrawal from various substances can cause psychiatric symptoms and/or mimic psychiatric disorders. Cessation of substance use after physical tolerance has developed (see Chapter 2) can cause behavior that closely resembles psychiatric disorders.

5. Psychiatric and substance abuse disorders can co-occur. One problem may prompt the emergence of the other, or the two may exist independently. Determining whether the disorders are related may be difficult.

6. Psychiatric symptoms can mimic behaviors caused by substance use. It is relatively easy, if you specialize in substance abuse, to misinterpret behaviors and symptoms of psychiatric problems as drug-induced. I have seen this happen frequently with parents who assume that their adolescent's odd or different behavior is drug-related, and by substance abuse professionals who assume that clients are in denial because they refused to admit to substance abuse problems to explain bizarre thoughts, emotions, or behaviors.

At this point, I need to insert an important cautionary note: Do not attempt to assess people's mental status if they are intoxicated. When it concerns a potential mental health diagnosis, be concerned about their drug use within the 48 hours prior to the session. If people have used drugs within 48 hours of the session, determine the kinds and doses of drugs used. If the dosage was high, delay the mental status screening because clients are still under the influence, even if they act sober. If you are not sure, ask! A simple question such as, "When's the last time you used?" can save a lot of guesswork and conjecture, and prevent an inaccurate determination of a potential mental illness.

Mental Status Screening Mental status screening is an organized way to examine issues such as clients' thoughts, perceptions, their grasp of a socially accepted "reality," orientation to the present, memory, appearance, and suicidal/homicidal thoughts, tendencies, and potential. As with other screening functions (see Chapter 7), it allows you to determine if people have symptoms or behaviors that might require immediate attention, although the results of this screening will not provide enough evidence to make a final mental health diagnosis. There are three primary areas to look at during a mental status screening: potential mood disorders, anxiety disorders, and thought or personality disorders (Shea, 1998; Zuckerman, 2000). Each is briefly explained below.

Mood Disorders To adequately assess mood and the potential for mood disorders, look for signs of depression, mania, bipolar disorder, and suicidality. You can use one or more of the screening instruments discussed in Chapter 7 for depression, or you can ask individuals to rate their own level of depression. To do this, have people describe their current mood on a scale between "ten" (best they have ever felt, like a million bucks) to "one" (worst they ever felt, suicidal). Generally, on a scale such as this, if clients report their mood as a five or below, it could indicate double depression (dysthmia, described in the latest version of the *DSM*) and depression. Below three, screen immediately for suicidality. If you suspect clients may be depressed, ask the following questions:

- Have you ever felt down?
- If so, what kind of feelings did you have? (i.e., helpless, hopeless, and/or depressed)
- Have you lost interest or pleasure in things you usually enjoy?
- Have you lost your ability to concentrate?
- Have you felt physically down? (i.e., fatigue, headaches, digestive problems, sleeplessness, etc.)

It is also important to consider gender when screening for mood disorders. For example, substance abuse and depression are reported more frequently by women who suffered childhood sexual abuse. Moreover, the severity of the abuse is directly related to the severity of adult mental health problems in women (Mullen et al., 1993). Child abuse (emotional or physical) and neglect, along with domestic violence (Miller & Downs, 1993; Miller, Downs, Gondoli, & Keil, 1989), contributes directly to substance abuse and depression in women (Miller, Downs, & Testa, 1993; Morris & Bihan, 1991).

Be especially attuned to the possibility of suicide. Always inquire about any history of suicidal thoughts and/or attempts by clients, family members, or friends. It is especially important to ask adolescent clients about suicide by friends or classmates, because they are susceptible to cluster suicides (van Wormer, Wells, & Boes, 2000). Gain an understanding of people's suicide history, including what led to the attempt(s), the chosen methods, and what stopped them from succeeding. Ask clients to compare their current feelings about life to how they felt in the past when they attempted suicide. In Chapter 7, we discussed a number of ways to screen for suicidality. Always be prepared to screen for evidence of suicidal thoughts, plans, and the potential for action (Shea, 1999).

When looking for evidence of manic episodes, ask clients about racing thoughts, periods when they are unable to sleep or eat, and impulsivity, especially related to substance use, spending, and/or sexuality (Zuckerman, 2000). Clients will describe these periods differently, often in lay terms that require you to help clarify what they meant. Keep in mind that a manic episode—like a depressive one—is only a potential issue if your clients were not intoxicated when their behavior intensified. Cocaine, amphetamines, and/or Ecstasy produce manic episodes, making it easy to misdiagnose a mood disorder. If it appears that your clients have experienced a non-drug-induced manic episode, also look for evidence of bipolar disorder.

Anxiety Disorders   The main problems to look for here include evidence of social anxiety disorder, panic disorder, agoraphobia, and post-traumatic stress disorder (PTSD), especially in people who have experienced violence or sudden loss, seen military combat, witnessed death or destruction, and been abused (Shea, 1998). Additionally, generalized anxiety disorder (GAD) is a common condition often found in substance-abusing clients (Shea, 1999). People with GAD are pathological worriers (American Psychiatric Association, 1994). For example, are your clients "driven" to succeed, future-oriented and controlling, complaining of constant worrying? If so, this does not mean that they have an addictive personality (Chapter 3), but it could indicate that your clients use drugs to mediate the intensity of the worry associated with GAD and panic associated with other anxiety disorders.

Related to PTSD, besides uncovering evidence of violence, collect detailed information about people's sexual history, including any evidence of sexual abuse and rape. In cases where abuse occurred, also look for signs of potential dissociation by asking about periods when your clients lose track of time, experience headaches, and/or have periods of extended memory loss (that are not substance induced). Again, if it appears that your clients experience periods of dissociation, remember that the side effects of certain drugs help people to dissociate. Simply because people have been abused and use drugs to dissociate (forget, escape, and cope) does not mean that they will experience dissociative symptoms when sober.

In addition to sexual history, also be prepared to discuss people's sexual orientation. This subject is one that some people would rather not discuss. To be competent and ethical, you must grow comfortable with your feelings about homosexuality, bisexuality, and gender transformation (see Chapter 11). If you find this difficult or are unwilling to address any negative feelings, seek immediate help from your supervisor or make arrangements to refer the client to another practitioner.

As part of a substance abuse assessment, it is important to explore sexual orientation because of its potential relationship to psychological and emotional well-being (van Wormer, Wells, & Boes, 2000), especially with regard to people's "out" status with friends, family, and colleagues. Substance abuse, chemical dependency, depression, and suicide are commonplace in gay and lesbian communities (Remafedi, Farrow, & Deisher, 1991). In fact, gay and lesbian teens are two to three times more likely to attempt and commit suicide than other youths

(Gibson, 1989). According to van Wormer, Wells, and Boes (2000), substance abuse, while being a commonly used method for gay, lesbian, bisexual, or transgendered (GLBT) persons to cope with a hostile social environment, also increases the potential for suicide (see Chapter 11 for treatment considerations).

Thought Disorders   Thought disorders are clinically defined as a flow of thought that may be haphazard, purposeless, illogical, apparently confused, incorrect, abrupt, and bizarre (American Psychiatric Association, 2000). These disorders are most frequently found in clients diagnosed with schizophrenia and/or organic brain damage. Five of the basic thought disorders are briefly described below to help you understand the various terms and their meanings when you find them on an agency's mental health screening form.

Thought disturbances include frequent and patterned deviations from rational, logical, or goal-directed thought. Hallucinations and delusions are the most common thought disturbances. Hallucinations are an apparent perception of an external object when no corresponding external object exists. These perceptions can be auditory, visual, tactile (touch), olfactory (smell), or gustatory (taste). Delusions are a false belief that arises without appropriate external stimulation and remains unshaken and fixed in the face of contradictory evidence. Do not forget to consider culture as part of this equation. What a European American social worker considers "rational and logical" may not mesh with what a recent immigrant believes, and goal-directed thought is not given as much weight in all cultures as it is given within the majority culture of the United States.

Disturbances in stream of thought are disruptions in the manner and rate of associations made in thinking. Some of the most common forms include blocking (sudden stop in the flow of thought or speech), intellectualization (brooding or anxious pondering about abstract, theoretical, or philosophical issues), tangential thinking (the goal of thought is never reached), perseveration (involuntary repetition of a specific goal or idea), incoherence (disorderly thinking), and flight of ideas (continuous, high-speed, and illogical flow of speech characteristic of manic episodes).

Additionally, look for potential thought and personality issues that existed before people began using drugs. Research evidence suggests that there may be certain cognitive-perceptual issues, beginning in early childhood, that are related to later onset of chemical dependency. For example, hyperactivity, poor impulse control, and antisocial behavior are considered childhood precursors of addictive substance use later in life (Barth, 2001; Goodwin, 1976; Kinney & Leaton, 1991; Mannuzza et al., 1993). While researchers are unable to determine the extent that these cognitive patterns relate to addictive behavior, it seems likely that clients with these problems could resort to self-medication with alcohol and other drugs as a way to cope.

Similarly, be alert for evidence of psychosis, including distorted thinking, delusions, hallucinations, and paranoid thoughts. If these issues are present, make sure your assessment is preliminary, because many of the desired side effects of drugs mimic the symptoms of thought disorders. Certain drugs are designed to cause delusions, hallucinations, and paranoia. As such, delay your commitment to a diagnosis—even if other professionals made the diagnosis previously—to ensure that people's symptoms are not drug-induced. The fact that a psychiatrist or social worker previously made a particular diagnosis does not necessarily mean it is correct.

Obsessive-compulsive disorder (OCD) is another common mental health problem among substance-abusing clients (Kuhn, Swartzwelder, & Wilson, 1998). The American Psychiatric Association (2000) states that more than 11 percent of the general population experiences OCD. This disorder is characterized by patterns of perfectionism, inflexibility, and repetitive thoughts and actions aimed at preventing or reducing distress, anxiety, or avoiding some dreaded event or situation. Symptoms include recurring thoughts, frequent hand washing, counting, checking, hoarding, physical behavior resembling tics, frequent thoughts about violence or sexual behavior, or constant praying and/or repeating words or phrases silently. The person experiencing OCD feels driven or compelled to carry out their particular obsession or compulsion (American Psychiatric Association, 1994). Again, if you suspect the possibility of OCD co-occurring with substance abuse, make sure any diagnosis is preliminary, or classified as a provisional diagnosis.

Before rushing to diagnose thought disorders, look for patterns of behavior. That is, clients should demonstrate their symptoms more than once, and in more than one way. For example, if people forget their thoughts in the middle of a sentence (as many of us do from time to time), make sure it is a pattern before deciding that they might be blocking thoughts. Although confusion of thought and thought disorders may indicate severe mental problems, take care when assessing these disorders. As stated above, some symptoms may be drug-induced, while others could reflect cultural differences between client and social worker. Instead of a thought disorder, could you possibly have misunderstood what your client's words, thoughts, and behaviors mean? While it has been said before, be careful, have patience, and seek consultation with your supervisor or experienced social workers when assessing these disorders. Remember that whatever you put down in writing on the final assessment report will follow a person for life, even if you were mistaken.

What to Look for   In this dimension, you will identify whether people have potential co-occurring disorders. Beyond making a simple substance abuse or mental health diagnosis, look for ways in which the disorders interact in daily life. For example, do you suspect that your clients use drugs to self-medicate? Make sure you screen for potential mental health issues, but do so in the context of patience and understanding, given that what may appear to be mental health disorders can easily be drug-induced. You can avoid costly mistakes by looking for symptoms that occur frequently, rather than one-time behaviors that, to the uneducated eye, could be mistaken for symptoms of mental health disorders. As is always the case during an assessment, if you suspect a serious mental health disturbance or if your clients are acting as if they may harm themselves or others, consult with your clinical supervisor and then make a referral to a licensed medical professional.

Key Questions When you have completed this dimension, you should be able to answer the following questions:

- What is your client's history of mental illness or other disorders, and how do these issues correspond with your client's substance use history in the context of his or her culture?

- Is there a family history of mental illness?

- Did your client present the potential for mood, anxiety, thought, or personality disorders during the mental health screening process, and if so, how do these symptoms correspond to the client's substance use?

- Is your client at risk for suicide? If so, what is his or her level of risk?

- Does your client currently take any prescribed medication for mental health issues, and if so, did you make a referral to a psychiatrist for a medication review?

- Is there anything in your client's presentation that requires an immediate referral for psychiatric services?

- What strengths and resources does your client exhibit with regard to this dimension?

Dimension 7: Family History and Structure

Since the importance of collecting a family history of substance use was covered in Dimension 3, the focus here is on the general history of family membership, relationships, and family functioning. As we discussed in Chapter 5, the family is the main unit of interaction, socialization, and learning. Its influence continues well beyond the time when a person emancipates and moves into the world. Ongoing family influence is especially common among substance abusers. In a landmark study about the efficacy of family therapy with adult opiate users, Stanton, Todd, and Associates (1982) discovered that adult opiate addicts maintain overly close emotional ties to their parents, even if the ties are not apparent. Others (Haley, 1976; Minuchin, 1974; Steinglass, 1980; Steinglass, Bennett, Wolin, & Reiss, 1987; and Kaufman, 1984) emphasize the importance of family relationships and interactions in substance abuse and chemical dependency. My clinical observations over the last 20 years support the centrality of family influence for chemically dependent clients of all ages.

There are many models of family therapy to help you organize your thinking about family structure and history (Price, 1996; Bowen, 1985; Madanes, 1981, 1984; Haley, 1976, 1980; de Shazer, 1985; Bergman, 1985; Berg & de Shazer, 1993; Minuchin, 1974; Minuchin & Fishman, 1981; O'Hanlon & Weiner-Davis, 1989; Palazzoli, Cirillo, Selvini, & Sorrentino, 1989; Whitaker & Keith, 1981). Whichever model, or combination of models, you choose to follow is not as relevant as the kind of information you collect before making final decisions about client problems, strengths, and needs.

For the purposes of a substance abuse assessment, in addition to whatever information your chosen model emphasizes, also collect information about family membership (who belongs to the family unit); demographics (marital status, residence, number of children, alive or deceased, along with dates of marriages, births, and deaths); mental and physical health; and relationships (Curtis, 1999;

Kaufman, 1984; Bepko & Krestan, 1985; Aponte & VanDeusen, 1981). Pertaining to relationships, learn about the quality of relationships, emotional and/or physical cutoffs, signs of unhealthy enmeshment, and so on. By using a method of interviewing called circular questioning, which is designed to elicit relationship information (Penn, 1982; Selvini, Boscolo, Cecchin, & Prata, 1980; Tomm, 1987), skilled interviewers can, by having family members respond to what other members say in the interview, quickly understand the many relationship patterns, subgroups, and coalitions that develop in families (Penn, 1982).

Style Tips for Circular Questioning

Circular questioning is a wonderful, time-tested approach to family interviewing. It allows skilled interviewers to quickly and powerfully assess family relationships. Below is a brief example of how circular questioning in a family interview might sound.

> *Social Worker:* John, what do you think your son's problems are?
>
> *John:* I think he's hooked on drugs!
>
> *Social Worker:* Sue, what do you think of your husband's opinion about your son's problems?
>
> *Sue:* I think he's wrong about that. I think Sonny is just too stressed about his work and he uses drugs to blow off steam. He's not hurting anybody.

> *Social Worker:* John, what do you think about what your wife just said?
>
> *John:* I think she's wrong! She's always protecting that worthless son of ours.

The next question, most likely, would be to ask Sonny for his opinion about what his parents just said about him. If the therapeutic relationship between the social worker and family is sound, he or she may even ask Sonny to comment on his parent's disagreement about the nature of his problems. Do they often disagree about him? If so, who usually wins? Then, the social worker would go back to the parents to get them to discuss Sonny's comments—and so on.

Advanced skill in circular questioning is an invaluable asset in family, individual, and group practice. You can use it with individuals as well as family groups. For example, you can ask your client to discuss what he believes his mother would say if she were there. In groups, the application should be obvious. How does one learn this skill? It is simple, really: practice. Think of any subject, and ask yourself as many questions as you can about the subject. Try to generate at least 20 different questions for every scenario . . . it can be done. Colleagues and I have spent hours asking each other 20 questions about almost anything. If you master this skill to the point that it becomes automatic, you will never find yourself "stuck" in session again.

Topic for Your Journal: Circular Questioning Exercise

Write down as many questions as you possibly can for the following topic that is often discussed during an assessment interview. Let's use our sample family (John, Sue, and Sonny) again.

You want to ask the family to explain why Sonny, at 25 years old, is chronically unemployed. Start now, and have fun with this exercise.

As we discussed in Chapter 5, you may want to frame family relationships into role configurations. Who, in the family, is the hero, scapegoat, lost child, and so on? Encourage families to participate in the process by having each label other family members according to their appointed role(s), giving examples of why they believe certain members fit certain role configurations. Circular questioning is an invaluable tool in this process.

Another area of interest during an assessment is the family's history of domestic violence, suicide, mental problems or illness, sexual abuse, and any other issues of relevance to clients (Johnson & Yanca, 2001). Clients, especially women (van Wormer, 1995), with a history of childhood sexual abuse or domestic violence tend to abuse substances; families with a history of violence and abuse (or, for that matter, ongoing abuse) also tend to have concurrent substance abuse issues (Mather & Lager, 2000). You should also be aware of potential children of alcoholics (COA) or codependency issues (Sher, 1991; Cermak, 1986; Norwood, 1985; Whitfield, 1984; Friel, Subby, & Friel, 1984) that may result from growing up and/or living in a substance-abusing or chemically dependent household.

It is important to grasp people's perceptions of their family, its members, and the influence of substance use, abuse, and/or chemical dependency on these beliefs and perceptions. People base their lives on their perceptions of people around them, what they believe the people around them think are their problems, severity of problems, and quality of relationships. Strive to get clients talking about their families, interrupting only to ask clarifying questions, or questions that elicit information about the quality and nature of relationships (Penn, 1982). Listen to their "story" as if you were listening to a family biography; look for the underlying stories, myths, beliefs, culture, messages, and hidden rules about conflict, emotions, support, and especially, substance use and abuse. Skilled interviewers encourage clients to tell stories, rather than expecting them to answer a series of "rapid-fire" questions designed to elicit the information needed to fill out assessment forms.

No matter how you choose to elicit family information, ultimately you should be able to compose a complete picture of where people fit in the scheme of multiple family relationships; whom they are close to, distant from, most similar to, most different from; and how people communicate. Moreover, gain a working understanding of the role that substance use, abuse, and chemical dependency plays in a particular family, and the relationship each member has to the issue (i.e., what function does substance use, abuse, and/or chemical dependency play in the family system?). Review our discussion in Chapter 5 of how substance abuse serves to keep families stable and intact at the expense of change and growth.

What to Look for How one looks at a family during a substance abuse assessment depends on which model or models of family therapy one is using. These family therapy models are often chosen because they are consistent with the cultural and personal perspectives of the social worker (McGoldrick, Preto, Hines, & Lee, 1991). For example, strategic and/or structural therapists using popular models developed by Haley (1976), Price (1996), Minuchin (1974), or Madanes

(1981) tend to see problems in families related to power imbalances between adult partners and children. Solution-focused therapists (Berg & Miller, 1994) believe families become stuck by focusing on their problems instead of realizing they already have the strengths to remedy the issues. Followers of Murray Bowen (1985) believe substance abuse problems, like all other problems of living, result from inappropriate cross-generational coalitions or unhealthy relationship patterns between, for example, parents and children, or single adults and their parents. What most of the seemingly endless models and theories of family therapy all have in common is a view that individual problems affect, and are affected by, relationships in people's families.

It is important to understand the nature of family relationships and how people fit into the patterns of relationships, including how substance abuse affects goodness-of-fit within the family. Your clients fit into their family relationship patterns, even if the fit is not apparent at first. As we discussed earlier, learn what roles people play in the context of their families, with whom in the family they are closest and most distant, and how people's substance abuse problems fit into the generational history of their families. For example, are your clients the first people in their families to have substance abuse problems, or are there long lines ahead of them? Think of the long term when assessing family information. Patterns involving relationships, attitudes, and behaviors often are transmitted horizontally and vertically across the generations. Rarely will you find contemporary behavior patterns by one family member that have not been preceded by others somewhere in the family system.

Genogram Preparation in Substance Abuse Assessment

I highly recommend constructing a three-generation genogram (McGoldrick & Gerson, 1985; Bowen, 1985), sometimes called a transgenerational diagram (Cermak, 1986), as a way to organize information gathering during the substance abuse assessment process. A genogram is a graphic illustration of a family system. It can be combined with an ecomap (Hartman, 1978) to include systemic relationships outside the family system. A genogram is easy to prepare, and it offers a holistic view of clients' family systems with an emphasis on relationships and patterns.

If you ask clients to participate in genogram construction, it can provide an absorbing activity to engage clients in their assessment process.

A marker board or large pad of paper and a set of colored markers are all you need to have family members drawing in their family history and revealing intimate details about family life and relationships during the process.

Comprehensive methods for constructing genograms are discussed in the literature (McGoldrick & Gerson, 1985; Bowen, 1985; Hartman, 1978), but you should try to develop your own system that includes information covering at least three generations (more, if necessary), encompassing extended kin and friends who play a significant role in the client's life now and have done so in the past.

The transgenerational transmission process may also signal the possibility that people's substance abuse problems have a genetic foundation. The problem with this concept is the fact that when people become convinced they are chemically dependent because of their genetic makeup, they may quickly come to believe their situation is hopeless, thus defeating the purpose of assessment and treatment. As we discussed at length in Chapter 3, genetic loading for chemical dependency has not been proven.

Substance abuse problems must be understood within the context of people's family systems. In discussing other dimensions, we will embed the individual and family into a wider context encompassing the local community and beyond. For now, the point is to learn to interview, assess, and interpret family information. I recommend that all clients, if possible, be interviewed with family members early and often during the assessment process.

Key Questions When you have completed this dimension, you should be able to answer the following questions:

- Did you complete a three-generation family genogram that includes information about demographics, membership, relationships, problems, strengths, and family structure (subsystems, boundaries, coalitions, etc.)?
- Do your clients fit within their family systems, and what types of boundaries exist between family members and between the family and outsiders? Do these patterns conform to, or deviate from, the family's cultural traditions?
- Is there any evidence of current or past abuse, and if so, how has it been addressed?
- How does the family handle (and at what cost to its members) the push and pull that occurs between long-term development and short-term stability?
- At what life cycle level is the family operating? How closely does it match the level at which it should be operating, and how much does it reflect the family's cultural traditions?
- What strengths and resources does your client exhibit with regard to this dimension?

Dimension 8: Community/Macro Context

As we discussed in Chapter 6, people live in communities of location (neighborhoods, cities, and rural or urban villages), identification (religion, culture, race, etc.), and affiliation (drug culture, professional, political/ideological, etc.), as well as the larger community (state, region, country, etc.). Helping clients to speak about the impact of their community contexts on their lives, choices, and lifestyles can be a difficult, yet enlightening endeavor.

Information in this dimension includes a description of people's living conditions, their neighborhoods, and their relationships with their communities and the people and institutions in these communities. You want to learn about people's unique interpretation of local cultures and the goodness-of-fit (or disconnect) with their cultures. Lastly, guide clients through a discussion of macro environmental influences including drug laws, policies, political mood, and public opinion and how these issues combine to affect their mindset and behavior.

Four sub-dimensions—culture, social class, social and relational life, and legal history and involvement—appropriately fit under the umbrella of the community/macro dimension. While each sub-dimension represents important areas of inquiry in its own right, it is also an important part of the wider community and macro context in which people live.

Local Community What should you learn about local communities during a substance abuse assessment? Begin by asking clients to describe their living conditions. Do they live in a house, apartment, or a shelter? Do they live alone, with family members, friends, or strangers? What is the atmosphere in their home, and what are their relationships with the people living there? Have your clients lived for a long time in their area, or are they relatively new? That is, how well do members of the local community know your clients, and what are the attitudes of these people towards them? The following case example illustrates why these questions are important.

CASE EXAMPLE The Man with a Bad Reputation

A former client was reported to Child Protective Services for allegedly physically abusing his seven-year-old son. During the first session, this man adamantly denied the allegations. After doing some interviewing about his community and history, I discovered some critical information that ultimately led to charges being dropped.

This particular man had lived in the same well-established neighborhood all of his life. After getting married, he purchased his family home and began raising his family in the same place where he was raised. As a youth, he had been viewed negatively by his family, the school system, and his neighbors. He was a substance abuser who was consistently in trouble for theft and, most notably, fighting. It seems that as a young man, my client possessed an explosive temper. His problems were well known by people in his local community, many of whom still either lived in the neighborhood or continued to teach in the local schools. In other words, he had a bad reputation.

However, by all accounts, over the years he had changed. He was no longer a troubled person with an explosive temper. He had grown into a calm and peaceful family man who worked hard and loved his family. The problem was that this information never seemed to reach the people in the community. They continued to view him as a troubled person with an explosive temper.

Therefore, when on a hot summer day he scolded his child in the front yard, picked him up abruptly, and carried him into the house in front of many neighbors, the stage was set for trouble. The next-door neighbor was a teacher at his son's school. Seeing the man scold his child (just like many parents) and believing that the man was a troubled person with an explosive temper, she called CPS based on his reputation rather than on the actual events that had occurred. In fact, the man did not abuse his son, but had appropriately, albeit loudly, disciplined the boy in an acceptable manner. The message of this incident is never to underestimate the value of information about your client's relationship to his immediate community.

After describing people's living conditions, broaden your view to include the surrounding environments. For example, does your client live in or around "drug houses"? Is the neighborhood safe or crime-ridden? Do others in the neighborhood take pride in their homes, or are the buildings run-down and the yards untended? Does your client's lifestyle fit with others in the community? Does your client live in the neighborhood "eyesore," or is the property maintained in accordance with neighborhood norms? Does your client feel supported through friendships, or are there few opportunities for social support? Does your client feel safe at night; can doors be left unlocked without fear of crime? Does your client interact with neighbors, or are people in the neighborhood isolated and protective? In a nutshell, what would it be like to live where your client lives?

Next, broaden your approach even further to the mezzo, or organizational, level. For example, what is the attitude of the local police toward your client's community? If it is a middle-class community, do the police and/or neighbors single your client out for negative attention? If it is a poorer community, will the police, fire department, or even pizza delivery operations respond to requests for service? Additionally, what community institutions and associations such as churches, block clubs, recreational outlets, stores, and other social outlets are available?

Related to systems of oppression and sense of belonging, are members of the community open, communicative, and accepting of difference; or closed, judgmental, and excluding toward people from your client's various communities of affiliation such as race, sexual orientation, class, and/or substance abusing lifestyle? This line of inquiry leads naturally into a discussion of people's culture.

Key Questions When you have completed this dimension, you should be able to answer the following questions:

- Do you have a complete picture of your client's local environment, in terms of location, conditions, social relationships, safety, and resources?

- What are the client's opinions about her or his environment, and what is the goodness-of-fit between your client and the local community? Does your client conform to the local environment, or is he or she seen as being different or odd, and why?

- How does your client interpret feedback from the local environments in terms of self, and a definition of self in comparison to others?

- What strengths and resources does your client exhibit with regard to this dimension?

Sub-Dimension 1: Cultural Context   Learning about cultural nuances is important in substance abuse assessment, treatment planning, and treatment (Lum, 1999). According to Pinderhughes (1989), there is no such thing as culture-free service delivery. Cultural differences between clients and social workers in terms of values, norms, beliefs, attitudes, lifestyles, and life opportunities affect every aspect of practice.

Many different concepts of culture are used in social work, sociology, and anthropology. Smelser (1992) considers culture a "system of patterned values, meanings, and beliefs that give cognitive structure to the world, provide a basis for coordinating and controlling human interactions, and constitute a link as the system is transmitted from one generation to another" (p. 11). Geertz (1973) regarded culture as simultaneously a product of and a guide to people searching for organized categories and interpretations that provide a meaningful experiential link to their social life. Building upon these two ideas, in this book we abide by the following definition of culture, borrowed from the Birmingham School (Willis, 1978), that I proposed elsewhere (Johnson, 2000):

> Culture is historical, bound up in traditions and practices passed through generations; memories of events—real or imagined—that define a people and their worldview. (Culture) is viewed as collective subjectivity, or a way of life adopted by a community that ultimately defines their worldview (p. 121).

Consistent with this definition, the collective subjectivity called culture is a pervasive force in the way people interact, believe, think, feel, and act in their social world. As we discussed in Chapter 6, culture plays a significant role in shaping how people view the world. As a historical force built—in part—upon ideas, definitions, and events passed through generations, culture also defines people's level of social acceptance by the wider community; shapes how they live, think, and act; and influences how they perceive others feel about them and how they view the world and their place in it. Thus, it is impossible to claim understanding in a client relationship without grasping your client's cultural foundations.

Helping clients discuss their attitudes, beliefs, and behaviors pertaining to substance use, abuse, and/or chemical dependency in the context of their culture—including their religious or spiritual belief systems—offers valuable information about their worldview, sense of social and spiritual connection, and/or practical involvement in their social world. Moreover, establishing connections between their culture and their substance-abusing lifestyle provides vital clues about people's belief systems, attitudes, expectations, and reasons for certain behaviors that cannot be understood outside the context of their culture.

Because many of us remember to ask about culture when clients are obviously different (i.e., different races, countries of origin, etc.), we often ignore difference with clients we wrongly consider to have the same cultural background that we do. For example, the search for differences between European Americans with Christian beliefs—if the social worker shares these characteristics—gets lost in mutual assumptions, based on the misguided belief that there is no difference that is important in their lives. The same is often true in many professional relationships where clients and social workers appear to have the same racial, cultural, or lifestyle foundations. You should always be interested in human differences, whether these differences are readily apparent or not. Work equally hard to understand the culture of people who appear similar to you as you would with people who are obviously from a different cultural, racial, ethnic, or religious background.

To examine culture is to take a comprehensive look into people's worldviews—to discover what they believe about the world and their places in it. It goes beyond race and ethnicity (although these are important issues) into how culture determines thoughts, feelings, and behaviors in daily life. This includes what culture says about substance use, abuse, and dependency; the impact of gender on these issues; and what it means to seek professional help (Appleby, Colon, & Hamilton, 2001; Leigh, 1998).

The larger questions to be answered are how clients interpret their culture; how the beliefs, attitudes, and behaviors are shaped by that interpretation; and how these cultural beliefs and practices affect daily life and determine lifestyle in the context of the larger community. Additionally, based on their cultural membership, beliefs, and practices, what are the potential and real barriers faced by your clients in the world? For many of our clients, the fact that they are part of non-majority cultures exposes them to issues generated by social systems of oppression such as racism, sexism, homophobia, and ethnocentrism.

Key Questions When you have completed this dimension, you should be able to answer the following questions:

- What are the different cultural communities (including religious and/or spiritual practices) that your client affiliates with, and how does your client interpret and practice cultural norms, practices, and behaviors in daily life?
- What does your client's culture and his or her own unique interpretation of culture say about substance use, abuse, or chemical dependency, its origins, help-seeking, and potential for change?
- How does your client fit within the larger culture of family, neighborhood, and community, and to what extent has she or he adopted the beliefs of the local drug subculture?
- What is your client's experience (including his or her family) with larger systems of oppression based on race, culture, ethnicity, gender, sexual orientation, or behavior?
- What strengths and resources does your client exhibit with regard to this dimension?

Sub-Dimension 2: Social Class Information about people's social class is directly related to information about their families, the goodness-of-fit between the person and environment, and the strengths, resources, and/or barriers in their communities. Social work practitioners and authors often overlook, gloss over, or ignore the impact of social class on people's problems and prospects for successful treatment. However, practitioners with a multi-systemic approach look upon social class as a potent social force to investigate (Mantsios, 1995). In fact, many believe that no other demographic factor explains so extensively the differences between people and/or groups (Lipsitz, 1997; Davis & Proctor, 1989). Among the many factors involved are social systems of domination and oppression in the United States (Appleby, Colon, & Hamilton, 2001).

In this text, social class represents a combination of income, education, occupation, prestige, and community, and it encompasses how these factors affect people's relative wealth and access to power (Boudon & Bourricaud, 1989). Where people fit into the social class system largely determines the effect various systems, policies, and laws have on their lives and their potential for advancement in society. Social class is "a position a person occupies within a (social) hierarchy" (Appleby, Colon, & Hamilton, 2001, p. 27). It shapes people's worldviews and prospects for self-determination.

To assess the impact of social class, gather information about income and income sources (i.e., job, professional position, welfare, or other nontraditional

sources, including illegal sources of income such as drug dealing and prostitution). Employment status can affect people's participation in an assessment and
treatment process, as well as help create a condition that adds to substance use
and/or abuse problems. For example, clients who are unemployed or lack job
skills or prospects may feel that they have nothing to strive for in their lives. Similarly, clients who are dissatisfied with their work or who demonstrate an unstable work history may be equally at risk for substance abuse (Denning, 2000).

Because future successes or failures rest heavily on people's ability to find
meaningful sources of income, assessing vocational skills is important. For clients
with regular employment histories, this task is simple and straightforward. It is
much more difficult when working with clients who lack work histories or have
earned most of their income from menial labor or illegal sources. In addition to
taking an employment history, also inquire about overall job-related skills, previous training, interests, and information pertaining to people's attitudes about
work. For those with spotty job histories, what competencies do they have that
could be useful for future employment or training? Do not forget to inquire
about military experience and/or job training programs completed while serving
time in jail or prison.

Do not overlook illegal activities—primarily drug selling—when searching
for vocational competencies. Drug dealers are not incompetent. They acquire
marketing, selling, and financial management skills to rival many in the legal
business world. Therefore, when assessing future potential you must work with
the skills, experience, and knowledge that clients bring to the assessment. If illegal activity is their only work experience, it would be a disservice to ignore skills
that might transfer into legal employment opportunities. If you object to this
idea, search your own attitude to see if you can discover why you believe it is
inconceivable that former criminals have marketable skills.

Transportation is another overlooked but important area to explore during an
assessment. In the United States, access to private transportation is so pervasive
that many people assume that everyone has an automobile and the resources to
keep it fueled and insured, but this is not the case. Moreover, do not falsely assume that safe, affordable, and reliable public transportation is available when it is
needed. For example, where I live, public transportation only operates until
6 p.m., meaning that people without a vehicle cannot work second or third shift
jobs unless they are willing to walk several miles to and from their jobs. The focus
of this investigation is on people's abilities to move about freely. Does your client
have a driver's license and/or a vehicle that operates? Can he or she move around
by bus, taxi, train, or bicycle? Many people without adequate transportation are
reluctant to discuss this topic, so you will have to ask. Again, depending upon
their answers to these questions, explore with people how a lack of transporta
tion contributes to their struggles.

You should also explore people's educational history, including information
about formal education, adult education, job training, and future plans for acquiring additional training. Be sure to spend time exploring people's attitudes,
experiences, and beliefs about their educational experiences. If clients have
dropped out of school or found education demeaning or difficult, explore their

reasons. Discover what values clients place on education and training. Additionally, include exercises (reading and writing) to determine their basic literacy skills. People suffering the pains of illiteracy become highly skilled at covering their inabilities. For example, one former client covered up his inability to read by asking others to read menus because he always seemed to forgot his glasses. Do not assume that people possess basic reading and writing skills simply because they are actively progressing in school or have even graduated from high school.

> We had a 17-year-old, African American male client in one of our programs who was a junior in high school. His semester grade reports stated that he was an average student, receiving a "C" average in most of his subjects. Soon after admission to the program for substance abuse and drug selling, we discovered that not only could he not read, but he was unable to write. This young man was illiterate. In a meeting with the school, we were informed that he was a "social promotion"; in other words, he had been passed to the next higher grade each year to keep him with peers of his own age and developmental level. The school never considered providing a tutor. After learning about this young man's situation, we developed a voluntary reading program that he participated in for the next 12 months, long after he had been successfully discharged from the program.

Another area to investigate is which, if any, social systems clients and families interact with regularly, such as child welfare, the courts, and foster care. From a person-in-environment approach (Germain & Gitterman, 1996; Karls & Wandrei, 1994a, 1994b), you must understand the role of various systems in people's lives and any social stigmas that tend to be associated with involvement in these systems. Look into the barriers and strengths associate with each system. Preparing an ecomap (Hartman, 1978) may be helpful in organizing this information.

Equally important are people's perceptions of their "place" in the world. How do your clients perceive their strengths and abilities in relation to others? Do they "measure up" to the expectations of significant others and their own dreams? Do they aspire to a different lifestyle, or are they satisfied with their present situation? Is their substance-abusing lifestyle compatible with the class position of their family of origin, or is it different? What do their families and/or significant others think about their lives? As in other dimensions, the specific details of income, education, etc., are not nearly as important as how clients view, perceive, or feel about themselves in comparison to others in their life and community. These issues determine goodness-of-fit between persons and their social environment.

Social class issues usually surface in the areas of life discussed above, leading clients to lose hope or simply resign themselves to their present circumstances. The class system is a pervasive force in life; when integrated into a person's worldview, it can lead one to believe that life is as good as it can be expected to get. Negative labels originating from the community, family, and/or the larger social system can become a "self-fulfilling prophecy," turning social and personal barriers into immovable forces that cannot be challenged, overcome, or sidestepped along the way to a different life. Do not underestimate the power of negative labels in the lives of your clients.

Key Questions When you have completed this dimension, you should be able to answer the following questions:

- With what social class level do your clients identify, and how does this compare to the social class positioning of their family, neighborhood, and community?

- What systems of oppression have your clients and their families confronted in their lives?

- What pressures do your clients feel and/or experience related to this dimension, and what is their experience with work, education, and other vehicles for improving one's position in the community?

- How do your clients make a living? Consider both legal and illegal sources of income.

- What strengths and resources does your client exhibit with regard to this dimension?

Sub-Dimension 3: Social-Relational Because human beings are social creatures who define themselves in relation to others (see Chapter 6), it is necessary to know something about people's ability to relate to others in their social environment. Are your clients capable of forming lasting relationships? Do they have close friends? Are close friendships even possible for them? How do they relate to others in group situations? Related specifically to substance abuse behavior, are your clients easily influenced by others, or are they independent thinkers? These are just some of the relationship issues that are important to understand during an assessment.

While inquiring about relationships, ask about loved ones (family and intimate relationships), friends, peers/supervisors in their work or school settings, and relationships with members of the same and opposite sex. Ask whether they prefer being in a one-on-one relationship or having groups of friends. In addition to knowing what types of relationships people maintain, you also want to explore the depth and quality of relationships and their feelings and attitudes about intimacy and closeness. Moreover, it is important to know if there have been changes in your client's social life since substance use escalated, especially related to intimate partners and long-term close friends. If people are moving toward chemical dependency, this progression often precludes them from maintaining close and intimate relationships with anyone who does not participate in their chemically dependent lifestyle.

Many people with substance abuse problems have difficulty forming and maintaining interpersonal relationships (Janzen & Harris, 1997). While clients may assert that their relationships are good, this claim is often untrue. For example, clients may make unreasonable demands on close friends; display explosive and unpredictable tempers; demand significant attention and support; refuse to accept critical feedback or confrontation without becoming aggressive; and have a history of "using" people to get their needs met—emotionally, sexually, and/or financially.

Some clients may have never experienced a meaningful interpersonal relationship. They may be loners who feel they neither need nor want interpersonal closeness, or they cannot seem to find and keep close relationships. These clients usually establish a pattern of rejecting people before they can be rejected. They are mistrusting and defensive, living by the creed that "I cannot befriend anyone stupid enough to have me as a friend." These clients will most often present as antagonistic in the assessment and/or practice setting, approaching you in the same defensive way that they approach others.

Some of your clients may not have shown signs of substance use or abuse until they joined certain social circles. If this is true, exploring relationship history may reveal a difficulty establishing close friendships until they were "accepted" by groups that center their lives around using and abusing substances. Perhaps they have come to believe that they are more "likable" or "sexy" when intoxicated. In people's minds, substance use and abuse can offer practical benefits in social circles. The same holds true for people's participation in recreational activities. It is common to learn that clients have given up all forms of healthy recreation in favor of substance-related activities. As the assessing social worker, work to understand patterns and trends. Have these changes—if they exist—occurred slowly and gradually, or was there a sudden change of lifestyle? How do your clients explain the fact that they have abandoned activities and associations they once enjoyed?

Key Questions When you have completed this dimension, you should be able to answer the following questions:

- How do your clients handle personal relationships with family, friends, and other associates? Do they have close, intimate relationships with others?

- Have there been changes in clients' relationship activities or recreational pursuits over time, and to what extent do these changes (if they exist) reflect their substance use history?

- What is their history and perspective about intimate relationships? How do they handle sexual relationships?

- What strengths and resources does your client exhibit with regard to this dimension?

Sub-Dimension 4: Legal History and Involvement In this dimension, you will explore people's legal history, including any information pertaining to arrests, convictions, the nature of their offenses, and punishments imposed on them. Do not focus only on offenses that are obviously drug-related, such as possession, selling, or drunken driving. Ask for a complete legal history, trying to make the connections, if they exist, between people's substance use, abuse, and involvement with the legal system.

Additionally, inquire about the legal involvement of family members and friends. This information can help you understand the social and cultural influences on their attitudes about the legal system and on being part of the legal system. Sometimes realizing that people, in their immediate social environments, have legal histories explains why certain clients do not seem to care about being arrested and/or spending time in jail or prison. In addition to providing clues about the individual's belief in the norms, values, and laws of our society, exploring a legal history in the context of people's family and social environment also lets you know about the degree to which criminal behavior is sanctioned in their world. It is difficult to convince people not to break the law if this behavior is sanctioned by those closest to them.

As in other dimensions, go beyond asking about the specifics of your clients' legal involvement and delve into their feelings, attitudes, and beliefs about themselves, their place in the world, and how multiple brushes with the law fit into their overall worldview. Do they feel that there are times when, despite social and moral sanctions against such behavior, illegal activity is justifiable? I am not speaking here about the most obvious cases of justifiable lawbreaking, such as killing in self-defense. Instead, try to find out whether clients believe there are circumstances that make it justifiable for a person to engage in activities such as prostitution, drug selling, or robbery. To increase your ability to understand your clients, write your own response to this question in your substance abuse journal.

In a strictly legal and moral sense, perhaps these acts cannot be justified. However, if these questions are placed within a broader social context that includes systems of oppression, the answers may change. For example, in one of our programs targeted at adolescent cocaine-sellers, we came to see these young offenders as entrepreneurs. They were doing the best they could, given their lowly place in the social hierarchy, to capture their slice of the so-called "American Dream." All of the clients in this program were African American or Latino males, from extremely low-income families. Most had been removed from school and had no family history of academic, social, or economic success to pattern their lives after. Given these characteristics and the traditional systems of oppression that have historically limited mainstream opportunities for many people, was their drug selling justifiable? Is their behavior not similar to others trying to make a worthwhile living by legal means?

Now, I am not recommending that you approve of illegal activities. We did not imply, state, or hint to the youths that selling crack cocaine was acceptable. In fact, our stance was just the opposite. However, to simply ignore the harsh realities imposed by systems of oppression and the broader social, economic, and political structure would have prevented us from understanding the attitudes, beliefs, and perspectives of our clients and the world they experienced every day. Again, as we discussed earlier, content (illegal acts) is not as important as process (working to understand a client's perspective) during assessment.

Key Questions When you have completed this dimension, you should be able to answer the following questions:

- What is your client's (including family and peer group) history of involvement with the criminal justice system, and what are her or his opinions about this in terms of self-identity?

- In what ways do national, state, or local drug laws and policies influence your client's present circumstances?

- What reasons, excuses, or explanations does your client give for problems with the legal system?

- What strengths and resources does your client exhibit with regard to this dimension?

What to Look for Pertaining to the community/macro dimension, seek answers to the broad question, "How do people see themselves in relation to their local community?" Do they believe that they "fit in," or do they sense—and respond to—being perceived as an outsider, or different from others? Each of the sub-dimensions (local community, culture, social class, social-relational, macro environment, and legal history) can yield answers to this question for each client. Asking clients to explain their responses by giving specific examples is often more critical than how they answer the original question. For example, if clients feel outside the mainstream, the reasons for this feeling will be found in their answers across the sub-dimensions, leading to a picture of what they think they should be like, and what, in fact, they perceive themselves to be in comparison to others.

Dimension 9: Motivation

In Chapter 4, we discussed the stages of motivation adopted from the transtheoretical model (Connors, Donovan, & DiClemente, 2001). Where people fit into the stages (precontemplation, contemplation, determination, action, maintenance, and relapse) offers clues about their level of motivation and how you should approach them during assessment and/or treatment. Take a few moments to review the discussion in Chapter 4 to refresh your memory about the specific indicators associated with the various stages of motivation.

Accurately assessing people's motivational levels is central to the substance abuse assessment process. Not only does it provide essential information, but it also informs you about the most effective approach to take during the assessment. Clients in the precontemplation stage should be approached differently from clients in the contemplation, determination, action, maintenance, or relapse stages. In all stages, you will need to concentrate on the quality of your relationship with your clients, especially those who present in the precontemplation and contemplation stages, if you intend to be successful in any substance abuse assessment or treatment processes.

Key Questions When you have completed this dimension, you should be able to answer the following questions:

- What was your client's level of motivation at the beginning of the assessment process, and on what criteria did you base this conclusion?
- What is your assessment of the client's level of motivation at the end of the assessment process, and on what criteria did you base this decision?
- Is there anything in your client's history and/or previous involvement with professional helpers that might explain his or her current level of motivation?
- What strengths and resources does your client exhibit with regard to this dimension?

Dimension 10: Diagnosis

Most clinical settings use the *Diagnostic and Statistical Manual of Mental Disorders* (*DSM*) (American Psychiatric Association, 1994, 2000) for codifying and labeling clinical diagnoses. The most recent version of the *DSM* (*DSM-IV-TR*) (American Psychiatric Association, 2000) is a revision of the *DSM-IV* (American Psychiatric Association, 1994). While additional codifying schemes are used for diagnosis (Karls & Wandrei, 1988, 1994a, 1994b; Appleby, Colon, & Hamilton, 2001), the *DSM* process is the most widely used format. Because of its prevalence and wide acceptance by practitioners, agencies, and funding sources, in this text we focus on its use as the primary mechanism for establishing a diagnosis.

The Person-in-Environment (PIE) assessment system (Karls & Wandrei, 1994b) was developed within the social work field in response to the medical orientation of the *DSM* process (Appleby, Colon, & Hamilton, 2001). It addresses the social work profession's unique need to integrate and understand the interrelationship between persons and their environment. While some believe that this system will be used extensively by social workers in the future (Appleby, Colon, & Hamilton, 2001), at present it is not. Therefore, because use of the PIE system has been slow to gain acceptance in the field, interested readers should investigate the efficacy of this process as outside reading.

Our discussion in these pages will not provide comprehensive training in *DSM* diagnostics. Here, we simply introduce you to the process, offering specific definitions and diagnostic criteria so that the information gathered during an assessment can be integrated into a usable, functional diagnosis of problems and conditions. It is clear that anyone intending to work in a clinical setting should become familiar with the *DSM* manual, including the initial chapters on the appropriate use of the system and how to record diagnoses appropriately. At the same time, I advise you to investigate other writings critical of the *DSM* system (Kirk & Kutchins, 1992; Appleby, Colon, & Hamilton, 2001) to ensure a well-rounded understanding of its efficacy and limitations in social work practice.

As mentioned earlier, diagnostic codes are just one aspect of the overall substance abuse assessment. These codes are by no means the be-all and end-all of client assessment, treatment planning, and treatment. In fact, these codes are used mainly to provide uniform terminology and to simplify record keeping (American Psychiatric Association, 2000). Use of diagnostic codes also benefits social workers and clients by facilitating third-party reimbursement. As a practical matter, use of the *DSM* diagnostic system is the primary way that social workers receive reimbursement and clients receive (ideally) the benefits from treatment services.

Despite the above caveats, many social workers and other professionals focus on the static event called a diagnosis, rather than the process for collecting the information needed to make a diagnosis useful. Diagnosis is not an end in itself, but the culmination of a process of client engagement leading to either treatment or successful referral for treatment. Think of a diagnosis as a snapshot of the client's condition at the moment of diagnosis. Instead of using it as a label that hangs like a two-ton weight around people's necks, it should be treated as one part of the overall assessment to determine what services people need at this moment in their lives. Given too much weight, *DSM* diagnoses can do more harm than good.

The Diagnostic Process   Figures 8.1 and 8.2 give the *DSM-IV-TR* diagnostic criteria for substance abuse and substance dependence. Study these criteria closely to learn the differences between the two, and compare the *DSM-IV-TR* diagnostic criteria to the definitions given of use, abuse, and addiction back in Chapter 1. Substance abuse is characterized by recurrent use leading to negative life consequences, while substance dependence does fit the definition of someone with a more pervasive pattern of substance abuse behavior.

You should know that the criteria listed in Figures 8.1 and 8.2 are general. In the *DSM,* the various drug categories discussed in Chapter 2, along with certain specific drugs in each category, have their own coding system specific to that particular category or drug. While the overall criteria for abuse and dependence are the same for each different drug and drug category, there are some differences. Where these occur, it is clearly noted in the *DSM.* Take the time to familiarize yourself with the chapter on substance use disorders in the *DSM.*

There are important qualitative differences between behaviors that qualify as substance abuse and those that qualify as substance dependence. The dosage people use or for how long they have used do not play a significant role in the differences between the two classifications. In fact, amounts used are not defined in either category. Therefore, a focus on how much people use, unless the dosage leads to medical problems (i.e., withdrawal), is irrelevant in this diagnostic scheme. If the difference does not involve quantity, how do we distinguish between substance abuse and substance dependence?

The major differences between the two diagnostic classifications are the addition of potential tolerance build-up (criteria 1 and 3), withdrawal (criterion 2),

---

A. A maladaptive pattern of substance use, leading to clinically significant impairment or distress, as manifested by one (or more) of the following, occurring within a 12-month period:
  (1) recurrent substance use resulting in a failure to fulfill major role obligations at work, school, or home (e.g., repeated absences or poor work performance related to substance use; substance-related absences, suspensions, or expulsions from school; neglect of children or household)
  (2) recurrent substance use in situations in which it is physically hazardous (e.g., driving an automobile or operating a machine when impaired by substance use)
  (3) recurrent substance-related legal problems (e.g., arrests for substance-related disorderly conduct)
  (4) continued substance use despite having persistent or recurrent social or interpersonal problems caused or exacerbated by the effects of the substance (e.g., arguments with spouse about consequences of intoxication, physical fights)
B. The symptoms have never met the criteria for Substance Dependence for this class of substance.

Source: Reprinted with permission from the *Diagnostic and Statistical Manual of Mental Disorders*, Fourth Edition, Text Revision. Copyright 2000 American Psychiatric Association.

FIGURE 8.1 *DSM-IV-TR* Diagnostic Criteria for Substance Abuse

A maladaptive pattern of substance use, leading to clinically significant impairment or distress, as manifested by three (or more) of the following, occurring at any time in the same 12-month period:

(1) tolerance, as defined by either of the following:
    (a) a need for markedly increased amounts of the substance to achieve intoxication or desired effect;
    (b) markedly diminished effect with continued use of the same amount of the substance.

(2) withdrawal, as manifested by either of the following:
    (a) the characteristic withdrawal syndrome for the substance;
    (b) the same (or closely related) substance is taken to relieve or avoid withdrawal symptoms.

(3) the substance is often taken in larger amounts or over a longer period than was intended.

(4) there is a persistent desire or unsuccessful efforts to cut down or control substance use.

(5) a great deal of time is spent in activities necessary to obtain the substance (e.g., visiting multiple doctors or driving long distances), use the substance (e.g., chain-smoking), or recover from its effects.

(6) important social, occupational, or recreational activities are given up or reduced because of substance use.

(7) the substance use is continued despite knowledge of having a persistent or recurrent physical or psychological problem that is likely to have been caused or exacerbated by the substance (e.g., current cocaine use despite recognition of cocaine-induced depression, or continued drinking despite recognition that an ulcer was made worse by alcohol consumption).

Source: Reprinted with permission from the *Diagnostic and Statistical Manual of Mental Disorders*, Fourth Edition, Text Revision. Copyright 2000 American Psychiatric Association.

FIGURE 8.2 *DSM-IV-TR* Diagnostic Criteria for Substance Dependence

loss of control (criteria 3 and 4), and lifestyle (criterion 5) as characteristics of substance dependence (see Figure 8.2). As we discussed in Chapter 1, chemical dependency involves, to one degree or another, each of these criteria.

In Figure 8.1, note that a diagnosis of substance abuse involves the potential for more short-term and sporadic negative life consequences. For example, according to *DSM-IV-TR,* a diagnosis of substance abuse relates more to social functioning than lifestyle. In Figure 8.1, criterion 1 pertains to major role obligations, criterion 2 to physical danger, criterion 3 to legal problems, and criterion 4 to continued use despite negative life consequences. There is no reference to loss of control, tolerance, or cravings. In fact, as the definition in Chapter 1 states, people who fit the diagnostic criteria for substance abuse are neither "addicted" nor are they destined to become addicts, even if they continue to use substances in the future.

There is another interesting difference between the two diagnostic classifications. This difference involves how the authors describe certain criteria in the *DSM-IV-TR* text. Notice that the authors use a number of adolescent-related examples to describe substance abuse and none to describe substance dependence. This distinction suggests, beyond the fact that the authors may believe that more adolescents are substance abusers than chemically dependent, the significant qualitative differences between the two classifications. That is, when you find clients who fit the criteria for substance dependence, there should be no doubt about its presence. You should not be left wondering if people fit the criteria—it should be clear. If you are uncertain, it means that they probably fit the criteria for substance abuse, you did not collect enough information, or you collected the wrong information to make an appropriate diagnosis.

Multiaxial Assessment Using *DSM*   Most social service agencies require social workers to know and use a "multiaxial assessment" format (American Psychiatric Association, 2000, p. 27). The multiaxial assessment process requires social workers to assess their clients on several axes (or areas). Each of the five axes refers to a different dimension of the client's life (see Figure 8.3). The multiaxial diagnostic process is demonstrated in the Sample Case History Report contained in Appendix B.

Axis I is the place to list people's presenting problems. These are usually the primary issues to be worked on during any course of treatment. Axis II comprises any personality disorders or other chronic, pervasive issues (i.e., mental retardation) that are present. These issues usually underlie the problems listed on Axis I.

Axis III is reserved for the identification of any medical issues that may be relevant and instrumental in people's Axis I problems. This is the place to note potential withdrawal illnesses and other medical concerns related to substance use.

Axes IV and V are the *DSM* system's attempt to incorporate the social and environmental aspects of people's present conditions. On Axis IV, any social or environmental issues are coded and listed that are directly or indirectly part of people's Axis I or II diagnoses. Axis V consists of your estimation of the client's Global Assessment Function, or GAF score. Here, the ability to function in daily life is estimated along a continuum from so-called "normal" to an inability to function. Global Assessment Function is assigned a numeric label that can have a lasting impact on people's lives; for example, this label can determine whether people receive treatment in outpatient or inpatient settings.

In this discussion, we focus on Axis I disorders because this is where you classify substance use and most co-occurring mental health problems. No doubt you have had (or will have) clients with diagnosed Axis II disorders. However, since our charge in this book is to consider substance abuse and, to a lesser extent, co-occurring mental health disorders, it is beyond our scope to provide a complete training in multiaxial diagnostics related to Axis II. Therefore, the discussion that

Axis I:	Clinical disorders and other conditions that may be a focus of clinical attention
Axis II:	Personality disorders and mental retardation
Axis III:	General medical conditions
Axis IV:	Psychosocial and environmental problems
Axis V:	Global assessment of functioning (GAF score)

Source: Reprinted with permission from the *Diagnostic and Statistical Manual of Mental Disorders*, Fourth Edition, Text Revision. Copyright 2000 American Psychiatric Association.

FIGURE 8.3 Five Axes of *DSM* Diagnostics

follows is a "short course" on making Axis I diagnostic decisions in substance abuse assessments. Previous discussions about family, community, and macro influences are used to determine Axis III and IV diagnostics.

As an assessing social worker, report all of the various disorders, except personality disorders (i.e., Schizophrenia, Borderline Personality Disorder, etc.) and mental retardation on Axis I. Axis I disorders are the primary clinical issues that your clients grapple with on a daily basis. In addition, list what the *DSM* (American Psychiatric Association, 2000) calls "Other Conditions That May Be a Focus of Clinical Attention" (p. 27) including most of the "V codes" such as bereavement (V62.82), occupational problems (V62.2), and phase of life problems (V62.89).

In the event that a client has more than one Axis I condition (i.e., substance abuse and major depression, substance dependence and eating disorders, etc.), each is reported on Axis I in order, beginning with the presenting problem. Below are two examples of how to list Axis I diagnoses. Example 1 describes a client with one Axis I diagnosis and Example 2 pertains to a client with two diagnoses (also see Appendix B).

Example 1

Axis I: 305.00—Alcohol Abuse

Example 2

Axis I: 305.00—Alcohol Abuse

          300.40—Dysthymic Disorder

Determining a client's diagnosis is relatively simple, provided you have collected the correct information about his or her life, lifestyle, and worldview. Before moving to diagnoses, make sure you are organized and prepared to make the appropriate decisions based on the client's life story. Each dimension and subdimension in the assessment process should be summarized, highlighting the specific points to consider in the final assessment (see Appendix B). For example, after completing the substance use history, you should write a short summary paragraph in the case history report showing which elements of the history pertain to the client's current condition ("current," according to the *DSM,* means within the past 12 months). After collecting and noting the client's lifetime history of substance use and thoroughly examining his attitudes, beliefs, and perspectives about his substance use, you might write a summary paragraph like the following:

> John has a long history of substance abuse, beginning more than 20 years ago. However, in the last year it appears that John, according to his statements, has escalated his use of alcohol such that he now reports drinking to intoxication daily, recurrent marital problems, job performance problems, drinking more now than he used to in order to reach intoxication, and two drinking and driving arrests within the past 6 months. It also appears that John spends a great deal of time thinking about and/or participating in his alcohol-involved lifestyle, including drinking, being at a local bar, and organizing his personal life to allow him the time and access to heavy drinking, at the expense of his family, job, and other social outlets.

Included within this summary paragraph, based on information gleaned from an assessment interview with John, are several specific diagnostic criteria from the *DSM-IV-TR*. When it is time to choose an appropriate diagnosis, simply re-read this section of your assessment report and compare the information with the diagnostic criteria for Substance Abuse first, and then if he meets those criteria, compare with Substance Dependence to see if he also meets those criteria (see Figures 8.1 and 8.2 and Appendix B).

Comparing John's current use and lifestyle to the criteria for Substance Abuse (Figure 8.1), we find that John meets all four of the major criteria for this category. He reported major role difficulties (criterion 1), recurrent use in hazardous situations (criterion 2), recurrent legal problems (criterion 3), and continued use despite the existence of these and other problems (criterion 4). As such, John meets the criteria for a diagnosis of Alcohol Abuse, by meeting one (or more) of the criteria listed. However, to make the diagnosis of Alcohol Abuse, according to the criteria, the client's symptoms must not also meet the criteria for Alcohol Dependence.

Therefore, the next step is to compare John's story with the criteria for Substance Dependence (Figure 8.2). Comparing John's situation to the criteria for Substance Dependence, we note that he reported needing to drink more to achieve the same level of intoxication (criteria 1a and b), but he did not suggest any issue with withdrawal, therefore he does not meet criterion 2. John reported escalated drinking in the past year (criterion 3), but he did not report trying to stop or cut down, meaning that he does not meet criterion 4. He reported spending a great deal of time with his use (criterion 5), giving up activities and relationships for drinking (criterion 6), and continuing to use alcohol despite the problems (criterion 7). Accordingly, because John meets three (or more) of the criteria for Alcohol Dependence, his diagnosis would be Axis I: 303.90—Alcohol Dependence.

This is a relatively simple process, unless or until you find a case where you did not collect enough information to make a clear diagnosis. How will you know when this happens? You will find yourself, while comparing client data to diagnostic criteria, making assumptions about "what must be true" given your experience or so-called knowledge of "substance abusers." Let's underscore this important point: when you look to the diagnostic criteria and are not clear where people fit, then you have not collected enough information. Do not diagnose anyone based on your assumptions or so-called experience and knowledge. This practice is a recipe for error.

For example, in John's case, you could reasonably suggest that he probably meets criterion 2 (withdrawal), because anybody who drinks that much will experience withdrawal symptoms when he stops drinking. Even if you know that this is true for most people, since John did not discuss it, it is either untrue for him or he was not asked about it. Therefore, either you should delay diagnosis to inquire about withdrawal, or you should not consider it as part of the diagnosis. If the social worker doing John's assessment followed the rule about referring all substance-abusing clients for a medical examination, then the possibility for withdrawal would be dealt with there, alleviating the need to base a diagnosis on assumption and experience. I repeat, if the information is not there, you cannot use it.

What do you do if you are unsure about a diagnosis and your supervisor, professor, or funding source demands an immediate codification? There are several ways to indicate uncertainty, relieving you of the need to diagnose something based on insufficient data. If you believe clients will ultimately meet the criteria for a particular diagnostic category, you can list the diagnosis, followed by the word "provisional." For example, if the assessing social worker believed John would meet the criteria for Alcohol Dependence with further information, he or she could have written for John:

Axis I: 303.90—Alcohol Dependence (provisional)

If you simply have inadequate information to make a diagnosis and are unsure that clients will ultimately meet the criteria for any diagnosis, use the diagnostic code 799.90. The code means that you do not have adequate information to make a diagnostic judgment about an Axis I disorder. It simply indicates that you are deferring judgment until a later time. For example, if the social worker was deeply unsure about John's status, he or she could have written:

Axis I: 799.90—Diagnosis Deferred

The final way to handle such cases is to utilize a V code. V codes are used when there are problems to consider, but these problems are not caused by an underlying mental disorder or you are unsure if the problems are attributable to such a disorder. For example, let's say that John did not meet the criteria for Alcohol Abuse or Alcohol Dependence, but he was experiencing marital problems and work problems. His social worker could have written:

Axis I: V62.2—Occupational Problem

          V61.1—Partner Relational Problem

Lastly, keep in mind that some people who appear for an assessment, even if forced into it, may not ultimately require a diagnosis. It is possible to run across clients who do not require an Axis I diagnosis, even if you have collected the appropriate information. Do not be afraid to use the code V71.09—No Diagnosis of Condition on Axis I if your client does not require a diagnosis. Why am I bringing up this possibility? Because there is often pressure to make a diagnosis. I know of agency directors and/or clinical supervisors who demand that social workers make diagnoses, suggesting that if the social workers "had only looked harder, they'd have been sure to find something." This practice is not only unethical but also morally inappropriate. The social work profession is built on the premise that we are to serve the best interests of each client, not the best interests of our agencies or agency directors.

By now, it should be clear that a conservative approach to diagnosis is best for all concerned. Realistically, while the diagnosis is only one part of the assessment process, it is what qualifies agencies and practitioners for reimbursement. The pressure to make a diagnosis, or in the case of substance abuse treatment, to make an appropriate diagnosis, can be intense. In this context, it is easy to forget that the numbers and letters you assign to people's behavior will follow them for the rest of their lives. To clients, a diagnosis means more than reimbursement—it is their life.

Take responsibility for making diagnoses seriously and humbly. Because of the seriousness of the issue and because diagnoses are often used to define people instead of their conditions, always pause before writing down those numbers and letters. In fact, I urge you to take this process so seriously that every diagnosis causes you to reflect deeply, even to the point of feeling unsettled by the responsibility. We are given the enormous responsibility of defining someone else's life, using means (*DSM*) that are highly subjective and based on criteria developed through questionable scientific methods (Kirk & Kutchins, 1992). If the diagnostic process does not make you pause and reflect—if it becomes so routine and depersonalized that it no longer matters to you—there is a higher potential for callous diagnoses, mistaken data, and inappropriate or ineffective treatment planning. If this description fits you, now may be the time to take an extended vacation or change positions.

To end this discussion, I will repeat something I said earlier. Do not focus on diagnostic skills, but strive to improve your relationship and interviewing skills. Development of these skills, rather than memorization of the *DSM,* will help to ensure that every diagnosis you give will be sensitively grounded in your client's life history and not based on assumptions, personal experience, stereotypes, or agency pressure. To see how diagnosis is inexorably linked to a multi-systemic assessment process, read the Sample Case History in Appendix B.

Key Questions When you have completed this dimension, you should be able to answer the following questions:

- Based on the entirety of the information collected during the assessment, does your client fit the criteria for a substance-related diagnosis, and if so, upon what specific criteria are you basing this decision?

- Based on the entirety of the information collected during the assessment, does your client fit the criteria for any other Axis I mental health diagnosis, and if so, upon what specific criteria are you basing this decision?

- What information do you still need to obtain to complete this dimension, and how will you gather it (e.g., from client, family, or psychiatric referral)?

- What strengths and resources does your client exhibit with regard to this dimension?

THE CASE HISTORY REPORT

After you have collected all the information in a substance abuse assessment, your job is to make sense of it by writing a report that communicates a multi-systemic understanding of the client's problems and strengths, as well as directions for the future. The case history report is a living document based on your interpretation of your client's life and history, culture and communities, and her or his place in these communities as determined by many factors, including race, ethnicity, gender, social class, and sexual orientation, to name a few. The case history report encompasses all of the information gathered during client interviews, as well as your responses to the series of questions given for each assessment dimension.

In preparing the case history report, you will use your working knowledge of people, systems, and substance abuse to look for connections between events and meanings not necessarily spoken by clients. This is your opportunity to demonstrate your special training and expertise in understanding person-in-environment (Karls & Wandrei, 1994a) and the workings of various social, governmental, and political systems in the lives of individuals and families at the local level. The case history report is not the place to casually or callously interpret people's life histories in a way designed to fit your particular personal or professional needs or satisfy your beliefs. Among other things, you must ensure that your interpretation is based on actual client information and not what you assume clients would have said if you had remembered to ask, or an altered version of their stories that often occurs when attempting to paraphrase people's actual words and meanings. This kind of bias occurs far too often, as described in the following example.

> I consulted in one substance abuse agency that assumed, before clients arrived, that they would have a co-occurring bipolar disorder in addition to chemical dependency. This notion was based on the presiding psychiatrist's personal belief that a preponderance of chemically dependent individuals had bipolar disorder. This psychiatrist informed me that it really did not matter whether clients demonstrated or discussed the appropriate symptoms, because they were all in denial and hid their symptoms well. I soon learned that in the previous year, nearly 75 percent of adult clients admitted to this particular inpatient substance abuse treatment program had been diagnosed and medicated for bipolar disorder.

To write a case history report that is accurate, understandable, and helpful, be concerned with what Goodall (2000, p. 12) and others (Denzin, 1996; Van Maanen, 1995) call the "crisis of representation." Taken from the research field of ethnography, the crisis of representation involves the way that professionals represent the words, stories, and experiences of people they interview. According to Goodall (2000),

> Because representation is literally about *re-presenting* a reality, which assumes a *correspondence between language used to create the representation and the reality that gets represented* . . . what counts as truth depends on where you are standing when you observe or participate in it, what you believe about it in the first place, and what you want to do with it—or who is paying you to do something with it—once you name it.
>
> "Who has the right to speak for a culture?" is very much a question about *who is entitled* to represent it. Furthermore, regardless of who represents it, or what is represented, cultures are *not* "out there" for inspection and amenable solely to received scientific truths. Rather, cultures are apprehended,

theorized, studied, explained, storied, and otherwise rendered *symbolic* through language. They are *constructed*. We locate (from the languages we collect through fieldwork) and invent (out of our own professional training and individual sensitivities) a language of contextual meanings for describing, analyzing, and storying a culture as we go along (pp. 12–13).

This explanation should sound familiar, assuming you have read all of the preceding chapters in this text. Just as your job is to understand clients' lives from their unique perspectives, so too must you accurately represent their lives and history in *their* case history reports. Just as it is your job to separate people's lives from your own, so too is it your job to separate their voices from your voice in the case history reports. The crisis of representation helps define and determine who has the right to define and label people's life stories. If I were to read your case history report, would it be easy for me to distinguish between passages where your clients were "talking" about their lives and passages where you were "talking" about what their behaviors mean in a professional context?

These distinctions may sound trivial and complicated, but attention to this area is consistent with social work values and ethics related to the right to self-determination and autonomy. This approach reverses the "normal" process of social work practice, which is designed to gradually depersonalize clients by using case numbers and professional lingo, referring to clients as "the client" instead of by name, and assigning diagnostic codes. Each step of the way, clients move from being living and breathing human beings, to computer or paper files containing approved numbers, letters, acronyms, and labels. For example, John Smith, a person who is dependent on alcohol, becomes case number 2134 with a diagnostic code of 303.90 and a GAF score of 50; he is an AOD client with potential PTSD and GAD, who you suspect was either a victim or a perp in a former life.

By now, you probably have surmised that depersonalization in practice is diametrically opposed to the process advocated here. At every step of the process, you have been encouraged to avoid depersonalization by developing the type of relationship that allows people to become even more human than they were the minute before they walked through your door. These efforts are all for naught, however, if you write case history reports in traditional and depersonalized ways. Take the same care to maintain people's humanness when writing about them as you did when talking with them.

When an outside person (supervisor, referral agent, probation officer, etc.) reads your case history report, the reader should get a real sense of the individual, as if reading the client's substance abuse biography. As the outside reader, I should be able to have a conversation with your clients about their lives, even if we have never met. Therefore, instead of calling a person "the client," use his or her name (i.e., "John said," "Sue reported") or, if you are assessing someone older than you are, or someone from a culture that values titles (i.e., older African American), refer to your client as Mr. Smith, Ms. Jones, or Dr. Alvarez. See Appendix B.

To resolve the crisis of representation, rely heavily on quotes, signifying when you are quoting directly or paraphrasing. It should be clear when people are speaking about themselves and when you are speaking about them. When you paraphrase, write that you are paraphrasing, and do not make it sound (consciously or unconsciously) as if your clients are speaking when you are speaking for them. Additionally, write in a way that clients can understand. The case history report is not a place to launch into a series of professional acronyms, social work jargon, or criticisms of people's lives or behaviors.

Never write anything in a case history report (or any client paperwork for that matter) that you would not want clients or their parents to read. It was standard practice in my agencies to give clients (and their parents, in the case of adolescents) a copy of their final case history report. Moreover, clients were given sufficient time and opportunity to discuss the findings and offer feedback about the conclusions before it became certified as a final report about their life. In qualitative research, this is called a member check, used to increase the validity of the researcher's findings (Berg, B., 1995; Lincoln & Guba, 1985). If researchers are concerned about validity, then you should be doubly concerned, since your reports will affect people's lives, often in dramatic ways. Therefore, allow people to read and respond to your final report. If you have carried out the process appropriately, nothing in the case history report should surprise them.

Involving your clients in the assessment process through an open discussion of the case history report is an integral part of a strengths-based approach to working with clients. It is based on the belief that despite having problems—even severe problems, at that—clients have the capacity, like people who are not clients, to be active agents in their own lives; to make their own decisions and assume responsibility for their lives. When you treat clients as functioning adults, dialogue can begin in earnest. Suddenly they will become more engaged in *their* helping process. Hence, their willingness to follow through on referral appointments will increase, as will their motivation to take action. When it comes to the case history report—no different from any other aspect of the assessment process—always strive to treat people as you would expect your children to be treated in a professional setting. Wouldn't you expect (or demand) the opportunity to read and discuss your child's assessment with the social worker? If your answer to this question is "yes," why should clients expect any less?

SUMMARY

In this chapter we looked at 10 dimensions that compose a comprehensive substance abuse assessment. This assessment structure is multi-systemic in nature, gleaning information about your client across the micro (individual and family), mezzo (organizational), and macro (local and broader community) spheres. We explored each dimension in significant detail, offering lines of inquiry and specific questions to ask yourself to ensure that you have collected the necessary information while ensuring that the assessment process proceeds in a way that will best serve your client. We also described how to prepare a case history report that furthers the collaborative and respectful spirit of the assessment process discussed in this text.

As we have described throughout this text, successful treatment begins with a comprehensive, multi-systemic assessment, built on the foundation of a trusting and open relationship between you and your client. While it is important to familiarize yourself with these dimensions of assessment, it is more important to develop the relationship skills discussed in Chapter 4. When you acquire these skills, you will also have acquired the foundation necessary to practice as a culturally competent social worker.

9

The Substance Abuse
Treatment System

By now, you should be familiar with the substance abuse assessment process. In the first eight chapters, we focused on how to perform a comprehensive, multi-systemic substance abuse assessment and write a case history report. Except for the opportunity to apply these concepts directly, performing these functions as part of your daily practice should no longer be a mystery.

In the remainder of the book, we explore the substance abuse treatment system, specific treatment approaches, and relapse prevention. My goal is to familiarize you with various approaches and methods used in substance abuse treatment, but our discussion here (as elsewhere in this text) will be geared primarily toward those who are not specializing in substance abuse. Therefore, our look into treatment will not be as thorough as it was for assessment. To do so would require a separate volume.

Nevertheless, it is important to familiarize yourself with the various methods and models used in substance abuse treatment. The more familiar you are with treatment, the more capable you will be of making an appropriate referral and supporting your clients through the treatment process; or the more effective you can become if you serve as the primary treatment provider. For some, these chapters may spark an interest in learning more about substance abuse treatment; perhaps you may even want to provide substance abuse treatment for your clients as part of your professional practice. Regardless of whether or not you choose to provide substance abuse treatment, understanding the treatment process will improve your professional practice.

To begin our look at substance abuse treatment, this chapter provides an overview of the treatment system. We explore the different levels of care available and the kinds of treatment provided at each level. In the next chapter (Chapter 10), we will delve more specifically into treatment methods, demonstrating how many of the models discussed in Chapter 3 are operationalized into specific treatment methods. We will discuss how to employ a multi-systemic approach to conceptualize, plan, and deliver services based on an ecological systems perspective.

While the total percentage of people receiving formal treatment from professional substance abuse treatment organizations (8%) represents only a small fraction of those estimated to have a substance abuse problem (27% of the population), substance abuse treatment is "big business" (Kessler et al., 1994). In fact, in the 1980s there were 7,759 professional substance abuse treatment centers treating an average of 734,000 individuals annually (NIDA/NIAAA, 1990). Obviously, substance abuse treatment programs involve many people, and the number of people who remain untreated each year far surpasses the number who receive treatment. The size and scope of the field make it even more imperative that you understand what occurs in substance abuse treatment centers, whether or not you treat (or strive to treat) clients for substance abuse.

LEVELS OF SUBSTANCE ABUSE TREATMENT

A wide variety of substance abuse treatment services are available, falling on a continuum from least restrictive to most restrictive. In the lexicon of substance abuse treatment, *level of care* refers to the amount of physical restriction at each specific level. For example, a client confined in an inpatient hospital program is participating in a higher level of care than a client participating in an outpatient group that meets weekly. Level of care is determined by the setting, not the specific type(s) of treatment provided in a setting. Clients may participate in group treatment sessions in both inpatient and outpatient programs. However, the inpatient setting makes it a higher level of care than outpatient care, because the client actually resides in the hospital while participating in the treatment.

There are six primary levels of care for both adults and adolescents, although some authors identify up to nine different levels (McNeese & DiNitto, 2000). These levels range from education and prevention services (early intervention) to medically managed intensive inpatient service (American Society of Addiction Medicine, 1996). While some clients require more than one level of care, others do not. The level of care continuum represents a comprehensive service delivery system that is designed to meet the personal needs of substance-abusing clients and their families. Below, we present the levels of care in order, from least restrictive to most restrictive.

Education/Prevention Services (Early Intervention)

Considered the least restrictive level of care, substance abuse education and/or prevention offers clients the chance to learn about the effects of substance abuse and chemical dependency in different dimensions of life. Providers of substance abuse education offer clients information about substance abuse and/or chemical dependency in the hope that knowledge about substance use, abuse, and addiction will help those who use or abuse substances to abstain, help those already abusing substances to avoid progressing to the chemically dependent stage, or prevent people from beginning to use substances in the first place.

More than a stand-alone level of care, didactic substance abuse education and/or psychoeducational interventions (participant/learner oriented activities) are part of nearly every level of care in the substance abuse field. Yet substance abuse education also represents a unique level of care. Whether education pertains to the effects of substances on the human body, the family, or other areas of involvement, providers often use some form of education as a way to engage clients in a helping process. I have found that as long as the educational information is accurate and presented in a way that allows clients to understand how it relates to their life, it can be an effective way to address misconceptions, present controversies, and—in higher levels of care—serve as part of a foundation for treatment and recovery.

As a stand-alone level of care, substance abuse education and psychoeducation are indicated when your client is not, according to your assessment, chemically dependent or has few, if any, immediate needs that require more intensive treatment, although there are exceptions to this general rule (see below). That is, clients who would normally not receive formal treatment are often appropriate for substance abuse education. Remember that people assessed and diagnosed as chemically dependent are not the only ones who may require some form of intervention. People categorized as substance abusers can, and often do, require some form of treatment to assist with the "fallout" from negative life consequences that result from their substance abuse, even if they abuse sporadically. For example, some clients may drink heavily only on weekends, but experience relationship problems. Their partners may strongly object to even one night of heavy drinking, putting stress on their relationships.

Not everyone requires treatment. Substance abuse, in and of itself, does not necessarily justify admission to treatment, and treatment that is more intensive does not necessarily lead to higher treatment success (Denning, 2000; Marlatt, 1996). For treatment to be helpful, individuals or families must be matched to the level of treatment indicated by their life history, and to a level commensurate with their level of motivation and willingness to participate. Moreover, the most important match to be made occurs between the treatment provider and client (Miller & Rollnick, 1991). Please read the discussion below about treatment matching.

Youths and Adolescents   Adolescents and children most often participate in stand-alone educational programs. For example, adolescents and young adults (especially college students) arrested for illegal possession of alcohol often must participate in substance abuse education (i.e., Minors in Possession programs) as a first-offense sentence. Most colleges and universities provide substance abuse education for students who violate alcohol or drug policies or laws, or for students who request help for substance abuse on campus. The same is true for high-school-age youths caught possessing alcohol or other drugs. If it is a first offense, they are usually referred to substance abuse education programs as the sole intervention.

Most public school districts in the United States expose students, as part of their education, to primary prevention programs that center on substance abuse education, values clarification, and peer-pressure refusal skills. An educational program is considered *primary prevention* if it is targeted at stopping substance use before it begins (Jung, 2001). For example, the Drug Abuse Resistance Education (DARE) program uses police officers in classrooms to teach a 17-lesson substance abuse education program to fifth- and sixth-grade students, with ten follow-up lessons in junior high and nine additional lessons in high school. Lessons include information about alcohol and other drugs, alternatives to drug use, resistance to peer pressure, refusal skills, decision-making, and self-esteem (DARE America, 1991).

The DARE program is the most widely known and, according to Ennett et al. (1994), the most widely used prevention program in the United States. It is not the only program available, however, or even the most effective one. In fact, DARE has been found to be an ineffective way to help young people avoid using substances later in life (Clayton, Cattarello, & Johnstone, 1996). Because of its publicity and governmental support, it is easy to assume that the DARE program is the only model available for early education to prevent substance abuse. It is not. Efforts to measure the effectiveness of drug education programs are controversial. Many researchers and other officials agree with Botvin and Botvin (1992) that "virtually all efforts to develop effective substance abuse prevention approaches have failed" (p. 910). It is not clear whether the prevention programs have failed because of programmatic issues, or whether faulty evaluation models were unable to correctly evaluate prevention programs. This controversy is not likely to be resolved any time soon.

DWI Schools   Substance abuse education groups or classes are also used for people convicted of first-offense drinking and driving (i.e., drunken driving school). These offenders are usually considered to have erred in judgment, as opposed to having significant substance abuse problems. Generally, these programs consist of films, lecture, and discussions about substance abuse and its effects on the human body and behavior.

First-offense drunken drivers sentenced to DWI schools often do not have significant or treatable substance abuse problems. However, this is not always the case. Some who are sentenced to DWI schools actually do have significant problems that have existed for years. Somehow, these individuals manage to avoid arrest and otherwise elude detection by the "system." As such, in some DWI schools, participants must complete an assessment as part of the program's requirement. Yet, my experience suggests that the "assessments" used in these programs are really nothing more than quick and easy screening instruments (i.e., Michigan Alcoholism Screening Test [MAST]). Many individuals still evade identification because of the inherent reliability and/or validity problems associated with these widely known screening instruments.

As we discussed in Chapter 7, screening instruments are helpful tools to indicate the possibility of substance use problems. Moreover, many social workers working in settings that do not specialize in substance abuse treatment may only have the capacity or mandate to use these screening instruments. If these are your circumstances, you can learn to augment items on screening instruments with additional questions to derive a more holistic and multi-systemic picture of your client's potential issues, instead of relying too heavily on the tool alone. Please review the discussion in Chapter 7 about this important subject.

Education as an Alternative for the "Resistant" Client There is yet another type of client who can benefit from educational programs. At first glance, this may seem an unlikely population to send to the least intensive and least restrictive level of care. In fact, many substance abuse professionals would not think to send this group for educational services alone, because of the perceived need for more intensive treatment. This population consists of clients at all levels of impairment, including the chemically dependent, whom you determine through the assessment as being unlikely to attend formal treatment options and/or twelve-step support groups because of low motivation. Substance abuse education can be a viable treatment option for clients with the most insurmountable level of personal denial: those who present in the precontemplation stage (Prochaska & DiClemente, 1986; DiClemente & Prochaska, 1985) of motivation (review Chapter 4). These clients are, in fact, among the best candidates for low-intensity, non-threatening educational programming (DiClemente, 1991) as a way to increase motivation and boost their willingness to accept help.

Why should this be the case, you ask? Shouldn't these clients be given the level of treatment intensity they need? Of course, they "should" be provided just that, but what if you know ahead of time that your client will not consider participating in, say, inpatient or residential services? What if, based on your assessment of motivation, you suspect that your clients will not attend even the most infrequent treatments with therapists of any ilk? What if, based on your assessment, your clients do not suspect that they have problems of any kind? Should you still refer to the more intensive treatment, knowing that he or she will not attend, or will have a bad experience? On the other hand, perhaps you could use the information ascertained in the comprehensive substance abuse assessment to provide the kind of service that might help increase motivation and, therefore, improve people's chances for treatment success.

Traditionally, clients such as the ones just described would have been labeled resistant, not ready for treatment, or not yet having "hit bottom." They would have been offered only one option, despite the counselor knowing that the intervention was destined to fail because of factors related to motivation. Ethically, this practice is marginally appropriate because the client actually needs a higher level of service intensity to achieve immediate sobriety. These practitioners are the ones who, in the absence of a comprehensive, multi-systemic substance abuse assessment, focus narrowly on substance use, frequency, and ultimately, the *DSM* diagnosis. By doing so, they ignore the "rest of the story." While the referral technically met people's needs based on substance use history, it did not meet their needs based on their life histories, including readiness to accept treatment.

Let us preview a discussion about treatment matching that comes later in this chapter. Treatment matching by modality or method was proven inconsequential (Project MATCH, 1997). I speculated that perhaps the hypothesis in the Project MATCH studies was incorrect, not the notion that certain clients would benefit from well-matched treatment services. I agree with others (Connors, Donovan, & DiClemente, 2001; Miller & Rollnick, 1991, 2002) who assert that for a match to be effective, not only must clients be matched to an appropriate method, but also to an appropriate practitioner *and* to a level of care suited to their motivation levels. Accordingly, even if you have the correct modality or method and the best fit personally with people, if they lack motivation to attend, treatment will most likely fail barring some unpredictable "miracle" occurring along the way. Clients must "show up" before they can be treated, a fact that is often overlooked in basic social work training. Low-intensity substance abuse education is non-threatening. Clients will often be happy to attend what they believe is nothing more than a "movie and popcorn," even when they are unwilling to attend any other form of professional or community help.

Therefore, instead of waiting for a miracle, perhaps a mediating step is needed to help clients move along the motivation continuum. This is where education as a beginning step for the most difficult clients can be helpful. I have found this strategy to also be effective with court-mandated clients. By providing or refer-ring mandated clients for low-intensity, non-threatening educational services, you can help create a context where a "miracle" can occur, instead of waiting and hoping for an act of spontaneous motivation. Decisions such as this take into account the complete substance abuse assessment, not just sections of it. Below we discuss the use of an organized "intervention" as another way of improving motivation during early intervention.

Education as a Component of Other Treatment Services As mentioned above, education, psychoeducation, and other forms of prevention (i.e., physical activities, social activities, etc.) are also an integral component of more intensive treatment modalities (i.e., residential, inpatient, and outpatient treatment). As part of these treatments, clients are often required to view films, attend lectures, participate in role-play activities, and make use of recreational outlets. These initiatives are designed to allow clients to learn about the effects of substances, help make a self-diagnosis (thereby improving motivation), and integrate new substance abuse knowledge with the other treatment activities for a more complete treatment effect (Center for Substance Abuse Treatment, 1995b; Jung, 2001). Examples of the various topics that may be presented during an educa-tional component of substance abuse education during treatment include the following:

- The disease concept
- Medical aspects of drugs
- Relapse prevention
- HIV and AIDS education
- Basic living skills
- Denial and other defenses
- Stress management
- Codependency

Additionally, many programs also offer educational and didactic activities for the client's family members and/or significant others. These sessions are designed to produce similar effects on family members and significant others as on individual clients. Some typical topics involved in family education include

- Codependency
- Family structure and boundaries
- Disease concept related to families
- Family roles
- Intergenerational nature of dependence
- The healthy family
- Sexual abuse education and prevention

Effectiveness of Educational Programs   As we stated earlier, researchers have been unable to prove that substance abuse education and/or prevention programs are effective in reducing substance use in the future. Hence, while education is a commonly used strategy during treatment, some have criticized it (Lewis, Dana, & Blevins, 1994) by saying,

> Many counselors assume, for instance, that 'educating clients about alcoholism' is a necessary and possibly even sufficient mechanism for engendering sobriety; yet one would be hard pressed to find real support for the generalization that the provision of factual information can be counted on to bring about desired changes in attitude or behavior (p. 18).

Furthermore, before exposing clients to educational programs, make sure to assess the learning style and capacity of the client. For example, Karacostas and Fisher (1993) found a higher-than-expected rate of learning disabled adolescents with potential substance abuse problems. Unless the educational delivery system matches your client's learning capacity and style, it will have little chance for success.

It is clear that substance abuse education, by itself, will not help people overcome substance abuse problems. As part of an early intervention program for people who do not have serious or persistent problems, or as a non-threatening way to engage poorly motivated clients, it may be beneficial. However, being "beneficial" is not the same as solving the problem(s) of substance use, abuse, and chemical dependency. That is, while early substance abuse education may help create a context for abstinence in children, it would be naive to believe—or even suggest—that a few hours of "just say no" in fifth or sixth grade will be powerful enough to overcome the social environment several years later. If you work from a multi-systemic approach, do not forget the complex environmental, familial, and personal issues that contribute to the decision to begin or continue using alcohol and other drugs. That is, do not expect more results than can reasonably be expected from substance abuse education. While many believe that "education is the key" to solving substance abuse problems, it is unreasonable to believe that it is the best or only way to address this significant cultural problem.

Intervention

The organized and formal process designed to help motivate individuals into accepting the need for substance abuse treatment is called an *intervention*. While an intervention is often used with individuals who are chemically dependent, I am placing it near the low end of the care spectrum because of its goal. The goal of an intervention is to interrupt the substance abuse and/or chemical dependency process *before* an individual "hits bottom"; thus, it is designed to serve a preventive function.

Beginning with Vernon Johnson (1973, 1986), a pioneer in the substance abuse treatment field, substance abuse treatment providers have searched for effective ways to motivate a chemically dependent client into getting treatment before he or she hits bottom. Hitting bottom, in this sense, means that people's problems escalate until they reach the inevitable conclusion of the disease process: death. To help people avoid this fate by "raising the bottom," Johnson (1986) developed a method to motivate chemically dependent clients to accept substance abuse treatment. Johnson's method, called an intervention, entails an organized confrontation of individuals by family members, close friends, employers, and others who are affected by the person's behavior. According to Johnson (1973),

> It became clear to us that it was not only pointless but also dangerous to wait until the alcoholic hit bottom. The crises everybody was trying to help him avoid could actually be employed to break through his defenses, by an act of intervention that could stop the downward spiral toward death. We came to understand that crises could be used to creatively bring about intervention (p. 3).

In the more general social work field, the word *intervention* usually means specific action taken by clients—often instigated by social workers—toward achieving their stated goals (Brill, 1998). In this context, an intervention is any action that helps clients to progress. Anderson (1992) defines intervention as the process for stopping people who are experiencing the harmful effects of substances. For example, grounding an adolescent who is caught drinking by his or her parents is an intervention. In the substance abuse field, the definition of intervention has taken on a narrower meaning. In this context, intervention is defined as a set of specific procedures used to motivate an individual to enter substance abuse treatment before he or she is individually "ready."

The Johnson Model of Intervention   The popular method known as the Johnson Model of Intervention is based on the disease model of addiction. It is designed to forcefully motivate a chemically dependent individual to enter treatment before he or she hits bottom and dies from the effects of the disease. According to Johnson (1973),

> It is a myth that alcoholics have some spontaneous insight and then seek treatment. Victims of this disease do not submit to treatment out of spontaneous insight—typically, in our experience they come to their recognition scenes through a buildup of crises that crash through their

almost impenetrable defense systems. They are forced to seek help; and when they don't, they perish miserably (p. 1).

The Johnson Model of Intervention is a dynamic, emotionally charged confrontation by significant others. As we discussed in Chapters 3 and 4, the disease model incorporates a belief that the denial systems of the chemically dependent are formidable, meaning that it is nearly impossible to motivate these persons to seek help without some element of force and emotional confrontation (Twerski, 1983; Anderson, 1987; Johnson, 1986). Hence, an intervention is focused to "counteract denial" (Anderson, 1987, p. 178) by disrupting people's psychological defense systems so that they will seek help at the moment of disruption, before having a chance to rationalize and/or restabilize in the hours and days following an intervention session. It is used to break through the denial system of chemically dependent persons by confronting the crises that they have caused through their behavior. The confrontation is performed by significant others in a chemically dependent person's life. It is hoped that the intervention process will "raise the bottom," leading the person to seek help earlier than they would do otherwise. To accomplish this feat, Johnson (1986) believed that chemically dependent persons need a clear view of reality, as presented by significant others in their lives:

> By *presenting reality*, we mean presenting facts about the person's behavior and things that have happened because of it. A *receivable way* is one that the person cannot resist because of its objective, unequivocal, and caring presentation (p. 61, italics original).

Although the Johnson Model is confrontational, it should not be confused with personal attacks or hostility, although this easily occurs if the helper is inexperienced in emotionally charged family and/or group settings, or the family decides against hiring a trained, outside helper to guide the process. Moreover, Johnson believed that the intervention process demonstrates caring and love by those who are willing to participate:

> In an intervention, confrontation means compelling the person to face the facts about his or her chemical dependency. . . . It is an attack upon the victim's wall of defenses, not upon the victim as a person . . . an intervention is an act of *empathy* rather than sympathy. You agree to take part in it out of the deep concern you feel for the chemically dependent person (Johnson, 1986, p. 62; italics original).

The Intervention Process   While Johnson (1986) developed his intervention process for lay people, it works best if the activity is orchestrated by a substance abuse professional with experience in group techniques and handling emotional interactions between family members. As you will see from descriptions of the process, interactions during an intervention often become heated and emotional— too much so for loved ones or other significant others to handle in a detached and caring manner. For an intervention to be successful, confrontation must be appropriate. It should not include the personal attacks and intense emotionality that inevitably occur between family members and close friends. Johnson (1986) outlines the following steps for planning and conducting an intervention:

1. The organizer, usually a significant other, locates two or more persons, "who are close to the victim and have witnessed his or her behavior while under the influence" (Johnson, 1986, p. 66) to participate in the intervention. The reason for having two or more people is for mutual support during the confrontation process. The person who instigates the intervention, along with the presiding professional, decides who should become part of the intervention team. From my clinical experience, the greater the number of people involved, the more dynamic is the intervention.

2. After the participants are chosen and agree to participate in the intervention, they develop a specific list of substance-related behaviors that they have personally witnessed. For each occurrence, participants describe what happened, when it happened, and how it affected the participant. These must be specific and detailed accounts, not generalized statements that can be disputed (e.g., "you are always high at work"). For example, a son might say, "Last week you were drunk at my game. When you yelled and screamed at my coach and the referees, you really embarrassed me . . . so much that I wanted to run and hide." Participants should write out these descriptions, to be read during the actual intervention meeting.

3. The intervention team should assemble and practice several times before actually meeting with the intervention target. This critical step ensures that participants maintain a tone and posture that are nonjudgmental, friendly, and slightly detached. Moreover, during practice sessions, participants should role-play different scenarios, practicing how to respond to each scenario depending on how the chemically dependent person reacts to the intervention.

4. Participants must also decide what action each will take if the chemically dependent person refuses to accept help at the conclusion of the intervention meeting. This is the point where many interventions "break down" (see case example below). Participants must be willing to follow through with the chosen action, or the intervention will not work and any future attempts at intervention will prove fruitless. Therefore, it is the professional facilitator's job to ensure that the actions are stern, serious, and yet reasonable.

   For example, if an employer says that the chemically dependent person will be terminated if he or she refuses help, then the employer must actually terminate him or her if treatment is refused. While this action might be reasonable and have a good chance of being carried out, having parents say that their 13-year-old son will be "out of the house" if he does not attend treatment is unrealistic. This is an area where you can be especially helpful. It is important that participants (especially parents or spouses/partners) not make idle threats that they will not or cannot legally implement, such as claiming that they will put their 13-year-old child out on the street if he does not participate in treatment.

5. One member of the intervention team is assigned to research various treatment options. For example, before the intervention meeting the team must

find out what services are available, whether there are openings, the costs involved, and insurance or other third-party funding options. All of the work will be jeopardized if the chemically dependent person agrees to enter treatment, only to discover that there are no openings in the local treatment center or that the client will be forced into bankruptcy in order to pay for services. The movement to treatment must be accomplished immediately after the intervention. Any delays in treatment entry will ruin any chances for a successful intervention.

6. At the scheduled time, participants meet and confront the chemically dependent person in the actual intervention meeting. This meeting should be introduced and led by the social worker. In it, each person reads his or her pre-written description of the issues created by the person's behavior, as well as any actions to be taken if the person refuses help. The chemically dependent person is allowed to respond at the end of the session, after all of the participants have finished. When the session is nearly complete, the chemically dependent person is asked to enter treatment immediately or face the consequences stated by the participants during the meeting. This is where the preparations made in step 5 pay off. If the client refuses treatment, each member of the intervention team must implement his or her consequences stated during the meeting, without exception, beginning immediately.

Effectiveness of Intervention   Our discussion of effectiveness must look at similar issues, since there are no studies of this specific process. A successful intervention results in the client entering treatment through social coercion. Therefore, a review of the literature about the success of coercive treatments is instructive in predicting the outcome of an intervention. There are a number of studies (e.g., Anglin, Brecht, & Maddahian, 1989; DeLeon, 1988; Goldkamp & Weiland, 1993) that claim that court-mandated clients do as well or better than do those who enter treatment voluntarily. Moreover, Matuschka (1985) stated, "treatment which carried a coercive element has been shown to have a higher cure ratio than treatment without a coercive element" (p. 209). Royce (1989) is very enthusiastic about the success of this type if intervention, claiming that when they are "properly done, interventions succeed 97 percent of the time in getting a person into treatment" (p. 234). Others, especially Miller and Rollnick (2002), believe otherwise.

While it is true that many successful clients were originally coerced into treatment, whether an intervention is successful in motivating people to participate in substance abuse treatment is debatable, and depends on those involved in the intervention. For example, I have seen this approach work well with adult middle-class male and female clients, but have found little success when the target of the intervention was an adolescent or young adult. Certainly, the decision to use an intervention depends on the commitment of potential intervention team members and a realistic assessment of the risks associated with the chemically dependent person disappearing, even for a short time, and perhaps becoming worse as a result. It is also determined by the degree to which the presiding social worker can assist the intervention team members to behave in a loving and empathetic way, instead of an angry and hostile manner.

CASE EXAMPLE   The "Easy" Judge

I was asked to lead an intervention by the family and friends of a 22-year-old chemically dependent male client. According to his parents and other family members, the client was unwilling to enter treatment, and he was approaching the point where his actions and lifestyle would lead to serious medical and legal consequences. The first step was to organize a meeting of the participants. His parents were asked to invite anyone who was intimately involved with their son and his chemical dependency. Twelve people attended the first organizational meeting, including one of their son's childhood friends and a prominent, local judge. As it turns out, the judge had a personal interest in the case, and had "gone easy" on the client during several previous court proceedings.

Over the next three weeks, the group met four times, with the final meeting consisting of a role-play of the actual intervention. Each participant was told that he or she must be willing and able to implement any consequences toward the client should he refuse to enter inpatient treatment. All agreed.

At the intervention meeting, family members and friends, including the judge, performed as planned. They all read their statements, pleaded with the client to enter treatment, and proposed personal consequences should the client refuse help. At the meeting's conclusion (three hours later), the client agreed to enter treatment. The parents, having prearranged an admission to a local inpatient treatment facility, whisked their son off to treatment that day.

Two weeks later, the group reconvened at the behest of the parents, to review the process and check on the client's progress. As it turned out, the client had walked out of treatment after one week. To their credit, the parents implemented the consequences, as did the rest of the participants except one: the judge. He had stated that if the client refused treatment or left early, he would re-impose a suspended jail sentence and place the client in jail for one year. When it came time to follow through, the judge refused, allowing the client "off the hook" one more time and thus rendering the intervention meaningless. The client continued to use drugs, and the parents continued to worry about the potential long-term consequences of his use.

This case study demonstrates the potential for good, as well as the difficulties involved in facilitating a successful intervention. Interventions can become an "all-or-nothing" proposition. That is, depending on the outcome, clients are admitted for treatment or they are not. Even if the client is admitted for treatment, nothing is guaranteed. If the client does not get treatment, trust between clients and their families and between clients and treatment providers is often diminished so significantly that another opportunity to intervene does not arise anytime soon. While there is little evidence to suggest that interventions are an effective method of preventing clients' problems from worsening, this method is widely accepted in the substance abuse field as an ethical way of trying to help. What is your opinion of the intervention process? This is another excellent topic for your substance abuse journal.

Twelve-Step Support Groups

The next level of service in the substance abuse field is referral to twelve-step support groups as the primary method of treatment. Alcoholics Anonymous (AA) is the most frequently used source of help for people with alcohol problems in the United States (Miller & McCrady, 1993). Approximately 10 percent of adults have attended at least one AA meeting, with two-thirds of these attending to support others and one-third for their own difficulties (Miller & McCrady, 1993; Zweben, 1995). In other words, more than 3 percent of all adults in the United States have attended at least one AA meeting because they thought that they might have a drinking problem (Godlaski, Leukefeld, & Cloud, 1997). Despite its widespread acceptance, AA is probably the least studied component of the substance abuse treatment industry (Jung, 2001). Supporters of the AA model believe it is the most effective means of treating chemical dependency, while many critics challenge this claim. Moreover, supporters believe that AA suffices as a primary treatment program (Peck, 1993; McCaul & Furst, 1994) while critics and others believe it is best used as a community support to supplement other professional treatment services (Lewis, Dana, & Blevins, 1988).

Despite the controversy that continues to surround AA and other programs based on the AA model [primarily Narcotics Anonymous (NA) and Al-Anon], for many clients it can become the most positive factor in achieving long-term abstinence, or recovery, from chemical dependency (Lewis, Dana, & Blevins, 1988). Hence, referring clients needing help with substance abuse and/or chemical dependency problems to twelve-step support groups either in lieu of professional treatment or as a supportive service for other professional treatment is appropriate, and for those who are chemically dependent, this type of referral is recommended.

While many substance abuse professionals require clients to attend twelve-step groups in addition to other forms of professional treatment, it is also appropriate to refer clients to a support group in lieu of attending professional treatment. I have often asked clients to attend support groups for 60 or 90 days before entering individual or family treatment. When these support groups are successful, your clients are able to establish a minimum foundation of abstinence prior to beginning work in other areas of life. Depending on people's level of motivation to engage in substance abuse treatment, referral to AA or NA only for a period can be an effective treatment strategy for clients who are willing to consider getting support, but not amenable to seeking professional help. Often, clients just entering the determination stage of motivation may be ready to explore sobriety, but not willing to enter therapy as a vehicle for this exploration.

Clients whose assessment suggests that they require only minimum or low-intensity services such as educational programs should not be referred to support groups. In other words, do not send someone to AA, NA, or any of the recovery-oriented support groups for educational purposes only. The only exception to this rule is if the meeting is an open or speakers meeting as a prelude to regular AA or NA attendance. Support groups such as AA and NA will not be helpful for people who do not have significant substance abuse problems, primarily because these clients will not find a personal connection with the basic tenets of AA that include "powerlessness," "disease," and lifetime abstinence. Moreover, despite the recent popularity of court-ordering clients to attend AA or NA meetings as part of their criminal sentence, this practice is not helpful (Clark, 1995; Humphreys & Moos, 1996).

Core Elements of the AA Model The original twelve-step program that provided the blueprint for similar groups is Alcoholics Anonymous. Founded in 1935 by two members of the Oxford Group (Bill W. and Bob S.), a fundamentalist Christian businessmen's group, AA began two years after national Prohibition ended. Many believe that the philosophical basis of AA is a direct extension of the political and religious beliefs that fueled the temperance movement (Bufe, 1991; Robertson, 1988). In subsequent years, AA meetings were instituted in nearly every community in the United States and in many countries around the world. In the United States, a person could theoretically attend a meeting every hour of every day during the year. Members, therefore, can always find a supportive atmosphere that practices a common set of beliefs and practices.

There are several core elements involved in the AA model. In the discussion below, these elements are presented to help you understand the twelve-step process. In addition, I recommend that you consider attending an open or speakers meeting offered by your local organization, locate and read organization literature, and search out longtime members to discuss the program and how it operates so that you truly understand what your clients can expect the first time they walk through the door of an AA, NA, or Al-Anon meeting. The more you know about how twelve-step programs operate, the more likely it is that your clients will actually attend and participate in AA or NA meetings.

The Twelve Steps AA and the related twelve-step programs operate on the core principles stated in AA's *Twelve Steps and Twelve Traditions* (1981). For clarity, I have divided the twelve steps into groups to help you better understand how AA and similar programs work.[*]

The first three steps help people accept the existence of substance abuse problems and surrender to the reality that their addiction is beyond personal control. These steps encourage people to accept and admit that they are unable to control their use or solve their problems without help. This goal helps to explain why AA members start every meeting by stating their name and label ("Hello, my name is Sam, and I'm an alcoholic"). After attending their first meeting, many students state that this process of self-definition is disempowering, contrary to the strengths perspective (Saleebey, 1997) in social work. However, according to AA philosophy, self-labeling is designed to have the opposite effect: to be, in fact, empowering. The process of publicly identifying oneself as an alcoholic or addict is a mechanism to overcome denial on a daily basis and introduces public accountability and positive peer pressure into the recovery process.

You will often hear members summarize the first three steps in the following way, "I can't, God can, I think I'll let Him (or Her)." There are three elements in

---

[*] The Twelve Steps are reprinted with permission of Alcoholics Anonymous World Services, Inc. (A.A.W.S.) Permission to reprint the Twelve Steps does not mean that A.A.W.S. has reviewed or approved the contents of this publication, or that A.A.W.S. necessarily agrees with the views expressed herein. A.A. is a program of recovery from alcoholism *only*—use of the Twelve Steps in connection with programs and activities which are patterned after A.A., but which address other problems, or in any other non-A.A. context, does not imply otherwise.

the process of gaining personal acceptance of one's problem and recognizing personal limitations, contained in the steps listed below:

Step 1:   We admitted that we were powerless over alcohol—that our lives had become unmanageable.

Step 2:   Came to believe that a Power greater than ourselves could restore us to sanity.

Step 3:   Made a decision to turn our will and our lives over to the care of God as we understood Him (Alcoholics Anonymous, 1981).

The next six steps (steps 4 through 9) are designed to help people make significant changes in their use and the lifestyles associated with use. While "working" these steps, people must confront and overcome many personal issues, or "defects of character" (Alcoholics Anonymous, 1981). Taken together, these steps help people make personal changes and, perhaps more importantly, confront the guilt and shame associated with past substance-abuse-related behaviors. Feelings of guilt and shame are often associated with how chemically dependent persons treated others during the time of their use (van Wormer, 1995).

For example, people may have stolen or borrowed money to buy drugs and never repaid it; mistreated lovers, partners, or parents; etc. This sequence of steps begins with an honest appraisal of the lifestyle and a public admission of these issues to a sponsor (see below). After identifying the issues and stating each publicly, individuals are expected to "make amends" for their actions, unless doing so would cause harm to self or others (i.e., contacting former victims of crimes committed, or a former drug dealer whom the individual "ripped off"). Steps 4 through 9 are as follows:

Step 4:   Made a searching and fearless moral inventory of ourselves.

Step 5:   Admitted to God, to ourselves, and to another human being the exact nature of our wrongs.

Step 6:   We were entirely ready to have God remove all of these defects of character.

Step 7:   Humbly asked Him to remove our shortcomings.

Step 8:   Made a list of all persons we had harmed, and become willing to make amends to them all.

Step 9:   Made direct amends to such people wherever possible, except when to do so would injure them or others (Alcoholics Anonymous, 1981).

The final three steps (steps 10 through 12) demand that individuals build on the foundation of change established earlier by continuing to confront daily shortcomings and taking steps to change issues that arise throughout the recovery process. Moreover, they are also expected to grow spiritually as a function of their recovery and to "carry the message" of the program to others in need of help. For example, members can carry the message by serving as a sponsor, giving public talks about their life and recovery, and helping to run meetings located inside of substance abuse treatment centers. Steps 10 through 12 are listed below.

Step 10: Continued to take personal inventory and when we were wrong, promptly admitted it.

Step 11: Sought through prayer and meditation to improve our conscious contact with God as we understood Him, praying only for knowledge of His will for us, and the power to carry that out.

Step 12: Having had a spiritual awakening as the result of these steps, we tried to carry this message to alcoholics, and to practice these principles in all our affairs (Alcoholics Anonymous, 1981).

The twelve steps are the cornerstone on which the entire program is built. The discussion that occurs in most closed meetings involves at least one of the steps, allowing members to learn how others have confronted and worked each step in their personal recovery. Anyone working as a professional in the substance abuse field is well served by knowing and understanding the steps, the philosophy and action that each step calls for, and the controversies that surround the steps and their application (Bufe, 1991; Marvel, 1995; Peck, 1993; Robertson, 1988).

Spirituality Clearly, the AA program places a high priority on spiritual growth and on the spiritual issues and problems experienced by many chemically dependent persons. M. Scott Peck (1993) believes that the twelve-step model is a program for spiritual growth. Next to the twelve steps, spirituality is the core of the AA model, helping members accept their personal limitations and surrender to the group for help and support. New members and students attending a meeting as part of a graduate course often mistake spirituality in AA as religion (Marvel, 1995). Alcoholics Anonymous makes a distinction between spirituality and religion (Berenson, 1987; Wallace, 1996) and it identifies with no specific religious group or doctrine (Alcoholics Anonymous, 1981).

If you reread the third step above, it clearly states that members are to recognize God *as we understand him (or her).* This refers to any God or "higher power" that the individual member wishes to use. For example, I have encouraged clients new to AA/NA who were unable to make a distinction between "higher power" and the God from a religious tradition they had rejected, to look upon the "power of the group" over aloneness as their higher power. I have heard clients say that their higher power was the memory of a dead relative; one client said he benefited from visualizing his motorcycle as his higher power. In other words, AA is based on a "whatever works" philosophy, not some traditional or recognized version of God or higher power.

Yet, depending upon the location and emphasis of a particular AA group in a particular location, the distinction between spirituality and religion can blur, making some participants uncomfortable with the proceedings. For example, recently two graduate students attended an AA "speakers meeting" in partial fulfillment of a course assignment. At the beginning of the meeting, instead of reading the normal serenity prayer, the group facilitator read a long passage from the Bible, thereby linking that particular AA meeting to the religious traditions that privilege the Bible over others. One student happened to be from a Buddhist tradition and was, as you might expect, offended. During a class discussion of the experience, she rightly stated that many clients would have been discouraged to attend that meeting based on the Bible reading.

Because it is so easy to misinterpret AA's spirituality for religion and/or because individual groups can become religious in nature, you will often have to discuss this issue with clients before or after a first meeting. Whether your clients have particular issues with organized religion, are unable to differentiate between religion and AA spirituality, or want to "use" the religious issue as an excuse for not attending, having these discussions can help overcome any resistance to AA or NA, often spelling the difference between successful and unsuccessful engagement. On many occasions over the years I have helped clients sort through this issue to help "clear the way" for AA and/or NA attendance.

To do this successfully, you must first understand the difference between religion and spirituality, familiarize yourself with the role of spirituality in AA and NA, and sort through your personal feelings, attitudes, and beliefs about the use of spirituality in the treatment process. As we have stated many times in this text, the first step is to understand self, before inadvertently (or purposefully) imposing your beliefs and attitudes onto clients needing help.

Sponsorship To help individuals accept and work the steps and to provide someone they can use as guide or mentor through the twelve-step process, new members are encouraged to locate a "sponsor" (McCrady & Delaney, 1995; Zweben, 1995). As important as sponsorship can be in the twelve-step process, it is often overlooked by new members and professional helpers. Professional substance abuse therapists and counselors often do not encourage their clients to find a sponsor because they may be unaware of the benefits or view this person as a threat to the therapeutic relationship. The former issue can be addressed through education and experience, while the latter simply indicates shortsightedness and probably reflects the professional person's own insecurities.

Sponsors are people who have successfully worked through the steps, having acquired several years of sobriety through a basic understanding of their own chemical dependency. Sponsors act as guides, confidants, and mentors to provide personal accountability for the member. They may be the people who guide members through the personal inventory in step 4, and the discussion of the contents of the inventory in step 5. It is their duty to take an interest in people's recovery, but not to take responsibility for it (McCrady & Irvine, 1989). That is, a sponsor must maintain boundaries and never lose sight of the possibility that the people they sponsor may relapse and/or leave the organization. Sponsors often use "tough love" (Peck, 1993) to ensure that responsibility for recovery remains with the new AA member.

Sponsorship is, in essence, an expression of step 12 where members are asked to "carry the message" of the program to others in need. Only those individuals who have reached the stage in their recovery where they can maintain boundaries and provide competent assistance to a new member should be considered as sponsors. As a professional who refers clients to AA, you should encourage each client to find a sponsor he or she can relate to, trust, and respect. Sponsors can be an invaluable "assistant" to the treatment process, although you will probably never meet them.

It is good practice to speak with your clients periodically about their sponsors, listening for what type of advice or assistance their sponsors are giving. There is not an "application process" in AA or NA for sponsorship; it is an informal part of the program, left to members to handle. Sometimes your clients will choose a sponsor who has not been "around" long enough. I recall many occasions in which a client and sponsor relapsed together, mainly because the sponsor was a relative newcomer and was not firmly grounded in his or her own recovery.

There are other instances where sponsors enter relationships for reasons beyond helping new members find sobriety. For example, occasionally new members (your clients) will become sexually involved with sponsors, etc. For this reason, most AA groups encourage members to have sponsors of the same sex (McCrady & Delaney, 1995). In the case of gay and lesbian clients, this "safeguard" will not apply. If you know your clients are gay or lesbian, discuss this issue openly. Perhaps, a sponsor of the opposite sex may be appropriate in these instances. However, it may be more helpful and appropriate to help your clients find a gay and lesbian AA or NA meeting so they can be assured of acceptance by the group and find a host of potential sponsors. Speak carefully with your clients about their choice of sponsor, how important the choice is, and how they should begin learning to screen the individuals they choose to have a relationship with in recovery.

Effectiveness of Twelve-Step Groups While many substance abuse professionals believe that regular attendance at AA or other twelve-step support groups is the single most effective component of a person's recovery (McCaul & Furst, 1994), formal outcome studies have, on the whole, failed to bear this out (Marvel, 1995). Whether studies have failed to prove effectiveness because the groups are ineffective or because these groups have rarely been studied (Watson et al., 1997) is debatable. It is true that little empirical research has been done to determine AA or NA's effectiveness or to identify which populations might find these programs most useful (Galanter, Castaneda, & Franco, 1991; McCaul & Furst, 1994). While many in the substance abuse profession believe that twelve-step groups are appropriate for everyone with a problem, others do not (Peele, 1998).

Similar to using educational or psychoeducational programs for difficult to engage clients, referring someone to a support group in lieu of professional treatment is a viable option. However, exercise this option with care because the perspective of these groups can sometimes be counterproductive. For example, for many women, traditional twelve-step approaches are not consistent with their treatment and personal needs. The same is also true for many people of color. Because of the prevalence of self-loathing, low self-esteem, and victimization experienced by many women and people of color as a result of a lifetime of discrimination and oppression in society, a twelve-step approach that relies on the acceptance of one's powerlessness can be problematic. According to Kasl (1990),

> The steps were formulated by a white, middle-class male in the 1930s; not surprisingly, they work to break down an overinflated ego, and put reliance on an all-powerful male God. But, most women suffer from a lack of healthy, aware ego, and need to strengthen their sense of self by affirming their own inner wisdom (p. 30).

Acceptance of one's powerlessness (surrender) over substances is supposed to bring relief from the battle to control one's use. Relinquishing the need to control one's use (and life) can bring immense relief to European American males taught to be in control. For women, people of color, and others socialized to be powerless in society, the demand to accept their powerlessness over one more issue in life can be overwhelming and counterproductive. Therefore, twelve-step support groups are not equally effective for all people. One way to solve this dilemma is to refer people to these groups who self-identify as being powerless or as having the disease of addiction.

Outpatient Treatment

Outpatient treatment in substance abuse means that clients live at home and attend scheduled sessions with outpatient therapists. These persons are assigned to therapists who meet with them at least once per week, although sessions can be more frequent in some cases (i.e., individual therapy and group therapy on different days, etc.), or less frequent, especially in the latter stages of treatment. As part of their involvement at this level, clients may participate in individual, group, or family therapy—or some combination of all three, depending upon the recommendation of the professional providing treatment and the resources available to the client. Clients in outpatient substance abuse treatment often simultaneously participate in twelve-step support groups such as AA or NA, and/or attend substance abuse education activities.

Outpatient treatment is a popular option. For example, McCaul and Furst (1994) stated that as many as 88 percent of those in treatment for substance abuse and/or chemical dependency are treated in outpatient programs. Why is outpatient treatment so popular? One reason is the cost involved. A typical 28-day inpatient treatment program can cost as much as $20,000 (Turbo, 1989), and longer-term residential programs, while the daily rate is usually lower than that of inpatient programs, can cost upwards of $50,000 because of the number of days in care. Second, outpatient treatment is more flexible (Turbo, 1989) and offers clients a less restrictive environment. Third, because clients remain at home, there is no reorientation period after treatment (Youngstrom, 1990). Fourth, while inpatient and residential treatment is usually time-limited, outpatient programs can last longer. Some claim that treatment should last at least one full year (Nace, 1987). In addition, clients are often referred to outpatient treatment for relapse prevention after completing inpatient or residential care.

Typically, clients suitable for outpatient treatment are those who have been assessed as substance abusers, or who have a number of related interpersonal, relationship, or family problems along with a substance abuse problem. Clients diagnosed as chemically dependent may also be amenable to traditional outpatient treatment if they do not have significant health problems, are not likely to experience acute withdrawal symptoms, and are capable of showing up regularly for appointments. To benefit from outpatient therapy, clients should be able to perform most social role functions, most of the time. In other words, they must have enough "control" over their lives to have the capacity to get to and from scheduled appointments as needed. Nace (1987) identified other criteria for determining whether outpatient treatment was appropriate. These include client motivation, the ability to discontinue use, social support, employment, lack of medical conditions, lack of severe mental illness, and treatment history (previous failures in outpatient and/or support group settings).

While traditional outpatient treatment is normally reserved for clients with less severe substance abuse problems, Jay Haley (1976, 1980) suggests that outpatient treatment should be used for even the most chronic clients. Haley believes that inpatient or residential care, because of its restrictive and protective nature, provides social control instead of treatment. He believes that clients do not improve if maintained in an institution or modality that focuses on social control. In these settings, it is difficult to know if clients are improving or simply acting as if they are improving in order to receive favorable reports from program personnel through compliance (see Chapter 4).

In the current era of managed care restrictions on third-party funding for inpatient or residential treatment, many outpatient service providers regularly see clients with severe or chronic chemical dependency. Unfortunately, as we have discussed before, in the substance abuse (and mental health) field, economic factors often dictate the treatment options that are available to clients.

Effectiveness of Outpatient Treatment Ultimately, the issue for providers, clients, policy makers, and third-party funders is the potential for successful treatment outcomes. Is there a significant difference in positive treatment outcomes between inpatient and outpatient settings? Many people assume that inpatient treatment is more effective because it is more intense, and that is what the public has been led to believe over the years (Peele, Brodsky, & Arnold, 1992). However, the empirical research does not bear out this assumption.

Miller and Hester (1986a) reviewed 26 controlled studies comparing the two treatment modalities and found that the more costly inpatient programs were not more effective than traditional outpatient programs, nor did inpatient programs of varying duration show differences in outcome. The most significant factor in successful treatment outcome, according to this review of treatment modalities, was length of time in treatment. Clients had a better chance of achieving long-term sobriety when they remained in treatment for a year or more. Given these findings, outpatient treatment is the level of care that allows clients to remain in treatment the longest, with the least disruption to daily life, at the lowest cost.

The discussion of outpatient treatment is shorter than others in this chapter, for good reason. In Chapter 10, we will discuss the primary methods and theories used to treat substance-abusing and chemically dependent clients on an outpatient basis. These theories (see Chapter 3) and methods (individual, group, family treatment) are the primary modalities used in outpatient treatment. Hence, to avoid redundancy, we leave this topic for Chapter 10.

Intensive Outpatient/Day Treatment

Until recently, clients requiring more intensive services than were available in an outpatient program were restricted to either inpatient or residential treatment, even if they had no physical or medical conditions to warrant such placements. Clients either had to disrupt their lives for a lengthy inpatient stay or struggle to maintain abstinence despite the lack of structure in outpatient treatment. No "in-between" level of care was available. Thus, clients often received too little treatment or too much treatment. In either case, clients received the only level of care available or that they could afford, leading to a system of care that was "all-or-nothing." For example, clients would receive high-intensity daily attention as inpatients, followed by low-intensity outpatient aftercare, or no formal aftercare at all beyond twelve-step support group attendance.

The all-or-nothing approach did not address the need for a gradual reduction in treatment intensity as clients are reoriented to living in their home environments. Moreover, clients with multiple needs (i.e., mental health, vocational, and educational) often had to travel to different agencies in order to receive the different services required. For example, it is still quite common for clients with co-occurring psychiatric disorders and substance abuse problems to receive psychiatric treatment at one site and substance abuse treatment at another (see Chapter 11).

Intensive outpatient or day treatment programs were originally designed to fill the aforementioned gaps in the treatment system by meeting the needs of clients whose assessed problems required more structure than traditional outpatient care, but not medically managed, 24-hour inpatient or residential care. Intensive outpatient treatment has become a generic name referring to a range of care that includes many treatment methods (i.e., individual, group, family, education). What occurs in an intensive outpatient program depends on the specific providers involved. The flexibility of this level of care allows providers to tailor services to meet the needs of various at-risk populations. In addition to the variation in services, coverage by third-party payers is also quite varied. Some insurance companies offer reimbursement for intensive outpatient treatment, while others do not.

Clients who are likely to benefit from intensive outpatient treatment include those who cannot manage their substance use as effectively as clients suited for traditional outpatient treatment, yet remain engaged in many life roles related to work, school, home, and family. These clients must be able to attend treatment sessions on a daily basis, returning home after each day's treatment. Hence, only clients unable to manage themselves or those who have medical or physical issues that require 24-hour care should be excluded from intensive outpatient treatment. However, I have found that clients with more significant role impairment can also be helped by intensive outpatient treatment. In a relatively few years, intensive outpatient programs have gained a reputation for effectively treating clients with relatively intact family systems and good psychosocial supports (Center for Substance Abuse Treatment, 1994).

Intensive outpatient treatment is especially helpful in aftercare for relapse prevention. Moreover, it can also serve clients with more chronic and severe problems, including those with co-occurring mental disorders (see Chapter 11). Either as a source of primary treatment or as a mid-level resource in a continuum of care that includes inpatient at the front end and traditional outpatient and support group attendance at the final stage of treatment, intensive outpatient treatment is a welcome addition to the substance abuse treatment system.

Intensive outpatient treatment is also an effective option for young people (adolescents) who lack parental supervision during the day or evening. In our adolescent substance abuse program, day treatment provided a needed adjustment period from intensive residential care with 24-hour supervision to traditional outpatient care that relied on parental and/or community supervision in the client's home environment. My program offered intensive outpatient treatment during the day (3:30 p.m. to 8 p.m.) for youths enrolled in school and in the morning (8 a.m. to 3 p.m.) for youths not attending school. Similarly, creative adult programs offer intensive outpatient programs at varied times throughout the day and evening, in order to address the needs of clients with different personal, family, and work schedules.

In an intensive outpatient program, clients attend treatment sessions daily (usually on weekdays, but often on weekends too) for three or more hours per day. Programs last anywhere from several weeks to several months, depending on program structure, client needs, and ability to pay for services. Clients participate in individual, group, family, and support group services on a daily basis. Programs also offer substance abuse education, vocational training and counseling, financial management, assertiveness training, relapse prevention, and psychiatric services, along with meals and nutritional counseling. The services offered during intensive outpatient treatment are the same as those available in an inpatient treatment setting. The only significant difference is the fact that intensive outpatient treatment is less disruptive to clients' lives. Clients receive intensive treatment while maintaining their life routines and carrying out their role obligations.

Intensive outpatient treatment provides clients with a high level of structure and intensity, while allowing them to process each day's activities over a longer period of time than with inpatient care. Clients remain engaged in their normal lives, making it possible for them to learn how to identify barriers and triggers and practice personal strategies to maintain abstinence on a daily basis. Thus, day treatment programs offer clients the opportunity to apply the knowledge and skills gained in treatment to daily life, and to process the results each day. Day treatment programs also are less expensive than inpatient care. Because of the lower cost, clients can receive several months of day treatment for less money than 28 days of inpatient treatment.

The major problem with intensive outpatient programs also pertains to their structure and format. Clients wanting to participate in this level of care must be motivated and be able to return to the treatment center daily, sometimes for weeks and months. It is challenging for intensive outpatient treatment providers to retain a stable client base, making the financial viability of these programs tenuous at best. The most successful and longstanding intensive outpatient programs are often attached to an inpatient program that provides financial support. While intensive outpatient treatment may be a more viable option than inpatient or residential care for most clients (excluding those with acute medical conditions), because of the administrative issues involved, this level of care is not widely available. It is particularly hard to find in rural communities.

Effectiveness of Intensive Outpatient Programs Unfortunately, there have been few, if any, outcome studies to determine the effectiveness of intensive outpatient programs. Since research suggests that length of time in treatment—not level of care—is the determining factor in treatment outcome (Cook, 1988; Miller & Hester, 1986a), it seems likely that combining the intensity of inpatient treatment with the flexibility and potential length of stay of outpatient treatment would be effective for many substance abuse clients. However, empirical research must be done before this statement can be counted as anything more than supposition.

Inpatient Treatment

Inpatient treatment for substance abuse is perhaps the best-known treatment method available. Almost everyone, whether treatment professional or layperson, has heard about inpatient or residential programs that last 28 days or longer. In fact, most people probably believe that this is the best, and perhaps the only, way to treat substance abuse and chemical dependency.

What is the difference between residential and inpatient treatment? Residential treatment centers are free-standing programs, while inpatient treatment is performed in a hospital-based environment. Clients needing medical intervention (i.e., for withdrawal syndrome, medication management, or other medical conditions) are best served, at least initially, in an inpatient setting. Most residential programs maintain referral agreements with medical personnel or facilities, but are not medical programs.

Inpatient and/or residential programs provide around-the-clock structure. This level of care offers clients intensive service and protection from the possibility of relapse. Clients reside in inpatient and residential programs for anywhere from three days to one year, depending on need, program structure, and client funding (third-party, public, or privately paid). Programming usually consists of individual, family, and group treatment, with a heavy emphasis on affiliation with twelve-step support groups and substance abuse education. Lengths of stay often depend on factors such as client motivation and reliability of outside support systems, chronicity of substance use history, and any medical or physical issues. Additionally, lengths of stay in inpatient or residential programs are often based on the funding source the client relies on to pay the high cost of care.

For many years, the typical length of stay in inpatient programs, based on the Minnesota Model (Larson, 1982), was 28 days. Although there is no basis in research for the belief that 28 days of inpatient treatment will produce better outcomes than other lengths of stay (Miller & Hester, 1986b), this was the industry standard. Many professionals and lay people alike began believing that 28 days of inpatient care were *required* for successful treatment; anything less was viewed as inadequate. In fact, the 28-day treatment period evolved primarily because of limits imposed by major health insurance carriers (Klar, 1987). Despite not being based on any research, the Minnesota Model has been the industry standard since the 1940s and 1950s. According to Cook (1988), the Minnesota Model "is an abstinence oriented, comprehensive, multiprofessional approach to treatment of the addictions, based upon the principles of Alcoholics Anonymous" (p. 625). While many third-party insurers have reduced benefits for inpatient treatment over the last 10 years, forcing programs to provide primary treatment in as short a period as seven days, many substance abuse professionals continue to believe that anything less than 28 days of inpatient treatment is inadequate. Similarly, before managed care became prevalent, many insurers would allow for up to 45 days of inpatient treatment for adolescent clients.

During the late 1980s, I developed an adolescent program that began with a 10-day residential stay designed primarily to assess the client and engage the family in treatment, followed by intensive outpatient care for three to six weeks and then traditional family and group-based outpatient treatment. At the time, the structure of this program contradicted the industry standard (unsupported by any research results) of 45 days of inpatient treatment followed mostly by twelve-step support group attendance. The idea of a continuum of care that reduced reliance on inpatient treatment was not well received, at least initially. Over time, primarily because of pressure from funding sources, our program design became the local standard, driving other programs for adolescents and adults to change or go out of business.

In addition to the treatment modalities discussed above, clients in longer-term residential treatment facilities also assume responsibility for the daily upkeep and operation of the program and facility. For example, in a therapeutic community setting, one group of clients is assigned to do the cleaning, while others cook, and so on. This is not the case for inpatient programs, where clients are treated as patients by hospital personnel.

Obviously, the major benefit of inpatient and residential care is structure. Living in a treatment center provides a structured and controlled environment in which clients can resist the urge to relapse because of the boundaries of the program. Moreover, clients have the opportunity to establish a beginning level of sobriety and form preliminary relationships with support group members before returning home.

This level of care also has problems, however. Because the structure is artificial—clients cannot relapse without leaving the program—clients do not learn how to deal with the stressors and triggers that exist in their home environment. Hence, until clients leave programs, it is impossible to predict how they will handle living drug-free in home environments that previously supported or tolerated chemically dependent behavior. Clients go through a process akin to "shock" treatment. They go from chemically dependent behavior to a structured life within the protective "bubble" of the hospital or treatment center. Then, after a few days, weeks, or months—with little warning and less preparation—clients are released back to their family and environment to "deal with it." The real world can quickly dispel the client's sense of self-efficacy and/or confidence in his or her abstinence. Although clients are able to remain abstinent within the inpatient or residential structure, they do not have the opportunity to practice new behaviors in their normal social environment. Without further planned aftercare, relapse is common (Denning, 2000).

Types of Inpatient/Residential Services Under the heading of inpatient or residential treatment, there are several variations in the type, intensity, and methods of treatment offered. While all of the programs require clients to disrupt their normal routines and live in a treatment facility or hospital, each of the inpatient or residential settings discussed below provides a different treatment experience.

Detoxification Programs For clients who have long and chronic histories of substance abuse or who have been abusing substances that are known to cause physical dependence, referral to a detoxification (detox) program is required. Although detoxification from alcohol or other drugs is not in itself considered a form of substance abuse treatment (Mattick & Hall, 1996; Miller & Hester, 1986a; National Academy of Sciences, 1990), many hospital-based inpatient programs have a detoxification unit, and non-medically-based residential programs maintain referral agreements with hospital-based detox units.

Detoxification programs are usually housed in hospitals. They are medically managed programs that offer a safe, humane place for clients to experience the often harsh and painful withdrawal process from drugs of abuse (Mattick & Hall, 1996). Detoxification is carried out under the supervision of a licensed physician who is trained in this area. The physician evaluates the client's needs and resources, and often provides medical management in the form of prescription medication to assist in the detoxification process while the client is an inpatient.

In recent years, however, many physicians have begun allowing clients to detoxify on an outpatient basis if the immediate threat to the client's life is not significant (Miller, Francis, & Holmes, 1988; Berg & Durbin, 1990; Mattick & Hall, 1996). For example, Abbott, Quinn, and Knox (1995) found that with careful screening, it was possible for more than 90 percent of all alcohol-dependent clients to be detoxified on an outpatient basis, also called "ambulatory detox" (National Academy of Sciences, 1990, p. 175) or "social detox" (Mattick & Hall, 1996). Regardless of whether detoxification is carried out on an inpatient or outpatient basis, its purpose is to closely monitor clients to ensure that no medical complications arise during withdrawal from their particular drug of choice, or combination of drugs, and to protect against immediate and possibly life-threatening relapse during the initial stages of withdrawal.

Clients are vulnerable to relapse early in the recovery process. This is especially true for clients who are dependent on opiates, depressants, and stimulant drugs. Moreover, when and if these clients relapse, they often take large doses of these drugs as a way to eliminate the negative effects of drug withdrawal. As such, another function of detoxification is to help clients avoid relapse and potential drug overdose (Miller, Francis, & Holmes, 1988). Clients at this stage, especially those withdrawing from stimulant dependence (cocaine, amphetamines, etc.) also can become potential suicide victims. Hence, another potential use of a detoxification program is to manage the potential for harm to self and others that often occurs early in the withdrawal process.

Two of the factors to consider when deciding whether your clients require formal detoxification services—either inpatient or outpatient—are their drugs of choice and the chronicity of their use history. As we discussed in Chapter 2, withdrawal from some drugs can cause severe, even life-threatening, conditions during detoxification. For example, withdrawal from most of the drugs categorized as depressants (alcohol, barbiturates, and benzodiazepines) can result in life-threatening seizures and other conditions that can lead to death. While there is little evidence that detoxification from opiates (heroin, etc.) causes significant medical danger, there is strong evidence that opiate-dependent clients who go through detoxification on an inpatient basis are more likely to stick with treatment after completing withdrawal (Mattick & Hall, 1996). As we have stated several times throughout this text, these decisions must ultimately be made in conjunction with a medical professional—yet another reason why referral for a complete physical examination during the assessment process is vital to competent substance abuse treatment (see Chapter 8).

Detoxification programs are usually part of the continuum of substance abuse treatment programs, but the research suggests that completion of a detoxification program is not a good indicator of participation in a treatment process after completing this phase (Miller & Rollnick, 1991). Moreover, detoxification programs are often misused by clients and treatment providers. For example, there are chemically dependent individuals who have gone through detoxification dozens of times, either to give themselves a place to live, or as a way to deal with pressures from family members and/or employers. Others check themselves into detoxification programs in order to hide from the police or to delay having to pay drug debts. It is up to the professionals responsible for admission into detoxification programs to ensure that valuable resources are not misused by clients with hidden agendas, as it were.

Controlling the admission process can become complicated, however. In many substance abuse treatment centers, the reimbursement rate for "detox" beds is three to five times higher than it is for regular substance abuse treatment beds. Hence, in programs across the country, clients admitted for inpatient or residential substance abuse treatment are initially placed in a "detox" bed even if their medical condition or use history does not warrant such a placement. In these circumstances, the social workers or other professionals responsible for admitting clients to detoxification programs undergo intense organizational pressure to take care of the program's "bottom line."

Therapeutic Communities The therapeutic community (TC) movement began in the late 1950s with the Synanon program and flourished throughout the 1960s and 1970s as a long-term, free-standing residential treatment option primarily for clients dependent on opiate drugs. Over the last 30 years, TCs have admitted clients dependent on drugs other than opiates, so much so that the majority of clients in therapeutic communities today are not opiate dependent (DeLeon, 1994).

While therapeutic communities have been around for over 40 years, there is no single model or program configuration that represents an "average" TC (DeLeon, 1989; National Academy of Sciences, 1990). Many different program models fall under the rubric of what has been called a therapeutic community. However, what all TCs have in common is long-term residential requirements. TC programs usually require clients to remain in the residential program for at least one year. Some TCs allow residents to remain in treatment for as long as three years, while others have begun limiting lengths of stay to six months or even shorter periods (DeLeon, 1989, 1994). For example, due to managed care restrictions placed on public funding for adult long-term residential care in Michigan, one TC began limiting clients referred through the Federal Bureau of Prisons and the Michigan Department of Corrections to 90 days of care. In recent years, managed care initiatives in both private and public third-party funding have changed the role and function of the therapeutic community as a long-term treatment option.

Most therapeutic communities operate on the theoretical and philosophical foundation that substance abuse is

> A deviant behavior, reflecting impeded personality development or chronic deficits in social, educational, and economic skills. The principal aim of the TC is a global change in lifestyle: abstinence from illicit substances, elimination of antisocial activity, development of employability, and prosocial attitudes (DeLeon, 1994, p. 392).

As stated above, to accomplish these goals, TCs have traditionally required rather lengthy periods in residence in the program. Such long-term treatment, according to the philosophy underlying the TC movement, is required for chronic chemically dependent individuals whose chemical dependency is complicated by elements of antisocial personality traits, mental disorders, or criminal involvement, sometimes called "social pathology" (ONDCP, 1990, p. 3). Providers of therapeutic community treatment fundamentally believe that chemical dependency is a holistic disorder that often requires stripping clients of the ego and personality that led to chemical dependency, and "rebuilding" them, as it were, with a more positive and prosocial ego and personality in order that they may achieve and maintain abstinence and become productive citizens.

Other characteristics of TC treatment include social and physical isolation from "old" friends, contacts, and locations, a structured living environment that includes regular and consistent confrontation and corrective behavioral feedback, a firm system of rewards and punishments, and a focus on self-examination and confession of past misdeeds. TCs usually operate on a "level system," whereby, as clients adjust and comply with the expectations of treatment, they move through various levels. Each subsequent level (usually four in all) allows for expanded personal privileges and responsibility within the community. At higher levels, clients are usually expected to work, either outside the program in an approved job, or inside as part of the community. For example, clients participate in housekeeping, cooking, and other daily functions needed to operate the program as a way of instilling and maintaining personal responsibility.

In many TCs, upper-level clients assume daily responsibilities for care and treatment of lower-level clients. This can lead to actual employment as paraprofessional counselors before and upon graduation from these programs (National Academy of Sciences, 1990). For example, in one TC upper-level clients were placed in charge of program supervision and security on third shifts; and many were appointed as the primary counselor for newly admitted clients as part of the new client's initiation into the program.

While many TCs employ professionally trained therapists and workers, most rely on so-called "life-experienced" or recovering counselors to carry out the bulk of the treatment offered. TC treatment generally focuses on group sessions led by upper-level clients and/or recovering professionals, with a heavy reliance on confrontation. Individual and family treatment is sometimes offered but is not central to the TC process. Aside from confrontational group treatment, TCs also rely heavily on education and often some form of vocational training. Treatment is, therefore, derived from a combination of confrontational group exposure, education, and personal responsibility. Behavior is immediately rewarded or punished as it occurs. As clients remain in this system for lengthy periods, their "old" traits, habits, beliefs, and behaviors are gradually replaced by new, more positive beliefs, values, and behaviors that occur through long-term immersion in a reinforcing milieu.

Traditionally, clients admitted to therapeutic community treatment were the most chronic and long-term chemically dependent. While this remains mostly true, today most clients find their way to TCs through the criminal justice system, primarily for substance-related crimes. That is, most clients admitted to therapeutic community treatment are sent to treatment in lieu of incarceration (jail or prison). It has been a long time since TCs were strictly reserved for the "hard-core" clientele, mainly because of the programs' need to keep their beds full of paying clients.

Over the years, typical TC treatment methods have caused controversy in the substance abuse field (Ausabel, 1983). Many TCs do not abide by the traditional disease model, and treatment methods are often considered harsh and demeaning (Lewis, Dana, & Blevins, 1988). For example, clients living in TCs were often given an assignment called an "awareness." An awareness is assigned by staff and/or upper-level residents when other residents act out in one of many ways. One local TC demanded that clients wear pajamas to group sessions if they were caught acting like "children," lie in a homemade coffin after a relapse, wear a toilet seat around their neck if caught using foul language, etc. The purpose of an awareness is to provide sufficient humiliation to help clients break through their system of personal denial. While these tactics were readily accepted in years past, more recently many began to disapprove. Certainly, not all TC programs use these tactics as part of everyday treatment. However, it is important to know that the therapeutic community treatment approach incorporates direct and often harsh confrontation, based on the idea that clients with substance abuse problems must be reborn into attitudes and belief systems that allow them to rejoin society as productive, drug-free, and crime-free citizens.

Effectiveness of Therapeutic Communities   Studies on the value of therapeutic communities in helping clients achieve long-term sobriety have had mixed results. For example, collectively TCs tend to experience significant client dropout rates. DeLeon (1994) stated that 30 to 40 percent of all clients admitted to a TC will drop out in the first 30 days of care, usually within the first 15 days ("Therapeutic Community," 1989). Further, over the course of treatment, a significant number of clients are asked to leave the program, often for breaking rules (Gelman et al., 1990). Ultimately, according to these numbers, only about 15 to 25 percent of all clients admitted for TC treatment ever successfully complete the program (DeLeon, 1994). In other words, 75 to 85 percent of all clients admitted to this level of care do not complete the program and therefore "cannot be distinguished from those . . . individuals who did not enter any substance abuse treatment modality" (National Academy of Sciences, 1990, p. 167).

While the statistics suggest that TCs are not the method of choice for many people, others believe that this model works well in cases when other methods do not (DeLeon, 1989, 1994; Peele, 1998; Yablonsky, 1967). After reviewing the data on TCs, one journal concluded that such programs were effective (ONDCP, 1990). That is, 80 percent of those clients who completed treatment remained drug-free. The National Academy of Sciences (1990) concluded that those who remained in treatment the longest were most likely to achieve sobriety. Similar to other levels of care, it seems that TCs work better for some clients than others. TCs offer a structured, strict, and highly accountable approach that requires clients to participate in direct and immediate confrontation, and sometimes humiliation, as a way of learning a new lifestyle. For those who are not able to benefit from this type of approach, referral to a TC is not advisable.

Halfway Houses   Under the heading of halfway houses, I include programs traditionally known as halfway houses, as well as three-quarter houses and missions. These programs are similar in structure and length-of-stay requirements (from several days up to several months) and in their demands that clients remain abstinent from substance use and contribute to the daily operation of the house. What separates these programs from therapeutic communities is the relative freedom residents have to engage and interact with the community outside the program. In fact, some programs in this category do not require clients to receive professional treatment. That is, many halfway and three-quarter houses only require

AA or NA attendance, while many missions simply require residents to attend religious services.

Halfway houses place clients "halfway" between treatment and full reintegration into their communities. Residents living in three-quarter houses are three-quarters reintegrated into the community, suggesting that they have more freedom and flexibility, along with fewer restrictions placed upon them and their interaction with "normal" life. Most of these programs require clients to work and contribute financially to the operation of the facility. Moreover, these programs also require that residents contribute to the daily operation of the house, including participation in daily domestic chores and, in some cases, participation in a resident or community governmental structure. While clients often become residents at halfway houses voluntarily, many houses are established to serve clients mandated by the criminal justice system. These programs usually require more stringent daily accountability checks, including random urine testing and weekly or daily participation in individual or group counseling, or daily AA and/or NA attendance.

Halfway houses may be publicly and/or privately funded. Some are funded entirely by residents' monthly payments. During the 1980s, halfway house programs were more prevalent than they are today, primarily because of the greater availability of public funds during that era. Today, while these programs continue to provide a valuable and needed resource, they are not as prevalent.

Halfway houses can be an effective resource for older adolescents who would otherwise become homeless without a structured place to live. For example, in a long-term residential program I used to operate, it was difficult to arrange housing for adolescents between 16 and 18 years old who did not have families to return to, or whose families and local environments were so violent or unsupportive that clients were certain to return to use. These clients were usually too old to be placed through foster care systems and too young to be turned loose on the streets to fend for themselves. Yet, because funding for halfway houses was sparse, these facilities were difficult, if not impossible, to locate. We tried unsuccessfully to raise seed funding for adolescent halfway houses.

Some halfway house programs hire professional staff to oversee daily operations and provide treatment and supportive services. However, most halfway houses are run either by residents through community government or by paraprofessional staff members who help with twelve-step support and manage the house operations on a daily basis. Often, the supervising manager of a halfway house lives on the premises and participates as a member of the community.

Clients appropriate for these programs are those with few, if any, social or financial resources, including employment and housing. These programs are especially appropriate for the recovering and motivated chronic chemically dependent person who has no job, home, or social support by which to sustain initial sobriety. For these clients, halfway houses serve as a critical link in the substance abuse treatment continuum. Halfway houses provide many clients, especially those who lack family support or financial resources, with opportunities to establish themselves in a relatively protected environment as they prepare to move back into life after treatment.

Effectiveness of Halfway Houses There is no outcome data that evaluates the effectiveness of halfway house programs or missions in helping clients achieve abstinence or remain drug-free. Since many of these programs exist outside the "mainstream" of substance abuse treatment, they tend to be overlooked and understudied. However, if length of time in treatment is a central factor in treatment success (Miller & Hester, 1986b), then it might be safe to suggest that halfway houses are probably an effective modality for clients needing long-term daily support in a drug-free environment. My clinical experience suggests that this is true in houses where professional staff provide management and daily treatment services (individual and group treatment). Nevertheless, until long-term empirical studies are completed, these conclusions remain anecdotal at best.

MAKING A REFERRAL
FOR SUBSTANCE ABUSE TREATMENT

Now that we have discussed the different levels of treatment that are available to clients with substance abuse problems, we can look into the process of making treatment referrals and explore various issues associated with this process. Before specifically discussing the referral process, however, we need to consider three issues that play a significant role in that process: least restrictive environment, treatment matching studies, and confidentiality. Following these discussions, we will look at ways to evaluate potential treatment providers and describe how to follow up with clients and providers after making a referral.

Least Restrictive Environment

The concept of least restrictive environment should be taken into account when referring clients to the appropriate level of substance abuse treatment. According to the ASAM PPC-2 (American Society of Addiction Medicine, 1996) and others (Doweiko, 1999; Jung, 2001; Klar, 1987), the concept of least restrictive environment states that clients should always be placed in a level of care that offers the least amount of physical and personal restriction, while maintaining the highest probability of success.

While this objective sounds good in theory, it is not always possible to follow these guidelines. For example, for the least restrictive environment criteria to work, there must be adequate treatment choices available in the client's geographic area, unless he or she has the resources to travel. According to the ASAM PPC-2 criteria, when the appropriate level of care is unavailable, you should refer to the next most intensive treatment option available (American Society of Addiction Medicine, 1996). That is, if clients fit the criteria for intensive outpatient treatment and none is available in their area, you should refer them to an inpatient treatment provider. This assumes that clients would not benefit from less restrictive settings, an assumption that my clinical experience suggests is not always correct. There are instances in which clients may benefit from traditional outpatient treatment instead of inpatient treatment, even when their assessments indicate that day treatment or intensive outpatient care was appropriate. In the end, base the level of care to which you refer people on your best understanding of the client's need and level of motivation, while seeking out the least restrictive environment. This is when it is appropriate to use professional judgment on behalf of clients and their families. Before making these judgments, however, consult with your clinical supervisor for advice, support, and direction.

The concept of least restrictive environment is a credible and reasonable criterion for making treatment referrals. To make it work on behalf of your clients, it is important to know the menu of services available in your geographic area, what type of funding options each provider accepts, what level of service the providers offer, and clients' funding resources. When available, always use the concept of least restrictive environment as a guide to placement. When certain levels of care are unavailable for some reason (funding, location, and so on), use your best clinical judgment in conjunction with your clinical supervisor.

Matching Treatment to Client Needs

As we have discussed throughout this text, clients who fit the diagnostic criteria for substance abuse and chemical dependency vary widely. In fact, no two clients who fit the same diagnostic criteria are identical. They have different lives, come from different circumstances, and have different needs. Clients neither come from the same backgrounds nor pass through the same stages as their substance abuse problems develop. Consequently, it makes sense that a single treatment method will not be suitable for every client. From this perspective, a "one-size-fits-all" approach to substance abuse treatment is ineffective and wasteful of scarce treatment resources (Miller & Hester, 1986b). Based on this idea, theorists developed a common-sense hypothesis of treatment matching in an attempt to discover whether different treatment methods work better for different clients based on their unique treatment needs. Clients would be screened for a number of personal issues in order to develop reliable categories that could be matched to particular treatment approaches. Accordingly, matching individual clients to programs using particular treatment methods would—if this hypothesis were correct—ensure that clients received the specific treatments that were best suited to the severity of their chemical dependency, thus improving treatment outcomes. There is plenty of room for improvement—most evaluation reports place substance abuse treatment success, defined as a continuous period of abstinence for upwards of one year post-treatment, at or below 10 percent (Jung, 2001).

Researchers set out to investigate this idea by conducting a series of studies in the late 1980s and 1990s. For example, one study (Kadden, Getter, Cooney, & Litt, 1989) found that alcohol-dependent clients benefited from being matched to either coping skills treatment or interactional group treatment. Another study (Cooney, Kadden, Litt, & Getter, 1991) found that clients mismatched with particular types of treatment were less successful than clients who were matched to particular treatments. Another study found that matching clients to particular treatments resulted in improved outcomes when abstinence was used as the primary outcome measure (Longabaugh, Wirtz, Beattie, Noel, & Stout, 1995). Initially, these results generated excitement about the potential for developing specific screening and assessment batteries to determine the best match for clients in need of substance abuse treatment (Babor, Kranzler, & Lauerman, 1989).

Unfortunately, a major evaluation (funded by the federal government) spanning eight years and including more than 900 clients randomly assigned to specific treatments found that overall treatment success rates did not significantly differ across the various treatment methods used in the study (Project MATCH, 1997). Researchers could not prove that treatment matching made a significant difference in treatment outcome. They also found that the interaction between specific treatment methods and types of alcoholism did not matter, although clients demonstrated progress in each of the treatment methods studied. As a result, some believe that the study created a ceiling effect, making it difficult to determine if any one of the methods was more effective than others for particular clients (Jung, 2001).

The evaluation did, however, produce some unexpected results. Researchers found that the severity of a client's psychiatric problems interacted significantly with specific treatments. For example, clients with less severe psychiatric symptoms were more successful in treatment based on a twelve-step approach than other methods. However, for clients reporting more severe psychiatric problems, there was no difference in outcome for various methods (Project MATCH, 1997).

Do the results of this study suggest that it makes no difference what method of treatment people participate in, as long as they participate? Do all treatments work the same? One of the most significant findings from the Project MATCH study was that most clients in the study, regardless of treatment assignment, showed improvement—a good sign for substance abuse treatment. Alternatively, was the study flawed? Perhaps the results are invalid because researchers did not establish a no-treatment control group, they used an all-male subject pool, and only three methods of treatment were offered (Jung, 2001).

One potential flaw in the study that was not discussed in the literature was the fact that it focused on treatment methods instead of more intangible factors involving the treatment providers, including issues related to diversity (Boyd-Franklin, 1989; Lee, 1994; Wilson, 1992). This study and the entire treatment matching movement assume that treatment methods make the difference, disregarding the potential influence of personal characteristics of the providers and the interaction between clients and individual providers in treatment settings.

The fact that no significant differences were found across methods is not surprising. Consistent with the thrust of this text and the literature about successful treatment outcomes (Harper & Lantz, 1996; Parham, 1993; Pinderhughes, 1989; Miller & Rollnick, 1991; Lantz, 1993; Lantz & Pegram, 1989; Luborsky et al., 1985), treatment methods mean less than how a treatment provider approaches and engages clients in a treatment setting. As stated earlier, clients do not trust and engage with techniques and methods, they trust and engage with (or distrust and remain detached from) people. Focusing on methods and overlooking provider characteristics refute the notion that individual characteristics, including race, gender, and other personal demographic information, have a significant impact on treatment outcome (Lum, 1999; Miller & Rollnick, 1991). Those in favor of treatment matching have concluded that the best variables to use for matching are not yet known (Mattson & Allen, 1991). Perhaps if the researchers had looked in a different direction and examined different variables, the benefits of treatment matching would have been more clear.

Confidentiality

The NASW Code of Professional Ethics (NASW, 2000) insists that individuals, groups, families, and communities seeking help from social workers are guaranteed a level of confidentiality. Specifically, professionals working with substance-abusing and chemically dependent clients should be aware of the portion of the *Federal Register* called "Confidentiality of Alcohol and Drug Abuse Patient Records" (42 CFR, Part 2). It details information that substance abuse professionals need to know to protect their clients and themselves. Moreover, while knowledge of the Code of Ethics and the specific requirements for substance abuse professionals is helpful, you (or your agency) should have good legal counsel available to discuss issues of confidentiality that will arise during daily substance abuse practice.

Generally, without prior permission, providers cannot reveal whether or not someone is a client in a substance abuse treatment facility or disclose any other information about them. Providing information to those outside the treatment program or requesting information from other sources generally requires people's written permission. Moreover, a release-of-information form may be required for you to communicate with people's partners or other family members, since you cannot assume that significant others know that your clients are in treatment.

Despite the above-mentioned safeguards, clients in treatment do not have the right to absolute confidentiality. That is, there is certain information that causes exceptions to confidentiality rules and regulations. Clients are afforded relative confidentiality, meaning that the most you can promise them is to act responsibly within the profession's Code of Ethics (NASW, 2000), adhere to existing laws, and follow agency policy concerning the handling of sensitive client information (Sheafor, Horejsi, & Horejsi, 2000). Relative confidentiality must always be explained to clients. For example, it is common in substance abuse treatment to have clinical records subpoenaed for court proceedings. Additionally, given the high correlation between substance abuse and child abuse and/or domestic violence (van Wormer, 1995), there may be occasions in which you will have to report information to the local authorities. During a medical emergency, which is another common occurrence in substance abuse treatment, you may release information to help save a client's life. The same is true when people pose a threat to self and others, as in cases of potential suicide or homicide.

Given the pressures and dilemmas often confronted in substance abuse practice over confidentiality, it is important to seek competent legal advice. It is also wise to remain in close contact with your clinical supervisor so that he or she can advise you about agency policy and the right to limited confidentiality that is afforded all clients in substance abuse practice.

Assessing Substance Abuse Treatment Providers

In addition to determining the appropriate level of care, during the referral process you must also decide which providers are best able to meet clients' treatment needs. In some locations, this is easy. Smaller cities, towns, and rural areas may have only one or two different providers who are qualified to perform substance abuse treatment services. To find alternatives, and different levels of care, clients would have to travel to the nearest metropolitan area. In most urban and suburban areas, however, there are various options based on location, transportation, funding (insurance, public funding, managed care), and goodness-of-fit between client and service provider. Choosing an appropriate provider is critical to the success of your clients, for reasons other than the effectiveness of one modality over others.

Most of the research involving treatment effectiveness suggests that the type of treatment is not a major factor in treatment effectiveness (Maisto & Carey, 1987; Miller & Hester, 1986a). In the past, some programs claimed success rates as high as 90 percent (Emrick & Hansen, 1983), while others found that only 7 percent of clients were successful (Polich, Armor, & Braiker, 1981). However, the former study was dismissed by researchers because of self-selection bias, which occurs when many people drop out of the study leaving only the most motivated and successful clients still participating at the end. As such, the results were based on only 10 percent of all of the original clients in the study. That is, the program was successful for 90 percent of a rather small segment consisting of 10 percent of the original client population. The second study mentioned above, conducted by the Rand Corporation, was based on random sampling of 474 clients who were followed for more than four years after primary treatment was completed, making it a more valid and reliable account of treatment success (or failure). As suggested by these two examples, it's always a good idea to use critical thinking skills and look closely at the particulars of any outcome study to determine if it is worthwhile.

Evaluation research further shows that the most widely used treatment methods were among the lowest in demonstrating effectiveness (Jung, 2001). Educational films, general addiction counseling, and psychotherapy—a main part of most treatment programs across the country—were among those treatment modalities with the lowest success rates. In contrast, studies evaluating brief interventions, social skills training, motivational enhancement, and community reinforcement demonstrated high effectiveness. Because there are no controlled studies to look at, it was not possible to evaluate AA in the same manner.

It is worth repeating that treatment success is enhanced by goodness-of-fit between clients and their treatment provider. Treatment success rates rise when clients feel hopeful and encouraged to participate in the treatment process. Instead of looking at providers for the modalities they employ, perhaps it would be better to look for providers who respect clients and are willing to individualize treatment planning and methods to address their clients' unique needs. It does not seem to matter which method, theory, model, or modality they use. What does matter is how individual providers engage clients in the treatment process.

Regardless of the answer to this and other questions, it is your job to become acquainted with local providers so that you can be aware of what these providers offer and the quality of their treatment services. I believe that an ethical social worker should not refer clients to treatment providers only on reputation, unless that program's reputation is confirmed by the referring social worker's own first-hand knowledge of their successes. In other words, do not refer clients to someone you have not met and spoken with about treatment methods and approaches. In good faith, you cannot encourage clients to follow through with treatment if you do not know whether it will be helpful. Do not wait for treatment failures or complaints before familiarizing yourself with local providers. Perhaps the most effective question to ask yourself about a local provider is, "Would I send my child, spouse, parent, or best friend to this particular treatment agency?" If the answer is no, why would you send clients there? Take a proactive approach to familiarizing yourself, and your agency, with the local treatment community. It will be worth the effort.

Beyond gaining familiarity with local referral sources, there are other factors to consider when referring a client for substance abuse services. These are discussed briefly below.

Provider Location   To ignore people's physical proximity to treatment providers is to practically guarantee high dropout rates. This is especially true if clients need any level of care other than inpatient or residential. For example, outpatient or intensive day treatment services require people to travel to and from treatment on a daily, multi-weekly, or weekly basis. To participate in an intensive outpatient program, clients must find transportation to and from the treatment center every day for several weeks, perhaps even months.

Location is not as important when considering an inpatient or residential program because people reside in these programs for designated periods. In fact, placing clients in residential or inpatient centers away from their home can discourage early withdrawal from the treatment program. However, this strategy has one major disadvantage. If the treatment center is too far from home, your clients' family members may be unable to participate in treatment, causing problems at discharge. A good referral is one in which your clients can participate, given their circumstances, transportation, and ability to travel. The closer and easier the trip, the more likely it is that people will continue with treatment.

Funding Sources   While numerous options are available to people with private health insurance or the personal wealth to pay for services, treatment options are scarce for the millions of people without insurance or the personal means to pay for services. However, there are federal, state, and local funds available in most areas to pay for substance abuse treatment, although these funds strictly limit the modality and/or providers available for referral. To make referrals that are appropriate to people's funding situations, you should take the time to familiarize yourself with the funding needs, requirements, and options for your clients, as well as which providers accept which types of funding.

You will need to do more than simply ask about insurance or other funding options. You should be aware of the various funding options and/or programs for which your clients might qualify, and be prepared to help them complete the appropriate paperwork so that they can receive the benefits available to them. Often, clients have no idea what options are available. This is our area of expertise. Therefore, having the appropriate knowledge and contacts will make treatment options available for clients who thought they had no choices at all.

Transportation In addition to considering location, you must determine whether clients have reliable and affordable modes of transportation to get to and from the service provider. Whether they own a car (assuming the client has a driver's license), have a friend or relative with a vehicle, or have access to reliable public transportation, it is important to assess this factor and make referrals accordingly. As stated above, the easier it is for clients to get to treatment, the more likely it is that they will attend. This is especially true for clients in the early stages of treatment, when they are ambivalent about committing to the process (Miller & Rollnick, 1991). Moreover, if you work with adolescent clients, do not assume that their parent(s) will drive them to and from treatment. Transportation—similar to funding—is an area that must be attended to if clients are to succeed in treatment. For example, in our adolescent day treatment program, we arranged free public bus vouchers for all of our clients. They rode the public buses to a drop-off point close to the center, where staff from the program picked them up in an agency vehicle and transported them to the center. There are various options available, and it is your job to ensure that clients benefit from these alternatives.

Goodness-of-Fit We have already mentioned treatment matching (Project MATCH, 1997). It is important to know the types of services that providers offer and how their offerings meet the unique needs of your clients. For example, if your client is a single mother with children, does the provider offer any special programming to address her unique needs? Such provisions are rare indeed. Moreover, the issue of selecting an appropriate treatment option for women is controversial. For example, it has been asserted that traditional treatment programs tend to be ineffective and perhaps even inappropriate for women because they were created by and for men (Van Den Bergh, 1991). Additionally, fewer women than men receive treatment for substance abuse disorders (National Institute on Alcohol Abuse and Alcoholism [NIAAA], 1990), and few aftercare programs address women's needs (Hughes, 1990). Women tend to seek help from providers other than those who specialize in treating substance abuse (Weisner & Schmidt, 1992). However, with a new emphasis on women's health and the addition of many female researchers attempting to gather information about women and substance abuse, information about women and chemical dependency is gradually becoming available.

If your client is a person of color, are there any social workers of color on staff? These are critically important issues to know when assessing the probability of treatment success. As stated above, this is where personal knowledge of particular programs and/or practitioners becomes invaluable to the referral process.

Follow-Up to Referral

If your primary job is to refer clients to substance abuse treatment providers, there is one remaining aspect to the assessment, planning, and referral process: follow-up. After deciding whether clients need treatment and determining which treatment providers are best suited to their needs, your final job is to follow up on the referral to see if people actually made it to their scheduled appointments.

Before we discuss this function, let us back up for a moment. If you are referring your clients for services, you should take steps to make sure that they actually schedule appointments or intake interviews. Similar to taking steps to ensure that they receive a medical examination, you have an obligation to see that clients make contact with treatment providers. I recommend calling the provider in the client's presence and scheduling the initial interview, or better yet, having your client schedule the appointment using the telephone in your office. When they make an appointment in your presence, it increases their sense of accountability, making it even more likely that they will attend the scheduled appointment. If you jot down the provider's telephone number for them to call later, there is a greater likelihood that the appointment will not be made. Therefore, the first step in the follow-up process is to make sure that the appointment is scheduled before your client leaves your office.

Second, before people leave your care, obtain a signed Release of Confidential Information form that allows you to contact service providers to check on their progress. Often, when you explain that the release will allow you to follow up on their progress, clients will be more likely to show up for the first session. If clients refuse to give you permission to follow up, instead of calling the provider, call your clients the morning of their scheduled appointments and after their appointments to increase accountability and positive pressure to attend.

If your clients do sign a release form (and most will do so), within a day or two after their scheduled appointment you will need to contact the provider to see if they actually appeared for the initial interview. Your next call should be to clients themselves. If they attended the session, ask them how it went and alleviate any fears, objections, or concerns about the treatment process. If they did not attend, you have one final opportunity to encourage future attendance. Either way, you can offer support, encouragement, and hope. If you engaged your clients as discussed in this text, your contribution during follow-up may help bridge the gap between their trust in you and lack of trust in a new provider. Your job here is not to contradict or intervene in people's treatment, but simply to offer encouragement and support for their efforts.

SUMMARY

In this chapter we began our discussion of substance abuse treatment. The majority of the work here focused on exploring the different levels of care in the substance abuse treatment system: education and early intervention; twelve-step support groups; outpatient treatment; intensive outpatient or day treatment; and various forms of inpatient and residential treatment. This information will be invaluable to you, regardless of whether you plan to provide substance abuse treatment or refer clients to other service providers following a multi-systemic substance abuse assessment.

This chapter ended with a discussion of various issues involved in making treatment referrals. We explored the concept of least restrictive care, the effectiveness of treatment matching, and issues involving confidentiality. Additionally, we discussed various criteria to employ when evaluating local treatment providers as possible referral sources for your substance-abusing clients.

10

Substance Abuse
Treatment Methods

Our focus in this chapter is on substance abuse treatment. Specifically, we will cover the information needed to begin the professional learning process of becoming a substance abuse treatment provider. After a brief presentation of general principles for substance abuse treatment, we will discuss treatment planning and several issues that pertain to this important task. Next, we will explore the four primary treatment modalities used to address substance abuse problems: individual, group, family, and community models. Our discussion will highlight the contributions of the models discussed in Chapter 3, while demonstrating how to treat clients using a multi-systemic approach that encompasses all of the specific models discussed earlier.

The chapter ends with a discussion of relapse prevention within the context of aftercare. Although it has been argued (and I agree) that all substance abuse treatment is a form of relapse prevention (Connors, Donovan, & DiClemente, 2001), we will explore how to help clients reintegrate and reorient themselves within their home communities as sober individuals after their primary treatment period has ended. My clinical experience suggests that a lack of long-term aftercare and relapse prevention is a leading cause of substance abuse treatment failure. Washton (1988) agrees with this observation, noting that relapse "has been the nemesis of addiction treatment for all types of chemical dependency problems" (p. 34). Hence, a comprehensive discussion of substance abuse treatment must emphasize the importance of providing aftercare services that help clients restructure their lives in order to maintain sobriety.

RECOVERY: THE HOLY GRAIL
OF SUBSTANCE ABUSE TREATMENT

Throughout this text, I have used the word "recovery" to describe the goal of substance abuse treatment. Whether recovery is accomplished by focusing initially on abstinence as a treatment objective or on achieving abstinence through a harm reduction approach (Denning, 2000), the ultimate goal of substance abuse treatment is to help clients participate in a recovery process. Recovery, as it is characterized here, is not a one-step process; it does not simply occur because your client abstains from all substance use. While one or two years of abstinence are the criteria most substance abuse programs use to gauge success, this is not "recovery" in a dynamic and holistic sense. Rather, recovery from chemical dependency is "a difficult, ongoing process, in which relapse back to active chemical use is a constant danger" (Doweiko, 1999, p. 399). Recovery involves transforming a person's lifestyle, attitudes, beliefs, and behaviors. Since the remainder of this chapter pertains to treatment, it will be helpful to define recovery first, because it is the ultimate goal of treatment. What does recovery look like, how will people know when they are in the recovery process, and what roles do we play in this process?

Several models of recovery are described in the literature, including the currently popular stages of change model (Connors, Donovan, & DiClemente, 2001), or transtheoretical model (Prochaska & DiClemente, 1982, 1984, 1986), which was discussed in Chapter 4 with regard to motivation. I adopted this model to assess client motivation during assessment and treatment, although it was originally developed to gauge progress toward recovery from tobacco addiction (Prochaska & DiClemente, 1982). Lichtenstein and Glasgow (1992) also presented a multi-stage model for recovery, based on the transtheoretical model. Another model of recovery, based largely on a twelve-step approach, was suggested by Nowinski (1996). In the first stage of this model, clients come to understand that will power alone will not guarantee recovery. In the second stage, clients become willing to do whatever it takes to make changes in their life, and they realize that they will need help with this process. The third stage occurs when clients take action, through either twelve-step support or professional assistance, to change their chemically dependent lifestyle or achieve abstinence.

Below, I offer a different, more holistic definition of recovery that goes well beyond abstinence. This definition is based on the professional literature and more than two decades of clinical experience with substance abuse clients of all ages. This model, while based in the work of others, has not been empirically tested. Rather than claim it as a version of the truth, I offer it as a way to further the discussion about the nature of recovery. When you are done reading and discussing this model, you may want to compare it to other models and record your thoughts in your substance abuse journal.

Back in Chapter 1, we discussed the qualitative differences between people diagnosed as substance abusers and those who are diagnosed as chemically dependent. I suggested that when a person "crosses the line" from abuse to dependence, substance use and everything associated with it becomes a lifestyle. More than a bad habit or irresponsible behavior, a chemically dependent lifestyle becomes an all-encompassing illness (see below) that dominates the life of the person who is chemically dependent. Substance use and the associated lifestyle become a fundamental aspect of self-identity. As you may recall, I stated that chemically dependent persons form a monogamous relationship with their drug(s) of choice.

Therefore, the goal of recovery from a chemically dependent lifestyle is to transform one's life to achieve a new self-identity that does not include substance use. Accomplishing this goal takes more than simply abstaining from substances. It requires massive and fundamental change in the way people view themselves and others. Recovery is not about abolishing personal traits that are defective, but about finding new and healthy ways of satisfying the needs that drugs fulfilled in the past. For example, many clients use cocaine as a way to overcome social difficulties or to feel sexually desirable. These desires are not flawed; it is the means used to accomplish them that is the problem. Therefore, for recovery to occur, these individuals will need not only to abstain from cocaine use but to find ways to meet these needs without chemical assistance.

Accordingly, recovery is a long-term—perhaps lifelong—process that begins when an individual chooses to abstain from substances. Recovery takes place in stages, although the impact and length of time in each stage differ among individuals. I suggest that there are four stages in the recovery process: abstinence, confrontation, growth, and transformation. While movement through the stages is not clean (meaning that people do fluctuate between the stages because of relapse), the stages are presented in linear fashion for clarity.

Stage One: Abstinence

The abstinence stage lasts as long as two years from the date of last use. The primary tasks of this stage involve learning to live from day to day without using chemicals. During this stage, individuals often relapse back to use. There are some clients who decide to abstain and then never relapse, but this is far from the norm. Some authors claim that the average chemically dependent individual will relapse as few as three or four times (Prochaska, DiClemente, & Norcross, 1992), while others claim that it takes perhaps as many as five to seven relapses before a person will be able to develop a consistent, daily pattern of abstinence (Brunton, Henningfield, & Solberg, 1994).

One goal in this stage is to minimize the damage (personal and social) caused by a relapse and to lengthen the time between relapses. Relapse is an expected and usual part of the early abstinence stage. Social support through twelve-step meetings and group treatment is invaluable during this stage of recovery. The ultimate purpose of this stage is for clients to reach the point where they are no longer responding to social triggers and drug cravings on a daily basis. This does not mean that the threat of relapse is gone. It only means that the individual learns to get through most days without experiencing or giving in to overwhelming cravings or urges to use. When this stage is complete, abstinence is no longer a minute-to-minute, hour-to-hour, or day-to-day struggle.

The treatment focus during this stage is on learning to remain abstinent on a daily basis, through social support, sponsorship, and group involvement. It will seem as if people's self-identities are fully involved with being sober, although they will not always be happy about it. In fact, it is normal and positive for clients in this stage to be fully involved in the process and to show signs of struggle and ambivalence (Miller & Rollnick, 2002) about abstinence. As we discussed in Chapter 4, this struggle is usually a sign of engagement in the abstinence process. It is appropriate for clients to focus as much of their efforts as possible on the difficult task of remaining abstinent, sometimes after years of chemical abuse.

It is generally inadvisable to expect clients to confront deeply held personal issues during the abstinence stage, although this process can begin as the client moves toward stage two. That is, if your client becomes willing and able to begin confronting personal issues beyond daily abstinence, this is a key indicator that he or she is progressing into stage two.

Stage Two: Confrontation

The second stage of recovery, lasting from the end of stage one up to as long as five years of consistent abstinence, is one in which clients are at high risk for relapse. During the confrontation stage, clients begin confronting and changing the personal, family, and social issues that contributed to their chemically dependent lifestyle. During this stage, clients will report almost daily confrontations with feelings, behaviors, and people associated with their past, often resulting in intense periods of shame and guilt. Here is an example:

> One of my clients had regularly engaged in sexual activities with gay men while he was cocaine dependent. Although he was primarily heterosexual when abstinent, he had experimented with gay sex as part of the effects of constant cocaine intoxication. One night when he was with a group of male friends, he bumped into a man with whom he'd had sexual contact. The man recounted the experiences to him in front of his new group of friends, who had not known that my client had engaged in sex with men. The intensity of this personal confrontation almost sent the client into relapse.

During the confrontation stage, recovering clients experience a developmental awakening similar to adolescence. They learn how to conduct adult relationships, assume responsibility for their actions, and explore lifestyles that do not include drugs and the people associated with their chemically dependent past. This is a time of growth and exhilaration, but it is also fraught with intense feelings. At this point, clients do not yet have a firm and confident sense of self beyond being a chemically dependent person. Often, this is the stage when clients begin exploring issues of abuse from their past, such as sexual abuse, rape, violence, and other personal and sexual issues that may have been part of, or preceded, their chemically dependent lifestyle. They begin confronting and working through familial issues and adult relationship issues, and they start to work on the difficult task of cleaning up the mess they made of their lives and reputation and the lives of those closest to them during their chemical dependency phase.

When you speak to people in the confrontation stage, they will appear to be enthralled with recovery, constantly telling their story to anyone who will listen, and relating everything in life back to tenets of the recovery process. Individuals in this stage go through a phase where they believe that anyone who uses substances is addicted. It is also during the confrontation stage that you will hear clients discussing their desire to become a counselor or social worker in order to help other chemically dependent persons. Clients engaged in the confrontation stage appear obsessed with the process of recovery.

Few signs of ambivalence are evident in the recovering person's daily presentation. However, do not be deceived. Each day can bring new issues to confront and along with it, a rapid return to ambivalent feelings about recovery and a high risk of relapse. You will often have to help clients discuss their ambivalence, even if they do not bring up the subject themselves. Continuing periods of ambivalence are common to the confrontation stage, especially early in the process. Because their public persona has become so immersed in the virtues of recovery, the possibility of ambivalence and relapse presents the recovering person with the threat of embarrassment. They may ask themselves, "How could I question my decision to recover, or consider relapse, after trumpeting the benefits of recovery to anyone who will listen?"

Ironically, it is during this highly sensitive and intense period that most clients are released from aftercare. As stated earlier, because of the emotional intensity often associated with the issues clients confront during this stage, they can easily relapse or have the urge to relapse even after three or more years of abstinence. Hence, clients often come to treatment just prior to, or immediately after, a relapse caused by the difficulties experienced during the confrontation stage. Clients and their support persons can benefit from individual, family, and group treatment approaches aimed at assisting them in working their way through these issues. Other interventions that are helpful and appropriate at this stage include training in dealing with stress, recognizing and coping with high-risk situations, and resolving conflicts. It is also important for clients to remain engaged in their social support network even when they begin feeling "better." Because of the nature of the confrontation stage, issues and feelings arise suddenly, often sending clients into a tailspin that could not have been predicted even minutes before it occurred. Therefore, work to keep your clients engaged in twelve-step groups and/or other recovery-oriented social supports, especially when you know they are in the confrontation stage, even when they claim that they feel "great."

When clients repeatedly demonstrate the ability to confront personal crises without teetering on the brink of relapse, they may be transitioning out of the confrontation stage.

Stage Three: Growth

By the time clients begin emerging from the emotional minefield of the confrontation stage, they should have established consistent, reliable, and positive social networks and be well on their way to confronting and handling the many personal and social issues involved with their previous lifestyle. At this point, lifestyle changes have begun in earnest. That is, they no longer see the same friends, frequent the same social settings, participate in the same recreational activities, or hold many of the same attitudes and beliefs they held during their chemical dependency period. Instead, they hold jobs and pay bills, take personal responsibility for their behavior and its consequences, and generally have a hopeful attitude toward the future. These individuals are beginning to establish productive and positive adult relationships, although intimacy may still present major challenges.

During the growth stage (five or more years of abstinence if they did the difficult, emotional work in the confrontation stage), individuals continue the process of lifestyle change. Their new way of life and worldview move them away from an identity consumed by their recovery, and toward a multi-faceted self-identity that includes their past as one element of self. That is, their new way of life without drugs and the associated lifestyle begins to feel "normal." No longer are these individuals surprised by success; during the growth stage they become functioning, responsible people living and thriving in the social world. In fact, when clients are in the growth stage, they will cease being aware of changes as they occur. New friends, jobs, responsibility, and respect become commonplace.

People's personal identities will slowly grow to encompass elements other than recovery and their experiences with chemical dependency. This does not mean that they will cease using social supports to stay in tune to their recovery needs, but it does mean that daily life does not involve constant attention to maintaining abstinence and recovery. A person who is in the growth stage of recovery is oriented toward the future, while appreciating lessons learned and hardships survived in the past. Clients in this stage are still susceptible to relapse, but it would take a catastrophic event to make this occur. For most who reach this stage, they no longer consider the option of using chemicals even when hardship occurs.

Treatment needs in this stage usually revolve around completing work remaining from the confrontation stage. These issues may involve childhood abuse, trauma, and/or adult relationship issues, especially problems with intimacy. Often, these individuals will appear for therapy about issues and problems in daily life, rather than concerns related directly to their recovery. Individual, relationship, and family therapy are the usual modes of treatment for clients needing help during the growth stage of recovery.

Stage Four: Transformation

When clients emerge from the growth stage, they have found the beginnings of a new lifestyle. Their new life does not involve substance use, and it may have been years since they last had a recognizable urge to use. When personal issues arise, these individuals now handle them in healthy ways, using social networks and personal skills developed through the recovery process. Clients who reach the transformation stage of recovery are no longer substance abuse clients. Instead, they are people who happen to have a history of chemical dependency.

Like everyone else, these individuals will continue to have problems to confront, but they now possess the skills and resources to handle life's challenges. While a part of their persona is still identified as recovering, their self-identity is holistic. That is, their past and the long and sometimes arduous process of recovery are but one aspect of self, along with all other experiences accumulated in a lifetime of living in the social world. How long does this final stage last? My experience suggests that on average, clients who have been consistently abstinent for seven to ten years and who have worked through the potential landmines in each stage can reach the point where their lives have truly been transformed.

The danger in presenting a stage model of recovery is that the linear description, imposed by the medium of text, can lead one to believe that individuals progress through the stages in a smooth and recognizable manner. While this is sometimes true, it is more often untrue. Clients bounce between the first two stages, and sometimes even from the growth stage—because of a relapse—back to earlier stages. However, as with other developmental models, it is appropriate to assume that if a client relapses in stages two, three, or four, it is because something was missed earlier, weakening the recovery foundation. Therefore, a relapse signals the need to discover which parts of the client's recovery foundation need work.

Recovery for the Substance Abuser

The four-stage recovery model applies to individuals diagnosed as chemically dependent. Clients who are diagnosed as substance abusers do not necessarily need to progress through the stages or transform their lifestyle. Moreover, these clients may not even need to achieve consistent abstinence (Peele, 1998; Nowinski, 1996). As you recall from Chapter 1, people who are substance abusers have not developed their use into a lifestyle. Their abuse patterns are still mostly behavioral patterns, causing negative life consequences that are problematic to the client and his or her significant others. Hence, substance abusers may not need to "recover," but change their behavior and thinking. These changes may be achieved through stress management sessions, family or relationship therapy, or group therapy aimed at dealing with the negative life consequences caused by use. For substance abusers, harm reduction appears to be the most appropriate treatment approach. If, along the way, these clients decide to abstain, all the better. A later section, Issues in Treatment Planning, explains how harm reduction principles are applied to substance abuse treatment.

GENERAL PRINCIPLES OF SUBSTANCE ABUSE TREATMENT

There are several general principles that guide substance abuse treatment. As with any statement of principles, these are not intended to serve as the final word on the subject. Practitioners supportive of one treatment model or another will have different opinions about these principles.

Chemical Dependency Is an Illness

Calling chemical dependency an illness is considerably different from calling it a disease. On this point, I agree with van Wormer (1995), who prefers to call chemical dependency an illness instead of a disease. In this context, an illness is a socio-psychological state that individuals subjectively experience because of their problems. According to van Wormer (1995), "The subjective level of illness makes this the term with more relevance to the social work focus on the person-in-the-environment and the interactional nature of the internal world of the human body and the world outside" (p. 42). Instead of worrying about a disease, treatment of chemical dependency should focus on the subjective experience of individuals, their significant others, and those who interact with these individuals in the social world. *Therefore, with chemically dependent clients, abstinence from all drugs of abuse is a necessary and appropriate treatment goal.* Despite this fact, it can be counterproductive to require clients to agree on this goal. This point will be discussed below.

Notice that I did not include substance abusers in the previous discussion. While it is true that individuals who have been assessed and diagnosed as substance abusers are experiencing negative life consequences, this does not mean that they have an illness or need to achieve lifetime abstinence in order to improve their lives. Certainly, there will be some clients at the extreme end of the abuse continuum for whom abstinence is appropriate as a treatment goal, and I am not saying that all clients whose behavior is assessed and diagnosed as abuse would not potentially benefit from a drug-free lifestyle. Nor am I advocating that clinical work focus on controlled use, or moderation management.

With clients who have been diagnosed as substance abusers, the issue of substance abuse may not even be explicitly addressed in the treatment goals, unless it becomes apparent to the client and provider that the abuse is significant and abstinence is needed as the treatment progresses. My clinical experience agrees with Peele's contention (1998) that people categorized as substance abusers often do not progress to the dependency stage. It is possible for many of these clients to work toward positive life changes without having to abstain from all substances for the remainder of their lives. *Therefore, with substance-abusing clients, abstinence may or may not be an appropriate primary treatment goal.*

Engagement Is Necessary for Successful Treatment

As we have discussed at length throughout this text, clients succeed in treatment when they are engaged with a social worker in a trusting and open relationship based on dialogue. To build such a relationship, you must possess effective communication skills and demonstrate worldview respect, hope, humility, trust, and empathy (see Chapter 4), within a culturally competent framework. By exhibiting these characteristics, you can engage clients as partners in treatment, eliciting responses and actions that enhance motivation and promote willingness to take action on their own behalf. Remember that clients do not engage with techniques or methods—they engage with human beings who also happen to be social workers.

A Multi-Systemic Approach Works Best

Approaching clients from a multi-systemic perspective allows you to design a treatment regimen that best suits your client's unique needs, issues, and strengths. A multi-systemic approach collects information from various contexts, including individual, familial, local community, and the macro environment, and uses this information to create a comprehensive approach to treatment. Key to working from this approach is familiarity with models and methods across the substance abuse practice spectrum. This means that you are able to provide individual, group, or family treatment, engage the client's local community if needed, and provide access to specialty services such as vocational, recreational, or spiritual counseling when appropriate. A multi-systemic approach is not wedded to a single theoretical or methodological school, but uses the appropriate theories and methods from several approaches to best meet a client's needs in treatment.

Aftercare Is Essential

A carefully designed aftercare plan is critical to long-term recovery. Chemical dependency treatment, especially when the client has a co-occurring disorder, is rarely amenable to brief intervention (Evans & Sullivan, 2001). That is, clients who achieve long-term recovery are normally those who remain engaged in a multi-faceted aftercare program for up to one year following discharge from primary treatment (Miller & Hester, 1986a; Miller & Rollnick, 2002). Clients assessed as substance abusers (especially adolescents) may have issues that are more amenable to brief forms of treatment (CSAT, 1999b). However, some form of follow-up contact is still necessary. Therefore, we must work to engage clients in a treatment process that provides the appropriate level of care and length of contact for each client.

Clients Need Help in Developing
a Social Support Network

As we discussed in Chapter 6, human beings are social creatures. Your clients found their way into substance abuse problems as individuals operating within the context of a social environment. The person-in-environment approach favored by the social work profession requires that social networks be considered not only during assessment, but in treatment and aftercare as well. It is my experience that clients often lack the normal social support systems that most people have in life—people or groups to call upon for support, guidance, and recreation. If the goal of treatment is to move toward the day when your client no longer needs treatment, then one of your primary tasks must be to help clients develop a network that supports their recovery and provides social and recreational outlets that replace key elements of the substance-abusing or chemically dependent lifestyle. That is, early in your relationship, begin insisting that clients rely on other people outside the treatment context for daily support. This support may come from twelve-step meetings, church groups, sober friends, family members, and other sources. As a treatment provider, you need to enlist the help of a social support network that will empower clients to successfully handle crises and stress without your assistance.

TREATMENT PLANNING

Before deciding on treatment approaches, you must learn to develop substance abuse treatment plans. Treatment plans are jointly constructed with clients and are designed to help keep both parties focused on the purpose of treatment. A collaboratively developed treatment plan also "help(s) catalyze progress toward change" (Perkinson & Jongsma, 1998, p 1). The plan takes into account the unique issues, problems, and resources of your particular client, and it is constructed in a collaborative way to ensure that your client feels a sense of ownership and control over its contents and implementation (Compton & Galway, 1994).

Treatment planning must be customized to meet the needs of individual clients. It should not be mass-produced (Perkinson & Jongsma, 1998), as I have seen in many large substance abuse treatment facilities. Individualized treatment plans offer clients a well reasoned, tailor-made plan that includes goals and strategies that serve to enhance their motivation (Miller & Rollnick, 1991) to follow through with treatment. Research in this area suggests that client participation in goal setting correlates with substance abuse treatment retention and success (Ojehagen & Berglund, 1989; Sanchez-Craig & Lei, 1986; Sobell, Sobell, Bogardis, Leo, & Skinner, 1992).

Effective, individualized treatment planning is built on the foundation provided by your assessment and case history report, which depends on client engagement. Furthermore, all future treatment efforts flow directly from the treatment plan, which provides a systemic mechanism to ensure that daily treatment methods are informed by the assessment (Perkinson & Jongsma, 1998). Similar to the assessment process, a treatment plan is not a static, one-time event in the life of a client. Effective treatment plans evolve over time to meet the ever-changing needs of your clients. Since clients are continually changing, treatment plans must be flexible enough to accommodate these changes.

Treatment Plan Format

Developing a treatment plan involves a logical series of steps that build on one another. As stated above, the foundation of any treatment plan is the data you collected from your client during an assessment interview. To that end, Figure 10.1 offers a simple format for treatment planning that can be modified to fit the needs of your individual practice context.

Of particular importance is the establishment of both long-term and short-term goals. Long-term goals consist of future-oriented, often broadly defined changes that your client decides are desirable. There is no definitive period that delineates "long-term." In fact, long-term goals can be accomplished after your client leaves treatment. For example, if clients establish a long-term goal of "lifetime sobriety," they do not have to remain in treatment for the rest of their lives and have this goal monitored by a substance abuse professional. While long-term goals are broadly defined, it is best if the prospects for reaching them are reasonable, while still making clients "stretch" in order to achieve success. Examples of long-term goals are given below:

Dr. Jones will achieve a consistent pattern of abstinence from all drugs of abuse.

Mrs. Smith will regularly attend NA meetings.

Mr. Jameson will reunite with his children and spouse.

Short-term goals, on the other hand, are very specific and measurable. In this sense, short-term goals are synonymous with "objectives." That is, short-term

Client: _____ Date: _____

Social worker: _____

I. Treatment Recommendation

  A. Modality: _____

  B. Program name: _____

  C. Type and frequency of counseling: _____

  D. Other supportive services and activities:

  _____

  _____

  _____

  E. Rationale for treatment recommendation (must be based on client assessment):

  _____

  _____

  _____

II. Goals and Tasks

  A. Long-term goals:

  _____

  _____

  _____

  B. Short-term goals (timeline defined by treatment context):

  Goals   *Tasks*

  1. _____   _____

  2. _____   _____

  3. _____   _____

  4. _____   _____

  C. Rationale for plan:

  _____

  _____

  _____

FIGURE 10.1 Treatment Planning Guide

goals represent time-limited, measurable statements of action that serve as stepping-stones toward achieving long-term goals (Miley, O'Melia, & DuBois, 1995). The sum total of short-term goals should "add up" to achievement of people's long-term goals. Short-term goals should be accompanied by a delineation of specific tasks that clients (and social workers, where appropriate) commit to performing in order to reach their short-term goals. For example, if your clients have long-term goals of becoming sober, their short-term goals might be to attend AA meetings four days per week, with associated tasks that include finding sponsors and attending group therapy in your office.

Short-term goals should be modest and attainable, allowing clients some degree of success and, therefore, improving their sense of motivation and self-efficacy as they accomplish a series of productive steps on their own behalf. They should be mutually agreed upon and within the resource capability of your client. For example, if a client cannot read, setting a short-term goal of reading AA materials is outside the resource capability of your client. However, reading these materials may work as a long-term goal, while taking literacy classes three nights per week or finding a sponsor to read the materials to her could serve as possible short-term goals.

The format offered in Figure 10.1 is only a guide to help conceptualize and develop treatment plans with your client. Most agencies use specific formats whose content is dictated by agency licensing or accreditation standards. While the specific formats used by particular agencies will vary, there are general categories of information that are required on most treatment plans. Siporin (1975) offered the following components needed to create treatment plans that are "multitarget, multilevel, and multiphasic in design" (p. 259). These components are listed below.

1. Broad (long-term) goals and concrete, measurable objectives (short-term goals).

2. A prioritization of short-term goals into immediate, intermediate, and long-term.

3. Strategies to use and actions to take to meet short-term goals (tasks).

4. Time frames for implementation.

5. An inventory of necessary resources such as financial, programs, or staff.

6. Clear division of responsibility for actions between client, social worker, and others.

7. Process for altering the plan.

I would add two more items to Siporin's list:

8. An inventory of client resources and strengths.

9. Evidence that your client has co-authored his or her own plan (beyond confirmatory signatures).

Perkinson and Jongsma (1998) also offer a format for treatment planning that is well conceived and easy to understand and follow. This format incorporates the following elements:

1. *Problem Selection.* Find and agree on the most significant problem(s) to be addressed (i.e., chemical dependency), secondary problems, and other problems that may have to be deferred.

2. *Problem Definition.* Define the problems chosen for action by your particular client.

3. *Goal Development.* Establish long-term, broadly defined goals. According to Perkinson and Jongsma (1998), goals are "aimed at replacing dysfunctional behaviors with adaptive ones in order to facilitate resolution of the target problem(s)" (p. 5).

4. *Objective Construction.* Objectives are the short-term goals discussed above. Objectives must be "stated in behaviorally measurable language" (Perkinson & Jongsma, 1998, p. 5). Moreover, what constitutes achievement of objectives must also be clearly stated, so that both your client and you know when significant progress has been made.

5. *Intervention Creation.* According to Perkinson and Jongsma (1998), interventions are "actions of the clinician designed to help the patient complete the objectives" (p. 6). Selecting appropriate interventions is crucial to client success.

Putting together such a detailed and specific plan of action requires the joint participation of clients and social workers. You should discuss all information pertaining to people's lives, allowing them to be involved in the process every step of the way. From the perspective of this text, clients identify reasonable life goals, and they have the right to veto suggested goals and to change goals at any time. Our job is to make suggestions, clarify ideas, discuss possible resources, and help clients to have the best possible opportunity to reach all of their goals, both short- and long-term.

Issues in Treatment Planning

The area of treatment planning presents social workers with two alternative approaches to consider: abstinence versus controlled use and harm reduction. In the following discussion, you are introduced to these approaches separately, as they pertain to planning for substance abuse treatment.

Treatment Goals: The Abstinence–Controlled Use Continuum This topic is especially difficult to discuss in so-called "mixed company"—i.e., groups that include those who believe abstinence is the only appropriate goal for treatment success and those who believe it is possible for clients to return to moderate or controlled substance use. People who believe in the disease model and its tenets, the most important of which are inevitable progression and loss of control (see Chapter 3), categorically insist that abstinence is the only way for clients to achieve success (Nathan, 1992). The ideology of AA clearly insists on abstinence as the only practical goal of substance abuse treatment. People advocating abstinence hold that it is dangerous for chemically dependent people to use substances at all, because they will lose control and, as a result, cause significant harm to themselves or others.

Others suggest that the "inevitable progression" scenario is not necessarily true. During the 1970s, several studies (Sobell & Sobell, 1973; Polich, Armor, & Braiker, 1981; Armor, Polich, & Stambul, 1978) drawing on earlier studies (Davies, 1962; Lovibond & Caddy, 1970) suggested that it was possible for alcoholics to achieve controlled drinking status. This controversy raged from the 1970s into the 1980s, as several studies showed that it was possible for some people to return to controlled substance use. These same studies also demonstrated that the longer people had been out of treatment, the closer were the rates of relapse between people whose treatment goal had been abstinence and those who had sought controlled use (Foy, Nunn, & Rychtarik, 1984; Rychtarik, Foy, Scott, Lokey, & Prue, 1987; Nordstrom & Berglund, 1987; Miller, Leckman, Delaney, & Tinkcom, 1992).

While the purpose of this discussion is not to exhaust the subject of abstinence versus controlled use, it is important to consider this topic as you prepare to assess and refer (or treat) people with substance abuse problems. These studies, and the resultant controversy, focused on whether it was possible for chemically dependent people to learn to use substances in moderation through treatment. This is an interesting topic. However, it is not necessarily relevant to our task here. Perhaps Jung (2001) put it best when he stated, "Whether recovering alcoholics *should* drink, even at a moderate level, and whether they *can* drink moderately are separate questions" (p. 441). For assessment and treatment, whether they can use substances is the more important issue to consider.

It is not important to decide whether clients should continue using; this is a moral question for you to solve for yourself. The relevant issues are whether clients can use substances during treatment and still make progress, and how you will respond to this issue when it arises, because it will. Many substance abuse professionals abide by the abstinence-only goal and refuse to allow clients into care, or to continue in care, if they admit to continued use, even if the use is less harmful than before. Further, many of these same professionals would not consider allowing a client to enter treatment if his or her primary motivation was to learn to drink or use drugs in nonabusive ways (Denning, 2000). This issue, therefore, goes directly to the heart of assessment and treatment planning.

Topic for Your Journal: Abstinence Versus Controlled Use

To effectively respond to client requests in this area, you must answer a few questions. First, is it acceptable for clients with substance abuse problems to set a treatment goal of moderate use instead of abstinence, and, if so, can or should we work with them? Second, is it possible for clients to improve their lives even if they continue to use alcohol or other drugs? Respond to these questions in your substance abuse journal, supporting your position with documentation and research.

Principles of Harm Reduction Harm reduction principles—the latest innovation in substance abuse treatment (Tatarsky, 1998)—provide an interesting context within which to address questions about treatment goals. A harm reduction approach is based on an international public health movement, similar to ones used to help with HIV/AIDS (needle exchanges), seat belt campaigns, antismoking campaigns, and vaccination programs. The primary principle of harm reduction as an approach to substance abuse is "to accept the fact that people do engage in high-risk behaviors and to commit to helping these people reduce the harm associated with their behavior" (Denning, 2000, p. 4). This approach has long been accepted in other areas of public health, but is relatively new to the substance abuse field. As you can imagine, harm reduction in the context of substance abuse treatment has many detractors, because it serves as a critique of the widely accepted disease model and abstinence-only approach.

In response to poor success rates in programs that employ traditional approaches to treating substance abuse (Marlatt, 1996), practitioners developed a harm reduction approach based on the following general tenets (Denning, 2000; Tatarsky, 1998; Marlatt & Tapert, 1993):

1. Practitioners should work closely with the stated goals of the client.
2. Access to treatment should be as barrier-free as possible.
3. There is no inevitable progression or inevitable loss of control.
4. Active substance abusers can and do participate in treatment.
5. Success is related to a client's level of self-efficacy.

According to this approach, clients are able to make progress in their lives while continuing to drink or use drugs. Harm reduction advocates do not suggest that clients should continue to drink—they may even believe clients should abstain—but they believe that it serves no purpose for the client, his or her family, community, or the larger society to refuse treatment simply because a person refuses to quit using drugs. Do you agree?

In this text, our goal is to engage clients around their problems, not insist on goals and outcomes that we believe are correct. As such, if a client is willing to engage with you around his or her substance use as the primary goal of treatment, then by all means, go forward. However, if your client believes that his or her child care problem, marriage, headaches, or childhood sexual abuse is more important than substance use, engage around those issues too. While you may believe that substance use causes your client's problems, your client may believe otherwise. Advocates of a harm reduction approach believe that clients can work toward abstinence as they progress on other issues, and that keeping people in treatment helps increase the client's motivation to work on their substance abuse issues in the future.

While some substance abuse professionals refuse to work with clients who are unwilling to immediately consider abstinence, others believe that ultimately the connections between other problems (i.e., job, relationship, health, etc.) and substance use will become obvious during the assessment and treatment process as clients continually "bump into" their substance abuse each time they begin making progress on the other issues. If chemical dependency is a disease, then continued use, relapse, and denial of the significance of their problems are part of the disease, although most traditional treatment programs seem to operate on a premise that ignores the theory they are supposed to believe. Hence, there is little value in trying to impose your ideology, beliefs, or methods on clients who are unwilling to see their problems as you believe they should. All that is sure to happen is that your clients will, after a short time, become someone else's clients or worse yet, get no help at all, creating an even bigger danger to themselves and others in their family or community.

SPECIFIC TREATMENT METHODS

In the following discussion, we will explore various treatment modalities used in the substance abuse field. Specifically, we will look at the role and function of individual, group, family, and community practice in substance abuse treatment. Our goal is to develop a multi-systemic approach that includes the skills necessary to use each method alone or in combination to provide a treatment approach that meets people's needs.

Individual Therapy/Counseling

Individual practice is part of most levels of care in substance abuse treatment. Clients participating in an inpatient, residential, intensive outpatient, or outpatient program may receive individual therapy as part of their treatment plan. Individual treatment has a number of benefits (Rounsaville & Carroll, 1997). It provides privacy and confidentiality, allowing clients to discuss sensitive and personal issues more freely than they could during group or family treatment. Individual treatment also provides a level of individualized care that is not available in other modalities and has advantages in dealing with certain types of problems (past abuse) or clients, especially those with co-occurring personality disorders (Rounsaville & Carroll, 1997).

Since you are preparing for a social work career, you either have had or will take courses on practice with individuals. Although it is beyond the scope of this text to discuss all the processes and theoretical approaches to individual therapy and counseling, there are a few general issues to consider as you prepare to work individually with substance-abusing clients.

According to Evans and Sullivan (2001), there is professional disagreement about the role helpers should assume in working with substance-abusing individuals. Psychotherapy that is more traditional relies on a therapist as a "blank screen for clients to project their issues onto, providing a forum for the therapist to identify and comment on the clients' issues" (Evans & Sullivan, 2001, p. 37). Borrowing from traditional psychodynamic approaches, psychotherapy is a process whereby a therapist assists clients to uncover and rectify issues of the past that help drive today's substance abuse behavior.

In contrast, the approach taken by most individual counselors working from a disease model is akin to the role of an AA or NA sponsor (see Chapter 9). This approach probably became prevalent because so many substance abuse counselors were in recovery themselves, and the role of sponsor conforms to the tenets of the disease model. From this perspective, "the ideal therapist is like the ideal sponsor: recovering, self-disclosing, available as needed, and the teacher/master to the client/pupil of how to do recovery in general and how to work the twelve-steps in particular" (Evans & Sullivan, 2001, p. 37).

There are two distinct phases of treatment that should serve to guide your behavior in individual treatment. Regarding the early phases of treatment, Doweiko (1999) said, "The general approach of individual and group therapy is to work through the addicted person's system of denial, while providing counseling designed to help the client learn how to face the problems of daily living *without chemicals*" (p. 384, italics in original). That is, in the early stages of individual treatment, before your client has established a pattern of abstinence, it is best to work vigorously on engagement, remaining in the here-and-now and trying to achieve the role and status of a quasi-sponsor, while not assuming the role of sponsor outside the context of treatment. Evans and Sullivan (2001) refer to this as an "*active but professional style*" with clients (p. 37, italics in original). Do not passively sit back and wait for the client to engage, but actively work toward engagement around the issues in daily life that are problematic to the client. For example, in early treatment work I focus entirely on helping clients overcome resistance to support group attendance, while gently yet consistently confronting their denial systems by identifying and discussing contradictions and discrepancies in their presentation. At this stage, it would be inappropriate to focus individual treatment on past abuses and/or familial issues that you believe underlie the client's substance-abusing behavior. If you focus on engaging the client early in the treatment process, there will be plenty of time to work on deeper issues later on.

During later stages of treatment, when clients have established a pattern of consistent abstinence and a social support network outside the context of therapy, your role may change. That is, you may switch from a here-and-now oriented, highly active approach to a more traditional psychotherapeutic approach that begins to identify issues from the past that impinge on the quality and the future of your client's recovery. For example, once your client establishes a pattern of abstinence, you may begin working through past trauma, abuses, or issues in your client's thought processes that lead him or her toward relapse. This is the stage when tactics from the cognitive-behavioral theories that focus on thinking and behavior, or as AA puts it, "stinking thinking" (van Wormer, 1995, p. 110), are appropriate. These techniques include the ABC model for identifying and avoiding high-risk environments (Evans & Sullivan, 2001), relaxation skills, stress management training, and parent education (Carroll, 1996).

Individual therapy is an excellent way to engage clients in treatment, and it provides a safe and confidential relationship as clients begin the recovery process. Moreover, individual therapy is also invaluable when clients need to begin confronting issues of abuse and trauma, especially those adult clients who have lived with these issues for many years. However, my experience suggests that for most clients, individual treatment is not effective as the only method of intervention, and is not especially helpful for most adolescent clients (see Chapter 11). For clients to find successful recovery and deal with the social and familial aspects of their lifestyle, group and family therapy is needed, particularly as clients begin moving toward the confrontation stage of recovery.

Group Therapy/Counseling

Over the years, group therapy has emerged as one of the most widely used treatment methods in the substance abuse field (Golden, Khantzian, & McAuliffe, 1994; Levy, 1997). It has surpassed individual therapy as the treatment method of choice and is used in nearly all substance abuse programs in the United States

(Stinchfield, Owen, & Winters, 1994). Group therapy is an essential component of an integrated, individualized approach to substance abuse treatment (Kaufman, 1994). Aside from the economic advantage of group therapy (Rounsaville & Carroll, 1997), there are a number of curative factors associated with group treatment that help distinguish it as a successful method of treatment in substance abuse (Connors, Donovan, & DiClemente, 2001; Yalom, 1995). Connors, Donovan, and DiClemente (2001) suggested that there are at least seven curative factors in group treatment that contribute to the behavior change process:

1. Many of the problems associated with substance abuse are interpersonal. The context of group treatment provides a realistic yet safe place to learn and practice new social skills.

2. Important aspects of social skills training, particularly modeling, rehearsal, and feedback, occur more powerfully in a group setting.

3. Group treatment provides an opportunity to capitalize on a number of features, including the instillation of hope, education, realization that the client is not alone with his or her problems, and modeling appropriate behaviors. The development of trust within a group setting appears to produce cognitive, affective, and behavioral changes.

4. Peer feedback allows clients the chance to observe and confront denial systems in themselves and others.

5. Rehearsal and feedback from peers are likely to have more impact on client behavior than feedback from a professional.

6. Participation in group treatment allows clients the chance to change social networks and to develop a meaningful support system.

7. Group treatment uses peer pressure and motivation to enhance individual commitment to recovery.

Groups have a number of important functions in substance abuse treatment, including education, therapy, and support (e.g., twelve-step groups). The skills necessary to lead successful treatment groups, like those in family therapy, must be learned and practiced under supervision. The ideal size of treatment groups is between six and 10 clients (Yalom, 1995). In addition to content, therapeutic groups should focus on here-and-now interactions and group process (Yalom, 1995). Group methods are based in a number of theories and models, and much of what occurs during relapse prevention and aftercare is accomplished in groups.

It is important for you to learn, understand, and know how to use group process to involve clients in the change process. It takes skill and practice to avoid turning group treatment into what I define as "individual therapy with an audience." That is, groups operate best when all members are talking to others, about self and others, in the here-and-now. To become a successful substance abuse practitioner, you will need to develop excellent group treatment skills. Be sure to take the group practice course as part of your professional social work training.

Family Therapy/Counseling

While the use of family therapy is on the rise in substance abuse treatment programs, it is not family therapy as you have probably learned about it in other courses. What is called family therapy in substance abuse treatment is usually little more than education about the disease concept and the family's role in the disease process. In some programs, families meet together with the substance-abusing member to vent their feelings and issues about the member's use. Despite an increasing number of programs at all levels of care claiming to perform family treatment, few actually utilize family therapy as a central part of the treatment process. This omission is ironic, given the centrality that the disease model gives to the family in relation to survival roles and intergenerational processes. Yet working with families in therapy is a crucial part of the substance abuse treatment process (Freeman, 1993). According to O'Farrell (1995):

> Many alcoholics have extensive marital and family problems . . . and positive family adjustment is associated with better alcoholism treatment outcomes at follow-up. . . . Marital and family problems may stimulate excessive drinking, and family interactions often help to maintain alcohol problems once they have developed. . . . Finally, even when recovery from the alcohol problem has begun, marital and family conflicts may often precipitate renewed drinking by abstinent alcoholics (p. 195).

There are three main functions of family therapy in substance abuse treatment. The first is education, discussed above. Besides education, family therapy is helpful as a way of engendering positive support for the substance-abusing member during recovery and during an intervention (see Chapter 9), and as the main unit of treatment that focuses on the family system as the primary substance abuse client. Whenever possible, try to include family members during a substance abuse assessment. Even if you do not intend to perform family therapy, it is useful to gain the family's assistance in preparing a comprehensive, multi-systemic assessment.

Most of the major family therapy models focus on treating the family as a system; however, it can be helpful to engage family members as support people for the recovering member. This is especially critical in the early stages of recovery, when abstinence is fragile. However, even when you are enlisting family members as support persons in recovery, it is important to recognize the issues, problems, and often deep-seated feelings of shame and resentment that many family members have toward their recovering member, and a false sense of responsibility they may feel for the substance abuser's behavior. For example, it is easy for family members to assume responsibility for the substance abuser's problem based on disease model education about survival roles, specifically the role of the so-called chief enabler (see Chapter 5) (Shorkey & Rosen, 1993). Some families will say that they have been "supporting" the substance abuser for years, now he or she must support the family. Hence, to overlook these issues in the name of supporting the client can lead to treatment failure.

More than simply providing a vehicle for involvement, family therapy with substance-abusing clients can and should be part of any substance abuse treatment regimen. Since, as we stated in Chapter 5, the family is the primary system for socialization, support, and learning, it seems obvious that we need to develop specific skills in family treatment and use these skills with substance abuse clients. To become a competent family therapist with substance-abusing clients demands attention, hard work, excellent supervision, and the support of peers and agency officials where you work. Jay Haley, a famous family therapist, once told me that it was necessary to work with 500 families under supervision before one could claim to be a family therapist. Whether this is true is open to debate, but it seems clear that family therapy skills are not easily learned and mastered.

As an overall framework for family therapy with substance abuse clients, Kaufman and Kaufman (1992) suggested the following approach:

> Treating the family of a substance abuser is a complicated process. Treatment takes place simultaneously on many levels. In meeting the needs of the family as an entity, the spouse subsystem, the sibling subsystem, and the individual needs of each person in the family must be considered. These three areas must interlock and work in harmony. Teaching and demonstrating effective parenting is an important aspect of treatment. Encouraging families to form positive social networks aids in the total treatment. Part of family therapy is the problem-solving process that occurs. I hope that these techniques become internalized so that the family maintains them throughout its lifetime (p. x).

There are many models of family therapy to utilize in substance abuse treatment. Most of these models are based in general systems theory, discussed in Chapter 5. A brief overview of a few of the more prominent models used in substance abuse treatment follows.

Disease Model The disease model looks at chemical dependency as a family disease, with the non-chemically dependent members defined as codependent. This label implies that codependent members possess many of the same traits observed in the chemically dependent member. Within this perspective, family treatment focuses on dysfunctional family roles, faulty communication, and family patterns in relation to the chemically dependent member (Curtis, 1999). However, family members are usually treated separately, and treatment involves education about the disease model and how chemical dependency affects the family. Family members are referred to twelve-step support groups such as Al-Anon, Adult Children of Alcoholics, and Alateen for ongoing support.

Family Systems Theory By far the largest group of family treatment models falls under the general heading of family systems theory. The tenets of systems theory in relation to families were discussed in Chapter 5 and relate primarily to family rules, family roles, boundaries and functioning (Evans & Sullivan, 2001), family cohesion (Steinglass et al., 1987), and the family life cycle. When family systems approaches are combined with theories of substance abuse, they provide relevant information about how substance abuse affects the family (Chaudron & Wilkinson, 1988). Also called "bridging theories" (Freeman, 1993, p. 3), family systems approaches highlight the connections among individuals (biological, social, and psychological), and between the individual, family, and community. These theories imply a positive view of human potential and the interactions that take place between these interdependent systems.

Under the heading of family systems approaches fall several prominent models of family treatment. These include strategic family therapy (Haley, 1976), structural family therapy (Minuchin, 1974), and intergenerational family therapy (Bowen, 1985), to name a few. Other authors and practitioners have developed family systems approaches based on combinations of the aforementioned models and theories of substance abuse (Kaufman, 1984; Dulfano, 1982; Steinglass et al., 1987; Wegscheider, 1981).

Recent developments in brief therapies have become popular, particularly the solution-focused approach (Berg, 1995; Berg & Miller, 1994; Berg & Reuss, 1998). Using this approach, the therapist helps the substance-abusing client recognize times when they were able to abstain from substances without help as a means to reinforce and change behavior. Future behavior is based on finding solutions to problem behaviors, with little time spent talking about the problem. Rather, treatment is focused on solutions that have already worked for the client in the past (Berg & Reuss, 1998).

The families of substance-abusing and chemically dependent clients can be difficult to engage in treatment. However, the extra effort to do so will pay off in overall treatment outcome. This is especially true for adolescents. In my adolescent substance abuse programs, we used family therapy as the primary method of treatment. While it was sometimes difficult to recruit the families, our success rates greatly improved when we were able to do so. If you cannot locate or recruit a client's family, it is still possible to base your work in the client's family system during individual treatment by including family information in all aspects of the treatment and targeting interventions to involve both the individual and family systems.

Community Practice

As we discussed in Chapter 6, to assess and properly treat clients with substance abuse problems you must have a working knowledge and understanding of their local community, and the policies, laws, and institutions in the macro system that influence their behavior and potential for recovery. In this textbook, we have focused on how to elicit and include this information when treating individuals and/or families. There are times when you, as the treating social worker, may have to include members of the community in your clients' treatment. For example, what do you do if your client has no family and is forced to live alone in a boarding house after completing primary treatment (inpatient or residential care)? What if the same client lives alone in a boarding house during primary treatment (intensive outpatient or outpatient)? The former case requires aftercare and relapse prevention, while the latter involves finding positive support to achieve a consistent pattern of abstinence.

Substance abuse treatment from a multi-systemic approach requires you to consider your client's community context when designing the treatment regimen. At the beginning of this chapter, I proposed five treatment principles in substance abuse practice. The fourth principle pertained to the need for a consistent and comprehensive aftercare program, while the fifth one discussed the need for positive social supports during all phases of the recovery process. Much of the community assessment and intervention you will undertake will involve fulfillment of these two principles. You will need to learn how to locate, recruit, and intervene in a client's local neighborhood, and how to involve family, extended kin, fictive kin, and other potential positive community members to provide the necessary support to a newly recovering person.

Here is an example of a case in which community intervention was essential for the client's recovery:

> During treatment of an adolescent substance abuse client, his parents complained that their son "did not have a chance" to quit drugs because of the drug house located in their neighborhood. After a lengthy discussion of their options, I asked if the parents would like to meet with interested neighbors to see what could be done within the community to rid the neighborhood of the drug house. The parents arranged a meeting at their home, and it was attended by more than 35 people. After a lengthy group session with the community members, a strategy was developed to empower the neighborhood residents to take action on their community's behalf. After three months of constant and persistent community pressure, the tenants of the drug house moved.

My students have often grumbled during this class discussion, "Who has the time for that?" My answer: treatment professionals interested in the long-term success of their clients can find a way to work this type of intervention into their schedules. Aside from travel time, the community group session described above did not require extra time on my part. We held the meeting at a time when I would have been meeting with the family anyway. The adolescent client, and many other adolescents in the neighborhood, attended the meeting, so treatment continued. Finding time was not a problem. In this case, the parents were correct. With a drug house in the neighborhood, their son had little chance of success. The other kids in the neighborhood faced the same problem. For treatment to be successful, community intervention was essential. Unfortunately, this aspect of treatment is often overlooked in the substance abuse field.

Little has been written about community practice methods designed specifically for substance abuse treatment. Even less has been written about how and when to engage the local community on behalf of a particular substance abuse client. A full discussion of community practice methods is well beyond the scope of this text. If you are interested in learning more about community practice, you can take a community practice course or look into the wealth of literature on general community practice methods (c.f., Brueggemann, 2001; Rivera & Erlich, 1998b; Freire, 1998, 1994; Gil, 1998; Etzioni, 1995; Haynes & Mickelson, 1997; Rothman, 1995a; Fellin, 1995; Poulin, 2000; Netting, Kettner, & McMurtry, 1998).

RELAPSE PREVENTION

One of the most frustrating and ubiquitous barriers to successful substance abuse treatment and recovery is the high likelihood of relapse by individuals recovering from dependence on drugs (Jung, 2001). It is common for clients to experience strong cravings for their drug of choice. These cravings are usually set off by personal or environmental triggers that remind the client, at some level, of their desire to use drugs. The temptation to resume use can be overwhelming for clients and perplexing to loved ones and friends who find the potential for relapse difficult to understand.

Many different labels have been given to a client's return to use after a period of abstinence. Jung (2001) uses the term *lapse* to connote a single return to use, and *relapse* to mean a series of lapses. Others, such as Fisher and Harrison (2000), refer to the former as a "slip" and the latter as a relapse. I find it most helpful to refer to any return to use after a commitment to abstinence as a relapse, although *lapse* accomplishes the same goal. To call a return to use a "slip" implies that the client was suddenly overpowered by external forces that were impossible to resist. That is, a slip connotes an event outside the client's control, much as it is beyond one's control not to fall when stepping on a patch of ice. While the disease model states that a person's use is outside personal control, this does not necessarily apply to use after a period of abstinence. As we will discuss later, minimizing the effects of a relapse in recovery often hinges on your client feeling empowered to take action to avoid triggers, deal with cravings, and thus control the desire to relapse. The term *slip* threatens the client's sense of self-efficacy.

As stated earlier, relapse is a common occurrence in substance abuse treatment. Relapses are so common that many suggest that this possibility should be introduced into the treatment dialogue very early in the process (Gorski, 1990, 1992, 1993; Gorski & Miller, 1986), although others believe that discussing relapse can actually trigger a relapse (Evans & Sullivan, 2001). Whatever strategy you take with regard to relapse, it is important to understand that regardless of the researcher, drug or drugs of choice, or population studied, it has become obvious that most substance abuse clients relapse at least once after primary treatment. That is, upwards of 70 percent relapse within the first year after primary treatment (Fisher & Harrison, 2000). If this is indeed the case, then somehow the near-inevitability of relapse must be directly addressed in primary treatment and become a central feature of any aftercare program.

Two primary models of relapse prevention are used in many treatment programs around the United States. The Cenaps Model was developed by Gorski (1990, 1992, 1993; Gorski & Miller, 1986) and has been widely used in treatment centers since the mid-1980s. With the disease model as its guiding foundation, this model approaches chemical dependency as a ". . . brain dysfunction . . . [that] disorganizes the preaddictive personality and causes social and occupational problems" (Gorski, 1990, p. 126). Since the disease is chronic and affects the brain, total abstinence is necessary. However, the Cenaps Model of relapse prevention also looks at issues related to personality, lifestyle, and family functioning.

In this model, only clients who have completed work on the "primary goals" of treatment are appropriate for relapse prevention work. The primary goals of treatment are listed below:

(1) the recognition that chemical dependency is a biopsychosocial disease;

(2) the recognition of the need for lifelong abstinence from all mind-altering drugs;

(3) the development and use of an ongoing recovery program to maintain abstinence;

(4) the diagnosis and treatment of other problems or conditions that can interfere with recovery (Gorski, 1990, p. 127).

Since Gorski believes that the Cenaps Model is for clients committed to recovery but having a difficult time maintaining abstinence, the number of clients viewed as being ready for relapse prevention are limited. According to the Cenaps Model, there are six steps in the recovery and relapse prevention process (Gorski, 1990, p. 128):

1. Abstaining from alcohol and other drugs.

2. Separating from people, places, and things that promote chemical use and establishing a social network that supports recovery.

3. Stopping compulsive self-defeating behaviors that suppress awareness of painful feelings and irrational thoughts.

4. Learning how to manage feelings and emotions responsibly, without resorting to compulsive behaviors or the use of chemicals.

5. Learning to change addictive-thinking patterns that create painful feelings and self-defeating behaviors.

6. Identifying and changing the mistaken core beliefs about self, others, and the world that promote the use of irrational thinking.

To accomplish its goals, the Cenaps Model uses a variety of procedures. Although it is based on the disease model, Gorski (1993) recommends using different models and approaches to treatment, including individual, group, and family therapy, along with techniques from cognitive-behavioral therapy in relapse prevention treatment. This model relies heavily on teaching clients to recognize triggers and plan responses to triggers that minimize the likelihood of relapse through a change in thinking and behavior.

The Cognitive-Social Learning Model of relapse prevention (Marlatt & Gordon, 1995) views addictive behavior not as a disease, but as "overlearned *habits* that can be analyzed and modified in the same manner as other habits" (Marlatt, 1985, p. 9; italics in original). This model is a combination of the social learning theory model and the cognitive-behavioral model, which were discussed more fully in Chapter 3. With regard to relapse prevention, Marlatt (1985) states that those who believe in this model

are particularly interested in studying the *determinants* of addictive habits, including situational and environmental antecedents, beliefs and expectations, and the individual's family history and prior learning experiences with the substance use activity. In addition, there is an equal interest in discovering the consequences of these behaviors, so as to better understand both the reinforcing effects that may contribute to increased use and the negative consequences that may serve to inhibit the behavior. . . . Attention is paid to the social and interpersonal reactions experienced by the individual before, during, and after engaging in an addictive habit and in the subsequent performance of the activity once the habit has become firmly established (pp. 9–10; italics in original).

Similar to Gorski's approach, this model relies on techniques from cognitive-behavioral and social learning theories to prevent relapse. However, it does not have a set of primary goals that a client must accomplish before being eligible for relapse prevention.

Treatment Issues

Given the literature on relapse prevention and the primacy it must be given in substance abuse treatment, the following issues should be addressed when planning a relapse prevention program for clients:

1. *Identify high-risk situations.* That is, what circumstances place clients at high risk for relapse? You will need to help clients to identify triggers in the environment and in their way of thinking that initiate the process of cravings. Gorski (1990) calls this a self-assessment, while the social learning model uses an individualized analysis of the client's use behavior over the previous year as a way of identifying high-risk situations (Marlatt, 1985). As we discussed earlier in this chapter, clients in the abstinence and confrontation stages of recovery are especially prone to relapse. Hence, during these phases it is important to help clients identify those issues and events that may trigger the overwhelming urge to use again.

2. *Develop strategies to cope with high-risk situations.* Once these situations have been identified, clients must develop coping strategies. Group treatment is helpful in this step, as clients can share experiences and strategies in a supportive and helpful manner. Gorski (1990) recommends that clients be assisted to cope at the situational-behavioral (changing people, places, and things), cognitive-affective (learning to manage feelings, thoughts, and behaviors that lead to use), and core issue (identifying and changing core beliefs about self and others) levels. Marlatt (1985) focuses on teaching clients alternative ways to handle high-risk situations by assigning homework that forces clients to practice these responses.

3. *Arrange for social support.* Help clients engage and remain in positive social support networks such as AA or NA, church, groups of supportive friends, and/or family. Group treatment is helpful in this area, as it exposes clients to a new support network. Family treatment can also be helpful in this regard.

4. *Use a multi-systemic holistic approach.* Consistent with the model of recovery presented in the beginning of this chapter and the multi-systemic approach

promoted in this text, efforts aimed toward relapse prevention must take a multi-systemic, holistic approach to be successful over the long term. The plan must consider issues related to the individual (recreation, relationships, health), family, local environment, and the macro environment.

5. *Discuss relapse prevention throughout treatment, beginning with the first session.* The goals of relapse prevention are to (1) keep the amount and duration of the relapse contained; (2) lengthen the time between relapses; (3) help clients place relapses into a positive context; and (4) retain clients in treatment after relapses occur. To accomplish these goals, it is appropriate to begin discussing the probability of relapse early in treatment in an attempt to reframe a relapse as a normal and regular part of the recovery process (i.e., two steps forward, one step back). It is vital to avoid giving clients the impression that a relapse signals failure, loss of all that has been gained, or a source of shame. If clients come to accept relapses as a normal part of the process, the four goals stated earlier can be met with minimal damage to the client's sense of self or level of self-efficacy.

SUMMARY

In this chapter, we took a close look at many specifics in substance abuse treatment, including a definition of recovery. You were also introduced to issues involved in developing comprehensive substance abuse treatment plans as a basis for treatment. Using the same multi-systemic approach to treatment that was advocated earlier for assessment, we looked at the various modalities used to provide substance abuse treatment (individual, group, family, and to a lesser extent, community practice). We also discussed how these modalities can and should be combined to form a comprehensive approach to substance abuse treatment.

The chapter ended with a discussion of relapse prevention as part of longer-term aftercare. Since research indicates that long-term success in recovery is related to longer lengths of time in treatment (Miller & Hester, 1986b), providing aftercare that focuses, in the first two stages of recovery (abstinence and confrontation), on relapse prevention is crucial if clients are to experience the rewards and growth associated with long-term recovery from a chemically dependent lifestyle.

11

Populations at Risk

In Chapter 9 we looked at the substance abuse treatment system and levels of care, and in Chapter 10 we explored treatment planning, treatment approaches, and relapse prevention. This chapter completes our discussion of substance abuse treatment by offering guidelines for treating people from various populations. Each of the at-risk populations discussed in this chapter (African Americans; Latino Americans; Native Americans; adolescents; older persons; gay, lesbian, bisexual, and transgendered persons; and persons with co-occurring disorders) has unique issues that demand special consideration in substance abuse treatment.

Throughout this text, we have emphasized that individual and group differences between clients—and between clients and social workers—must be accounted for when planning and providing substance abuse assessment and treatment. In Chapter 4, we discussed culturally competent practice as it pertains to client engagement, assessment, and treatment. In this chapter, we discuss treatment issues for various populations-at-risk. The information should prove helpful when you are working with clients who belong to one or more of these groups.

The descriptions and issues discussed below should never be used to stereotype clients or to gloss over the process of getting to know each client. Although a comprehensive discussion of the treatment issues for every population-at-risk is beyond the scope of this book, this brief overview will acquaint you with some of the general issues involved so you will at least know what information you need to learn before working with clients from these populations.

AFRICAN AMERICANS

African Americans are not a monolithic group, but they do share a common cultural heritage rooted in a history of slavery, northern migration, urban living, the civil rights movement, and the continuing undercurrent of racism in American society (Wright, 2001; Rogan, 1986). The patterns of substance use and abuse that exist today among African Americans are influenced by both history and current social conditions. Neither influence can be ignored if your goal is to engage and treat African American people. Wright (2001) lists the following reasons for contemporary substance use and abuse patterns among African Americans:

Racism and internalized oppression. For African Americans, racism and internalized oppression can damage self-confidence and block the development of a healthy self-image. Therefore, many African Americans experience impaired achievement and performance.

Double consciousness. African Americans often have difficulty establishing a healthy self-concept, primarily because they are forced to live in a racist society that demands a double consciousness: the awareness of being a Black person in a White society (Bell & Evans, 1981). The stress of living within this dual reality can be overwhelming, and it can make it difficult for clients to trust social services and substance abuse treatment practitioners.

Poverty and violence. According to the 1990 census, more than 33 percent of African Americans were living in poverty compared to 10 percent of European Americans (Queralt, 1996). Poverty increases the likelihood of violence, and it limits life chances and restricts opportunities for positive living conditions. Over the last 20 years, violence, initiated by alcohol and other drug use and abuse and correlated with drug sales, has wracked many African American communities across the United States. In some families, drugs sales have become a means of economic support, as well as a way to enhance one's self-image in the community (Whitehead, Patterson, & Kaljee, 1994). At the same time, according to Wright (2001), substance abuse and criminal behavior within some segments of the African American population has created another stereotype that serves to undermine substance abuse treatment and prevention strategies.

Lack of positive role models. African American substance abusers have limited access to positive role models. Because of the exodus of middle-class African Americans to the suburbs, many urban communities lack the type of positive influence that enhances a sense of community and forbids certain behaviors (Wilson, 1987; Brisbane, 1992). This lack of role models is also evident in many AA and NA groups. African Americans are usually underrepresented in these programs, leading many new clients to become discouraged by the lack of African American recovering people who can relate to their experiences.

Advertising. Many African American communities are inundated with advertising that links drinking with social power and influence (Wright, 2001), creating an atmosphere that encourages substance use and abuse. Since many African Americans do not or cannot relocate to other areas, they are often disadvantaged in treatment and aftercare by the environmental influences that present many triggers for use in daily life.

Ideology of conspiracy. According to Wright (2001), the unfulfilled promises of equal opportunity instilled by the civil rights movement perpetuate feelings of anger and resentment in African American communities. Rumors of FBI drugs sales in African American communities during the 1960s and 1980s, along with unequal treatment of African Americans and European Americans by law enforcement and the courts, have fostered feelings of hopelessness about self-improvement among many African American individuals.

Treatment Issues

Given that most substance abuse treatment is based on European American values (Philleo, Brisbane, & Epstein, 1995), there are a number of barriers to overcome when trying to provide comprehensive substance abuse treatment to African American clients. If you work toward becoming a culturally competent practitioner, as described in Chapter 4, these barriers should not be insurmountable. If you belong to the dominant culture, however, many of the following issues are likely to exist below the level of your conscious awareness. As we have stated many times before, it behooves you to continually review your own beliefs and values, searching out, discussing, and working through hidden and unconscious issues about African American clients before beginning to work with this population. Briefly, Wright (2001) lists the following barriers to substance abuse treatment that must be overcome for treatment to have a chance at success: culturally biased diagnostic tools, biased European American clinicians, clinicians' fear of African American rage, and covert prejudice and racism.

When considering work with African American substance abuse clients, you will need to be aware of the respect given to elders in most African American families and communities. Respect can be demonstrated in a number of ways: by addressing your client by his or her title (Mr., Mrs., Ms., Dr.) until given permission to do otherwise; by requesting personal information in private; and by understanding the nature of European American privilege. According to Wright (2001), there are several ways that you can increase your level of cultural competence and engage African American clients in substance abuse treatment. These principles are listed below.

1. *Recognize that an Afrocentric perspective values the interpersonal relationship between people above all other motivations for change.* That is, African Americans engage with human beings, not therapeutic techniques, models, or methods.

2. *Express genuine interest in your client's culture, and become familiar with cultural norms.* Regardless of how much you think you know about African American culture, African American clients know more about their culture than you do. Even if you are African American, your clients still know more than you do about their unique interpretation and application of their cultural norms. As stated earlier (Chapter 8), do not assume you know people's culture simply because you share the same racial identity.

3. *Rid yourself of assumptions of racial and cultural identity based on appearance.* As I have stated many times, do not base your approaches with clients on assumptions. If you are not sure about something, ask your client about it. When you make assumptions, you are likely to fall into the trap of stereotyping.

4. *Ask the client how he or she self-identifies culturally* (Gordon, 1993). People interpret culture individually, and they do not necessarily conform to the norms

reported in group-level social surveys. Discover how each client interprets culture and how this interpretation affects his or her daily life.

5. *Be willing to learn and understand the words used by your client.* As discussed in Chapter 4, it is your task to adjust to clients, rather than forcing or demanding that clients adjust to you.

6. *Be patient when gathering personal information.* Because of past betrayals of trust, many African American clients are wary of helpers and the context of professional helping. Have patience and take time to build the relationship. Personal information will be disclosed over time, not all at once.

7. *Solicit the client's definition of family, and believe it.* The client's family is likely to be broad enough to include extended and/or fictive kinship relations. Most African Americans prize familial relations and broadly define family membership.

8. *Never use words that describe family members in a derogatory manner.* Actually, this statement should apply to everybody you treat. It does not matter what you think about people's family members, so keep your beliefs and comments to yourself if you hope to engage African American clients in a trusting professional relationship.

9. *Recognize the role of elders by inviting them to participate in the assessment and/or treatment process.* For example, invite respected elders to attend the session with the client, whether they happen to be parents, extended kin, or fictive kin. Clients often value the advice and support of elders from the family and/or community when it pertains to personal issues such as substance abuse. The role of elders in the client's life should be identified during the comprehensive substance abuse assessment discussed in Chapter 8.

For a compelling look into the world of African American women and the lingering effects of a history of enslavement, together with contemporary racism and sexism, please take time to read the essay by Lois Smith Owens in Appendix C. Not only will you find Smith Owens' prose powerful and moving, but this essay provides dramatic insight into the dynamics of substance abuse within this population, offering implications for assessment and treatment.

LATINO AMERICANS

Also known as Hispanic populations, the groups that are collectively known as Latino Americans vary so much that it is difficult to generalize treatment principles. The three major subgroups of Latino Americans are Mexican Americans, Puerto Ricans, and Cuban Americans (Rothe & Ruiz, 2001; Alvarez & Ruiz, 2001; Medina, 2001). Each group has a unique history, ancestry, socio-economic experience, and relationship with American society. In addition to speaking a common language, however, these groups also share some common themes of Latin American heritage that often transcend the differences mentioned above.

Community surveys in many Latin American countries indicate a high level of alcohol use, especially among males (Smart & Mora, 1986). In many of these communities, there is an association between heavy drinking and *machismo*, a concept that will be explored below (Rothe & Ruiz, 2001). Excessive drinking by women is frowned upon in most of these countries. A survey of drinking patterns across the three major Latino groups in the United States found that Mexican American males included the highest percentage of heavy drinkers and abstainers, while Cuban and Puerto Rican males showed a more moderate use pattern (Caetano, 1986). Women in all three groups favored abstinence or drank lightly. Among the Mexican American population, cultural attitudes showed greater tolerance of drinking by females with increasing levels of acculturation into the norms of American society (Canino, Burman, & Caetano, 1992).

Pertaining to the use and abuse of other drugs, the Substance Abuse and Mental Health Services Administration's (1993) National Household Survey on Drug Abuse found that overall, 5.9 percent of the Latino population in the United States used illicit drugs. However, because these surveys merge data from all three Latino groups into one group known as "Hispanic," it is difficult to identify the percentages of use in each of the groups (Alvarez & Ruiz, 2001).

Treatment Issues

Most authors state that substance abuse treatment need not vary for members of the three major Latino populations in the United States (Rothe & Ruiz, 2001; Alvarez & Ruiz, 2001; Medina, 2001). That is, clients from these populations can successfully be subjected to many of the same treatment approaches used in working with members of other ethnic groups. Based on the professional literature and my own clinical experience, however, I have found the following issues to be important when treating Latino clients:

1. *Language.* Treatment providers should either speak Spanish or have translators available. Even if a particular family appears acculturated or has been in the United States for several generations, some members of the family may speak mostly Spanish, or Spanish may be their language of choice when discussing personal matters. Performing treatment through a translator is difficult at best. Thus, if your clients use Spanish as their chosen language, either refer them to a colleague who is fluent in Spanish, or learn Spanish yourself.

2. *Build trust by respecting the client's confidentiality and dignity.* When Latino clients first present for treatment, explain the issue of confidentiality to the client's full satisfaction. Your task at this point is to engender as much trust as possible to promote dialogue and personal disclosure. Many Latino clients have been exposed to anti-immigration legislation, leading to a distrust of American institutions, and you may see clients who are in the country illegally (Alvarez & Ruiz, 2001). Most importantly, it is crucial to be nonjudgmental about the client's substance abuse, conveying respect, warmth, and empathy at all times. According to Sanchez and Mohl (1992), these qualities affect Latino client retention in treatment more than all other factors.

Because the concept of *personalismo* is so prominent in Latino culture (Martinez, 1993), especially with Mexican American clients, it may influence the type of therapist these clients are willing to trust. *Personalismo* describes a tendency to be attracted to informality in social conversation (Alvarez & Ruiz, 2001). Hence, Latino clients may be more likely to trust and cooperate with a social worker who seems approachable and "easy-going." Similarly, Latino clients place considerable importance on preserving their sense of dignity. You should avoid any comments that may challenge the client's dignity and honor. This includes the use of confrontation in treatment. If confrontation is to be used in treatment, you will need to explain its purpose and function to clients beforehand to avoid the appearance of insulting their character.

3. *Utilize cognitive approaches in treatment.* According to Alvarez and Ruiz (2001), clinicians may find it helpful to "engage the client in therapy that is practical, active, and problem solving in its orientation and consistent with the realities of living in deprived socioeconomic circumstances" (p. 128). Cognitive-behavioral approaches that target faulty thinking and teach stress management and coping skills are typical of approaches found to be successful with Latino clients. These approaches can be used effectively in individual and/or group treatment.

4. *Role of machismo.* The concept that demarcates gender identity in Latino men, known as *machismo*, has been defined as "a set of traits possessed by the male that include bravery, strength, and, most important, being a good provider to his family" (Alvarez & Ruiz, 2001, p. 125). You will need to be aware of this cultural emphasis, but you must also be careful to avoid falling into traps caused by blind stereotyping. There is considerable variation as to the degree to which Latino American males identify with *machismo*. In accord with the concept of *machismo*, however, many Latino males do not ascribe to a disease model of chemical dependency, instead choosing to believe in a moral model (Chapter 3) that attributes chemical dependency to personal weakness. Many males will not present for substance abuse treatment because of this belief system.

Another aspect of *machismo* that you may see in treatment is the belief that drinking alcohol without displaying signs of intoxication or loss of control is evidence of a man's strength, which is often measured by the amount of liquor he can drink. Because drinking is strongly associated with *machismo*, you must assess this cultural belief system closely and be prepared to deal with it directly, but in a culturally competent and respectful manner, during treatment.

NATIVE AMERICANS

Native American people should not be thought of as a monolithic group with similar norms, values, cultural practice, and behaviors. In fact, the differences between tribes can be as great as the differences between people from different countries. Each tribe has its own history, culture, language, and values, as well as its own specific historical and contemporary relationship with the dominant European American society (Weaver, 2001). Some Native people have assimilated into the values, norms, and beliefs of the dominant society, while others maintain their own languages, ways of life, and a strong belief in the inherent sovereignty of their tribe as an independent "nation" that is outside the jurisdiction of United States law.

The 1990 census counted nearly two million Native people living in the United States (U.S. Bureau of the Census, 1993). Weaver (2001) contends that census data undercount the population because many Native people identify primarily as citizens of Native nations and resist being counted by what they consider to be a foreign government. The U.S. government currently recognizes the existence of more than 500 Native nations or tribes within its borders. The four largest nations, the Cherokee, Navajo, Chippewa/Ojibway, and Sioux (Lakota/ Dakota/Nakota), each have more than 100,000 people (Weaver, 2001).

Regarding substance abuse, over the years the literature has painted a bleak picture. Almost all reports about alcohol and other drug abuse and rates of chemical dependency have been negative. Fisher and Harrison (2000) reported that Native Americans are at higher risk than European Americans in the categories of fair to poorer health status, medical costs, binge drinking, cigarette smoking, being overweight, and having diabetes. Additionally, these same authors report that Native American women fare poorer than males in almost all of the categories.

The Native American relationship with alcohol has been mitigated by the historical events of forced relocation of tribes, separation of children from their families to attend remote and often abusive boarding schools, and the infiltration of disease (and alcohol) from European American settlers and soldiers. Together, these experiences have resulted in varying degrees of physical and cultural genocide (Maracle, 1993). Over the years, many theories have been developed in an attempt to explain the influence of historical factors on Native American substance abuse. One of the most prominent theories is categorized as a sociocultural explanation (Young, 1991). This theory states that Native Americans continue to mourn the loss of their heritage and culture and are reacting to the stresses of assimilation and the demands to integrate into mainstream European American society. According to this theory, alcohol is used to anesthetize the pain caused by hundreds of years of physical and cultural genocide.

At the same time, some authors caution against putting too much faith in theories and data about Native people, primarily because of the stereotypes and bias that exist about substance abuse and Native Americans. According to Weaver (2001):

> The fact that so much has been written about substance abuse and Native Americans suggests a belief that something about substance abuse in this population is qualitatively different than it is in other populations. Some authors have written about a distinctive style of "Indian drinking" . . . and others have pointed to historical and cultural factors unique to Native people that may be related to substance abuse. . . . However, it is stereotypical to rigidly apply any singular explanatory model or treatment philosophy to all Native people. Like other backgrounds, Native people use and abuse substances for a variety of reasons. Myths surrounding Native Americans and

substance abuse must be critically examined before successful prevention and intervention efforts can be developed (p. 78).

Treatment Issues

The following issues should be considered when treating Native people with substance abuse problems:

1. *Develop treatment regimens that are specifically tailored to each client.* According to Weaver (2001), it is often assumed that culturally grounded programs are the most effective for Native clients. While many Native clients may benefit from this type of programming, others will not. Please refer to the discussion of cultural assessment in Chapter 8.

2. *The disease model may or may not be an effective approach with Native clients.* For example, according to Edwards and Edwards (1988), forcing a Native client to admit to being an alcoholic may be counterproductive because of sensitivity to negative labeling. However, according to Weaver (2001), many Canadian Natives have benefited from programs that combine twelve-step recovery with elements of local Native cultures. Do not insist on using the same approach for every client.

3. *In some Native communities, there is strong bias against treatment by "outsiders."* According to Weaver (2001), solutions and treatments may be accepted more readily if they "come from within, as in Natives helping other Natives through telling their stories" (p. 89).

4. *Familiarize yourself with local Native traditions, cultures, and healing practices.* Do not hesitate to refer clients to Native healers and ceremonies for help. You must be able to relinquish stereotypical ideas about various Native cultures and culturally based interventions that will seem foreign to you as a practicing social worker.

5. *Display respect for clients and work toward engagement rather than labeling.* Always be respectful of culture, elders, customs, and a Native client's apparent unwillingness to participate with a non-Native social worker.

GAY, LESBIAN, BISEXUAL, AND TRANSGENDERED (GLBT) PERSONS

Rates of chemical dependency among gay, lesbian, bisexual, and transgendered (GLBT) persons are higher than among the general population. Most studies estimate that 30 to 35 percent of all GLBT persons abuse substances, with a similar level among both sexes (Sandmaier, 1992; Kus, 1988). While some believe that a new culture of sobriety is developing among lesbians (Faderman, 1991), overall the chemical dependency rates for GLBT populations are four to five times higher than heterosexual populations (van Wormer, 1995). Gay bars and clubs are central to the social fabric of gay life; cocaine, methamphetamines, and other dangerous drugs are readily available in after-hours clubs frequented by gay men (van Wormer, Wells, & Boes, 2000). Unique to this population is the fact that heavy alcohol consumption and the associated problems continue across the life span rather than diminishing with age (van Wormer, Wells, & Boes, 2000):

> One possible explanation for homosexual men is that they do not "settle down" as readily and are freer to spend more time drinking. Another factor relating to their substance abuse is the tendency of sexual minorities to use mind-altering chemicals to break down their sexual inhibitions; such inhibitions or hang-ups are related to sexuality that is out of step with societal norms (p. 143).

Among other factors to look for when working with GLBT populations are high rates of suicide (discussed in Chapter 7) and eating disorders (van Wormer, 1995). According to van Wormer (1995), approximately 22 percent of women and 18 percent of men suffer from serious eating disorders.

While GLBT persons have gained greater social acceptance in recent years, according to van Wormer (1995), "a counterresistance has impeded progress" (p. 186). Violence against GLBT persons has never been higher, promoted through a backlash of homophobia (Comstock, 1991). This backlash results in GLBT persons becoming alienated from family, church, and society, closing many of the much-needed avenues of social support. According to Hartman (1993), the violence, hatred, and anger directed against GLBT persons indicates the depth and pervasiveness of homophobia in American society. Social stigma can be an especially difficult barrier to substance abuse treatment for persons in these groups.

Treatment Issues

Based on the discussion above and the professional treatment literature, I offer the following issues to consider when treating GLBT persons with substance abuse problems. These issues and suggestions must be considered holistically, in the context of other issues that may be involved because of your client's membership in other populations as well (e.g., African American gay man, adolescent lesbian woman, and so on). Generally, substance abuse treatment proceeds in the same modalities and methods used with heterosexual clients. However, there are specific issues to consider that are specific to members of these groups. It is important to realize that in nearly every treatment setting, some of your clients will be GLBT persons. Compared to the 10 percent to 12 percent of the public who seek some form of treatment for substance abuse, a staggering 42 percent of GLBT persons do so (van Wormer, Wells, & Boes, 2000).

1. *Client engagement is crucial.* While engagement is important for every client, with GLBT clients it is essential. Most treatment centers and agencies are predominantly heterosexual, making many GLBT clients unwilling or afraid to reveal their sexual identity. Hence, you must first perform the necessary self-work (see Chapter 4) to deal with any lingering issues of homophobia or stereotypes about GLBT persons before proceeding. That is, you must have a self-awareness of your own sexual orientation and empathy for the human condition that

includes sexual orientations different from your own. With clients, make it clear that you are open to discussing sexual orientation and will not impose your beliefs onto your clients. Van Wormer (1995) suggests displaying gay AA meeting literature in your office as a sign of openness and acceptance.

2. *Understand that treatment will take place within the context of larger systems.* You cannot treat a GLBT person without understanding and considering the impact of homophobia on your client's behavior and belief system. As with racial and ethnic minorities, GLBT persons live in a world that is predominately hostile to them. As such, accepting self and their sexual orientation, along with the extent of their problems, is a central part of any treatment process. According to van Wormer, Wells, and Boes (2000),

> Coming to grips with one's sexual and romantic attractions to same-sex individuals in a hostile societal environment often results in scrutinizing the meaning of these desires in order to determine the strength or extent of one's drive for a gay or lesbian union. During the process, people frequently try to enforce heterosexuality to avoid becoming and perhaps identifying with a sexual minority. Such persons may act out sexually, withdraw, immerse themselves in a fundamentally conservative religion or bargain with God, invest in denial, attempt or commit suicide, or attempt to change their sexual orientation (p. 109).

Accordingly, a multi-systemic approach that includes information about living as a sexual minority in a hostile environment must be central to the treatment process. In this context, the promise of confidentiality and trust is paramount. For fear of reprisal, hostility, or other perceived risks, GLBT clients may not be willing to discuss their sexual orientation to any degree until the issues of confidentiality and your ability to demonstrate sensitivity to the prevailing hostile social context have been discussed and resolved.

3. *Help clients to develop positive and accepting social support networks.* Treatment should focus on helping GLBT substance abuse clients to connect with positive social support networks that are accepting of their sexual orientation. In many larger metropolitan areas, there are gay and lesbian chapters of AA and NA, as well as emerging networks of recovering persons. Because of the social issues discussed above, GLBT substance abuse clients desperately need to form social groups and social mixing outlets that do not include alcohol and other drugs. In some areas, these outlets are being established. In the city where I live, several coffee shops and bookstores have opened that cater to GLBT persons. Like all clients, GLBT persons need social settings where they can relax, feel accepted, openly and honestly own their self-identity, and meet interesting people.

In a related issue, because of the fear (rightly) of not being accepted as GLBT persons, many will not engage with a heterosexual therapist (van Wormer, Wells, & Boes, 2000). In fact, you may currently be seeing GLBT clients and not even know it, because they refuse to "come out" in your presence. Accordingly, maintain a list of respectable GLBT social workers who are available to provide individual, group, and family treatment for substance abuse and associated issues. Often, to help a client relax, these social workers will "come out" to their clients to clear the way for open and frank discussion of the issues.

4. *Do not try to change your client's sexual orientation.* Nor should you insist that your clients "come out" beyond the degree to which they are comfortable. While many have tried and even claimed to be successful at changing their sexual orientation, there has never been a documented case of a person successfully changing his or her sexual identity (van Wormer, Wells, & Boes, 2000). In fact, to attempt to change a client's sexual orientation would be in violation of the NASW Code of Professional Ethics, because to do so would infringe upon clients' right to self-determination and autonomy. This practice also runs contrary to accepted wisdom regarding sexual orientation. That is, the American Psychological Association clearly states that homosexuality is not a mental disorder and that treatment to change one's sexual orientation is unwarranted. If you find that your personal beliefs and attitudes do not allow you to respect a GLBT person's right to be GLBT, you must refer the client to someone else immediately.

ADOLESCENTS

Treating adolescents for substance abuse problems presents unique challenges. However, the substance abuse field has been relatively slow to acknowledge these challenges. Most adolescents are treated in programs based on models designed for European American adult males. That is, there are few adolescent programs in the United States designed to address the special developmental needs and issues that adolescent clients present in substance abuse treatment (Peele, 1998). Typically, adolescents are treated according to the disease model, which stresses acceptance of a lifelong disease, abstinence, and consistent attendance at twelve-step meetings. Below, we look at why these practices, which are so prevalent in substance abuse treatment, are inappropriate for most adolescents, especially those under the age of 17 years old. These methods of treatment continue despite the fact that authors such as Royce (1989) claim that merely applying an adult program to adolescents is ineffective and unethical.

Having spent nearly 20 years treating adolescent substance abuse clients in all levels of care, I have found that adolescent substance abuse treatment requires a shift in thinking and approach if it is to be successful. In fact, the very definition of success must also be changed from lifetime abstinence to success in other areas of life. In response to a funding source's need for us to justify our "unusual" treatment methods, in 1994, I surveyed the parents of more than 1000 former adolescent substance abuse clients in my agency (Johnson, 1994). The survey was intended to clarify parents' opinions of our family approach and short-term methods. However, parent responses to other items on the survey were more telling. Of the parents who responded to the survey, more than 79 percent reported that they considered the treatment successful, although 72 percent reported that their son or daughter had used substances since leaving treatment. I also asked parents to define the criteria they used to determine treatment success.

When the results were tallied, I generated a list of the top 20 criteria parents used to determine treatment success, and abstinence from alcohol and other drugs was seventeenth on the list, behind issues such as success in school, being home on time, and treating parents with respect. This was a survey of parents who had admitted their adolescent into substance abuse treatment. The results of this survey suggested that the definition of success with adolescent substance abusers is not necessarily abstinence. It can (and should) encompass much more.

There are several unique issues to consider when treating adolescent substance abuse clients (CSAT, 1995b). First, for most adolescent clients, the disease model approach is irrelevant. It is difficult to convince adolescents that they are "powerless" over substances or that they have a disease and that they can never use again for the rest of their lives (Fisher & Harrison, 1993). Furthermore, twelve-step programs are also usually irrelevant for most adolescents until they reach the age of 18 or older. Below this age, adolescents cannot relate to the stories of older recovering people. In addition, the meeting structure is developmentally inconsistent with adolescence. How many 15- or 16-year-olds do you know who would be able to speak about themselves for three minutes and then listen intently and empathetically to other people's stories for the next hour or more? My experience suggests that until an adolescent reaches about 18 years of age, he or she will not benefit from AA or NA attendance.

Second, most adolescents who enter treatment are not chemically dependent, according to the *DSM* definition or the definition proposed in this text. Hence, the majority of adolescent clients' use patterns fall somewhere along the abuse continuum. To apply disease model concepts or intensive individual treatment in a hospital or residential facility would be incompatible with the level of problems most adolescent clients present in an assessment.

Third, adolescents do not have the same right to self-determination that adults possess. That is, in most adolescent cases, problems must be considered within the context of the family. After treatment, unless there is a documented case of abuse or neglect, the adolescent must return home to live with his or her family. For this reason, the family should be treated along with the adolescent. The following example shows why the family needs to be included when working with adolescent clients:

> I once had a 15-year-old client who was brought in for an assessment by his father and stepmother. He had been smoking marijuana daily and drinking on weekends. He was failing school, had been arrested twice for theft and vandalism, and had stolen his father's car several times. Looking at this case individually, it would be easy to determine that this child had at least a diagnosis of substance dependence, along with a probable co-occurring adolescent behavioral diagnosis. However, when he was interviewed with his family, his story became more complicated.
>
> His biological mother was a long-term alcoholic who refused to see him. His stepmother had been abstinent for one year and was separated from his father "because of the son." Since his stepmother had entered the family 10 years earlier, she had stated aloud that the boy was "no good" and predicted that he would be in prison someday. She had told him that she "hated" him and that he was the reason for his father's first divorce and

would ultimately cause her marriage to end too. The father refused to confront the stepmother. The client's older sister was anorexic, and his two younger stepbrothers had behavior problems.

This case illustrates how complicated it can become to accurately assess and diagnose adolescent substance abuse. Did the boy have a disease that was caused by individual behavior, or was he merely trying to cope with living in a hostile environment? Would it do him any good to label him an addict, place him in the hospital, and invite the family to watch educational films about the disease model? I doubt it.

Treatment Issues

From the discussion above, I offer the following issues to consider when contemplating how to provide substance abuse treatment for adolescent clients.

1. *Choose the least restrictive setting.* Unless the child has no place to reside, inpatient or residential treatment is usually not required. Hence, rigidly apply the least restrictive setting criteria in the case of adolescent clients, favoring less intensive options over the more intensive treatment options.

2. *Opt for family and group treatment.* Because of the issues discussed above, family and group therapy are best suited to adolescent treatment needs. Family treatment (not education) should be the primary method, with group treatment used as an adjunctive method to support and encourage individual behavior change. The family should be integrally involved in the treatment process at every turn: assessment, planning, treatment, and aftercare. Therefore, if you want to work with adolescent substance abusers, you need to become a skilled family therapist. Group therapy allows adolescents to work on social skills development and supports a change of peers, which will be needed if most adolescents are to change their behavior significantly (van Wormer, 1995).

Contrary to what some others believe (Doweiko, 1999; Evans & Sullivan, 2001; Connors, Donovan, & DiClemente, 2001), I maintain that individual therapy for most adolescents is not helpful in the substance abuse treatment context. If individual work is needed, you should serve more as a mentor than a therapist. Exceptions include adolescents who have suffered abuse, incest, violence, or who have suicidal ideation. However, once these issues have been broached individually, it is helpful to move the client to a supportive group setting for further treatment.

3. *Establish appropriate treatment goals.* I placed this issue third, not because it is the third most important, but because it must be discussed in the context of item 2 above. If you believe the results of the survey discussed earlier, whatever goals are agreed upon for adolescent treatment must be jointly authored by parents and the adolescent, although primarily by the parents. Do not assume that abstinence is the goal of the parents, but do assume that it will not be the adolescent's goal. Therefore, whatever needs to be approached in treatment must be agreed upon by the parents, and not forced upon them by a well-meaning but misguided substance abuse worker.

4. *Parents will always be more important to the client than you are.* No matter where or from what family conditions your clients originate, you will never reach the

stage where you become more important to adolescent clients than their parents. This point may sound obvious, but many practitioners working with adolescents begin to act as if they are more central to the adolescent's life than the parents. How does this show up in practice?

First, it shows when you choose to exclude family members from treatment. Perhaps you think the parents are poor role models or that they do not care about your client. Keep in mind that excluding parents or guardians from treatment means that there are people important to your client "out there" who have the capacity to diminish or render irrelevant the work you perform with your client. Parents want to feel important to the treatment, even if they do not act that way. If you choose to exclude them, many times they will say to their child, "That therapist does not know what she is talking about. You can use some pot at home."

Second, it shows if you disparage or discount parents or family members in front of adolescent clients. No matter how "bad" or "evil" you believe parents may be, do not convey these feelings to the adolescent. If your client disparages his or her parents, you can simply respond reflectively to clarify the feelings, instead of agreeing. My experience suggests that regardless of how an adolescent *says* he or she feels about parents, as soon as the therapist agrees, the adolescent immediately begins defending them.

Also, be careful of the messages you send to parents about their abilities. For example, if parents admit their adolescent for treatment, do not say, "Don't worry, folks, we can fix this problem." What message does this send? "Parents, you've tried and failed, so now let the experts do what you have been unable to do for years: help your child." This can be an especially difficult problem in inpatient or residential treatment. In fact, for adolescents and families, inpatient and/or residential treatment presents a dilemma. Parents who feel like failures admit their child into a mysterious program hoping that the child will improve. For the most part, parents are excluded from the treatment until or unless that child is expelled or graduates successfully. Then, if the successful adolescent leaves the program and acts up, the parents are left to wonder if they have done something wrong. Hence, they feel excluded and discounted.

In our adolescent programs, we tried to overcome this built-in problem in residential treatment in the following way:

> Parents, guardians, or whoever was the legally responsible adult in the client's life was included every step of the way in treatment. These adults participated in all planning, decision-making, and interventions, throughout the treatment process. The adults were so integral to the treatment that if and when their child acted out in the program, the adults were called (day or night) to come into the program and deal with their child, with staff support. If parents needed to stay the night to be with their child, this was allowed. Thus, we never removed the adolescent from the care and attention of the parents; instead, we enlisted them fully in the treatment process.

Third, it shows when you become angry or upset when your adolescent client does not do what you think he or she should do. If your client agrees to abstinence as a goal, and then uses in the week between sessions, be careful not to act as if the client has "let you down." This is an easy trap to fall into, but one that must be avoided. Above all, your client is not your child, and you do not have the right to scold or punish for what you consider inappropriate behavior or lying.

Working with adolescents in substance abuse treatment takes unique skills and approaches. The dynamics of this treatment are different from substance abuse work with adults. As you can see from this discussion, the successful adolescent treatment provider must have a variety of skills. If you want to work in this area, hone your group and family skills, as well as your personal beliefs and attitudes about substance abuse, treatment, and families.

OLDER PERSONS

The elderly are routinely underrepresented in substance abuse treatment programs (Jung, 1994). However, as the "graying of America" continues and the Baby Boom generation becomes older, it has become increasingly important to understand substance abuse among the elderly. Underrepresentation in the literature may be due to social and economic barriers to entering treatment, lack of recognition of problems by older clients and their families, or failure of treatment providers to understand the potential for substance abuse problems in older persons. Nevertheless, according to Abrams and Alexopoulos (1987), "more than 20 percent of patients admitted to a psychiatric facility over the age of 65 could be considered drug dependent" (p. 822). The Center for Substance Abuse Treatment (CSAT, 1998) estimates that more than 17 percent of people over the age of 60 abuse alcohol or other drugs.

Despite the growing population of older adults, substance abuse providers remain largely silent on this issue. There are several potential reasons for this silence. First, health care providers, including social workers, tend to overlook substance abuse among older people, mistaking the symptoms for those of dementia, depression, or other problems common to older adults. Second, older adults are more likely to hide their substance abuse and less likely to seek help. Third, many relatives of older adults, particularly adult children, are ashamed of the problem and choose not to address it. Perhaps another reason for the silence is that most substance abuse providers are not equipped to handle the specific needs of older adult clients with substance abuse problems.

Older adults who are involved with substance abuse behavior tend to abuse alcohol along with prescription and over-the-counter medications (CSAT, 1998). Adults age 65 and older consume more prescribed medication and over-the-counter medications than any other age group in the United States. More than half who use these drugs report adverse drug reactions leading to hospitalization (Chastain, 1992). Approximately 85 percent of all adults over 65 reportedly suffer from one or more chronic diseases or conditions, and an estimated 83 percent of these adults take at least one prescription medication (Ray, Thapa, & Shorr, 1993). A large share of these prescriptions are for psychoactive drugs that carry the potential for abuse and dependence.

Treatment Issues

Based on a review of the substance abuse treatment literature specific to older adults, the following five features should be incorporated into treatment with this group (Schonfeld & Dupree, 1995):

1. *Treat older adults in age-specific settings.* Provide age-specific group treatment that is supportive and non-confrontational, designed to build or reinforce the client's sense of self-efficacy.

2. *Demonstrate respect for older clients.* That is, give older clients the respect that they deserve and expect as an elder in the community. One way to do this is to refer to people by title instead of first names (i.e., Mr. Smith, Mrs. Jones).

3. *Take a broad, holistic, and multi-systemic approach to treatment that includes age-specific medical care, as well as addressing psychological and social issues.* When assessing older clients, watch for issues of depression, loneliness, and loss (i.e., death of a spouse, retirement, loss of skills and/or independence). A primary focus should be on rebuilding the client's social support network and self-efficacy.

4. *Plan treatment that is flexible and maintained at a pace and with expectations appropriate for an older client.* Also, be prepared to address gender issues with older clients who may or may not abide by current gender ideas or roles.

5. *Above all, you must have an interest in working with this population.* Beyond that, to be competent in this area it is important to stay informed regarding the issues of older adulthood and to recognize the needs that older clients may bring to the treatment process.

PERSONS WITH
CO-OCCURRING DISORDERS

As we discussed in Chapter 8, the assessment and treatment needs of clients with co-occurring mental health disorders and substance abuse problems differ significantly from the treatment needs of clients with either a mental health or substance abuse problem. In such cases, a "one-size-fits-all" approach does not work. Similarly, neither the mental health nor substance abuse treatment systems can provide adequate treatment alone for both problems. The following discussion includes issues for consideration that are clinically relevant in a substance abuse treatment context. Readers who are interested in more detailed and thorough training in mental health diagnosis and treatment can find that information elsewhere. In this text, my goal is to help you understand that clients with a substance abuse or chemical dependency problem and a co-occurring mental health disorder require different and more integrated services than do clients with a singular diagnosis of substance abuse or chemical dependence.

As we stated in Chapter 8, your first step should be to determine if, in fact, a co-occurring mental health diagnosis exists. This task is complicated by the fact that the effects of many drugs mimic a mental health disorder, making it hard to discriminate between mental health disorders, mental health disorders caused by substance use, and/or behaviors that appear to be mental health disorders that are simply the aftereffects of substance use, abuse, or dependence. I urge you to take a moment to review the discussion in Chapter 8 before moving forward. That information will be extremely helpful as you attempt to place the following treatment discussion into context.

Over the years, conventional boundaries between single-focus agencies (i.e., either substance abuse or mental health) have impeded the progress of clients with co-occurring disorders (Baker, 1991). Hence, treating clients effectively for co-occurring disorders represents a challenge to the traditional treatment systems and prevailing notions about social work education and training. For example, most graduate schools of social work encourage, if not require, students to specialize either by modality or field of practice, while agencies adhere to singular foci regarding client populations and/or fields of practice. Many social agencies and schools of social work have yet to make changes to accommodate clients with co-occurring disorders. Therefore, both the treatment and educational systems encourage the type of focus that often leads to clinical misinterpretation and/or failure to recognize or consider the possibility that a second (or third) disorder may, in fact, exist.

Beyond the difficulty of providing care that specifically addresses both categories of problems, the misinterpretation of co-occurring disorders and/or failure to identify a co-occurring psychiatric disorder often is a detriment to treatment. For example, the symptoms of a co-occurring psychiatric disorder are often misinterpreted by substance abuse professionals as poor or incomplete "recovery" from chemical dependency. Psychiatric disorders may interfere with clients' ability and motivation to participate in substance abuse treatment and may impede their ability or willingness to adhere to substance abuse treatment guidelines. These clients are often labeled resistant and "not ready for treatment" by substance abuse professionals when they often have good reason for their behavior.

For example, individuals suffering from anxiety disorders may fear and/or resist attending support group or group therapy sessions. Depressed clients may be too unmotivated and lethargic to participate in treatment. Those with psychotic or manic symptoms may exhibit bizarre behavior and poor personal relations in treatment, especially in groups. Clients whose substance use is the primary way of suppressing psychiatric symptoms (self-medication) may not achieve and/or maintain abstinence in the time frame or with the consistency that substance abuse professionals prefer. I know of many instances in which substance abuse professionals—even today—consider clients with psychiatric disorders as failing to achieve abstinence because they take prescribed medication to treat those disorders. I have witnessed substance abuse professionals instructing these clients to stop using their prescribed medications in order to find "recovery" and labeling any use of prescribed medication as a relapse. Unfortunately, failure to identify co-occurring psychiatric symptoms or disorders often ends with a client being removed or barred from treatment at a time when he or she is most vulnerable.

The many possible combinations of co-occurring disorders vary along important dimensions, such as severity, chronicity, disability, and degree of impairment.

For example, two disorders may be similar in severity (agoraphobia and cocaine dependence), or one may be more severe (i.e., major depression and alcohol abuse). The severity of both problems may (and often does) change over time. There is no single combination of co-occurring disorders; in fact, there is tremendous variability among them. However, as we discussed in Chapters 1 and 8, clients with mental health disorders are at an increased risk for developing substance abuse problems, and clients with substance abuse problems have a greater risk for mental health problems (Anthony, Warner, & Kessler, 1997; Regier et al., 1990). More than 50 percent of the people who use or abuse substances have experienced psychiatric symptoms significant enough to fulfill diagnostic criteria for a psychiatric disorder (Regier et al., 1990), although many of the symptoms may be substance related and not represent an independent condition.

From a substance abuse treatment perspective, clients with a co-occurring mental health disorder experience more severe and chronic medical, social, and emotional problems than other clients (CSAT, 1995a) and are more difficult to engage in assessment and treatment (Denning, 2000). Profiles of clients with co-occurring disorders consistently demonstrate that they are more or differently disabled and require more services than clients with a single issue. Because these clients have at least two disorders, they are vulnerable to both substance use relapse and a worsening of the mental health condition. Further, relapse with substances often leads to psychiatric decompensation, and worsening of psychiatric symptoms often leads to relapse with substances. Hence, relapse prevention treatment must be specifically designed for clients with co-occurring disorders.

Clients with a co-occurring disorder often have more crises and progress more gradually in treatment. These clients have higher rates of homelessness, legal problems, and medical issues, often needing more frequent and longer-lasting hospitalizations, and have more frequent emergency room visits (Center for Substance Abuse Treatment, 1995a). For example, clients with schizophrenia are twice as likely to experience episodes of violence and suicide if they simultaneously abuse street drugs (Anthony, Warner, & Kessler, 1997).

The treatment and social needs of clients with co-occurring disorders differ depending on the type and severity of the disorders. They are less able to navigate between, engage in, and remain engaged in treatment services. Therefore, treatment must be suited to the client's personal needs and characteristics, often across the various treatment systems. Moreover, abstinence from substance use may not be appropriate for these clients, suggesting that a harm reduction approach, instead of a disease model approach, may be more appropriate (Center for Substance Abuse Treatment, 1995a).

Treatment Issues

As you should be aware by now, the prevailing attitudes and beliefs about how to treat clients with co-occurring disorders are changing. As professionals within the substance abuse and mental health fields have become increasingly aware that clients with co-occurring disorders require flexibility with regard to ideas and methods about substance abuse treatment, various attempts have been made to account for the special needs of this population (Baker, 1991; Minkoff & Drake,

1991; Ries & Consensus Panel Chair, 1994). As a social worker interested in treating clients with substance abuse problems or mental illness, it is essential to learn how to provide treatment to this complex and significantly at-risk population.

According to Baker (1991), attempts to address the needs of this population reflect philosophical differences between substance abuse and mental health fields about the nature of co-occurring disorders, as well as differing opinions regarding the best way to treat them. They also reflect the limitations of available resources and differences in treatment responses for problems of varying severity. Three primary approaches have been taken to treat clients with co-occurring disorders: sequential treatment, parallel treatment, and integrated treatment. Our discussion will focus on the third approach.

Integrated Treatment   An integrated model of treatment combines elements of both substance abuse and mental health treatments into a unified and comprehensive treatment program designed specifically for clients with co-occurring disorders (CSAT, 1995a). In this model, professionals are cross-trained in substance abuse and mental health treatments, and often utilize case management as a way of monitoring and supporting clients through various substance abuse and mental health crises as they occur. One provider or program provides the primary treatment for both the substance abuse and mental health problems at the same time, as part of a comprehensive treatment approach. If and when outside services are required, such as psychiatric evaluation and medication, vocational counseling, credit counseling, or legal services, the primary provider serves as case manager, seeing to it that the client receives the services he or she requires as part of the overall comprehensive treatment approach (Evans & Sullivan, 2001).

Based on the professional literature and my own clinical experience, I have assembled the following list of issues to consider when treating persons with co-occurring substance abuse problems and mental health disorders. Keep in mind that these issues must be considered in the context of other groups and communities to which the client belongs (i.e., racial, ethnic, age, sexual orientation).

1. *Implement a dual recovery approach* (Evans & Sullivan, 2001). This approach can best be described as a recovery-oriented approach for both the substance abuse and mental health disorder(s). According to Evans and Sullivan (2001),

> The priority for early stages of recovery from chemical dependency is simply maintaining abstinence, and typically, the interventions rely on frequent AA meetings . . . Later chemical dependency work relies on step work to achieve positive aspects of health through addressing issues such as guilt, fear, and resentment. Similarly, the priority in the early stages of recovery from psychiatric disorders is simply maintaining stability, and typically, interventions rely on case management, a structured lifestyle, and acceptance of the need to manage the disorder. Later mental health work relies on skills training and psychotherapy to achieve positive functioning through addressing issues such as grief at having an illness, establishing intimacy, and operating as a prosocial member of society (p. 29).

2. *Base treatment on the disease model.* For many persons with co-occurring disorders, the disease model provides a nonjudgmental rationale for the need to abstain from drugs, and it helps clients to reframe their sense of self from being bad to being ill. Simultaneously, this approach reinforces education about the nature of their second illness, the mental health disorder. The disease model also provides a long-term and consistent mechanism to help guard against relapse, and it allows these clients an opportunity to explore the existential and spiritual issues that persons with co-occurring disorders often face.

3. *Use a variety of treatment modalities.* Clients with co-occurring disorders are treated in individual, group, and family therapy. According to Evans and Sullivan (2001), a cognitive-behavioral approach to treatment is most effective as an adjunct to disease model approaches. This approach, which can be performed in all three treatment modalities, focuses on thinking and action. Cognitive-behavioral therapy is especially good at relapse prevention and teaching new coping mechanisms for life stressors.

4. *Attend to the basics first.* As we discussed in Chapter 8 pertaining to substance abuse assessment, always attend to your client's most immediate crisis first, before moving into treatment. That is, look for potential emotional, psychological, or physical issues early in your contact, to ensure that your client has these needs met by the appropriate professionals. After these issues have been stabilized and addressed, you can begin formal treatment planning to address the co-occurring disorders.

SUMMARY

In this chapter we explored issues to consider when treating people from a variety of populations, including African Americans; Latino Americans; Native Americans; gay, lesbian, bisexual, and transgendered (GLBT) persons; adolescents; older adults; and persons with co-occurring disorders. While several issues were presented that are unique to each population, it is important to remember our discussion about an individual's participation and identification with multiple communities (Chapter 6). That is, clients do not identify with only one group; instead, they belong to many. Therefore, you must work to combine approaches and considerations in a way that will meet the needs of each client. No single approach based on the needs of one group will suffice. This integration of issues and approaches is the hallmark of a comprehensive and multi-systemic approach to substance abuse treatment, as discussed throughout this text.

A P P E N D I X A

Substance Abuse Assessment/ Case History Format

The following assessment/case history format is based on the assessment dimensions discussed in Chapter 8. As a reader and purchaser of this text, you are permitted to use this form in any way you see fit pertaining to substance abuse practice.

Guide for use: Each dimension requires data, narrative, and a short summary of the relevant issues to consider in the final assessment. To save space, I have left little room between dimensions for writing. If you choose to use this format in practice, the form will need to be modified to allow sufficient space under each dimension to complete an assessment properly.

Client name: Date of first contact:

Social worker: Date completed:

Dimension 1: Client description, presenting problem, and context of referral

A. Brief description of client:

B. Chief complaint and symptoms by client and others present:

C. Context of the referral, precipitating events, facts, and dates:

D. Issues and strengths to consider:

Dimension 2: Treatment history

A. Substance abuse treatment (places, dates, modality, problem—self and family members):

B. Client attitude toward treatment (outcome, counselor/therapist, etc.):

C. Mental health treatment (places, dates, modality, problem—self and family members):

D. Attitudes about previous treatment(s):

E. Issues and strengths to consider:

Dimension 3: Substance use history

A. Lifetime substance use history (Complete table. Explain in narrative.):

Substance	Frequency	Dose (avg.)	Age at first use	Age at last use	Route of Admin.	Overdose

B. Drugs used in previous 30 days:

C. Top three drugs of choice:

D. Drug mixing:

E. Longest period of abstinence:

F. Narrative (include attitudes and beliefs about use):

G. Issues and strengths to consider:

Dimension 4: Medical history

Issues and strengths to consider:

Dimension 5: Basic needs

Issues and strengths to consider:

Dimension 6: Psychological and emotional functioning
Mental status screening (check all that apply)

A. General appearance:

1. Physical appearance: ___neat ___clean ___unkempt ___older ___younger ___appropriate
2. Attitude:

___cooperative	___negative	___suspicious	___inaccessible
___shy	___frank	___hostile	___sensitive
___uncooperative	___quiet	___polite	___provocative
___resentful	___irritable	___submissive	___indifferent
___serious	___defensive	___tense	___preoccupied
___detached			

B. Behavioral functioning:

1. Motor activity: ___normal ___slow ___hyperactive
   ___restless ___tremors ___agitation
   ___other: _____
2. Gait: ___normal ___stooped ___awkward ___staggering
3. Posture: ___normal ___rigid ___limp ___gesturing

C. Speech:

___normal ___spontaneous ___slow ___hesitant ___rapid
___stutter ___pressured ___soft ___loud ___slurred
___monotonous ___emotional ___mumbled ___threatening
___other: _____

D. Emotional functioning:

1. Mood: ___euphoric ___depressed ___anxious ___angry
2. Affect: ___appropriate ___inappropriate ___flat ___broad
   ___constricted ___blunted ___euphoric

E. Thought process:

___appropriate ___blocking ___preservation
___incoherent ___circumstantiality ___flight of ideas
___loose association ___distractible
___other: _____

F. Thought content:

___appropriate ___obsessions ___compulsions ___preoccupied
___guilt ___suicidal ___homicidal ___somatic concerns
___ideas of reference/influence ___thought control ___thought broadcasting
___paranoia
___delusions (___persecutory ___somatic ___grandiosity)

G. Perceptions:

Hallucinations: __auditory   __visual   __tactile   __none

H. Cognitive functions:

1. Consciousness: __alert   __confused   __clouded

                                 __stuporous   __apathetic

2. Orientation: __normal   __defective (time, place, person)

3. Memory: __normal   __defective (__remote __recent __now)

4. Attention/concentration: __normal   __impaired

I. General knowledge (estimated):   __average   __below average

                                                                  __above average

J. Intellectual function (estimated):   __average   __below average

                                                                  __above average

K. Insight: __good   __fair   __poor

L. Judgment: __good   __fair   __poor (explain)

Mental status impressions (potential mood, anxiety, thought, or personality disorders: results of any screening tools):

Issues and strengths to consider:

Dimension 7: Family history and structure (attach a three-generation genogram):

Issues and strengths to consider:

Dimension 8: Community/macro context

A. Local community:

Issues and strengths to consider:

B. Cultural context:

Issues and strengths to consider:

C. Social class:

Issues and strengths to consider:

D. Social-relational:

Issues and strengths to consider:

E. Legal history:

Issues and strengths to consider:

Dimension 9: Motivation (stage of motivation and justification):

Issues and strengths to consider:

Dimension 10: Diagnosis

Axis I:

Axis II:

Axis III:

Axis IV:

Axis V:

Justification:

Narrative assessment (Include all relevant issues and strengths to compose a multi-systemic description of the client's life.):

Sample Substance
Abuse Assessment/
Case History Report

Client name: Jim

Social worker: George

Date of first contact: 0/0/00

Date completed: 0/0/00

Dimension 1: Client description, presenting problem, and context of referral

A. Brief description of client: Jim is a 26-year-old Caucasian male, dressed casually and neatly. He appeared well groomed and maintained appropriate eye contact. Jim appeared polite but anxious during this session, at times perspiring and glancing quickly around the room. Jim appeared alone for this assessment. His spouse was invited but did not attend.

B. Chief complaint and symptoms by client and others present: Jim stated that his "life is out of control" at this time. He complained that his spouse and family insist that his drug use (cocaine) is the reason, but he denies this. He says that he has always been a "nervous sort" and that lately (in the last six months) his nerves have "gotten worse." Jim said that if his spouse were in the sessions, she would blame his behavior on cocaine and alcohol abuse. When asked, he stated that his parents would agree. Jim stated that all he wants from therapy is to learn to "relax and enjoy life again" and that he is not sure that his "occasional" use of cocaine and alcohol "to relax" is a problem.

C. Context of the referral, precipitating events, facts, and dates: Jim claims that he chose to come in for an assessment and "therapy" and that this decision was not made with any outside pressure, yet he pointed out that there is a discrepancy between what he believes are his problems and what his spouse and family believe are the problems. He also stated that his spouse "encouraged" him to come for therapy, but that he did not feel as if he was being forced into it. Jim said he chose to come for therapy today, after experiencing "four sleepless nights and several arguments with his spouse" over his drug use and financial issues.

D. Issues and strengths to consider: Jim is a well-spoken man who appears to have family support and encouragement to attend therapy. He claims to be a nervous person, and appears unwilling to consider his use of cocaine and alcohol as a part of his "nervous" condition. There appears to be disagreement between Jim and his family over the definition of his problems, suggesting that perhaps he presented for therapy under more duress than he was willing to admit during a first session.

Dimension 2: Treatment history

A. Substance abuse treatment (places, dates, modality, problem—self and family members): Jim stated that he was a client in residential substance abuse treatment for alcohol and marijuana use when he was 16 years old, resulting from problems in school attendance and a history of status offenses as a juvenile (see legal history). His treatment lasted six months and was followed by a recommendation to attend AA meetings (which he did not attend).

B. Client attitude toward treatment (outcome, counselor/therapist, etc.): When asked, Jim stated that the treatment was a "joke." He believed that he had "no business" in a residential treatment program, given that his drug use was minimal at the time. He said that the program insisted that he admit to having a disease, and that he refused for a time. Jim then claimed that he finally admitted to having a disease, because that was the only way he was ever going to complete the program and go home. He said that "there is no way in hell" that he had a disease then, or now for that matter. He said that he liked one of the counselors, but most of them were "lame-ass former dope fiends" who thought everyone who used drugs was a junkie.

Jim reported that his father was in inpatient treatment several years ago for alcoholism, and that he had not drunk since that time (five years). His father is a current AA member, and his mother and wife now attend Al-Anon. He also stated that his paternal grandfather probably could have used treatment for alcoholism, but never attended.

C. Mental health treatment (places, dates, modality, problem—self and family members): Jim reports no history of treatment for mental health problems. His mother was on "some kind of medication" for depression for many years before his father quit drinking. There were no reports of other family members attending mental health treatment.

D. Attitudes about previous treatment(s): Jim stated that his mother's experience with medication for depression was excellent. It helped her "feel much better" and allowed her to function during the time his father was drinking.

E. Issues and strengths to consider: There is a history of positive familial experiences with substance abuse and mental health treatment, suggesting that Jim will receive appropriate support for any therapy. Conversely, Jim learned to comply with treatment as a way of "getting by" in an experience that he remembers as "lame-ass." Therefore, it may be difficult to engage Jim in serous treatment because he may be inclined to find ways to comply in order to make a positive impression on the therapist, program staff, and his family. Additionally, Jim made it clear that he was not open to talk of the disease model, which may be indications of denial or a leftover poor attitude caused by inappropriate treatment at a young age.

Dimension 3: Substance use history

A. Lifetime substance use history (Complete table. Explain in narrative.):

Substance	Frequency	Dose (avg.)	Age at first use	Age at last use	Route of Admin.	Overdose
Alcohol (beer)	Daily	3–6 cans	12	NA	Drink	No
Alcohol (liquor)	2–3 x's/week	2–3 shots/use	12	NA	Drink	No
Cocaine (powder)	2–3 x's/week	$\frac{1}{4}$oz/week	23	NA	Snort/smoke	No
Marijuana	1–2 x's/month	1 joint	13	NA	Smoke	No
LSD	1 x/week	1 tab	14	18	Oral	Yes
Speed	2–3 x's/week	1–2 pills	14	23	Oral	No
Nicotine	Daily	1 can per day	19	NA	Chewing	No

B. Drugs used in previous 30 days: Jim reported drinking on a daily basis and having used cocaine the day before this session. He also chews tobacco on a daily basis. In the 48 hours prior to the session, Jim drank 12 cans of beer and snorted at least 3 grams of powder cocaine, along with use of nicotine.

C. Top three drugs of choice: Jim claims that cocaine, alcohol, and LSD are his drugs of choice, although he quit using LSD when he was 18 years old after a "bad trip." However, he says that he would do LSD again if he weren't fearful of another bad trip.

D. Drug mixing: Jim constantly mixes three drugs: cocaine, alcohol, and nicotine. This mixture presents no clear and present health dangers. There is no evidence that Jim mixes any other depressant drugs with alcohol at this time, as he reports that he does not take prescription medication.

E. Longest period of abstinence: Jim reports that he has been abstinent for no longer than 24 hours since he was 12 years old, the age at which he began using alcohol and other drugs.

F. Narrative (include attitudes and beliefs about use): Jim began using substances at 12 years old, and has been using on a regular basis since that time (14 years). His use is regular and consistent; he stated that he has not been abstinent for more than 24 hours since he was 12. This suggests that Jim has used quite regularly, even at a young age. Moreover, he has used a mixture of drugs since that time. Based on his substance use history, while he has not used a plethora of different drugs, it appears that Jim finds certain drugs and mixtures that he likes and stays with them. He stopped using LSD, a drug he used weekly for five years, only after experiencing a bad trip. This experience has made Jim afraid of LSD, despite his liking of the drug. Another interesting indicator is that he used speed (amphetamines) until age 23, when he began using cocaine, suggesting that stimulant drugs satisfy his needs better than other drugs. He reports that "90%" of his cocaine use is powder cocaine, but occasionally he will smoke crack cocaine for a new experience. When asked, Jim admitted that the amount of cocaine used each week has increased in the last year, and that he often does not feel as good as he once did when using cocaine.

Jim states that he has "no problem" with his substance use, and that he is unashamed of it, even though his wife and parents are against it. While he knows how destructive alcohol can be because of his father's experience, he claims that he is not a "drunk" who "needs it" everyday. When asked about his daily use, Jim claimed that he uses to relax and have fun, but does not "need it" to survive. When asked if he thought he had a drug problem, Jim stated, "No, I don't have a problem." However, he did say that he had thought about it before deciding that he "didn't need it, so I couldn't have a problem."

G. Issues and strengths to consider: Jim's use is regular and consistent, and the effects of his drugs of choice, especially cocaine and nicotine, can cause the kind of "nervous" issues that Jim presents. Given his history of use and the amount, frequency, and doses used currently, we must look closely to determine whether Jim has a more significant problem than he is willing to admit. Yet, despite his refusal to admit to drug issues, Jim admittedly has considered the possibility, which could be positive later in treatment if it is determined that he has a treatable substance use problem. He appears to be a thoughtful person, willing at least to "glance" at his personal behavior and habits in a critical manner.

Dimension 4: Medical history

Jim reports no recurrent medical issues or problems. He has never had surgery, nor been hospitalized for any illness or disease up to this point in his life.

Issues and strengths to consider: While he reports no medical issues, because of the frequency of drug use and his "nervous" issues, it is appropriate to refer Jim to his physician for a complete physical examination.

Dimension 5: Basic needs

Jim lives in his home (which he owns) with his wife and two children. He appears to be meeting his personal and family basic needs on a daily basis.

Issues and strengths to consider: Jim has a stable place to live, a supportive spouse, and two young children that he appears to adore. The family income seems sufficient to provide for the basic needs of his growing family, although one has to wonder where he finds the financial resources to afford his rather expensive cocaine use and what impact this has on the provision of his family's basic needs and financial well-being.

Dimension 6: Psychological and emotional functioning
Mental status screening (check all that apply)

A. General appearance:

1. Physical appearance: __X__ neat __X__ clean ___unkempt ___older ___younger
    __X__ appropriate

2. Attitude: __X__ cooperative   ___negative   ___suspicious   ___inaccessible
                 ___shy   ___frank   ___hostile   ___sensitive

___uncooperative   ___quiet   X polite   ___provocative

___resentful   ___irritable   ___submissive   ___indifferent

X serious   X defensive   X tense   ___preoccupied

___detached

B. Behavioral functioning:

1. Motor activity: ___normal   ___slow   ___hyperactive

   X restless   ___tremors   X agitation

   ___other: _____

2. Gait: X normal   ___stooped   ___awkward   ___staggering

3. Posture: X normal   ___rigid   ___limp   ___gesturing

C. Speech:

___normal   ___spontaneous   ___slow   ___hesitant   X rapid

___stutter   ___pressured   ___soft   ___loud   ___slurred

___monotonous   X emotional   ___mumbled   ___threatening

___other: _____

D. Emotional functioning:

1. Mood: ___euphoric   ___depressed   X anxious   ___angry

2. Affect: X appropriate   ___inappropriate   ___flat   ___broad

   ___constricted   ___blunted   ___euphoric

E. Thought process:

X appropriate   ___blocking   ___preservation

___incoherent   ___circumstantiality   ___flight of ideas

___loose association   ___distractible   ___other: _____

F. Thought content:

X appropriate   ___obsessions   ___compulsions   ___preoccupied

___guilt   ___suicidal   ___homicidal   ___somatic concerns

___ideas of reference/   ___thought control   ___thought   ___paranoia
influence   broadcasting

___delusions (___persecutory ___somatic ___grandiosity)

G. Perceptions:

Hallucinations: ___auditory   ___visual   ___tactile   X none

H. Cognitive functions:

1. Consciousness: X alert   ___confused   ___clouded

   ___stuporous   ___apathetic

2. Orientation: X normal   ___defective (time, place, person)

3. Memory: X normal   ___defective (___remote ___recent ___now)

4. Attention/concentration: ___normal   X impaired

I. General knowledge (estimated): <u>X</u> average ___below average ___above average

J. Intellectual function (estimated): <u>X</u> average ___below average ___above average

K. Insight: ___good   <u>X</u> fair   ___poor

L. Judgment: ___good   <u>X</u> fair   ___poor (explain)

Mental status impressions (potential mood, anxiety, thought, or personality disorders: results of any screening tools): Jim presents as a cooperative and polite, yet serious person who becomes defensive when discussing the possibility of having substance abuse problems. His mood is anxious, and he moves between agitated and restless presentation during the session, to being listless and resigned in presentation. He complains of being "nervous" often and that his life is out of control. This could be a sign of an anxiety disorder, such as bipolar disorder; however, it could also be side effects of the drugs he uses on a near daily basis. Jim denies any thoughts of suicide or homicide, now or in the past. Should indications surface that his issues with anxiety predated his drug use, or exist independently of his drug use, Jim will be referred to Dr. Consultant for a psychiatric evaluation.

Issues and strengths to consider: Jim is thoughtful, cooperative, with fair insight, and average to above average intelligence. He appears to want help with his anxiety issues, and seems capable of thinking critically about his life and problems.

Dimension 7: Family history and structure
(attach a three-generation genogram):

Jim is the eldest son of his parents, both of whom are living. He has two younger sisters: one is 23 years old and in college, and the other is 18 years old and living at home. His father is a recovering alcoholic who has been an AA member for five years, and his mother attends Al-Anon. Jim claims that his relationships are close with his family members, although they have been strained lately because of his father's insistence that he has a drug problem. Neither of Jim's sisters abuses drugs, according to Jim.

His wife (Marie) is the only child of two living parents. She is a part-time secretary, working two days per week. According to Jim, there is no history of substance abuse or mental health problems in her family. Her family is close to the children, and has expressed their belief that Jim has problems and needs help. Jim believes that his mother-in-law has influenced Marie's opinion of his use over the last few months, and blames his mother-in-law for some of the troubles between Marie and himself.

Jim and Marie have two young children: a boy (Jim Jr.) who is four years old, and a girl (Ann-Marie) who is two. Jim and Marie have been married five years, and both pregnancies were planned. He reports that he "loves" his kids and wife, and would not want to see anything happen to break up his family. His relationship with his wife has been strained lately, over his drug use and recent evidence of sexual problems. According to Jim, Marie has been uninterested in sex, and at times, he has been unable to perform. Jim claims that he has not had extramarital affairs and is loyal to his wife. When asked why Marie did not come to this session, Jim claims that they could not arrange child care.

Jim's grandparents are all deceased. However, he claims that his paternal grandfather had drinking problems that contributed to his death. (See attached genogram).

Issues and strengths to consider: It appears that Jim has a strong and supportive family that is willing to support any efforts he may make toward change. Because of a family history of substance abuse dating at least three generations, Jim's family knows this issue and, with his father's five-year recovery in AA, understands the recovery process. While there is current friction because of Jim's unwillingness to accept the family's definition of his problems, they are a close group. His in-laws appear to also be supportive, although Jim is not sure of this. He currently blames his mother-in-law for influencing Marie into believing that he has a drug problem. It remains to be seen how the relationship between Jim and his wife's family plays in treatment. There is a need to include Marie and, perhaps, his family in the treatment process. Perhaps, if Jim remains in treatment, there also may come a time when the in-laws will be needed in treatment as well. Because his dad was an alcoholic, it will be important to consider the ramifications of growing up in an alcoholic household on Jim's past and present behavior.

Dimension 8: Community/macro context

A. Local community: Jim and Marie live in a middle-class neighborhood that is a mixture of young and older families. They have lived in this home and neighborhood for three years. He claims that his neighbors are friendly but distant, and that is "OK" with him. He has befriended one neighbor, who he likes to "party" with on occasion. This particular neighbor, according to Jim, has become his sole source for cocaine. He finds the neighborhood safe and supportive of young families, but is unsure what his neighbors would think about him if they knew he was seeing a social worker. He states that many of his neighbors would not understand.

Issues and strengths to consider: Jim lives in a stable neighborhood that is a safe and positive environment for raising a family. While he does not participate in neighborhood events, he appears comfortable with his home and community. An issue to consider is the friend in the neighborhood who is his cocaine supplier and what impact this may have if Jim should decide to work on his drug use. Moreover, Jim is not sure that his neighbors would be supportive of him and his family if they discovered that he used drugs regularly.

B. Cultural context: Jim is a European American male of Italian descent, although he admits that he has no connection to his Italian heritage. His wife is also Italian, and her family, according to Jim, does practice and abide by some of their Italian traditions, especially Catholicism. Jim attends church only to appease his wife and "to be a good role model" for his children. He believes that the people in his church are "hypocrites" who act "pious" on Sunday, then return home and act differently. He denies any religious or spiritual beliefs, claiming that he is a self-reliant man who does not need God or some other person telling him how to live his life.

Jim claims that he has never been one to "fit in" with groups, that he likes to be alone or with a small group of people. He claims that he fits best with the few friends that he can "relax" and "party" with, because they understand how tense he is and what his use does to make his life easier. Jim claims that his wife was once someone whom he could relax with, but that has changed recently. He claims that "nobody really knows me" and that he just wants to be left alone to live and "provide for his family." Jim's major daily goals are to "work, love his kids, and relax." According to Jim, the only way that he has "ever" found to relax is through substance use.

Issues and strengths to consider: Despite the supportive family, Jim believes he does not fit in, and that few people understand him. Unfortunately, the only people that Jim believes do understand him are his using friends. He is removed from the church and the connection this could bring to his wife, and seems to believe that he is a loner, who does not have a place in his daily world. He claims that he wants to be left alone. These feelings and beliefs could be the result of his intensely hanging on to the belief that he does not have a substance abuse problem, or it could be a longstanding set of beliefs generated by being a child of an alcoholic father.

C. Social class: Jim is the son of a middle-class schoolteacher and has established, along with his wife, a middle-class existence. There appear to be few, if any, hurdles that Jim must confront on a daily basis to live. Jim has been employed as a car salesperson for six years, having worked in the same dealership since he began his career. He stated that he is the "wonder boy," in that he leads the dealership in new car sales each year, bringing home more than $100,000 annually. When asked, Jim admitted to working when high on cocaine, and that sometimes it made him a better salesman because it "relaxes" him. He claims that his boss has asked him not to drink at lunch during work, but there are no employment problems "to speak of." He graduated from high school in 1994, and said that he never had the desire to go to college.

Issues and strengths to consider: It appears that Jim is firmly entrenched in the middle class with a wife and two children. He provides for his family and does not seem to be overly concerned with financial status or other symbols of success. With the exception of his substance use and what appears to be impending marital and family disruption, Jim's family and income are consistent with his lifestyle. Yet, he makes considerable money for someone living in the way that his family does. This could explain how he supports his cocaine use. Jim spends approximately $1000 per month on cocaine. It is unclear whether his family has adjusted to this expenditure and lives accordingly, the family has financial troubles that Jim has not stated, or he has other sources of income that he has not mentioned.

D. Social-relational: According to Jim, he has few friends that he is close to. Jim also stated that he has never been someone to be in groups, instead preferring to have one or two "buddies" that he is comfortable with. He states that he was once a good athlete and enjoyed golf after high school. However, he quit golfing three years ago and has not participated in sports of any kind since that time. He says that his goal, when not working, is to relax and "be calm" and that he is able to do that with the friends that he currently has—all substance users. In fact, Jim states that he cannot remember the last time when his friends were together that they did not party. When asked about this, he became agitated, saying "there's nothing wrong with a few of the guys hanging out and getting high."

Issues and strengths to consider: Jim has few social supports and a lack of recreational outlets beyond using substances. He claims that this is how he prefers it. In the past, he had interests in sports and golf, but has since given these activities up, apparently in favor of using drugs to "relax" and work. Should Jim engage in treatment, finding a social support system that includes alternative ways to relax will be important to the future of treatment.

E. Legal history: As a juvenile, Jim was arrested at least five times for status offenses, including truancy, curfew violations, and two minor-in-possession-of-alcohol charges. As an adult, Jim has been arrested for drunk driving once, in 1998. He was given a suspended sentence, one-year probation, and a restricted driver's license. He claims that the arrest was the most embarrassing moment of his life, and vowed never to be arrested again. When asked, Jim admitted that he continues to drink and drive, but that now he "knows how to get away with it."

Issues and strengths to consider: Jim has no current legal involvement and seems to have been affected at some emotional level by his DWI in 1998, although he remains at-risk for another arrest. The possibility of further arrest may provide a mechanism for discussing his substance use in the future.

Dimension 9: Motivation (stage of motivation and justification):

While Jim refuses to admit that he has a substance abuse problem, he has "thought about it" at times. Therefore, currently Jim is teetering between the precontemplation and contemplation stage of motivation. He does appear to have a significant denial system in place, pertaining to his "need" for drugs to relax, while at the same time claiming that he doesn't "need" drugs to survive. When this discrepancy was pointed out to him, he claimed that the need to relax was different from the need to survive.

Issues and strengths to consider: Jim has considered the possibility of having a drug problem, and he does not become hostile or closed when asked personal and revealing questions. However, he has a history of being compliant in treatment to get by, so it is important to pay close attention to his level of engagement and to take steps to include others as a way of verifying Jim's story and progress in treatment. He will not be amenable to direct confrontation, but seems to respond well to gentle confrontation such as the times that I pointed to discrepancies in his story, and will not respond to labeling or disease model discussions, at least early in treatment.

Dimension 10: Diagnosis

Axis I: 304.20, cocaine dependence without physiological dependence. 303.90, alcohol dependence (rule out physiological dependence). 799.9, diagnosis deferred (292.89, cocaine-induced anxiety disorder).

Axis II: V71.09, no diagnosis.

Axis III: None.

Axis IV: Marital problems, sexual problems, family-of-origin relational problems, and discord with spouse's family.

Axis V: 65 (current).

Justification: On Axis I, client meets criteria 1, 3, 5, 6, and 7 (three required) for cocaine and alcohol dependence. Although there is no evidence that the client is physiologically dependent on cocaine, this is a concern with his alcohol use because of the frequency, amount, and years of use. Any consideration of an anxiety disorder is deferred until it can be decided whether his symptoms are cocaine-induced or an indication of an independent disorder requiring treatment. Jim does not present indications of an Axis II or Axis III condition. Jim is experiencing significant family and marital disruption because of his use, and apparent refusal to admit a problem and seek help. On Axis V, Jim deserves a GAF score of 65, as he is experiencing moderate role disruption and other symptoms presently.

Narrative assessment (Include all relevant issues and strengths to compose a multi-systemic description of the client's life.):

Jim presented as a well-spoken man who appears to have family support and encouragement to attend therapy. He claims to be a nervous person, and appears unwilling to consider his use of cocaine and alcohol as a part of his "nervous" condition. There appears to be disagreement between Jim and his family over the definition of his problems, suggesting that perhaps he presented for therapy under more duress than he was willing to admit during a first session.

There is a history of positive familial experiences with substance abuse and mental health treatment, suggesting that Jim will receive appropriate support for any therapy. Conversely, Jim learned to comply with treatment as a way of "getting by" in an experience that he remembers as "lame-ass." Therefore, it may be difficult to engage Jim in serous treatment because he may be inclined to find ways to comply in order to make a positive impression on the therapist, program staff, and his family. Additionally, Jim made it clear that he was not open to talk of the disease model, which may be indications of denial or a leftover poor attitude caused by inappropriate treatment at a young age.

Jim began using substances at 12 years old, and has been using on a regular basis since that time (14 years). His use is regular and consistent; he stated that he has not been abstinent for more than 24 hours since he was 12. This suggests that Jim has used quite regularly, even at a young age. Moreover, he has used a mixture of drugs since that time. Based on his substance use history, while he has not used a plethora of different drugs, it appears that Jim finds certain drugs and mixtures that he likes and stays with them. He stopped using LSD, a drug he used weekly for five years, only after experiencing a bad trip. This experience has made Jim afraid of LSD, despite his liking of the drug. Another interesting indicator is that he used speed (amphetamines) until age 23, when he began using cocaine, suggesting that stimulant drugs satisfy his needs better than other drugs. He reports that "90%" of his cocaine use is powder cocaine, but occasionally he will smoke crack cocaine for a new experience. When asked, Jim admitted that the amount of cocaine used each week has increased in the last year, and that he often does not feel as good as he once did when using cocaine.

Jim states that he has "no problem" with his substance use, and that he is unashamed of it, even though his wife and parents are against it. While he knows how destructive alcohol can be because of his father's experience, he claims that he is not a "drunk" who "needs it" everyday. When asked about his daily use, Jim claimed that he uses to relax and have fun, but does not "need it" to survive. When asked if he thought he had a drug problem, Jim stated, "No, I don't have a problem." However, he did say that he had thought about it before deciding that he "didn't need it, so I couldn't have a problem."

Jim's use is regular and consistent, and the effects of his drugs of choice, especially cocaine and nicotine, can cause the kind of "nervous" issues that Jim presents. Given his history of use and the amount, frequency, and doses used currently, we must look closely to determine whether Jim has a more significant problem than he is willing to admit. Yet, despite his refusal to admit to drug issues, Jim admittedly has considered the possibility, which could be positive later in treatment if it is determined that he has a treatable substance use problem. He appears to be a thoughtful person, willing at least to "glance" at his personal behavior and habits in a critical manner.

While he reports no medical issues, because of the frequency of drug use and his "nervous" issues, it is appropriate to refer Jim to his physician for a complete physical examination.

Jim has a stable place to live, a supportive spouse, and two young children that he appears to adore. The family income seems sufficient to provide for the basic needs of his growing family, although one has to wonder where he finds the financial resources to afford his rather expensive cocaine use and what impact this has on the provision of his family's basic needs and financial well-being.

Jim presents as a cooperative and polite, yet serious person who becomes defensive when discussing the possibility of having substance abuse problems. His mood is anxious, and he moves between agitated and restless presentation during the session, to being listless and resigned in presentation. He complains of being "nervous" often and that his life is out of control. This could be a sign of an anxiety disorder, such as bipolar disorder; however, it could also be side effects of the drugs he uses on a near daily basis. Jim denies any thoughts of suicide or homicide, now or in the past. Should indications surface that his issues with anxiety predated his drug use, or exist independently of his drug use, Jim will be referred to Dr. Consultant for a psychiatric evaluation.

It appears that Jim has a strong and supportive family that is willing to support any efforts he may make toward change. Because of a family history of substance abuse dating at least three generations, Jim's family knows this issue and, with his father's five-year recovery in AA, understands the recovery process. While there is current friction because of Jim's unwillingness to accept the family's definition of his problems, they are a close group. His in-laws appear to also be supportive, although Jim is not sure of this. He currently blames his mother-in-law for influencing Marie into believing that he has a drug problem. It remains to be seen how the relationship between Jim and his wife's family plays in treatment. There is a need to include Marie and, perhaps, his family in the treatment process. Perhaps, if Jim remains in treatment, there also may come a time when the in-laws will be needed in treatment as well. Because his dad was an alcoholic, it will be important to consider the ramifications of growing up in an alcoholic household on Jim's past and present behavior.

Jim lives in a stable neighborhood that is a safe and positive environment for raising a family. While he does not participate in neighborhood events, he appears comfortable with his home and community. An issue to consider is the friend in the neighborhood who is his cocaine supplier and what impact this may have if Jim should decide to work on his drug use. Moreover, Jim is not sure that his neighbors would be supportive of him and his family if they discovered that he used drugs regularly.

Despite the supportive family, Jim believes he does not fit in, and that few people understand him. Unfortunately, the only people that Jim believes do understand him are his using friends. He is removed from the church and the connection this could bring to his wife, and seems to believe that he is a loner, who does not have a place in his daily world. He claims that he wants to be left alone. These feelings and beliefs could be the result of his intensely hanging on to the belief that he does not have a substance abuse problem, or it could be a longstanding set of beliefs generated by being a child of an alcoholic father.

It appears that Jim is firmly entrenched in the middle class with a wife and two children. He provides for his family and does not seem to be overly concerned with financial status or other symbols of success. With the exception of his substance use and what appears to be impending marital and family disruption, Jim's family and income are consistent with his lifestyle. Yet, he makes considerable money for someone living in the way that his family does. This could explain how he supports his cocaine use. Jim spends approximately $1000 per month on cocaine. It is unclear whether his family has adjusted to this expenditure and lives accordingly, the family has financial troubles that Jim has not stated, or he has other sources of income that he has not mentioned.

Jim has few social supports and a lack of recreational outlets beyond using substances. He claims that this is how he prefers it. In the past, he had interests in sports and golf, but has since given these activities up, apparently in favor of using drugs to "relax" and work. Should Jim engage in treatment, finding a social support system that includes alternative ways to relax will be important to the future of treatment.

As a juvenile, Jim was arrested at least five times for status offenses, including truancy, curfew violations, and two minor-in-possession-of-alcohol charges. As an adult, Jim has been arrested for drunk driving once, in 1998. He was given a suspended sentence, one-year probation, and a restricted driver's license. He claims that the arrest was the most embarrassing moment of his life, and vowed never to be arrested again. When asked, Jim admitted that he continues to drink and drive, but that now he "knows how to get away with it."

Jim has no current legal involvement and seems to have been affected at some emotional level by his DWI in 1998, although he remains at-risk for another arrest. The possibility of further arrest may provide a mechanism for discussing his substance use in the future.

Jim has considered the possibility of having a drug problem, and he does not become hostile or closed when asked personal and revealing questions. However, he has a history of being compliant in treatment to get by, so it is important to pay close attention to his level of engagement and to take steps to include others as a way of verifying Jim's story and progress in treatment. He will not be amenable to direct confrontation, but seems to respond well to gentle confrontation such as the times that I pointed to discrepancies in his story, and will not respond to labeling or disease model discussions, at least early in treatment.

While I have diagnosed Jim, based on the data he presented during this assessment, as cocaine and alcohol dependent, with potential cocaine-induced anxiety disorders, Jim presents as a man currently unwilling to address these issues directly. More preliminary work at developing trust in the professional relationship is necessary before Jim's motivation to address his substance abuse issues will increase.

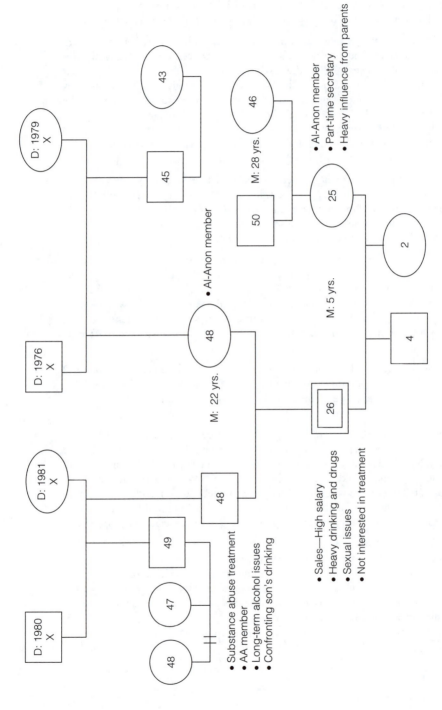

Family Genogram (Case Example for Appendix B)

African American Women: Oppression, Depression, Rage, and Self-Medication

LOIS SMITH OWENS

Author's note: *Professor Lois Smith Owens argues that substance abuse among African American women derives from the lingering legacy of enslavement and racism. Employing a structural, community-based perspective, Smith Owens suggests substance use provides a way for African American women to self-medicate in the face of constant, pervasive, and intergenerational depression.*

Smith Owens takes us to the heart of oppression as it relates to African American women, their lives, fears, and the stereotypes projected on them. Her essay underscores the relationship between clients' culture, class, community, and the larger social systems in which they live. Things may not always be as they first appear.

African American women find themselves at the core of a contradiction: American history demanded that they perform heroically while the dominant culture consistently, systematically demeaned them. For more than 300 years Africans (certainly not yet Americans) lived in slavery; another century locked them in Jim Crow, segregation, and Black codes. One need only consult American employment rates and average wages by race in America to see that discrimination is hardly a thing of the past. I believe African American women internalized the contradictory messages of the culture, its demeaning stereotypes, and its physical violence into self-hatred. Is it surprising, then, that some self-medicate to ease pain and rage?

Analysts readily acknowledge that constant pain, unrequited struggle, rejection, and oppression lead to chronic, severe depression and substance abuse. That description encapsulates the African American experience. One might argue that African American women suffer from Post Traumatic Stress Disorder (PTSD), but "post" would be a misleading term. America's cultural messages, its images of Black women, its enforced poverty and capitalist values continue to inflict stress and must be considered in any substance abuse assessment of African American women. But I want to give you more than an academic list of factors for assessment. I want you to glimpse the pain in the faces of African American women; I want you to hear the rage in their voices. I want you to see it, hear it, feel it, be touched by it.*

Authorities note (and practice verifies) that African American women experience difficulty securing substance abuse treatment. The following list indicates some of the reasons:

1. Inability to pay for treatment
2. Reliance on alcohol and illicit drugs to deal with daily stresses
3. High percentage of adolescent mothers
4. Regular use of drugs by male partner
5. Fear of admission resulting in loss of children
6. Fear of reprisal and/or unjust treatment in the criminal justice system
7. Personal shame as a by-product of their drug problem
8. Inability to stay free of alcohol or drugs
9. Lack of social supports, including male partners and family members
10. Poor or low educational level
11. Inability to obtain employment at a reasonable living wage level
12. Strong need for job training
13. Lack of treatment opportunities suitable for women's needs (mainly child rearing)
14. Lack of adequate child care
15. Lack of access to transportation
16. High levels of depression

While the analysts agree on these problems, they are less ready to understand that all are linked ineradicably to slavery and racism. Consider the following messages that the dominant American culture has sent, and continues to send, to African American women:

"Know your place."

"Understand that you are invisible."

"Understand that whatever power you have can be removed in a heartbeat."

"Know that your Black skin is unattractive."

"Know that your worth and value as a Black woman is less than a White woman's."

---

* I will offer little scientific evidence for my claims. No science can help you face the brutal rage and depression when you (and perhaps your client) stumble upon it for the first time.

"Understand that even to your Black man, you will often be considered less desirable than White women."

"Know that Black men have been put to death because of White women."

"Know that your children are not your own."

"Know and understand that your body is not your own."

"Understand that your Black man cannot protect you."

"Know that your BLACKNESS IS SINFUL AND UGLY, and the primary reason for your life of constant debasement."

Consider, as well, the images the culture perpetuates with its language. African American women are the Welfare Mother, the Illegitimate Mother, the Queen of the Nile, the Hootchie Momma, the Nigger Whore, the Crackhead Bitch, but never Lady. Magazines and movies demonstrate that their behinds are too large, their lips too thick, their hair too kinky.* Combine these words with long-standing characterizations of African Americans as savage, primitive, lazy, and backward, and you will understand some of the pain. According to Meri Danquah, author of *Willow Weep For Me*, "The main stereotype of black women is that they are the ever-nurturing 'mammies' of the nation. The upshot is that 'when a black woman suffers from a mental disorder, the overwhelming opinion is that she is weak. And weakness in a black woman is intolerable'" (http://www.sistahspace.com/WeepingWillows/seekhelp.html).

Central to the question of African American women's rage are the cultural images of their sexuality. They are the sexual exotics, the forbidden fruit—yet they are the despised sluts as well. And this perception derives again from slavery. African women had to be strong, had to stand up to the Massa, be raped by the Massa, but still continue. Oddly, through their sexuality and perceived vulnerability, these women could manipulate the Massa and often the Mistress of the house as well. After all, who protected their men by hiding them from those who would maim or kill them? African women endured the rapes and humiliation to save their families, yet they had been violated—and even their endurance and strength could not gainsay society's image of them as the master's whore.

James Baldwin would delve into much the same theme in his short story "Going to Meet the Man" (1965). An impotent white sheriff regularly arrests African American women to rape them, his desire stimulated by the emasculation and lynching of a black man in his youth. "Come on, sugar," he says to his wife at the end of the story, "I'm going to do you like a nigger, just like a nigger, come on, sugar, and love me just like you'd love a nigger." The sheriff, a symbolic representative of the dominant White culture, clearly views African American women as more sexually desirable than his wife but must humiliate and abuse them in order to maintain control of his own social values and self esteem.

---

* Ironically, some White women enhance their lips and behinds with collagen while searching for "permanent" curls.

Over time, African American women internalized this contradiction; they were programmed to devalue themselves. And often, this belief system was passed down from generation to generation by Mommas and Grandmommas. Additionally, according to Dr. Constance Dunlap, advisor to the National Women's Health Resource Center, depression can also be a hereditary trait caused by a person's chemical makeup: "If there is a history of depression in a person's family, they are at risk of suffering from this illness. People can also become depressed if there are certain 'dysfunctions' in a family that cause an individual to have trouble working through difficult situations" (http://www.geocities.com/~cullars/jan-feb00/depression.htm).

Inextricably linked to the cycle of rape was the fact that their men could *not* defend them. It is important to understand that their men did not belong to them, but to their masters; their men lacked the education, knowledge, and ability to combat a racist system, and therefore, often did not possess the tools or strategies needed to engage in struggle. African American women's enslaved ancestors learned that their men could not protect them or even their own daughters from the master's sexuality. Again, while the enslaved African male was unable to provide for, protect, and shelter even his own family, the enslaved woman often performed these roles, for she was perceived as vulnerable because her femaleness made her less threatening.

Currently, many African Americans are economically disadvantaged and lack the resources to move forward. It is equally apparent that many African Americans live in crime-ridden ghetto-colonies established by the economic inequities maintained by a capitalistic system. The individual is never guaranteed economic security. African American women, denied education and other opportunities, are reduced to "fend[ing] for themselves." When they rebel against the system which refuses them quality of life, taking solace in alcohol or drugs, they are branded criminal. Or worse, they may take more ferocious action, selling drugs themselves to "gain some of the goods unequally distributed. . . ."

The dominant society brands these acts the immorality of the poor. It finds that the poor in America deserve to be poor because they are lazy ("Why don't they get a job?"), self-indulgent ("All they do is get high."), and, no doubt, deficient in mental capacity ("Why would anybody take dope?"). In short the poor are the principal cause of American social and criminal problems. When the society combines such ideology with continuing racism and prevailing stereotypes, it (society) discovers the ultimate scapegoat in the African American.

This ideology produces yet another "bonus" for the majority. One might expect that the structural nature of crime and poverty would elicit some sympathy for the criminal victims. Instead, according to Reiman (2001), "My suspicion is that it produces or at least reinforces the reverse: *hostility toward the poor*" (p. 172). Reiman (2001) further states:

> Undoubtedly, waiting for the opportunity to snatch away the worker's meager gains serves also to deflect opposition away from the upper classes. A politician who promises to keep working-class communities free of Blacks and the prisons full of them can get votes even if the major portion of his or

her policies amount to continuation of the favored treatment of the rich at their expense. (p. 171)

It is more comfortable to blame welfare mothers for society's budget shortfalls than to question its institutions. It is far easier to lock up street criminals than to pursue corporate felons. It is much more reassuring to abhor and punish drug users than to understand them. And it's certainly a lot simpler to throw them in jail than it is to treat them.

Unfortunately, many African American women have been conditioned to accept these same social notions of right and wrong. Programmed by a past which punished any revolt against cultural values with pain and death, the African psyche internalized rage and pain in order to survive. Wilson (1990) states:

> [I]nternalization refers to the process whereby a subject as the result of conditioning, exposure to certain types of information, definitions and interpretations of reality, deliberately restricted experiences and opportunities, observational learning and imitation, fantasies and other incentives as manipulated by certain influential persons or groups, comes to incorporate into his active belief, behavioral, and evaluative systems, the values, attitudes and lifestyles characteristic of such persons and groups. Negative internalization occurs when the values, mores, etc., are introjected by the internalizing subject in such ways as to cause him to behave maladaptively or self-destructively.
>
> Driven by unconscious internalization of White racist attitudes and behavior, or his deluded acceptance of their seeming correctness, the African American relinquishes control over his or her temper, moral judgments and sense of proportions. He becomes the plaything of his impulses, raw emotions, and desires; feeling compelled to behave in ways that leave him or her able to offer transparent rationalizations, or for which he can offer no explanation except to say: "I just did it—I don't know why. I don't mean to do it. It just happens." (pp. 55–57)

Similarly, introjection, according to Wilson (1990), refers to the process by which an individual incorporates and accepts the prohibitions, values, attitudes, and commands of others as her own, even when this works against her interests. Wilson further states,

> The dominant White community, by controlling the rhythm of Black community life, controls to a significant extent the setting and experiences of Black people, their self-perception and perception of reality. The dominant White community, by means of projection, acts in ways that organize the motivational systems of the Black community so that those systems are a functional reflection of the White community's psycho political needs. Introjective projection onto the African community occurs when that community accepts and internalizes the stereotypical characterization of itself as projected by another. (p. 61)

No doubt, the White community will find such concepts difficult to comprehend. Perhaps explaining these concepts to women who actively live out their own script of self-hatred will prove equally troublesome. However, this writer strongly believes that it is possible to teach a group of people that they have—because of history—learned to hate themselves; that their Mommas, Grandmommas, and Great Grandmommas believed (were programmed and conditioned to believe) that they were inherently inferior to the dominant White group. And I believe it is also possible to teach that group that some of their shame and rage could turn to pride if they considered the strength of their female ancestors—that their enslaved Great Grandmommas endured the violence of assault and that their Grandmommas and Mommas have survived America's legal and social obstacles through their persistent attention to family and community.

The devalued state of the African American women's life experiences is best described in fiction. Fiction allows storytelling with room for emotional expression that—unfortunately—is not allowed in most academic writing. The fictional narrator can be honest: relating and reliving the pain and travail of what it means to be an African American woman in America, to bear 500 years of marginalization as a human being, not just as a woman. The fictional author allows us to participate in the emotions of the characters. Therefore, fiction can demonstrate the devalued state of the African woman repeated throughout American history.

For example, Patricia J. Williams (1990) demonstrates how her own mother internalized and introjected White values as she discusses her daughter's "white" blood:

> . . . Mother was asking me not to look to her as a role model. She was devaluing that part of herself that was not Harvard and refocusing my vision to that part of herself that was hard-edged, proficient, and Western. She hid the lonely, black, defiled-female part of herself and pushed me forward as the projection of a competent self, a cool rather than despairing self, a masculine rather than a feminine self. I took this secret of my blood into the Harvard milieu with both the pride and the shame with which my mother had passed it along to me. I found myself in the situation described by Marguerite Duras, in her novel *The Lover:* "We're united in a fundamental fate, the fact that [we] are our mother's children, the children of a candid creature murdered by society. We're on the side of society which has reduced her to despair. Because of what's been done to our mother, so amiable, so trusting, we hate life, we hate ourselves." (p. 20)

The mother represses her own identity, passing the same attitude to her daughter, ultimately resulting in self-hatred.

At another level, Alice Randall's *The Wind Done Gone* tells of the longing that the enslaved Black Child of the Massa feels as she watches her white "sister" gain access to the breast that has been denied her:

> She was old enough to walk. She walked right past me, past Lady, she walked right past Lady and me, over to Mammy, reached up up for Mammy and *my Mama* reached down to pull [other] up onto her hip. Other reached into the top of Mammy's dress and pulled out my mother's breast. "I want some titty-tip," she said, and I ached in some place I didn't know I had, where my heart should have been but wasn't. I've come to believe that was the very first time I ever felt my soul, and it was having a spasm. It clinched again, pushing the

air out of me in a hiccup. I flushed in a rage of possession as those little white hands drew the nipple toward the little pink mouth, then clasped on.

Randall lets us see how early rejection and the devalued state are recognized by even the youngest of the enslaved female children.

Pecola, an older female child in Toni Morrison's *The Bluest Eye*, perceives herself to be black and ugly as she approaches a store counter to buy penny candy:

> The gray head of Mr. Yacobowski looms up over the counter. He urges his eyes out of his thoughts to encounter her. Blue eyes. Blear-dropped. Slowly, like Indian summer moving imperceptibly toward fall, he looks toward her. Somewhere between retina and object, between vision and view, his eyes draw back, hesitate, and hover. At some fixed point in time and space he senses that he need not waste the effort of a glance. He does not see her, because for him there is nothing to see. How can a fifty-two-year-old white immigrant store-keeper with the taste of potatoes and beer in his mouth, his mind honed on the doe-eyed Virgin Mary, his sensibilities blunted by a permanent awareness of loss, *see* a little black girl?

The African American girl learns early that she is invisible and that she must accept and, if necessary, demonstrate that she welcomes her place in the society.

Lalita Tademy writes of an adolescent girl-woman's menarche (particularly important for slaves because the onset of menses determined adulthood). In *Cane River*, thirteen-year-old Suzette speaks with her young Mistress of her rape by the Master:

> "Aunt Francoise told me about the baby," she said, her words clipped.
>
> There was nothing for Suzette to say. She removed Oreline's gray-and-black-plaid dress from the armoire.
>
> "Why did you go with him?"
>
> "I can only do what I am told, Mam'zelle."
>
> "How long has it been going on? Since he came to Cane River?"
>
> The on-the-edge pitch Suzette recognized from childhood was mixed with something new.
>
> "He found me alone at Christmastime," Suzette said tiredly.
>
> "What did you do to make him come to you?"
>
> "He followed me, I did nothing. I was wearing my christening dress."
>
> Suzette didn't know why she had added the last part. As if what she was wearing mattered.
>
> "Did you want to make a baby with him?" Oreline pushed.
>
> "No."
>
> "Did you tell him that?"
>
> "No."
>
> "If you didn't want this to happen, why didn't you say anything?"
>
> "I don't know."

"Why didn't you tell me?"

"I don't know Mam'zelle." (And then) . . .

"What could you have done?" Suzette asked, her tongue heavy and dull.

"What could anyone have done?"

Ironically, Suzette's mother questions her about the pregnancy and affirms the values of the oppressor:

"The world didn't start with you, Suzette. I've been through it. In
Virginia, with the Master's son, before coming here. . . . This is what our
life is, baby girl."

Such literary texts represent devalued life in its rawest form—a litany of voices telling the same story for centuries: you don't count, you don't matter, and you don't exist. Voices of your Momma, your Grandmomma, your master, your mistress, your sister, the world—YOU ARE NOTHING—but you better be something!

Women of other races and ethnicities have struggled to find their place in this man's world. Worldwide, women are the victims of domestic violence and religious persecution. Systematically, methodically, they have been excluded from a quality of life accorded only to men.

However, the African American woman's experience has differed significantly. From the very beginning, America designated her different: *She was Black.* She was dark and dank, mysterious and primitive; covertly desired while perceived as ugly; needed while fertile but rejected when worn. Like black Kleenex, she was snotted into and disposed into a place where she became nothing and no longer existed. Now, African American women are work-worn and "tired of being tired of being tired." They no longer need to be told that "you are what you are because of who you are." They need to understand that their history has determined who and what they are. They need to cry out, wail their pain and rage with Sojourner Truth: "Ain't I a woman?"

Is it any wonder then that rage, internalized self-hatred, pain and confusion confound African American women? Do they self-medicate? Or are they "Colored girls who have considered suicide"? African American women have mastered the art of surviving in spite of the entirety of their history. They are no longer the village herb women, mixing magic potions and herbs; they lost those recipes while being sold from plantation to plantation. They just get high. . . .

Nonetheless, the last stanza of Mari Evans' poem, "I Am a Black Woman," reminds us of how those women strive to live lives of strength and resilience. Thus, in spite of the dichotomy, in spite of the contradictions of the American culture, African American women continue to chant their mantra of survival:

I am a black woman,
Tall as a cypress,
Strong, beyond all definition
Still defying time and circumstance
Assailed, impervious, indestructible,
Look on me,
And be renewed.

References

Abbott, A. A. (1994). Substance abuse and the feminist perspective. In N. Van Den Bergh (Ed.), *Feminist practice in the 21st century*. Washington, DC: National Association of Social Workers, pp. 258–277.

Abbott, P. J., Quinn, D., & Knox, L. (1995). Ambulatory medical detoxification for alcohol. *American Journal of Drug and Alcohol Abuse, 21,* 549–564.

Abrams, R. C., & Alexopoulos, G. (1987). Substance abuse in the elderly: Alcohol and prescription drugs: Over-the-counter and illegal drugs. *Hospital and Community Psychiatry, 39,* 822–823.

Acevedo, G., & Morales, J. (2001). Assessment with Latino/Hispanic communities and organizations. In R. Fong & S. Furuto (Eds.), *Culturally competent practice: Skills, interventions, and evaluations* (pp. 147–162). Boston: Allyn & Bacon.

Ackerman, R. J. (1989). *Perfect daughters: Adult daughters of alcoholics.* Deerfield Beach, FL: Health Communications.

Aguilera, D. C., & Messick, J. M. (1982). *Crisis intervention: Theory and methodology* (4th ed.). St. Louis: Mosby.

Akers, R. L. (1977). *Deviant behavior: A social learning approach* (2nd ed.). Belmont, CA: Wadsworth.

Akers, R. L. (1992). *Drugs, alcohol, and society: Social structure, process, and policy.* Belmont, CA: Wadsworth.

Alcoholics Anonymous. (1981). *Twelve steps and twelve traditions.* New York: AA World Services, Inc.

Allen, J. P., & Columbus, M. (Eds.). (1995). *Assessing alcohol problems: A guide for clinicians and researchers.* Bethesda, MD: National Institute on Alcohol Abuse and Alcoholism.

Alvarez, L. R., & Ruiz, P. (2001). Substance abuse in the Mexican American population. In S. L. A. Straussner (Ed.), *Ethnocultural factors in substance abuse treatment* (pp. 111–137). New York: Guilford Press.

American Heart Association. (1999). Cigarette and tobacco smoke: Biostatistical fact sheets [online]. Available: http://www.americanheart.org/statistics

American Psychiatric Association. (1994). *Diagnostic and statistical manual of mental disorders* (4th ed.). Washington, DC: Author.

American Psychiatric Association. (1995). Practice guidelines for the treatment of patients with substance use disorders: Alcohol, cocaine, opioids. *American Journal of Psychiatry, 152* (11, suppl.).

American Psychiatric Association. (2000). *Diagnostic and statistical manual of mental disorders* (4th ed.-TR). Washington, DC: Author.

American Society of Addiction Medicine. (1996). Patient Placement Criteria (2nd ed.) [online]. Available: http://www.asam.org/ppc/ppc2.htm

Amodeo, M., Schofield, R., Duffy, T., Jones, K., Zimmerman, T., & Delgado, M. (1997). *Social work approaches to alcohol and other drug problems: Case studies and teaching tools.* Alexandria, VA: Council on Social Work Education.

Amoureus, M. P. S. R., van den Hurd, A. A., Schippers, G. M., & Breteler, M. H. M. (1994). The Addiction Severity Index in penitentiaries. *International Journal of Offender Therapy & Comparative Criminology, 38,* 309–318.

Anderson, E. (1990). *Streetwise: Race, class, and change in an urban community.* Chicago: University of Chicago Press.

Anderson, G. L. (1987). *When chemicals come to school.* Greenfield, WI: Community Recovery Press.

Anderson, J. Z. (1992). Stepfamilies and substance abuse: Unique treatment considerations. In E. Kaufman & P. Kaufman (Eds.), *Family therapy of drug and alcohol abuse* (2nd ed., pp. 172–189). Boston: Allyn & Bacon.

Anderson, R. E., & Carter, I. (1984). *Human behavior in the social environment: A social systems approach* (3rd ed.). New York: Aldine.

Anglin, M. D., Brecht, M. L., & Maddahian, E. (1989). Pretreatment characteristics and treatment performance of legally coerced versus voluntary methadone maintenance admissions. *Criminology, 27,* 537–557.

Annis, H. M., & Chan, D. (1983). The differential treatment model: Empirical evidence from a personality typology of adult offenders. *Criminal Justice and Behavior, 10,* 159–173.

Anthony, J. C., Arria, A. M., & Johnson, E. O. (1995). Epidemiological and public health issues for tobacco, alcohol, and other drugs. In J. M. Oldham & M. B. Riba (Eds.), *Review of Psychiatry* (Vol. 14). Washington, DC: American Psychiatric Press.

Anthony, J. C., Warner, L. A., & Kessler, R. C. (1997). Comparative epidemiology of dependence on tobacco, alcohol, controlled substances, and inhalants: Basic findings from the national comorbidity survey. In G. A. Marlatt & G. R. Vandenbos (Eds.), *Addictive behaviors: Readings on etiology, prevention, and treatment* (pp. 3–39). Washington, DC: American Psychological Association.

Aponte, H. J. (1994). *Bread and spirit: Therapy with the new poor.* New York: Norton.

Aponte, H. J., & VanDeusen, J. M. (1981). Structural family therapy. In A. S. Gurman & D. P. Kniskern (Eds.), *Handbook of family therapy* (Vol. I, pp. 310–360). New York: Brunner/Mazel.

Appleby, G. A. (2001). Dynamics of oppression and discrimination. In G. A. Appleby, E. Colon, & J. Hamilton (Eds.), *Diversity, oppression, and social functioning: Person-in-environment assessment and intervention* (pp. 36–52). Boston: Allyn & Bacon.

Appleby, G. A., Colon, E., & Hamilton, J. (Eds.). (2001). *Diversity, oppression, and social functioning: Person-in-environment assessment and intervention.* Boston: Allyn & Bacon.

Armor, D. J., Polich, J. M., & Stambul, H. B. (1978). *Alcoholism and treatment.* New York: Wiley.

Arnstein, R. L. (1984). Young adulthood: Stages of maturity. In D. Offer & M. Sabshin (Eds.), *Normality and the life cycle: A critical integration* (pp. 108–144). New York: Basic Books.

Ausabel, D. P. (1983). Methadone maintenance treatment: The other side of the coin. *International Journal of the Addictions, 18,* 851–862.

Avis, J. M. (1985). The politics of functional family therapy: A feminist critique. *Journal of Marital and Family Therapy, 11,* 127–138.

Avis, J. M. (1996). Deconstructing gender in family therapy. In F. P. Piercy, D. H. Sprenkle, J. Wetchler, & Associates (Eds.), *Family therapy sourcebook* (2nd ed.). New York: Guilford Press.

Babor, T. F., de la Fuente, J. R., Saunders, J., & Grant, M. (1992). *The Alcohol Use Disorders Identification Test (AUDIT): Guidelines for use in primary health care.* Geneva: World Health Organization.

Babor, T. F., Kranzler, H. R., & Lauerman, R. J. (1989). Early detection of harmful alcohol consumption: Comparison of clinical, laboratory, and self-report screening procedures. *Addictive Behaviors, 14,* 139–157.

Baker, F. (1991). *Coordination of alcohol, drug abuse, and mental health services* (TIP #4). Washington, DC: Office of Treatment Improvement, Alcohol, Drug Abuse, and Mental Health Administration.

Baldwin, J. (1965). *Going to meet the man.* New York: Dial Press.

Bandura, A. (1969). *Principles of behavior modification.* New York: Holt, Rinehart & Winston.

Bandura, A. (1977). *Social learning theory.* Englewood Cliffs, NJ: Prentice-Hall.

Bandura, A. (1986). *Social foundations of thought and action: A social cognitive theory.* Englewood Cliffs, NJ: Prentice-Hall.

Barker, R. L. (1999). *The social work dictionary* (4th ed.). Washington, DC: NASW Press.

Barry, C. T. (1998). *Treatment for methamphetamine abuse disorders.* Presented at the Methamphetamine Interagency Task Force Federal Advisory Committee Meeting, Washington, DC.

Barth, R. P. (2001). Research outcomes of prenatal substance exposure and the need to review policies and procedures regarding child abuse reporting. *Child Welfare: Journal of Policy, Practice, and Program, LXXX* (2), 275–296.

Bauman, Z. (1995). *Life in fragments: Essays in postmodern morality.* Oxford: Blackwell.

Beattie, M. (1987). *Codependent no more: How to stop controlling others and start caring for yourself.* New York: Harper/Hazelden.

Beck, A. T., Ward, C., Mendelson, M., Mock, J., & Erbaugh, J. (1961). An inventory for measuring depression. *Archives of General Psychiatry, 4,* 561–571.

Beck, A. T., & Weishaar, M. (2000). Cognitive therapy. In R. J. Corsini & D. Wedding (Eds.), *Current psychotherapies* (6th ed., pp. 241–272). Itasca, IL: F. E. Peacock.

Beck, A. T., Wright, F. D., Newman, C. F., & Liese, B. S. (1993). *Cognitive therapy of substance abuse.* New York: Guilford.

Becker, H. S. (1963). *Outsiders: Studies in the sociology of deviance.* New York: Free Press.

Becker, H. S. (1967). History, culture, and subjective experience: An exploration of the social basis of drug-induced experiences. *Journal of Health and Social Behavior, 8,* 163–176.

Becker, H. S., & McCall, M. M. (1990). *Symbolic interactionism and cultural studies.* Chicago: University of Chicago Press.

Bell, P., & Evans, J. (1981). *Counseling the black client: Alcohol use and abuse in black America.* Minneapolis, MN: Hazelden.

Bennett, L. W. (1995). Substance abuse and the domestic assault of women. *Social Work, 40,* 760–771.

Bepko, C., & Krestan, J. A. (1985). *The responsibility trap: A blueprint for treating the alcoholic family.* New York: Free Press.

Berenson, D. (1987). Alcoholics Anonymous: From surrender to transformation. *The Family Therapy Networker, 11* (4), 25–31.

Berg, B. (1995). *Qualitative research methods for the social sciences* (2nd ed.). Boston: Allyn & Bacon.

Berg, B. J., & Durbin, W. R. (1990). Economic grand rounds: Why 28 days? An alternative approach to alcoholism treatment. *Hospital & Community Psychiatry, 41,* 1175–1178.

Berg, I. K. (1995). Solution-focused brief therapy with substance abusers. In A. M. Washton (Ed.), *Psychotherapy and substance abuse: A practitioner's handbook* (pp. 223–242). New York: Guilford Press.

Berg, I. K., & de Shazer, S. (1993). Making numbers talk: Language in therapy. In S. Friedman (Ed.), *The new language of change.* New York: Guilford Press.

Berg, I. K., & Miller, S. (1994). *Working with the problem drinker: A solution-focused approach.* New York: Norton.

Berg, I. K., & Reuss, N. (1998). Solution-focused brief therapy: Treating substance abuse. *Current Thinking and Research in Brief Therapy, 2,* 57–83.

Bergman, J. (1985). *Fishing for barracuda.* New York: Norton.

Best, S., & Kellner, D. (1991). *Postmodern theory: Critical interrogations.* New York: Guilford Press.

Bierut, L. J., Dinwiddie, S. E., Begleiter, H., Crowe, R. R., Hesselbrock, V.,

Nurnberger, J. I., Jr., Porjesz, B., Schuckit, M. A., & Reich, T. (1998). Familial transmission of substance dependence: Alcohol, marijuana, cocaine, and habitual smoking. *Archives of General Psychiatry, 55,* 982–988.

Black, C. (1981). *It will never happen to me.* New York: Ballantine.

Bloch, D. S. (1999). Adolescent suicide as a public health threat. *Journal of Child and Adolescent Psychiatric Nursing, 12,* 26–33.

Blume, S. B. (1986). Women and alcohol. *Journal of the American Medical Association, 256,* 1467–1469.

Blume, S. B. (1992). Alcohol and other drug problems in women. In J. H. Lowinson, P. Ruiz, & R. B. Millman (Eds.), & J. G. Langrod (Assoc. Ed.), *Substance abuse: A comprehensive textbook* (2nd ed., pp. 861–867). Baltimore: Williams & Wilkins.

Blume, S. B. (1994). Gender differences in alcohol-related disorders. *Harvard Review of Psychiatry, 2,* 7–14.

Blumer, H. (1969). *Symbolic interactionism: Perspective and method.* Englewood Cliffs, NJ: Prentice-Hall.

Botvin, G. J., & Botvin, E. M. (1992). School-based and community-based prevention approaches. In J. H. Lowinson, P. Ruiz, & R. B. Millman (Eds.), & J. G. Langrod (Assoc. Ed.), *Substance abuse: A comprehensive textbook* (2nd ed., pp. 910–927). Baltimore: Williams & Wilkins.

Boudon, R., & Bourricaud, F. (1989). *A critical dictionary of sociology.* Chicago: University of Chicago Press.

Bowen, M. (1985). *Family therapy in clinical practice.* New York: Jason Aronson.

Bower, B. (1997). Alcoholics synonymous: Heavy drinkers of all stripes may get comparable help from a variety of therapies. *Science News, 151,* 62–63.

Boyd-Franklin, N. (1989). *Black families in therapy.* New York: Guilford Press.

Boyd-Franklin, N. (1993). Race, class, and poverty. In F. Walsh (Ed.), *Normal family processes* (2nd ed., pp. 361–376). New York: Guilford Press.

Brady, K., & Lydiard, R. (1992). Bipolar affective disorder and substance abuse. *Journal of Clinical Psychopharmacology, 12,* 178–228.

Braithwaite, J. (1989). *Crime, shame, and reintegration.* Cambridge, UK: Cambridge University Press.

Brehm, S. S., & Brehm, J. W. (1981). *Psychological reactance: A theory of freedom and control.* New York: Academic Press.

Brill, N. I. (1998). *Working with people: The helping process* (6th ed.). New York: Longman.

Brisbane, F. (1992). *Working with African Americans: The professional's handbook.* Chicago: HRDI International.

Brown, L. S., & Alterman, A. (1992). African Americans. In J. H. Lowinson, P. Ruiz, & R. B. Millman (Eds.), & J. G. Langrod (Assoc. Ed.), *Substance abuse: A comprehensive textbook* (2nd ed.). Baltimore: Williams & Wilkins.

Brown, L. S., Alterman, A. I., Rutherford, M. J., & Cacciola, J. S. (1993). Addiction Severity Index scores for four racial/ethnic and gender groups of methadone maintenance patients. *Journal of Substance Abuse, 5,* 269–279.

Brown, R. L., Leonard, T., Saunders, L. A., & Papasoulioutis, O. (1997). A two-item screening test for alcohol and other drug problems. *Journal of Family Practice, 44,* 151–160.

Brown, S. (1985). *Treating the alcoholic: A developmental model of recovery.* New York: Wiley.

Browne, C., & Mills, C. (2001). Theoretical frameworks: Ecological model, strengths perspective, and empowerment theory. In R. Fong & S. Furuto (Eds.), *Culturally competent practice: Skills, interventions, and evaluations.* Boston: Allyn & Bacon.

Brueggemann, W. G. (2001). *The practice of macro social work.* Belmont, CA: Wadsworth.

Brunswick, A., Messeri, P., & Titus, S. (1992). Predictive factors in adult substance abuse: A prospective study of African American adolescents. In M. Glantz & R. Pickens (Eds.),

Vulnerability to drug abuse (pp. 419–472). Washington, DC: American Psychological Association.

Brunton, S. A., Henningfield, J. E., & Solberg, L. I. (1994). Smoking cessation: What works best? *Patient Care, 25,* 89–115.

Buck, J. A. (1999). Effects of the Mental Health Parity Act of 1996. Center for Mental Health Services [online]. Available: http://www.mentalhealth.org/cmhs/ManagedCare/Parity/ParityActsEffcts.asp

Buck, J. A., Teich, J. L., Umland, B., & Stein, M. (1999). Behavioral health benefits in employer-sponsored health plans, 1997. *Health Affairs, 18* (2), 67–78.

Buck, J. A., & Umland, B. (1997). Covering mental health and substance abuse services. *Health Affairs, 16* (4), 120–126.

Bufe, C. (1991). *Alcoholics Anonymous: Cult or cure?* San Francisco: See Sharp Press.

Caetano, R. (1986). Patterns and problems of drinking among U.S. Hispanics. In *Report of the secretary's task force on black and minority health* (Vol. 7: Chemical dependency and diabetes). Washington, DC: U.S. Department of Health and Human Services.

Campbell, J. W. (1992). Alcoholism. In R. J. Ham & P. D. Sloane (Eds.), *Primary care geriatrics* (2nd ed.). Boston: Mosby.

Canino, G., Burman, A., & Caetano, R. (1992). The prevalence of alcohol abuse and/or dependence in two Hispanic communities. In J. Helzer & G. Canino (Eds.), *Alcoholism in North America, Europe, and Asia* (pp. 131–153). New York: Oxford University Press.

Carpenter, J. (1994). Finding people in family therapy. *Dulwich Centre Newsletter, 1,* 32–38.

Carroll, K. M. (1996). Relapse prevention as a psychosocial treatment: A review of controlled clinical trials. *Clinical and Experimental Psychopharmacology, 4,* 46–65.

Carter, B., & McGoldrick, M. (1988). Overview: The changing family life cycle—A framework for family therapy.

In B. Carter & M. McGoldrick (Eds.), *The changing family life cycle: A framework for family therapy* (2nd ed., pp. 3–28). New York: Gardner Press.

Cartwright, A. K. J. (1981). Are different therapeutic perspectives important in the treatment of alcoholism? *British Journal of Addiction, 76,* 347–361.

Castro, F. G., Barrington, E. H., Sharp, E. V., Dial, L. S., Wang, B., & Rawson, R. (1992). Behavioral and psychological profiles of cocaine users upon treatment entry: Ethnic comparisons. *Drugs and Society, 6,* 231–251.

Cattarello, A. M., Clayton, R. R., & Leukefeld, C. G. (1995). Adolescent alcohol and drug abuse. In J. M. Oldham & M. B. Riba (Eds.), *Review of Psychiatry* (Vol. 14). Washington, DC: American Psychiatric Press.

Center for Substance Abuse Research, University of Maryland. (1997). Methamphetamine use in the western United States: An in-depth look. *CESAR Fax, 6* (29).

Center for Substance Abuse Treatment. (1994). *Intensive outpatient treatment for alcohol and other drug abuse* (TIP #8). Rockville, MD: U.S. Department of Health and Human Services.

Center for Substance Abuse Treatment. (1995a). *Assessment and treatment of patients with coexisting mental illness and alcohol and other drug abuse* (TIP #9). Rockville, MD: U.S. Department of Health and Human Services.

Center for Substance Abuse Treatment. (1995b). *Guidelines for the treatment of alcohol and other drug abusing adolescents* (TIP #4). Rockville, MD: U.S. Department of Health and Human Services.

Center for Substance Abuse Treatment. (1997). *Proceedings of the National Consensus Meeting on the use, abuse, and sequelae of abuse of methamphetamine with implications for prevention, treatment, and research.* DHHS Pub. No. (SMA) 96–8013. Rockville, MD: CSAT, Substance Abuse and Mental Health Services Administration, U.S. Department of Health and Human Services.

Center for Substance Abuse Treatment. (1998). *Substance abuse among older adults* (TIP #26). Rockville, MD: U.S. Department of Health and Human Services.

Center for Substance Abuse Treatment. (1999a). *Treatment for stimulant use disorders* (TIP #33). Rockville, MD: U.S. Department of Health and Human Services.

Center for Substance Abuse Treatment. (1999b). *Brief interventions and brief therapies for substance abuse* (TIP #34). Rockville, MD: U.S. Department of Health and Human Services.

Centers for Disease Control and Prevention. (1998). Targeting tobacco use: The nation's leading cause of death [online]. Available: http://www.cdc.gov/tobacco

Cermak, T. L. (1986). *Diagnosing and treating co-dependence: A guide for professionals who work with chemical dependents, their spouses, and children.* Center City, MN: Hazelden.

Charon, J. M. (1998). *Symbolic interactionism: An introduction, an interpretation, and integration* (6th ed.). Upper Saddle River, NJ: Prentice-Hall.

Chassin, L., Curran, P. J., Hussong, A. M., & Colder, C. R. (1996). The relation of parent alcoholism to adolescent substance use: A longitudinal follow-up study. *Journal of Abnormal Psychology, 105,* 70–80.

Chastain, S. (1992, Feb./March). The accidental addict. *Modern Maturity.*

Chaudron, C. D., & Wilkinson, D. A. (1988). *Theories on alcoholism.* Toronto: Addiction Research Foundation.

Clark, C. M. (1995). Alcoholics Anonymous. *The Addiction Newsletter, 2,* 9–22.

Clayton, R. R., Cattarello, A. M., & Johnstone, B. M. (1996). Effectiveness of Drug Abuse Resistance Education (DARE): 5-year follow-up results. *Preventive Medicine, 25,* 307–318.

Cloninger, C. R., Gohman, M., & Sigvardsson, S. (1981). Inheritance of alcohol abuse: Cross fostering analysis of adopted men. *Archives of General Psychiatry, 38,* 861–868.

Cloninger, C. R., Sigvardsson, S., & Gohman, M. (1996). Type I and Type II alcoholism: An update. *Alcohol Health & Research World, 20* (1), 18–23.

Cloward, R., & Ohlin, L. (1961). *Delinquency and opportunity.* Glencoe, IL: Free Press.

Cohen, A. P. (1985). *The symbolic construction of community.* New York: Tavistock Publications and Ellis Horwood Limited.

Combrinck-Graham, L. (1983). The family life cycle and families with young children. In H. Liddle (Ed.), *Clinical implications of the family life cycle.* Rockville, MD: Aspen Systems.

Combrinck-Graham, L. (1985). A model for family development. *Family Process, 24,* 139–150.

Combrinck-Graham, L. (1988). Adolescent sexuality in the family life cycle. In C. Falikov (Ed.), *Family transitions.* New York: Guilford Press.

Community Epidemiology Work Group. (1998). *Epidemiologic trends in drug abuse, December 1997.* NIH Pub. No. 98-4297. Rockville, MD: National Institute on Drug Abuse.

Compton, B. R., & Galway, B. (1994). *Social work processes* (5th ed.). Pacific Grove, CA: Brooks/Cole.

Comstock, G. D. (1991). *Violence against lesbians and gay men.* New York: Columbia University Press.

Connors, G. J., Donovan, D. M., & DiClemente, C. C. (2001). *Selecting and planning interventions: Substance abuse treatment and the stages of change.* New York: Guilford Press.

Cook, C. H. (1988). The Minnesota Model in the management of drug and alcohol dependency: Miracle or myth? Part I: The philosophy and the programme. *British Journal of Addiction, 83,* 620–631.

Cook, P. J. (1981). The effects of liquor taxes on drinking, cirrhosis and auto accidents. In M. H. Moore & D. R. Gerstein (Eds.), *Alcohol and alcohol policy: Beyond the shadow of Prohibition* (pp. 255–285). Washington, DC: National Academy Press.

Cook, R. T. (1998). Alcohol abuse, alcoholism, and damage to the immune system—A review. *Alcoholism, Clinical and Experimental Research, 22,* 1927–1942.

Cooney, N. L., Kadden, R. M., Litt, M. D., & Getter, H. (1991). Matching alcoholics to coping skills or interactional therapies: Two-year follow-up results. *Journal of Consulting and Clinical Psychology, 59,* 598–601.

Cooney, N. L., Zweben, A., & Fleming, M. F. (1995). Screening for alcohol-related problems and at-risk drinking in health-care settings. In R. K. Hester & W. R. Miller (Eds.), *Handbook of alcoholism treatment approaches: Effective approaches* (2nd ed., pp. 45–60). Boston: Allyn & Bacon.

Cooper, M. L., Russell, M., & George, W. H. (1988). Coping, expectancies, and alcohol use: A test of social learning formulations. *Journal of Abnormal Psychology, 97,* 218–230.

Corcoran, J. J., & Fischer, J. (1987). *Measures for clinical practice: A sourcebook.* New York: Free Press.

Corse, S. J., Zanis, D., & Hirschinger, N. B. (1995). The use of the Addiction Severity Index with people with severe mental illness. *Psychiatric Rehabilitation Journal, 19,* 9–18.

Cowger, C. D. (1992). Assessment of client strengths. In D. Saleebey (Ed.), *The strengths perspective in social work practice* (pp. 139–147). New York: Longman.

Cowger, C. D. (1994). Assessing client strengths: Clinical assessment for client empowerment. *Social Work, 39* (3), 262–267.

Cowley, G., & Underwood, A. (1997, Dec. 29). A little help from serotonin. *Newsweek,* 78–81.

Creager, C. (1989, July/Aug.). SASSI test breaks through denial. *Professional Counselor, 65.*

Cross, T. L., Bazron, B. J., Dennis, K. W., & Isaacs, M. R. (1989). *Toward a culturally competent system of care: A monograph on effective services for minority children who are severely emotionally disturbed* (Vol. 1). Washington, DC: CASSP Technical Assistance, Georgetown University Child Development Center.

Cruse, J. R. (1989). *Painful affairs: Looking for love through addiction and codependency.* Deerfield Beach, FL: Health Communications.

Curtis, O. (1999). *Chemical dependency: A family affair.* Pacific Grove, CA: Brooks/Cole.

DARE America. (1991). *D.A.R.E. will teach over 5 million children drug resistance skills in 1991.* Los Angeles: Author.

Davidson, K. M. (1993). The relationship between alcohol dependence and depression. *Alcohol and Alcoholism, 28,* 147–155.

Davidson, R., Rollnick, S., & MacEwan, I. (Eds.). (1991). *Counseling problem drinkers.* London: Tavistock/Routledge.

Davies, D. L. (1962). Normal drinking in recovered alcohol addicts. *Journal of Studies on Alcohol, 23,* 94–104.

Davis, L. E., & Proctor, E. K. (1989). *Race, gender, and class: Guidelines for practice with individuals, families, and groups.* Englewood Cliffs, NJ: Prentice-Hall.

Davis, L. V. (1996). Role theory and social work treatment. In F. J. Turner (Ed.), *Social work treatment: Interlocking theoretical approaches* (4th ed., pp. 581–600). New York: Free Press.

Dawes, R. M. (1994). *House of cards: Psychology and psychotherapy built on myth.* New York: Free Press.

De Maria, W. (1992). On the trail of a radical pedagogy for social work education. *British Journal of Social Work, 22* (3), 231–252.

de Shazer, S. (1985). *Keys to solutions in brief therapy.* New York: Norton.

de Shazer, S. (1988). *Clues: Investigating solutions in brief therapy.* New York: Norton.

Decker, K. P., & Ries, R. K. (1993). Differential diagnosis and psychopharmacology of dual disorders. *Psychiatric Clinics of North America, 16,* 703–718.

Del Boca, F. K., & Hesselbrock, M. N. (1996). Gender and alcoholic subtypes. *Alcohol Health and Research World, 20* (1), 56–62.

DeLeon, G. (1988). Legal pressure in therapeutic communities. In C. G Leukfeld & F. M. Tims (Eds.), *Compulsory treatment of drug abuse: Research and clinical practice* (NIDA Research Monograph No. 86, pp. 160–177). Rockville, MD: National Institute on Drug Abuse.

DeLeon, G. (1989). Psychopathology and substance abuse: What is being learned from research in therapeutic communities. *Journal of Psychoactive Drugs, 21* (2), 177–188.

DeLeon, G. (1994). Therapeutic communities. In M. Galanter & H. D. Kleber (Eds.), *Textbook of substance abuse treatment.* Washington, DC: American Psychiatric Press.

Denning, P. (2000). *Practicing harm reduction psychotherapy: An alternative approach to addictions.* New York: Guilford Press.

Denzin, N. K. (1987). *The alcoholic self.* Beverly Hills, CA: Sage.

Denzin, N. K. (1992). *Symbolic interactionism and cultural studies: The politics of interpretation.* Oxford: Blackwell.

Denzin, N. K. (1996). *Interpretive ethnography.* Walnut Creek, CA: Alta Mira Press.

DiClemente, C. C. (1991). Motivational interviewing and the stages of change. In W. R. Miller & S. Rollnick (Eds.), *Motivational interviewing: Preparing people to change addictive behavior* (pp. 191–202). New York: Guilford Press.

DiClemente, C. C., & Hughes, S. O. (1990). Stages of change profiles in outpatient alcoholism treatment. *Journal of Substance Abuse, 2,* 217–235.

DiClemente, C. C., & Prochaska, J. O. (1985). Processes and stages of change: Coping and competence in smoking behavior change. In S. Shiffman & T. A. Wills (Eds.), *Coping and substance abuse.* New York: Academic Press.

Dimeff, L. A., & Marlatt, G. A. (1995). Relapse prevention. In R. H. Hester & W. R. Miller (Eds.), *Handbook of alcoholism treatment approaches* (2nd ed., pp. 176–194). Needham Heights, MA: Allyn & Bacon.

Dixon, S., & Sands, R. (1983). Identity and the experience of crisis. *Social Casework, 64,* 223–230.

Doweiko, H. E. (1993). *Concepts of chemical dependency.* Pacific Grove, CA: Brooks/Cole.

Doweiko, H. E. (1999). *Concepts of chemical dependency* (4th ed.). Pacific Grove, CA: Brooks/Cole.

Drake, R. E., McHugo, G. J., & Biesanz, J. C. (1995). The test-retest reliability of standardized instruments among homeless persons with substance use disorders. *Journal of Studies on Alcohol, 56,* 161–167.

Dreger, R. M. (1986). Does anyone really believe that alcoholism is a disease? *American Psychologist, 37,* 322.

Drug Enforcement Administration. (1997). *Drugs of abuse.* Arlington, VA: U.S. Department of Justice.

Dulfano, C. (1982). *Families, alcoholism, and recovery.* Center City, MN: Hazelden.

Duvall, E. (1957). *Family development.* Philadelphia: Lippincott.

Edwards, E. D., & Edwards, M. E. (1988). Alcoholism prevention/treatment and Native American youth: A community approach. *Journal of Studies on Alcohol, 54,* 172–177.

Elkin, M. (1984). *Families under the influence: Changing alcoholic patterns.* New York: Norton.

Ellis, A. (2000). Rational emotive behavior therapy. In R. J. Corsini & D. Wedding (Eds.), *Current psychotherapies* (6th ed., pp. 168–204). Itasca, IL: F. E. Peacock.

Ellis, A., McInerney, J., DiGiuseppe, R., & Yeager, R. (1988). *Rational-emotive therapy with alcoholics and substance abusers.* New York: Pergamon.

Ellis, C., & Bochner, A. P. (1996). *Composing ethnography: Alternative forms of qualitative writing.* Walnut Creek, CA: Alta Mira.

Emrick, C. D., & Hansen, J. (1983). Assertions regarding effectiveness of treatment for alcoholism: Fact or fantasy? *American Psychologist, 38,* 1078–1088.

Engels, F. (1972). *The origin of the family, private property, and the state* (E. Burke, ed.). New York: International.

Engle, K. B., & Williams, T. K. (1972). Effect of an ounce of vodka on alcoholics' desire for alcohol. *Quarterly*

Journal of Studies on Alcohol, 33, 1099–1105.

Ennett, S. T., Rosenbaum, D. P., Flewelling, R. L., Bieler, G. S., & Bailey, S. L. (1994). Long-term evaluation of drug abuse resistance education. *Addictive Behaviors, 19,* 113–125.

Erlich, J. L., & Rivera, F. G. (1998). Introduction. In F. G. Rivera & J. L. Erlich (Eds.), *Community organizing in a diverse society* (3rd ed.). Boston: Allyn & Bacon.

Eshleman, J. R. (1994). *The family* (7th ed.). Boston: Allyn & Bacon.

Ettore, E. (1992). *Women and substance use.* New Brunswick, NJ: Rutgers University Press.

Etzioni, A. (Ed.). (1995). *New Communitarian thinking: Persons, virtues, institutions, and communities.* Charlottesville, VA: University Press of Virginia.

Evans, G., & Farberow, N. L. (1988). *The encyclopedia of suicide.* New York: Facts on File.

Evans, K., & Sullivan, J. M. (2001). *Dual diagnosis: Counseling the mentally ill substance abuser* (2nd ed.). New York: Guilford Press.

Ewing, J. A. (1984). Detecting alcoholism: The CAGE questionnaire. *Journal of the American Medical Association, 252,* 1905–1907.

Ewing, J. A., & Rouse, B. A. (1974). Alcohol sensitivity and ethnic background. *American Journal of Psychiatry, 131,* 206–210.

Faderman, L. (1991). *Odd girls and twilight lovers.* New York: Columbia University Press.

Falk, J. L. (1981). The environmental generation of excessive behavior. In S. J. Mule (Ed.), *Behavior in excess.* New York: Free Press.

Falk, J. L. (1983). Drug dependence: Myth or motive? *Pharmacology, Biochemistry, and Behavior, 19,* 385–391.

Falk, J. L., Dews, P. B., & Schuster, C. R. (1983). Commonalities in the environmental control of behavior. In P. K. Levison, D. R. Gerstein, & D. R. Maloff (Eds.), *Commonalities in substance abuse and habitual behavior.* Lexington, MA: Lexington.

Famularo, R., Kinscherff, R., & Fenton, T. (1992). Parental substance abuse and the nature of child maltreatment. *Child Abuse and Neglect, 16,* 475–483.

Fellin, P. (1995). *The community and the social worker* (2nd ed.). Itasca, IL: F. E. Peacock.

Fine, M. (1994). Working the hyphens: Reinventing self and other in qualitative research. In N. K. Denzin and Y. S. Lincoln (Eds.), *Handbook of qualitative research.* Thousand Oaks, CA: Sage.

Fingarette, H. (1988). *Heavy drinking: The myth of alcoholism as a disease.* Berkeley, CA: University of California.

Fischbach, G. D. (1992). Mind and brain. *Scientific American, 267* (3), 48–57.

Fischer, J. (1973). An eclectic approach to therapeutic casework. In J. Fischer (Ed.), *Interpersonal helping: Emerging approaches for social work practice* (pp. 317–335). Springfield, IL: Charles C. Thomas.

Fishbein, D. H., & Pease, S. E. (1996). *The dynamics of drug abuse.* Boston: Allyn & Bacon.

Fisher, G. L., & Harrison, T. C. (1993). The school counselor's role in relapse prevention. *The School Counselor, 41,* 120–125.

Fisher, G. L., & Harrison, T. C. (2000). *Substance abuse: Information for school counselors, social workers, therapists, and counselors* (2nd ed.). Boston: Allyn & Bacon.

Fisher, R., & Karger, H. J. (1997). *Social work and community in a private world.* White Plains, NY: Longman.

Fong, R. (2001). Culturally competent social work practice: Past and present. In R. Fong & S. Furuto (Eds.), *Culturally competent practice: Skills, interventions, and evaluations* (pp. 1–10). Boston: Allyn & Bacon.

Fong, R., & Furuto, S. (Eds.). (2001). *Culturally competent practice: Skills, interventions, and evaluations.* Boston: Allyn & Bacon.

Fossum, M. A., & Mason, M. J. (1986). *Facing shame: Families in recovery.* New York: Norton.

Fowler, R. C., Rich, C. L., & Young, D. C. (1986). San Diego suicide study, II: Substance abuse in young cases. *Archives of General Psychiatry, 43,* 962–965.

Foy, D. W., Nunn, L. B., & Rychtarik, R. G. (1984). Broad-spectrum behavioral treatment for chronic alcoholics: Effect of training controlled drinking skills. *Journal of Consulting and Clinical Psychology, 52,* 218–230.

Frank, P., & Golden, G. (1992). Blaming by naming: Battered women and the epidemic of codependence. *Social Work, 37,* 5–6.

Frankel, M. (1992). Suicide: Highest in wide-open spaces. *American Demographics, 14,* 9.

Frankl, V. (1973). *The doctor and the soul.* New York: Vintage Books.

Freeman, E. M. (Ed.). (1993). *Substance abuse treatment: A family systems perspective.* Newbury Park, CA: Sage.

Freire, P. (1973/1998). *Education for critical consciousness.* New York: Continuum.

Freire, P. (1994). *Pedagogy of hope.* New York: Contiuum.

Freire, P. (1996). *Letters to Christina: Reflections on my life and work.* New York: Routledge.

Freire, P. (1998). *Pedagogy of freedom: Ethics, democracy, and civic courage.* Lanham, MD: Rowan & Littlefield.

Frezza, M., DiPadova, C., Pozzato, G., Terpin, M., Baraona, E., & Lieber, C. S. (1990). High blood alcohol levels in women: The role of decreased gastric alcohol dehydrogenase activity and first-pass metabolism. *New England Journal of Medicine, 322,* 95–99.

Fried, A. (1997). *McCarthyism: The great American red scare: A documentary history.* New York: Oxford University Press.

Friel, J., Subby, R., & Friel, L. (1984). *Codependence and the search for identity.* Pompano Beach, FL: Health Communications, Inc.

Galanter, M., Castaneda, R., & Franco, H. (1991). Group therapy and self-help groups. In R. J. Frances & S. I. Miller (Eds.), *Clinical textbook of addictive disorders.* New York: Guilford Press.

Galper, J. (1980). *Social work practice: A radical approach.* Englewood Cliffs, NJ: Prentice-Hall.

Gambrill, E. (1997). *Social work practice: A critical thinker's guide.* New York: Oxford University Press.

Garvin, C. D., & Tropman, J. E. (1992). *Social work in contemporary society.* Englewood Cliffs, NJ: Prentice-Hall.

Gaston, L. (1990). The concept of the alliance and its role in psychotherapy: Theoretical and empirical considerations. *Psychotherapy, 27,* 143–153.

Geertz, C. (1973). *The interpretation of cultures: Selected essays.* New York: Basic Books.

Gelman, D., Underwood, A., King, P., Hager, M., & Gordon, J. (1990). Some things work! *Newsweek, CXVI* (13), 78–81.

Gelso, C. J., & Hayes, J. A. (1988). *The psychotherapy relationship: Theory, research, and practice.* New York: Wiley.

Germain, C. B. (1981). The ecological approach to people-environment transactions. *Social Casework, 62* (6), 323–331.

Germain, C. B. (1991). *Human behavior and the social environment: An ecological view.* New York: Columbia University Press.

Germain, C. B., & Gitterman, A. (1996). *The life model of social work practice* (2nd ed.). New York: Columbia University Press.

Gibelman, M., & Schervish, P. (1993). *Who we are: The social work labor force.* Washington, DC: NASW.

Gibson, P. (1989). Gay male and lesbian youth suicide. Alcohol, Drug Abuse, and Mental Health Administration, *Report of the secretary's task force on youth suicide.* (Vol. 3: Prevention and interventions in youth suicide). DHHS Pub. No. (ADM) 89–1623. Washington, DC: Superintendent of Documents, U.S. Government Printing Office.

Giddens, A. (1991). *Modernity and self-identity: Self and society in the late modern age.* Stanford, CA: Stanford University Press.

Giddens, A. (1993). *New rules of sociological method* (2nd ed.). Cambridge: Polity Press.

Gil, D. G. (1998). *Confronting injustice and oppression: Concepts and strategies for social workers.* New York: Columbia University Press.

Gilligan, C. (1982). *In a different voice: Psychological theory and women's development.* Cambridge, MA: Harvard University Press.

Gil-Rivas, V., Fiorentine, R., Anglin, M. D., & Taylor, E. (1997). Sexual and physical abuse: Do they compromise drug treatment outcomes? *Journal of Substance Abuse Treatment, 14,* 351–358.

Giordano, J., & Carini-Giordano, M. A. (1995). Ethnic dimensions in family treatment. In R. H. Mikesell, D-D. Lusterman, & S. H. McDaniel (Eds.), *Integrating family therapy: Handbook of family psychology and systems theory.* Washington, DC: American Psychological Association.

Giroux, H. A. (1997). *Pedagogy and the politics of hope: Theory, culture, and schooling.* Boulder, CO: Westview Press.

Glaser, E. M., Abelson, H. H., & Garrison, K. N. (1983). *Putting knowledge to use: Facilitating the diffusion of knowledge and the implementation of planned change.* San Francisco: Jossey-Bass.

Glasser, W. (1965). *Reality therapy: A new approach to psychiatry.* New York: Harper & Row.

Godlaski, T. M., Leukefeld, C., & Cloud, R. (1997). Recovery: With and without self-help. *Substance Use and Misuse, 32,* 621–627.

Golden, S. J., Khantzian, E. J., & McAuliffe, W. E. (1994). Group therapy. In M. Galanter & H. D. Kleber (Eds.), *The American Psychiatric Press textbook of substance abuse treatment* (pp. 303–314). Washington, DC: American Psychiatric Press.

Goldenberg, I., & Goldenberg, H. (2000). *Family therapy: An overview* (5th ed.). Belmont, CA: Brooks/Cole.

Goldkamp, J. S., & Weiland, D. (1993). *Assessing the impact of Dade County's Felony Drug Court.* Washington, DC: National Institute of Justice.

Goldman, M. S., Del Boca, F. K., & Darkes, J. (1999). Alcohol expectancy theory: The application of cognitive neuroscience. In K. E. Leonard & H. T. Blaine (Eds.), *Psychological theories of drinking and alcoholism* (2nd ed., pp. 203–246). New York: Guilford Press.

Goldner, V. (1985). Feminism and family therapy. *Family Process, 24,* 13–47.

Gomory, T. (1997). Does the goal of preventing suicide justify placing suicidal clients in care? NO. In E. Gambrill & R. Pruger (Eds.), *Controversial issues in social work ethics, values, and obligations* (pp. 70–74). Boston: Allyn & Bacon.

Goodall, H. L. (2000). *Writing the new ethnography.* Lanham, MD: Alta Mira.

Goode, E. (1989). *Drugs in American society* (3rd ed.). New York: Knopf.

Goodwin, D. (1976). *Is alcoholism hereditary?* New York: Oxford University Press.

Goodwin, D. W., & Warnock, J. K. (1991). Alcoholism: A family disease. In R. J. Frances & S. I. Miller (Eds.), *Clinical textbook of addictive disorders.* New York: Guilford Press.

Googins, B. (1984). Avoidance of the alcoholic client. *Social Work, 29,* 161–166.

Gordon, J. U. (1993). A culturally specific approach to ethnic minority young adults. In E. M. Freeman (Ed.), *Substance abuse treatment: A family systems perspective* (pp. 71–99). Newbury Park, CA: Sage.

Gordon, V., & Ledray, L. (1986). Growth-support intervention for the treatment of depression in women of middle years. *Western Journal of Nursing Research, 8,* 263–283.

Gorski, T. T. (1990). The Cenaps model of relapse prevention: Basic principles and procedures. *Journal of Psychoactive Drugs, 22,* 125–133.

Gorski, T. T. (1992, July/Aug.). Creating a relapse prevention program in your treatment center. *Addiction & Recovery,* 16–17.

Gorski, T. T. (1993, March/April). Relapse prevention: A state-of-the-art overview. *Addiction & Recovery,* 25–27.

Gorski, T. T., & Miller, M. M. (1986). *Staying sober: Guide to relapse prevention.* Independence, MO: Herald House.

Gottfredson, M., & Hirschi, T. (1990). *A general theory of crime.* Stanford, CA: Stanford University Press.

Gravitz, H., & Bowden, J. (1987). *Recovery: A guide for adult children of alcoholics*. New York: Simon & Schuster.

Gray, M. C. (1995). Drug abuse. In *Encyclopedia of social work* (Vol. 1, pp. 795–803). Washington, DC: NASW Press.

Greene, G. J., Jensen, C., & Jones, D. H. (1999). A constructivist perspective on clinical social work practice with ethnically diverse clients. In P. Ewalt, E. M. Freeman, A. E. Fortune, D. L. Poole, & S. L. Witkin (Eds.), *Multicultural issues in social work: Practice and research* (pp. 3–16). Washington, DC: NASW Press.

Grilly, D. M. (1994). *Drugs and human behavior* (2nd ed.). Boston: Allyn & Bacon.

Grinspoon, L. (1993). Update on cocaine. *Harvard Mental Health Letter, 10,* 1–4.

Hack, T. (1995). Suicide risk and intervention. In D. Marlin & A. Moore (Eds.), *First steps in the art of intervention.* Pacific Grove, CA: Brooks/Cole.

Hagan, T., & Smail, D. (1997). Power-mapping, I: Background and basic methodology. *Journal of Applied and Community Psychology, 7* (4), 257–267.

Haley, J. (1973). *Uncommon therapy: The psychiatric techniques of Milton H. Erickson, M.D.* New York: Norton.

Haley, J. (1976). *Problem-solving therapy* (2nd ed.). San Francisco: Jossey-Bass.

Haley, J. (1980). *Leaving home.* New York: McGraw-Hill.

Hall, W., & Sannibale, C. (1996). Are there two types of alcoholism? *Lancet, 348,* 1258.

Halloway, M. (1991, March). Rx for addiction. *Scientific American,* 94–103.

Hanson, B. G. (1995). *General systems theory: Beginning with wholes.* Washington, DC: Taylor & Francis.

Hanson, G., & Venturelli, P. J. (1995). *Drugs and society* (4th ed.). Boston: Jones and Bartlett.

Hanson, G., & Venturelli, P. J. (1998). *Drugs and society* (5th ed.). Boston: Jones and Bartlett.

Hardcastle, D. A., Wenocur, S., & Powers, P. R. (1997). *Community practice: Theories and skills for social workers.* New York: Oxford University Press.

Hare-Mustin, R. T. (1978). A feminist approach to family therapy. *Family Process, 17,* 181–194.

Hare-Mustin, R. T. (1987). The problem of gender in family therapy theory. *Family Process, 26,* 15–27.

Harper, K. V., & Lantz, J. (1996). *Cross-cultural practice: Social work practice with diverse populations.* Chicago: Lyceum Books.

Hartman, A. (1978). Diagrammatic assessment of family relationships. *Social Casework, 8,* 467–474.

Hartman, A. (1993). Out of the closet: Revolution and backlash. *Social Work, 38,* 245–246, 360.

Harvard Mental Health Letter. (1992). Addiction—Part II. *Harvard Mental Health Letter, 9* (5), 1–4.

Hawkins, C. A. (1997). Disruption of family rituals as a mediator of the relationship between parental drinking and adult adjustment in offspring. *Addictive Behaviors, 22,* 219–231.

Hawley, D. R., & deHaan, L. (1996). Toward a definition of family resilience: Integrating lifespan and family perspectives. *Family Process, 35,* 283–298.

Haynes, K. S., & Mickelson, J. S. (1997). *Affecting change: Social workers in the political arena* (3rd ed.). New York: Longman.

Heath, A. W., & Stanton, M. D. (1998). Family-based treatment: Stages and outcomes. *Clinical textbook of addictive disorders* (2nd ed., pp. 496–520). New York: Guilford Press.

Hepworth, D. H., Rooney, R. H., & Larsen, J. (1997). *Direct social work practice: Theory and skills* (5th ed.). Pacific Grove, CA: Brooks/Cole.

Hersen, M., & Bellack, A. S. (1976). *Behavioral assessment: A practical handbook.* New York: Pergamon.

Hewitt, J. P. (1997). *Self and society: A symbolic interactionist social psychology* (7th ed.). Boston: Allyn & Bacon.

Hilgard, E. R., & Bower, G. H. (1975). *Theories of learning* (4th ed.). Englewood Cliffs, NJ: Prentice-Hall.

Hill, S. Y. (1995). Vulnerability to alcoholism in women. In M. Galanter (Ed.),

Recent developments in alcoholism (Vol. 12). New York: Plenum Press.

Hillard, J. R. (1995). Predicting suicide. *Psychiatric Services, 46,* 223–225.

Hirschfield, R. M. A., & Davidson, L. (1988). Risk factors for suicide. In A. J. Frances & R. E. Hales (Eds.), *Review of Psychiatry* (Vol. 7). Washington, DC: American Psychiatric Association Press.

Hirschi, T. (1969). *Causes of delinquency.* Berkeley, CA: Sage.

Hobe, P. (1990). *Lovebound: Recovering from an alcoholic family.* New York: New American Library.

Holsems, C. A. (1998). *Chemical dependency: A systems approach.* Boston: Allyn & Bacon.

Homan, M. S. (1999). *Rules of the game: Lessons learned from the field of community change.* Pacific Grove, CA: Brooks/Cole.

Howe, G. (1981). The ecological approach to permanency planning: An interactionist perspective. *Child Welfare, 42,* 291–301.

Hudson, W. (1992). *Walmyr Assessment Scales.* Tempe, AZ: Walmyr.

Hughes, T. L. (1990). Evaluating research on chemical dependency among women: A women's health perspective. *Family and Community Health, 13,* 35–46.

Hughes, W. (1996). The case for parity in mental health insurance through a single-payer plan. *Psychiatric Rehabilitation Journal, 20* (1), 33–36.

Humphreys, K., & Moos, R. H. (1996). Reduced substance-abuse-related health care costs among voluntary participants in Alcoholics Anonymous. *Psychiatric Services, 47,* 709–713.

Hystad, N. (1989). *The Alcohol Use Profile.* Two Harbors, MN: Chemical Dependency Publications.

Inaba, D. S., Cohen, W. E., & Holstein, M. E. (1997). *Uppers, downers, all arounders: Physical and mental effects of drug abuse* (3rd ed.). Ashland, OR: Cinemed, Inc.

Inciardi, J. A., & McElrath, K. (1995). *The American drug scene: An anthology.* Los Angeles: Roxbury Publishing.

Ireland, T., & Widom, C. S. (1994). Childhood victimization and risk for alcohol and drug arrests. *International Journal of the Addictions, 29,* 235–274.

Ivanoff, A. M., & Reidel, M. (1995). Suicide. In R. L. Edwards (Ed.), *Encyclopedia of social work* (19th ed., Vol. 3, pp. 2358–2372). Washington, DC: NASW Press.

Jacobs, M. R., & Fehr, K. (1987). *Addiction Research Foundation's drugs and drug abuse: A reference text* (2nd ed.). Toronto: Addiction Research Foundation.

Janis, I. L. (1971, Nov.). Group-think. *Psychology Today,* 43–46.

Janis, I. L. (1982). Counteracting the adverse effects of concurrence-seeking in policy-planning groups: Theory and research perspectives. In H. Brandstatter, J. H. Davis, & G. Stocker-Kreichgauer (Eds.), *Group decision making.* New York: Academic Press.

Janzen, C., & Harris, O. (1997). *Family treatment in social work practice* (3rd ed.). Itasca, IL: F. E. Peacock.

Jarvik, M. (1990). The drug dilemma: Manipulating the demand. *Science, 250,* 387–392.

Jellinek, E. M. (1946). Phases in the drinking history of alcoholics: Analysis of a survey conducted by the official organ of Alcoholics Anonymous. *Quarterly Journal of Studies on Alcohol, 7,* 1–88.

Jellinek, E. M. (1952). Phases of alcohol addiction. *Quarterly Journal of Studies on Alcohol, 13,* 637–684.

Jellinek, E. M. (1960). *The disease concept of alcoholism.* New Haven: Hillhouse Press.

Jennings, L., & Skovhodt, T. M. (1999). The cognitive, emotional, and relational characteristics of master therapists. *Journal of Counseling Psychology, 46,* 3–11.

Jensen, G. A., Rost, K., Burton, R. P. D., & Bulycheva, M. (1998). Mental health insurance in the 1990s: Are employers offering less to more? *Health Affairs, 17* (3), 201–208.

Jessor, R., & Jessor, S. L. (1977). *Problem behavior and psychological development.* New York: Academic Press.

Johanson, C. E., & Uhlenhuth, E. H. (1981). Drug preference and mood in humans: Repeated assessment of d-amphetamine. *Pharmacology, Biochemistry, and Behavior, 14,* 159–163.

Johnson, D. W. (1997). *Reaching out: Interpersonal effectiveness* (6th ed.). Boston: Allyn & Bacon.

Johnson, J. L. (1994). *Adolescent substance abuse treatment outcome: A parent's view.* Unpublished manuscript.

Johnson, J. L. (2000). *Crossing borders— confronting history: Intercultural adjustment in a post-Cold-War world.* Lanham, MD: University Press of America.

Johnson, L. C., & Yanca, S. J. (2001). *Social work practice: A generalist approach* (7th ed.). Boston: Allyn & Bacon.

Johnson, V. E. (1973). *I'll quit tomorrow.* New York: Harper & Row.

Johnson, V. E. (1986). *Intervention: How to help someone who doesn't want help. A step-by-step guide for families and friends of chemically dependent persons.* Minneapolis, MN: Johnson Institute Books.

Johnston, L. D., O'Malley, P. M., & Bachman, J. G. (1998). *National survey results on drug abuse from the Monitoring the Future study, 1975–1997.* Rockville, MD: National Institute on Drug Abuse.

Jones, J. M. (1991). Psychological models of race: What have they been and what should they be? In J. D. Goodchilds (Ed.), *Psychological perspectives on human diversity in America.* Washington, DC: American Psychological Association.

Julien, R. M. (1998). *A primer of drug action: A concise, nontechnical guide to the actions, use and side effects of psychoactive drugs* (8th ed.). New York: W. H. Freeman and Company.

Jung, J. (1994). *Under the influence: Alcohol and human behavior.* Pacific Grove, CA: Brooks/Cole.

Jung, J. (2001). *Psychology of alcohol and other drugs: A research perspective.* Thousand Oaks, CA: Sage.

Kadden, R. M., Getter, H., Cooney, N. L., & Litt, M. D. (1989). Matching alcoholics to coping skills or interactional therapies: Posttreatment results. *Journal of Consulting and Clinical Psychology, 57,* 698–704.

Kahn, P. (1996). Gene hunters close in on elusive prey. *Science, 271,* 1352–1354.

Kahn, S. (1991a). *How people get power: Organizing oppressed communities for action.* Washington, DC: National Association of Social Workers.

Kahn, S. (1991b). *Organizing: A guide for grassroots leaders.* Washington, DC: National Association of Social Workers.

Kaiser, D. (1996). Not by chemicals alone: A hard look at "psychiatric medicine." *Psychiatric Times, XIII* (12), 41–44.

Kamerman, S. B. (1998). Fields of practice. In M. Mattaini, C. Lowery, & C. Meyer (Eds.), *The foundations of social work practice: A graduate text* (2nd ed.). Washington, DC: National Association of Social Workers.

Kaminer, Y., Bukstein, O. G., & Tarter, R. E. (1991). The Teen Addiction Severity Index: Rationale and reliability. *International Journal of Addictions, 26,* 219–226.

Kandel, D. B. (1978). Homophily, selection, and socialization in adolescent friendships. *American Journal of Sociology, 84,* 427–436.

Kandel, D. B., & Adler, I. (1982). Socialization into marijuana use among French adolescents: A cross-cultural comparison with the United States. *Journal of Health and Social Behavior, 23,* 295–309.

Kanter, J. S. (Ed.). (1985). *Clinical issues in treating the chronic mentally ill.* San Francisco: Jossey-Bass.

Kaplan, H. I., & Sadock, B. J. (1990). *Pocket handbook of clinical psychiatry.* Baltimore: Williams & Wilkins.

Karacostas, D. D., & Fisher, G. L. (1993). Chemical dependency in students with and without learning disabilities. *Journal of Learning Disabilities, 26,* 491–495.

Karls, J., & Wandrei, K. (1988). *Person in environment: A system for describing, classifying, and coding problems of social functioning.* Silver Spring, MD: NASW.

Karls, J., & Wandrei, K. (1994a). *Person-in-environment system: The PIE classification* system for social functioning problems. Washington, DC: NASW.

Karls, J., & Wandrei, K. (1994b). *PIE manual: Person-in-environment system: The PIE classification system for social functioning*. Washington, DC: NASW.

Karpel, M. A., & Strauss, E. S. (1983). *Family evaluation*. New York: Gardner Press.

Kasl, C. D. (1990, Nov./Dec.). The twelve-step controversy. *Ms.*, 30–31.

Kassel, J. D., & Shiffman, S. (1992). What can hunger teach us about drug craving? A comparative analysis of the two constructs. *Advances in Behaviour Research and Therapy, 14,* 141–147.

Kaufman, E. (1984). *Power to change: Family case studies in the treatment of alcoholism*. New York: Gardner Press.

Kaufman, E. (1994). *Psychotherapy of addicted persons*. New York: Guilford Press.

Kaufman, E., & Kaufman, P. (1992). From psychodynamic to structural to integrated family treatment of chemical dependency. In E. Kaufman & P. Kaufman (Eds.), *Family therapy of drug and alcohol abuse* (2nd ed., pp. 34–45). Boston: Allyn & Bacon.

Kaufman, G. (1992, Feb.). Shame. *The Atlantic Monthly, 53.*

Keith-Lucas, A. (1972). *The giving and taking of help*. Chapel Hill, NC: University of North Carolina Press.

Keller, M. (1972). On the loss-of-control phenomenon in alcoholism. *British Journal of Addiction, 67,* 153–166.

Kemp, S. P., Whittaker, J. K., & Tracey, E. M. (2002). Contextual social work practice. In M. O'Melia & K. K. Miley (Eds.), *Pathways to power: Readings in contextual social work practice*. Boston: Allyn & Bacon.

Kender, K. S., Heath, A. C., Neale, M. C., Kessler, R. C., & Eves, J. (1992). A population-based twin study of alcoholism in women. *Journal of the American Medical Association, 268,* 1877–1882.

Kerr, B. (1994). Review of the Substance Abuse Subtle Screening Inventory. In J. C. Conoley & J. C. Impara (Eds.), *The supplement to the eleventh mental measurements yearbook* (pp. 249–251). Lincoln, NE: University of Nebraska Press.

Kessler, R. C., McGonagle, K. A., Zhao, S., Nelson, C. B., Eschelman, S., Wittchen, H. U., & Kandler, K. S. (1994). Lifetime and 12-month prevalence of DSM-III-R psychiatric disorders in the United States. *Archives of General Psychiatry, 51,* 8–19.

Kinney, J., & Leaton, G. (1991). *Loosening the grip*. St. Louis: Times Mirror/ Mosby.

Kirk, J., & Miller, M. (1986). *Reliability and validity in qualitative research*. Beverly Hills, CA: Sage.

Kirk, S. A., & Kutchins, H. (1988). Deliberate misdiagnosis in mental health practice. *Social Science Review, 62,* 225–237.

Kirk, S. A., & Kutchins, H. (1992). *The selling of DSM: The rhetoric of science in psychiatry*. New York: Aldine De Gruyter.

Kirst-Ashman, K. K., & Hull, G. H., Jr. (1999). *Understanding generalist practice* (2nd ed.). Chicago: Nelson-Hall.

Klar, H. (1987). The setting for psychiatric treatment. In A. J. Frances & R. E. Hales (Eds.), *American Psychiatric Association annual review* (Vol. 6, pp. 336–352). Washington, DC: American Psychiatric Association.

Knipe, E. (1995). *Culture, society, and drugs: The social science approach to drug use*. Prospect Heights, IL: Waveland Press.

Kozol, J. (1991). *Savage inequalities: Children in America's schools*. New York: Crown Publishers.

Kretzmann, J. P., & McKnight, J. L. (1993). *Building communities from the inside out: A path toward finding and mobilizing a community's assets*. Chicago: ACTA Publications.

Kuhn, C., Swartzwelder, S., & Wilson, W. (1998). *Buzzed: The straight facts about the most used and abused drugs from alcohol to ecstasy*. New York: Norton.

Kurtz, P. D., Gaudin, J. M., Howing, P. T., & Wodarski, J. S. (1993). The consequences of physical abuse and neglect on the school-age child: Mediating factors. *Children and Youth Services Review, 15,* 85–104.

Kus, R. (1988). Alcoholism and non-acceptance of gay self: The critical link. *Journal of Homosexuality, 15,* 25–41.

Kutchins, H., & Kirk, S. (1988). The business of diagnosis: DSM-III and clinical social work. *Social Work, 33,* 215–220.

Kutchins, H., & Kirk, S. (1995). Should DSM be the basis for teaching social work practice? No! *Journal of Social Work Education, 31* (2), 159–165.

Lafferty, P., Beutler, L. E., & Crago, M. (1989). Differences between more and less effective psychotherapists: A study of select therapist variables. *Journal of Consulting and Clinical Psychology, 57,* 76–80.

Lamb, J. M. (1990). The suicidal adolescent. *Nursing, 90,* 72–76.

Landry, M. J., Smith, D. E., and Steinberg, J. R. (1991). Anxiety, depression, and substance use disorders: Diagnosis, treatment, and prescribing practices. *Journal of Psychoactive Drugs, 23* (4), 397–416.

Lantz, J. (1993). *Existential family therapy.* Northvale, NJ: Jason Aronson.

Lantz, J., & Pegram, M. (1989). Cross-cultural curative factors and clinical social work. *Journal of Independent Social Work, 4,* 55–68.

Larsen, E. (1985). *Stage II recovery: Life beyond addiction.* Minneapolis, MN: Winston Press.

Larson, K. K. (1982). Birthplace of "The Minnesota Model." *Alcoholism, 3* (2), 34–35.

Lasagna, L., von Felsinger, J. M., & Beecher, H. K. (1954). A study of the placebo response. *American Journal of Medicine, 16,* 770–779.

Lasch, C. (1994). *The revolt of the elites and the betrayal of democracy.* New York: Norton.

Lauer, R. H., & Handel, W. T. (1983). *Social psychology: The theory and application of symbolic interactionism.* Englewood Cliffs, NJ: Prentice-Hall.

Lee, J. A. B. (1994). *The empowerment approach to social work practice.* New York: Columbia University Press.

Lehman, A. F., Myers, C. P., & Corty, E. (1989). Assessment and classification of patients with psychiatric and substance abuse syndromes. *Hospital and Community Psychiatry, 40* (10), 1019–1030.

Leibenluft, E. (1994). A research agenda for women's mental health. *Journal of Women's Health, 3,* 377–382.

Leigh, J. W. (1998). *Communicating for cultural competence.* Boston: Allyn & Bacon.

Lender, M. E. (1981). The disease concept of alcoholism in the United States: Was Jellinek first? *Digest of Alcoholism Theory and Application, 1* (1), 25–31.

Lennard, H. L., Epstein, L. J., Bernstein, A., & Ransom, D. (1971). *Mystification and drug misuse.* San Francisco: Jossey-Bass.

Leo, J. (1990). The it's-not-my-fault syndrome. *U.S. News & World Report, 109* (12), 16.

Leshner, A. I. (1997, Oct.). Addiction is a brain disease, and it matters. *Science,* 45–47.

Lesieur, H. R., & Blum, S. B. (1992). Modifying the Addiction Severity Index for use with pathological gamblers. *American Journal on Addictions, 1,* 240–247.

Levin, J. D. (1990). *Alcoholism: A bio-psycho-social approach.* New York: Hemisphere.

Levinthal, C. F. (1999). *Drugs, behavior, and modern society* (2nd ed.). Boston: Allyn & Bacon.

Levy, M. (1997). Group therapy in addictive and psychiatric disorders. In N. S. Miller (Ed.), *The principles and practice of addictions in psychiatry* (pp. 384–391). Philadelphia: Saunders.

Lewis, J. A., Dana, R. Q., & Blevins, G. A. (1988). *Substance abuse counseling.* Pacific Grove, CA: Brooks/Cole.

Lewis, J. A., Dana, R. Q., & Blevins, G. A. (1994). *Substance abuse counseling: An individualized approach* (2nd ed.). Pacific Grove, CA: Brooks/Cole.

Lichtenstein, E., & Glasgow, R. E. (1992). Smoking cessation: What we have learned over the past decade. *Journal of Consulting and Clinical Psychology, 60,* 518–526.

Liddle, H. A. (1991). Training and supervision in family therapy: A comprehensive and critical analysis. In A. S. Gurman & D. P. Kniskern (Eds.), *Handbook of family therapy* (Vol. II, pp. 638–697). New York: Brunner/Mazel.

Lieber, C. S. (1994). Susceptibility to alcohol-related liver injury. *Alcohol and Alcoholism, 2* (suppl.), 315–326.

Lieberman, M. A., Yalom, I. D., & Miles, M. B. (1973). *Encounter groups: First facts.* New York: Basic Books.

Lincoln, Y. S., & Guba, E. G. (1985). *Naturalistic inquiry.* Beverly Hills, CA: Sage.

Lipsitz, G. (1997). Class and class consciousness: Teaching about social class in public universities. In A. Kumar (Ed.), *Class issues.* New York: New York University Press.

Longabaugh, R., Wirtz, P. W., Beattie, M. C., Noel, N., & Stout, R. (1995). Matching treatment focus to patient social investment and support: 18-month follow-up results. *Journal of Consulting and Clinical Psychology, 63,* 296–307.

Longres, J. F. (2000). *Human behavior in the social environment* (3rd ed.). Itasca, IL: F. E. Peacock.

Lovibond, S., & Caddy, G. (1970). Discriminated aversive control in the moderation of alcoholics' drinking behavior. *Behavior Therapy, 1,* 437–444.

Lowery, C. T. (1998). Social work with families. In M. A. Mattaini, C. T. Lowery, & C. H. Meyer (Eds.), *The foundations of social work practice: A graduate text* (2nd ed., pp. 165–187). Washington, DC: NASW Press.

Luborsky, L., McLellan, A. T., Woody, G. E., O'Brien, C. P., & Auerbach, A. (1985). Therapist success and its determinants. *Archives of General Psychiatry, 42,* 602–611.

Lukas, S. E., Sholar, M., Lundahl, L. H., Lamas, X., Kouri, E., Wines, J. D., Kragie, L., & Mendelson, J. H. (1996). Sex differences in plasma cocaine levels and subjective effects after acute cocaine administration in human volunteers. *Psychopharmacology, 125* (4), 346–354.

Lum, D. (1999). *Culturally competent practice.* Pacific Grove, CA: Brooks/Cole.

MacCannell, D. (1976). *The tourist: A new theory of the leisure class.* New York: Schocken Books.

Madanes, C. (1981). *Strategic family therapy.* San Francisco: Jossey-Bass.

Madanes, C. (1984). *Behind the one-way mirror.* San Francisco: Jossey-Bass.

Maher, J. J. (1997). Exploring alcohol's effects on liver function. *Alcohol Health & Research World, 21,* 5–12.

Maisto, S. A., & Carey, K. B. (1987). Treatment of alcohol abuse. In T. D. Nirenberg & S. A. Maisto (Eds.), *Developments in the assessment and treatment of addictive behaviors* (pp. 173–212). Norwood, NJ: Ablex.

Maisto, S. A., Carey, K. B., & Bradizza, C. M. (1999). Social learning theory. In K. Leonard & H. Blane (Eds.), *Psychological theories of drinking and alcoholism* (2nd ed., pp. 106–163). New York: Guilford Press.

Maisto, S. A., Galizio, M., & Connors, G. J. (1995). *Drug use and abuse* (2nd ed.). Fort Worth, TX: Harcourt Press.

Mallinckrodt, B. (1993). Session impact, working alliance, and treatment outcome in brief counseling. *Journal of Counseling Psychology, 40,* 25–32.

Malone, K. M., Hass, G. L., Sweeney, J. A., & Mann, J. J. (1995). Major depression and the risk of attempted suicide. *Journal of Affective Disorders, 8,* 173–185.

Manning, M. C. (2001). Culturally competent assessments of African American communities and organizations. In R. Fong & S. Furuto (Eds.), *Culturally competent practice: Skills, interventions, and evaluations.* Boston: Allyn & Bacon.

Mannuzza, S., Klein, R., Bessler, A., Malloy, P., & La Padula, M. (1993). Adult outcome of hyperactive boys. *Archives of General Psychiatry, 50,* 565–576.

Mantsios, G. (1995). Class in America: Myths and realities. In S. P. Rothenberg (Ed.), *Race, class, and gender in the United States: An integrated study* (3rd ed., pp. 131–143). New York: St. Martin's Press.

Maracle, B. (1993). *Crazywater: Native voices on addiction and recovery*. Toronto: Penguin Books.

Mark, D., & Faude, J. (1997). *Psychotherapy of cocaine addiction: Entering the interpersonal world of the cocaine addict*. Northvale, NJ: Aronson.

Marlatt, G. A. (1982). Relapse prevention: A self-controlled program for the treatment of addictive behaviors. In R. B. Stuart (Ed.), *Adherence, compliance and generalization in behavioral medicine*. New York: Brunner/Mazel.

Marlatt, G. A. (1995). Relapse prevention: Theoretical rationale and overview of the model. In G. A. Marlatt & J. R. Gordon (Eds.), *Relapse prevention: Maintenance strategies in the treatment of addictive behaviors* (pp. 3–70). New York: Guilford Press.

Marlatt, G. A. (1996). Harm reduction: Come as you are. *Addictive Behaviors, 21,* 779–788.

Marlatt, G. A., Demming, B., & Reid, J. B. (1973). Loss-of-control drinking in alcoholics: An experimental analogue. *Journal of Abnormal Psychology, 81,* 223–241.

Marlatt, G. A., & Gordon, J. R. (Eds.). (1995). *Relapse prevention: Maintenance strategies in the treatment of addictive behaviors*. New York: Guilford Press.

Marlatt, G. A., & Miller, W. R. (1984). *Comprehensive drinking profile*. Odessa, FL: Psychological Assessment Resources.

Marlatt, G. A., & Rohsenow, D. J. (1980). Cognitive processes in alcohol use: Expectancy and the balanced placebo design. In N. K. Mello (Ed.), *Advances in substance abuse* (Vol. 1). Greenwich, CT: JAI Press.

Marlatt, G. A., & Tapert, S. F. (1993). Harm reduction: Reducing the risks of addictive behaviors. In J. Baer, A. Marlatt, & R. J. McMahon (Eds.), *Addictive behaviors across the life span: Prevention, treatment, and policy issues* (pp. 243–273). Newbury Park, CA: Sage.

Martinez, C. (1993). Psychiatric care of Mexican Americans. In A. C. Gaw (Ed.), *Culture, ethnicity, and mental illness* (pp. 431–462). Washington, DC: American Psychiatric Press.

Marvel, B. (1995). AA's "higher power" challenged. *St. Paul Pioneer Press, 147* (44), 4A.

Maslow, A. H. (1970). *Motivation and personality*. New York: Harper & Row.

Mather, J. H., & Lager, P. B. (2000). *Child welfare: A unifying model of practice*. Belmont, CA: Brooks/Cole.

Mathias, R. (1995). Novelty seekers and drug abusers tap same brain reward system, animal studies show. *NIDA Notes, 10* (4), 1–5.

Mattick, R. P., & Hall, W. (1996). Are detoxification programs effective? *Lancet, 347,* 97–100.

Mattson, M. E., & Allen, J. P. (1991). Research on matching alcoholic patients to treatments: Findings, issues, and implications. *Journal of Addictive Diseases, 11,* 33–49.

Mattson, S. N., & Riley, E. P. (1998). A review of the neurobiological deficits in children with fetal alcohol syndrome or prenatal exposure to alcohol. *Alcoholism, Clinical and Experimental Research, 22,* 279–294.

Matuschka, E. (1985). Treatment, outcomes, and clinical evaluation. In T. E. Bratter & G. C. Forrest (Eds.), *Alcoholism and substance abuse: Strategies for clinical intervention* (pp. 193–224). New York: Free Press.

McCaul, M. D., & Furst, J. (1994). Alcoholism treatment in the United States. *Alcohol Health & Research World, 18,* 253–260.

McCrady, B. S. (2001). Foreword. In G. J. Connor, D. M. Donovan, & C. C. DiClemente, *Selecting and planning interventions: Substance abuse treatment and the stages of change* (pp. viii–x). New York: Guilford Press.

McCrady, B. S., & Delaney, S. I. (1995). Self-help groups. In R. K. Hester & W. R. Miller (Eds.), *Handbook of alcoholism treatment approaches* (2nd ed.). New York: Allyn & Bacon.

McCrady, B. S., & Irvine, S. (1989). Self-help groups. In R. K. Hester &

W. R. Miller (Eds.), *Handbook of alcoholism treatment approaches.* New York: Pergamon Press.

McGinnis, J. M., & Foege, W. H. (1993). Actual causes of death in the United States. *Journal of the American Medical Association, 270,* 2207–2212.

McGoldrick, M. (1989). Ethnicity and the family life cycle. In E. A. Carter & M. McGoldrick (Eds.), *The changing family life cycle: A framework for family therapy.* Boston: Allyn & Bacon.

McGoldrick, M., Preto, N. G., Hines, P. M., & Lee, E. (1991). Ethnicity and family therapy. In A. S. Gurman & D. P. Kniskern (Eds.), *Handbook of family therapy* (Vol. II, pp. 546–582). New York: Brunner/Mazel.

McGue, M. (1997). A behavioral-genetic perspective on children of alcoholics. *Alcohol Health and Research World, 21,* 210–217.

McLaren, P. (1995). *Critical pedagogy and predatory culture: Oppositional politics in a postmodern era.* London: Routledge.

McLaren, P., & Leonard, P. (1996). *Paulo Freire: A critical encounter.* New York: Routledge.

McLellan, A. T., Alterman, A., Metzger, D., Grissom, G., Woody, G., Luborsky, L., & O'Brien, C. (1997). Similarity of outcome predictors across opiate, cocaine, and alcohol treatments: Role of treatment services. In G. Marlatt & G. Vandenbos (Eds.), *Addictive behaviors: Readings on etiology, prevention, and treatment* (pp. 718–758). Washington, DC: American Psychological Association.

McLellan, A.T., Kushner, H., Metzger, D., Peters, F. (1992). The fifth edition of the Addiction Severity Index. *Journal of Substance Abuse Treatment, 9,* 199–213.

McLellan, A. T., Luborsky, L., Cacciola, J., & Griffith, J. (1985). New data from the Addiction Severity Index: Reliability and validity in three centers. *Journal of Nervous and Mental Disorders, 173,* 412–423.

McLellan, A.T., Luborsky, L., O'Brien, C. P., Woody, G. E. (1980). An improved diagnostic instrument for substance abuse patients: The Addiction Severity Index. *Journal of Nervous and Mental Disorders, 168,* 26–33.

McLellan, A. T., Randall, M., Joseph, N., & Alterman, A. I. (1991). Using the ASI to compare cocaine, alcohol, opiate and mixed substance abusers. In L. Harris (Ed.), *Problems of drug dependence 1989.* NIDA Research Monograph, Washington, DC: U.S. Government Printing Office.

McMahon, M. O. (1994). *Advanced generalist practice with an international perspective.* Englewood Cliffs, NJ: Prentice-Hall.

McNeese, C. A., & DiNitto, D. M. (2000). *Chemical dependency: A systems approach* (2nd ed.). Englewood Cliffs, NJ: Prentice-Hall.

McRoy, R. G., Aguilar, M. A., & Shorkey, C. T. (1993). A cross-cultural treatment approach for families with young children. In E. M. Freeman (Ed.), *Substance abuse treatment: A family systems perspective* (pp. 23–47). Newbury Park, CA: Sage.

Mead, G. H. (1962). *Mind, self, and society from the standpoint of a social behaviorist.* Chicago: University of Chicago Press.

Medina, C. (2001). Toward an understanding of Puerto Rican ethnicity and substance abuse. In S. L. A. Straussner (Ed.), *Ethnocultural factors in substance abuse treatment* (pp. 137–164). New York: Guilford Press.

Melek, S. P., & Pyenson, B. (1996). Premium rate estimates for a mental health parity provision to S.1028, "The Health Insurance Reform Act of 1995" [online]. Available: http://www.ambha.org/Reports/cost.htm

Mello, N. K. (1988). Effects of alcohol abuse on reproductive function in women. In M. Galanter (Ed.), *Recent developments in alcoholism* (Vol. 6, pp. 253–276). New York: Plenum.

Merikangas, K. R. (1990). Genetic epidemiology of alcoholism. *Psychological Medicine, 20,* 1–22.

Merton, R. K. (1938). Social structure and anomie. *American Sociological Review, 3,* 672–682.

Merton, R. K. (1957). *Social theory and social structure.* Glencoe, IL: Free Press.

Metzger, L. (1988). *From denial to recovery: Counseling problem drinkers, alcoholics, and their families*. San Francisco: Jossey-Bass.

Meyer, C. (1993). *Assessment in social work practice*. New York: Columbia University Press.

Meyer, R. E. (1986). How to understand the relationship between psychopathology and addictive disorders: Another example of the chicken and the egg. In R. E. Meyer (Ed.), *Psychopathology and addictive disorders*. New York: Guilford Press.

Meyers, D. G. (1996). *Social psychology* (5th ed.). New York: McGraw-Hill.

Miley, K. K., O'Melia, M., & DuBois, B. L. (1995). *Generalist social work practice: An empowering approach*. Boston: Allyn & Bacon.

Miller, B. A., & Downs, W. R. (1993). The impact of family violence on the use of alcohol by women. *Alcohol Health and Research World, 17,* 137–143.

Miller, B. A., Downs, W. R., Gondoli, D. M., & Keil, A. (1989). The role of childhood sexual abuse in the development of alcoholism in women. *Violence and Victims, 2,* 157–172.

Miller, B. A., Downs, W. R., & Testa, M. (1993). Interrelationships between victimization experiences and women's alcohol use. *Journal of Studies on Alcohol* (Vol. II, Suppl.), 109–117.

Miller, D. (1967). *Individualism: Personal achievement and the open society*. Austin, TX: University of Texas Press.

Miller, G. A. (1983). *Substance Abuse Subtle Screening Inventory*. Bloomington, IN: SASSI Institute.

Miller, J. G. (1965). Living systems: Basic concepts. *Behavioral Science, 10,* 193–237.

Miller, N. S. (1994). Psychiatric comorbidity: Occurrence and treatment. *Alcohol Health and Research World, 18,* 261–264.

Miller, N. S. (1997). *The Substance Abuse Subtle Screening Inventory-3*. Spencer, IN: Spencer Evening World.

Miller, S. I., Francis, R. J., & Holmes, D. J. (1988). Use of psychotropic drugs in alcoholism treatment: A summary. *Hospital & Community Psychiatry, 39,* 1251–1252.

Miller, W. R. (1983). Motivational interviewing with problem drinkers. *Behavioural Psychotherapy, 1,* 147–172.

Miller, W. R., & Baca, L. M. (1983). Two-year follow-up of bibliotherapy and therapist-directed controlled drinking training for problem drinkers. *Behavior Therapy, 14,* 441–448.

Miller, W. R., & Hester, R. K. (1986a). The effectiveness of alcoholism treatment: What research reveals. In W. R. Miller & N. Heather (Eds.), *The addictive behaviors: Process of change* (pp. 121–174). New York: Plenum.

Miller, W. R., & Hester, R. K. (1986b). Matching problem drinkers with optimal treatments. In W. R. Miller & N. Heather (Eds.), *The addictive behaviors: Process of change* (pp. 175–203). New York: Plenum.

Miller, W. R., & Hester, R. K. (1995). Treatment for alcohol problems: Toward an informed eclecticism. In R. K. Hester & W. R. Miller (Eds.), *Handbook of alcoholism treatment approaches: Effective alternatives* (2nd ed., pp. 1–11). Boston: Allyn & Bacon.

Miller, W. R., & Kurtz, E. (1994). Models of alcoholism used in treatment: Contrasting AA and other perspectives with which it is often confused. *Journal of Studies on Alcohol, 55,* 159–166.

Miller, W. R., Leckman, A. L., Delaney, H. D., & Tinkcom, M. (1992). Long-term follow-up of behavioral self-control training. *Journal of Studies on Alcohol, 53,* 249–261.

Miller, W. R., & Marlatt, G. A. (1984). *Manual for the Comprehensive Drinker Profile*. Odessa, FL: Psychological Assessment Resources.

Miller, W. R., & McCrady, B. S. (1993). The importance of research on Alcoholics Anonymous. In B. S. McCrady & W. R. Miller (Eds.), *Research on Alcoholics Anonymous*. New Brunswick, NJ: Rutgers Center of Alcohol Studies.

Miller, W. R., & Munoz, R. F. (1982). *How to control your drinking* (Rev. Ed.). Albuquerque, NM: University of New Mexico Press.

Miller, W. R., & Rollnick, S. (1991). *Motivational interviewing: Preparing people to change addictive behavior.* New York: Guilford Press.

Miller, W. R., & Rollnick, S. (2002). *Motivational interviewing: Preparing people to change addictive behavior* (2nd ed.). New York: Guilford Press.

Miller, W. R., & Sovereign, R. G. (1989). The check-up: A model for early intervention in addictive behaviors. In T. Loberg, W. R. Miller, P. E. Nathan, & G. A. Marlatt (Eds.), *Addictive behaviors: Prevention and early intervention* (pp. 219–231). Amsterdam: Swets & Zeitlinger.

Miller, W. R., Taylor, C. A., & West, J. C. (1980). Focused versus broad-spectrum behavior therapy for problem drinkers. *Journal of Consulting and Clinical Psychology, 48,* 590–601.

Miller, W. R., Westerberg, V. S., & Waldron, H. B. (1995). Evaluating alcohol problems in adults and adolescents. In R. K. Hester & W. R. Miller (Eds.), *Handbook of alcoholism treatment approaches: Effective alternatives* (2nd ed.). New York: Allyn & Bacon.

Mills, C. W. (1959). *The sociological imagination.* London: Oxford University Press.

Minkoff, K., & Drake, R. E. (Eds.). (1991). *Dual diagnosis of major mental illness and substance disorder.* San Francisco: Jossey-Bass.

Minuchin, S. (1974). *Families and family therapy.* Cambridge, MA: Harvard University Press.

Minuchin, S., & Fishman, H. C. (1981). *Family therapy techniques.* Cambridge, MA: Harvard University Press.

Monk, G. (1997). How narrative therapy works. In G. Monk, J. Winslade, K. Crocket, & D. Epston (Eds.), *Narrative therapy in practice: The archaeology of hope* (pp. 3–31). San Francisco: Jossey-Bass.

Moody, H. R. (2000). *Aging: Concepts and controversies* (3rd ed.). Thousand Oaks, CA: Pine Forge Press.

Moore-Kirkland, J. (1981). Mobilizing motivation: From theory to practice. In A. N. Maluccio (Ed.), *Promoting competence in clients: A new/old approach to social work practice* (pp. 27–54). New York: Free Press.

Moos, R. H., Finney, J. W., & Gamble, W. (1985). The process of recovery from alcoholism, II: Comparing spouses of alcoholic patients and matched community controls. In E. M. Freeman (Ed.), *Social work practice with clients who have alcohol problems* (pp. 292–314). Springfield, IL: Charles C. Thomas.

Morris, P. A., & Bihan, S. M. (1991). Aftercare: Its role in primary and secondary recovery of women from alcohol and other drug dependence. *International Journal of the Addictions, 26,* 546–549.

Morse, R. M., & Flavin, D. K. (1992). The definition of alcoholism. *Journal of the American Medical Association, 268,* 1012–1014.

Mullally, R. P. (1993). *Structural social work: Ideology, theory, and practice.* Toronto: McClelland and Stewart.

Mullen, P. E., Martin, J. L., Anderson, J. C., Romans, S. E., & Herbison, G. P. (1993). Childhood sexual abuse and mental health in adult life. *British Journal of Psychiatry, 163,* 721–732.

Murphy, C. M., & O'Farrell, T. J. (1996). Marital violence among alcoholics. *Current Directions in Psychological Science, 5,* 183–186.

Murphy, G. E., Wetzel, R. D., Robins, E., & McEvoy, L. (1992). Multiple risk factors predict suicide in alcoholism. *Archives of General Psychiatry, 49,* 459–463.

Musto, D. F. (1999). *The American disease: Origins of narcotic control* (3rd ed.). New York: Oxford University Press.

Nace, E. P. (1987). *The treatment of alcoholism.* New York: Brunner/Mazel.

Najavits, L. M., & Strupp, H. H. (1994). Differences in the effectiveness of psychodynamic therapists: A process-outcome study. *Psychotherapy, 31,* 114–123.

Narcotics Anonymous. (1986). *Narcotics Anonymous.* New York: World Services.

Nash, J. M. (1997). Why do people get hooked? *Time* (May), 68–76.

Nathan, P. E. (1992). Peele hasn't done his homework—again: A response to "Alcoholism, politics, and bureaucracy: The consensus against controlled-drinking therapy in America." *Addictive Behaviors, 17,* 63–65.

National Academy of Sciences. (1990). *Treating drug problems* (Vol. 1). Washington, DC: National Academy Press.

National Association of Social Workers (2000). *Code of Ethics of the National Association of Social Workers.* Washington, DC: Author.

National Center on Addiction and Substance Abuse. (1996). *Substance abuse and the American woman.* New York: National Center on Addiction and Substance Abuse.

National Institute of Mental Health. (1997). *Parity in coverage of mental health services in an era of managed care: An interim report to Congress.* Rockville, MD: NIMH.

National Institute on Alcohol Abuse and Alcoholism. (1990). *National household survey on drug abuse: Population estimates, 1988.* (DHHS Publication No. ADM 89-1638). Washington, DC: U.S. Department of Health and Human Services, Public Health Services, Alcohol, Drug Abuse, and Mental Health Administration.

National Institute on Drug Abuse. (1999). *Drug abuse and addiction research: 25 years of discovery to advance the health of the public.* Rockville, MD: National Institute on Drug Abuse [online]. Available: http://www.drugabuse.gov

National Institute on Drug Abuse/National Institute on Alcohol Abuse and Alcoholism (NIDA/NIAAA). (1990). *National drug and alcoholism treatment unit survey (NDATUS) 1989: Main findings report.* Rockville, MD: Author.

Nestler, E. J., & Aghajanian, G. K. (1997). Molecular and cellular basis of addiction. *Science, 278,* 58–63.

Nestler, E. J., Fitzgerald, L. W., & Self, D. W. (1995). Neurobiology. In J. M. Oldham & M. B. Riba (Eds.), *Review of psychiatry* (Vol. 14). Washington, DC: American Psychiatric Press.

Netting, F. E., Kettner, P. M., & McMurtry, S. L. (1993). *Social work macro practice* (2nd ed.). New York: Longman.

Netting, F. E., Kettner, P. M., & McMurtry, S. L. (1998). *Social work macro practice* (3rd ed.). New York: Longman.

Nichols, M. P., & Schwartz, R. C. (1991). *Family therapy: Concepts and methods* (2nd ed.). Boston: Allyn & Bacon.

Nordstrom, G., & Berglund, M. (1987). A prospective study of successful long-term adjustment in alcohol dependence: Social drinking vs. abstinence. *Journal of Studies on Alcohol, 48,* 95–103.

Norwood, R. (1985). *Women who love too much.* Los Angeles: Jeremy P. Tarcher.

Nowinski, J. (1996). Facilitating 12-step recovery from substance abuse and addiction. In F. Rotgers, D. S. Keller, & J. Morgenstern (Eds.), *Treating substance abuse.* New York: Guilford Press.

Oakes, G. (1994). *The imaginary war: Civil defense and American Cold War culture.* New York: Oxford University Press.

O'Farrell, T. J. (1995). Marital and family therapy. In R. K. Hester & W. R. Miller (Eds.), *Handbook of alcoholism treatment approaches: Effective alternatives* (2nd ed., pp. 195–220). Boston: Allyn & Bacon.

Office of Substance Abuse Prevention. (1989). Alcohol, Drug Abuse, and Mental Health Administration. *Message and material review* (RPO726). Washington, DC: U.S. Government Printing Office.

O'Hanlon, B., & Wilk, J. (1987). *Shifting contexts: The generation of effective psychotherapy.* New York: Guilford Press.

O'Hanlon, W., & Weiner-Davis, M. (1989). *In search of solutions: A new direction in psychotherapy.* New York: Norton.

Ojehagen, A., & Berglund, M. (1989). Changes in drinking goals in a two-year outpatient alcoholic treatment program. *Addictive Behaviors, 14,* 109.

Olsen, L. J. (1995). Services for substance-abuse-affected families: The Project

Connect experience. *Child and Adolescent Social Work Journal, 12,* 183–196.

ONDCP gives rundown on treatment approaches. (1990). *Alcoholism & Drug Abuse Week, 2* (26), 3–5.

Orford, J. (1985). *Excessive appetites: A psychological view of addictions.* New York: Wiley.

Pages, K. P., Russo, J. E., Roy-Byrne, P. P., Ries, R., & Crowley, D. S. (1997). Determinants of suicidal ideation: The role of substance use disorders. *Journal of Clinical Psychiatry, 66,* 533–540.

Palazzoli, M. S., Cirillo, S., Selvini, M., & Sorrentino, A. (1989). *Family games.* New York: Norton.

Palfai, T., & Jankiewicz, H. (1997). *Drugs and human behavior* (2nd ed.). Dubuque, IA: W. C. Brown.

Pantoja, A., & Perry, W. (1998). Community development and restoration: A perspective and case study. In F. G. Rivera & J. L. Erlich (Eds.), *Community organizing in a diverse society* (3rd ed., pp. 220–242). Boston: Allyn & Bacon.

Pardeck, J. T., Murphy, J. W., & Choi, J. M. (1994). Some implications of postmodernism for social work practice. *Social Work, 39* (4), 343–346.

Parham, T. A. (1993). *Psychological storms: The African American struggle for identity.* Chicago: African American Images.

Patterson, B. W., Williams, H. L., McLean, G. A., Smith, L. T., & Schaffer, K. W. (1987). Alcoholism and family history of alcoholism: Effects on visual and auditory event-related potentials. *Alcohol, 4,* 265–269.

Payne, M. (1997). *Modern social work theory* (2nd ed.). Chicago: Lyceum Books.

Peck, M. S. (1993). *Further along the road less traveled.* New York: Simon & Schuster.

Peele, S. (1985/1998). *The meaning of addiction: An unconventional view.* San Francisco: Jossey-Bass.

Peele, S., Brodsky, A., & Arnold, M. (1992). *The truth about addiction and recovery.* New York: Simon & Schuster.

Pellegrini, A. (1992). S(h)ifting the terms of hetero/sexism: Gender, power, homophobias. In W. J. Blumenfeld (Ed.), *Homophobia: How we all pay the price* (pp. 39–56). Boston: Beacon Press.

Penn, P. (1982). Circular questioning. *Family Process, 21,* 267–280.

Perkinson, R. R., & Jongsma, A. E., Jr. (1998). *The chemical dependence treatment planner.* New York: Wiley.

Petersen, D. R. (1987). The role of assessment in professional psychology. In D. R. Petersen & D. B. Fishman (Eds.), *Assessment for decisions* (pp. 5–43). New Brunswick, NJ: Rutgers University Press.

Petraitis, J., Flay, B. R., & Miller, T. Q. (1995). Reviewing theories of adolescent substance use: Organizing pieces in the puzzle. *Psychological Bulletin, 117,* 67–86.

Philleo, J., Brisbane, F. L., & Epstein, L. G. (1995). *Cultural competence for social workers: A guide for alcohol and other drug abuse prevention professionals working with ethnic/racial communities.* Rockville, MD: U.S. Department of Health and Human Services, Public Health Service, Substance Abuse and Mental Health Services Administration, Center for Substance Abuse Prevention.

Phillips, D. C. (1987). *Philosophy, science, and social inquiry: Contemporary methodological controversies in social science and related fields of research.* New York: Pergamon Press.

Pickens, R. W., Svikis, D. S., McGue, M., Lykken, D. T., Heston, L. L., & Clayton, P. J. (1991). Heterogeneity in the inheritance of alcoholism: A study of male and female twins. *Archives of General Psychiatry, 48,* 19–28.

Pincus, A., & Minahan, A. (1973). *Social work practice: Model and method.* Itasca, IL: F. E. Peacock.

Pinderhughes, E. (1989). *Understanding race, ethnicity, and power: The key to efficacy in clinical practice.* New York: Free Press.

Pittman, F. (1987). *Turning points: Treating families in transition and crisis.* New York: Norton.

Polich, J. M., Armor, D. J., & Braiker, H. B. (1981). *The course of alcoholism: Four years after treatment.* New York: Wiley.

Pollock, V. E., Schneider, L. S., Gabrielli, W. F., & Goodwin, D. W. (1987). Sex of parent and offspring in the transmission of alcoholism: A meta-analysis. *Journal of Nervous and Mental Disease, 175,* 668–673.

Poole, D. L. (1999). Politically correct or culturally competent? In P. Ewalt, E. M. Freeman, A. E. Fortune, D. L. Poole, & S. L. Witkin (Eds.), *Multicultural issues in social work: Practice and research* (pp. 259–264). Washington, DC: NASW Press.

Popper, K. R. (1994). *The myth of the framework: In defense of science and rationality.* Edited by M. A. Notturno. New York: Routledge.

Postman, N. (1976). *Crazy talk, stupid talk.* New York: Delacorte.

Poulin, J. (2000). *Collaborative social work: Strengths-based generalist practice.* Itasca, IL: F. E. Peacock.

Powell, B. J., Read, M. R., Penick, E. C., Miller, N. S., & Bingham, S. F. (1987). Primary and secondary depression in alcoholic men: An important distinction. *Journal of Clinical Psychiatry, 48,* 98–101.

Price, J. A. (1996). *Power and compassion: Working with difficult adolescents and abused parents.* New York: Guilford Press.

Pritchard, C., Cotton, A., Bowen, D., & Williams, R. (1998). A consumer study of young people's views on their educational social worker: Engagement as a measure of an effective relationship. *British Journal of Social Work, 28,* 915–938.

Prochaska, J. O., & DiClemente, C. C. (1982). Transtheoretical therapy: Toward a more integrative model of change. *Psychotherapy: Theory, Research, and Practice, 19,* 276–288.

Prochaska, J. O., & DiClemente, C. C. (1984). *The transtheoretical approach: Crossing traditional boundaries of therapy.* Homewood, IL: Dow Jones/Irwin.

Prochaska, J. O., & DiClemente, C. C. (1986). Toward a comprehensive model of change. In W. R. Miller & N. Heather (Eds.), *Treating addictive behaviors: Processes of change* (pp. 3–27). New York: Plenum Press.

Prochaska, J. O., DiClemente, C. C., & Norcross, J. C. (1992). In search of how people change. *American Psychologist, 47,* 1102–1114.

Proctor, C. D., & Groze, V. K. (1994). Risk factors for suicide among gay, lesbian, and bisexual youth. *Social Work, 39,* 504–512.

Project MATCH Research Group. (1997). Matching alcoholism treatments to client heterogeneity: Project MATCH post-treatment drinking outcomes. *Journal of Studies on Alcohol, 58,* 7–29.

Queralt, M. (1996). *The social environment and human behavior: A diversity perspective.* Boston: Allyn & Bacon.

Ragg, D. M. (2001). *Building effective helping skills: The foundation of generalist practice.* Boston: Allyn & Bacon.

Ramsey, P. (1965). The transformation of ethics. In P. Ramsey (Ed.), *Faith and ethics: The ideology of H. Richard Niebuhr.* New York: Harper and Row.

Rand Corporation. (1997). Research on managed care for psychiatric disorders [online]. Available: http://www.nami.org/update/insparity.html

Raskin, M. S., & Daley, D. C. (1991). Assessment of addiction problems. In M. S. Raskin & D. C. Daley (Eds.), *Treating the chemically dependent and their families.* Newbury Park, CA: Sage.

Rauch, J. B., Sarno, C., & Simpson, S. (1991). Screening for affective disorders. *Families in Society, 72,* 602–609.

Ray, O., & Ksir, C. (1993). *Drugs, society, & human behavior* (6th ed.). St. Louis, MO: Mosby.

Ray, W. A., Thapa, P. B., & Shorr, R. I. (1993). Medications and the older driver. *Clinics in Geriatric Medicine, 9,* 413–438.

Reader's Digest. (January 1987). Can cocaine conquer America? New York: Reader's Digest, 31–38.

Reandeau, S. G., & Wampold, B. E. (1991). Relationship of power and involvement to working alliance: A multiple-case sequential analysis of brief therapy. *Journal of Counseling Psychology, 38,* 107–114.

Reed, B. G. (1987). Developing women-sensitive drug dependency treatment services: Why so difficult? *Journal of Psychoactive Drugs, 19,* 533–540.

Regan, T. J. (1990). Alcohol and the cardiovascular system. *Journal of the American Medical Association, 264,* 377–381.

Regier, D. A., Farmer, M. E., Rae, D. S., Locke, B. Z., Keith, S. J., Judd, L. L., & Goodwin, F. K. (1990). Comorbidity of mental disorders with alcohol and other drug abuse: Results from the Epidemiologic Catchment Area (ECA) study. *Journal of the American Medical Association, 264* (19), 2511–2518.

Reiman, J. (2001). *The rich get richer and the poor get prison: Ideology, class, and criminal justice.* Needham Heights, MA: Allyn & Bacon.

Remafedi, G., Farrow, J. A., & Deisher, R. W. (1991). Risk factors for attempted suicide in gay and bisexual youth. *Pediatrics, 87* (6), 869–875.

Restak, R. (1994). *Receptors.* New York: Bantam Books.

Restak, R. (1995). *Brainscapes.* New York: Hyperion Press.

Ridgeway, I. R., & Sharpley, C. F. (1991). Multiple measures for the prediction of counselor trainee effectiveness. *Canadian Journal of Counseling, 24,* 165–177.

Ries, R., & Consensus Panel Chair. (1994). *Assessment and treatment of patients with coexisting mental and alcohol and other drug abuse* (Treatment Improvement Protocol Series No. 9). U.S. Department of Health and Human Services, Center for Substance Abuse Treatment, Publication No. [SMA] 94-2078.

Rivera, F. G., & Erlich, J. L. (1998a). A time of fear; a time of hope. In F. G. Rivera & J. L. Erlich (Eds.), *Community organizing in a diverse society* (3rd ed., pp. 1–24). Needham Heights, MA: Allyn & Bacon.

Rivera, F. G., & Erlich, J. L. (Eds.). (1998b). *Community organizing in a diverse society* (3rd ed.). Needham Heights, MA: Allyn & Bacon.

Robertson, N. (1988). *Getting better: Inside Alcoholics Anonymous.* New York: William Morrow and Company.

Robins, L. N., Davis, D. H., & Goodwin, D. W. (1974). Drug use by U.S. army enlisted men in Vietnam: A follow-up on their return home. *American Journal of Epidemiology, 99,* 235–249.

Robins, L. N., Helzer, J. E., Hesselbrock, M., & Wish, E. (1975). Narcotic use in Southeast Asia and afterward. *Archives of General Psychiatry, 32,* 955–961.

Robins, L. N., Helzer, J. E., Hesselbrock, M., & Wish, E. (1980). Vietnam veterans three years after Vietnam: How our study changed our view of heroin. In L. Brill & C. Winick (Eds.), *The yearbook of substance use and abuse* (Vol. 2). New York: Human Sciences Press.

Rogan, A. (1986). Recovery from alcoholism: Issues for black and Native-American alcoholics. *Alcohol Health and Research World, 2,* 42–44.

Rogers, C. (1957). The necessary and sufficient conditions of therapeutic personality change. *Journal of Consulting Psychology, 21,* 99–103.

Rojek, C. (1986). The "subject" in social work. *British Journal of Social Work, 16* (1), 65–77.

Rothe, E. M., & Ruiz, P. (2001). Substance abuse among Cuban Americans. In S. L. A. Straussner (Ed.), *Ethnocultural factors in substance abuse treatment* (pp. 97–110). New York: Guilford Press.

Rothman, J. (1995a). Approaches to community intervention. In J. Rothman, J. L. Erlich, & J. E. Tropman (Eds.), *Strategies of community intervention* (5th ed.). Itasca, IL: F. E. Peacock.

Rothman, J. (1995b). Introduction. In J. Rothman, J. L. Erlich, & J. E. Tropman (Eds.), *Strategies of community intervention* (5th ed.). Itasca, IL: F. E. Peacock.

Rothman, J., & Sager, J. S. (1998). *Case management: Integrating individual and community practice* (2nd ed.). Boston: Allyn & Bacon.

Rounsaville, B. J., & Carroll, K. M. (1997). Individual psychotherapy. In

J. H. Lowinson, P. Ruiz, R. B. Millman, & J. G. Langrod (Eds.), *Substance abuse: A comprehensive textbook* (3rd ed., pp. 430–439). Baltimore: Williams & Wilkins.

Roy, A. (1993). Risk factors for suicide among adult alcoholics. *Alcohol Health & Research World, 17,* 133–136.

Royce, J. (1989). *Alcohol problems and alcoholism.* New York: Free Press.

Ryan, N., Puig-Antich, J., Ambrosini, P., Rabinovich, H., Robinson, D., Nelson, B., Ivenger, S., & Twomey, J. (1987). The clinical picture of major depression in children and adolescents. *Archives of General Psychiatry, 44* (11), 854–861.

Rychtarik, R. G., Foy, D. W., Scott, T., Lokey, L., & Prue, D. M. (1987). Five-six year follow-up broad spectrum behavioral treatment for alcoholism: Effects of training controlled drinking skills. *Journal of Consulting and Clinical Psychology, 55,* 106–108.

Saari, C. (1991). *The creation of meaning in clinical social work.* New York: Guilford Press.

Saleebey, D. (Ed.) (1997). *The strengths perspective in social work practice* (2nd ed.). New York: Longman.

SAMHSA. (1998). *National Household Survey on Drug Abuse.* DHHS Pub. No. SMA 98-3200. Rockville, MD: Substance Abuse and Mental Health Services Administration [online]. Available: http://www.samhsa.gov

Sanchez, E. G., & Mohl, P. C. (1992). Psychotherapy with Mexican-American patients. *American Journal of Psychiatry, 149,* 626–630.

Sanchez-Craig, M., & Lei, H. (1986). Disadvantages of imposing the goal of abstinence on problem drinkers: An empirical study. *British Journal of Addiction, 81,* 505–512.

Sandmaier, M. (1992). *The invisible alcoholics: Women and alcohol.* Blue Ridge Summit, PA: TAB Books.

Satel, S. L., Kosten, T. R., Schuckit, M. A., & Fischman, M. W. (1993). Should protracted withdrawal from drugs be included in the DSM-IV? *American Journal of Psychiatry, 150,* 695–704.

Satir, V. M. (1964). *Conjoint family therapy: A guide to theory and technique.* Palo Alto, CA: Science and Behavioral Books.

Satir, V. M. (1972). *People making.* Palo Alto, CA: Science and Behavioral Books.

Saunders, J. B., Aasland, O. G., Babor, T. F., de la Fuente, J. R., & Grant, M. (1993). Development of the Alcohol Use Disorders Identification Test (AUDIT): WHO collaborative project on early detection of persons with harmful alcohol consumption. II. *Addiction, 88,* 791–804.

Savage, S. R. (1993). Opium: The gift and its shadow. *Addiction & Recovery, 13* (1), 38–39.

Sayette, M. A. (1999). Cognitive theory and research. In K. E. Leonard & H. T. Blane (Eds.), *Psychological theories of drinking and alcoholism* (2nd ed., pp. 247–291). New York: Guilford Press.

Schamess, G. (1996). Who profits and who benefits from managed mental health care? *Smith College Studies in Social Work, 60,* 209–220.

Schonfeld, L., & Dupree, L. W. (1995). Treatment approaches for older problem drinkers. *International Journal of the Addictions, 30,* 1819–1842.

Schuckit, M. A. (1986). Primary male alcoholics with histories of suicide attempts. *Journal of Studies on Alcohol, 47,* 78–81.

Schuckit, M. A. (1995). *Drug and alcohol abuse: A clinical guide to diagnosis and treatment* (4th ed.). New York: Plenum Press.

Schuckit, M. A., Klein, J., Twitchell, G., & Smith, T. (1994). Personality test scores as predictors of alcoholism almost a decade later. *American Journal of Psychiatry, 151,* 1038–1042.

Schuckit, M. A., Smith, T. L., Anthenelli, R., & Irwin, M. (1993). Clinical course of alcoholism in 636 male inpatients. *American Journal of Psychiatry, 150,* 786–792.

Schwartz, R. H. (1987). Marijuana: An overview. *The Pediatric Clinics of North America, 34,* 305–317.

Segal, R., & Sisson, B. V. (1985). Medical complications associated with alcohol use and the assessment of risk of physical damage. In T. E. Bratter & G. G. Forrest (Eds.), *Alcoholism and substance abuse: Strategies for clinical intervention*. New York: Free Press.

Selzer, M. L. (1971). The Michigan alcohol screening test: The quest for a new diagnostic instrument. *American Journal of Psychiatry, 27,* 1653–1658.

Selvini, M. P., Boscolo, L., Cecchin, G., & Prata, G. (1980). Hypothesizing—circularity—neutrality: Three guidelines for the conductor of the session. *Family Process, 19* (1), 3–12.

Sernau, S. (2001). *Worlds apart: Social inequalities in a new century*. Thousand Oaks, CA: Pine Forge Press.

Sexias, F. (1975). Alcohol and its drug interactions. *Annals of Internal Medicine, 83,* 86–92.

Shader, R. I. (1994). A perspective on contemporary psychiatry. In *Manual of psychiatric therapeutics* (2nd ed.). Boston: Little, Brown.

Shea, S. C. (1998). *Psychiatric interviewing: The art of understanding* (2nd ed.). Philadelphia: W. B. Saunders.

Shea, S. C. (1999). *The practical art of suicide assessment: A guide for mental health and substance abuse counselors*. New York: Wiley.

Sheafor, B. W., Horejsi, C. R., & Horejsi, G. A. (2000). *Techniques and guidelines for social work practice* (5th ed.). Boston: Allyn & Bacon.

Sher, K. J. (1991). *Children of alcoholics: The critical appraisal of theory and research*. Chicago: University of Chicago Press.

Sher, K. J. (1997). Psychological characteristics of children of alcoholics. *Alcohol Health and Research World, 21,* 247–254.

Sherer, R. A. (1998). Annual and lifetime limits to mental health care thwart intent of parity act. *Mental Health Economics, 2* (4) [online]. Available: http://www.mentalhealth.org/cmhs/ManagedCare/Parity/bibliography.htm

Shoptaw, S., Frosch, D., Rawson, R. A., & Ling, W. (1997). Cocaine abuse counseling as HIV prevention. *AIDS Education and Prevention, 9* (6), 511–520.

Shorkey, C. T., & Rosen, W. (1993). Alcohol addiction and codependency. In E. M. Freeman (Ed.), *Substance abuse treatment: A family systems perspective* (pp. 100–122). Newbury Park, CA: Sage.

Shulman, L. (1999). *The skills of helping individuals, families, groups, and communities* (4th ed.). Itasca, IL: F. E. Peacock.

Siegel, B. S. (1989). *Peace, love, and healing*. New York: Harper & Row.

Sigvardsson, S., Gohman, M., & Cloninger, R. (1996). Replication of the Stockholm adoption study. *Archives of General Psychiatry, 53,* 681–687.

Sing, M., Hill, S., Smolkin, S., & Heiser, N. (1998). *Substance abuse insurance benefits*. Center for Mental Health Services, Office of Managed Care. DHHS Pub. No. SMA 98-3205. Rockville, MD: U.S. Government Printing Office.

Singer, M. T., & Wynne, L. C. (1965). Thought disorder and family relations of schizophrenics. IV: Results and implications. *Archives of General Psychiatry, 12,* 201–212.

Siporin, M. (1975). *Introduction to social work practice*. New York: Macmillan.

Siporin, M. (1980). Ecological systems theory in social work. *Journal of Sociology and Social Welfare, 7,* 507–532.

Sisney, E. K. (1991). The relationship between social support and depression in recovering chemically dependent nurses. *Image, 25,* 107–112.

Skinner, H. A. (1982). The Drug Abuse Screening Test. *Addictive Behaviors, 7,* 363–371.

Sklar, H. (1995). *Chaos or community? Seeking solutions, not scapegoats for bad economics*. Boston: South End Press.

Skog, O. J., & Duckert, F. (1993). The development of alcoholics' and heavy drinkers' consumption: A longitudinal study. *Journal of Studies on Alcohol, 54,* 178–188.

Smart, R., & Mora, M. E. (1986). Alcohol-control policies in Latin America and other countries. In T. Babor (Ed.), *Alcohol and culture: Comparative perspectives from Europe and America* (pp. 211–218). New York: New York Academy of Sciences.

Smelser, N. J. (1992). Culture: Coherent or incoherent. In R. Munch & N. J. Smelser (Eds.), *Theory of culture*. Berkeley, CA: University of California Press.

Smith, D. E. (1990). *The conceptual practices of power: A feminist sociology of knowledge*. Boston: Northeastern University Press.

Smith, D. E., Wesson, D. R., & Tusel, D. J. (1989). *Treating opiate dependency*. Center City, MN: Hazelden.

Smith, S. G. T., Touquet, R., Wright, S., & Das Gupta, N. (1996). Detection of alcohol misusing patients in accident and emergency departments: The Paddington alcohol test (PAT). *Journal of Accident & Emergency Medicine, 13,* 308–312.

Sobell, L. C., Sobell, M. B., & Ward, E. (Eds.). (1980). *Evaluating alcohol and drug abuse treatment effectiveness*. Elmsford, NY: Pergamon Press.

Sobell, M. B., & Sobell, L. C. (1973). Alcoholics treated by individualized behavior therapy: One-year treatment outcome. *Behavior Research Therapy, 11,* 599–618.

Sobell, M. B., Sobell, L. C., Bogardis, J., Leo, G. I., & Skinner, W. (1992). Problem drinkers' perceptions of whether treatment goals should be self-selected or therapist selected. *Behavior Therapy, 23,* 43–52.

Soderstrom, C. A., Trifillis, A. L., Shankar, B. S., & Clark, W. E. (1988). Marijuana and alcohol use among 1023 trauma patients: A prospective study. *Archives of Surgery, 123,* 733–737.

Speer, D. C. (1979). Family systems: Morphostasis and morphogenesis, or is homeostasis enough? *Family Process, 9,* 259–278.

Stanton, M. D. (1997). The role of family and significant others in the engagement and retention of drug-dependent individuals. In L. S. Onken, J. D. Blaine, & F. J. Boren (Eds.), *Beyond the therapeutic alliance: Keeping the drug-dependent individual in treatment* (pp. 157–180). Rockville, MD: National Institute on Drug Abuse.

Stanton, M. D., Todd, T., & Associates. (1982). *The family therapy of drug abuse and addiction*. New York: Guilford Press.

Steinglass, P. (1980). A life history model of the alcoholic family. *Family Process, 19,* 211–226.

Steinglass, P., Bennett, L. A., Wolin, S. J., & Reiss, D. (1987). *The alcoholic family*. New York: Basic Books.

Stinchfield, R., Owen, P. L., & Winters, K. C. (1994). Group therapy for substance abuse: A review of the empirical evidence. In A. Fuhriman & G. M. Burlinggame (Eds.), *Handbook of group psychotherapy: An empirical and clinical synthesis* (pp. 458–488). New York: Wiley.

Storgaard, H., Nielsen, S. D., & Gluud, C. (1994). The validity of the Michigan Alcoholism Screening Test (MAST). *Alcohol and Alcoholism, 29,* 493–502.

Strom, K. (1992). Reimbursement demands and treatment decisions: A growing dilemma for social workers. *Social Work, 37* (5), 398–403.

Stuart, R. B. (1980). *Helping couples change: A social learning approach to marital therapy*. New York: Guilford Press.

Sturm, R. (1997). How expensive is unlimited mental health care coverage under managed care? *Journal of the American Medical Association, 278,* 1553–1557.

Sturm, R., Zhang, W., & Schoenbaum, M. (1999). How expensive are unlimited substance abuse benefits under managed care? *Journal of Behavioral Health Services, 26* (2), 203–210.

Substance Abuse and Mental Health Services Administration (SAMHSA). (1993). *1991–1993 National Household Survey on Drug Abuse*. Washington, DC: U.S. Government Printing Office.

Swan, G. E., Carmelli, D., & Cardon, L. R. (1997). Heavy consumption of cigarettes, alcohol, and coffee in male twins. *Journal of Studies on Alcohol, 58,* 182–190.

Szasz, T. C. (1972). Bad habits are not diseases: A refutation of the claim that alcoholism is a disease. *Lancet, 319,* 83–84.

Szasz, T. C. (1974). *The myth of mental illness: Foundations of a theory of personal conflict.* New York: Harper & Row.

Szasz, T. C. (1988). A plea for the cessation of the longest war in the twentieth century—the war on drugs. *Humanistic Psychologist, 162* (2), 314–322.

Szasz, T. C. (1991). Diagnoses are not diseases. *Lancet, 338,* 1574–1576.

Szasz, T. C. (1994). *Cruel compassion: Psychiatric control of society's unwanted.* New York: Wiley.

Szasz, T. C. (1996). The war on drugs is lost. *National Review, XLVIII* (2), 45–47.

Szasz, T. C. (1997). Save money, cut crime, get real. *Playboy, 44* (1), 129, 190.

Tatarsky, A. (1998). An integrated approach to harm reduction psychotherapy: A case of problem drinking secondary to depression. *In Session: Psychotherapy in Practice, 4,* 9–24.

Teichart, N. W. (1996). Booze, drugs spell trouble for kids. In H. Wilson (Ed.), *Drugs, society, and behavior* (14th ed., pp. 155–157). Guilford, CT: Dushkin/McGraw-Hill.

Therapeutic community research yields interesting results. (1989). *The Addiction Letter, 5* (1), 2.

Tomm, K. (1987). Interventive interviewing. Part II: Reflexive questioning as a means to enable self-healing. *Family Process, 26,* 167–183.

Toneatto, T., Sobell, L. C., Sobell, M. B., & Leo, G. I. (1991). Psychoactive substance use disorder (alcohol). In M. Hersen & S. M. Turner (Eds.), *Adult psychotherapy and diagnosis* (2nd ed.). New York: Wiley.

Torrey, E. (1986). *Witch doctors and psychiatrists.* New York: Harper & Row.

Tracey, E. M., & Whittaker, J. K. (1990). The social network map: Assessing social support in clinical practice. *Families in Society, 71,* 461–470.

Treadway, D. (1989). *Before it's too late: Working with substance abuse in the family.* New York: Norton.

Treadway, D. (1990). Codependency: Disease, metaphor, or fad? *Family Therapy Networker, 14* (1), 39–43.

Treatment Research Institute. (1990). The Addiction Severity Index manual and question by question guide [online]. Available: http://www.tresearch.org

Turbo, R. (1989). Drying out is just a start: Alcoholism. *Medical World News, 30* (3), 56–63.

Twerski, A. J. (1983). Early intervention in alcoholism: Confrontational techniques. *Hospital and Community Psychiatry, 34,* 1027–1030.

Uhl, G. R., Persico, A. M., & Smith, S. S. (1992). Current excitement with D_2 dopamine receptor gene alleles in substance abuse. *Archives of General Psychiatry, 49,* 157–160.

U.S. Bureau of the Census. (1993). *We the . . . First Americans.* Washington, DC: U.S. Government Printing Office.

U.S. Bureau of the Census. (1995). *Statistical abstract of the United States: 1995* (115th ed.). Washington, DC: U.S. Government Printing Office.

U.S. General Accounting Office. (1990). *Drug exposed infants: A generation at risk.* Washington, DC: U.S. General Accounting Office.

U.S. Sentencing Commission. (1997). *Special report to the Congress: Mandatory minimum penalties in the federal criminal justice system.* Washington, DC: U.S. Government Printing Office.

Vaillant, G. E. (1983). *The natural history of alcoholism: Causes, patterns, and paths to recovery.* Cambridge, MA: Harvard University Press.

Vaillant, G. E. (1990). We should retain the disease concept of alcoholism. *Harvard Medical School Mental Health Letter, 9* (6), 4–6.

Valle, S. K. (1981). Interpersonal functioning of alcoholism counselors and treatment outcome. *Journal of Studies on Alcohol, 42,* 783–790.

Van Den Bergh, N. (1991). Having bitten the apple: A feminist perspective on addictions. In N. Van Den Bergh (Ed.),

Feminist perspective on addictions. New York: Springer.

Van Maanen, J. (1995). *Representation in ethnography.* Thousand Oaks, CA: Sage.

van Wormer, K. (1987). Training social work students for practice with substance abusers: An ecological approach. *Journal of Social Work Education, 23* (2), 47–56.

van Wormer, K. (1995). *Alcoholism treatment: A social work perspective.* Chicago: Nelson-Hall.

van Wormer, K., Wells, J., & Boes, M. (2000). *Social work with lesbians, gays, and bisexuals: A strengths perspective.* Boston: Allyn & Bacon.

von Bertalanffy, L. (1971). *General systems theory: Foundations, development, application.* London: Allen Lane.

Wachtel, E. F., & Wachtel, P. L. (1986). *Family dynamics in individual psychotherapy.* New York: Guilford Press.

Walborn, F. S. (1996). *Process variables: Four common elements of counseling and psychotherapy.* Pacific Grove, CA: Brooks/Cole.

Walker, S. (1998). *Sense and nonsense about crime and drugs: A policy guide* (4th ed.). Belmont, CA: Wadsworth.

Walker, S. (2001). *Sense and nonsense about crime and drugs: A policy guide* (5th ed.). Belmont, CA: Wadsworth.

Wallace, J. (1989). A biopsychosocial model of alcoholism. *Social Casework, 70* (6), 325–332.

Wallace, J. (1996). Theory of 12-step oriented treatment. In F. Rotgers, D. S. Keller, & J. Morgenstern (Eds.), *Treating substance abuse.* New York: Guilford Press.

Walsh, F. (1996). The concept of family resilience: Crisis and challenge. *Family Process, 35,* 261–281.

Warren, R. (1972). *The community in America* (2nd ed.). Chicago: Rand McNally.

Washton, A. M. (1988). Preventing relapse to cocaine. *Journal of Clinical Psychiatry, 49* (suppl.), 34–38.

Watson, C. G., Hancock, M., Gearhart, L. P., Mendez, C. M., Maloyrth, P., & Raden, M. (1997). A comparative outcome study of frequent, moderate, occasional, and nonattenders of Alcoholics Anonymous. *Journal of Clinical Psychology, 53,* 209–214.

Weaver, H. N. (1999). Indigenous people in a multicultural society: Unique issues for human services. In P. Ewalt, E. M. Freeman, A. E. Fortune, D. L. Poole, & S. L. Witkin (Eds.), *Multicultural issues in social work: Practice and research* (pp. 85–95). Washington, DC: NASW Press.

Weaver, H. N. (2001). Native Americans and substance abuse. In S. L. A. Straussner (Ed.), *Ethnocultural factors in substance abuse treatment* (pp. 77–96). New York: Guilford Press.

Wegscheider, S. (1981). *Another chance: Hope and health for the alcoholic family.* Palo Alto, CA: Science and Behavioral Books.

Wegscheider-Cruse, S. (1985). *Choicemaking for co-dependents, adult children and spirituality seekers.* Palo Alto, CA: Public Health Communications.

Weisner, C., & Schmidt, L. (1992). Gender disparities in treatment for alcohol problems. *Journal of the American Medical Association, 268,* 1872–1876.

West, C. (1999). Black strivings in a twilight civilization. In C. West (Ed.), *The Cornel West Reader* (pp. 87–118). New York: Basic Books.

Westermeyer, J. (1992). Cultural perspectives: Native Americans, Asians, and new immigrants. In J. H. Lowinson, P. Ruiz, & R. B. Millman (Eds.), & J. G. Langrod (Assoc. Ed.), *Substance abuse: A comprehensive textbook* (2nd ed., pp. 890–896). Baltimore: Williams & Wilkins.

Westermeyer, J. (1996). Alcoholism among new world peoples: A critique of history, methods, and findings. *American Journal of Addictions, 5* (2), 110–123.

Whitaker, C. A. (1989). *Midnight musings of a family therapist.* New York: Norton, 1989.

Whitaker, C. A., & Keith, D. V. (1981). Symbolic-experiential family therapy. In A. S. Gurman & D. P. Kniskern (Eds.), *Handbook of family therapy* (Vol. 1, pp. 187–225). New York: Brunner/Mazel.

White, H. R., Bates, M., & Johnson, V. (1990). Social reinforcement and alcohol consumption. In M. Cox (Ed.), *Why people drink* (pp. 233–261). New York: Gardner Press.

Whitehead, R. L., Patterson, J., & Kaljee, L. (1994). The "hustle": Socioeconomic deprivation, urban trafficking, and low-income: African-American male gender identity. *Pediatrics, 93,* 1050–1054.

Whitfield, C. (1984). Co-alcoholism: Recognizing a treatable disease. *Family and Community Health, 7,* 16–25.

Whitfield, S. J. (1991). *The culture of the Cold War.* Baltimore: Johns Hopkins University Press.

Wilkinson, D. A., & LeBreton, S. (1986). Early indications of treatment outcome in multiple drug users. In W. R. Miller & N. Heather (Eds.), *Treating addictive behaviors: Processes of change* (pp. 239–261). New York: Plenum Press.

Williams, P. J. (1990). Chapter One. In M. R. Malson (Ed.), *Black women in America.* Chicago: University of Chicago Press.

Willis, P. (1978). *Profane culture.* London: Routledge & Kegan Paul.

Willoughby, A. (1984). *The alcohol troubled person: Known and unknown.* Chicago: Nelson-Hall.

Wilson, A. M. (1992). *Awakening the natural genius of black children.* New York: Afrikan World Info-systems.

Wilson, G. T. (1981). The effect of alcohol on human sexual behavior. In N. K. Mello (Ed.), *Advances in substance abuse* (Vol. 2). Greenwich, CT: JAI Press.

Wilson, S. N. (1990). *Black on black violence.* New York: Afrikan World Information Systems.

Wilson, W. J. (1987). *The truly disadvantaged: The inner city, the underclass, and public policy.* Chicago: University of Chicago Press.

Wing, D. M. (1995). Transcending alcoholic denial. *Image, 27,* 121–126.

Winslade, J., Crocket, K., & Monk, G. (1997). The therapeutic relationship. In G. Monk, J. Winslade, K. Crocket, & D. Epston (Eds.), *Narrative therapy in practice: The archaeology of hope* (pp. 53–81). San Francisco: Jossey-Bass.

Winslade, J., & Smith, L. (1997). Countering alcoholic narratives. In G. Monk, J. Winslade, K. Crocket, & D. Epston (Eds.), *Narrative therapy in practice: The archaeology of hope* (pp. 158–192). San Francisco: Jossey-Bass.

Winter, G. (1966). *Elements for a social ethic: The role of social science in public policy.* New York: Macmillan.

Woititz, J. (1983). *Adult children of alcoholics.* Deerfield Beach, FL: Health Communications.

Wolf-Reeve, B. S. (1990). A guide to the assessment of psychiatric symptoms in the addictions treatment setting. In D. F. O'Connell (Ed.), *Managing the dually diagnosed patient.* New York: Haworth Press.

Wright, E. M. (2001). Substance abuse in African American communities. In S. L. A. Straussner (Ed.), *Ethnocultural factors in substance abuse treatment* (pp. 31–51). New York: Guilford Press.

Yablonsky, L. (1967). *Synanon: The tunnel back.* Baltimore: Penguin.

Yablonsky, L. (1989). *The therapeutic community: A successful approach for treating substance abusers.* New York: Gardner Press.

Yalom, I. (1995). *The theory and practice of group psychotherapy* (4th ed.). New York: Basic Books.

Young, T. (1991). Native American drinking: A neglected subject of study and research. *Journal of Drug Education, 21,* 65–72.

Young, T. (1994). Environmental modification in clinical social work: A self-psychological perspective. *Social Science Review, 68,* 202–218.

Youngstrom, N. (1990). Debate rages on: In- or outpatient? *APA Monitor, 21* (10), 19.

Zimmer, L., & Morgan, J. P. (1997). *Marijuana myths, marijuana facts.* New York: Lindesmith Center.

Zinberg, N. E. (1972). Heroin use in Vietnam and the United States. *Archives of General Psychiatry, 26,* 550–557.

Zinberg, N. E. (1974). The search for rational approaches to heroin use. In P. G. Bourne (Ed.), *Addiction*. New York: Academic Press.

Zinberg, N. E. (1984). *Drug, set, and setting: The basis for controlled intoxicant use*. New York: Yale University Press.

Zuckerman, E. L. (2000). *Clinician's thesaurus: A guidebook for writing psychological reports* (5th ed.). New York: Guilford.

Zung, W. (1965). A self-rating depression scale. *Archives of General Psychiatry, 12,* 63–70.

Zweben, J. E. (1995). Integrating psychotherapy and 12-step approaches. In A. M. Washton (Ed.), *Psychotherapy and substance abuse*. New York: Guilford Press.

Index

AA. *See* Alcoholics Anonymous
Abandonment, fear of, 150
Abstinence
   controlled use vs., 296–297
   information from clients about, 208
   recovery process and, 286–287
Abuse
   definition of, 9–10
   dependency vs., 11–13
   emotional, 150
   misuse vs., 8
   physical, 151, 214
   sexual, 150, 214, 215, 220
   See also Substance abuse
Accidents, substance-related, 15
Action stage of change, 120–121
Adaptive roles, 137–138
Addiction
   definition of, 10
   disease model of, 5–6, 76–83
   genetic link to, 68–71, 128–129
   models of, 56–91
   traditional concept of, 10–11
   See also Chemical dependency
Addiction Severity Index (ASI), 187–188
Addictive personality, 70
Administering drugs. *See* Drug administration methods
Adolescents, 320–324
   educational programs for, 247–248
   gender-biased treatment of, 19
   intensive outpatient treatment for, 266
   parental substance abuse and, 150–151
   substance abuse among, 20–21, 320–322
   suicide rates for, 193
   treatment issues for, 322–324
Adult Children of Alcoholics (ACOA), 76, 132, 303
Adverse life events, 195
Advertising, 80, 311
African Americans, 310–313
   chemical dependency among, 22
   drug laws and, 172, 174
   substance abuse among, 21, 311–312, 349–356

treatment issues for, 312–313
twelve-step programs and, 263
women's issues for, 349–356
Aftercare, 292
Age
   first use assessment and, 206
   substance abuse issues and, 20–21
   treatment specific to, 325
AIDS, 49, 191, 210
Al-Anon, 131, 257, 303
Alateen, 303
Alcohol, 37
   intended use criterion and, 8
   mixing drugs and, 32–33
Alcoholics Anonymous (AA), 256–263
   core elements of, 258
   disease model and, 80, 82, 131
   effectiveness of, 262–263
   family members and, 131, 132
   moral model and, 63
   professional helpers and, 179
   spirituality and, 88, 260–261
   sponsorship in, 261–262
   twelve steps of, 258–260
   visiting meetings of, 78–79
   See also Twelve-step support groups
Alcohol industry, 80
Alcoholism
   diagnosis of, 238
   disease model of, 77
   drug abuse vs., 58
   genetic link to, 68–69, 128–129
   screening test for, 184–186
   suicide risk and, 195
Alcohol use
   accidents/deaths related to, 15
   anti-drug legislation and, 173
   family history of, 209
   gender issues and, 18–19
   Latinos and, 314, 315
   major effects of, 38–39
   Native Americans and, 316
   pregnancy and, 20
   trends in, 14–15
   withdrawal symptoms from, 39–40
   See also Substance abuse
Alcohol Use Disorders Identification Test (AUDIT), 189
Alcohol Use Profile, 189

Alzheimer's Disease, 24
Ambulatory detox, 269
American Medical Association (AMA), 76
American Psychiatric Association (APA), 217, 233
American Society of Addiction Medicine (ASAM), 275
Amotivational syndrome, 46
Amphetamines, 41, 42
Anti-anxiety medications, 37
Anti-Drug Abuse Act
   of 1986, 171–173
   of 1988, 173–174
Anxiety disorders, 215–216
ASI (Addiction Severity Index), 187–188
Assessment, 181–183, 200–244
   basic needs, 211–212, 339
   case history report and, 240–243, 331–348
   community, 222–232, 342–344
   cultural, 224–226, 342–343
   definition of, 182–183
   diagnosis and, 196–197, 233–240, 344–345
   dimensions of, 200–201
   family, 147–151, 218–222
   importance of, 181–182
   interpersonal relationship, 229–230, 343
   legal history, 230–232, 343–344
   macro context, 222–232
   medical history, 210–211
   motivation, 118–122, 232, 344
   multiaxial, 236–240
   narrative, 345–347
   operating principles of, 198–199
   presenting problem and, 201–202
   psychological/emotional, 212–218
   referral context and, 202
   screening vs., 183–184
   social class, 226–229, 343
   steps in process of, 201–240
   substance abuse history, 205–210
   suicide risk, 195
   summary of, 199, 243–244
   treatment history, 204–205
   See also Screening
Associations, community, 164–165

At-risk populations. *See* Populations at risk
Attack therapy, 122
Attention deficit hyperactivity disorder (ADHD), 41
AUDIT (Alcohol Use Disorders Identification Test), 189
Awareness assignments, 272–273
Axes of *DSM* diagnostics, 236, 237, 239

Bad habits, 74, 79
Bad reputation, 223
Bad trips, 52
Baldwin, James, 351
Bandura, Albert, 71
Barbiturates, 37–38
Basic needs assessment, 211–212, 339
Bauman, Zygmunt, 103
Beck Depression Inventory (BDI), 192
Behavioral health care, 175
Behavioral tolerance, 36
Beliefs
     community, 163–164
     core, 75
     understanding your own, 57–58
Benzodiazepines, 38
Biological factors
     genetic link to addiction and, 68–70, 128–129
     multi-systemic approach and, 86–87
Biological model, 68–71
Biopsychosocial model, 85
Bisexuals, 317–320
     substance abuse among, 317–320
     treatment issues for, 318–320
Blood alcohol levels (BAL), 31, 173
Bluest Eye, The (Morrison), 355
Boundaries, family, 134–135
Bowen, Murray, 221
Brain chemistry, 69–70
Bridging theories, 303

Caffeine, 41–42
CAGE test, 186–187
Cane River (Tademy), 355
Cannabis, 44–47
     drugs in category of, 45
     major effects of, 45–46
     overdose symptoms of, 46–47
     routes of administration for, 45
     tolerance to, 47
     withdrawal symptoms from, 47
Case history report, 236, 240–243
     completed sample of, 336–348
     crisis of representation and, 241–242
     format for writing, 331–348
     showing to clients, 243
Categories of drugs. *See* Drug categories
Cenaps Model of relapse prevention, 306–307
Census Bureau, 193, 316
Center for Substance Abuse Prevention (CSAP), 173
Center for Substance Abuse Treatment (CSAT), 173, 324

Centers for Disease Control and Prevention, 15
Central nervous system (CNS), 70
     depressant drugs, 37–40
     stimulant drugs, 44–47
Challenges of substance abuse practice, 1–4
     personal challenges, 3–4
     professional challenges, 2–3
Change
     dilemma of, 124–125
     family stability and, 136–137
     stages of, 118–122
Chemical dependency
     abstinence and, 286–287, 291
     abuse distinguished from, 11–13
     age as factor in, 20–21
     definition of, 10, 11
     diagnosis of, 233–240
     disease model of, 5–6, 76–83
     experience of, 26–27
     family systems and, 139–145
     genetic link to, 68–71, 128–129
     illness of, 290–291
     models of, 56–91
     recovery from, 284–290
     social class and, 22–23
     See also Addiction
Chemical inhalants. *See* Inhalants
Chemically dependent families, 139–145
     characteristics of, 139–141
     family survival roles in, 141–145
Chemically dependent person role, 141–142
Chief enabler role, 142
Child abuse, 150, 214, 215, 220
Child Protective Services (CPS), 60–61, 174, 223
Children
     educational programs for, 247–248
     parental substance abuse and, 150–151
     See also Adolescents
Children of alcoholics (COA), 220
Chippers, 50
Chronic phase of alcoholism, 77
Circular questioning, 219
CISA-AR test, 189
Civil rights movement, 311
Classifying drugs. *See* Drug categories
Class issues. *See* Social class
Class knowledge, 3
Class shame, 149
Client behaviors
     alternative explanations for, 126
     compliance vs. engagement and, 125–126
     evasive clients and, 124
     intoxicated clients and, 202–204
     resistant clients and, 249–250
Client engagement, 92–127
     art of, 93–94
     assessment and, 198
     client motivation and, 118–122
     communication skills and, 94–105
     compliance and, 125–126

confrontation and, 122–123
cultural competence and, 105–106
definition of, 93
denial and, 115–117
dialogue and, 95–97
dilemma of change and, 124–125
empathy and, 114–115
evasive behavior and, 124
GLBT clients and, 318–319
hopefulness and, 108–109
humility and, 109–112
important characteristics for, 106–115
individual therapy and, 299–300
self-exploration and, 103–105
special issues in, 115–126
stages of change and, 118–122
summary of, 126–127
treatment process and, 291
trust and, 112–114
worldview respect and, 107–108
Clinical Institute Withdrawal Assessment for Alcohol Scale-Revised (CISA-AR), 189
Clinical specialization, 58–60
CNS depressants, 37–40
     major effects of, 38–39
     overdose symptoms of, 39
     routes of administration for, 38
     tolerance to, 39
     types of, 37–38
     withdrawal symptoms of, 39–40
CNS stimulants, 40–44
     major effects of, 42
     overdose symptoms of, 43
     routes of administration for, 42
     tolerance to, 44
     types of, 40–42
     withdrawal symptoms of, 44
Cocaine, 40–41
     attractiveness of, 43
     case example of withdrawal symptoms, 11
     drug abuse laws and, 171–173
     scary myths about, 16
Codependency, 76, 87, 148–149, 220
Coercion, 255
Cognitive-behavioral model, 74–75, 87–88, 300, 315, 329
Cognitive processes, 72
Cognitive-Social Learning Model of relapse prevention, 307–308
Communication skills, 94–105
     dialogue and, 95–97
     self-exploration and, 103–105
     semiotic of communication and, 97–102
     tourism metaphor and, 102–103
     See also Client engagement
Community, 153–165
     assessment of, 222–232, 342–344
     belief systems of, 163–164
     definitions of, 66, 155
     geographic, 163
     local, 161–162, 223–224
     power of, 153–154
     resources available in, 164–165
     self and, 160–161

symbolic interactionism and, 155–161
therapeutic, 271–273
treatment process and, 304–305
values of, 164
See also Macro influences
Community mental health centers, 2–3
Community model, 65–68, 89
Community practice, 26, 304–305
Compliance, 125
Comprehensive Drinking Profile, 189
Comprehensive Drug Abuse Prevention and Control Act (1970), 169–171
Confidentiality, 278–279
Confrontation
dealing with denial through, 122–123, 253
intervention process and, 253
recovery process and, 287–288
Conspiracy ideology, 311–312
Contemplation stage of change, 119–120
Controlled Substances Act (1970), 169–171
Controlled use, 296–297
Co-occurring disorders, 325–329
substance abuse and, 325–327
treatment issues for, 327–329
Cool down rooms, 52
Coping deficits model, 73
Core beliefs, 75
Cost-sharing issues, 176
Counseling
family, 302–304
group, 300–301
individual, 299–300
Crack cocaine, 40–41
drug abuse laws and, 171–173
media portrayal of, 174
Crisis of representation, 241–242
Cross-generational coalitions, 134
Cross-tolerance, 36
Crucial phase of alcoholism, 77
Cuban Americans, 313–315
Cultural competence, 105–106
Culture, 21
assessment of, 224–226, 342–343
communication and, 97–98
definition of, 225
functional families and, 136
tourism metaphor and, 102–103

Dangerous drugs, 171
Danquah, Meri, 351
DARE program, 248
"Date rape" drug, 38
Day treatment programs, 265–267
Deaths, substance-related, 15
Defense mechanisms, 87, 115, 116
Delirium tremens (DTs), 39
Delusions, 216
Denial, 115–117
confrontation and, 122–123, 253
definition of, 116
dilemma of change and, 124–125
intervention process and, 253
minimization as, 116–117

projection as, 117
rationalization as, 117
Dependency
abuse distinguished from, 11–13
physiological vs. psychological, 10–11
See also Chemical dependency
Depersonalization, 242
Depressants. *See* CNS depressants
Depression
hopelessness and, 109
screening clients for, 191–193, 214
substance abuse and, 17, 109
suicide and, 193, 195
Determination stage of change, 120
Detoxification programs, 269–270
Diagnosis, 233–240
assessment and, 196–197, 233–240, 344–345
codifying schemes for, 233
conservative approach to, 239–240
multiaxial assessment and, 236–240
process of, 234–236
Diagnostic and Statistical Manual of Mental Disorders (DSM), 233–240
based on disease model, 197
depression symptoms in, 192
multiaxial assessment using, 236–240
substance abuse criteria, 8, 9, 234–235
substance dependence criteria, 234–235
Dialogue, 95–97, 112
Differential reinforcement, 71–72
Dilemma of change, 124–125
Disease model, 5–6, 76–83
basic tenets of, 78
controversy about, 79
co-occurring disorders and, 329
dogma of, 83
evaluation of, 80
family therapy and, 303
gateway drugs and, 82
inevitable progression and, 81–82
loss of control and, 82–83
origins of, 77
powerlessness and, 80–81
public opinion about, 80
Domestication, 96
Domestic violence, 151, 214, 220
Dosage
drug variability and, 32
substance use assessment and, 206
Double consciousness, 311
Downers, 37
Driving while intoxicated (DWI), 9
DWI schools, 248–249
Drug Abuse Resistance Education (DARE), 248
Drug administration methods, 33–35
inhalation, 34
injection, 34
oral, 33–34
smoking, 34
snorting, 35
See also Routes of administration

Drug categories, 36–55
cannabis, 44–47
CNS depressants, 37–40
CNS stimulants, 40–44
hallucinogens, 50–53
inhalants, 53–55
opiates, 47–50
Drug Enforcement Administration (DEA), 168, 169
Drug-Free Schools and Communities Act (1989), 173
Drug laws, 167–174
Anti–Drug Abuse Acts, 171–174
Comprehensive Drug Abuse Prevention and Control Act, 169–171
Federal Sentencing Reform Act, 171
impact on substance abuse practice, 174
public opinion and, 167–169
Drug mixing
assessing patterns of, 208
variability and, 32–33
Drug schedules, 170
Drug tolerance, 10, 35–36
Drug use
accidents/deaths related to, 15
age factors and, 20–21, 206
alcohol use vs., 58
assessment of recent, 207
countering misinformation about, 29
family history of, 209
favorite substances and, 207–208
"intended use" criterion and, 8
pregnancy and, 20
trends in, 13–15
See also Substance abuse
Drug variability, 29–33
dosage and, 32
drug mixing and, 32–33
environmental/situational factors and, 31
individual factors and, 30–31
Dual recovery approach, 328
Dunlap, Constance, 352
DWI schools, 248–249
Dysfunctional families, 138, 139

Early intervention, 246–251
Eating disorders, 17
Eclecticism, 59–60
Ecological systems theory, 84–86
Ecomap, 162–163, 221
Economic class. *See* Social class
Ecstasy, 51, 52
Education, 246–251
DWI schools and, 248–249
effectiveness of, 251
prevention services and, 246–251
resistant clients and, 249–250
social class assessment and, 227–228
substance abuse factors and, 22
treatment services and, 250–251
See also Treatment
Education for Critical Consciousness (Freire), 96

Effects of drugs
  cannabis, 45–46
  CNS depressants, 38–39
  CNS stimulants, 42
  hallucinogens, 51–52
  inhalants, 54
  opiates, 48–49
Elderly. See Older adults
Emotional abuse, 150, 214
Emotional functioning assessment, 212–218, 339–341
Empathy, 114–115
Employment
  community conditions for, 161
  social class assessment and, 227
  substance abuse and, 22
Enabling behavior, 87, 142, 148
Engagement. See Client engagement
Enmeshed families, 134
Environmental factors
  drug variability and, 31
  multi-systemic approach and, 89–90
Epidemiologic Catchment Area Study, 17
Equal opportunity, 311
Ethics, NASW Code of, 64, 278, 320
Ethnicity, 21
Ethnography, 241
European Americans, 21
Evans, Mari, 356
Evasive behavior, 124

Families, 128–152
  adaptation to chemical dependency in, 137–138
  assessment of, 147–151, 218–222
  characteristics of chemically dependent, 139–141
  codependency in, 148–149
  definitions of, 130–131
  domestic violence in, 151
  emotional abuse in, 150
  functional, 135–136
  genetic link to addiction in, 68–70, 128–129
  life cycle of, 145–147
  multi-systemic approach and, 88
  need for understanding, 128–130
  parental substance abuse in, 150–151
  resilience of, 138–139
  sexual abuse in, 150
  shame in, 149–150
  stability and change in, 136–137
  substance abuse treatment and, 131–132
  summary of, 151–152
  survival roles in, 141–145
  systems view of, 132–135
  twelve-step programs and, 131, 132, 303
Family history, 88, 151, 209, 218–222, 341–342
Family life cycle, 145–147
  assessment of, 147
  summary chart of, 146
Family mascot role, 144–145

Family practice, 25
Family scapegoat role, 143–144
Family structure, 135, 341–342
Family survival roles, 141–145
  chemically dependent person, 141–142
  chief enabler, 142
  family mascot, 144–145
  family scapegoat, 143–144
  hero, 142–143
  lost child, 144
Family systems, 132–135
  boundaries and, 134–135
  definition of, 133
  structure and, 135
  subsystems and, 133–134
  survival roles in, 141–145
Family therapy, 302–304
  adolescents and, 322
  disease model of, 303
  gender issues in, 135–136
  systems theory in, 130–131, 132–135, 303–304
Favorite substances, 207–208
Fear of authority, 149
Federal Register, 278
Federal Sentencing Reform Act (1984), 171
Fetal alcohol syndrome (FAS), 18
Fields of practice, 23–26
  definition of, 24
  substance abuse issues and, 24–26
Fine, Michelle, 96
First-order change, 86
First use of drugs, 206
Flashbacks, 52
Following-up referrals, 282–283
Ford, Henry, 157
Freire, Paulo, 65, 95–97, 112, 126
Frequency of use, 206
Freud, Sigmund, 40
Functional families, 135–136
Funding treatment, 281

Gateway drugs, 82
Gay men, 317–320
  substance abuse among, 317–318
  suicide rates for, 193, 215–216
  treatment issues for, 318–320
  twelve-step sponsorship for, 262
Gender issues
  family therapy models and, 135–136
  mood disorders and, 214
  pharmacology and, 31
  substance abuse and, 18–20
  suicide risk and, 194
  treatment options and, 282
  twelve-step programs and, 263
Generalized anxiety disorder (GAD), 215
Genetics
  addiction linked to, 68–71, 86
  family alcoholism and, 128–129
Genograms, 221, 348
Geographic community, 163
Gerontology, 24
GLBT (gay, lesbian, bisexual, transgendered) persons, 317–320

substance abuse among, 317–318
  treatment issues for, 318–320
Global Assessment Function (GAF), 236
Goals
  relapse prevention, 309
  treatment, 293–295, 296–297, 322
Goodness-of-fit, 281–282
Group therapy, 123, 300–301, 322
Growth stage of recovery, 288–289
Guilt, 149

Habitual use, 10
Haley, Jay, 136, 303
Halfway houses, 273–275
  characteristics of, 273–274
  effectiveness of, 275
Hallucinations, 216
Hallucinogens, 50–53
  major effects of, 51–52
  overdose symptoms of, 52
  routes of administration for, 51
  tolerance to, 53
  types of, 51
  withdrawal symptoms from, 53
Harm reduction, 290, 297–298
Hashish, 45
Health insurance plans
  mental health services and, 176–177
  substance abuse treatment and, 178, 281
Health problems
  client history of, 210–211
  screening clients for, 190–191
Helper attractiveness, 109
Helping professionals
  characteristics of effective, 106–115
  cultural competence of, 105–106
Hepatitis, 49, 191
Heroin, 48, 168, 169
Hero role, 142–143
High-risk situations, 308
Hispanics. See Latino Americans
History, client
  family, 88, 151, 209, 218–222, 341–342
  legal, 230–232, 343–344
  medical, 210–211, 339
  sexual, 215
  substance abuse, 205–210, 338–339
  treatment, 204–205, 337–338
Hitting bottom, 252
HIV infection, 49, 191, 210
Holistic approach, 308–309
Homophobia, 318
Homosexuals, 317–320
  substance abuse among, 317–318
  suicide rates for, 193, 215–216
  treatment issues for, 318–320
  twelve-step sponsorship for, 262
Hope, 108–109
Hot seat, 122
Huffing, 54
Human diversity, 21

Humility, 109–112
    language and, 111–112
    self-exploration of, 111
Hypnotics, 37

Illegal activities, 227, 231–232
Illegal drugs
    clients involved in selling, 227, 231
    "intended use" criterion and, 8
Illiteracy, 228
Illness
    chemical dependency as, 290–291
    See also Disease model
Immune system problems, 210
Income
    social class assessment and, 226–227
    substance abuse and, 22
Individual therapy, 299–300
Industrial solvents, 54
Inhalants, 53–55
    major effects of, 54
    overdose symptoms of, 54
    routes of administration for, 54
    tolerance to, 54
    types of, 54
    withdrawal symptoms from,
        54–55
Inhaling drugs, 34
Injecting drugs, 34
Inpatient treatment, 267–269
    detoxification programs and,
        269–270
    length of stay for, 267–268
    outpatient treatment vs., 263, 264
    residential programs vs., 267
    structure of, 268–269
    types of, 269–275
    See also Residential treatment
        programs
Institutions, community, 164–165
Integrated treatment, 328
"Intended use" criterion, 8
Intensive outpatient treatment,
    265–267
    benefits of, 265–266
    effectiveness of, 267
    structure and format of, 266–267
Interactionist approach, 85
Intergenerational family therapy, 304
Internalization process, 353
Interpersonal relationships
    assessment of, 165, 229–230, 343
    triangulated, 134
    See also Families
Intervention, 252–256
    case example of, 256
    early, 246–251
    effectiveness of, 255–256
    Johnson Model of, 252–253
    process of, 253–255
    treatment plan and, 296
    See also Treatment
Intoxicated clients, 202–204
Intravenous (IV) administration of
    drugs, 34
Introjection process, 353
Involuntary clients
    confrontation and, 122
    suicide prevention and, 194

Jail, chosen over treatment, 113–114
Jellinek, E. M., 76, 77, 80, 83
Job issues. *See* Employment
Johnson, Vernon, 252
Johnson Model of Intervention,
    252–253
Journal of substance abuse, 4

Language
    humility and, 111–112
    treatment issues and, 314
Lapse, 306
Latino Americans, 313–315
    substance abuse among, 21, 314
    treatment issues for, 314–315
Least restrictive environment,
    275–276, 322
Legal issues
    client assessment and, 230–232,
        343–344
    drug laws and, 47, 167–174
Lesbians, 317–320
    substance abuse among, 317–318
    suicide rates for, 193, 215–216
    treatment issues for, 318–320
    twelve-step sponsorship for, 262
Level of care, 246
Level system in TCs, 272
Life cycle of families, 145–147
Life-experienced counselors, 272
Limbic system, 70
Literacy skills, 228
Local community, 161–162, 223–224
Location of treatment providers, 280
Long-term goals, 293
Loss of control, 82–83
Lost child role, 144
LSD (lysergic acid diethylamide),
    51–53
    See also Hallucinogens

Machismo, 314, 315
Macro influences, 153–180
    assessment of, 222–232
    communities and, 153–165
    drug laws and, 167–174
    multi-systemic framework
        and, 90
    oppression and, 165–167
    public opinion and, 168–169
    social work practice and,
        175–180
    substance abuse treatment and,
        165–168
    summary of, 180
Madanes, Cloe, 136
Maintenance stage of change, 121
Managed care, 132, 178
Manic episodes, 215
Marijuana, 44–47
    history of, 45
    legalization of, 47
    major effects of, 45–46
    tolerance to, 47
    trends in use of, 14
    withdrawal symptoms from, 47
    See also Cannabis
Marital status, 194
Marker, 98–99

Marxist tradition, 66
Mascots, family, 144–145
Maslow's hierarchy of needs, 190
MAST (Michigan Alcoholism
    Screening Test), 184–186
Mead, George Herbert, 158
Media
    disease model and, 80
    drug use portrayed in, 174
Medical problems
    client history of, 210–211, 339
    screening clients for, 190–191
Medical social work, 25
Medications
    abuse of, 324
    over-the-counter, 38, 324
Member check, 243
Mental health disorders. *See*
    Psychiatric disorders
Mental Health Parity Act (MHPA),
    176
Mental status screening, 213–217,
    339–341
    of anxiety disorders, 215–216
    of mood disorders, 214–215
    of thought disorders, 216–217
Methadone, 49
Methamphetamine, 41, 42
Methcathinone, 42
Mexican Americans, 313–315
Michigan Alcoholism Screening Test
    (MAST), 184–186
Mills, C. Wright, 67, 91
Minimization, 116–117
Minnesota Model, 268
Misuse, abuse vs., 8
Mixing drugs. *See* Drug mixing
Modeling, 72, 73
Models of chemical dependency,
    56–91
    biological model, 68–71
    clinical specialization and, 58–60
    cognitive-behavioral model,
        74–75
    community model, 65–68
    disease model, 76–83
    moral model, 62–65
    multi-systemic approach, 84–90
    personal perspectives and, 57–58
    social learning theory model,
        71–74
    summary of, 84, 90–91
Monitoring the Future study, 13, 14
Mood disorders, 214–215
Moral model, 62–65, 176, 177
Morphine, 48
Morrison, Toni, 355
Mothers Against Drunk Driving
    (MADD), 15, 173
Motivation, assessing in clients,
    118–122, 232, 344
Mucous membranes, 35
Multiaxial assessment, 236–240
Multi-systemic approach, 84–90
    biological dimension of, 86–87
    family dimension of, 88
    foundations of, 84–86
    macro dimension of, 90
    practice framework for, 86–90

psychological dimension of, 87–88
religious/spiritual/existential
     dimension of, 88–89
social/environmental dimension
     of, 89–90
treatment process and, 291–292

Narcotics Anonymous (NA), 63,
     78–79, 257
     See also Alcoholics Anonymous
Narrative assessment, 345–347
National Academy of Sciences, 273
National Association of Social
     Workers (NASW), Code of
     Professional Ethics, 64, 278, 320
National Comorbidity Study, 16
National Institutes of Health, 46
National Institute on Alcohol Abuse
     and Alcoholism (NIAAA), 18, 282
National Institute on Drug Abuse, 46
National Women's Health Resource
     Center, 352
Native Americans, 315–317
     community model and, 65
     substance abuse among, 21,
          316–317
     traditional values of, 160
     treatment issues for, 317
Needs assessment, 211–212, 339
Negative life consequences, 6–7
Nicotine, 42
Nixon administration, 169
Normative shame, 149

Objectives, 296
Obsessive-compulsive disorder
     (OCD), 217
Office of National Drug Control
     Policy, 173
Older adults, 324–325
     substance abuse among, 324
     treatment issues for, 325
"One-hit" addiction, 16
Ontological vocation, 96
Opiates, 47–50
     major effects of, 48–49
     overdose symptoms of, 49
     routes of administration for, 48
     tolerance to, 49–50
     types of, 48
     withdrawal symptoms from, 50
Oppression
     Freire's description of, 95–96
     internalized in African
          Americans, 311
     structural and historical systems
          of, 165–167
Orally administering drugs, 33–34
Organic brain damage, 216
Outpatient treatment, 263–267
     clients suitable for, 264
     detoxification as, 269
     effectiveness of, 264–265
     inpatient treatment vs., 263, 264
     intensive, 265–267
Overdose history, 207
Overdose symptoms
     of cannabis, 46–47
     of CNS depressants, 39

of CNS stimulants, 43
of hallucinogens, 52
of inhalants, 54
of opiates, 49
Over-the-counter medications, 38, 324
Oxford Group, 258

Parents
     adolescent treatment programs
          and, 322–324
     substance abuse of, 150–151
Peck, M. Scott, 260
People of color
     chemical dependency among, 22
     treatment options and, 282
     twelve-step programs and, 263
Personal challenges, 3–4
Personalismo, 315
Personality, addictive, 70
Person-in-Environment (PIE)
     assessment, 233
Pharmacology, 28–55
     drug categories and, 36–55
     gender issues and, 31
     misinformation about, 29
     routes of administration and,
          33–35
     summary of, 55
     tolerance and, 35–36
     variability and, 29–33
Phenylpropanolamine, 42
Physical problems
     client history of, 210–211
     screening clients for, 190–191
Physical tolerance, 35
Physiological dependency, 11
     See also Chemical dependency
Plans, treatment, 292–298
Populations at risk, 310–329
     adolescents, 320–324
     African Americans, 310–313,
          349–356
     co-occurring disorders and,
          325–329
     GLBT persons, 317–320
     Latino Americans, 313–315
     Native Americans, 315–317
     older persons, 324–325
     summary of, 329
     See also Risk factors
Positive role models, 311
Post-traumatic stress disorder (PTSD),
     215, 349
Potency, 32
Poverty, 311, 352
Power, 166
Powerlessness, 263
Power-mapping, 167
Praxis, 92
Prealcoholic phase of alcoholism, 77
Precontemplation stage of change,
     118–119
Pregnancy, 20
Presenting problem, 201–202, 336
Presenting reality, 253
Prevention
     relapse, 306–309
     substance abuse, 246–251
     suicide, 194

Price, Jerome, 147
Primary prevention, 248
Prison, chosen over treatment, 113–114
Problem definition, 296
Problem-posing dialogue, 96–97
Problem selection, 295
Prodromal phase of alcoholism, 77
Professional challenges, 2–3
Professional treatment resources, 164
Prohibition era, 131, 169
Projection, 117
Project MATCH, 249, 277
Providers of treatment, 279–282
     assessment of, 279–280
     following-up with, 282–283
     funding sources for, 281
     goodness-of-fit with, 281–282
     location of, 280, 281
Pseudo ailments, 76
Psychiatric disorders
     anxiety disorders, 215–216
     assessment of, 212–218
     co-occurring, 325–329
     mood disorders, 214–215
     social work and, 25
     substance abuse and, 17–18, 213,
          325–329
     thought disorders, 216–217
Psychobiological perspective, 197
Psychoeducational interventions, 247
Psychological dependency, 11
     See also Chemical dependency
Psychological factors
     assessment of, 212–218, 339–341
     multi-systemic approach and,
          87–88
Psychological tolerance, 36
Public opinion
     disease model and, 80
     drug laws and, 167–169
Public transportation, 227
Puerto Ricans, 313–315

Qualitative research, 94, 243
Questioning, circular, 219

Race, 21
Racism, 166, 311
Randall, Alice, 354
Rational Emotive Therapy (RET), 75
Rationalization, 117
Rationalizing precontemplators, 119
Reagan administration, 169
Reality therapy, 75
Rebellious precontemplators, 119
Reciprocal determinism, 72
Recovery, 78, 284–290
     abstinence stage of, 286–287
     aftercare and, 292
     confrontation stage of, 287–288
     co-occurring disorders and, 326,
          328
     growth stage of, 288–289
     models of, 285
     overview of, 284–286
     stages in process of, 286–290
     substance abuse workers in,
          178–180
     transformation stage of, 289–290

Referrals, 275–278
    context of, 202, 336–337
    follow-up process for, 282–283
    least restrictive environment
      concept and, 275–276
    matching treatments to needs via,
      276–277
Reimbursement policies, 175–177
Relapse, 306
    abstinence stage and, 286
    change process and, 121
    co-occurring disorders and, 327
    dependence following, 78
    depressant drugs and, 40
    detoxification and, 270
    prevention of, 306–309
    risk factors for, 308
Relationships
    assessment of, 165, 229–230, 343
    triangulated, 134
    See also Families
Release-of-information form, 278, 282
Religion
    moral model and, 64
    multi-systemic approach and,
      88–89
    twelve-step programs and, 88–89,
      260–261
Reluctant precontemplators, 118
Reports, case history, 236, 240–243,
    331–348
Representation, crisis of, 241–242
Reproductive problems, 46, 210–211
Residential treatment programs,
    267–275
    adolescents in, 323
    detoxification programs, 269–270
    group confrontation in, 122–123
    halfway houses, 273–275
    inpatient treatment vs., 267
    length of stay in, 267–268
    structure of, 268–269
    therapeutic communities,
      271–273
    types of, 269–275
    See also Inpatient treatment
Resigned precontemplators, 119
Resilience, family, 138–139
Resistant clients, 249–250
Resources, community, 164–165
Respect, worldview, 107–108
Risk factors
    for relapse, 308
    for suicide, 194–195
    See also Populations at risk
Ritalin, 41
Rogers, Carl, 109
Rohypnol, 38
Role models, 311
Roles, family, 141–145, 220
Routes of administration, 33–35, 207
    for cannabis, 45
    for CNS depressants, 38
    for CNS stimulants, 42
    for hallucinogens, 51
    for inhalants, 54
    for opiates, 48
    See also Drug administration
      methods

SASSI-3 screening tool, 188
Satir, Virginia, 141
Scapegoats, family, 143–144
"Scary drug of the year" designation, 16
Schedules of drugs, 170
Schizophrenia, 216, 327
Schools
    DWI (drunken driving), 248–249
    substance abuse education in,
      247–248
Screening, 183–196
    assessment vs., 183–184
    depression, 191–193, 214
    instruments used for, 184–189,
      209
    mental status, 213–217
    physical problems, 190–191
    substance-abuse-related problems,
      189–196
    suicidal ideation, 193–196, 214
    summary of, 199
    See also Assessment
Screening instruments, 184–189, 209
    ASI, 187–188
    AUDIT, 189
    CAGE, 186–187
    CISA-AR, 189
    MAST, 184–186
    SASSI, 188
Second-order change, 86
Sedatives, 37
Self
    community and, 160–161
    others and, 157–158
    social, 156–157
Self-determination, 158–160, 321
Self-efficacy, 72
Self-esteem, 123, 150
Self-exploration, 103–105
Self-fulfilling prophecy, 228
Self-medication, 213, 217
Semiotic of communication, 97–102
Sexual abuse, 150, 214, 215, 220
Sexual history, 215
Sexual orientation, 215, 318–319, 320
Shame, 149–150
Short-term goals, 293–295
Sight involvement, 99
Sign, 98
Situational factors, 31
Situational shame, 149
Slip, 306
Smith Owens, Lois, 313, 349–356
Smoking drugs, 34
Snorting drugs, 35
Social class
    assessment of, 226–229, 343
    chemical dependency and, 22–23
    definition of, 226
    shame related to, 149
    substance abuse and, 22
Social coercion, 255
Social detox, 269
Social dimension, 89–90
Social environment, 31
Social learning theory (SLT), 71–74,
    87–88
Social network map, 162–163
Social relationships, 165, 229–230

Social self, 156–157
Social support networks, 292,
    308, 319
Social systems, 228
Social work
    clinical specialization in, 58–60
    code of ethics in, 64, 278, 320
    fields of practice in, 24–26
    macro influences on, 175–180
    substance abuse issues in, 23–26
Social workers
    cultural competence of, 105–106
    important characteristics of,
      106–115
    roles in substance abuse field,
      177–178
Solution-focused therapy, 221, 304
Speed (drug), 40
Spirituality
    multi-systemic approach and,
      88–89
    twelve-step programs and, 88–89,
      260–261
    See also Religion
Sponsorship, 261–262
Stability
    chief enablers and, 142
    family change and, 136–137
State of being, 197
Stereotypes, 106, 351
Stimulants. See CNS stimulants
Strategic family therapy, 304
Strengths perspective, 67, 139
Structural family therapy, 304
Students Against Drunk Driving
    (SADD), 15
Substance abuse
    abstinence from, 208
    accidents/deaths related to, 15
    age as factor in, 20–21
    assessment of, 200–244
    at-risk populations and, 310–329
    chemical dependency vs., 11–13
    client's history of, 205–210,
      338–339
    definition of, 9–10
    diagnosis of, 233–240
    family history of, 209, 220
    favorite substances for, 207–208
    gender issues and, 18–20
    human diversity and, 21
    key terms related to, 4–13
    pregnancy and, 20
    problems related to, 189–196
    psychiatric disorders and, 17–18,
      213
    screening instruments for,
      184–189
    social class and, 22–23
    trends in, 13–15
Substance Abuse and Mental Health
    Services Administration
    (SAMSHA), 14, 173, 314
Substance abuse journal, 4
Substance abuse practice
    challenges of, 1–4
    client engagement in, 92–127
    impact of anti-drug legislation
      on, 174

Substance abuse practice (continued)
multi-systemic framework for, 86–90
recovering counselors in, 178–180
reimbursement policies in, 175–177
role of social workers in, 177–178
Substance abusers
challenges of working with, 1–4
drug abusers vs. alcoholics, 58
recovery for, 290
Substance Abuse Subtle Screening Inventory-3 (SASSI-3), 188
Substance abuse treatment. *See* Treatment
Subsystems, family, 133–134
Suicide, 193–196
case example of, 194
depression and, 193, 195
risk factors for, 194–195
screening for risk of, 193–196, 214
Symbolic interactionism (SI), 155–161
self and community, 160–161
self and others, 157–158
self-determination, 158–160
social self, 156–157
Symptoms. *See* Overdose symptoms; Withdrawal symptoms
Synanon program, 122, 271
Systems of oppression, 165–167
Systems theory, 84–86
family therapy and, 130–131, 132–135
multi-systemic approach and, 84–90

Tademy, Lalita, 355
Teen Addiction Severity Index (T-ASI), 187
THC, 45, 46
Theory, 59
Therapeutic communities (TCs), 271–273
characteristics of, 271–272
controversial methods of, 272–273
effectiveness of, 273
length of stay in, 271
Therapy
family, 130–136, 302–304
group, 300–301
individual, 299–300
Thought disorders, 216–217
Three-generation genogram, 221
Tobacco use
chemical dependency and, 16, 42
pregnancy and, 20
Tolerance, 10, 35–36
to cannabis, 47
to CNS depressants, 39
to CNS stimulants, 44
to hallucinogens, 53
to inhalants, 54
to opiates, 49–50
Tough love, 261
Tourism metaphor, 102–105

Tranquilizers, 37
Transformation stage of recovery, 289–290
Transgendered persons, 317–320
substance abuse among, 317–318
treatment issues for, 318–320
Transgenerational diagrams, 221
Transportation issues, 227, 280, 281
Transtheoretical model, 118, 232, 285
Treadway, David, 79
Treatment, 245–309
aftercare and, 292
at-risk populations and, 310–329
client engagement and, 291
client's history of, 204–205, 337–338
community resources for, 164
confidentiality and, 278–279
detoxification, 269–270
education and, 246–251
following-up referrals for, 282–283
funding sources for, 281
gender-biased, 19
general principles of, 290–292
goals of, 293–295, 296–297, 322
goodness-of-fit, 281–282
inpatient, 267–269
integrated model of, 328
intensive outpatient, 265–267
intervention and, 252–256
least restrictive environment for, 275–276, 322
levels of care in, 246–275
location/transportation issues, 280, 281
matching to client needs, 276–277
methods of, 299–305
multi-systemic approach to, 291–292
outpatient, 263–265
planning, 292–298
prevention services and, 246–251
prison chosen over, 113–114
providers of, 279–282
recovery process and, 284–290
referrals for, 275–278
relapse prevention and, 306–309
residential, 267–275
role of families in, 131–132
social support and, 292
summary of, 283, 309
twelve-step groups and, 256–263
Treatment matching, 249–250
Treatment methods, 299–305
community practice, 304–305
family therapy, 302–304
group therapy, 300–302
individual therapy, 299–300
Treatment planning, 292–298
goals of, 296–297
harm reduction principles and, 297–298
plan format for, 293–296
Triangulated relationships, 134
Trips, hallucinogenic, 52
Trust, 112–114, 314

Truth, Sojourner, 356
Tuberculosis, 49, 191, 210
Tuning-in, 94
Twelve-step support groups, 256–263
core elements of, 258
effectiveness of, 262–263
family members and, 131, 132, 303
overview of steps in, 258–260
reasons for visiting, 78–79
recovery model based on, 285
spirituality and, 88–89, 260–261
sponsorship in, 261–262
See also Alcoholics Anonymous
Type I/Type II alcoholism, 69

Uppers, 40
Urinalysis, 189
Use
abuse vs., 8
definition of, 6–9

Validity, 243
Valliant, George, 81, 83
Values, community, 164
Variability. *See* Drug variability
V codes, 237, 239
Vicarious learning, 72
Vietnam veterans, 31
Violence
domestic, 151, 214, 220
poverty and, 311
Vocational skills assessment, 227

Walmyr Scales, 189, 192
War on Drugs, 5, 13, 169
Wegscheider, Sharon, 141
Welfare recipients, 174, 353
Whitaker, Carl, 129
Williams, Patricia J., 354
Willow Weep for Me (Danquah), 351
Wind Done Gone, The (Randall), 354
Withdrawal symptoms, 10–11
of cannabis, 47
of CNS depressants, 39–40
of CNS stimulants, 44
of hallucinogens, 53
of inhalants, 54–55
of opiates, 50
Women
African American, 349–356
family therapy models and, 135–136
substance abuse problems of, 18–20
treatment options for, 282
twelve-step programs and, 263
See also Gender issues
Women's Christian Temperance Union (WCTU), 8
Work issues. *See* Employment
World Health Organization (WHO), 189
Worldview respect, 107–108

Zung Self-Rating Depression Scale, 192